A Guide to the Study of the PENTECOSTAL MOVEMENT

by
CHARLES EDWIN JONES

Volume One: Parts I and II

ATLA Bibliography Series, No. 6

The Scarecrow Press, Inc.
and
The American Theological Library Association
Metuchen, N.J., & London
1983

ACKNOWLEDGMENTS

To a greater degree than scholars in other areas, the bibliographer incurs debts that not even he can credit. He is debtor to innumerable benefactors: collectors who saved materials everyone else thought were ephemeral, and librarians who knew the insides of reference tools and who valued accurate, full citations. He is indebted to these and many, many more. A partial list of my creditors includes the following librarians and scholars: David William Faupel and Melvin Dieter of Asbury Theological Seminary; Alfreda Hanna, Geraldine Huhnke, and Anna Belle Laughbaum of Bethany Nazarene College; Esther Schandorff of Point Loma College; Gerald Flokstra of Central Bible College; Murl Winters of Southwestern Assemblies of God College; Kenneth Rowe of Drew University; Elizabeth Schumann and William McLoughlin of Brown University; and W. J. Hollenweger of the University of Birmingham. Wayne Warner and Alice Reynolds Flower of the General Council of the Assemblies of God and Vinson Synan of the Pentecostal Holiness Church provided notable assistance. Library resources of the following institutions proved invaluable: Emmanuel College, Lee College, Central Bible College, Oral Roberts University, the Assemblies of God Graduate School, North Central Bible College, the Southwestern Assemblies of God College, Oklahoma City Southwestern College, Zion Bible Institute, Moody Bible Institute, Gordon-Conwell Theological Seminary, Central State University, the University of Oklahoma, Clarion State College, Asbury College, Asbury Theological Seminary, Nazarene Theological Seminary, Bethany Nazarene College, Point Loma College, North Park Theological Seminary, Garrett Theological Seminary, Episcopal Divinity School, Boston University School of Theology, Union Theological Seminary, Harvard Divinity School, Andover-Newton Theological School, Providence College, Barrington College, and Brown University. The burden of research was lightened immeasurably by the help and hospitality of the following: James and Nancy Barcus, Donald Dayton, Richard Gould, Martin and Sandra Hamburg, Walter Stitt and Karen Gagnon, John and Linda Leax, Richard Huibregtse, David and Carlynn Reed, David and Kathryn Faupel, Patrick Henry Reardon, Russell and Carol Lundy, Florence Lundy, and Kenneth Scheffel.

Library of Congress Cataloging in Publication Data

Jones, Charles Edwin, 1932-
    A guide to the study of the Pentecostal movement.

    (ATLA bibliography series ; no. 6)
    Includes index.
    1. Pentecostalism--Bibliography. 2. Pentecostal
churches--Bibliography. I. Title. II. Series.
Z7845.P4J66 1983 [BR1644] 016.2708'2 82-10794
ISBN 0-8108-1583-4

TO
Beverly and Karl,
who stopped short of despair
that I would ever finish.

EDITOR'S FOREWORD

The American Theological Library Association Bibliography Series is designed to stimulate and encourage the preparation and publication of reliable bibliographies and guides to the literature of religious studies in all of its scope and variety. Each compiler is free to define his field, make his own selections, and work out internal organization as the unique demands of his subject indicate. We are pleased to publish this guide to the literature of Pentecostalism as number six in our series.

Charles Edwin Jones holds a Ph. D. degree from the University of Wisconsin in the field of American Religious Studies, specializing in the Holiness Movement in American Methodism. He has held library positions in St. Paul School of Theology, Kansas City; Park College, Parkville, Missouri; the University of Michigan; Houghton College; and Brown University. He also has served as archival consultant for the Billy Graham Evangelistic Association, Bethany Nazarene College, and the Pentecostal Holiness Church. Dr. Jones previously taught in the School of Library Science of Clarion State College in Clarion, Pennsylvania and currently resides in Oklahoma City, Oklahoma.

Kenneth E. Rowe
Drew University Library
Madison, New Jersey

FOREWORD

Pentecostal Research: Problems and Promises

The study of the Pentecostal movement has been and still is hindered by a number of difficulties.

The first one is that it has always been presented as a North American phenomenon that started in the U.S.A. and from there conquered the whole world. It thus fits into the general contemporary view of American missions, American films, American business life, and American culture engulfing the whole world.

In the case of the Pentecostal movement this picture is only partly true. The distortion is due to the fact that more research on this topic has been done by Americans than by anyone else. Furthermore, the printed material that the American Pentecostals themselves produce is considered to be internationally representative. However-- to take just a few examples--Brazilian Pentecostalism is far more important than American Pentecostalism; the small Swiss Pentecostal periodical is older than any American Pentecostal periodical still in existence; the Russian, Indonesian or many of the African Pentecostal churches are theologically, politically, liturgically, and ethically so far removed from American Pentecostalism that Americans would find it difficult to recognize in them their fellow Pentecostals.

To overcome this difficulty the researcher has either to concentrate on one country or culture or--in the case of a worldwide overview--he needs to operate in several languages. Because Pentecostalism is a strongly indigenized folk religion, it does not use the cultural medium of English for its liturgy, theology, and religious communication (this applies, of course, to countries with a predominantly non-English culture). English literature that comes from these

vii

parts of the world is written either by expatriates or with a view to adapting the presentation to an English-speaking readership. In either case it is hardly representative of the countries in question.

The second difficulty which a researcher into Pentecostalism encounters is the fact that Pentecostalism is either presented as a white man's religion or--if the overwhelming black and brown majority in Pentecostalism is taken into account--it is dismissed as a religion that is not yet fully mature and worthy of theological investigation.

This impediment can only be overcome by careful field research, tape recordings, and an analysis of the oral forms of theology which prevail in the worldwide Pentecostal community. Such research is now being undertaken and will lead the way to a deeper understanding not only of Pentecostalism but of all forms of oral Christianity. In particular it will help us to understand the structure and tradition of New Testament oral Christianity which, in my opinion, has been so admirably researched by form-criticism. As far as I can see, however, nobody has yet asked the obvious question: How is it that the structures of oral theology, in the case of both New Testament Christianity and Pentecostalism, have been such adaptable missionary tools?

The third difficulty which a researcher into Pentecostalism meets is the unspoken but nevertheless strong assumption that Pentecostalism is properly represented by the two major types of Pentecostalism, namely those that Charles Edwin Jones calls the "baptistic bodies" and those that he calls the "Wesleyan-Arminian bodies." The Pentecostal researcher will be greatly helped by the inclusion of the "Oneness Groups" and the "Signs-Following Groups" in this bibliography.

The fourth problem for a Pentecostal researcher is the fact that it becomes more and more difficult to separate a religious from a non-religious experience (e.g., in art or in human relations), and a Christian from a non-Christian experience. It is still thought to be much easier to separate Christian ideas from non-Christian. Whether that is true or not, I do not know. But one thing is sure:

a movement that relies so heavily on experiences--on experiencing the Holy Spirit, salvation, healing, prayer, visions, the fellowship of the believers--is challenged by experiences of a similar intensity and significance which do not occur within a strictly Christian context.

Dr. Charles E. Jones' Guide to the Study of the Pentecostal Movement is an important, long-awaited and useful first step in the direction of overcoming the outlined difficulties. I have no doubt that it will become a standard companion for all who work in this field.

Dr. Walter J. Hollenweger
Professor of Mission
The University of Birmingham,
England
October 1979

BRIEF TABLE OF CONTENTS

FULL TABLE OF CONTENTS

xii

xiii

xix

INTRODUCTION

"The religion of the poor is not a poor religion." Used first by
W. J. Hollenweger as the title of an article on Latin American
Pentecostalism, this statement might as appropriately be applied to
the Pentecostal movement as a whole. The material scarcity in
which the movement originated seemed in some uncanny way to augment the richness of its spiritual character. Poverty has been an
important factor both in the internal development of Pentecostalism
and in the reactions of outsiders to it.

One area in which the poverty of the Pentecostal movement
was especially crucial was in the nature and quantity of the written
record that it produced. Initially, scarce resources and fear that
intellectual analysis might impede the work of the Holy Spirit caused
Pentecostals to limit publishing output to periodicals, doctrinal polemics, and personal testimonies.

From without, disdain for the poor and sectarian rivalry pre-
determined published comment. Early attention centered on sensational personalities and emotional meetings, particularly on such
bridge-burning practices as tongues-speaking and faith healing.
Spokesmen for groups from which early Pentecostals had originally
come, particularly Holiness and Fundamentalist commentators, at-
tempted to refute Pentecostal teachings. Other religionists and secular
scholars largely ignored them. When alluded to at all, Pentecostals
were called "Holy Rollers" and "Tongues People," almost as if these
were proper names.

Stigmatized by their economic condition and religious beliefs,
Pentecostals ministered to the displaced rural and foreign born of
the inner cities and declining farm areas, balancing the poverty of
their life-situations with their religious experiences. Divided doc-

trinally into at least four irreconcilable camps, they shared, nevertheless, in a peculiar fraternity of isolation which transcended ideological differences.

This informal fraternity remained intact until the post-World War II era, when growing prosperity afforded Pentecostals life-comforts and educational advantages rarely dreamed of before. To some extent, the feeling of kinship survived even the strengthened denominationalism and newly-sharpened doctrinal polemics of a better-educated leadership. Acceptance of traditional Pentecostal beliefs and practices by Charismatic elements in mainline Protestant and Roman Catholic churches also emphasized the common identity of traditional Pentecostals.

Yet, racial and doctrinal divisions remain. Most Pentecostal congregations and denominations are racially segregated. There is also little organizational communication over racial lines, even less between denominations holding conflicting doctrinal views. The official silence between Trinitarian and Oneness groups, for instance, is almost total. The Guide will recognize both the informal unity and the formal dividedness of the movement.

This bibliography is organized in four parts. Part I is devoted to literature of the movement without reference to doctrinal tradition. Part II classifies works by doctrinal emphasis: Wesleyan-Arminian, which is subdivided into Holiness-Pentecostal and Signs-Following groups; and Finished Work of Calvary or Baptistic, which is in turn subdivided into Trinitarian and Oneness bodies. Each of the sub-movements in Part II, i.e., Holiness-Pentecostal, Signs-Following, etc., is prefaced by an introduction tracing historical development and doctrinal emphases, and followed by non-denominational literature of the sub-movement. This material is followed, in turn, by an historical sketch and bibliography for each denomination or other body associated with the particular sub-movement. Part III, SCHOOLS, includes the names of Bible schools, colleges and seminaries with locations, sponsorship, and related bibliography. Part IV, BIOGRAPHY, is devoted to works on individuals--an asterisk (*) indicates a non-Pentecostal--who are participants or critics of the movement. Works by Pentecostal authors on non-religious subjects are also included.

The internal organization of each category in Parts I and II is uniform. General introductory, apologetic and sociological works are followed by subject bibliography in alphabetical order, i.e., "--BIBLIOGRAPHY," etc. In these sections collective biography is listed under "--BIOGRAPHY." Under "--DOCTRINAL AND CONTRO-VERSIAL WORKS" are listed works by Pentecostal writers, followed in some categories by "--NON-PENTECOSTAL AUTHORS" for works critical of Pentecostal beliefs. Under "--HISTORY AND STUDY OF DOCTRINES" are placed works by either Pentecostal or non-Pentecostal writers that attempt objective analysis and are designed to prove neither the truth or falsity of the teachings treated. A geographical sequence arranged by continent, country, province, and city completes the listing in each category.

Approaches to subjects and authors not possible through the regular organization of the Guide are available through the Index. References there are to entry numbers, which precede each biblio-graphical and biographical entry. An approach to racial and national minorities, occupational groups, and women is available under such Index entries as Negroes; West Indians in Great Britain; Italian-Americans; Evangelists; Actors and actresses; and Women. Authors not affiliated with Pentecostal denominations have been identified when possible by denomination or denominational tradition, for example, Nazarene authors, Baptist authors.

Inclusion of a group in the Guide indicates a relationship at some point to the Pentecostal movement. This does not imply, how-ever, that glossolalia was stressed by that group at all times or in all places, nor does it indicate commitment to any one teaching, such as tongues-speaking as the initial evidence of the baptism of the Holy Spirit.

Unfortunately, because of poverty in many developing countries and because of the acquisition policies of American and British li-braries, the published record that has been gathered in libraries ac-cessible to me is overwhelmingly in Western languages, particularly

English. For other materials one must continue to supplement this Guide with W. J. Hollenweger's monumental dissertation, Handbuch der Pfingstbewegung.

BOOKS

ABD	American Psychological Association. Biographical directory.
ACWW	American Catholic who's who.
AGOS	Agrimson. Gifts of the Spirit and the body of Christ.
AHAOAF	Apostolic Faith Mission. A historical account of the Apostolic Faith.
AJNSIT	Adams. Jesus never spoke in tongues.
AMD	American medical directory.
AMS	American men of science.
AMWS	American men and women of science.
AMWS/MS	American men and women of science. The medical sciences.
APABD	American Psychiatric Association. Biographical directory of fellows and members.
ASTS	Apostolic Faith Mission. Saved to serve.
ATF	Atter. The third force.
AVOD	Anderson. Vision of the disinherited.
AWW	Academic who's who.
BACFBTR	Boon. The Anglican Church from the bay to the Rockies.
BCFY	Brooklyn. Ridgewood Pentecostal Church. Commemorating fifty years of God's blessing and faithfulness.
BDNM	Biographical directory of Negro ministers.
BDOD	Buckingham. Daughter of destiny.
BFUWM	Basham. Face up with a miracle.
BHOMM	Barclay. History of Methodist missions.
BHPM	Bloch-Hoell. The Pentecostal Movement.
BIE	Bach. The inner ecstasy.
BMOT	Basham. The miracle of tongues.
BRTP	Bach. Report to Protestants.
BSFH	Brumback. Suddenly from heaven.
BTHS	Bruner. A theology of the Holy Spirit.
CA	Contemporary authors.
CAD	Canadian almanac and directory.
CAP	Contemporary authors (permanent series).
CB	Current biography.
CCD	Crockford's clerical directory.
CCM	Cheek. Cherished memories.

CETCP	Crayne. Early 20th century Pentecost.
CFYISOK	Chambers. Fifty years in the service of the King.
CGP	Calley. God's people.
CHCGH	Cowen. A history of the Church of God (Holiness).
CLMA	Conn. Like a mighty army moves the Church of God.
CMIB	Cash. Man in black.
CMOM	Chambers. The measure of a man.
CNJC	Conn. The new Johnny Cash.
CPH	Crayne. Pentecostal handbook.
CPHC	Campbell. The Pentecostal Holiness Church, 1898-1948.
CR	Celebrity register.
CSFPP	Campbell. Stanley Frodsham, prophet with a pen.
CSSIA	Clark. Small sects in America.
CUWS	Clanton. United we stand.
CWTSHT	Conn. Where the saints have trod.
CWW	Canadian who's who.
DAB	Dictionary of American biography.
DAS	Directory of American scholars.
DBL	Dansk biografisk leksikon.
DBS	Directory of British scientists.
DBWS	Durasoff. Bright wind of the Spirit.
DHOFIA	Dollar. A history of fundamentalism in America.
DMS	Directory of medical specialists.
DNB	Dictionary of national biography.
DPBIC	Durasoff. Pentecost behind the Iron Curtain.
DTAOF	Damboriena. Tongues as of fire.
DWM	Denham. Wonderful miracles wrought by the mighty hand of God.
ECD	Episcopal clerical directory.
EMCM	Encyclopedia of modern Christian missions.
EPOP	Ewart. The phenomenon of Pentecost.
EWM	Encyclopedia of world Methodism.
FGFG	Flower. Grace for grace.
FMOM	Freeman. Missions on the March.
FOF	Facts on file.
FPIC	Flora. Pentecostalism in Columbia.
FSTUR	Full Gospel Business Men's Fellowship International. Steps to the upper room.
FSYOPB	Flower. Seventy years of Pentecostal blessing.
FTINS	Foster. Think it not strange.
FTPF	Ferguson. T. P. Ferguson.
FWSF	Frodsham. With signs following.
GFIIH	Geiger. Further insights into holiness.
GHPAW	Golder. History of the Pentecostal Assemblies of the World.
GM	Gaines. Marjoe.
GNRC	Glock. The new religious consciousness.
GPM	Gee. The Pentecostal movement.
GPPC	Gerlach. People, power, change.
GRG	Gardiner. Radiant glory.

GWAD	Geiger. The word and the doctrine.
GWAF	Gee. Wind and flame.
HATAP	Harrell. All things are possible.
HCM	Hamilton. The charismatic movement.
HHAG	Harrison. A history of the Assemblies of God.
HHSCC	Hilson. History of the South Carolina Conference of the Wesleyan Methodist Church of America.
HJHI	Humphrey. J. H. Ingram.
HMIML	Humbard. Miracles in my life.
HMORBH	Hayes. Memoirs of Richard Baxter Hayes.
HOSDAG	Hoover. Origin and structural development of the Assemblies of God.
HP	Hollenweger. The Pentecostals.
HPBBAW	Hollenweger. Pentecost between black and white.
HWATS	Hoekema. What about tongue-speaking?
HWGWB	Harrison. When God was black.
HWSABM	Harrell. White sects and black men in the recent South.
IWW	International who's who.
JPD	Jernigan. Pioneer days of the Holiness Movement in the Southwest.
KISOK	Kidson. In the service of the King.
KMA	Knight. Ministry aflame.
KPF	Kendrick. The promise fulfilled.
KWGHW	Kulbeck. What God hath wrought.
LGLS	Lindsay. The Gordon Lindsay story.
LHM	Lalive d'Epinay. Haven of the masses.
LIE	Leaders in education.
LLITW	Lamson. Lights in the world.
LMGSS	Lillenas. Modern gospel song stories.
LMWHFH	Lindsay. Men who heard from heaven.
LOAH	Larden. Our Apostolic heritage.
LTAT	Lebsack. Ten at the top.
LTSIH	Lindsay. They saw it happen.
LTSTUS	La Barre. They shall take up serpents.
LV	Lamson. Venture!
MATS	Menzies. Anointed to serve.
MAWCSM	Metcalf. American writers and compilers of sacred music.
MCAC	McLeister. Conscience and commitment.
MCV	McClurkan. Chosen vessels.
MDP	Meyers. Divine power.
MEOAR	Melton. The encyclopedia of American religions.
MFATALW	Marston. From age to age a living witness.
MFCASOA	Mathison. Faiths, cults and sects of America.
MFIP	Montgomery. Fire in the Philippines.
MGTT	Minneapolis. Gospel Tabernacle. 1968 trumpet.

MGWD   Miller. Grappling with destiny.
MHLD   Martindale-Hubbell law directory.
MHODIUS   Mead. Handbook of denominations in the United
              States.
MHOPDIUS   Moore. Handbook of Pentecostal denominations in
              the United States.
MIDBNB   Mesquita. Istória dos Batistas no Brasil.
MIS   Meloon. Ivan Spencer.
MLMR   Manuel. Like a mighty river.
MP   Morris. The preachers.
MPC   Moon. The Pentecostal Church.
MPE   Miller. Pentecost examined.
MPFPP   Middlebrook. Preaching from a Pentecostal perspec-
              tive.
MSITBA   Metz. Speaking in tongues; a Biblical analysis.
MSITLTAI   Mills. Speaking in tongues; let's talk about it.
MSOG   Missen. The sound of a going.
MSOML   McPherson. The story of my life.
MUHW   Montgomery. Under His wings.

NCAB   National cyclopedia of American biography.
NCASOC   Neve. Churches and sects of Christendom.
NCDOCWM   Neill. Concise dictionary of the Christian world
              mission.
NP   Nichol. Pentecostalism.
NPU   Nazarene pulpit.
NSS   Nickel. The Shakarian story.
NYT   New York Times.

OCDOWC   O'Brien. Corpus dictionary of Western churches.
OFT   Orr. The flaming tongue.
OYMA   Outstanding young men of America.

PCEPAC   Peters. The contribution to education by the Pente-
              costal Assemblies of Canada.
PDOJ   Preece. Dew on Jordan.
PEOPE   Palmer. Explosion of people evangelism.
PLCFP   Parham. The life of Charles F. Parham.
POT   Preachers of today.
POWW   Perkin. Our world witness.
PPIB   Piepkorn. Profiles in belief.

RC   Roberts. The call.
RHAFY   Ross. History and formative years of the Church of
              God in Christ.
RHDWE   Roberts. His darling wife, Evelyn.
RLACG   Read. Latin American church growth.
RLOA   Religious leaders of America.
RO   Robinson. Oral.
RPFC   Rasnake. Pentecost fully come.
RSBR   Rasnake. Stones by the river.
RSG   Ridout. Spiritual gifts.
RTOTR   Robertson. That old-time religion.
RWSISTC   Runyon. What the Spirit is saying to the churches.

SAOPCO	Synan. Aspects of Pentecostal-Charismatic origins.
SCAOA	Spence. Charismatism: awakening or apostasy.
SCC	Smith. Contemporary conversions.
SCHG	Shumway. A critical history of glossolalia.
SCUH	Smith. Called unto holiness.
SEC	Synan. Emmanuel College.
SEOFCWM	Stambler. Encyclopedia of folk, country and western music.
SFH	Simson. The faith healer.
SFLF	Smith. Flames of living fire.
SFOPC	Stemme. The faith of a Pentecostal Christian.
SHPM	Synan. The Holiness-Pentecostal Movement.
SHPOE	Shakarian. The happiest people on earth.
SHUMC	Storms. History of the United Missionary Church.
SOTP	Synan. The Old-Time Power.
SPONP	Spittler. Perspectives on the new Pentecostalism.
SPRCDE	Standard & Poor's Register of corporations, directors and executives.
SSH	Steele. Storming heaven.
SSO	Sanford. Sealed orders.
STCR	Swaggart. To cross a river.
STOMAA	Samarin. Tongues of men and angels.
STSWOT	Sherrill. They speak with other tongues.
SUT	Smith. The unknown tongue.
TCERK	Twentieth century encyclopedia of religious knowledge.
TDOOP	Thomas. The days of our pilgrimage.
THH	Trance, healing, and hallucination.
THOHTS	Thomas. The history of Holmes Theological Seminary.
WAOG	Winehouse. The Assemblies of God.
WED	Webster's biographical dictionary.
WCH	World Christian handbook.
WEAGW	Ward. Elder A. G. Ward.
WFNF	Willems. Followers of the new faith.
WJ	Winley. Jesse.
WLOPAC	Wagner. Look out! The Pentecostals are coming.
WMDCB	Wallace. Macmillan dictionary of Canadian biography.
WNTCB	West. The New Testament church book.
WPOS	Wilson. Patterns of sectarianism.
WQFPAO	Wittlinger. Quest for piety and obedience.
WSAS	Wilson. Sects and society.
WSML	White. The story of my life and the Pillar of Fire.
WUYYC	Wiens. Unto you and to your children.
WW	Who's who.
WWBA	Who's who among Black Americans.
WWIA	Who's who in America.
WWIACUA	Who's who in American college and university administration.
WWIAE	Who's who in American education.
WWIAM	Who's who in American Methodism.
WWIAP	Who's who in American politics.
WWIC	Who's who in the clergy.
WWICA	Who's who in colored America.

WWICO	Who's who in consulting.
WWIE	Who's who in the East.
WWIFO	Who's who in football.
WWIFR	Who's who in France.
WWIG	Who's who in Germany.
WWIM	Who's who in Methodism.
WWIMC	Who's who in the Methodist Church.
WWIMW	Who's who in the Midwest.
WWIN	Who's who in the Netherlands.
WWIR	Who's who in religion.
WWIW	Who's who in the West.
WWIWO	Who's who in the world.
WWOAW	Who's who of American women.
WWWA	Who was who in America.
WWWCH	Who was who in church history.
YHFH	Yeomans. Healing from heaven.
YOAACC	Yearbook of American and Canadian churches.
YOAC	Yearbook of American churches.
ZRMCA	Zaretsky. Religious movements in contemporary America.

CHURCHES

AAGA	General Assembly of the Apostolic Assemblies.
AAOOLASJC	Apostolic Assembly of Our Lord and Saviour Jesus Christ.
ABEA	Anchor Bay Evangelistic Association.
AC	Apostolic Church.
AChrGID	Arbeitsgemeinschaft der Christen-Gemeinden in Deutschland.
ACIC	Apostolic Church in Canada.
ACOJC	Apostolic Church of Jesus Christ.
ACOPOC	Apostolic Church of Pentecost of Canada.
AChrA	Association of Christian Assemblies.
AdChrC	Advent Christian Church.
ADI	Assembles di Dio d'Italia.
AF	Apostolic Faith.
AFM	Apostolic Faith Mission.
AGA	Asambleas de Dios en la Argentina.
AGAu	Assemblies of God in Australia.
AGB	Assembléias de Deus do Brasil.
AGF	Assemblées de Dieu en France.
AGGC	Assemblies of God, General Council.
AGGI	Assemblies of God in Great Britain and Ireland.
AGK	Assemblies of God in Korea.
AGNZ	Assemblies of God in New Zealand.
AGP	Assemblies of God of the Philippines.

AGQ	Assemblies of God, Queensland.
AGSA	Assemblies of God in South Africa.
AGSSA	Apostoliese Geloof Sending van Suid-Afrika.
AMA	Apostolic Ministerial Alliance.
AME	African Methodist Episcopal Church.
AngCC	Anglican Church of Canada.
AOFMAC	Association of Fundamental Ministers and Churches.
AOHCG	Apostolic Overcoming Holy Church of God.
APeA	Association of Pentecostal Assemblies.
APeCA	Association of Pentecostal Churches of America.
Bapt	Baptist churches.
BiChr	Bible Christians.
BiSC	Bible Standard Churches.
BiWCOLJCWW	Bible Way Churches of Our Lord Jesus Christ World Wide.
BM	Bethany Mission.
BPN	Broederschap van Pinkstergemeenten in Nederland.
Br	Brethren churches.
BrC	Brethren Church.
BrIChrC	Brethren in Christ Church.
Cath	Catholic Church.
CathAC	Catholic Apostolic Church.
CBr	Church of the Brethren.
CChr	Church of Christ.
CChr (S)	Church of Christ (Scientist)
CE	Church of England.
CEI	Chiesa Evangelica Internazionale.
CG (A)	Church of God (Anderson, In.)
CG (C)	Church of God (Cleveland, Tn.)
CG (G)	Church of God (Guthrie, Ok.)
CG (GA)	Church of God (General Assembly)
CG (H)	Church of God (Holiness)
CG (IE)	Churches of God (Indiana Eldership)
CG (JA)	Church of God (Jerusalem Acres)
CG (R)	Church of God (Rodgers)
CG (SIE)	Churches of God (Southern Indiana Eldership)
CGAF	Church of God of the Apostolic Faith.
CGBF	Church of God by Faith.
CGFBJC	Church of God Founded by Jesus Christ.
CGIC	Church of God in Christ.
CGICI	Church of God in Christ, International.
CGII	Churches of God in Ireland.
CGINA (GE)	Churches of God in North America (General Eldership)
CGMA	Church of God of the Mountain Assembly.
CGOMA	Church of God of the Original Mountain Assembly.
CGOP	Church of God of Prophecy.
CGUA	Church of God of the Union Assembly.
CGWH	Church of God, World Headquarters.
CGWSFA	Church of God with Signs Following After.
CHC	Calvary Holiness Church.

ChrA	Christian Assembly.
ChrAC	Christ Apostolic Church.
ChrC	Christian Church.
ChrCathC	Christian Catholic Church.
ChrCNA	Christian Church of North America.
ChrG	Christlicher Gemeinschaftsverband GmbH Mülheim/Ruhr.
ChrCGI	Christ Gospel Churches International.
ChrMA	Christian and Missionary Alliance.
ChrNC	Christian Nation Church.
ChrRC	Christ Revival Church.
ChrRef	Christian Reformed Church.
ChrU	Christian Union.
CJ	Church of Jesus.
CJCLDS	Church of Jesus Christ of Latter-Day Saints.
CLG	Church of the Living God.
CLJCAF	Church of the Lord Jesus Christ of the Apostolic Faith.
CN	Church of the Nazarene.
COLJCAF	Church of Our Lord Jesus Christ of the Apostolic Faith.
Cong	Congregational churches.
CongCr	Congregacão Cristã do Brasil.
CongHC	Congregational Holiness Church.
CongM	Congregational Methodist Church.
COPe	Church of Pentecost.
CPeC	Calvary Pentecostal Church.
CS	Church of Scotland.
CSI	Church of South India.
DChr	Disciples of Christ (Christian Church)
DVeC	Deutsche Volksmission entschiedener Christen.
EAOHCG	Ethiopian Apostolic Overcoming Holy Church of God.
EChrW	Elbethel Christian Work.
ECJC	Emmanuel's Church in Jesus Christ.
EEB	Elim Evangelistic Band.
EF	Elim Fellowship.
EFGA	Elim Foursquare Gospel Alliance.
EHC	Emmanuel Holiness Church.
EJSSTAPSK	Eglise de Jesus-Christ sur la terre par le prophète Simon Kimbangu.
EMA	Elim Missionary Assemblies.
EMF	Elim Ministerial Fellowship.
EMIB	Evangelische Missionsgesellschaft in Basel.
EPeA	Elim Pentecostal Alliance.
EPeC	Elim Pentecostal Church.
Epis	Protestant Episcopal Church in the United States of America.
Ev	Evangelical churches.
EvANA	Evangelical Association of North America.
EvCCOA	Evangelical Covenant Church of America.
EvChrIAS	Evangelical Christians in the Apostolic Spirit.
EvFCOA	Evangelical Free Church of America.
EvRef	Evangelical and Reformed Church.
EvUBr	Evangelical United Brethren Church.

FBHAOA	Fire-Baptized Holiness Association of America.
FBHC	Fire-Baptized Holiness Church.
FBHCG	Fire-Baptized Holiness Church of God.
FBHCGOA	Fire-Baptized Holiness Church of God of the Americas.
FChrA	Fellowship of Christian Assemblies.
FGC	Full Gospel Church.
FGFCMI	Full Gospel Fellowship of Churches and Ministers Int.
FGT	Full Gospel Testimony.
FM	Free Methodist Church of North America.
FMALAOKCM	Fundamental Ministerial and Laymen's Association of Kansas City, Missouri.
FPeCOUSAC	Finnish Pentecostal Churches of the United States and Canada.
Frd	Society of Friends.
FrGC	Free Gospel Church.
FrWBapt	Free-Will Baptist Church.
FT	Faith Tabernacle.
GCAC	Gold Coast Apostolic Church.
GGF	Grace Gospel Fellowship.
GOrtho	Greek Orthodox Church.
H	Holiness churches.
HATex	Holiness Association of Texas.
HBapt	Holiness Baptists.
HC	Holiness Church.
HCChr	Holiness Church of Christ.
HCG	Holiness Church of God.
HCGIJN	Holiness Church of God in Jesus' Name.
HChrC	Holiness Christian Church.
HOGWICLG-PAGOT	House of God, Which is the Church of the Living God, the Pillar and Ground of the Truth.
HOPFAP	House of Prayer for All People.
HY	Herättäjä-Yhdistys.
I	Independent.
IAEAMA	International Apostolic Evangelistic and Missionary Assc.
IAG	Independent Assemblies of God.
IAGI	Independent Assemblies of God, International.
IAHC	International Apostolic Holiness Church.
IAHUC	International Apostolic Holiness Union and Churches.
IAHUPL	International Apostolic Holiness Union and Prayer League.
ICCLA	Iglesias Cristianas, Concilio Latino-Americano.
ICFG	International Church of the Foursquare Gospel.
IDPePR	Iglesia de Dios Pentecostal de Puerto Rico.
IEPeBPC	Igreja Evangélica Pentecostal "Brasil para Cristo"
IEPeC	Iglesia Evangélica Pentecostal de Chile.
IFundCA	Independent Fundamental Churches of America.
IHC	Independent Holiness Church.
IHM	International Holiness Mission.
IM	Iglesia Metodista.
IMA	International Ministerial Association.
IMN	Iglesia Metodista Nacional.

IMPe	Iglesia Metodista Pentecostal.
IndHC	Independent Holiness Church.
IPeA	International Pentecostal Assemblies.
IPeCC	Italian Pentecostal Church of Canada.
IPeCChr	International Pentecostal Church of Christ.
IPeChl	Iglesia Pentecostal de Chile.
IWN	Iglesia Wesleyana Nacional.
JW	Jehovah's Witnesses.
KEV	Kristian Evangel'skoy Very.
KPeC	Kristova Pentekostna Crkva u FNR Jugoslaviji.
LHOLAPACMA	Latter House of the Lord for All People and Church of the Mountain, Apostolic.
Luth	Lutheran Church.
M	Methodist Church (United States)
MBrIChr	Mennonite Brethren in Christ.
MCA	Metropolitan Church Association.
MCHCOA	Mount Calvary Holy Church of America.
ME	Methodist Episcopal Church.
Menn	Mennonite churches.
MES	Methodist Episcopal Church, South.
Meth	Methodist churches.
MIPe	Misión Iglesia Pentecostal.
MisC	Missionary Church.
MPC	Methodist Protestant Church.
NAGK	Nihon Assemblies of God Kyodan.
NDSTOCCU	National David Spiritual Temple of Christ Church Union, U.S.A.
NIPeMU	National and International Pentecostal Missionary Union.
NPY	Norske Pinsevenners Ytremisjon.
NTCChr	New Testament Church of Christ.
NTCG	New Testament Church of God.
OBiEA	Open Bible Evangelistic Association.
OBiSC	Open Bible Standard Churches.
ObiSEA	Open Bible Standard Evangelistic Association.
(O) CG	(Original) Church of God.
OMS	Oriental Missionary Society.
Ortho	Eastern Orthodox churches.
PB	Philadelphia-Bewegung.
PBr	Plymouth Brethren.
Pe	Pentecostal churches.
PeAC	Pentecostal Assemblies of Canada.
PeAJC	Pentecostal Assemblies of Jesus Christ.
PeAN	Pentecostal Assemblies of Newfoundland.
PeAUSA	Pentecostal Assemblies of the U.S.A.
PeAW	Pentecostal Assemblies of the World.
PeC	Pentecostal Church, Incorporated.
PeCAFA	Pentecostal Churches of the Apostolic Faith Association.

PeCAu	Pentecostal Church of Australia.
PeCChr	Pentecostal Church of Christ.
PeCG	Pentecostal Church of God.
PeCGOA	Pentecostal Church of God of America.
PeCJC	Pentecostal Church of Jesus Christ.
PeCN	Pentecostal Church of the Nazarene.
PeEvC	Pentecostal Evangelical Church.
PeFBHC	Pentecostal Fire-Baptized Holiness Church.
PeFWBapt	Pentecostal Free-Will Baptist Church.
PeHC	Pentecostal Holiness Church.
PeHCC	Pentecostal Holiness Church of Canada.
PeM	Pentecostal Mission
PeMA	Pentecostal Ministerial Alliance.
PenlM	Peniel Missions.
PeU	Pentecostal Union.
PF	Pillar of Fire Church.
PHC	Pilgrim Holiness Church.
PlyBr	Plymouth Brethren.
PM	Primitive Methodist Church.
Pres	Presbyterian Church.
Prot	Protestant churches.
RCOOL	Refuge Churches of Our Lord.
Ref	Reformed churches.
RefBapt	Alliance of the Reformed Baptist Church.
RefCIA	Reformed Church in America.
RefPres	Reformed Presbyterian Church.
RLDS	Reorganized Church of Jesus Christ of Latter Day Saints.
SA	Salvation Army.
SDAd	Seventh-Day Adventist Church.
SDBapt	Seventh Day Baptist Church.
SFM	Svenska Fria Missionen.
SP	Schweizerische Pfingstmission.
SPeA	Southern Pentecostal Association.
SSS	Soul Saving Station for Every Nation Christ Crusaders of America.
TCAKOGIC	Triumph the Church and Kingdom of God in Christ.
(T) CG	(Tomlinson) Church of God.
TPres	Tabernacle Presbyterian Church.
UAFC	United Apostolic Faith Church.
UB	United Brethren in Christ.
UCC	United Church of Canada.
UCChr	United Church of Christ.
UCJChr	United Church of Jesus Christ.
UFGAMS	United Free Gospel and Missionary Society.
UFMCC	Universal Fellowship of Metropolitan Community Churches.
UHCOA	United Holy Church of America.
UHOPFAP	United House of Prayer for All People.
UM	United Methodist Church.

UMisC	United Missionary Church.
Unit	Unitarian Church.
Univ	Universalist Church.
UPeC	United Pentecostal Church.
V eC	Volksmission entschiedener Christen.
V H	Voice of Healing.
WC	Wesleyan Church.
WCC	World Council of Churches.
WFMA	World's Faith Missionary Association.
WM	Wesleyan Methodist Connection (or Church) of America.
WM (Eng.)	Wesleyan Methodist Connection (England)
WOC	World Church.
YT	Yahvah Temple.
ZEF	Zion Evangelistic Fellowship.

LIBRARIES

ABH	Samford University, Birmingham, Al.
ArU	University of Arkansas, Fayetteville.
AU	University of Alabama, University.
AzFU	Northern Arizona University, Flagstaff.
C	California State Library, Sacramento.
CaBVaU	University of British Columbia, Vancouver.
CaBViP	Provincial Library, Victoria, B.C.
CaBViPA	Provincial Archives Library, Victoria, B.C.
CaMWU	University of Manitoba, Winnipeg.
CaOHM	McMaster University, Hamilton, Ont.
CaOKQ	Queen's University, Kingston, Ont.
CaOONL	National Library of Canada, Ottawa.
CaOTK	Knox College, Toronto.
CaOTP	Toronto Public Library, Toronto.
CAzPC	Azusa Pacific College, Azusa, Ca.
CBBD	Berkeley Baptist Divinity School, Berkeley, Ca.
CBDP	Church Divinity School of the Pacific, Berkeley, Ca.
CBGTU	Graduate Theological Union, Berkeley, Ca.
CBPac	Pacific School of Religion, Berkeley, Ca.
CBPL	Pacific Lutheran Theological Seminary, Berkeley, Ca.
CCC	Claremont Graduate School and University Center, Claremont, Ca.
CCmS	Southern California College, Costa Mesa.
CCSC	School of Theology at Claremont, Claremont, Ca.
CFlS	California State University, Fullerton.
CFS	California State University, Fresno.
CLamB	Biola Library, La Mirada, Ca.
CLgA	Alma College, Los Gatos, Ca.
CLolC	Loma Linda University, Loma Linda, Ca.
CLSU	University of Southern California, Los Angeles.

CLU	University of California, Los Angeles.
CMlG	Golden Gate Baptist Theological Seminary, Mill Valley, Ca.
CoD	Denver Public Library, Denver.
CoDCB	Conservative Baptist Theological Seminary, Denver.
CoDU	University of Denver, Denver.
CoHi	State Historical Society of Colorado, Denver.
CoU	University of Colorado, Boulder.
CPFT	Fuller Theological Seminary, Pasadena, Ca.
CSaT	San Francisco Theological Seminary, San Anselmo, Ca.
CSdP	Point Loma College, San Diego.
CSfCI	California Institute of Asian Studies, San Francisco.
CSluSP	California Polytechnic State University, San Luis Obispo.
CSmH	Henry E. Huntington Library, San Marino, Ca.
CSt	Stanford University, Stanford, Ca.
CStoC	University of the Pacific, Stockton, Ca.
CtHC	Hartford Seminary Foundation, Hartford, Ct.
CtU	University of Connecticut, Storrs.
CtY	Yale University, New Haven, Ct.
CtY-D	Yale University, New Haven, Ct. Divinity School.
CU	University of California, Berkeley.
CU-B	University of California, Berkeley. Bancroft Library.
CU-S	University of California, San Diego.
CU-SC	University of California, Santa Cruz.
DAU	American University, Washington.
DCU	Catholic University of America, Washington.
DeU	University of Delaware, Newark.
DHU	Howard University, Washington.
DLC	Library of Congress, Washington.
DNLM	National Library of Medicine, Washington.
DWT	Wesley Theological Seminary, Washington.
FMU	University of Miami, Coral Gables, Fl.
FTaSU	Florida State University, Tallahassee.
FU	University of Florida, Gainesville.
GA	Atlanta Public Library, Atlanta.
GASU	Georgia State University, Atlanta.
GDC	Columbia Theological Seminary, Decatur, Ga.
GEU	Emory University, Atlanta.
GEU-T	Emory University, Atlanta. Candler School of Theology.
GStG	Georgia Southern College, Statesboro.
GU	University of Georgia, Athens.
HU	University of Hawaii, Honolulu.
IaAS	Iowa State University of Science and Technology, Ames.
IaDmD	Drake University, Des Moines, Ia.
Ia-HA	Iowa State Department of History and Archives, Des Moines.

IaU	University of Iowa, Iowa City.
ICJ	John Crerar Library, Chicago.
ICMB	Moody Bible Institute, Chicago.
ICMcC	McCormick Theological Seminary, Chicago.
ICN	Newberry Library, Chicago.
ICNPT	North Park Theological Seminary, Chicago.
ICRL	Center for Research Libraries, Chicago.
ICT	Chicago Theological Seminary, Chicago.
ICU	University of Chicago, Chicago.
IDfT	Trinity Evangelical Divinity School, Deerfield, Il.
IdPI	Idaho State University, Pocatello.
IEG	Garrett-Evangelical Theological Seminary, Evanston, Il.
IEN	Northwestern University, Evanston, Il.
IGreviC	Greenville College, Greenville, Il.
IKON	Olivet Nazarene College, Kankakee, Il.
IMunS	Saint Mary of the Lake Seminary, Mundelein, Il.
In	Indiana State Library, Indianapolis.
InAndC	Anderson College, Anderson, In.
InIB	Butler University, Indianapolis.
InIT	Christian Theological Seminary, Indianapolis.
InLP	Purdue University, Lafayette, In.
InNd	University of Notre Dame, Notre Dame, In.
InRE	Earlham College, Richmond, In.
InU	Indiana University, Bloomington.
InWinG	Grace Theological Seminary and College, Winona Lake, In.
IRA	Augustana College, Rock Island, Il.
ISC	Concordia Theological Seminary, Springfield, Il.
IU	University of Illinois, Urbana.
IWW	Wheaton College, Wheaton, Il.
KMK	Kansas State University, Manhattan.
KPT	Kansas State College, Pittsburg.
KU	University of Kansas, Lawrence.
KU-RH	University of Kansas, Lawrence. Regional History Department.
KWiU	Wichita State University, Wichita.
KyLoL	Louisville Presbyterian Seminary, Louisville.
KyLoS	Southern Baptist Theological Seminary, Louisville.
KyLxCB	Lexington Theological Seminary, Lexington, Ky.
KyU	University of Kentucky, Lexington.
KyWA	Asbury College, Wilmore, Ky.
KyWAT	Asbury Theological Seminary, Wilmore, Ky.
L	British Museum, London.
LE	London School of Economics and Political Science.
LNB	New Orleans Baptist Theological Seminary, New Orleans, La.
LU	University of London.
MB	Boston Public Library, Boston.
MBCo	Countway Library of Medicine, Boston.

MBtS	St. John's Seminary, Brighton, Ma.
MBU	Boston University.
MBU-T	Boston University. School of Theology.
MCE	Episcopal Divinity School, Cambridge, Ma.
McHB	Boston College, Chestnut Hill, Ma.
MCW	Weston School of Theology, Cambridge, Ma.
MH	Harvard University, Cambridge, Ma.
MH-AH	Harvard University, Cambridge, Ma. Andover-Harvard Theological Library.
MiBsA	Andrews University, Berrien Springs, Mi.
MiD	Detroit Public Library, Detroit.
MiD-B	Detroit Public Library, Detroit. Burton Historical Collection.
MiEM	Michigan State University, East Lansing.
MiMtpT	Central Michigan University, Mount Pleasant.
MiU	University of Michigan, Ann Arbor.
MiU-H	University of Michigan, Ann Arbor. Michigan Historical Collections.
MnCS	St. John's University, Collegeville, Mn.
MnHi	Minnesota Historical Society, St. Paul.
MnManBS	Bethany Lutheran Theological Seminary, Mankato, Mn.
MNtcA	Andover Newton Theological School, Newton Center, Ma.
MnU	University of Minnesota, Minneapolis.
MoKN	Nazarene Theological Seminary, Kansas City, Mo.
MoSCEx	Christ Seminary--Seminex, St. Louis.
MoSCS	Concordia Seminary, St. Louis.
MoSpA	Assemblies of God Graduate School, Springfield, Mo.
MoSpCB	Central Bible College, Springfield, Mo.
MoSpS	Southwest Missouri State College, Springfield.
MoSU	St. Louis University, St. Louis.
MoSU-D	St. Louis University, St. Louis. School of Divinity.
MSohG	Gordon-Conwell Theological Seminary, South Hamilton, Ma.
MoU	University of Missouri, Columbia.
MoWgK	Saint Louis Roman Catholic Theological (Kenrick) Seminary, Webster Groves, Mo.
MoWgT	Eden Theological Seminary, Webster Groves, Mo.
MWenhG	Gordon College, Wenham, Ma.
MWollE	Eastern Nazarene College, Wollaston, Ma.
N	New York State Library, Albany.
NB	Brooklyn Public Library, Brooklyn.
Nbu	Buffalo and Erie County Public Library, Buffalo.
NbU	University of Nebraska, Lincoln.
NBuG	Buffalo and Erie County Public Library, Buffalo. Grosvenor Reference Division.
NBuHi	Buffalo and Erie County Historical Society, Buffalo.
NBuU	State University of New York at Buffalo, Buffalo.
NcC	Public Library of Charlotte and Mecklenburg County, Charlotte, N.C.
NcD	Duke University, Durham, N.C.
NcGrE	East Carolina University, Greenville, N.C.
NcGU	University of North Carolina, Greensboro.
NcU	University of North Carolina, Chapel Hill.

NcWfSB	Southeastern Baptist Theological Seminary, Wake Forest, N.C.
NdU	University of North Dakota, Grand Forks.
NEsM	Mount St. Alphonsus Seminary, Esopus, N.Y.
NHou	Houghton College, Houghton, N.Y.
NIC	Cornell University, Ithaca, N.Y.
NjMD	Drew University, Madison, N.J.
NjP	Princeton University, Princeton, N.J.
NjPT	Princeton Theological Seminary, Princeton, N.J.
NjR	Rutgers University, New Brunswick, N.J.
NN	New York Public Library, New York.
NNBS	Biblical Seminary in New York, New York.
NNC	Columbia University, New York.
NNG	General Theological Seminary of the Protestant Episcopal Church, New York.
NNMR	Missionary Research Library, New York.
NNU	New York University, New York.
NNUT	Union Theological Seminary, New York.
NNU-W	New York University, N.Y. Washington Square Library.
NR	Rochester Public Library, Rochester, N.Y.
NRCR	Colgate Rochester Divinity School, Rochester, N.Y.
NRU	University of Rochester, Rochester, N.Y.
NSyL	Le Moyne College, Syracuse, N.Y.
NSyU	Syracuse University, Syracuse, N.Y.
NvU	University of Nevada, Reno.
O	Ohio State Library, Columbus.
OBlC	Bluffton College, Bluffton, Oh.
OC	Public Library of Cincinnati and Hamilton County, Cincinnati.
OCH	Hebrew Union College, Cincinnati.
OCl	Cleveland Public Library, Cleveland.
OClW	Case Western Reserve University, Cleveland.
OClWHi	Western Reserve Historical Society, Cleveland.
OCoE	Evangelical Lutheran Theological Seminary, Columbus.
OCU	University of Cincinnati, Cincinnati.
ODaStL	St. Leonard College, Dayton, Oh.
ODaTS	United Theological Seminary, Dayton, Oh.
ODM	Methodist Theological School in Ohio, Delaware.
ODW	Ohio Wesleyan University, Delaware.
OHi	Ohio Historical Society, Columbus.
Ok	Oklahoma Department of Libraries, Oklahoma City.
OkBetC	Bethany Nazarene College, Bethany, Ok.
OkEG	Phillips University, Enid, Ok. Graduate Seminary.
OKentU	Kent State University, Kent, Oh.
OkEP	Phillips University, Enid, Ok.
OkOk	Oklahoma County Libraries, Oklahoma City.
OkS	Oklahoma State University, Stillwater.
OkTOr	Oral Roberts University, Tulsa.
OkTU	University of Tulsa, Tulsa.
OkU	University of Oklahoma, Norman.
OMtvN	Mount Vernon Nazarene College, Mount Vernon, Oh.
OO	Oberlin College, Oberlin, Oh.
Or	Oregon State Library, Salem.

OrP	Library Association of Portland, Portland, Or.
OrPW	Western Evangelical Seminary, Portland, Or.
OrPWB	Western Conservative Baptist Theological Seminary, Portland, Or.
OrPWP	Warner Pacific College, Portland, Or.
OrU	University of Oregon, Eugene.
OSteC	University of Steubenville, Steubenville, Oh.
OSW	Wittenberg University, Springfield, Oh.
OT	Toledo-Lucas County Public Library, Toledo, Oh.
OU	Ohio State University, Columbus.
OUrC	Urbana College, Urbana, Oh.
OWorP	Pontifical College Josephinum, Worthington, Oh.
PGL	Lutheran Theological Seminary, Gettysburg, Pa.
PGraM	Messiah College, Grantham, Pa.
PLT	Lancaster Theological Seminary of the United Church of Christ, Lancaster, Pa.
PP	Free Library of Philadelphia, Philadelphia.
PPDrop	Dropsie College for Hebrew and Cognate Learning, Philadelphia.
PPEB	Eastern Baptist Theological Seminary, Philadelphia.
PPFr	Friends' Free Library of Germantown, Philadelphia.
PPi	Carnegie Public Library, Pittsburgh.
PPiPT	Pittsburgh Theological Seminary, Pittsburgh.
PPiU	University of Pittsburgh, Pittsburgh.
PPLT	Lutheran Theological Seminary, Philadelphia.
PPT	Temple University, Philadelphia.
PPULC	Union Library Catalogue of Pennsylvania, Philadelphia.
PPWe	Westminster Theological Seminary, Philadelphia.
PSt	Pennsylvania State University, University Park.
PU	University of Pennsylvania, Philadelphia.
RBaB	Barrington College, Barrington, R. I.
RP	Providence Public Library, Providence, R. I.
RPB	Brown University, Providence, R. I.
RPPC	Providence College, Providence, R. I.
RPRC	Rhode Island College, Providence.
RU	University of Rhode Island, Kingston.
ScCoT	Lutheran Theological Southern Seminary, Columbia, S. C.
ScDwE-T	Erskine Theological Seminary, Due West, S. C.
ScGBJ	Bob Jones University, Greenville, S. C.
ScU	University of South Carolina, Columbia.
SdSifB	North American Baptist Seminary, Sioux Falls, S. D.
SdU	University of South Dakota, Vermillion.
T	Tennessee State Library and Archives, Nashville.
TJoS	East Tennessee State University, Johnson City.
TMH	Harding Graduate School of Religion, Memphis, Tn.
TNJ	Joint University Libraries, Nashville.
TNJ-R	Joint University Libraries, Nashville. Vanderbilt School of Religion.
TNL	David Lipscomb College, Nashville.
TSewU	University of the South, Sewanee, Tn.

TU	University of Tennessee, Knoxville.
TxAuE	Episcopal Theological Seminary of the Southwest, Austin, Tx.
TxDaM	Southern Methodist University, Dallas.
TxDaM-P	Southern Methodist University, Dallas. Perkins School of Theology.
TxDaTS	Dallas Theological Seminary and Graduate School, Dallas.
TxFS	Southwestern Baptist Theological Seminary, Fort Worth, Tx.
TxFTC	Texas Christian University, Fort Worth.
TxHR	Rice University, Houston.
TxHU	University of Houston, Houston.
TxLoL	Le Tourneau College, Longview, Tx.
TxLT	Texas Tech University, Lubbock.
TxSaT	Trinity University, San Antonio.
TxU	University of Texas, Austin.
TxViHU	University of Houston, Victoria Center, Victoria, Tx.
TxWaS	Southwestern Assemblies of God College, Waxahachie, Tx.
TxWB	Baylor University, Waco, Tx.
UU	University of Utah, Salt Lake City.
ViHarEM	Eastern Mennonite College, Harrisonburg, Va.
ViRU	University of Richmond, Richmond, Va.
ViRUT	Union Theological Seminary, Richmond, Va.
ViU	University of Virginia, Charlottesville.
ViW	College of William and Mary, Williamsburg, Va.
Wa	Washington State Library, Olympia.
WaE	Everett Public Library, Everett, Wa.
WaS	Seattle Public Library, Seattle.
WaSp	Spokane Public Library, Spokane, Wa.
WaU	University of Washington, Seattle.
WHi	State Historical Society of Wisconsin, Madison.
WPlaU	University of Wisconsin, Platteville.
WU	University of Wisconsin, Madison.

PLACES

Afr.	Africa	Beds.	Bedfordshire
Ak.	Alaska	Belg.	Belgium
Al.	Alabama	Braz.	Brazil
Ar.	Arkansas	Bucks.	Buckinghamshire
Argen.	Argentina		
Arm.	Armenia	Ca.	California
Austl.	Australia	Carms.	Carmarthenshire
Az.	Arizona	Ch.	China
		Co.	Colorado
B. C.	British Columbia	Col.	Colombia

C. R.	Costa Rica		Newf.	Newfoundland
Ct.	Connecticut		N. H.	New Hampshire
			N. J.	New Jersey
D. C.	District of Columbia		N. M.	New Mexico
De.	Delaware		Nor.	Norway
Derbys.	Derbyshire		N. S.	Nova Scotia
Devon.	Devonshire		N. S. W.	New South Wales
Dorset.	Dorsetshire		Nv.	Nevada
			N. Y.	New York
Eg.	Egypt		N. Z.	New Zealand
Fl.	Florida		O. F. S.	Orange Free State
Fr.	France		Oh.	Ohio
			Ok.	Oklahoma
Ga.	Georgia		Ont.	Ontario
Ger.	Germany		Or.	Oregon
Glos.	Gloucestershire		Oxon.	Oxfordshire
Gr.	Greece			
Guat.	Guatemala		Pa.	Pennsylvania
			P. E. I.	Prince Edward Island
Hants.	Hampshire		Phil.	Philippines
Hi.	Hawaii		Pol.	Poland
			P. R.	Puerto Rico
Ia.	Iowa			
Id.	Idaho		Q.	Queensland
Il.	Illinois			
In.	Indiana		R. I.	Rhode Island
Ire.	Ireland			
I. T.	Indian Territory		Sask.	Saskatchewan
			S. C.	South Carolina
Ks.	Kansas		S. D.	South Dakota
Ky.	Kentucky		Son.	Sonora
			Swed.	Sweden
La.	Louisiana		Swit.	Switzerland
Lanarks.	Lanarkshire			
Lancs.	Lancashire		Tasm.	Tasmania
Lincs.	Lincolnshire		Tn.	Tennessee
			Tvl.	Transvaal
Ma.	Massachusetts		Tx.	Texas
Md.	Maryland			
Me.	Maine		Ut.	Utah
Mi.	Michigan			
Middx.	Middlesex		Va.	Virginia
Mn.	Minnesota		Vict.	Victoria
Mo.	Missouri		Vt.	Vermont
Monms.	Monmouthshire			
Ms.	Mississippi		W. I.	West Indies
Mt.	Montana		Wi.	Wisconsin
			Worcs.	Worcestershire
N. B.	New Brunswick		W. Va.	West Virginia
N. C.	North Carolina		Wy.	Wyoming
N. D.	North Dakota			
Ne.	Nebraska		Yorks.	Yorkshire

PART I: PENTECOSTAL MOVEMENT

The Pentecostal movement as a whole includes a wide range of beliefs and practices, though it presents for outsiders a unity that belies its true diversity. This unity centers on Pentecostal stress on tongues-speech and physical healing. A large body of literature produced by proponents and critics of the movement and addressed to non-sectarian elements within the movement and to outsiders is listed below. The denominational affiliation of some writers is known; of others, unknown. This, however, is not the determining factor for inclusion here. Rather, works placed here purport to speak for or about the movement as a whole.

01 Baldwin, James, 1924-
     Go tell it on the mountain. New York, Knopf, 1953. 303p.
    A novel. DLC

02 Barnes, Douglas F.
     Charisma and religious leadership: an historical analysis,
    by Douglas F. Barnes. In Journal for the Scientific Study of
    Religion, 17 (Mar. 1978), 1-18.

03 Barratt, Thomas Ball, 1862-1940.
     In the days of the latter rain. London, Simpkin, Marshall,
    1909. viii, 124p. L

04 Barratt, Thomas Ball, 1862-1940.
     In the days of the latter rain. Rev. ed. London, Elim Publishing Co., 1928. 222p. L, TxWaS

05 Bauman, Louis Sylvester, 1875-
     The tongues movement, by Louis S. Bauman. Winona Lake,
    Ind., Brethren Missionary Herald Co., c1963. 47p.

06 Beckmann, David M.
     Trance: from Africa to Pentecostalism [by] David M. Beckmann. In CTM, 45 (Jan. 1974), 11-26.

07 Bianchi, Eugene Carl, 1930-
     Ecumenism and the Spirit-filled communities [by] Eugene C.
    Bianchi. In Thought, 41 (Fall 1966), 390-412.

08 Bloch-Hoell, Nils, 1915-
     Den Hellige ånd i Pinsebevegelsen, den Charismatiske

Bevegelse og i Jesus-Vekkelsen, av Nils E. Bloch-Hoell. In Norsk Teologisk Tidsskrift, 77:2 (1976), 75-86.

09 Boisen, Anton Theophilus, 1876-1965.
    Economic distress and religious experience; a study of the Holy Rollers [by] Anton T. Boisen. In Psychiatry, 2 (May 1939), 185-194.

10 Boisen, Anton Theophilus, 1876-1965.
    Religion and hard times: a study of the Holy Rollers, by Anton T. Boisen. In Social Action, 5 (Mar. 15, 1939), 8-35.

11 Boisen, Anton Theophilus, 1876-1965.
    Religion and hard times: a study of the Holy Rollers [by] Anton T. Boisen. In Schuler, E. A., ed. Outside readings in sociology. New York, c1952, p. 430-439.

12 Boisen, Anton Theophilus, 1876-1965.
    Religion in crisis and custom; a sociological and psychological study, by Anton T. Boisen. New York, Harper & Brothers, 1955. xv, 271p. "Economic distress as social crisis": p. 71-94.

13 Braden, Charles Samuel, 1887-
    Churches of the dispossessed, by Charles S. Braden. In Christian Century, 61 (Jan. 26, 1944), 108-110.

14 Braden, Charles Samuel, 1887-
    Sectarianism run wild [by] Charles S. Braden. In Anderson, W. K., ed. Protestantism; a symposium. Nashville, 1944, 110-122.

15 Brewster, Percy S.
    The spreading flame of pentecost [by] P. S. Brewster. London, Elim Publishing House, 1970. ix, 135p. L

16 Briem, Efraim, 1890-1946.
    Den moderna pingstroerelsen. Stockholm, Svenska Kyrkans Diakonistyrelses Bokfoerlag, 1924. 352p. MH-AH

17 Canty, George
    Pentecostalist hesitations. In Frontier, 11 (Winter 1968/ 1969), 264-266.

18 Carter, Richard
    That old-time religion comes back. In Coronet, 43 (Feb. 1958), 125-130.

19 Chinn, Jack J., 1917-
    May we Pentecostals speak? [By] Jack J. Chinn. In Christianity Today, 5 (July 17, 1961), 8-9.

20 Cohn, Werner, 1926-

A movie of experimentally-produced glossolalia. In Journal for the Scientific Study of Religion, 6 (Fall 1967), 278.

20a Cohn, Werner, 1926-
Personality, Pentecostalism, and glossolalia: a research note on some unsuccessful research. In Canadian Review of Sociology and Anthropology, 5 (Feb. 1968), 36-39.

21 Conn, Charles William, 1920-
A spiritual explosion, by Charles W. Conn. In Christian Life, 28 (July 1966), 30-31, 54.

22 Courtney, Howard Perry, 1911-
Present-day evidences of Christ's return, by Howard P. Courtney. In Christian Life, 28 (July 1966), 34-35.

23 Crayne, Richard
Pentecostal handbook. Morristown, Tenn., 1963. 113p. TxWaS

24 Damboriena, Prudencio, 1913-
The Pentecostal fury. In Catholic World, 202 (Jan. 1966), 217-223.

25 Darst, Stephen, 1933-
The theology of joy. In Nation, 213 (Nov. 1, 1971), 440, 442-443.

26 Davies, Horton, 1916-
Centrifugal Christian sects [by] Horton Davies, Charles S. Braden [and] Charles W. Ranson. In Religion in Life, 25 (Summer 1956), 323-358.

27 Davies, Horton, 1916-
The challenge of the sects. Rev. and enlarged ed. Philadelphia, Westminster Press, 1962, c1961. 176p. First published in 1954 under title: Christian deviations. Account of Pentecostalism: p. 83-98. DLC

28 Davies, Horton, 1916-
Christian deviations: the challenge of the sects. Rev. and enlarged ed. London, SCM Press, 1961. 176p. Account of Pentecostalism: p. 83-98. ICU

29 Davies, Horton, 1916-
Christian deviations: the challenge of the new spiritual movements. Philadelphia, Westminster Press, 1965. 144p. "A revised edition of the challenge of the sects." "Pentecostalism": p. 26-37.

30 Davies, Horton, 1916-
Pentecostalism, threat or promise? In Expository Times, 76 (Mar. 1965), 197-199.

31 Davison, Leslie, 1906-1972.
    A conscious awareness. In Frontier, 14 (Nov. 1971), 235-
    238.

32 Dayton, Donald Wilber, 1942-
    The Holiness and Pentecostal churches: emerging from cul-
    tural isolation [by] Donald W. Dayton. In Christian Century,
    96 (Aug. 15, 1979), 786-792.

33 Dayton, Donald Wilber, 1942-
    Wesleyan tug-of-war on Pentecostal link [by] Donald W. Day-
    ton. In Christianity Today, 23 (Dec. 15, 1978), 43. On four-
    teenth annual meeting of the Wesleyan Theological Society in
    Mount Vernon, Ohio, in November.

34 Du Plessis, David Johannes, 1905-
    A Pentecostal and the ecumenical movement [by] David du
    Plessis. In Runyon, T. H. , ed. What the Spirit is saying to
    the churches. New York, 1975, 91-103.

35 Du Plessis, David Johannes, 1905-
    The world Pentecostal movement, by David J. du Plessis.
    In Coxill, H. W. , ed. World Christian handbook, 1968. Nash-
    ville, c1967, 15-18.

36 Ecke, Karl, 1886-1952.
    Die Pfingstbewegung, ein Gutachten von kirchlicher Seite.
    n. p. , Selbstverlag des Verfassers, 1950. 15p.

37 Ecke, Karl, 1886-1952.
    Sektierer oder Wertvolle Bruder? Randglossen zu einem
    Sektenbuch. n. p. , Selbstverlag des Verfassers, 1951. 7p.

38 Ecke, Karl, 1886-1952.
    Skandal im Hause Gottes; oder die seibte Sekte des Verderbens?
    n. p. , Selbstverlag des Verfassers, 1951. [4]p.

39 Edel, Eugen, 1872-1951.
    Der Kampf um die Pfingstbewegung. Mülheim/Ruhr, E. Hum-
    burg, 1949. 63p.

40 Edel, Eugen, 1872-1951.
    Der Kampf um die Pfingstbewegung. Altdorf bei Nürnberg,
    Missionsbuchhandlung und Verlag, 1966. 56p.

41 Eisenlöffel, Ludwig, 1928-
    Ein Feuer auf Erden: Einfuhrung in Lehre und Leben der
    Pfingstbewegung. Erzhausen bei Dramstadt, Leuchter-Verlag,
    1965. 147p.

42 Fischer, Harold Arthur
    Progress toward world fellowship of the various Pentecostal
    groups. Forth Worth, Tx. , 1950. vi, 80ℓ. Thesis (M. A.)--
    Texas Christian University. TxFTC

43 Fleming, Thomas J., 1927-
Miracles of faith healing, by T. F. James. In Cosmopolitan,
145 (Dec. 1958), 34-41. Comments on Pentecostal healers Jack
Coe, Oral Roberts, Aimee Semple McPherson and Charles Price:
p. 38-39.

44 Förster, Herbert
Die Pfingstbewegung und ihr Verhaltnis zur Okumene. In
Evangelische Missionszeitschrift, 20:3 (1963), 115-121.

45 Forbes, James Alexander, 1935-
A Pentecostal approach to empowerment for Black liberation,
by James A. Forbes, Jr. Rochester, N. Y., 1975. [139]ℓ.
Thesis (D. Min.)--Colgate Rochester Divinity School. NRCR

46 Gaustad, Edwin Scott, 1923-
Historical atlas of religion in America. New York, Harper &
Row, 1962. xii, 179p. "Holiness and Pentecostal bodies":
p. 121-126.

47 Gaver, Jessyca (Russell), 1915-
Pentecostalism. New York, Award Books, c1971. 286p.
VIU, WHi, TxWaS

48 Gee, Donald, 1891-1966.
All with one accord. Springfield, Mo., Gospel Publishing
House, 1961. 61p. TxWaS

49 Gee, Donald, 1891-1966.
Toward Pentecostal unity. Springfield, Mo., Gospel Publishing House, 19--. 61p. (Radiant books.) First published in
1961 under title: All with one accord. KyWAT

50 Gerlach, Luther Paul, 1930-
Corporate groups and movement networks in urban America
[by] Luther P. Gerlach. In Anthropological Quarterly, 43 (July
1970), 123-145. "The House of Deliverance Pentecostal church
group": p. 127-134.

51 Gerlach, Luther Paul, 1930-
Five factors crucial to the growth and spread of a modern
religious movement [by] Luther P. Gerlach and Virginia H. Hine.
In Journal for the Scientific Study of Religion, 7 (Spring 1968),
23-40. Based on study of Pentecostal churches in Minneapolis
and St. Paul, Haiti, Jamaica, Colombia and Mexico.

52 Gerlach, Luther Paul, 1930-
People, power, change; movements of social transformation
[by] Luther P. Gerlach and Virginia H. Hine. Indianapolis,
Bobbs-Merrill, 1970. xxiii, 257p. Comparison of the Pentecostal
and Black Power movements. DLC, MCE, MH

53 Gibeau, Dawn
Pentecostals, conservatives growing fast; liberals lose.

In National Catholic Reporter, 9 (Jan. 12, 1973), 1-2.

54 Gilmore, Susan Kay
    Personality differences between high and low dogmatism
    groups of Pentecostal believers [by] Susan K. Gilmore. In
    Journal for the Scientific Study of Religion, 8 (Spring 1969),
    161-164. Study of a group drawn from three Pentecostal con-
    gregations in a city in northwestern United States.

55 Green, Hollis Lynn, 1933-
    Understanding Pentecostalism. Cleveland, Tenn., Pathway
    Press, c1970. 26p.

56 Hamilton, Michael Pollock, 1927-
    The charismatic movement. Edited by Michael P. Hamilton.
    Grand Rapids, Mich., Eerdmans, 1975. 196p. and phonodisc
    (2 s. 5 1/2 in. 33 1/3 rpm. microgroove) in pocket. Essays
    by Dennis J. Bennett, James C. Logan, Krister Stendahl, George
    H. Williams, Edith Waldvogel, Josephine Massyngberde Ford,
    John P. Kildahl, Lawrence N. Jones, Nathan L. Gerrard, Ray-
    mond W. Davis, and Frank Benson. DLC, KyWAT, MCE, RPB,
    TxWaS

57 Hart, Larry Douglas, 1947-
    Problems of authority in Pentecostalism, by Larry Hart. In
    Review and Expositor, 75 (Spring, 1978), 249-266.

58 Hébert, Gérard
    Les sectes évangéliques et pentecôtistes. In Relations, 20
    (Nov. 1960), 282-285.

59 Hickman, James T.
    Let's find Pentecostal balance, by James T. Hickman. In
    Eternity, 25 (Apr. 1974), 16-17. On relations between Pente-
    costals and non-Pentecostals.

60 Hinders, J. T.
    Pentecostalism, by J. T. Hinders and E. J. Martoch. In
    Nuntius Aulae, 4 (1961), 158-168.

61 Hine, Virginia (Haglin), 1920-
    Bridge-burners: commitment and participation in a religious
    movement [by] Virginia H. Hine. In Sociological Analysis, 31
    (Summer 1970), 61-66.

62 Hine, Virginia (Haglin), 1920-
    The deprivation and disorganization theories of social move-
    ments [by] Virginia H. Hine. In Zaretsky, I. I., ed. Religious
    movements in contemporary America. Princeton, N.J., c1974,
    646-661.

63 Hine, Virginia (Haglin), 1920-
    Personal transformation and social change: the role of com-

mitment in a modern religious movement.   Minneapolis, 1969.
248, 9ℓ.   MnU

64   Hollenweger, Walter Jacob, 1927-
     Black Pentecostal concept: Interpretations and variations, by
     Walter J. Hollenweger. Geneva, World Council of Churches,
     Department on Studies in Evangelism, 1970. 70p. (Concept,
     special issue no. 30.)

65   Hollenweger, Walter Jacob, 1927-
     Charisma and oikoumene [by] Walter J. Hollenweger. In
     One in Christ, 7:4 (1971), 324-343.

66   Hollenweger, Walter Jacob, 1927-
     Handbuch der Pfingstbewegung, von Walter J. Hollenweger.
     Zürich, 1966. 3v. in 10. Inaug.-Diss.--Zürich.
         Contents: 1. Hauptt.   Sektierer oder Enthusiasten?
     2. Hauptt.   Die einzelnen Pfingstgruppen, nach geographischen
     Gesichtsspunkten gegliedert: [1] Africa; [2] Nordamerika;
     [3] Lateinamerika; [4] Asien, Australian und Oceanien; [5]-[6]
     Europa. 3. Hauptt.   Kommentierte Bibliographie, Kurzbio-
     graphien: [1] Einfuhrung in den III. Hauptteil; [2] Selbstdarstel-
     lungen; [3] Frembddarstellungen, Selbst- und Frembddarstellungen
     der Heilingungsbewegung.   Uebrige Spezialliteratur.
         Microfilm (positive). 3 reels   35 mm.   Reproduced for
     the American Theological Library Association Microtext Project
     by Department of Photoduplication, University of Chicago, 1968.
     IEG, MH-AH, NjMD

67   Hollenweger, Walter Jacob, 1927-
     Pentecost between black and white; five case studies on Pente-
     cost and politics [by] Walter J. Hollenweger. Belfast, Christian
     Journals Ltd., 1974. 143p. DLC, MCE, KyWAT

68   Hollenweger, Walter Jacob, 1927-
     The Pentecostal movement and the World Council of Churches,
     by Walter J. Hollenweger. In Ecumenical Review, 18 (July
     1966), 310-320.

69   Hollenweger, Walter Jacob, 1927-
     Pentecostalism and black power, by Walter J. Hollenweger.
     In Theology Today, 30 (Oct. 1973), 228-238.

70   Hollenweger, Walter Jacob, 1927-
     Pentecostalism and the third world, by Walter J. Hollenweger.
     In Dialog, 9 (Spring 1970), 122-129.

71   Hollenweger, Walter Jacob, 1927-
     Pfingstbewegung und Ökumene, von Walter J. Hollenweger.
     In Ökumenische Rundschau, 17:1 (1968), 57-59.

72   Hollenweger, Walter Jacob, 1927-
     Die Pfingstkirchen; Selbstarstellungen, Dokumente, Kommentare.

Hrsg. von Walter J. Hollenweger. Stuttgart, Evangelisches
Verlagswerk, 1971. 480p. (Die Kirchen der Welt [Reihe A
Bd. 7.]) DLC, MH-AH.

73 Hollenweger, Walter Jacob, 1927-
    Redécouvrir le pentecôtisme [par] Walter J. Hollenweger.
    In Communion, 24:1 (1970), 74-78.

74 Holsteen, Melbourne Edward
    Controlled resistance to change in a Pentecostal church.
    Minneapolis, 1968.   iii, 181ℓ.   Thesis (M. A.)--University of
    Minnesota.   MnU

75 Homrighausen, Elmer George, 1900-
    Pentecostalism in the third world, by E. G. Homrighausen.
    In Theology Today, 26 (Jan. 1970), 446-448.

76 Huffman, Jasper Abraham, 1880-1970.
    Profile of a modern Pentecostal movement, by Jasper A.
    Huffman.   Elkhart, Ind. , Bethel Publishing, c1968.   36p.
    Traces relationship between the Holiness and the Pentecostal
    movements.

77 Humburg, Emil, 1874-
    Was ist die Pfingsbewegung?   Mülheim/Ruhr, 1910.   16p.

78 Hutten, Kurt, 1901-
    Pfingstbewegen und Ökumene, von K. Hutton.   In Ökumenische
    Rundschau, 12:4 (1963), 221-228.

79 Keene, Gertrude Beckett
    Distinctive social values of the Pentecostal churches.   Los
    Angeles, 1938.   v, 96ℓ.   Thesis (M. A.)--University of Southern
    California.   CLSU

80 Kendrick, Klaude, 1917-
    The Pentecostal movement: hopes and hazards.   In Christian
    Century, 80 (May 8, 1963), 608-610.

81 Lidman, Sven, 1882-1960.
    Pingstvackalsens hemlighet.   Stockholm, A. Bonnier, 1926.   48p.

82 Linderholm, Emanuel, 1872-1937.
    Pingströrelsen dess förutsättningar och uppkomst ekstas, under
    och apokalyptik i Bibel och nytida folkreligiositet.   Stockholm, A.
    Bonniers, 1924.   315p.   MH-AH

83 Litell, Franklin Hamlin, 1917-
    Free churches and the Pentecostal challenge.   In Journal of
    Ecumenical Studies, 5 (Winter 1968), 131-132.

84 McLoughlin, William Gerald, 1922-
    Is there a third force in Christendom?   [By] William G.
    McLoughlin.   In Daedalus, 96 (Winter 1967), 43-68.

85	McLoughlin, William Gerald, 1922-
	Is there a Third Force in Christendom? [By] William G.
	McLoughlin. In McLoughlin, W. G. , ed. Religion in America.
	Boston, 1968, 45-72.

86	Martin, William Curtis, 1937-
	The God-hucksters of radio, by William C. Martin. In
	Atlantic, 225 (June 1970), 51-56.

86a	Meeting in the air. [Motion picture]
	WGBH-TV, 1974. 28 min. sd. color. 16mm. (Religious
	America.) DLC

87	Meyer, Donald Burton, 1923-
	The positive thinkers; a study of the American quest for
	health, wealth and personal power from Mary Baker Eddy to
	Norman Vincent Peale, by Donald Meyer. Garden City, N. Y. ,
	Doubleday, 1965. 358p. Includes a few references to Pente-
	costal churches. DLC, MCE, MSohG

88	Miracles of tongues and tones.
	In Independent, 66 (June 24, 1909), 1410-1411. Includes
	account of Spirit-inspired piano playing.

89	Molland, Einar, 1908-
	Christendom; the Christian churches, their doctrines, consti-
	tutional forms, and ways of worship. London, A. R. Mowbray,
	1959. xiv, 418p. Translation of Konfesjonskunnskap; kristen-
	hetens troshekjennelser og kirkesamfunn. "The Pentecostalists":
	p. 300-304. RPB

90	Molland, Einar, 1908-
	Christendom; the Christian churches, their doctrines, constitu-
	tional forms, and ways of worship. New York, Philosophical
	Library, 1959. xiv, 418p. Translation of Konfesjonskunnskap;
	kristenhetens troshekjennelser og kirkesamfunn. "The Pente-
	costalists": p. 300-304. DLC, MNtcA

91	Molland, Einar, 1908-
	Konfesjonskunnskap; kristenhetens troshekjennelser og kirke-
	samfunn. 2. rev. utg. Oslo, Land og Kirke, 1961. 352p.
	Includes Pentecostalists. CU

92	Murray, James Stirling
	What we can learn from the Pentecostal churches [by] J. S.
	Murray. In Christianity Today, 11 (June 9, 1967), 10-12.

93	Neve, Juergen Ludwig, 1865-1943.
	Churches and sects of Christendom, by J. L. Neve. Rev.
	ed. Blair, Neb. , Lutheran Publishing House, c1944. 509p.
	"The Holiness and Pentecostal organizations": p. 360-376.
	RPB

94	Newbigen, James Edward Lesslie, bp. , 1909-

Die Pfingstler und die Ökumenische Bewegung, von Lesslie Newbigen. In Ökumenische Rundschau, 13:4 (1964), 323-326.

95   Olila, James Howard
     Pentecostalism: the dynamics of recruitment in a modern socio-religious movement. Minneapolis, 1968. 57ℓ. Thesis (M. A.)--University of Minnesota. MnU

96   Packard, Vance Oakley, 1914-
     The status seekers; an exploration of class behavior in America and the hidden barriers that affect you, your community, your future, by Vance Packard. New York, D. McKay Co., 1959. 376p. "The long road from Pentecostal to Episcopal": p. 194-206. DLC

97   Pattison, Edward Mansell, 1933-
     Ideological support for the marginal middle class: faith healing and glossolalia [by] E. Mansell Pattison. In Zaretsky, I. I., ed. Religious movements in contemporary America. Princeton, N. J., c1974, 418-455.

98   Paulk, Earl Pearly, 1927-
     Your Pentecostal neighbor, by Earl P. Paulk. Cleveland, Tenn., Pathway Press, 1958. 237p. DLC, TxWaS

99   Pelletier, Joseph
     The Pentecostal renewal. In Liguorian, 59 (Aug. 1971), 27-29.

100 Pentecost revisited.
     In Christianity Today, 12 (Nov. 24, 1967), 39. On proposed evaluation of the Pentecostal movement being endorsed by the General Council of the Assemblies of God.

101 Quebedeaux, Richard, 1944-
     The wordly evangelicals. New York, Harper & Row, 1978. xii, 189p. Includes Pentecostals.

102 Reed, David Arthur, 1941-
     Pentecostalism and the ecumenical movement since 1948, by David A. Reed. Newton Centre, Mass., 1969. 42ℓ. Student paper--Andover Newton Theological School. MNtcA

103 Roebling, Karl
     Pentecostals around the world [by] Karl Roebling. Photos. by the author. Hicksville, N. Y., Exposition Press, c1978. 120p. DLC

104 Rooth, Richard Arlen
     Social structure in a Pentecostal church. Minneapolis, 1967. 101ℓ. Thesis (M. A.)--University of Minnesota. MnU.

105 Salisbury, William Seward

Religion in American culture, a sociological interpretation, by W. Seward Salisbury. Homewood, Ill. , Dorsey Press, 1964. ix, 538p. "Third-force Protestantism": p. 157-174.

106   Schram, Neva
Jesus died for Pentecostals too! In Christian Herald, 99 (Feb. 1976), 39-41.

107   Schwartz, Gary H. , 1936-
Sect ideologies and social status [by] Gary Schwartz. Chicago, University of Chicago Press, 1970. x, 260p. Based on thesis (Ph. D.)--Brandeis University, 1968. Study of Pentecostals and Seventh-Day Adventists. DLC

108   Schwartz, Gary H. , 1936-
Social status and religious ideology; a study of two types of Urban religious sects. Waltham, Mass. , 1968. iii, 286ℓ. Thesis (Ph. D.)--Brandeis University. Study of Pentecostals and Seventh-Day Adventists. MWalB

109   Smolchuck, Fred
What is a Pentecostal? Rev. ed. Dearborn, Mich. , Assemblies of God, Michigan District, 1975. 13p. First ed. published in 1965. "Originally appeared ... in the Detroit News. " KyWAT

110   Sorem, Anthony Milton
Some secular implications of the Pentecostal denomination. Minneapolis, 1969. v, 86ℓ . Thesis (M. A.)--University of Minnesota. MnU

111   Steinbeck, John, 1902-1968.
The grapes of wrath. New York, Viking Press, c1939. 473p. A major character in this novel on the Dust Bowl immigration to California is Jim Casy, a backslidden Pentecostal preacher.

112   Studd, George B. , 1861-1946.
My convictions as to the Pentecostal movement, irreverently called "The tongues, " by George B. Studd. Los Angeles, 1910. 8p.

113   Synan, Harold Vinson, 1934-
Charismatic bridges [by] Vinson Synan. Ann Arbor, Mich. , Word of Life, 1974. xv, 57p. On the relation between traditional Pentecostalism and Neo-Pentecostalism.

114   Synan, Harold Vinson, 1934-
Shaking up the Pentecostals [by] Vinson Synan. In Christianity Today, 20 (Jan. 2, 1976) 37. On meeting of the Society for Pentecostal Studies in Ann Arbor, Michigan in December. Includes comment on the attack of Timothy L. Smith on the use of glossolalia.

115   Theyssen, Gerd W.
       Pfingstgemeinden im Ökumenischen Rat. In Junge Kirche,
       24 (1963), 73-77.

116   Tinney, James Stephen
       Pentecostals refurbish the Upper Room [by] James S. Tin-
       ney. In Christianity Today, 10 (Apr. 1, 1966), 47-48.

117   The "Tongue" movement.
       In Independent, 66 (June 10, 1909), 1286-1289. By an un-
       named contributor in Hong Kong.

118   Torrey, Reuben Archer, 1856-1928.
       Is the present "tongues" movement of God? Answered by
       R. A. Torrey. Los Angeles, Biola Book Room, 19--. [11]p.

119   Webster, Douglas, 1920-
       The Pentecostals. In Churchman, 86 (Winter 1972), 290-
       292.

120   Whalen, William Joseph, 1926-
       The Pentecostals, by William J. Whalen. In U.S. Catholic,
       32 (Feb. 1967), 12-16.

121   Wilmore, Gayraud S.
       Black religion and Black radicalism, by Gayraud S. Wilmore.
       Garden City, N.Y., Doubleday, 1972. xiii, 344p. (The C. Eric
       Lincoln series on Black religion.) On Black Pentecostal
       churches: p. 210-215. DLC

122   Wilson, Bryan Ronald, 1926-
       Religious sects: a sociological study [by] Bryan Wilson.
       London, Weidenfeld & Nicolson, 1970. 256p. (World univer-
       sity library.) DLC

123   Wilson, Bryan Ronald, 1926-
       Religious sects: a sociological study [by] Bryan Wilson.
       New York, McGraw-Hill, 1970. 256p. (World university li-
       brary.) DLC

124   Womack, David Alfred, 1933-
       The wellsprings of the Pentecostal movement, by David A.
       Womack. Written in cooperation with the Committee on Ad-
       vance for the General Council of the Assemblies of God.
       Springfield, Mo. , Gospel Publishing House, 1968. 96p. DLC,
       MSohG, TxWaS

125   Zimmerman, Thomas Fletcher, 1912-
       Plea for the Pentecostalists [by] Thomas F. Zimmerman.
       In Christianity Today, 7 (Jan. 4, 1963), 11-12.

125a   Zimmerman, Thomas Fletcher, 1912-
       Priorities & beliefs of Pentecostals [by] Thomas F. Zimmer-

man. In Christianity Today, 25 (Sept. 4, 1981), 36-37.

126 Zimmerman, Thomas Fletcher, 1912-
     Rags to riches, by Thomas F. Zimmerman. In Christian
     Life, 28 (July 1966), 32-33, 55-56.

127 Zimmerman, Thomas Fletcher, 1912-
     The reason for the rise of the Pentecostal movement [by]
     Thomas F. Zimmerman. In Synan, H. V. , ed. Aspects of
     Pentecostal-Charismatic origins. Plainfield, N. J. , 1975, 5-13.

128 Zimmerman, Thomas Fletcher, 1912-
     Where is the "third force" going? [By] Thomas F. Zimmer-
     man. In Christianity Today, 4 (Aug. 1, 1960), 15-16, 18.

                       --BIBLIOGRAPHY

129 Faupel, David William, 1944-
     The American Pentecostal movement; a bibliographical es-
     say, by David W. Faupel. Wilmore, Ky. , B. L. Fisher Li-
     brary, Asbury Theological Seminary, 1972. 56p. (Occasional
     bibliographical papers of the B. L. Fisher Library, 2.) "Re-
     vised version of the text published originally in the 1972 Pro-
     ceedings of the American Theological Library Association. "
     KyLxCB, KyWAT, MNtcA, TxWaS

130 Faupel, David William, 1944-
     Bibliography on eschatology. Wilmore, Ky. , B. L. Fisher
     Library, Asbury Theological Seminary, 1970. 59,12ℓ . In-
     cludes Pentecostal publications. KyWAT

131 Hollenweger, Walter Jacob, 1927-
     Handbuch der Pfingstbewegung, von Walter J. Hollenweger.
     Zürich, 1966. 3v. in 10. Inau. -Diss. --Zürich.
     Contents: 1. Hauptt. Sektierer oder Enthusiasten?
     2. Hauptt. Die einzelnen Pfingstgruppen, nach geographi-
     schen Gesichtsspunkten gegliedert: [1] Afrika; [2] Nordamerika;
     [3] Lateinamerika; [4] Asien, Australien und Oceanien; [5]-[6]
     Europa. 3. Hauptt. Kommentierte Bibliographie, Kurzbio-
     graphien: [1] Einfuhrung in den III. Hauptteil; [2] Selbstdar-
     stellungen; [3] Frembddarstellungen, Selbst- und Frembddarstel-
     lungen der Heiligungsbewegung. Uebrige Spezialliteratur.
     Microfilm (positive). 3 reels 35 mm. Reproduced for
     the American Theological Library Association Microtext Project
     by Department of Photoduplication, University of Chicago, 1968.
     IEG, MH-AH, NjMD

132 Hollenweger, Walter Jacob, 1927-
     Literatur von und über die Pfingst bewegung (Weltkonferenzen,
     Holland, Belgien), von Walter J. Hollenweger. In Nederlands
     Theologisch Tijdschrift, 18 (Apr. 1964), 289-306.

133 Hollenweger, Walter Jacob, 1927-
     Literatur von und über die Pfingsbewegung (Weltkonferenzen,
     Holland, Belgien), von Walter J. Hollenweger. Wageningen,
     H. Veenman und Zonen, 1964. 17p. Reprinted from Meder-
     lands Theologisch Tijdschrift, 18 (Apr. 1964), 289-306.

134 Journal of Pentecostal literature.
     1- 1975- Fort Pierce, Fla.

135 McDonnell, Kilian, 1921-
     New dimensions in research on Pentecostalism. In Worship,
     45 (Apr. 1971), 214-219.

136 Martin, Ira Jay, 1911-
     Glossolalia, the gift of tongues; a bibliography [by] Ira J.
     Martin, III. Cleveland, Tenn. , Pathway Press, 1970. 72p.
     DLC, MSohG

137 Melton, John Gordon, 1942-
     A reader's guide to the church's ministry of healing, by
     J. Gordon Melton. Evanston, Ill. , Academy of Religion and
     Psychical Research, 1973. 75p. Includes Pentecostal publi-
     cations. KyWAT

138 Mills, Watson Early, 1939-
     Literature on glossolalia [by] Watson E. Mills. In Journal
     of the American Scientific Affiliation, 26 (Dec. 1974), 169-173.

139 Mills, Watson Early, 1939-
     Speaking in tongues--a classified bibliography, by Watson E.
     Mills. Franklin Springs, Ga. , Society for Pentecostal Studies,
     1974. 66p.

140 Stotts, George Raymond, 1929-
     Pentecostal archival material, its nature and availability,
     with emphasis on the Southwest, by George R. Stotts. Spring-
     field, Mo. , 1974. 20ℓ. "A paper presented to the Church
     History Section, the American Academy of Religion, SW Region,
     Austin College, Sherman, Texas, March 15-16, 1974. " CCSC

141 Tinder, Donald George, 1938-
     The Holy Spirit from Pentecost to the present: book survey
     [by] Donald Tinder. In Christianity Today, 19 (May 19, 1975),
     11-12, 16, 18, 20.

          --BIOGRAPHY

142 Crayne, Richard
     Pentecostal handbook. Morristown, Tenn. , 1963.   113p.
     TxWaS

143 Harrell, Irene (Burk), comp. 1927-

God ventures: true accounts of God in the lives of men.
Waco, Tex. , Word Books, 1970. 131p.

144 Harrell, Irene (Burk), comp. 1927-
God ventures: true accounts of God in the lives of men.
Plainfield, N. J. , Logos International; London, Good Reading,
c1970. 131p.

145 Hollenweger, Walter Jacob, 1927-
Handbuch der Pfingstbewegung, von Walter J. Hollenweger.
Zürich, 1966. 3v. in 10. Inaug. -Diss. --Zürich.
Contents: 1. Hauptt. Sektierer oder Enthusiasten?
2. Hauptt. Die einzelnen Pfingstgruppen, nach geographischen
Gesichtsspunkten gegliedert: [1] Afrika; [2] Nordamerika;
[3] Lateinamerika; [4] Asien, Australien und Oceanien; [5]-[6]
Europa; 3. Hauptt. Kommentierte Bibliographie, Kurzbio-
graphien: [1] Einfuhrung in den III. Hauptteil; [2] Selbstdar-
stellungen der Heilingungsbewegung. Uebrige Spezialliteratur.
Microfilm (positive). 3 reels. 35mm. Reproduced for the
American Theological Library Association Microtext Project by
Department of Photoduplication, University of Chicago, 1968.
IEG, MH-AH, NjMD

146 Lindsay, Gordon, 1906-1973.
Men who changed the world. Dallas, Voice of Healing Publishing Co. , 19--. 219p.

147 Lindsay, Gordon, 1906-1973, comp.
Men who heard from heaven; sketches from the life stories
of evangelists whose ministries are reaching millions, as told
by themselves. Compiled by Gordon Lindsay. Dallas, Voice
of Healing Publishing Co. , c1953. vi, 165p. TxWaS

148 Lindsay, Gordon, 1906-1973.
They saw it happen. Dallas, Christ for the Nations, 1972.
47p. KyWAT

149 Morris, James, 1926-
The preachers. Illustrations by Tom Huffman. New York,
St. Martin's Press, 1973. x, 418p. Includes biographies of
A. A. Allen, Oral Roberts, C. W. Burpo and Kathryn Kuhl-
man. DLC

--CATECHISMS AND CREEDS

150 Barratt, Thomas Ball, 1862-1940.
Kiongozi katika neno la Mungu. Ledetråd i Guda ord [av]
T. B. Barratt. Omarbeidet av Osvald Orlien. Chuo hiki
kimefasirika katika lugha ya Kinorvêga kwa lugha ya Kiswahili
na P. Langseth. Oslo, Filadelfiaforlaget, 1951. 63p. DLC

151 Gentile, Ernest B. , 1929-

Charismatic catechism, by Ernest B. Gentile. Harrison,
Ark. , New Leaf Press, 1977. 199p.

152   Gentile, Ernest B. , 1929-
God and His word [by] Ernest B. Gentile. 2d ed. , rev.
and enlarged. Hong Kong, Asian Outreach; San Jose, Calif. ,
Gospel Temple, 1971. 199p.

153   Gruits, Patricia Doris (Beall), 1923-
Understanding God; a catechism of Christian doctrine, by
Patricia D. Gruits. Detroit, Evangel Press, c1962. 328p.
Cover title.

154   Gruits, Patricia Doris (Beall), 1923-
Understanding God, by Patricia Beall Gruits. 2d ed.
[Monroeville, Pa.] Whitaker Books, 1972. 422p.

155   Purdie, James Eustace
567 Christian answers, by J. E. Purdie. Kisumu, Kenya,
Evangel Publishing House, c1972. 94p.

--CLERGY

156   Gaxiola, Manuel Jesús, 1927-
The Pentecostal ministry [by] Manuel J. Gaxiola. In Inter-
national Review of Mission, 66 (Jan. 1977), 57-63. On Latin
America.

157   Hollenweger, Walter Jacob, 1927-
Ordination: Pentecostal [by] W. J. Hollenweger. In Davies,
J. G. , ed. A dictionary of liturgy and worship. New York,
1972, 295-296.

158   Saracco, J. Norberto
The type of ministry adopted by the Pentecostal churches
in Latin America [by] J. Norberto Saracco. In International
Review of Mission, 66 (Jan. 1977), 64-70.

159   Wilson, Bryan Ronald, 1926-
Pentecostalist minister: role conflicts and status contradic-
tions [by] Bryan R. Wilson. In American Journal of Sociology,
64 (Mar. 1959), 494-504; reprinted in Wilson, B. R. , ed.
Patterns of sectarianism; organization and ideology in social
and religious movements. London, 1967, p. 138-157.

--CONGRESSES

-- --EUROPEAN PENTECOSTAL CONFERENCE

(Stockholm, 1939)

160 European Pentecostal Conference, Stockholm, 1939.
     Europeiska Pingstkoferensen i Stockholm den 5-12 juni 1939.
     Tal, samtal och predikningar. Stockholm, Förlaget Filadelfia,
     1939. 436p.

                 -- --PENTECOSTAL WORLD CONFERENCE

161 Fischer, Harold Arthur
     Progress toward world fellowship of the various Pentecostal
     groups. Fort Worth, 1950. vi, 80ℓ. Thesis (M. A.)--Texas
     Christian University. TxFTC

                     (3d, London, 1952)

162 Pentecostal World Conference, 3d, London, 1952.
     World Pentecostal Conference, 1952: a brochure setting
     forth interesting aspects of the great world-wide Pentecostal
     revival and the third World Conference of Pentecostal Churches.
     Compiled and edited by H. W. Greenway in collaboration with
     Donald Gee [and] Ian Macpherson. London, British Pentecostal
     Fellowship, 195-. 76p.

                   (4th, Stockholm, 1955)

163 Pentecostal World Conference, 4th, Stockholm, 1955.
     Världspingstkonferensen i Stockholm den 13-20 juni 1955; i
     ord och bild. Stockholm, Förlaget Filadelfia, 1955. 150p.
     MH-AH

                   (5th, Toronto, 1955)

164 Pentecostal World Conference, 5th, Toronto, 1955.
     Discursos evangélicos: proferidos na quinta convenção mun-
     dial dos Pentecostais em Toronto, Canadá, 14 a 21 de setem-
     bro de 1958. Editodos por Donald Gee. Rio de Janeiro,
     Libros Evangélicos, 1960. 224p. Translation of Messages
     preached at the fifth triennial Pentecostal World Conference.

165 Pentecostal World Conference, 5th, Toronto, 1958.
     Messages preached at the fifth triennial Pentecostal World
     Conference, held in the Coliseum Arena, Exhibition Grounds,
     Toronto, Canada, from September 14-21, 1958, edited by
     Donald Gee. Toronto, Advisory Committee for the Conference
     by Testimony Press, c1958. xxiv, 188p. Cover title: The
     fifth World Pentecostal Conference. DLC, TxWaS

                   (6th, Jerusalem, 1961)

166 Pentecostal World Conference, 6th, Jerusalem, 1961.
     Addresses presented at the sixth Pentecostal World Confer-
     ence, Jerusalem, Israel, May 19th to 21st, 1961. Toronto,
     Testimony Press, c1961. 60p.

167 Gilbert, Arthur, 1926-
     Pentecost among the Pentecostals. In Christian Century,
     78 (June 28, 1961), 794. American rabbi's critique of the
     1961 Pentecostal World Conference in Jerusalem.

168 Henry, Carl Ferdinand Howard, 1913-
     Pentecostal meeting makes Holy Land history [by] C. F. H. H.
     In Christianity Today, 5 (May 22, 1961), 737, 740. On sixth
     Pentecostal World Conference, held in Jerusalem in May.

                    (8th, Rio de Janeiro, 1967)

169 Pentecostal World Conference, 8th, Rio de Janeiro, 1967.
     O Espírito Santo glorificando a Cristo. Anais da oitava
     conferência mundial Pentecostal, 18 a 23 de Julho de 1967,
     Rio de Janeiro. Coordenacão de Emilio Conde. Rio de
     Janeiro, 196-. 198p.

170 Pentecostal tongues & converts.
     In Time, 90 (July 28, 1967), 64. On Pentecostal World
     Conference, Rio de Janeiro.

171 Pentecostals in Rio.
     In Christianity Today, 11 (August 18, 1967), 49. On the
     eighth Pentecostal World Conference, held in Rio de Janeiro
     in July.

                    (10th, Seoul, 1973)

172 The Spirit in Asia.
     In Time, 102 (Oct. 8, 1973), 102. On the tenth Pentecostal
     World Conference, held in Seoul.

                    (11th, London, 1976)

173 Synan, Harold Vinson, 1934-
     The Pentecostal tide is coming in [by] Vinson Synan. In
     Christianity Today, 21 (Nov. 5, 1976), 78-80. On the eleventh
     Pentecostal World Conference in London in September.

                    (12th, Vancouver, 1979)

174 Mackey, Lloyd
     Pentecostals proliferate and bridge barriers. In Christianity
     Today, 23 (Nov. 2, 1979), 61-63. On twelfth Pentecostal World
     Conference held in Vancouver, British Columbia in October.

               --CONTROVERSIAL LITERATURE

175 Bartleman, Frank, 1871-1935.
     A voice in the wilderness. Los Angeles, 19--. [12]p.
     Caption title.

175a Drew, Ralph Earl
    Hey, you're stealing our stuff. In Christian Life, 39 (July
    1977), 25-26, 67. The charismatic movement: an unbiased
    look.

176 Elsom, John R.
    Pentecostalism versus the Bible; or, The tongues movement
    and why I left it, by John R. Elsom. Los Angeles, Wetzel
    Publishing Co. , c1937. 60p. NcD

177 Fiorentino, Joseph, 1912-
    The new Pentecost and the old. Woburn, Mass. , 1971.
    16p.

178 Gause, Rufus Hollis, 1925-
    Issues in Pentecostalism [by] R. Hollis Gause. In Spittler,
    R. P. , ed. Perspectives on the new Pentecostalism. Grand
    Rapids, Mich. , 1976, 106-116.

179 Hughes, Ray Harrison, 1924-
    The new Pentecostalism: perspective of a classical Pente-
    costal administrator [by] Ray H. Hughes. In Spittler, R. P. ,
    ed. Perspectives on the new Pentecostalism. Grand Rapids,
    Mich. , 1976, 166-180.

180 Hughes, Ray Harrison, 1924-
    A traditional Pentecostal look at the new Pentecostals [by]
    Ray H. Hughes. In Christianity Today, 18 (June 7, 1974),
    6-10.

181 Kendrick, Klaude, 1917-
    The Pentecostal movement: hopes and hazzards. In Chris-
    tian Century, 80 (May 8, 1963), 608-610.

182 Richards, William Thomas Henry
    Pentecost is dynamite [by] W. T. H. Richards. Nashville,
    Abingdon Press, c1972. 94p. MBU-T, TxWaS

183 Robinson, Wayne Austin, 1937-
    I once spoke in tongues, by Wayne A. Robinson. Atlanta,
    Forum House, 1973. 144p. DLC

184 Robinson, Wayne Austin, 1937-
    I once spoke in tongues [by] Wayne A. Robinson. New
    York, Pillar Books, 1975, c1973. 128p.

185 Spence, Othniel Talmadge, 1926-
    Charismatism: awakening or apostasy? By O. Talmadge
    Spence. Greenville, S. C. , Bob Jones University Press, 1978.
    xi, 266p. DLC

186 Spence, Othniel Talmadge, 1926-
    A Pentecostal speaks to Pentecostalists, by O. Talmadge

Spence. In Faith for the Family, 1 (Sept. /Oct. 1973), 4-8.

--DEVOTIONAL LITERATURE

187   Bible. English. Selections. 1967. Authorized.
      The rhyming Bible. Compiled by Gordon Lindsay. Dallas,
      Christ for the Nations, 1970, c1967. 3v. in 1.

188   Caldwell, Louis Oliver, 1935-
      Good morning, Lord; devotions for college students [by]
      Louis O. Caldwell. Grand Rapids, Mich. , Baker Book House,
      1971. [64]p. DLC

189   Flower, Alice (Reynolds), 1890-
      From under the threshold (Ezekiel 47:1); devotional heart
      talks. Framingham, Mass. , Christian Workers' Union, 1936.
      110p.

190   Hembree, Charles Ron, 1938-
      Devotions for everyday living [by] Charles R. Hembree.
      Grand Rapids, Mich. , Baker Book House, 1971. [64]p.
      (Good morning, Lord) DLC

191   Hembree, Charles Ron, 1938-
      Voice of the turtledove [by] Charles R. Hembree.   Grand
      Rapids, Mich. , Baker Book House, 1971. 140p. DLC

192   Hillary, Derrick
      Our Lord's fiancée: portraits and profiles. Hong Kong,
      World Outreach Publishers, 1969. 254p.

193   Pethrus, Lewi, 1884-1974.
      Julen harold; illustrated kalender tugoandra argangen, re-
      digerad av Lewi Pethrus och G. E. Söderholm. Stockholm,
      Filadelfia, 1937. 159p. WaE

194   Pethrus, Lewi, 1884-1974.
      Under den högstes beskärm. 2. uppl. Bromma, 1966.
      402p. DLC

195   Richards, William Thomas Henry, 1916-1974.
      God's great promises: fifty-two Bible promises, one for
      each week of the year [by] W. T. H. Richards. Nashville,
      Abingdon Press, 1973. 127p.

196   Roberts, Oral, 1918-
      Prayers for seed-faith living. Tulsa, 1970. 127p.

197   Robinson, Martha (Wing), 1874-1936.
      Kleinode göttlicher Weisheit. [Brooklyn, N. Y. , 19--] 1v.
      (unpaged) Translation of Treasures of wisdom. "Diese Aus-
      wahl von Zitaten aus Schriften und Predigten von M. W.

Robinson wurde von Herrn und Frau Gordon P. Gardiner zu-
sammengestellt. "

198 Robinson, Martha (Wing), 1874-1936.
       Treasures of wisdom. [Brooklyn, N. Y. , 19--] 1v. (unpaged)
       Compiled by Mr. and Mrs. Gordon P. Gardiner.

199 Warner, Wayne Earl, 1933-
       Devotions for servicemen [by] Wayne E. Warner.   Grand
       Rapids, Mich. , Baker Book House, 1971. 64p. (Good morn-
       ing, Lord) DLC

--DOCTRINAL AND CONTROVERSIAL WORKS

200 Allen, Asa Alonso, 1911-1970.
       The curse of madness; or, Has America gone mad?   Mira-
       cle Valley, Ariz. , 19--. 83p. "Special pictorial supplement:
       18 pictures of demons as seen and drawn by a demon pos-
       sessed woman. "--p. 53-71. MnCS

201 Allen, Asa Alonso, 1911-1970.
       Demon possession today, by A. A. Allen.   Lamar, Colo. ,
       A. A. Allen Revivals, c1953. 157p. TxWaS

202 Allen, Asa Alonso, 1911-1970.
       Demon possession today and how to be free.   Hereford,
       Ariz. , A. A. Allen Publications, c1953. 160p. OBlC

203 Allen, Asa Alonso, 1911-1970.
       Divorce the lying demon; a new approach to an old problem.
       Miracle Valley, Ariz. , 19--. 21p. MnCS

204 Allen, Asa Alonso, 1911-1970.
       God will heal you, by A. A. Allen.   Miracle Valley, Ariz. ,
       195-. 60p.

205 Allen, Asa Alonso, 1911-1970.
       God's guarantee to heal you, by A. A. Allen.   Lamar,
       Colo. , c1950. 168p. TxWaS

206 Allen, Asa Alonso, 1911-1970.
       The man whose number is six-sixty-six, by A. A. Allen.
       Dallas, c1953. 40p. TxWaS

207 Allen, Asa Alonso, 1911-1970.
       Miracles today, by A. A. Allen.   Dallas, 19--. 65p.
       TxWaS

208 Allen, Asa Alonso, 1911-1970.
       The price of God's miracle working power; sequel to God's
       guarantee to heal you....   Lamar, Colo. , 1950. 122p.
       CLamB

209   Allen, Asa Alonso, 1911-1970.
        Prisons with stained glass windows, by A. A. Allen.   Mira-
      cle Valley, Ariz., A. A. Allen Revivals, c1963.   115p.

210   Allen, Asa Alonso, 1911-1970.
        Receive ye the Holy Ghost, by A. A. Allen.   Lamar, Colo.,
      1950.   32p.   TxWaS

211   Allen, Asa Alonso, 1911-1970.
        Receive ye the Holy Ghost, by A. A. Allen.   Miracle Valley,
      Ariz., 19--.   40p.

212   Allen, John Harden, 1847-1930.
        Judah's sceptre and Joseph's birthright; or, The royal family
      and the many nations of Israel, by J. H. Allen.   Portland,
      Ore., 1902.   377p.   "The great bulk of Israelites are not the
      Jews": p. 71.   DLC

213   Allen, John Harden, 1847-1930.
        Judah's sceptre and Joseph's birthright; an analysis of the
      prophecies of scripture in regard to the royal family of Judah
      and the many nations of Israel, by J. H. Allen.   4th ed.
      Boston, A. A. Beauchamp, 1917.   377p.   "The great bulk of
      Israelites are not the Jews": p. 71.   CaBVaU, CoD, CoDU,
      DLC, NNUT, OCH, OrP, WaS

214   Allen, John Harden, 1847-1930.
        The national number and heraldry of the United States of
      America.   Boston, A. A. Beauchamp, 1919.   83p.   DLC, MiU,
      NN, WaS

215   Allen, John Harden, 1847-1930.
        The national rebirth of Judah, by J. H. Allen.   Boston,
      A. A. Beauchamp, 1920.   125p.   DLC, MiU, PPDrop

216   Allen, John Harden, 1847-1930.
        The spirit man; or, The hidden man of the heart: a work
      on pneumatology and psychology showing the Biblical distinctions
      between the soul and the spirit of man, and the harmony of
      these with the objective and the subjective man of science, by
      J. H. Allen.   Los Angeles, Press of the Grafton Publishing
      Corporation, c1915.   232p.   DLC

217   Anderson, E. Howard
        Receive the Holy Spirit and power.   How you can receive
      the gift of the Holy Spirit and power by faith.   By E. Howard
      Anderson.   Stamford, Conn., 196-.   64p.

218   Armstrong, Hart Reid, 1912-
        All things for life, by Hart R. Armstrong.   Wichita, Kan.,
      Defenders of the Christian Faith, c1969.   94p.

219   Armstrong, Hart Reid, 1912-

The beast, by Hart R. Armstrong. Kansas City, Mo.,
Defenders of the Christian Faith, c1967. 64p.

220 Armstrong, Hart Reid, 1912-
He is risen! By Hart R. Armstrong. Wichita, Kan., Defenders of the Christian Faith, c1969. 31p.

221 Armstrong, Hart Reid, 1912-
How great thou art! By Hart R. Armstrong. Wichita, Kan.,
Defenders of the Christian Faith, c1975. 34p.

222 Armstrong, Hart Reid, 1912-
The impossible events of Bible prophecy, by Hart R. Armstrong. Wichita, Kan., Defenders of the Christian Faith,
c1975. 94p.

223 Armstrong, Hart Reid, 1912-
Primer of prophecy, by Hart R. Armstrong. Wichita, Kan.,
Defenders of the Christian Faith, 1970-1971. 3v.

224 Armstrong, Hart Reid, 1912-
The rebel, by Hart R. Armstrong. Kansas City, Mo., Defenders of the Christian Faith, c1967. 64p.

225 Armstrong, Hart Reid, 1912-
The seven churches of Revelation, by Hart R. Armstrong.
Wichita, Kan., Defenders of the Christian Faith, c1974. 79p.

226 Armstrong, Hart Reid, 1912-
To those who are left, by Hart R. Armstrong. Kansas City,
Mo., Defenders of the Christian Faith, 19--. 64p.

227 Armstrong, Hart Reid, 1912-
What will happen to the United States? [By] Hart Armstrong.
Kansas City, Mo., Defenders of the Christian Faith, c1969.
55p. WiH

228 Armstrong, Hart Reid, 1912-
Why I believe in the Bible? By Hart R. Armstrong. Kansas City, Mo., Defenders of the Christian Faith, c1971. 62p.

229 Austin-Sparks, T.
What is man? By T. Austin-Sparks. Cloverdale, Ind.,
Ministry of Life, 19--. 110p.

230 Axelsson, Henry
Andens gaavor. Stockholm, Förlaget Filadelfia, 1958. 103p.
MH-AH

231 Axelsson, Henry
De femeente ... het huis van God. Rotterdam/Leeuwarden,
Stichting Volle Evangelie Lectuur, 1958. 53p. Translation of
Guds församling.

231a Bachman, Delbert Strader
       The truth that makes us free, by Delbert S. Bachman.
       Lebanon, N.J., 1944. 12p.

232   Baker, H. A.
       Demons, by H. A. Baker. _____, Yünnan, 19--.
       90p. CLamB

233   Baker, H. A.
       Demons, by H. A. Baker. Youngstown, Ohio, Christ Mis-
       sionary Society, 19--. 100p.

234   Baker, H. A.
       Devils and dupes, by H. A. Baker. _____, Yünnan,
       19--. 234p. CLamB

235   Baker, H. A.
       Devils and dupes, by H. A. Baker. Youngstown, Ohio,
       Christ Missionary Society, 19--. 234p.

236   Baker, H. A.
       Healing in Jesus, by H. A. Baker. Youngstown, Ohio,
       Christ Missionary Society, 19--. 68p.

237   Baker, H. A.
       Heaven and the angels, by H. A. Baker. Minneapolis,
       Osterhus Publishing House, 19--. 262p. CLamB

238   Baker, H. A.
       The three worlds, by H. A. Baker. Minneapolis, Osterhus
       Publishing House, 19--. 420p. CLamB, OCl

239   Baker, H. A.
       The three worlds, by H. A. Baker. Youngstown, Ohio,
       Christ Missionary Society, 19--. 420p.

240   Baker, H. A.
       Visiones mas alla del velo. Callaom, Peru, W. L. Hunter,
       1952. 120p. Translation of Visions beyond the veil.

241   Baker, H. A.
       Visions beyond the veil, by H. A. Baker. Youngstown,
       Ohio, Christ Missionary Society, 19--. 122p.

242   Baker, H. A.
       Visions beyond the veil, by H. A. Baker. Minneapolis,
       Osterhus Publishing House, 19--. 122p. CLamB

243   Balliet, Emil Alexander, 1911-1977.
       Who will win the war in the Middle East--Israel, Egypt, or
       Russia? By Emil Balliet and Morris Cerullo. San Diego,
       World Evangelism, 1970. 60p.

244   Barham, Wendell S.
       Simple steps to the baptism of the Holy Spirit, by W. S.
       Barham. San Antonio, Tex., 19--. 19p. TxWaS

245   Barker, Harold P.
       Christ's vicar, by Harold P. Barker. Kilmarnock, Scot.,
       J. Ritchie, 19--. 176p.

246   Barker, Harold P.
       Understanding the Holy Spirit, by Harold P. Barker. West-
       chester, Ill., Good News Publishers, 1959. 63p.

247   Barratt, Thomas Ball, 1862-1940.
       Hinter Tod unc Grab. Gibt es eine Hölle? Aus dem Nor-
       wegischen übers, und erweitert von Otto Witt. Reisach, Kreis
       Heilbronn; Württemberg, Verlag Deutsche Volksmission Ent-
       schiedener Christen, 1948. 72p. DLC

248   Barratt, Thomas Ball, 1862-1940.
       In the days of the latter rain. London, Simpkin, Marshall,
       1909. viii, 124p. L

249   Barratt, Thomas Ball, 1862-1940.
       In the days of the latter rain. Rev. ed. London, Elim
       Publishing Co., 1928. 222p. L

250   Barratt, Thomas Ball, 1862-1940.
       To seekers after "The promise of the Father," by T. B.
       Barratt. Bedford, Eng., 1911. 32p.

251   Bartleman, Frank, -1956.
       A treasure chest: nuggets of gold. 2d ed. Los Angeles,
       1927. 28p.

252   Baur, Benjamin A.
       Spiritual experiences every Christian ought to receive, by
       Benjamin A. Baur. Rochester, N.Y., Glad Tidings Publishing
       Society, 19--. 124p.

253   Baxter, W. J. Ern
       The measure of faith, by W. J. Ern Baxter. Detroit,
       Evangel Press, 1951. 15p.

254   Beall, James Lee, 1924-
       Adoption and sonship, by James L. Beall. Detroit, Bethesda
       Missionary Temple, 19--. 30p. (Galatians series, 4) Cover
       title.

255   Beall, James Lee, 1924-
       All things under His feet. Detroit, Bethesda Missionary
       Temple, 19--. 38p. (The eternal purposes of God, 4) Cover
       title.

256 Beall, James Lee, 1924-
        Are you headed for a storm? Detroit, Bethesda Missionary
     Temple, 19--. 34p. Cover title. On Jonah.

257 Beall, James Lee, 1924-
        Building a new faith. Detroit, Bethesda Missionary Temple,
     19--. 38p. Cover title.

258 Beall, James Lee, 1924-
        Can moderns believe in miracles? Detroit, Bethesda Mis-
     sionary Temple, 19--. 38p. Cover title. At head of title:
     A miracle is an event completely out of the ordinary natural
     sequence of events.

259 Beall, James Lee, 1924-
        Dangers of delving into demonology. Detroit, Bethesda
     Missionary Temple, 19--. 38p. Cover title.

260 Beall, James Lee, 1924-
        Dead or alive. Detroit, Bethesda Missionary Temple,
     19--. 38p. Cover title.

261 Beall, James Lee, 1924-
        Depression. Detroit, Bethesda Missionary Temple, 19--.
     39p. Cover title.

262 Beall, James Lee, 1924-
        The devices of satan, by James L. Beall. Detroit, Bethesda
     Missionary Temple, 19--. 23p. (The manifestation of the sons
     of God, 3) Cover title.

263 Beall, James Lee, 1924-
        Election and predestination: a universe with divine order.
     Detroit, Bethesda Missionary Temple, 19--. 34p. (The eter-
     nal purposes of God, 1.) Cover title.

264 Beall, James Lee, 1924-
        Enlightened and understanding eyes. Detroit, Bethesda Mis-
     sionary Temple, 19--. 38p. (The eternal purposes of God, 3.)
     Cover title.

265 Beall, James Lee, 1924-
        The female of the species. Detroit, Bethesda Missionary
     Temple, 19--. 38p. Cover title.

266 Beall, James Lee, 1924-
        Filled with the fullness of God. Detroit, Bethesda Mission-
     ary Temple, 19--. 38p. Cover title.

267 Beall, James Lee, 1924-
        Find the rock. Detroit, Bethesda Missionary Temple, 19--.
     38p. Cover title.

268 Beall, James Lee, 1924-
The fire and the dove. Detroit, Bethesda Missionary Temple, 19--. 39p. Cover title.

269 Beall, James Lee, 1924-
The four horsemen of Revelation, by James L. Beall. Detroit, Bethesda Missionary Temple, 19--. 33p. Cover title.

270 Beall, James Lee, 1924-
The gifts of the Holy Spirit, by James L. Beall. Detroit, Bethesda Missionary Temple, 19--. 29p. Cover title.

271 Beall, James Lee, 1924-
Give yourself away. Detroit, Bethesda Missionary Temple, 19--. 34p. Cover title.

272 Beall, James Lee, 1924-
Glimpses of the kingdom. Detroit, Bethesda Missionary Temple, 19--. 33p. Cover title.

273 Beall, James Lee, 1924-
The grace of God, by James L. Beall. Detroit, Bethesda Missionary Temple, 19--. 30p. Cover title.

274 Beall, James Lee, 1924-
Grow up! By James L. Beall. Detroit, Bethesda Missionary Temple, 19--. 23p. Cover title.

275 Beall, James Lee, 1924-
The guidance of God. Detroit, Bethesda Missionary Temple, 19--. 38p. Cover title.

276 Beall, James Lee, 1924-
The heart of healing: lessons in caring. Detroit, Bethesda Missionary Temple, 19--. 38p. Cover title.

277 Beall, James Lee, 1924-
Heaven: what is it? Detroit, 19--. 33p. Cover title.

278 Beall, James Lee, 1924-
Hell, what is it? Detroit, Bethesda Missionary Temple, 19--. 30p. Cover title.

279 Beall, James Lee, 1924-
In the twinkling of an eye. Detroit, Bethesda Missionary Temple, 19--. 39p. Cover title.

280 Beall, James Lee, 1924-
Israel, the nations, and the church, by James L. Beall. Detroit, Bethesda Missionary Temple, 19--. 27p. Cover title.

281 Beall, James Lee, 1924-

The joy of belonging to God. Detroit, Bethesda Missionary Temple, 19--. 38p. Cover title.

282   Beall, James Lee, 1924-
The judgment seat of Christ, by James Beall. Detroit, Bethesda Missionary Temple, 19--. 23p. Cover title.

283   Beall, James Lee, 1924-
Law & grace, by James L. Beall. Detroit, Bethesda Missionary Temple, 19--. 34p. (Galatians series, 2.) Cover title.

284   Beall, James Lee, 1924-
The laying on of hands. Detroit, Bethesda Missionary Temple, 19--. 27p. (New Testament church series, 5.) Cover title.

285   Beall, James Lee, 1924-
Learning creative prayer. Detroit, Bethesda Missionary Temple, 19--. 38p. Cover title.

286   Beall, James Lee, 1924-
The life-style of the kingdom. Detroit, Bethesda Missionary Temple, 19--. 34p. Cover title. At head of title: There is a way to live and a way not to live. The universe will back only one way.

287   Beall, James Lee, 1924-
Living at your best. Detroit, Bethesda Missionary Temple, 19--. 39p. Cover title.

288   Beall, James Lee, 1924-
The local church. Detroit, Bethesda Missionary Temple, 19--. 27p. (New Testament church series, 1.) Cover title.

289   Beall, James Lee, 1924-
The Lord's Supper. Detroit, Bethesda Missionary Temple, 19--. 38p. Cover title.

290   Beall, James Lee, 1924-
Lucifer, his pride and folly, by James L. Beall. Detroit, Bethesda Missionary Temple, 19--. 25p. (The manifestation of the sons of God, 1.) Cover title.

291   Beall, James Lee, 1924-
Men & angels, by James L. Beall. Detroit, Bethesda Missionary Temple, 19--. 31p. (The manifestation of the sons of God, 2.) Cover title.

292   Beall, James Lee, 1924-
The ministry of tithing. Detroit, Bethesda Missionary Temple, 19--. 38p. Cover title.

293 Beall, James Lee, 1924-
     The ministry of women, by James L. Beall. Detroit,
     Bethesda Missionary Temple, 19--. 25p. (New Testament
     church series, 3.) Cover title.

294 Beall, James Lee, 1924-
     The ministry of worship & praise, by James L. Beall.
     Detroit, Bethesda Missionary Temple, 19--. 30p. (New
     Testament church series, 4.) Cover title.

295 Beall, James Lee, 1924-
     The New Testament ministry of the evangelist. Detroit,
     Bethesda Missionary Temple, 19--. 30p. Cover title.

296 Beall, James Lee, 1924-
     The New Testament ministry of the pastor. Detroit,
     Bethesda Missionary Temple, 19--. 30p. (Ministry gifts, 4.)
     Cover title.

297 Beall, James Lee, 1924-
     New Testament priesthood. Detroit, Bethesda Missionary
     Temple, 19--. 19p. Cover title.

298 Beall, James Lee, 1924-
     Observations of the now generation. Detroit, Bethesda Mis-
     sionary Temple, 197-. 27p. Cover title.

299 Beall, James Lee, 1924-
     One body in Christ. Detroit, Bethesda Missionary Temple,
     19--. 38p. Cover title.

300 Beall, James Lee, 1924-
     One new man. Detroit, Bethesda Missionary Temple, 19--.
     38p. Cover title.

301 Beall, James Lee, 1924-
     Our present dilemma: sons vs. fathers. Detroit, Bethesda
     Missionary Temple, 19--. 38p. Cover title.

302 Beall, James Lee, 1924-
     "Peace on earth," who says? Detroit, Bethesda Missionary
     Temple, 19--. 22p. Cover title.

303 Beall, James Lee, 1924-
     The revelation of grace, by James Beall. Detroit, Bethesda
     Missionary Temple, 19--. 26p. (Galatians series, 1.) Cover
     title.

304 Beall, James Lee, 1924-
     Rise and be healed. Detroit, Bethesda Missionary Temple,
     19--. 38p. Cover title.

305 Beall, James Lee, 1924-

Rise to newness of life; a look at water baptism.   Detroit,
Evangel Press, 1974.   ix, 149p.

306   Beall, James Lee, 1924-
        Salvation, by J. L. Beall. Detroit, Bethesda Missionary
        Temple, 19--. 24p. Cover title.

307   Beall, James Lee, 1924-
        The seal of redemption: the Holy Spirit. Detroit, Bethesda
        Missionary Temple, 19--. 38p. (The eternal purposes of God,
        2.) Cover title.

308   Beall, James Lee, 1924-
        The 7 churches of Revelation, by J. L. Beall. Detroit,
        Bethesda Missionary Temple, 19--. 2v. Cover title.

309   Beall, James Lee, 1924-
        The seven pillars of faith. Detroit, Bethesda Missionary
        Temple, 19--. 37p. Cover title.

310   Beall, James Lee, 1924-
        Spots, blemishes, and deceptions. Detroit, Bethesda Mis-
        sionary Temple, 19--. 39p. Cover title.

311   Beall, James Lee, 1924-
        "Stewards of the mysteries of God."   (1 Cor. 4:1) Detroit,
        Bethesda Missionary Temple, 19--. 2v. Cover title.

312   Beall, James Lee, 1924-
        Striving for mastery, by James L. Beall. Detroit, Bethesda
        Missionary Temple, 19--. 2v.

313   Beall, James Lee, 1924-
        Suicide. Detroit, Bethesda Missionary Temple, 19--. 38p.
        Cover title.

314   Beall, James Lee, 1924-
        Understanding sin: What is it? What sins can be forgiven?
        The unpardonable sin. The sin unto death. Does God keep an
        account of our sins? Detroit, Bethesda Missionary Temple,
        19--. 37p. Cover title.

315   Beall, James Lee, 1924-
        The unity of the local church. Detroit, Bethesda Missionary
        Temple, 19--. 35p. (New Testament church series, 2.)
        Cover title.

316   Beall, James Lee, 1924-
        The unsearchable riches of Christ. Detroit, Bethesda Mis-
        sionary Temple, 19--. 36p. Cover title.

317   Beall, James Lee, 1924-
        Water baptism: command or elective? Detroit, Bethesda

Missionary Temple, 19--. 38p. Cover title.

318   Beall, James Lee, 1924-
        What in the world is going on? Detroit, Bethesda Mission-
      ary Temple, 19--. 31p. Cover title.

319   Beall, James Lee, 1924-
        Where do we go from here? Detroit, Bethesda Missionary
      Temple, 19--. 34p. Cover title.

320   Beall, James Lee, 1924-
        Who changed the sabbath? Detroit, Bethesda Missionary
      Temple, 19--. 38p. Cover title.

321   Beall, James Lee, 1924-
        The whole man. Detroit, Bethesda Missionary Temple,
      19--. 34p. Cover title.

322   Beall, James Lee, 1924-
        The work of the Holy Spirit, by J. L. Beall. Detroit,
      Bethesda Missionary Temple, 19--. 26p. Cover title.

323   Beall, James Lee, 1924-
        The world church. Detroit, Bethesda Missionary Temple,
      19--. 27p. Cover title.

324   Beall, James Lee, 1924-
        The world, the flesh, and the devil. Detroit, Evangel
      Press, 19--. 38p. Cover title.

325   Beall, James Lee, 1924-
        Would you like to be a transformed person? Detroit,
      Bethesda Missionary Temple, 19--. 31p. Cover title.
      At head of title: A person who is himself a problem cannot
      himself deal with his own problems. Would you like some
      answers to life?

326   Beck, Johanne
        Vekten; Kristendom paa videvanke. Oslo, 1959. 80p.
      MH-AH

327   Bevington, Guy C.
        Remarkable miracles [by] G. C. Bevington. Plainfield, N.J.,
      Logos International, c1973. 209p. (A Logos classic.) First
      published under title: Remarkable incidents and modern mira-
      cles through prayer and faith. DLC

328   Bible. English. 1963. Authorized.
        Dake's annotated reference Bible: the Holy Bible, containing
      the Old and New Testaments of the Authorized or King James
      version text ... and a complete concordance and cyclopedic in-
      dex, by Finis Jennings Dake. Atlanta, Dake Bible Sales, 1963.
      944, 324, 131p. DLC

329   Bible.   English.   Selections.   1960.   Authorized.
       The healing scriptures, compiled by Oral Roberts.   Tulsa,
       Oral Roberts Evangelistic Association, c1960.   48p.

330   Bible.   O. T. Daniel.   English.   1968.   Authorized.
       The Book of Daniel and the book of the Revelation of Jesus
       Christ, with personal commentary by Oral Roberts.   Authorized
       (King James) version.   Tulsa, Oral Roberts Evangelistic Asso-
       ciation, 1968.   126p.

331   Bible.   N. T.   English.   1961.   Authorized.
       Dake's annotated reference Bible: the New Testament (with
       the addition of Daniel, Psalms and Proverbs).   By Finis J.
       Dake.   Grand Rapids, Mich., Zondervan Publishing House,
       1961.   488p.   DLC, MH-AH, PPWe

332   Bible.   N. T.   Gospels.   English.   1967.   Authorized.
       The four Gospels and the Acts of the Apostles, with per-
       sonal commentary by Oral Roberts.   Tulsa, Oral Roberts
       Evangelistic Association, 1967.   254p.

333   Björkquist, Curt
       Fornkristna martyrer.   Stockholm, Filadelfia, 1944.   223p.
       DLC

334   Blossom, Willis W.
       The gift (dorea) of the Holy Spirit; what is the gift of the
       Holy Spirit and how obtained?   [By] Willis W. Blossom.   Rev.
       ed.   Madison, Wisc., 1925.   230p.   DLC

335   Bodie, Mary M.
       The biography of the King: gospel of Matthew, by Mary M.
       Bodie.   2d ed.   Kansas City, Mo., Grace and Glory, 19--.
       150p.

336   Bodie, Mary M.
       The book of sanctification; or, Lessons in Leviticus, by
       Mary M. Bodie.   Kansas City, Mo., Grace and Glory, 1970.
       100p.

337   Bodie, Mary M.
       Christendom found wanting; or, Stirring studies in Judges,
       by Mary M. Bodie.   2d ed.   Kansas City, Mo., Grace and
       Glory, 1957.   108p.   "Given as a series of ... addresses ...
       at a 'Grace and Glory Camp Meeting' in Topeka, Kansas,
       August 15th to 25th, 1918. "

338   Bodie, Mary M.
       The correction of the sons of God; lessons in Collossians
       [sic], by Mary M. Bodie.   Kansas City, Mo., Grace and Glory,
       19--.   134p.

339   Bodie, Mary M.

Discourses on Daniel, the interpreter of dreams, by Mary
M. Bodie. 3d ed. Kansas City, Mo., Grace and Glory, 1952.
109p.

340 Bodie, Mary M.
The exodus of the sons of God; studies in Romans, by Mary
M. Brodie. 4th ed. Kansas City, Mo., Grace and Glory,
1963. 79p. Written in 1918.

341 Bodie, Mary M.
An exposition of Zechariah, the man of visions, by Mary M.
Bodie. Kansas City, Mo., Grace and Glory, 19--. 146p.
"Given ... in 1925 in The Tabernacle in Kansas City, Mo., in
a series of addresses."

342 Bodie, Mary M.
The gleaner and the queen; meditations on Ruth and Esther,
by Mary M. Bodie. Kansas City, Mo., Grace and Glory, 1926.
124p.

343 Bodie, Mary M.
The heavenlies; live lessons in Joshua, by Mary M. Bodie.
Kansas City, Mo., Grace and Glory, 1961. 115p.

344 Bodie, Mary M.
Lessons from the gospel by John: the glory gospel, by Mary
M. Bodie. Kansas City, Mo., Grace and Glory, 1941. 142p.
First "appeared in Grace and Glory as a serial from April
1935 to April 1937."

345 Bodie, Mary M.
Lessons in Genesis, by Mary M. Bodie. Kansas City, Mo.,
Grace and Glory, 1955-1956. 2v. Cover title.

346 Booth-Clibborn, Arthur Sydney, 1855-1939.
Blood against blood. 2d ed. New York, G. H. Doran Co.,
1914. 168p. MH, NN

347 Booth-Clibborn, Arthur Sydney, 1855-1939.
Blood against blood. 3d ed. New York, C. C. Cook, 1916.
176p. DLC, MiU, NIC

348 Booth-Clibborn, William E.
The baptism in the Holy Spirit: a personal testimony, by
William Booth-Clibborn. Stockport, Cheshire, J. Nelson Parr,
1929. 35p.

349 Bosworth, Fred Francis, 1877-1956.
Af denne grund; eller, Hvorfor mange er svage og mange
dør fortidlig. Medforfatterens tilladelse oversat fra engelsk
ved Lise B. Henning Hommefoss. Minneapolis, Oversoettererens
forlag, 1921. 31p.

34 Guide to the Pentecostal Movement

350 Bosworth, Fred Francis, 1877-1958.
Deshalb. Leonberg, Württ, Philadelphia Verlag, 19--.
32p.

351 Branham, William, 1909-1965.
Conduct, order, doctrine of the church [by] William Marrion
Branham. Jeffersonville, Ind., Spoken Word Publications,
1973. 510p.

351a Branham, William, 1909-1965.
An exposition of the seven church ages, by William Marrion
Branham. Jeffersonville, In., 19--. 381p.

352 Brewster, Percy S.
Pentecostal doctrine. Editor: P. S. Brewster. Cheltenham,
Glos., Grenehurst Press, c1976. 400p. KyWAT

353 Brewster, Percy S.
The spreading flame of pentecost [by] P. S. Brewster.
London, Elim Publishing House, 1970. ix, 135p. L

354 Britton, Bill
Jesus, the pattern son, by Bill Britton. Springfield, Mo.,
1966. 77p.

355 Brooks, Noel, 1914-
The place of faith in sickness and health. Nelson, Lancs.,
Coulton, 19--. 16p.

356 Brown, Victor Gordon, 1914-
The church, historical and contemporary [by] Victor G.
Brown. Peterborough, Ont., College Press, c1966. x, 251p.
DLC, OkEG

357 Brumback, Carl, 1917-
"What meaneth this?" A Pentecostal answer to a Pentecostal
question. Springfield, Mo., Gospel Publishing House, c1947.
352p. DLC, NNUT, TxWaS

358 Burkett, Dewey
Studies in His rest and the former and latter rain. Sheldon,
Iowa, J. Groot, 19--. 59p.

359 Burton, William Frederick Padwick, 1886-1971.
Mafundijyo a ku mukanda wa Leza. Elizabethville, 1948.
100p. L

360 Burton, William Frederick Padwick, 1886-1971.
Safe eternally [by] W. F. P. Burton. Johannesburg, Dis-
tributed by D. Fischer, 196-. 76p. OkTOr

361 Burton, William Frederick Padwick, 1886-1971.
Signs following [by] W. F. P. Burton. n.p., 196-. 47p.

362 Burton, William Frederick Padwick, 1886-1971.
     What mean ye by these stones? Bible talks on the Lord's
     table. London, Victory Press, 1947. 96p. L

363 Buxton, Clyne W.
     The Bible says you may expect these things [by] Clyne W.
     Buxton. Old Tappan, N.J., F. H. Revell Co., 1973. 160p.
     Half title: Expect these things. DLC

364 Caldwell, William A.
     The charismatic translation: 1 Corinthians 12-14, by William
     Caldwell. Tulsa, Front Line Evangelism, c1968. 83p.

365 Caldwell, William A.
     Lying spirits, by William Caldwell. Tulsa, Front Line
     Evangelism, c1964. 55p.

366 Caldwell, William A.
     Meet the healer, by William Caldwell. Tulsa, Miracle
     Moments Evangelistic Association, 1965. 96p. TxWaS

367 Caldwell, William A.
     Meet the healer, by William Caldwell. Tulsa, Front Line
     Evangelism, c1965. 96p.

368 Caldwell, William A.
     Pentecostal baptism, by William A. Caldwell. Tulsa, Mira-
     cle Moments Evangelistic Association, c1963. 96p. TxWaS

369 Caldwell, William A.
     Pentecostal baptism, by William A. Caldwell. Tulsa, Front
     Line Evangelism, 1974, c1963. 96p. TMH

370 Caldwell, William A.
     Power, the baptism in the Holy Spirit: key to miracle
     power, gateway to spiritual gifts, pattern for worldwide evan-
     gelism, by William Caldwell. Tulsa, Front Line Evangelism,
     c1972. 24p. Abridgment of Pentecostal baptism.

371 Caldwell, William A.
     Running away from home, by William Caldwell. Tulsa,
     Front Line Evangelism, c1966. 22p.

372 Caldwell, William A.
     When the world goes boom, by William A. Caldwell. Tulsa,
     Miracle Moments Evangelistic Association, 1965. 54p.

373 Caldwell, William A.
     Wonderful things, by William Caldwell. Tulsa, Front Line
     Evangelism, c1971. 24p.

374 Canada, A. G.
     Divine healing. Falcon, N.C., Falcon Publishing Co., 19--.
     16p. Cover title.

375   Cantelon, Willard, 1915-
         The new world money system.   Independence, Mo. , Gospel
      Tract Society, 197-.   16p.

376   Canty, George
         In my Fahter's house; Pentecostal expositions of major
      Christian truths.   Foreword by W. G. Hathaway.   Greenwood,
      S. C. , Attic Press, c1969.   128p.

377   Canty, George
         What's going on?   The George Canty viewpoint.   Cheltenham,
      Grenehurst Press, 1977.   iv, 116p.   DLC

378   Carter, Herbert Franklin, 1933-
         The spectacular gifts: prophecy, tongues, interpretations,
      by Herbert Carter.   n. p. , 19--.   44p.

379   Carter, Howard, 1891-1971.
         The gifts of the Holy Spirit.   London, Defoe Press, 1946.
      148p.

380   Carter, Howard, 1891-1971.
         Questions and answers on the gifts of the Spirit.   Slough,
      Bucks. , Ambassador Productions, 1946.   134p.

381   Carter, Howard, 1891-1971.
         Questions et réponses sur les dons spirituels.   Paris, Viens
      et Vois, 1967.   180p.

382   Cathcart, William, 1893-
         The glory of Christ revealed in charismatic ministry.   New
      York, Vantage Press, c1979.   xiv, 256p.

383   Cerullo, Morris, 1931-
         Key to spiritual success.   San Diego, World Evangelism,
      1965.   32p.

384   Cerullo, Morris, 1931-
         The new anointing.   San Diego, World Evangelism, c1975.
      147p.   KyWAT

385   Cerullo, Morris, 1931-
         The new anointing is here.   Special ed.   San Diego, World
      Evangelism, c1972.   45p.   On cover: Handbook for the harvest.

386   Cerullo, Morris, 1931-
         Seven steps to victory for body, soul, and spirit.   San Diego,
      World Evangelism, 1955.   32p.

387   Cerullo, Morris, 1931-
         Spiritual breakthrough in prophecy.   San Diego, World
      Evangelism, 1971.   30p.   Cover title: Breakthrough in proph-
      ecy.

388 Cerullo, Morris, 1931-
        Two men from Eden. San Diego, M. C. W. E., Inc.,
     c1977. v, 148p.

389 Cerullo, Morris, 1931-
        What does this mean? San Diego, World Evangelism, c1976.
     viii, 139p. KyWAT

390 Cerullo, Morris, 1931-
        Wind over the 20th century. San Diego, World Evangelism,
     1973. 67p.

391 Chawner, C. Austin, 1903-1964.
        Timhaka ta Xikwembu. 2d ed. Nelspruit, E. Tvl., 1952.
     85p. L

392 Clarke, Robert
        The Christ of God. London, Victory Press, 1949. 164p.

393 Coe, Jack, 1918-1956.
        Wilt thou be made whole? Dallas, Herald of Healing, 19--.
     46p. TxWaS

394 Coe, Juanita (Scott)
        On being a real Christian, by Juanita Coe. Dallas, Challenge
     Press, 1963. 26p. KyWAT

395 Coe, Juanita (Scott)
        What God will do for you, by Juanita Coe. Dallas, Coe
     Foundation, 19--. 28p. OkTOr

396 Coe, Juanita (Scott)
        Where revival is born! By Juanita Coe. Dallas, Loftin-
     Shepherd Ptg. & Litho., 19--. 32p. OkTOr

397 Copley, A. S.
        The arrangement of the ages, including ranks in the resur-
     rection [by] A. S. Copley. Kansas City, Mo., Grace and
     Glory, 19--. 32p.

398 Copley, A. S.
        The blessed hope of the sons of God; lessons in Thessalonians,
     by A. S. Copley. Kansas City, Mo., Grace and Glory, 19--.
     52p.

399 Copley, A. S.
        The blessed hope of the sons of God; lessons in Thessalonians,
     by A. S. Copley. 2d ed. Kansas City, Mo., Grace and Glory,
     1931. 95p.

400 Copley, A. S.
        The church of Christ founded: spiritual-studies in the Acts,
     by A. S. Copley. Kansas City, Mo., Grace and Glory, 19--.
     95p.

401 Copley, A. S.
     The divine order of the sons of God; lessons in Corinthians,
     by A. S. Copley. Kansas City, Mo., Grace and Glory, 19--.
     65p.

402 Copley, A. S.
     The exaltation of the sons of God; lessons on Ephesians,
     by A. S. Copley. Kansas City, Mo., Grace and Glory, 19--.
     192p. OkTOr

403 Copley, A. S.
     The heavenly courtship; or, Solomon's Song of Songs.   3d
     ed. Kansas City, Mo., Grace and Glory, 1951. 72p.   First
     ed. published in 1918.

404 Copley, A. S.
     The Holy Spirit, by A. S. Copley. Kansas City, Mo.,
     Grace and Glory, 19--. 16p. OkTOr

405 Copley, A. S.
     The Holy Spirit: the one baptism, the anointing, personal
     and practical, by A. S. Copley. Kansas City, Mo., Grace
     and Glory, 19--.   48p.

406 Copley, A. S.
     How to receive, by A. S. Copley. Kansas City, Mo.,
     Grace and Glory, 19--. 6p. OkTOr

407 Copley, A. S.
     The liberty of the sons of God; lessons in Galatians, by
     A. S. Copley. Kansas City, Mo., Grace and Glory, 1970.
     60p. "Lessons given ... first ... in Oak Hill Tabernacle,
     Indianapolis, Indiana, in 1914. "

408 Copley, A. S.
     The revelation of Jesus anointed to John, by A. S. Copley.
     Kansas City, Mo., Grace and Glory, 1960.   105p.

409 Copley, A. S.
     This is that, by A. S. Copley. Kansas City, Mo., Grace
     and Glory, 19--. 16p. OkTOr.

410 Cossum, William Henry, 1863-
     Mountain peaks of prophecy and sacred history, by W. H.
     Cossum. Chicago, Evangel Publishing House, c1911.   195p.
     DLC.

411 Cowing, Lawrence Albert, 1877-
     The glory plain; an advanced Pentecostal theology, by Law-
     rence A. Cowing. Robbinsdale, Minn., Printed by the Bible
     Friend Publishing Co., c1934. 64p. DLC

412 Crayne, Richard

The church.   Morristown, Tenn. , 1957.   78p.

413   Crayne, Richard
        The church.   2d ed.   Morristown, Tenn. , 1959.   81p.
      KyWAT

414   Crayne, Richard
        Holy Ghost power from on high.   3d ed.   Morristown,
      Tenn., 19--.   51p.   Cover-title.

415   Culpepper, Richard Weston
        How you too can receive your healing, by R. W. Culpepper.
      Bellflower, Calif. , 1955.   34p.   OkTOr

416   Culpepper, Richard Weston
        How you too can receive your healing, by R. W. Culpepper.
      Bellflower, Calif. , 19--.   45p.   TxWaS

417   Culpepper, Richard Weston
        Pentecost is not a denomination.   Dallas, 19--.   29p.
      OkTOr

418   Dake, Finis Jennings, 1902-
        The anti-Christ will not rule America or be a world dictator.
      Atlanta, Bible Research Foundation, c1955.   32p.   Cover title.
      KyWAT

419   Dake, Finis Jennings, 1902-
        Bible truths unmasked.   Atlanta, Bible Research Foundation,
      1950.   128p.

420   Dake, Finis Jennings, 1902-
        Foundation studies of scripture; or, Dispensational truth:
      a book for the classroom and home.   4th ed.   Bristol, Tenn.,
      c1941.   248p.

421   Dake, Finis Jennings, 1902-
        God's plan for man; contained in fifty-two lessons, one for
      each week of the year.   Atlanta, 1949.   26 pts in 1 v.   DLC

422   Dake, Finis Jennings, 1902-
        God's plan for man; contained in fifty-two lessons, one for
      each week of the year.   Lawrenceville, Ga., Dake Bible Sales,
      c1949.   1018p.

423   Dake, Finis Jennings, 1902-
        The key to the world's storehouse of wisdom.   Atlanta,
      19--.   16p.

424   Dake, Finis Jennings, 1902-
        The plan of the ages; the Bible on canvas.   Lawrenceville,
      Ga., c1949.   2 fold. ℓ.

425   Dake, Finis Jennings, 1902-
        The rapture and the second coming of Christ.   Lawrence-
      ville, Ga., Dake Bible Sales, c1977.   119p.

426   Dake, Finis Jennings, 1902-
        Revelation expounded; or, Eternal mysteries simplified: a
      book for the classroom and the home.   Tulsa, c1931.   256p.
      DLC

427   Dake, Finis Jennings, 1902-
        Revelation expounded; or, Eternal mysteries simplified ...
      a book for the classroom and the home.   2d ed.   Atlanta,
      1949.   366p.   DLC

428   Dake, Finis Jennings, 1902-
        Revelation expounded; or, Eternal mysteries simplified ...
      a book for the classroom and the home.   2d, enlarged ed.
      Lawrenceville, Ga., Dake Bible Sales, c1950.   320p.

429   Dake, Finis Jennings, 1902-
        The truth about sin and sanctification.   Bristol, Tenn.,
      c1946.   64p.

430   Dake, Finis Jennings, 1902-
        The truth about the baptism in the Holy Spirit.   Atlanta,
      Bible Research Foundation, 1967.   32p.

431   Dake, Finis Jennings, 1902-
        The two future world empires: world wars, world rulers,
      world changes.   Atlanta, Bible Research Foundation, c1955.
      32p.   Cover title.   KyWAT

432   Dangerfield, Dorothea
        Homely talks on divine healing.   London, Victory Press,
      1931.   x, 129p.   L, TxWaS

433   Daoud, Mounir Azia
        Difference between miracles and healings: time required
      for each, why many are not healed, when should we die?
      [By] Evangelist and Mrs. M. A. Daoud.   n.p., 1955.   31p.
      OkTOr

434   Daoud, Mounir Aziz
        Divine healing for all, by M. A. Daoud.   Dallas, Voice of
      Miracles and Missions, c1955.   157p.   TxWaS

435   Daoud, Mounir Aziz
        Faith: how to receive it, how to exercise it, by M. A.
      Daoud.   Dallas, 1955.   31p.   OkTOr

436   Daoud, Mounir Azia
        Sickness: is it from God or the Devil?   By M. A. Daoud.
      Dallas, Voice of Miracles and Missions, 1955.   28p.   OkTOr

437 Dacud, Mounir Azia
      Undeniable proofs: God's will is to heal today! By Evan-
      gelist and Mrs. M. A. Daoud. n.p., 19--. 31p. OkTOr

438 Darms, Anton
      Divine healing in the scriptures. Dallas, T. V. H. Pub-
      lishing Co., 19--. 146p. TxWaS

439 Daugherty, Bob
      New Testament teaching on tongues. Rossville, Ga., 19--.
      11p.

440 Deem, Fred, 1867-
      One reason why doubting "if" prayers for healing are not
      answered. Dayton, Ohio, J. J. Scruby, 19--. 19p. TxWaS

441 Demarest, Victoria (Booth-Clibborn), 1890-1982.
      The Holy Spirit [by] Victoria Booth-Clibborn Demarest.
      Norfolk, Va., Demarest Book Concern, c1923. 85p.

442 Doering, Alma Emma, 1878-
      His way out, by Alma E. Doering. 3d ed. Philadelphia,
      Office of the "Unevangelized," 1943. 64p. At head of title:
      "Come with me and look from the top" (Canticles 4:8) and find
      His way out. First ed. published in 1936.

443 Douglas, John Elwood
      Jerusalem and Israel in Bible prophecy [by] John E. Douglas,
      Sr. Dallas, World Missionary Evangelism, c1967. 28p.

444 Douglas, John Elwood
      Let your women keep silent: what does it mean? By John
      E. Douglas, Sr. and Edith C. Douglas. Dallas, 1958. 64p.
      TxDaTS

445 Douglas, John Elwood
      This is the rest and refreshing! Dallas, 1960. 32p.
      OkTOr

446 Dowell, Buford
      The Holy Spirit baptism; or, The miracle working power of
      God for you. Spiritual gifts: how to obtain and operate them.
      San Diego, 19--. 61p. Cover title.

447 Duffield, Guy Payson, 1909-
      Handbook of Bible lands, by Guy P. Duffield. Glendale,
      Calif., G/L Regal Books, 1969. 186p. DLC

448 Duncan, Philip B.
      The Pentecostal path, by Philip B. Duncan. n.p., 19--.
      44p.

449 Du Plessis, David Johannes, 1905-

Glossolalia, by David J. du Plessis. Oakland, Calif.,
19--. 15p.

450   Ecke, Karl, 1886-1952.
      Der Durchbruch des Urchristentum infolge Luthers Reforma-
      tion. Nürnberg, Süddeutscher Missionsverlag, 195-. 131p.

451   Ecke, Karl, 1886-1952.
      Das Ratsel der Taufe; ein Wort zur Verständigung Gütersloh,
      C. Bertelsmann, 1952. 27p. (Alte und neue Wege zur leben-
      digen Gemeinde, 3) DLC, ICU, MH

452   Ecke, Karl, 1886-1952.
      Der reformierende Protestismus; Streiflichter auf die Ent-
      wicklung lebendiger Gemeinde von Luther bis heute. Gütersloh,
      G. Bertelsmann, 1952. 52p. (Alte und neue Wege zur leben-
      digen Gemeinde, 2.) DLC, NjPT, OU

453   Erickson, Clifton O.
      Supernatural deliverance, by Clifton O. Erickson. Wenatchee,
      Wash., c1950. 88p. TxWaS

454   Eusebius, Pamphili, bp. of Caesarea.
      Miracles, signs and wonders. Compiled from the Ecclesias-
      tical history of Eusebius, by Thea F. Jones. Cleveland, Tenn.,
      Healing Today, 19--. 62p.

455   Ferris, Alexander James, 1907-
      Armageddon is at the doors. Keston, Kent., Eng., A. J.
      Ferris, 1934. 88p. This second edition comprises "Armaged-
      don is at the doors" and "Signs of the end of this age," pub-
      lished 1935 in two separate volumes. NN

456   Ferris, Alexander James, 1907-
      Britain-America revealed as Israel. 8th ed. London, 1941.
      62p. Cover-title: Great Britain and the U.S.A. revealed as
      Israel: the new order. First published under title: God's
      education of the Anglo-Saxon race. MH

457   Ferris, Alexander James, 1907-
      The British Commonwealth and the United States of America
      foretold in the Bible. Bexhill, Sussex, 1937. 95p. MH

458   Ferris, Alexander James 1907-
      Deliverance from Russia, how it will come. London,
      Blackheath Publishers, 1947. 91p. DLC

459   Ferris, Alexander James, 1907-
      Germany's doom foretold. (Companion volume to "When
      Russia bombs Germany" ...) London, Marshall Press, 1942.
      48p. DLC

460   Ferris, Alexander James, 1907-

The jubilee, 1957-1958; eight lectures delivered in Ireland during 1954, and recorded on electro-magnetic tapes. London, 1954. 141p. DLC

461 Ferris, Alexander James, 1907-
     Palestine for Jew or Arab? London, Marshall Press, 1946. 61p. DLC

462 Ferris, Alexander James, 1907-
     The resurrection of the twelve apostles. London, Marshall Press, 1955. 128p. IEG

463 Ferris, Alexander James, 1907-
     The Revelation unveiled. London, Blackheath Park, 1952. 192p. CLamB

464 Ferris, Alexander James, 1907-
     When Russia bombs Germany, by A. J. Ferris. 5th ed. London, Marshall Press, 1942. 80p. NN

465 Ferris, Alexander James, 1907-
     When Russia invades Palestine; or, "Zechariah's end-of-the-age message to the Anglo-Saxon-Israel peoples, as in Zech. 12 to 14." London, 1939. 99p. CLamB

466 Finney, Charles Grandison, 1792-1875.
     A digest of ... Finney's Systematic theology; thirty-six lectures. Sweet Home, Ore., J. W. Jepson, 1970. 67p.

467 Finney, Charles Gradison, 1792-1875.
     Power from on high; a selection of articles on the Spirit-filled life. London, Victory Press, 1944. 79p. L

468 Follette, John Wright, 1883-1966.
     This wonderful venture called Christian living. Asheville, N.C., distributed by Follette Books, 1974. 83p. DLC

469 Follette, John Wright, 1883-1966.
     The threefold witness of God; God's objective in the outpouring of the Holy Spirit. Asheville, N.C., Follette Books, 1973. 32p.

470 Foster, Kenneth Neill, 1935-
     I believe in tongues, but - [by] K. Neill Foster. Eastbourne, Sussex, Victory Press, 1976. 160p. First published in 1975 under title: Help! I believe in tongues.

471 Franklin, A. P.
     Party or country? An argument against socialism. London, Staples Press, 1947. 145p. DLC

472 Frodsham, Stanley Howard, 1882-1969.
     The Spirit-filled life; a word to those who desire to live a

vistorious life. Grand Rapids, Mich., W. B. Eerdmans Publishing Co., 1948. 81p.

473 Frodsham, Stanley Howard, 1882-1969.
    The Spirit-filled life; a word to those who desire to live a
    victorious life. Grand Rapids, Mich., W. B. Eerdmans Pub-
    lishing Co., 1952. 88p. TxWaS

474 Gardiner, Gordon P., 1916-
    Concerning spiritual gifts, by Gordon P. Gardiner. Wauke-
    gon, Ill., C. Hofflander, 19--. 50p.

475 Gardner, Velmer J.
    The God of miracles lives today, by Velmer J. Gardner.
    Wenatchee, Wash., c1950. 127p. TxWaS

476 Gardner, Velmer J.
    The God of miracles lives today! By Velmer J. Gardner.
    2d ed. Springfield, Mo., 1954, c1950. 96p.

477 Gardner, Velmer J.
    The God of miracles lives today! By Velmer J. Gardner.
    Orange, Calif., Velmer J. Gardner Evangelistic Association,
    1954. 96p. OkTOr

478 Gardner, Velmer J.
    Healing for you, by Velmer J. Gardner. Springfield, Mo.,
    1952. 32p. OkTOr

479 Gardner, Velmer J.
    Healing for you, by Velmer J. Gardner. Dallas, Voice of
    Healing, c1952. 32p. TxWaS

480 Gardner, Velmer J.
    "I spent Saturday night in the devil's house"; an exposure [!]
    of Father Divine. Springfield, Mo., Velmer Gardner Evangel-
    istic Association, c1952. 47p. OkTOr

481 Gardner, Velmer J.
    The reality, results, receiving of the Holy Spirit, by Velmer
    J. Gardner. 2d ed. Los Angeles, Full Gospel Businessmen's
    Fellowship International, 1968, c1954. 47p.

482 Goodwin, J. R.
    The Holy Spirit's three gifts of utterance [by] Reverend and
    Mrs. J. R. Goodwin. Pasadena, Tex., Faith-in-Depth, 1974.
    32p. (Spiritual house series, 4)

483 Gorman, Samuel
    The coming world ruler. London, Victory Press, 1944.
    viii, 184p. DLC

484 Gorman, Samuel

Two phases or one? Christ's second advent. London, Victory Press, 1946. 40p. L

485 Gossett, Don, 1929-
Courageous Christians. Blaine, Wa., Cloverdale, B.C.,
Bold Living, 19--. 31p. OkTOr

485a Gossett, Don, 1929-
Praise power. Cloverdale, B.C. Bold Bible Missions,
19--. 28p.

486 Grant, Walter Vinson, 1913-
The acts of the Holy Spirit: 1. Manifestations; 2. Operations;
3. Demonstrations. By W. V. Grant. Dallas, Faith Clinic,
19--. 31p. Cover title.

487 Grant, Walter Vinson, 1913-
The anointing of power: how you may have power to heal
the sick. Dallas, Grant's Faith Clinic, 19--. 32p. OkTOr

488 Grant, Walter Vinson, 1913-
Casting out devils for preachers, teachers and seekers, by
W. V. Grant. Dallas, Faith Clinic, 19--. 99p.

489 Grant, Walter Vinson, 1913-
The coming world-wide revival, by W. V. Grant and David
Nunn. Dallas, Faith Clinic, 19--. 32p.

490 Grant, Walter Vinson, 1913-
Confirming the word, by W. V. Grant. Dallas, Faith Clinic,
19--. 31p.

491 Grant, Walter Vinson, 1913-
The curse and the cure, by W. V. Grant. Dallas, Faith
Clinic, 19--. 32p.

492 Grant, Walter Vinson, 1913-
Desire spiritual gifts, by W. V. Grant. Dallas, Grant's
Faith Clinic, 19--. 30p.

493 Grant, Walter Vinson, 1913-
Discerning of spirits and other gifts, by W. V. Grant.
Dallas, Grant's Faith Clinic, 19--. 32p.

494 Grant, Walter Vinson, 1913-
Divine healing answers! By W. V. Grant. Waxahachie,
Tex., Southwestern Bible Institute Press, 1952. 2v.

495 Grant, Walter Vinson, 1913-
85 things you should know about the gift of prophecy. Dallas,
Grant's Faith Clinic, 19--. 32p. OkTOr

496 Grant, Walter Vinson, 1913-

Faith cometh; or, How to get faith, by W. V. Grant. Malvern, Ark., 19--. 100p.

497 Grant, Walter Vinson, 1913-
Faith for finance, by W. V. Grant. Dallas, Grant's Faith Clinic, 19--. 32p.

498 Grant, Walter Vinson, 1913-
Freedom from evil spirits; how to be set free from depression, recession, and repression, by W. V. Grant. Dallas, Grant's Faith Clinic, 19--. 32p.

499 Grant, Walter Vinson, 1913-
Freedom from obsession and oppression, by W. V. Grant. Dallas, Grant's Faith Clinic, 19--. 31p.

500 Grant, Walter Vinson, 1913-
From rags to riches; or, Clothed with humility, by W. V. Grant. Dallas, Grant's Faith Clinic, 19--. 49p.

501 Grant, Walter Vinson, 1913-
The fruit of the Spirit. Dallas, Grant's Faith Clinic, 19--. 48p. OkTOr

502 Grant, Walter Vinson, 1913-
The gift of faith, by W. V. Grant. Malvern, Ark., 19--. 30p.

503 Grant, Walter Vinson, 1913-
The gift of faith, by Walter V. Grant. Dallas, Grant's Faith Clinic, 19--. 30p.

504 Grant, Walter Vinson, 1913-
Gifts of healing, by W. V. Grant. Malvern, Ark., 19--. 32p.

505 Grant, Walter Vinson, 1913-
Gifts of healing, by W. V. Grant. Dallas, Grant's Faith Clinic, 197-. 36p. (Faith books) Cover title.

506 Grant, Walter Vinson, 1913-
Gifts of the Spirit in the home, by W. V. Grant. Dallas, Grant's Faith Clinic, 19--. 32p.

507 Grant, Walter Vinson, 1913-
The great dictator: the man whose number is 666, by W. V. Grant. Dallas, Grant's Faith Clinic, 19--. 31p.

508 Grant, Walter Vinson, 1913-
The hand of the healer, by W. V. Grant. Dallas, Grant's Faith Clinic, 19--. 32p.

509 Grant, Walter Vinson, 1913-

Healing and health: faith tonic, by W. V. Grant. Malvern, Ark., 19--. 32p.

510   Grant, Walter Vinson, 1913-
Health and healing. Dallas, Grant's Faith Clinic, 19--. 32p. OkTOr

511   Grant, Walter Vinson, 1913-
How spiritual gifts operate. Dallas, Grant's Faith Clinic, 19--. 32p.

512   Grant, Walter Vinson, 1913-
How to receive the Holy Spirit baptism, by W. V. Grant. Dallas, Voice of Healing, 19--. 100p. TxWaS

513   Grant, Walter Vinson, 1913-
How to receive without asking. Dallas, Grant's Faith Clinic, 19--. 29p.

514   Grant, Walter Vinson, 1913-
How you may have a double portion, by W. V. Grant. Dallas, Grant's Faith Clinic, 19--. 32p.

515   Grant, Walter Vinson, 1913-
If you need the Holy Ghost. Dallas, Grant's Faith Clinic, 19--. [32]p. OkTOr

516   Grant, Walter Vinson, 1913-
The last step to healing. Dallas, Grant's Faith Clinic, 19--. 28p. OkTOr

517   Grant, Walter Vinson, 1913-
The master key to revival: the last move of God. Dallas, Grant's Faith Clinic, 19--. 32p. OkTOr

518   Grant, Walter Vinson, 1913-
Maybe you have a thorn in the flesh. Dallas, Grant's Faith Clinic, 19--. 31p. OkTOr

519   Grant, Walter Vinson, 1913-
Men from the moon in America: Did they come in a Russian satellite? By W. V. Grant. Dallas, Grant's Faith Clinic, 195-. 31p. Cover title. DLC

520   Grant, Walter Vinson, 1913-
Men in the flying saucers identified: not a mystery! [by] W. V. Grant. Dallas, Grant's Faith Clinic, 195-. 32p. Cover title. DLC

521   Grant, Walter Vinson, 1913-
More than conquerors: killing the lions. Dallas, Grant's Faith Clinic, 19--. 32p. OkTOr

522   Grant, Walter Vinson, 1913-
         The 9 spiritual gifts and how to receive them, by W. V.
      Grant. Dallas, Grant's Faith Clinic, 19--. 1v. (unpaged)

523   Grant, Walter Vinson, 1913-
         One God, one baptism, by W. V. Grant. Dallas, 19--.
      14p. OkTOr

524   Grant, Walter Vinson, 1913-
         Power from on high. Dallas, Grant's Faith Clinic, 19--.
      [32]p. OkTOr

525   Grant, Walter Vinson, 1913-
         Power to discern disease. Dallas, Grant's Faith Clinic,
      19--. 32p. OkTOr

526   Grant, Walter Vinson, 1913-
         Present day outpouring. Dallas, Grant's Faith Clinic,
      19--. 32p.

527- Grant, Walter Vinson, 1913-
  8   Putting women in their place. Dallas, Grant's Faith Clinic,
      19--. 32p. OkTOr

529   Grant, Walter Vinson, 1913-
         The real revival of restoration. Dallas, Grant's Faith
      Clinic, 19--. 48p. OkTOr

530   Grant, Walter Vinson, 1913-
         Receive ye the Holy Ghost instantly! Dallas, Grant's Faith
      Clinic, 19--. 32p. OkTOr

531   Grant, Walter Vinson, 1913-
         The seven keys to the kingdom, by W. V. Grant. Dallas,
      Grant's Faith Clinic, 19--. 32p.

532   Grant, Walter Vinson, 1913-
         Signs following your ministry, by W. V. Grant. Dallas,
      Grant's Faith Clinic, 19--. 31p.

533   Grant, Walter Vinson, 1913-
         Spiritual gifts and how to receive them. For teachers-
      instructors, for Spirit-filled Christians, by W. V. Grant.
      Dallas, Grant's Faith Clinic, 1952. 100p.

534   Grant, Walter Vinson, 1913-
         Spiritual gifts and how to receive them. For teachers-
      instructors, for Spirit-filled Christians, by W. V. Grant.
      Waxahachie, Tex., Southwestern Bible Institute Press, c1952.
      97p. TxWaS

535   Grant, Walter Vinson, 1913-
         The truth about faith healers. Dallas, Grant's Faith Clinic,
      19--. 32p. OkTOr

536 Grant, Walter Vinson, 1913-
     The two witnesses. Dallas, Grant's Faith Clinic, 19--.
     32p. OkTOr

537 Grant, Walter Vinson, 1913-
     The weapons of our warfare: the vocal gifts, regulation
     and demonstration. Dallas, Grant's Faith Clinic, 19--. 32p.
     OkTOr

538 Grant, Walter Vinson, 1913-
     When prayer fails. Dallas, Grant's Faith Clinic, 19--.
     31p. OkTOr

539 Grant, Walter Vinson, 1913-
     The will of God concerning you! Dallas, Grant's Faith
     Clinic, 19--. 31p. OkTOr

540 Groves, H. W.
     Miracle healing, by H. W. Groves. Tulsa, 19--. 107p.

541 Grubb, Paul N.
     The end time revival. Memphis, Tenn., 19--. 90p.

542 Gustafsson, Harald
     Bibelns laera om den Helige Ande. Stockholm, Förlaget
     Filadelfia, 1959. 54p. MH-AH

543 Gustafsson, Harald
     Brinnande budskap. Stockholm, Förlaget Filadelfia, 1957.
     179p. MH-AH

544 Gustafsson, Harald
     Budskap från Uppenbarelseboken. Stockholm, Förlaget
     Filadelfia, 1961. 96p. MH-AH

545 Gustafsson, Harald
     Pingsteld och Pilgrimsliv. Örebro, Evangeliipress, 1959.
     102p.

546 Gustafsson, Harald
     Samhaellsproblem och andlig vaeckelse. Stockholm, Förlaget
     Filadelfia, 1959. 32p.

547 Guyon, Jeanne Marie (Bouvier de La Motte), 1648-1717.
     Madame Guyon; an autobiography. Abridged by Anna C.
     Reiff. Chicago, Evangel Publishing House, 1911. 269p. DLC

548 Hagin, Kenneth E., 1917-
     Concerning spiritual gifts, by Kenneth E. Hagin. Tulsa,
     1974. 96p.

549 Hagin, Kenneth E., 1917-
     Exceedingly growing faith [by] Kenneth E. Hagin. Tulsa,
     Kenneth E. Hagin Evangelistic Association, c1973. 126p.

550 Hagin, Kenneth E. , 1917-
         The gift of prophecy, by Kenneth Hagin. 5th ed. Tulsa,
     Kenneth Hagin Evangelistic Association, 1975. 31p.

551 Hagin, Kenneth E. , 1917-
         God's medicine, by Kenneth E. Hagin. 3d ed. Tulsa,
     Kenneth Hagin Ministries, 1977. 32p. (Faith library publica-
     tions.) OkTOr

551a Hagin, Kenneth E. , 1917-
         Healing belongs to us, by Kenneth E. Hagin. Tulsa, 19--.
     30p.

552 Hagin, Kenneth E. , 1917-
         The Holy Spirit and His gifts, by Kenneth Hagin. Tulsa,
     19--. 114p.

553 Hagin, Kenneth E. , 1917-
         I believe in visions [by] Kenneth E. Hagin. Old Tappan,
     N. J. , F. H. Revell Co. , 1972. 126p. DLC

554 Hagin, Kenneth E. , 1917-
         The interceding Christian, by Kenneth Hagin. 3d ed. Tulsa,
     1973. 32p.

555 Hagin, Kenneth E. , 1917-
         The origin and operation of demons, by Kenneth E. Hagin.
     6th ed. Tulsa, Kenneth E. Hagin Evangelistic Association,
     1974. 32p. (Satan, demons, and demon possession series, 1.)

556 Hagin, Kenneth E. , 1917-
         Seven steps to receiving the Holy Spirit, by Kenneth E.
     Hagin. Tulsa, 19--. 29p. Cover title: Seven vital steps to
     receiving the Holy Spirit.

557 Hagin, Kenneth E. , 1917-
         The woman question [by] Kenneth E. Hagin. Tulsa, Kenneth
     E. Hagin Evangelistic Association, c1975. 93p.

558 Hall, Franklin
         Atomic power with God with fasting and prayer. New ed.
     Phoenix, c1973. 63p. First published in 1946.

558a Hall, Franklin
         Because of your unbelief. Phoenix, Hall Deliverance Founda-
     tion, 1968. 44p.

559 Hall, Franklin
         Because of your unbelief. Phoenix, Hall Deliverance Founda-
     tion, c1975. 42p.

560 Hall, Franklin
         The fasting prayer. San Diego, Calif. , 1947. 222p.

561   Hall, Franklin
        The fasting prayer.   3d ed.   Phoenix, c1967.   195p.

562   Hall, Franklin
        Glorified fasting: the ABC of fasting.   San Diego, Calif.,
        1948.   64p.

563   Hall, Franklin
        Glorified fasting: the ABC of fasting.   Rev. ed.   Phoenix,
        c1973.   63p.

564- Hall, Franklin
   5   The return of immortality; 5 books in one and with revisions
        of former UFO volumes.   Phoenix, Hall Deliverance Foundation,
        c1976.   80p.   "This volume replaces books I, II, III and IV,
        flying saucers booklets. "

566   Harris, Leo
        God heals today; a sound scriptural basis for divine healing
        today: the secrets of a faith for the miraculous, inspiring
        testimonies of modern healing miracles.   Fullarton, S. Austl.,
        Crusader Publications, 19--.   64p.

567   Harris, Leo
        Pentecostal truth triumphant!   Reply to The Pentecostal
        error, by Cyril H. Maskrey.   Fullarton, S. Austl., Crusader
        Publications, 19--.   1v. (unpaged)

568   Harvey, William Lee, 1880-
        Christianity in action; a lawyer's search for Christian reality.
        Make deeds of your creeds.   Translate God's word into matters
        of practice.   By William L. Harvey.   San Bernardino, Calif.,
        Franklin Press, c1953.   131p.   CLamB, CLSU

569   Harvey, William Lee, 1880-
        God's master plan for man; describing God's process trans-
        forming natural man into sons of God.   By William L. Harvey.
        San Bernardino, Calif., Franklin Press, c1956.   142p.   CLamB

570   Hassenzahl, George M.
        The day of the Lord, by Geo. M. Hassenzahl.   Springfield,
        Mo., Bill Britton, 196-.   47p.

571   Hastie, Eugene N.
        The triumphant church [by] Eugene N. Hastie.   Perry, Iowa,
        1971.   [23]p.   Cover title.

572   Hawtin, George R.
        Church government, by George and Ernest Hawtin.   North
        Battleford, B.C., Los Angeles, Calif., 19--.   84p.

573   Hembree, Charles Ron, 1938-
        Fruits of the Spirit [by] Charles R. Hembree.   Grand

Rapids, Mich. , Baker Book House, 1969.   128p.   TxWaS

574   Hembree, Charles Ron, 1938-
        Pocket of pebbles; inspirational thoughts on the fruits of the
      Spirit [by] Charles R. Hembree.   Grand Rapids, Mich. , Baker
      Book House, 1969.   128p.   DLC

575   Hembree, Charles Ron, 1938-
        Rehearsal for heaven [by] Ron Hembree.   Grand Rapids,
      Mich. , Baker Book House, 1977.   161p.

576   Henry, Carl
        Christ, the great physician; miracles and healing in the
      twentieth century.   Oakland, Calif. , c1946.   160p.   TxWaS

577   Henry, Carl
        Exploits of faith, miracles and healing in the twentieth cen-
      tury.   Oakland, Calif. , c1946.   160p.   TxWaS

578   Hicks, B. R.
        And God made woman, by B. R. Hicks.   Jeffersonville,
      Ind. , Christ Gospel Press, 1973.   228p.

579   Hicks, Roy H.
        The Pentecostal faith: answer to all generations, by Roy H.
      Hicks.   Surrey, B. C. , Word of Faith Fellowship, 19--.   100p.
      (L. I. F. E. Bible College of Canada.   Alumni lectureship, c1969.)

580   Isensee, Frank E.
        Words of wisdom from the pen of Frank Isensee.   Long
      Beach, Ca. , Belmont Shore Printing Co. , 19--.   39p.   Cover
      title.

581   Iverson, Sylva F.
        Releasing the power within, by Sylva F. Iverson.   Portland,
      Ore. , 19--.   93p.

582   Jackson, Gayle, 1913-
        Divine deliverance.   Sikeston, Mo. , c1951.   184p.   TxWaS

583   Jaggers, Orval L.
        Everlasting spiritual and physical health, by O. L. Jaggers.
      Dexter, Mo. , 1949.   162p.   TxWaS

584   Jaggers, Orval L.
        Omnipotence is yours; or, How Diety places Himself in the
      lives of men, by O. L. Jaggers.   Dexter, Mo. , c1949.   112p.
      TxWaS

585   Jenkins, Leroy, 1935-
        How you can receive your healing.   Delaware, Ohio, Leroy
      Jenkins Evangelistic Association, 1966.   88p.   OkTOr

586- Jenkins, Leroy, 1935-
  7   Power for abundant living.   Delaware, Ohio, Leroy Jenkins
       Evangelistic Association, 1965.   32p.   OkTOr

588   Johnson, Phil
       How to obtain and retain your healing.   Tulsa, Pentecostal
       Publications, c1949.   63p.   TxWaS

589   Jones, Thea F. , 1920-
       The mistakes of Satan.   n. p. , 19--.   93p.

590   Jones, Thea F.
       What's in the manger?   By Thea Jones.   Philadelphia,
       Philadelphia Evangelistic Centre, 19--.   87p.   OkTOr

591   King, Charlotte Marie
       Glimpses of the overcoming life.   East Providence, R. I. ,
       Zion Publishers, 1966.   113p.

592   Kingston, Charles John Ewart
       The coming of Christ--and after, by Charles J. E. Kingston.
       London, Victory Press, 1929.   vii, 142p.   CCmS

592a   Kingston, Charles John Ewart
       The coming of Christ--and after; or, What the future holds,
       by Charles J. E. Kingston.   Rev. and enl. ed.   London, Vic-
       tory Press, 1939.   178p.   MoSpA

592b   Kingston, Charles John Ewart
       Fulness of power, by Charles J. E. Kingston.   London,
       Victory Press, c1939.   225p.   TxWaS

593   Kirban, Salem
       Christian Science.   Huntingdon Valley, Pa. , 1974.   59p.
       DLC

594   Kirban, Salem
       Doctrines of devils; exposing the cults of our day.   Hunting-
       don Valley, Pa. , 1970- .   v. 1- .   DLC

595   Kirban, Salem
       Jehovah's Witnesses.   Huntingdon Valley, Pa. , c1972.   77p.
       DLC

596   Kirban, Salem
       Kirban's prophecy New Testament, including Revelation
       visualized, King James version.   Huntingdon Valley, Pa. ,
       c1973.   873, 480p.   DLC

597   Kirban, Salem
       Prophecy New Testament series.   Huntingdon Valley, Pa. ,
       1972- .   v. 1- .   DLC

598 Kirban, Salem
     Questions frequently asked me on prophecy. Huntingdon
     Valley, Pa. , 1972. 63p.

599 Kirban, Salem
     20 reasons why this present earth may not last another 20
     years. Huntingdon Valley, Pa. , 1973. 191p. DLC

600 Kirban, Salem
     What in the world will happen next? Huntingdon Valley,
     Pa. , 1974. 64p. DLC

601 Kirby, Gilbert Walter
     The question of healing; some thoughts on healing and suf-
     fering. Edited by Gilbert W. Kirby. London, Victory Press,
     1967. 95p. Essays by Donald Gee, C. J. E. Lefroy, Gilbert
     W. Kirby, Kenneth Prior, Geoffrey R. King, Derek J. Prime
     and Paul S. Rees. RPB

602 Kirby, Gilbert Walter
     "Remember, I am coming soon!" Revelation 22:7 (N. E. B.)
     A symposium edited by Gilbert W. Kirby. London, Victory
     Press, 1964. 86p. CLgA: CLamB, L

603 Klink, Otto J.
     Is there a God? Answering the American Association for
     the Advancement of Atheism. Redlands, Calif. , Christian Book
     and Bible Rooms, 1949. 36p.

604 Krust, Christian Hugo
     Was wir glauben, lehren und bekennen; unter Mitarbeit des
     Hauptbrüdertages, herausgegeben von Christian Krust. Altdorf
     bei Nürnberg, Missionsbuchhandlung und Verlag, 1963. 164p.

605 Lachat, William
     La Réception et l'Action du Saint-Esprit. Neuchatel, Dela-
     chaux & Niestlé, c1953. 65p. MH-AH, TxDaM-P

606 Lancaster, John
     In spirit and in truth: principles for Pentecostal people.
     Cheltenham, Glos. , Grenehurst Press, 1977. 138p.

607 Lancaster, John
     The Spirit-filled Church. Cheltenham, Glos. , Grenehurst
     Press, 1973. 91p.

607a Lawrie, R. Paulaseer
      Heavenly Canaan [by] R. Paulaseer. Tirunelveli, India,
      P. Lawrie Publications, 197-. 484p. (Thunder series, 7B.)
      OkTOr

607b Lawrie, R. Paulaseer
      The hidden manna [by] R. Paulaseer Lawrie. Tirunelveli,

India, P. Lawrie Publications, 197-. 75p. (Thunder series, 3.) OkTOr

607c Lawrie, R. Paulaseer
It is possible to overcome death in this generation; or, The feast of the tabernacles [by] R. Paulaseer Lawrie. Tirunelveli, India, P. Lawrie Publications, 197-. 97p. (Thunder series, 2.) OkTOr

607d Lawrie, R. Paulaseer
The last trump, by R. Paulaseer Lawrie. Tirunelveli, India, 19--. 398p. CCmS

607e Lawrie, R. Paulaseer
Son of man: message to the bride [by] R. Paulaseer Lawrie. Tirunelveli, India, R. P. Lawrie Publications, 196-. 48p. OkTOr

608 Lewis, W. G.
Divine guidance, by W. G. Lewis. n. p. , 19--. 214p.

609 Lidman, Sven, 1882-1960.
Fjäril och vilddjur, en bok om liv och nåd. Stockholm, A. Bonnier, 1947. 282p. DLC

610 Lidman, Sven, 1882-1960.
Forganggelsens traler och frihetens soner; tankar om nod, nad och nodvandighet. 2. Uppl. Stockholm, A. Bonnier, 1928. 307p. CLU

611 Lidman, Sven, 1882-1960.
Från Coventry till Bethlehem; en bok om frälsning i stormen. Stockholm, A. Bonnier, 1942. 276p. MnU, WaU

612 Lidman, Sven, 1882-1960.
Guds eviga nu; en bok om vägen, sanningen och livet. Stockholm, A. Bonnier, 1947. 328p. CU

613 Lidman, Sven, 1882-1960.
Ingen lurar Gud; sett, tänkt och talat. Stockholm, A. Bonnier, 1945. 244p. NNC

614 Lidman, Sven, 1882-1960.
Människan och tidsandan. Stockholm, A. Bonnier, 1932. 236p. Reprinted from various sources. NN

615 Lidman, Sven, 1882-1960.
På resan genom livet; sett och tänkt. 6. uppl. Stockholm, A. Bonnier, 1936. 320p. NN

616 Lidman, Sven, 1882-1960.
Uppenbarat; en bok om andlig verklighet. Stockholm, A. Bonnier, 1943. 253p. MnU

617   Lidman, Sven, 1882-1960.
      Utvald av Gud; en själs lovsång.   Stockholm, A. Bonnier,
      1940.   269p.   MnU

618   Lidman, Sven, 1882-1960.
      Var inte förskräckt!   Sett, tänkt och talat.   Stockholm, A.
      Bonnier, 1939.   301p.   DLC, L

619   Lindblad, Frank V.
      The Spirit which is from God, by Frank Lindblad.   Seattle,
      19--.   229p.

620   Lindsay, Gordon, 1906-1973.
      After Vietnam--what?   Dallas, Christ for the Nations, 1973.
      33p.

621   Lindsay, Gordon, 1906-1973.
      All about the gift of faith.   Dallas, Voice of Healing Pub-
      lishing Co. , 1963.   64p.   (Gifts of the Spirit, 5.)

622   Lindsay, Gordon, 1906-1973.
      All about the gift of the word of knowledge.   Dallas, Voice
      of Healing Publishing Co. , 1963.   30p.

623   Lindsay, Gordon, 1906-1973.
      All about the gift of working of miracles.   Dallas, Voice of
      Healing Publishing Co. , 1963.   71p.   (Gifts of the Spirit, 7.)

624   Lindsay, Gordon, 1906-1973.
      All about the gifts of the Spirit.   Dallas, Voice of Healing,
      1962.   62p.

625   Lindsay, Gordon, 1906-1973.
      All about the gifts of the Spirit.   Dallas, Christ for the
      Nations, 1971.   63p.   (Gifts of the Spirit, 1.)   MnCS

626   Lindsay, Gordon, 1906-1973.
      Amazing discoveries in the words of Jesus.   Shreveport,
      La. , Voice of Healing Publishing Co. , c1951.   119p.   DLC

627   Lindsay, Gordon, 1906-1973.
      American presidents and their destiny.   Dallas, Voice of
      Healing, 1960.   31p.

628   Lindsay, Gordon, 1906-1973.
      Answers to the difficult questions concerning divine healing.
      Dallas, Voice of Healing Publishing Co. , 1960.   25p.

629   Lindsay, Gordon, 1906-1973.
      Answers to the difficult questions concerning divine healing.
      Dallas, Christ for the Nations, 1971.   25p.   TxWaS

630   Lindsay, Gordon, 1906-1973.

Apostles, prophets, and governments. Dallas, Christ for the Nations, 1975. 57p. Reprint of 195- ed.

631 Lindsay, Gordon, 1906-1973.
Apostles, prophets, and governments--are they in the church today? Dallas, Voice of Healing Publishing Co., 195-. 32p.

632 Lindsay, Gordon, 1906-1973.
Baptism of the Holy Spirit. Dallas, Voice of Healing Publishing Co., 1964. 92p. "Prepared for World correspondence course." OkTOr

633 Lindsay, Gordon, 1906-1973.
The baptism of the Holy Spirit. Dallas, Christ for the Nations, 1971. 93p. (Gifts of the Spirit, 10.)

634 Lindsay, Gordon, 1906-1973.
Bible days are here again; divine healing for today and God's plan for ending sickness. Shreveport, La., 1949. 190p. CLamB, TxWaS

635 Lindsay, Gordon, 1906-1973.
Bible days are here again; divine healing for today and God's plan for ending sickness. Dallas, Voice of Healing Publishing Co., 19--. 190p. Reprint of 1949 ed.

636 Lindsay, Gordon, 1906-1973.
The Bible is a scientific book. Dallas, Christ for the Nations, 1971. 63p.

637 Lindsay, Gordon, 1906-1973.
The Bible secret of divine health. Dallas, Christ for the Nations, 1968. 25p. TxWaS

638 Lindsay, Gordon, 1906-1973.
The blueprints of God. Portland, Ore., Cosbys--printers, c1940. v. 1- . DLC, Or

639 Lindsay, Gordon, 1906-1973.
The book of Revelation made easy. Dallas, Christ for the Nations, 197-. 513p. On cover: Revelation series.

640 Lindsay, Gordon, 1906-1973.
Christ, the great physician. Dallas, Christ for the Nations, 1967. 27p. TxWaS

641 Lindsay, Gordon, 1906-1973.
The crucifixion. Dallas, Christ for the Nations, 1969. 64p. (Life of Christ series, 15.) OkTOr

642 Lindsay, Gordon, 1906-1973.
Crusade for world fellowship. Dallas, Voice of Healing Publishing Co., 19--. 105p.

643   Lindsay, Gordon, 1906-1973.
      Daniel's 70 weeks. Dallas, Christ for the Nations, 1969.
      45p. (The prophecies of Daniel series, 3.)

644   Lindsay, Gordon, 1906-1973.
      The days of Christ and the apostles. Dallas, Voice of
      Healing Publishing Co. , 1963. 85p. "Prepared for the World
      correspondence course. "

645   Lindsay, Gordon, 1906-1973.
      The death cheaters. Dallas, Christ for the Nations, 1971.
      36p.

646   Lindsay, Gordon, 1906-1973.
      Difficult questions about the Bible answered. Dallas, Christ
      for the Nations, 1971. 33p.

647   Lindsay, Gordon, 1906-1973.
      Evolution--the incredible hoax. Christ or gorilla, which?
      Dallas, Voice of Healing, 1960. 23p.

648   Lindsay, Gordon, 1906-1973.
      Evolution--the incredible hoax. 2d ed. Dallas, Voice of
      Healing, 1963. 23p. MnCS

649   Lindsay, Gordon, 1906-1973.
      Evolution--the incredible hoax. Dallas, Christ for the Na-
      tions, 1973. 23p.

650   Lindsay, Gordon, 1906-1973.
      The facts about the seventh-day. Dallas, Voice of Healing
      Publishing Co. , 1964. 32p. "Prepared for the World corre-
      spondence course. "

651   Lindsay, Gordon, 1906-1973.
      48 signs in the land of Israel. Dallas, Voice of Healing
      Publishing Co. , 1965. 48p. Cover title: 48 signs in the land
      of Israel of the soon coming of Christ. "Prepared for the
      World correspondence course. "

652   Lindsay, Gordon, 1906-1973.
      49 strange facts about the Bible. n. p. , 19--. 34p.

653   Lindsay, Gordon, 1906-1973.
      Forty signs of the soon coming of Christ. Dallas, Voice
      of Healing, 19--. 63p.

654   Lindsay, Gordon, 1906-1973.
      40 things you've always wanted to know about death and the
      hereafter. Dallas, Christ for the Nations, 1972. 32p.

655   Lindsay, Gordon, 1906-1973.
      The gift of discerning of spirits. Dallas, Voice of Healing

Publishing Co., 1963.   39p.

656   Lindsay, Gordon, 1906-1973.
        The gift of discerning of spirits.   Dallas, Christ for the
      Nations, 1972.   39p.   (Gifts of the Spirit, 4.)   "Prepared for
      the World correspondence course."

657   Lindsay, Gordon, 1906-1973.
        The gift of prophecy and the gift of interpretation of tongues.
      Dallas, Voice of Healing Publishing Co., 1964.   64p.   (Gifts
      of the Spirit, 8.)   "Prepared for the World correspondence
      course."

658   Lindsay, Gordon, 1906-1973.
        The gift of prophecy--the true and the false.   Dallas, Christ
      for the Nations, 1968.   36p.

659   Lindsay, Gordon, 1906-1973.
        The gift of prophecy--the true and the false.   Dallas, Christ
      for the Nations, 1971.   36p.   (Gifts of the Spirit, 12.)

660   Lindsay, Gordon, 1906-1973.
        The gifts of healing.   Dallas, Voice of Healing Publishing
      Co., 1963.   29p.

661   Lindsay, Gordon, 1906-1973.
        The gifts of healing.   Dallas, Christ for the Nations, 1970.
      29p.   (Gifts of the Spirit, 6.)

662   Lindsay, Gordon, 1906-1973.
        Gifts of the Spirit.   Dallas, Christ for the Nations, 1975.
      28p.

663   Lindsay, Gordon, 1906-1973.
        God's answer to puzzling cases.   Dallas, Voice of Healing,
      1956.   52p.

664   Lindsay, Gordon, 1906-1973.
        God's master key to prosperity.   Dallas, Christ for the
      Nations, 1975.   72p.   First published in 1959 under title:
      God's master key to success and prosperity.   KyWAT

665   Lindsay, Gordon, 1906-1973.
        God's master key to success and properity.   Dallas, Voice
      of Healing Publishing Co., 1959.   61p.   MnCS

666   Lindsay, Gordon, 1906-1973.
        God's plan of the ages, as revealed in the wonders of Bible
      chronology.   Dallas, Christ for the Nations, 1971.   254p.

667   Lindsay, Gordon, 1906-1973.
        The great day of the Lord and the seven trumpets.   Dallas,
      Voice of Healing, 19--.   p. 97-127.   (The book of Revelation

made easy, 4.) Cover title.

668   Lindsay, Gordon, 1906-1973.
      The great tribulation. Dallas, Voice of Healing Publishing
      Co. , 1957.   117p.

669   Lindsay, Gordon, 1906-1973.
      Hades--abode of the unrighteous dead. Dallas, Christ for
      the Nations, 1968.   32p.

670   Lindsay, Gordon, 1906-1973.
      How can you be healed? Dallas, Christ for the Nations,
      19--.   31p.   TxWaS

671   Lindsay, Gordon, 1906-1973.
      How to find the perfect will of God. Dallas, Christ for the
      Nations, 1972.   36p.

672   Lindsay, Gordon, 1906-1973.
      How to receive the baptism in the Holy Spirit. Dallas,
      Christ for the Nations, 19--.   30p.

673   Lindsay, Gordon, 1906-1973.
      How to receive your healing. Shreveport, La. , c1949.
      28p.   TxWaS

674   Lindsay, Gordon, 1906-1973.
      How to receive your healing. Dallas, Voice of Healing,
      19--.   27p.   OkTOr

675   Lindsay, Gordon, 1906-1973.
      How you can be healed; or, All about divine healing. Dallas,
      Winning the Nations Crusade, 19--.   29p.   OkTOr

676   Lindsay, Gordon, 1906-1973.
      How you can have divine health. Dallas, Christ for the
      Nations, 1971.   27p.   TxWaS

677   Lindsay, Gordon, 1906-1973.
      How you may become a successful Christian. Dallas,
      Christ for the Nations, 1972.   31p.

678   Lindsay, Gordon, 1906-1973.
      Increase your prayer power tenfold. Dallas, Christ for the
      Nations, 1977.   31p.   Reprint of 1972 ed.   OkTOr

679   Lindsay, Gordon, 1906-1973.
      Is Jesus the son of God? Dallas, Christ for the Nations,
      19--.   31p.

680   Lindsay, Gordon, 1906-1973.
      Is the healing revival from heaven or men? Dallas, Voice
      of Healing Publishing Co. , 19--.   60p.   TxWaS

681 Lindsay, Gordon, 1906-1973.
     Jeane Dixon: prophetess or psychic medium?   Dallas,
     Voice of Healing Publishing Co., 1966.   30p.

682 Lindsay, Gordon, 1906-1973.
     The judgment throne and the seven seals.   Dallas, Voice of
     Healing Publishing Co., 196-. p. 73-96. (The book of Reve-
     lation made easy, 3.)

683 Lindsay, Gordon, 1906-1973.
     Life after death; or, Where are the dead?   Dallas, Voice
     of Healing Publishing Co., 1956.   114p.

684 Lindsay, Gordon, 1906-1973.
     Ministry of angels.   Dallas, Christ for the Nations, 19--.
     28p.

685 Lindsay, Gordon, 1906-1973.
     Moses and his contemporaries.   Dallas, Voice of Healing
     Publishing Co., 1964.   32p.   (Through the Bible series, 12.)

686 Lindsay, Gordon, 1906-1973.
     The mystery of the flying saucers in the light of the Bible.
     Dallas, Voice of Healing Publishing Co., 1953.   94p.   C LamB,
     TxWaS

687 Lindsay, Gordon, 1906-1973.
     One year to live.   Dallas, Christ for the Nations, 1972.
     36p.

688 Lindsay, Gordon, 1906-1973.
     Paradise: abode of the righteous dead.   Dallas, Voice of
     Healing Publishing Co., 1967.   32p.   "Prepared for the World
     correspondence course."

689 Lindsay, Gordon, 1906-1973.
     Prayer and fasting; the master key to the impossible.
     Dallas, Voice of Healing Publishing Co., 1957.   67p.   C LamB

690 Lindsay, Gordon, 1906-1973.
     Prayer that moves mountains.   Dallas, Christ for the Na-
     tions, 1971-1973.   2v. in 1.

691 Lindsay, Gordon, 1906-1973.
     Prayer to change the world.   Dallas, Voice of Healing Pub-
     lishing Co., 195-.   2v.

692 Lindsay, Gordon, 1906-1973.
     Present world events in the light of prophecy.   Shreveport,
     La., Voice of Healing Publishing Co., c1951.   125p.

693 Lindsay, Gordon, 1906-1973.
     Present world events in the light of prophecy.   4th ed.

Dallas, Voice of Healing Publishing Co., 1951.   124p.

694   Lindsay, Gordon, 1906-1973.
      The race for the moon in the light of the scriptures.
      Dallas, Christ for the Nations, 1969.   32p.

695   Lindsay, Gordon, 1906-1973.
      The rapture. Dallas, Christ for the Nations, 1968.   40p.

696   Lindsay, Gordon, 1906-1973.
      The rapture and the second coming of Christ. Dallas,
      Voice of Healing, 196-.   p. 225-256.   (The book of Revelation
      made easy, 8.)   Cover title.

697   Lindsay, Gordon, 1906-1973.
      The real reason why Christian are sick, and how they may
      get well. Dallas, Voice of Healing Publishing Co., 195-.
      97p.   TxWaS

698   Lindsay, Gordon, 1906-1973.
      The real reason why Christians are sick, and how they may
      get well. Dallas, Christ for the Nations, 1971.   97p.

699   Lindsay, Gordon, 1906-1973.
      The resurrection of Jesus Christ. Dallas, Christ for the
      Nations, 1970.   48p.   (The life of Christ series, 17.)

700   Lindsay, Gordon, 1906-1973.
      The riddle of the flying saucers. Dallas, Voice of Healing
      Publishing Co., 1966.   31p.   "Prepared for the World corre-
      spondence course. "

701   Lindsay, Gordon, 1906-
      The riddle of the flying saucers. Kitchener, Ont., Galaxy
      Press, 1972.   [31]p.   DLC

702   Lindsay, Gordon, 1906-1973.
      The riddle of the flying saucers. Dallas, Christ for the
      Nations, 1973.   31p.

703   Lindsay, Gordon, 1906-1973.
      Satan, fallen angels and demons. Dallas, Christ for the
      Nations, 197-.   29p.

704   Lindsay, Gordon, 1906-1973.
      Satan, fallen angels and demons; how to have power over
      them. Dallas, Voice of Healing Publishing Co., 19--.   161p.

705   Lindsay, Gordon, 1906-1973.
      The second coming of Christ. Dallas, Christ for the Na-
      tions, 1974.   28p.   Reprint of 1970 ed.

706   Lindsay, Gordon, 1906-1973.

The secret of prayer that moves mountains. Dallas, Voice of Healing Publishing Co. , 1955. 122p.

707 Lindsay, Gordon, 1906-1973.
The seven churches of prophecy. Dallas, Voice of Healing Publishing Co. , 1961-196-. 2v. (64p.) (The book of Revelation made easy, 1-2.)

708 Lindsay, Gordon, 1906-1973.
7 master keys to triumphant Christian living. Dallas, Christ for the Nations, 19--. 39p.

709 Lindsay, Gordon, 1906-1973.
Should a Christian smoke? Dallas, Voice of Healing, 1963. 58p. "Prepared for the World correspondence course. "

710 Lindsay, Gordon, 1906-1973.
Should Christians attend the movies? Dallas, Voice of Healing Publishing Co. , 1964. 36p. "Prepared for the World correspondence course. "

711 Lindsay, Gordon, 1906-1973.
Should Christians drink alcohol? Dallas, Voice of Healing, 19--. 32p.

712 Lindsay, Gordon, 1906-1973.
Signs of the soon coming of Christ. Dallas, Christ for the Nations, 19--. 31p.

713 Lindsay, Gordon, 1906-1973.
The signs of the times in the heavens. Dallas, Voice of Healing Publishing Co. , 1966. 32p. "Prepared for the World correspondence course. "

714 Lindsay, Gordon, 1906-1973.
Sorcery in America. Dallas, Christ for the Nations, 1973-1977. 4v. KyWAT

715 Lindsay, Gordon, 1906-1973.
The story of Daniel. Dallas, Christ for the Nations, 1969. 39p. (Prophecies of Daniel series, 1.)

716 Lindsay, Gordon, 1906-1973.
Strange facts about Adolph Hitler. Portland, Ore. , Anglo-Saxon Christian Association, c1942. 38p. (Blueprints of God series.) OrU

717 Lindsay, Gordon, 1906-1973.
Thirty Bible reasons why Christ heals today. Dallas, Christ for the Nations, 1971. 36p. TxWaS

718 Lindsay, Gordon, 1906-1973.
30 objections to speaking in other tongues and the Bible

answer. Dallas, Christ for the Nations, 1968. 36p.

719   Lindsay, Gordon, 1906-1973.
      Thunder over Palestine; or, The holy land in prophecy.
      Dallas, Voice of Healing Publishing Co. , 195-.   123p.

720   Lindsay, Gordon, 1906-1973.
      The tragedy of Bishop Pike. Dallas, Christ for the Nations
      Publishing Co. , 1970.   36p.   OkTOr

721   Lindsay, Gordon, 1906-1973.
      The tribulation temple and the three woes. Dallas, Voice
      of Healing, 1961.   p. 129-160.   (The book of Revelation made
      easy, 5.) Cover title.

722   Lindsay, Gordon, 1906-1973.
      25 objections to divine healing and the Bible answers.
      Dallas, Voice of Healing Publishing Co. , 1966.   32p.   OkTOr

723   Lindsay, Gordon, 1906-1973.
      21 reasons why Christians should speak in other tongues.
      Dallas, Voice of Healing Publishing Co. , 1959.   26p.

724   Lindsay, Gordon, 1906-1973.
      21 reasons why Christians should speak in other tongues.
      Dallas, Christ for the Nations, 1972.   26p.   (Gifts of the
      Spirit, 9.) Reprint of 1959 ed.

725   Lindsay, Gordon, 1906-1973.
      21 signs fulfilled in Israel since the Six Day War. Dallas,
      Christ for the Nations, 1971.   39p.

726   Lindsay, Gordon, 1906-1973.
      20 things most people don't know about Bible giving. Dallas,
      Christ for the Nations, 19--.   31p.

727   Lindsay, Gordon, 1906-1973.
      22 questions most frequently asked by the unsaved. Dallas,
      Christ for the Nations, 1970.   39p.

728   Lindsay, Gordon, 1906-1973.
      The two witnesses. Dallas, Voice of Healing, 196-.
      p. 161-192.   (The book of Revelation made easy, 6.) Cover
      title.

729   Lindsay, Gordon, 1906-1973.
      The Vietnam war in prophecy. Dallas, Christ for the Na-
      tions Publishing Co. , 1966.   36p.

730   Lindsay, Gordon, 1906-1973.
      The visions of Daniel. Dallas, Christ for the Nations Pub-
      lishing Co. , 1969.   35p.   (Prophecies of Daniel series, 2.)

731   Lindsay, Gordon, 1906-1973.
      The way to eternal life. Dallas, Christ for the Nations,
      1969. 28p.

732   Lindsay, Gordon, 1906-1973.
      What the Bible says about marriage, divorce and remarriage.
      Dallas, Voice of Healing Publishing Co. , 1962. 63p. "Adapted
      to the World correspondence course of the Voice of Healing. "

733   Lindsay, Gordon, 1906-1973.
      Why do the righteous suffer? Dallas, Christ for the Nations
      Publishing Co. , 1968. 52p. Reprint of 1956 ed. MnCS,
      TxWaS

734   Lindsay, Gordon, 1906-1973.
      Why do they do it? Dallas, Christ for the Nations, 1972.
      62p. On suicide.

735   Lindsay, Gordon, 1906-1973.
      Why some are not healed. Dallas, Christ for the Nations,
      1967. 31p. TxWaS

736   Lindsay, Gordon, 1906-1973.
      Why the Bible is the Word of God. Dallas, Christ for the
      Nations, 1972. 30p.

737   Lindsay, Gordon, 1906-1973.
      Will the Antichrist come out of Russia? Dallas, Voice of
      Healing, 1966. 32p. OkTOr

738   Lindsay, Gordon, 1906-1973.
      The word of knowledge. Dallas, Christ for the Nations,
      1971. 30p. (Gifts of the Spirit, 3.) "Prepared for the World
      correspondence course. "

739   Lindsay, Gordon, 1906-1973.
      The word of wisdom. Dallas, Voice of Healing Publishing
      Co. , 1963. 32p.

740   Lindsay, Gordon, 1906-1973.
      The world today in prophecy. Dallas, Voice of Healing Pub-
      lishing Co. , 1953. 130p.

741   Litzman, Warren Lee
      The cross in the change from the temporal to the eternal.
      Dallas, Berean Press, 1966. 22p. Reprinted from Life in
      the Spirit. OkTOr

742   Litzman, Warren Lee
      Pentecostal truths.   Waco, Tex. , Litzman Pentecostal Cam-
      paigns, 1956. 78p.

743   Litzman, Warren Lee

Pentecostal truths. 3d ed. Waxahachie, Tex., Litzman
Pentecostal Campaigns, 1959. 78p.

744   Lowery, Thomas Lanier
        The baptism of the Holy Ghost. Cleveland, Tenn., T. L.
        Lowery Evangelistic Association, 19--. 67p. OkTOr

745   Lowery, Thomas Lanier
        Christ your healer. Cleveland, Tenn., T. L. Lowery
        Evangelistic Association, 19--. 112p.

746   Lowery, Thomas Lanier
        Come quickly, Lord Jesus! Cleveland, Tenn., Lowery
        Publications, 1966. 104p.

747   Lowery, Thomas Lanier
        Demon possession. Cleveland, Tenn., T. L. Lowery
        Evangelistic Association, 1970. 60p.

748   Lowery, Thomas Lanier
        The end of the world. Cleveland, Tenn., Lowery Publica-
        tions, 1969. 136p.

749   Lowery, Thomas Lanier
        The Holy Spirit at work. Cleveland, Tenn., Lowery Pub-
        lications, 1965. 96p.

750   Lowery, Thomas Lanier
        The power of faith. Cleveland, Tenn., T. L. Lowery
        Evangelistic Association, 19--. 52p.

751   Lowery, Thomas Lanier
        Prophets from hell: my visit to Father Divine's heaven;
        Christian Science; Jehovah's Witnesses; the antichrist of
        prophecy and tribulation. Cleveland, Tenn., 19--. 40p.

752   Lowery, Thomas Lanier
        Seven steps to health and happiness. Cleveland, Tenn.,
        T. L. Lowery Evangelistic Association, 1963. 30p.

753   Lowery, Thomas Lanier
        The trends of communism. Cleveland, Tenn., Lowery
        Publications, 1965. 90p.

754   Lowery, Thomas Lanier
        The troubled waters: divine healing instructions, by T. L.
        Lowery. Galax, Va., 19--. 79p.

755   Lowery, Thomas Lanier
        The unpardonable sin. n.p., 19--. 36p.

756   Lowery, Thomas Lanier
        Youth should know. Cleveland, Tenn., T. L. Lowery

Evangelistic Association, 19--.   40p.

757   Lowry, Cecil John
         Christ's brethren, by Cecil J. Lowry.   Oakland, Calif. ,
      1950.   60p.   NN

758   Lowry, Cecil John
         The coming tribulation, by Cecil J. Lowry.   Grand Rapids,
      Mich. , Zondervan Publishing House, c1943.   114p.   CLamB

759   Lowry, Cecil John
         Whither Israeli?   Oakland, Calif. , c1955.   69p.   NN

760   Lund, Eric, 1852-1933.
         Hermenéutica; o sea, Reglas de interpretación de la Sagradas
      Escrituras, por E. Lund.   San Antonio, Tex. , Casa Evangélica
      de Publicaciones, 194-.   95p.   DLC

761   Lund, Eric, 1852-1933.
         Hermeneutics; or, The science and art of interpreting the
      Bible, by Eric Lund.   Translated from the Spanish by P. C.
      Nelson.   Enid, Okla. , Printed by the Southwestern Press,
      c1934.   140p.   DLC

762   Lund, Eric, 1852-1933.
         Hermeneutics; or, The science and art of interpreting the
      Bible, by Eric Lund.   Translated from the Spanish by P. C.
      Nelson.   2d ed. , with numerous notes, a new chapter and an
      appendix and scripture index by the translator.   Enid. Okla. ,
      Southwestern Press, 1938.   159p.   DLC

763   Lund, Eric, 1852-1933.
         Hermeneutics; or, The science and art of interpreting the
      Bible, by Eric Lund.   Translated from the Spanish by P. C.
      Nelson.   3d rev. ed. , with numerous notes, new chapters and
      an appendix and a scripture-index by the translator.   Enid,
      Okla. , Southwestern Press, 1941.   207p.   DLC, PPDrop

764   McWhirter, James
         The Bible and war.   London, Covenant Publishing Co. , 1940.
      24p.   L

765   McWhirter, James
         Britain and Palestine in prophecy.   London, Methuen, 1937.
      185p.   DLC, L

766   McWhirter, James
         Is Christ coming?   London, Methuen, 1940.   viii, 102p.
      L, MH

766a Maltby, H. S.
         The reasonableness of hell, the new earth, the Pentecostal
      movement, etc.   Santa Cruz, Ca. , 1913.   99p.

767   Mattsson-Boze, Joseph D. , 1905-
       Tro som förflyttar berg: om bönens och fastans storal-
       betydelse för väckelsen och v'art andliga liv [av] Jos. D.
       Mattsson-Boze. Stockholm, Filadelfia, 1950. 107p.

767a   Meaux, Larry
       Why I should have the baptism of the Holy Spirit (and why
       some do not receive), by Larry Meaux with George Clouse.
       Winnie, Tx. , Goodnews Fellowship, c1979. 47p.

768   Merritt, Stephen, 1843-1917.
       En time med Sammy Morris, av Stephen Merrit og T. C.
       Reade. Oslo, Filadelfia-forlaget, 194-. 32p. (Time biblio-
       teket, nr. 2) IU

769   Montgomery, Carrie (Judd), 1858-
       Secrets of victory. Compiled by Sadie A. Cody. Oakland,
       Calif. , Office of Triumphs of Faith, 1921. 168p. CU-B,
       TxWaS

770   Montgomery, Granville Harrison, 1903-1966.
       Enemies of the cross, by G. H. Montgomery. Dallas,
       Challenge Press, 19--. 64p. OkTOr

771   Montgomery, Granville Harrison, 1903-1966.
       I predict; things which must shortly come to pass, by
       G. H. Montgomery. Wichita, Kan. , Mertmont Publishing
       Co. , 1963. 63p. CLamB

772   Montgomery, Granville Harrison, 1903-1966.
       The moon, music, and this mad world, by G. H. Mont-
       gomery. Kansas City, Mo. , Defenders of the Christian Faith,
       1966. 24p.

773   Montgomery, Granville Harrison, 1903-1966.
       Tomorrow's world, by G. H. Montgomery. Kansas City,
       Mo. , Defenders of the Christian Faith, 1967. 80p.

774   Murray, Andrew, 1828-1917.
       The full blessing of Pentecost: the one thing needful.
       London, Victory Press, 1944. viii,97p. L

775   Myers, W. L.
       Does God call women to preach? By W. L. Myers. Rock-
       mart, Ga. , c1948. 63p.

776   Myers, W. L.
       Does Paul forbid speaking in tongues? Evangelist John R.
       Rice says, "Yes"; Pastor W. L. Myers says, "No." Rock-
       mart, Ga. , c1948. 68p.

777   Ness, Henry H.
       The baptism with the Holy Spirit: what is it? By Henry

H. Ness. Haywood, Calif., Evangelism Crusaders, 196-.
28p. OkTOr

778 Nunn, David Oliver
     The Bible secret to believing faith, by David O. Nunn.
     Dallas, Bible Revival Evangelistic Association, 19--. 39p.
     TxWaS

779 Nunn, David Oliver
     The coming world ruler. Dallas, David Nunn revivals,
     19--. 32p.

780 Nunn, David Oliver
     The confession of sin. Dallas, Bible Revivals, 19--. 32p.

781 Nunn, David Oliver
     Declaration faith, by David O. Nunn. Dallas, Bible Revival
     Evangelistic Association, 19--. 80p. KyWAT

782 Nunn, David Oliver
     Disciples prayer. Dallas, Bible Revival Evangelistic Asso-
     ciation, 19--. 47p.

783 Nunn, David Oliver
     God's dynamic trio: faith, healing, miracles. Dallas,
     Bible Revival Evangelistic Association, 19--. 32p.

784 Nunn, David Oliver
     God's gifts: wisdom, knowledge, discerning of spirits.
     Dallas, Bible Revival Evangelistic Association, 19--. 30p.

785 Nunn, David Oliver
     God's golden hour of power, by David Nunn. Dallas,
     19--. 32p. TxWaS

786 Nunn, David Oliver
     God's law of health and wealth, by David O. Nunn. Dallas,
     Bible Revivals, Inc., 19--. 32p. TxWaS

787 Nunn, David Oliver
     Jesus, the healer divine. Dallas, 19--. 32p. TxWaS

788 Nunn, David Oliver
     Judgment must begin at the house of God. Dallas, Bible
     Revivals, 19--. 29p.

789 Nunn, David Oliver
     The key to spiritual gifts. Dallas, David Nunn Revivals,
     19--. 30p.

790 Nunn, David Oliver
     Manifestation of the Spirit; the three glorious gifts of utter-
     ance: diverse kinds of tongues, interpretation of tongues,

interpretation of tongues, prophecy. Dallas, Bible Revival
Evangelistic Association, 19--. 32p.

791 Nunn, David Oliver
        Prayer power. Dallas, Bible Revival Evangelistic Associa-
     tion, 19--. 32p.

792 Nunn, David Oliver
        The promise, power, purpose of Pentecost, by David Nunn.
     Dallas, 19--. 47p. TxWaS

793 Nunn, David Oliver
        Wonderful Jesus. Dallas, Bible Revival Evangelistic Asso-
     ciation, 19--. 30p.

794 Osborn, Tommy Lee, 1923-
        Black gold; pictorial, by T. L. Osborn. Tulsa, 1957. 1v.
     (unpaged) CM1G

795 Osborn, Tommy Lee, 1923-
        Divine healing through creative word power, by T. L. Os-
     born. Tulsa, 19--. 76p.

796 Osborn, Tommy Lee, 1923-
        Divine healing through infinite light power, by T. L. Osborn.
     Tulsa, 19--. 104p.

797 Osborn, Tommy Lee, 1923-
        Divine healing through revelation faith power, by T. L.
     Osborn. Tulsa, 19--. 128p.

798 Osborn, Tommy Lee, 1923-
        Divine healing through six methods of power, by T. L.
     Osborn. Tulsa, 1949. 78p.

799 Osborn, Tommy Lee, 1923-
        Divine healing through word confession power, by T. L.
     Osborn. Tulsa, 19--. 96p.

800 Osborn, Tommy Lee, 1923-
        Faith's testimony, by T. L. Osborn. Tulsa, c1956. 53p.
     TxWaS

801 Osborn, Tommy Lee, 1923-
        Faith's testimony; the important secret of confession un-
     veiled and how to keep your healing, by T. L. Osborn. 3d
     ed. Tulsa, 1962, c1956. 86p. CM1G

802 Osborn, Tommy Lee, 1923-
        Frontier evangelism with miracles of healing, by T. L.
     Osborn. Tulsa, 1955. 102p.

803 Osborn, Tommy Lee, 1923-

Frontier evangelism: God's indispensable method for world evangelism, by T. L. Osborn. 2d ed. Tulsa, c1955. 126p. First published in 1955 under title: Frontier evangelism with miracles and healing. CMlG

804   Osborn, Tommy Lee, 1923-
Geloofs getuigenis, het belangrijke geheim van bet bilijden ontsluierd en hoe uw genezing te behouden. Rotterdam, Osborn's Boek- en Filmdepot, 1958. 76p. Translation of Faith's testimony. DNLM

805   Osborn, Tommy Lee, 1923-
Healing en masse, by T. L. Osborn. Tulsa, c1956. 54p. TxWaS

806   Osborn, Tommy Lee, 1923-
Healing en masse, by T. L. Osborn. Tulsa, 1958. 123p. CMlG

807   Osborn, Tommy Lee, 1923-
Healing from Christ, by T. L. Osborn. Tulsa, 1955. 70p.

808   Osborn, Tommy Lee, 1923-
Healing from Christ [by] T. L. Osborn. 12th ed. Tulsa, Osborn Foundation, 1971, c1955. 69p. KyWAT

809   Osborn, Tommy Lee, 1923-
Healing the sick, by T. L. Osborn. Tulsa, c1955. 239p. TxWaS

810   Osborn, Tommy Lee, 1923-
Healing the sick and casting out devils, by T. L. Osborn. Tulsa, 1941. 275p.

811   Osborn, Tommy Lee, 1923-
Healing the sick and casting out devils. The message and ministry of a Bible disciple now living. Christ's power of attorney exercised today. The faith adventures of Evangelist T. L. Osborn. Tulsa, 1950. 285p. DLC, TxWaS

812   Osborn, Tommy Lee, 1923-
Healing the sick and casting out devils. The message and ministry of a Bible disciple now living. Christ's power of attorney exercised today. Sermons and faith adventures of Evangelist T. L. Osborn. 3d ed. , rev. and enl. Tulsa, c1953. 299p.

813   Osborn, Tommy Lee, 1923-
How to be born again [by] T. L. Osborn. Tulsa, Osborn Foundation, c1977. 160p. KyWAT

814   Osborn, Tommy Lee, 1923-

How to receive miracle healing [by] T. L. Osborn.   Tulsa,
Osborn Foundation International, 1977.   222p.   KyWAT

815   Osborn, Tommy Lee, 1923-
      Kolme avainta Apostolien tekoihin.   Suomentanut Taito Seila.
      Helsinki, Kuva ja sana, 1961.   48p.   Translation of Three
      keys to the book of Acts.   MH

816   Osborn, Tommy Lee, 1923-
      The purpose of Pentecost [by] T. L. Osborn.   3d ed.
      Tulsa, 1962.   22p.   OkTOr

817   Osborn, Tommy Lee, 1923-
      The purpose of Pentecost, by T. L. Osborn.   8th ed.
      Tulsa, Osborn Foundation, 19--.   121p.   OkTOr

818   Osborn, Tommy Lee, 1923-
      Seven steps to receive healing from Christ, by T. L. Os-
      born.   Tulsa, c1955.   57p.   TxWaS

819   Osborn, Tommy Lee, 1923-
      Three keys to the book of Acts, by T. L. Osborn.   3d ed.
      Tulsa, 1963.   75p.

820   Osborn, Tommy Lee, 1923-
      Zeven stappen om genezing van Christus te oatvangen: een
      keur van de goddelijke genezingswaarheden, welke geloof en
      bevrijding aan nonderdduizenden lijders over de gehele wereld
      gehracht hebben.   Rotterdam, Osborn's Boek--en Filmdepot,
      1958.   75p.   Translation of Seven steps to receive healing
      from Christ.   DNLM

821   Paino, Paul E.
      Tne Bible reasons for the ministry of tongues, by Paul E.
      Paino.   Fort Wayne, Ind. , Calvary Temple, 197-.   [24]p.
      (Bible truth series) KyWAT

822   Parr, John Nelson, 1888-1976.
      Death's mystery solved, by J. Nelson Parr.   Leamington,
      Warwicks. , Full Gospel Publishing House, 1944.   40p.   L

823   Paul, Jonathan, 1853-1931.
      Ihr werdet die Kraft des Heiligen Geistes empfangen; ein
      Zeugnis von Taufe mit dem Heiligen Geist und Feuer.   Nürn-
      berg, Christlicher Verlag, 195-.   224p.   Abridged.

824   Paulk, Earl Pearly, 1927-
      Divine runner [by] Earl P. Paulk, Jr.   Atlanta, Cross
      Roads Publications, c1978.   142p.

824a Paulk, Earl Pearly, 1927-
      Your Pentecostal neighbor, by Earl P. Paulk.   Cleveland,
      Tenn. , Pathway Press, 1958.   237p.   DLC, TxWaS

825 Pearson, Leonard Thomas
Through the Holy Land: a fascinating tour with the Bible in hand. London, Victory Press, 1937. viii, 127p. L

826 Perkins, Jonathan Elsworth, 1889-
The biggest hypocrite in America, Gerald L. K. Smith unmasked. Introd. by Meade McClanahan. Los Angeles, American Foundation, 1949. 152p. DLC

827 Pethrus, Lewi, 1884-1974.
Heilszekenheid. Stockholm, Förlaget Filadelfia, 1953. 15p. Translation of Fralsingsvisshet.

828 Pethrus, Lewi, 1884-1974.
Pa Bibelns mark. Stockholm, Forlaget Filadelifa, 1937. 1v. (93p.) No more published.

829 Pethrus, Lewi, 1884-1974.
Secret of success, by Lewi Pethrus. Translated by Paul B. Peterson. Chicago, Philadelphia Book Concern, 19--. 93p.

830 Pethrus, Lewi, 1884-1974.
Urkristna kraftkällor. 14. uppl. Stockholm, 1948. 127p. L

831 Pethrus, Lewi, 1884-1974.
The wind bloweth where it listeth, by Lewi Pehtrus. Translated by Harry Lindblom. Chicago, Philadelphia Book Concern, 1938. 1v. (93p.) (On Bible grounds) No more published. Translation of Pa Bibeln mark, pt. 1: Vinden Blaser Vart den Vill. DLC, CLamB

832 Pethrus, Lewi, 1884-1974.
The wind bloweth where it listeth, by Lewi Pethrus. Translated by Harry Lindblom. 2d ed. Chicago, Philadelphia Book Concern, 1945. 1v. (93p.) No more published. Translation of Pa Bibelns mark, pt. 1: Vinden Blaser Vart den Vill.

833 Pethrus, Lewi, 1884-1974.
The wind bloweth where it listeth, by Lewi Pethrus. Translated by Harry Lindblom. Minneapolis, Bethany Fellowship, 1968, c1945. v, 93p. Translation of Pa Bibelns mark, pt. 1: Vinden Blaser Vart den Vill.

834 Petrelli, Giuseppe
Heavenward: book I, The Holy Spirit; book II, Receiving the kingdom; book III, Partakers of the divine nature. New York, 1953. 303p. DLC

835 Petrelli, Giuseppe
The law of the Spirit. Syracuse, N. Y., House of Prayer, 19--. 51p.

836   Phillips, Frederic B.
          Is war Christian? By Frederic B. Phillips. London, Vic-
      tory Press, 1936. viii,108p. L

837   Pirolo, Nicholas, -1946.
          Babylon, political and ecclesiastical, showing characteristics
      of anti-Christ and false prophet, considering Mussolini and the
      Pope with their respective, "Vv il Duce" and "Vicarius Filii
      Dei," 666.   Milwaukee, Word and Witness Publishing Co.,
      1937.   109p.   On cover: The Pope, Mussolini, Babylon, 666.
      DLC

838   Pirolo, Nicholas, -1946.
          The Roman system of religion, is [!] effects upon the na-
      tions, the churches, the home and the individual. Chicago,
      Word and Witness Publishing Co., 1942. 82p. DLC, OCU

839   Poole, Ralph A.
          Healing, our divine heritage, by Ralph A. Poole. Corpus
      Christi, Tex., Christian Triumph Press, c1952. 80p. TxWaS

840   Pope, Willard H.
          Revelation rightly divided; written so that you can understand
      it. By Willard H. Pope and Gerald S. Pope. 2d ed. Tulsa,
      County Office Supply Co., c1947. 143p. CSaT

841   Pottinger, Robert E.
          Heal the sick, by Robert E. Pottinger. La Verne, Calif.,
      El Comino Press, c1973. 130p.

842   Price, Charles Sydney, 1887-1947.
          The battle of Armageddon. Pasadena, Calif., Charles S.
      Price Publishing Co., c1938. 119p. DLC

843   Price, Charles Sydney, 1887-1947
          The end of the world and you, by Charles S. Price. Pasa-
      dena, Calif., Charles S. Price Publishing Co., c1939. 112p.
      CLamB

844   Price, Charles Sydney, 1887-1947.
          The great physician, by Charles S. Price. Winnipeg, Man.,
      DeMontport Press, c1924. 98p.

845   Price, Charles Sydney, 1887-1947.
          The meaning of faith, by Charles S. Price. Pasadena,
      Calif., 1936. 78p.

846   Price, Charles Sydney, 1887-1947.
          Miracles: being an account of miraculous healings in the
      Charles S. Price evangelistic campaigns. Seattle, 1930. 160p.

847   Price, Charles Sydney, 1887-1947.
          Mussolini: is he the anti-Christ? With introductory chap-

ters on Nebuchadnezzar's image, by Charles S. Price. Seattle, Charles S. Price Publishing Co., c1929. 101p.

848 Price, Charles Sydney, 1887-1947.
The next war. Pasadena, Calif., C. S. Price Publishing Co., c1936. 79p. DLC

849 Price, Charles Sydney, 1887-1947.
The sick are healed [by] Charles S. Price. Pasadena, Calif., C. S. Price Publishing Co., 1939. 63p.

850 Price, Charles Sydney, 1887-1947.
Spiritual and physical health, by Charles S. Price. Pasadena, Calif., 1946. 174p. TxWaS

851 Pridgeon, Charles Hamilton, 1863-1932.
Faith and prayer, by C. H. Pridgeon. Pittsburgh, Evangelization Society of the Pittsburgh Bible Institute, 1928. xi, 151p. DLC

852 Pridgeon, Charles Hamilton, 1863-1932.
Is hell eternal; or, Will God's plan fail? By Charles H. Pridgeon. New York, Funk & Wagnalls, 1920. 333p. DLC, OCl, OO, UU, ViU, Wa

853 Pridgeon, Charles Hamilton, 1863-1932.
Is hell eternal; or, Will God's plan fail? By Charles H. Pridgeon. 3d ed. Pittsburgh, Evangelization Society of the Pittsburgh Bible Institute, 1931, c1920. xiii, 327p.

854 Prince, Derek
Pentecost. Chicago, Faith Tabernacle, 19--. 3v.

855 Ramsey, Vic
Why I pray for the sick. Great Yarmouth, Norfolk, Vic Ramsey Evangelistic Association, 1958. 23p. L

856 Richards, William Thomas Henry, 1916-1974.
Pentecost is dynamite [by] W. T. H. Richards. Nashville, Abingdon Press, c1972. 94p. MBU-T, TxWaS

857 Richey, Eloise May
Crumbs from the master's table. Houston, Richey Evangelistic Association, 19--. 69p. TxWaS

858 Roberts, Oral, 1918-
The baptism with the Holy Spirit and the value of speaking in tongues today. Tulsa, 1964. 96p. KyLxCB, MH-AH, TxWaS, KyWAT

859 Roberts, Oral, 1918-
Christ in every book of the Bible. Tulsa, 1965. 95p.

860   Roberts, Oral, 1918-
      A daily guide to miracles and successful living through seed-
      faith.   Tulsa, Pinoak Publications, 1975.   367p.

861   Roberts, Oral, 1918-
      Deliverance from fear and from sickness.   Tulsa, 1954.
      94p.   DLC, TxWaS

862   Roberts, Oral, 1918-
      Deliverance from fear and from sickness.   Rev. ed.   Tulsa,
      1967, c1954.   96p.

863   Roberts, Oral, 1918-
      The drama of the end-time.   Tulsa, 1963.   95p.

864   Roberts, Oral, 1918-
      Exactly how you may receive your healing--through faith;
      including a heart-to-heart talk on your salvation.   Tulsa,
      Oral Roberts Evangelistic Association, 1958.   64p.   DLC,
      TxWaS

865   Roberts, Oral, 1918-
      Expect a new miracle every day.   Tulsa, Oral Roberts
      Evangelistic Association, 1963.   63p.   CMlG

866   Roberts, Oral, 1918-
      Faith against life's storms.   Tulsa, 1957.   95p.   NjPT

867   Roberts, Oral, 1918-
      God is a good God; believe it and come alive.   Indianapolis,
      Bobbs-Merrill, 1960.   188p.   DLC

868   Roberts, Oral, 1918-
      God is a good God; believe it and come alive.   Kingswood,
      Eng. , World's Work, 1961.   220p.   L

869   Roberts, Oral, 1918-
      God's formula for success and prosperity, edited by Oral
      Roberts and G. H. Montgomery.   Tulsa, 1956.   158p.   DLC

870   Roberts, Oral, 1918-
      God's formula for success and prosperity, ed. by the edi-
      torial staff, Abundant life magazine.   Rev. ed.   Tulsa, Abun-
      dant Life Publications, 1966.   128p.   First ed. by O. Roberts
      and G. H. Montgomery, published in 1956.   DLC

871   Roberts, Oral, 1918-
      Healing for the whole man.   Tulsa, 1965.   61p.

872   Roberts, Oral, 1918-
      The healing stream.   Tulsa, Oral Roberts Evangelistic
      Association, 1959.   70p.   OkTOr

873 Roberts, Oral, 1918-
    The healing stream. Tulsa, 1960, c1959. 71p. Revision of 1959 ed.

874 Roberts, Oral, 1918-
    The Holy Spirit in the now. Tulsa, c1974. 2v.

875 Roberts, Oral, 1918-
    How to be personally prepared for the second coming of Christ. Tulsa, c1967. 64p.

876 Roberts, Oral, 1918-
    How to find your point of contact with God. Tulsa, c1962. 63p.

877 Roberts, Oral, 1918-
    How to find your point of contact with God. Tulsa, 1966, c1962. 63p. Revision of 1962 ed.

878 Roberts, Oral, 1918-
    If you need healing do these things. Tulsa, c1947. 130p.

879 Roberts, Oral, 1918-
    If you need healing do these things. Rev. ed. Tulsa, Healing Waters, Inc. , c1950. 130p.

880 Roberts, Oral, 1918-
    If you need healing do these things. 2d, rev. ed. Tulsa, Oral Roberts Evangelistic Association, 1957. 126p. DLC

881 Roberts, Oral, 1918-
    If you need healing do these things. 2d, rev. ed. Tulsa, 1965. 92p. DNLM

882 Roberts, Oral, 1918-
    If you need healing do these things. 4th, rev. ed. Tulsa, 1969. 57p.

883 Roberts, Oral, 1918-
    Life takes on new meaning when you expect a miracle every day. Rev. ed. Tulsa, Oral Roberts Evangelistic Association, 1969. 63p. First ed. published in 1963 under title: Expect a miracle every day.

884 Roberts, Oral, 1918-
    The miracle book; God made miracles for you, and you for miracles. Tulsa, Pinoak Publications, 1972. 275p. Sequel to Miracle of seed-faith. KyWAT

885 Roberts, Oral, 1918-
    Miracle of seed-faith. Tulsa, Oral Roberts Evangelistic Association, 1970. 168p. Sequel: The miracle book.

886   Roberts, Oral, 1918-
         My blessing pact covenant with God [by] Oral and Evelyn
         Roberts.   Tulsa, Oral Roberts Evangelistic Association, c1969.
         48p.

887   Roberts, Oral, 1918-
         101 questions and answers on healing and salvation.   Tulsa,
         1968.   95p.

888   Roberts, Oral, 1918-
         Raising the roof for victory.   Tulsa, c1964.   64p.

889   Roberts, Oral, 1918-
         Seed-faith commentary on the Holy Bible.   Tulsa, Pinoak
         Publications, 1975.   272p.

890   Roberts, Oral, 1918-
         Seven divine aids for your health.   Tulsa, 1960.   79p.
         DLC

891   Roberts, Oral, 1918-
         This is your abundant life in Jesus Christ; Bible studies in
         Abundant life.   Rev. ed.   Tulsa, Abundant Life Publications,
         1961.   126p.

892   Roberts, Oral, 1918-
         Your healing problems and how to solve them.   Tulsa,
         1966.   93p.

893   Robinson, Charles Elmo, 1867-1954.
         His glorious church.   London, Victory Press, 1932.   vi,
         181p.   L

894   Robinson, Charles Elmo, 1867-1954.
         Praying to change things, being a presentation of rules,
         principles and warnings; intended to teach lowly and common-
         place men how to pray effectively.   By Chas. E. Robinson.
         Dayton, Ohio, J. J. Scruby, c1925.   117p.   DLC

895   Robinson, Charles Elmo, 1867-1954.
         Praying to change things, being a presentation of rules,
         principles and warnings; intended to teach lowly and common-
         place men how to pray effectively.   By Chas. E. Robinson.
         London, Victory Press, 1930.   vii,103p.   L

896   Robinson, J.
         The Holy Spirit.   n.p., Evangel Bible Correspondence
         School, 19--.   120p.

897   Sabiers, Karl George, 1917-
         The amazing story how archaeology proves how the Bible is
         true.   Los Angeles, Robertson Publishing Co., c1943.   89p.
         (Christian study course series.)   CLamB

898   Sabiers, Karl George, 1917-
         Astounding new discoveries [by] Karl G. Sabiers. Los
      Angeles, Robertson Publishing Co. , c1941. 171p. DLC

899   Sabiers, Karl George, 1917-
         Astounding new discoveries.   Toronto, Numerica Unlimited,
      194-. 24p. OCH

900   Sabiers, Karl George, 1917-
         Astounding new discoveries; thousands of amazing facts dis-
      covered beneath the very surface of the original Bible text.
      Los Angeles, Christian Books for the World, c1948. 24p.
      DLC

901   Sabiers, Karl George, 1917-
         A comparison of world religions, by Karl G. Sabiers.
      Los Angeles, Robertson Publishing Co. , 1944. 92p.

902   Sabiers, Karl George, 1917-
         How the Bible came down through the centuries, from its
      ancient manuscripts to our modern printed copies, by Karl G.
      Sabiers. Los Angeles, Robertson Publishing Co. , c1943.
      92p. (Christian study course series, 23.) NN

903   Sabiers, Karl George, 1917-
         Where are the dead?   The Bible answer, fundamental!
      Orthodox! By Karl G. Sabiers. Hollywood, Calif. , c1938.
      111p. "First edition. " DLC

903a Säw, Ivar
         Sigynerpredikanten Gipsy Smith; til norsk ved Knut Knutsen.
      Oslo, Filadelfiaforlaget, 1947. 66p. DLC

904   Schneider, Karl, 1896-1967.
         Die Geistesgaben. Basel, Mission fuer das volle Evangelium,
      1958. 38p. MH-AH, OkTOr

904a Schoch, David E.
         The precious blood, by David E. Schloch.   Long Beach, Ca. ,
      Bethany Missionary Association, 1975, c1965. 30p. Cover
      title.   "Second printing. "

904b Schoch, David E.
         Sarah: a picture of the restored church as seen in Genesis
      20 [by] David E. Schoch.   Long Beach, Ca. , Bethany Missionary
      Association, 197-. 26p.

905   Schrader, Anna
         Prophecies of the ages; given by the spirit of prophecy to
      Anna Schrader. Dallas, Christ for the Nations, 19--. v. 1- .

906   Scruby, John James, 1863- , ed.
         Gems of truth on divine healing, by John J. Scruby.

Dayton, Ohio, 19--.   3v.   TxWaS

907 Scruby, John James, 1863-
        The great tribulation, the church's supreme test.   Dayton,
     Ohio, c1933- . v. 1- . DLC

908 Scruby, John James, 1863-
        Need believers die?   A reply to Rev. Donald Gee of London,
     England, by John J. Scruby.   Dayton, Ohio, 194-.   179,16p.
     "A supplement to The redemption of the body, a present attain-
     ment by faith. "

909 Scruby, John James, 1863-
        The redemption of the body, a present attainment by faith,
     by John J. Scruby.   Rev. and enl. ed.   Dayton, Ohio, 194-.
     641p.

910 Sisson, Elizabeth, 1843-
        Foregleams of glory; resurrection papers; faith reminis-
     cences; in Trinity college.   Chicago, Evangel Publishing House,
     1912.   201p.   DLC

911 Skibsted, Werner
        Sannheten om tungetalen.   Oslo, Filadelfiaforlaget, 1947.
     55p.   DLC

912 Smith, David R.
        Fasting, a neglected discipline, by David R. Smith.   Wash-
     ington, Pa. , Christian Literature Crusade, 1973, c1954.   96p.

912a Spittler, Russell Paul, 1931-
        Cults and isms; twenty alternates to evangelical Christianity,
     by Russell P. Spittler.   Grand Rapids, Mi. , Baker Book House,
     1962.   143p.   DLC

913 Springer, Rebecca Ruter
        Within the gates.   Edited by Gordon Lindsay.   Dallas,
     Christ for the Nations, 1973.   60p.   First published under the
     title: Intra muros.

914 Squire, Frederick Henry, 1904-1962.
        Divine healing today, by Fred H. Squire.   London, Victory
     Press, 1954.   86p.   NjPT

915 Squire, Frederick Henry, 1904-1962.
        Fruit or leaves?   Soul winning--the Christian's form of na-
     tional service, by Frederick H. Squire.   London, Edinburgh,
     Marshall, Morgan & Scott, 1940.   96p.   L

916 Squire, Frederick Henry, 1904-1962.
        The healing power of Christ, by Frederick H. Squire.
     Southend-on-Sea, Essex, Full Gospel Publishing House, 1935.
     71p.   (Full gospel series)   L

917 Squire, Frederick Henry, 1904-1962.
     Is water baptism necessary? By Frederick H. Squire.
     Southend-on-Sea, Essex, Full Gospel Publishing House, 194-.
     11p. L

918 Squire, Frederick Henry, 1904-1962.
     The personality, ministry and baptism of the Holy Spirit,
     by Frederick H. Squire. Southend-on-Sea, Essex, Full Gospel
     Publishing House, 194-. 23p. L

919 Squire, Frederick Henry, 1904-1962.
     The revelation of the Holy Spirit, by Fredk. H. Squire.
     Leamington Spa, Warwicks. , Full Gospel Publishing House,
     19--. 63p. MnManBS

920 Stewart, Donald Lee, 1939-
     Fakes, frauds, and fools. Miracle Valley, Ariz. , Don
     Stewart Evangelistic Association, 1972. 53p. DLC

921 Stewart, Paul W.
     Body ministry, by Paul W. Stewart and Barbara Franzen.
     Detroit, Evangel Press, 1955. 96p. (Harvest rain series, 4.)

922 Stewart, Paul W.
     The body of Christ, by Paul W. Stewart and Barbara Fran-
     zen. Detroit, Evangel Press, 1954. 108p. (Harvest rain
     series, 3.)

923 Stewart, Paul W.
     Confirmation, by Paul W. Stewart and Barbara Franzen.
     Detroit, Evangel Press, 1954. 116p. (Harvest rain series,
     2.)

924 Stewart, Paul W.
     The grace of God, by Paul W. Stewart and Barbara Franzen.
     Detroit, Evangel Press, 1955. 101p. (Harvest rain series,
     5.)

925 Stewart, Paul W.
     Impartation, by Paul W. Stewart and Barbara Franzen.
     Detroit, Evangel Press, 1954. 109p. (Harvest rain series,
     1.)

926 Stiles, John Edwin
     The gift of the Holy Spirit, by Jack E. Stiles. Burbank,
     Calif. , 196-. 156p.

927 Stiles, John Edwin
     The gift of the Holy Spirit, by J. E. Stiles. Old Tappan,
     N. J. , Revell, 1971. 127p. DLC, KyWAT, MH-AH, MSohG

928 Stiles, John Edwin
     How to receive the Holy Spirit, by J. E. Stiles. Oakdale,
     Calif. , 1949. 20p.

929   Strand, Egil
          Mennesker.   Oslo, Filadelfiaforlaget, 1948.   126p.   DLC

929a Stranges, Frank Ernest, 1927-
          Danger from the stars; a warning from Frank E. Stranges.
      Van Nuys, Ca. , I. E. C. , Inc. , 196-.   14ℓ .   Cover title.
      DLC

929b Stranges, Frank Ernest, 1927-
          Flying saucerama, by Frank E. Stranges.   New York,
      Vantage Press, 1959.   115p.   DLC, NN, O

929c Stranges, Frank Ernest, 1927-
          My friend from beyond earth, by Frank E. Stranges.
      Kitchener, Ont. , Galaxy Press, 1972.   [24]p.   DLC

929d Stranges, Frank Ernest, 1927-
          My friend from beyond earth, by Frank E. Stranges.   New,
      rev. enl. ed.   Van Nuys, Ca. , I. E. C. , Book Division, 1974.
      63p.   IU

929e Stranges, Frank Ernest, 1927-
          New flying saucerama, by Frank E. Stranges.   4th ed.
      Glendale, N. Y. , International Evangelism Crusades, 1966.
      117p.   First ed. published in 1959 under title: Flying saucer-
      ama.   DLC

929f Stranges, Frank Ernest, 1927-
          Stranger at the Pentagon, by Frank E. Stranges.   Van Nuys,
      Ca. , I. E. C. , Inc. , Book Division, 1967.   v, 201p.   DLC

930   Stroup, John, 1853-1929.
          What God can do.   South Solon, Oh. , 1913.   136p.

931   Sumrall, Lester Frank, 1913-
          The cup of life, by Lester Sumrall.   Nashville, Sceptre
      Books, c1980.   180p.

932   Sumrall, Lester Frank, 1913-
          Demons: the answer book [by] Lester Sumrall.   Nashville,
      T. Nelson, c1979.   139p.   DLC

933   Sumrall, Lester Frank, 1913-
          Hypnotism, divine or demonic?   South Bend, Ind. , Lester
      Sumrall Evangelistic Association, 19--.   30p.   OkTOr

934   Sumrall, Lester Frank, 1913-
          Is one world possible?   By Lester F. Ward.   n. p. , 195-.
      32p.

935   Sumrall, Lester Frank, 1913-
          Living free [by] Lester Sumrall.   Nashville, Tenn. , Sceptre
      Books, c1979.   175p.   DLC

936 Teuber, Andrew S.
Tongues of fire, by Andrew S. Teuber. n. p., 1966. 32p.

937 Törnberg, Allan, 1907-1956.
Stötestenen; några ord till stod och hjälp for dem som söka
eller tvivla. Stockholm, Fritze, 1956. 95p. MH

938 Tolson, Billy Joe
The Antichrist: satan's messiah [by] Billy J. Tolson. New
York, Carlton Press, c1978. 64p.

939 Tolson, Billy Joe
The golden book of theology [by] Billy J. Tolson. Hicks-
ville, N. Y., Exposition Press, c1979. 88p.

940 Tubby, C. S.
The time of the end: unmistakable signs of Christ's coming,
by C. S. Tubby. 3d ed., revised, improved, illustrated.
Stevensville, Ont., 19--. 117p.

941 Ulonska, Reinhold
Nahe und doch so fern. Erzhausen, Leuchter-Verl., 1971.
71p.

942 Wärenstam, Eric, 1905-
Amerika och Gud. Stockholm, Förlaget Filadelfia, 1958.
175p. MH-AH, NN

943 Wärenstam, Eric, 1905-
James Hudson Taylor, mannen som vågade. Stockholm,
Filadelfia, 1947. 107p. (Kämpar i Guds här, 2.) CtY-D,
NN

944 Wärenstam, Eric, 1905-
John Wesley; landsvägariddaren som vackte England. Stockholm, Förlaget Filadelfia, 1949. 93p. (Kämpar i Guds här,
5.) DLC, NNUT

945 Wärenstam, Eric, 1905-
Judafolkets väg; den historiska bakgrunden, framtidsperspek-
tivet. Jönköping, Hall, 1949. 24p. DLC

946 Wärenstam, Eric, 1905-
Messias: Messiastro och Messiahsforvätan inom judendom
och kristendom. Stockholm, Förlaget Filadelfia, 1953. 187p.
MH-AH

947 Wärenstam, Eric, 1905-
Mayflower och pilgrimerna. Stockholm, Förlaget Filadelfia,
1957. 232p. DLC, MH, MnU, NN, WHi

948 Wärenstam, Eric, 1905-
Varför hatar man judarna? Jönköping, Hall, 1950. 61p.
DLC, NN

949   Wallis, Arthur R.
      God's chosen fast; a spiritual and practical guide to fasting,
      by Arthur R. Wallis.   London, Victory Press, 1968.   119p.
      L

950   Wallis, Arthur R.
      God's chosen fast, by Arthur Wallis.   London, Victory
      Press, 1969.   119p.   A reduced photographic reprint of the
      edition of 1968.   L

951   Wallis, Arthur R.
      Into battle; a manual of the Christian life, by Arthur Wallis.
      Eastbourne, Victory Press, 1973.   122p.   DLC

952   Wallis, Arthur R.
      Pray in the Spirit: the work of the Holy Spirit in the min-
      istry of prayer, by Arthur Wallis.   Eastbourne, Victory Press,
      1970.   126p.

953   Warnock, George H.
      The feast of tabernacles, by George H. Warnock.   Spring-
      field, Mo., B. Britton, 1951.   122p.

954   Watkins, Mamie
      The baptism in the Holy Spirit made plain.   Greensburg,
      Pa., Manna Christian Outreach, c1975.   128p.   DLC, ViRUT

955   Watts, Newman
      God heals.   London, Victory Press, 19--.   95p.   TxWaS

956   The way of unity: baptism of the Holy Ghost and gifts in the
      church.   Winton, Hants., Eng., K. F. Publications, 1956.
      [8]p.

957   Wells, Robert J.
      Be filled with the Spirit, by Robert J. Wells.   Sacramento,
      Calif., Bethel Temple, 1950.   47p.

958   West, Jack
      The day death died.   Stow, Ohio, New Hope Press, 1974.
      106p.

959   Whitmire, Charles D., ed.
      Behold He cometh!   n.p., 19--.   20p.

960   Whyte, Harry Archibald Maxwell
      Bible baptisms, by H. A. Maxwell Whyte.   Scarborough,
      Ont., 1971.   36p.

961   Whyte, Harry Archibald Maxwell
      Charismatic gifts, by H. A. Maxwell Whyte.   Scarborough,
      Ont., 19--.   32p.

962 Whyte, Harry Archibald Maxwell
       Charismatic gifts, by H. A. Maxwell Whyte. 3d ed. Scar-
     borough, Ont., 1970. 32p.

963 Whyte, Harry Archibald Maxwell
       Dominion over demons, by H. A. Maxwell Whyte. Toronto,
     Booksellers and Church Bookroom, 196-. 38p.

964 Whyte, Harry Archibald Maxwell
       The emerging church, by H. A. Maxwell Whyte. Scar-
     borough, Ont., 1971. 46p.

965 Whyte, Harry Archibald Maxwell
       The prophetic word, by H. A. Maxwell Whyte. Scarborough,
     Ont., 1971. 34p.

966 Wight, Fred Hartley, 1899-
       Jesus Christ--His pre-existence, deity, humanity and minis-
     try, by Fred H. Wight and Karl G. Sabiers. Los Angeles,
     Robertson Publishing Co., 1944. 92p. (Christian study course
     series, 13.) DLC

967 Willitts, Ethel R.
       The Holy Spirit, by Ethel R. Willitts. Chicago, 19--. 31p.

968 Willitts, Ethel R.
       The second coming of Christ, by Ethel R. Willitts. n.p.,
     19--. 32p.

969 Woodworth-Etter, Maria Beulah (Underwood), 1844-1924.
       Questions and answers on divine healing, by Mrs. M. B.
     Woodworth-Etter. Revised and enlarged, together with scrip-
     tures on the subject, to which is added a brief account of God's
     call and remarks regarding the new tabernacle. Indianapolis,
     192-. 40p.

970 Wyatt, Evelyn
       The believer's heritage. Los Angeles, Wings of Healing,
     c1965. 32p. KyWAT

971 Wyatt, Evelyn
       Healing unlimited. Los Angeles, Wings of Healing, 1968.
     32p.

972 Wyatt, Evelyn
       The place called "There." Los Angeles, Wings of Healing,
     1965. 32p.

973 Wyatt, Thomas, -1964.
       The work of demons. 3d ed. Portland, Ore., Wings of
     Healing, 1948, c1946. 32p.

974 Zaiss, Herman, -1956.

Das Abendmahl. Marburg a. d. Lahn, Rathmann, 1959.
63p. MH-AH

975 Zaiss, Herman, -1956.
Gottes Imperativ; sei gesund! Die Bibel als Schlussel zu
einem gesunden Leben der Freude und Kraft; eine biblische
Therapie. 2. Aufl. Marburg, Rathmann, 1958. 100p.
(Veröffentlichung Nr. 2 der Schriftenreihe "Die Aktualität des
lebendigen Wortes. ") DNLM

-- --NON-PENTECOSTAL AUTHORS

976 Åberg, Zander
Har Pingstvännerna Rätt? Ett ord i andedopsfrågan. Stockholm, Missionsförbundets, 1956. 127p. MH-AH

977 Adams, Moody Paul, 1931-
Jesus never spoke in tongues, by Moody Adams. Baker,
La., c1974. 94p.

978 Allen, Stuart
Tongues speaking today: a mark of spirituality or deception?
London, Berean Publishing Trust, 1971. 8p.

979 American Lutheran Church. Commission on Evangelism.
A report on glossolalia (speaking in tongues). Minneapolis,
196-. 6ℓ. MoSCS

980 Andersen, Hans Jörgen
The "ABC" of Acts 2:4: glosse-tongues, by Hans J. Andersen. Los Angeles, c1926. 64p. DLC

981 Andersen, Robert F.
A study of the theology of the Episcopalians, the Lutherans,
and the Pentecostals on the charismata of the Holy Spirit, es-
pecially as manifested in speaking in tongues and healing, by
Robert F. Andersen. Springfield, Ill., 1964. v, 67ℓ. Thesis
(B. D.)--Concordia Theological Seminary. ISC

982 Anderson, Sir Robert, 1841-1918.
Spirit manifestations and "The gift of tongues. " 3d ed.
London, Evangelical Alliance & Marshall Bros., 1909. 36p.
Includes criticism of the Irvingites. L

983 Anderson, Sir Robert, 1851-1918.
Spirit manifestations and "The gift of tongues. " 4th ed.
Glasgow, 1909. 32p. Includes criticism of the Irvingites.
PPDrop, PPULC

984 Anderson, Sir Robert, 1841-1918.
Spirit manifestations and "the gift of tongues. " Neptune,
N. J., Loizeaux Brothers, 19--. 31p. Cover title. KyWAT,
MoWgT

985 Averill, R. L.
      The Apostolic Faith movement, by R. L. Averill. In Holi-
      ness Evangel, 1 (Jan. 1, 1907)

986 Averill, R. L.
      The "tongues" people as I saw them, by R. L. Averill.
      In Pentecostal Advocate, 10 (Jan. 10, 1907).

987 Axup, Edward J.
      The truth about Bible tongues, by Edward J. Axup. Stock-
      ton, Calif., 1933. 44p. CAzPC

988 Bales, James David, 1915-
      The Holy Spirit and the Christian, by James D. Bales.
      Shreveport, La., Lambert Book House, c1966. 147p. "The
      miraculous gifts of the Spirit": p. 15-36.

989 Bales, James David, 1915-
      Miracles or mirages? By James D. Bales. Austin, Tex.,
      Firm Foundation Publishing House, c1956. 279p.

990 Banks, William L.
      Questions you have always wanted to ask about tongues,
      but.... [By] William L. Banks. Chattanooga, Tenn., AMG
      Publishers, 1978. 79p.

991 Barnhouse, Donald Grey, 1895-1960.
      Finding fellowship with Pentecostals. In Eternity, 9 (Apr.
      1958), 8-10.

992 Barr, James
      Fundamentalism. Philadelphia, Westminster Press, c1978.
      vii, 379p. "Pentecostalism and the like": p. 207-209. DLC

993 Bauman, Louis Sylvester, 1875-
      The modern tongues movement, examined and judged in the
      light of the scripture and in the light of its fruits, by Louis S.
      Bauman. 3d ed. Long Beach, Calif., A. S. Pearce, 1941.
      38p. First ed. published in 1930.

994 Bauman, Louis Sylvester, 1875-
      The tongues movement, by Louis S. Bauman. Winona Lake,
      Ind., Brethren Missionary Herald Co., c1963. 47p.

995 Baxter, Robert, 1802-1889.
      Narrative of facts concerning the unknown tongues and super-
      natural manifestations in members of the Rev. Edward Irving's
      congregation and other individuals, and formerly in the writer
      himself--manifestations preceding the establishment of the Catho-
      lic Apostolic Church. London, Prophetic News Office and Beth-
      shan Bookroom, 1908. 48p. At head of title: Speaking in
      tongues. Written and first published in 1832.

996   Belew, Pascal Perry, 1894-
            The gift of tongues, by P. P. Belew. In Herald of Holi-
       ness, 6 (Oct. 17, 1917), 4.

997   Belew, Pascal Perry, 1894-
            Light on the tongues question, by Pascal P. Belew. Kan-
       sas City, Mo., Nazarene Publishing House, 1926. 64p.
       CSdP, MoKN

998   Bishop, Albert E.
            Tongues, signs, and visions, not God's order for today,
       by A. E. Bishop. With introduction by C. I. Scofield. Chi-
       cago, Bible Institute Colportage Association, c1920. 24p.
       ICMB

999   Blackwelder, Boyce W., 1913-
            Thirty errors of modern tongues advocates, by Boyce W.
       Blackwelder. In Vital Christianity, 94 (May 26, 1974), 9-10.

1000   Blaney, Harvey Judson Smith, 1905-
            Speaking in unknown tongues: the Pauline position by Har-
       vey J. S. Blaney. Kansas City, Mo., Beacon Hill Press,
       1973. 24p. "First printing."

1001   Boer, Harry R.
            The Spirit: tongues and message [by] Harry R. Boer.
       In Christianity Today, 7 (Jan. 4, 1963), 6-7.

1002   Boggs, Wade Hamilton, 1916-
            Faith healing and the Christian faith [by] Wade H. Boggs,
       Jr. Richmond, John Knox Press, 1956. 216p. DLC, MCE,
       RBaB

1003   Boggs, Wade Hamilton, 1916-
            Faith healing cults, by Wade H. Boggs, Jr. In Interpreta-
       tion, 11 (Jan. 1957), 55-70.

1004   Bostrom, Fred W.
            House built upon the sand; Christian Science examined, so-
       cialism reviewed, Pentecostal Movement tested, by Fred W.
       Bostrom. Los Angeles, 1921. 409p. DLC

1005   Bosworth, Fred Francis, 1877-1958.
            "Do all speak with tongues?" (1 Cor. 12:30); an open let-
       ter to the ministers and saints of the Pentecostal Movement,
       by F. F. Bosworth. Dallas, 19--. 24p.

1006   Brethren in Christ Church. Board of Bishops.
            The gift of tongues. [Nappanee, Ind., 19--] folder (8p.)
       "Written by David E. Climenhaga, bishop of the Central Con-
       ference, for the Board of Bishops, Brethren in Christ Church."

1007   Brooks, Delos Ferdinand, 1845-1935.

What was the only work of God performed in believers at
Pentecost? or, No new language given at Pentecost. Albany,
N. Y., 19--. 16p. CSdP

1008   Brown, Charles Ewing, 1883-1971.
       The confusion of tongues, by Charles E. Brown. Ander-
       son, Ind., Gospel Trumpet Co., 1949. 31p. ("Paper mes-
       senger" series.)

1009   Brown, John Elward, 1879-1957.
       Will Pentecost be repeated? By John E. Brown. Siloam
       Springs, Ark., John Brown University Press, 1935. 250p.

1010   Bruner, Frederick Dale
       A theology of the Holy Spirit; the Pentecostal experience
       and the New Testament witness. Grand Rapids, Mich., Eerd-
       mans, 1970. 390p. Based on thesis (Th. D.)--Hamburg,
       1963. DLC

1011   Bruner, Frederick Dale
       A theology of the Holy Spirit; the Pentecostal experience
       and the New Testament witness. London, Hodder and Stough-
       ton, 1971. 390p. Based on thesis (Th. D.)--Hamburg, 1963.
       DLC

1012   Buck, E. Parker
       The true Bible teaching versus the unknown tongue theory,
       by E. Parker Buck. Brooksville, Fla., Printed by Transyl-
       vania Bible School, Freeport, Pa., 19--. 32p.

1013   Buck, E. Parker
       The true Bible teaching versus the unknown tongue theory,
       by E. Parker Buck. [Marion, Ind., Wesley Press], 1962.
       32p. Reprint.

1014   Budd, William H.
       The Bible gift of tongues vs. the modern gift of unknown
       tongues, by William H. Budd. Louisville, Ky., Pentecostal
       Publishing Co., 1909. 16p. Cover title. "Sermon ...
       preached at the Bonnie, Ill., holiness camp meeting, Aug. 17,
       1909. KyWA, KyWAT

1015   Burdick, Donald Walter, 1917-
       Tongues: to speak or not to speak, by Donald W. Burdick.
       Chicago, Moody Press, 1969. 94p. (Christian forum books.)
       CAzPC, PPiPT

1016   Burgess, W. J.
       Glossolalia: speaking in tongues, by W. J. Burgess.
       Little Rock, Ark., Baptist Publications Committee, c1968.
       64p.

1017   Burns, J. Lanier

A reemphasis on the purpose of sign gifts [by] J. Lanier
Burns. In Bibliotheca Sacra, 132 (July 1975), 242-249.

1018   Byrum, Russell Raymond, 1888-
        Holy Spirit baptism and the second cleansing, by Russell
        R. Byrum. Anderson, Ind., Gospel Trumpet Co., c1923.
        107p. "The evidence of the baptism": p. 29-31. DLC

1019   Caldwell, Wayne Eugene
        The fruit and gifts of the Holy Spirit, by Wayne E. Cald-
        well. Edited by Armor D. Peisker. Marion, Ind., Wesley
        Press, c1979. iii, 204p.

1020   Callen, Barry L.
        A Biblical perspective on tongues, by Barry Callen. In
        Vital Christianity, 99 (Jan. 21, 1979), 9-10; 99 (Feb. 11,
        1979), 9-10.

1021   Carradine, Beverly, 1848-1931.
        A box of treasure. Chicago, Christian Witness Co.,
        c1910. 336p. "The Upper Room and tongues": p. 78-85.
        IKON, OkBetC

1022   Carter, Charles Webb, 1905-
        The Bible gift of tongues, by Charles W. Carter. Syra-
        cuse, N.Y., Wesley Press, 1952. 44p.

1023   Carter, Charles Webb, 1905-
        The person and ministry of the Holy Spirit, a Wesleyan
        perspective. Grand Rapids, Mich., Baker Book House, 1974.
        355p. DLC

1024   Cate, B. F.
        The nine gifts of the Spirit are not in the church today;
        or, The answer to the modern tongues and healing movements,
        by B. F. Cate. Des Plaines, Ill., Regular Baptist Press,
        c1956. 62p.

1025   Chalfant, Morris
        Unknown tongues--tomfoolery or not? Danville, Ill.,
        196-. 58p.

1026   Chapman, James Blaine, 1884-1947.
        Questions answered, by J. B. Chapman. In Herald of
        Holiness, 11 (July 19, 1922), 2; 11 (Jan. 3, 1923), 3; 13
        (Jan. 7, 1925), 6.

1027   Chapman, James Blaine, 1884-1947. Questions and answers.
        In Herald of Holiness, 15 (June 9, 1926), 12.

1028   Chapman, James Blaine, 1884-1947.
        Editorial comments, by J. B. Chapman. In Herald of
        Holiness, 16 (June 8, 1927), 4.

1029   Chapman, James Blaine, 1884-1947.
           The question box. In Herald of Holiness, 23 (Aug. 11,
       1934), 12; 12 (Aug. 25, 1934), 13; 25 (Feb. 20, 1937), 12;
       27 (Sept. 24, 1938), 13; 28 (Aug. 19, 1939), 12; 32 (Dec. 6,
       1943), 11; 32 (Feb. 28, 1944), 2, 11; 34 (Feb. 25, 1946), 8;
       36 (Apr. 21, 1947), 10-11.

1030   Chapman, James Blaine, 1884-1947.
           Sanctification and the baptism with the Holy Ghost.   In
       Herald of Holiness, 13 (Feb. 4, 1925), 2.   Editorial.

1031   Chesnut, Lawrence James
           True Bible tongues, their proper place and use in the
       church, by Lawrence J. Chesnut.   Oklahoma City, 1948.
       96p.   CAzPC, OrPWP

1032   Church, John Robert, 1899-
           Which is right? One, two or three works of grace? Is
       speaking with tongues a sign of the baptism with the Spirit?
       By John R. Church.   Louisville, Ky., Pentecostal Publishing
       Co., 19--.   94p.   KyWAT, MoKN

1033   Coppin, Enoch, 1896-
           "The Holy Spirit"; Pentecostalism's travesty and imitation.
       Palmerston North, N.Z., 1964.   48p.   CLamB

1034   Coppin, Enoch, 1896-
           The Pentecostalist Spirit-baptism.   Levin, N.Z., K. B.
       H. Print, 1955.   32p.   ("Wolves in sheep's clothing series,"
       3.)   CLamB

1035   Corlett, David Shelby, 1894-1979.
           Speaking in other tongues, by D. Shelby Corlett.   In
       Herald of Holiness, 28 (Apr. 29, 1939), 4; 28 (May 6, 1939),
       4-5.   Symbols of Pentecost, 4.   Editorial.

1036   Corlett, David Shelby, 1894-1979.
           Symbols of Pentecost, by D. Shelby Corlett.   Kansas City,
       Mo., Nazarene Publishing House, 1939.   24p.

1037   Corlett, David Shelby, 1894-1979.
           Tongues at Corinth, by D. Shelby Corlett.   In Herald of
       Holiness, 28 (May 13, 1939), 4-5.   (Symbols of Pentecost, 5.)
       Editorial.

1038   Cox, J. L.
           Tongues theory, by J. L. Cox.   In Herald of Holiness, 6
       (June 27, 1917), 4-5.

1039   Cox, Thomas Benton, 1868-
           Getting "it": Pentecostalism, McPhersonism, divine heal-
       ing; their errors laid bare under the scapel of a medical doc-
       tor.... By T. B. Cox.   Lawndale, Calif., 1927.   70p.
       NNUT

1040   Cox, Thomas Benton, 1868-
         Getting "it": Pentecostalism, McPhersonism, divine
healing; their error and dangers.   In three parts.   By T. B.
Cox.   Lawndale, Calif., c1927.   80p.   CLamB

1041   Crockett, Horace Leeds,   -1951.
         Conversations on "the tongues," by H. L. Crockett.
Louisville, Ky., Pentecostal Publishing Co., c1929.   163p.
DLC

1042   Dallas, W. F.
         The third blessing or the unknown tongues, by W. F.
Dallas.   In Holiness Evangel, 3 (Apr. 14, 1909)

1043   Dallmeyer, Heinrich
         Die Zungenbewegung: ein Beitrag zu ihrer Geschichte
und eine Kennzeichnung ihres Geistes.   Lindhorst, Adastra-
Verlag, 1924.   143p.   L, MH-AH

1044   Dallmeyer, Heinrich
         Die Zungenbewegung: ein Beitrag zu ihrer Geschichte und
eine Kennzeichnung ihres Geistes.   2. Aufl.   Langenthal,
Swit., 19--.   143p.

1045   Davies, John Mathias, 1895-
         Pentecost and today: tongues and healing, by J. M.
Davies.   Kansas City, Kan., Walterick Pub., 19--.   63p.
MWenhG

1046   De Haan, Martin Ralph, 1891-1965.
         Holy Spirit baptism.   Grand Rapids, Mich., Radio Bible
Class, c1964.   32p.   (Studies in Acts booklet, 1.)   Cover
Title.

1047   De Haan, Martin Ralph, 1891-1965.
         Pentecost and after.   Grand Rapids, Mich., Radio Bible
Class, c1964.   32p.   (Studies in Acts booklet, 2.)   Cover
title.

1048   De Haan, Martin Ralph, 1891-1965.
         Pentecost and after, by M. R. De Haan.   Grand Rapids,
Mich., Zondervan Publishing House, 1964.   184p.   DLC,
MSohG

1049   De Haan, Martin Ralph, 1891-1965.
         Speaking in tongues: four messages delivered by M. R.
De Haan over the coast to coast Mutual and ABC networks.
Grand Rapids, Mich., Radio Bible Class, 196-.   29p.   OkTOr

1050   De Haan, Richard W., 1923-
         Speaking in tongues; a series of four messages delivered
over a special network of leading radio stations throughout the
world, by Richard W. De Haan.   Grand Rapids, Mich., Radio

Bible Class, c1967.   32p.   UU

1051   De Haan, Richard W. , 1923-
          Speaking in tongues, by Richard W. De Haan.   In Hillis,
          D. W. , ed.   Is the whole body a tongue?   Grand Rapids,
          Mich. , c1974, 53-77.

1051a Dillow, Joseph C.
          Speaking in tongues [by] Joseph Dillow.   Grand Rapids,
          Mi. , Zondervan Publishing House, 1975.   191p.   DLC,
          KyWAT

1052   Dixon, Amzi Clarence, 1854-1925.
          Speaking with tongues, by A. C. Dixon.   Chicago, Bible
          Institute Colportage Association, 19--.   28p.   TxFS

1053   Dollar, George William, 1917-
          Church history and the tongues movement, by George W.
          Dollar.   In Bibliotheca Sacra, 120 (Oct. -Dec. 1963), 316-321.
          A symposium on the tongues movement.

1054   Dominian, Jacob
          A psychological evaluation of the Pentecostal movement,
          by J. Dominian.   In Expository Times, 87 (July 1976), 292-
          297.

1055   Dominian, Jacob
          A psychological evaluation of the Pentecostal movement,
          by J. Dominian.   In Fountain, 43 (Jan. 18, 1978), 3, 7; 43
          (Jan. 25, 1978), 2-3; 43 (Feb. 1, 1978), 2-3.   Reprint from
          Expository Times, 87 (July 1976).

1056   Duewel, Wesley Luelf, 1916-
          The Holy Spirit and tongues, by Wesley L. Duewel.
          Winona Lake, In. , Light and Life Press, 1974.   xv, 135p.
          PGraM

1057   Dunn, James Douglas Grant, 1939-
          Baptism in the Holy Spirit; a re-examination of the New
          Testament teaching on the gift of the Holy Spirit in relation
          to Pentecostalism today [by] James D. G. Dunn.   London,
          SCM Press, 1970.   viii, 248p.   (Studies in Biblical theology,
          2d ser. , 15.)   "A revised form of the [author's] thesis ...
          1968. "   DLC, MSohG

1058   Dunn, James Douglas Grant, 1939-
          Baptism in the Holy Spirit; a re-examination of the New
          Testament teaching on the gift of the Spirit in relation to
          Pentecostalism today [by] James D. G. Dunn.   Naperville,
          Ill. , A. R. Allenson, 1970.   vii, 248p.   (Studies in Biblical
          theology, 2d ser. , 15.)   TxWaS

1059   Dunn, James Douglas Grant, 1939-

Baptism in the Holy Spirit; a reexamination of the New
Testament teaching on the gift of the Holy Spirit in relation
to Pentecostalism today [by] James D. G. Dunn. Philadelphia, Westminster Press, 1977, c1970. vii, 248p. DLC

1060   Earle, Ralph, 1907-
        Pentecost: what does it mean? In Herald of Holiness,
        64 (Jan. 29, 1975), 8-9.

1061   Eggenberger, Oswald, 1923-
        Evangelischer Glaube und Pfingstbewegung, mit besonderer
        Beruecksichtigung der Verhaeltnisse in der Schweiz. Zollikon,
        Evangelischer Verlag, 1956. 61p. (Schriftenreihe zur Sek-
        tenkunde, 1.) MH-AH

1062   Eggenberger, Oswald, 1923-
        Die Geistestaufe in der gegenwärtigen Pfingstgewegung.
        In Theologische Zeitschrift, 11 (July-Aug. 1955), 272-295.

1063   Elsom, John R.
        Pentecostalism versus the Bible; or, The tongues move-
        ment and why I left it, by John R. Elsom. Los Angeles,
        Wetzel Publishing Co., c1937. 60p. NcD

1064   Epp, Theodore H., 1907-
        Gifts of the Spirit, by Theodore H. Epp. Lincoln, Neb.,
        Back to the Bible Publication, 1954. 93p.

1065   Epp, Theodore H., 1907-
        The use and abuse of tongues, by Theodore H. Epp and
        John I. Paton. Lincoln, Ne., Back to the Bible Broadcast,
        c1963. 47p. "Revision of certain portions of Gifts of the
        Spirit, copyright 1954."

1065a   Epp, Theodore H., 1907-
        The use and abuse of tongues, by Theodore H. Epp and
        John I. Paton. In Hillis, D. W., ed. Is the whole body a
        tongue? Grand Rapids, Mich., c1974, 31-52.

1066   Fife, Eric S.
        Power for the impossible, by Eric Fife. In His, 23
        (Mar. 1963), 1-4.

1067   Frame, Raymond
        Something unusual. In His, 24 (Dec. 1963), 18-20, 25-
        28, 30.

1068   Gaebelein, Arno Clemens, 1861-1945.
        The healing question; an examination of the claims of
        faith-healing and divine healing systems in the light of the
        scriptures and history. New York, Publication Office "Our
        Hope," c1925. 132p. DLC, DNLM, NcC, OrU, NN, PPWe,
        MSohG

1069   Galloway, E. B.
          Latter day peril, by E. B. Galloway. In Pentecostal
       Advocate, 14 (Apr. 27, 1911).

1070   Gauss, J. H.
          God's truth versus man's theories; Bible deliverance from
       Satan's deceits, by J. H. Gauss. St. Louis, Faithful Words
       Pub. Co., 19--. 286p. "Pentecostalism": p. 162-173. PPWe

1071   Gauss, J. H.
          God's truth versus man's theories; Bible deliverance from
       Satan's deceits, by J. H. Gauss. Rev. ed. St. Louis,
       Frederick Printing Co., 19--. 314p. "Pentecostalism":
       p. 188-199.

1072   Gift of tongues.
          In Pentecostal Advocate, 10 (Mar. 14, 1907).

1073   Godbey, William Baxter, 1833-1920.
          Current heresies, by W. B. Godbey. Cincinnati, God's
       Revivalist Office, 19--. 46p. "The tongue movement": p. 20-
       28. OkBetC

1074   Godbey, William Baxter, 1833-1920.
          Pentecost, by W. B. Godbey. Cincinnati, God's Revi-
       valist Office, 19--. 31p. On the "Tongues movement":
       p. 14-17.

1074a Godbey, William Baxter, 1833-1920.
          Tongue movement, satanic, by W. B. Godbey. Zare-
       phath, N.J., Pillar of Fire, 1918. 36p. (The Godbey
       series.) IEG

1075   Goodwin, John Wesley, 1869-1945.
          The miracle of Pentecost; or, The evidence by speaking
       in tongues, by J. W. Goodwin. Kansas City, Mo., Nazarene
       Publishing House, 192-. 22p. Cover title. OkBetC

1076   Gosey, S. B.
          The tongues delusion, by S. B. Gosey. In Herald of
       Holiness, 8 (Aug. 6, 1919), 5.

1077   Greathouse, William Marvin, 1919-
          Who is the Holy Spirit? [By] William M. Greathouse.
       Kansas City, Mo., Nazarene Publishing House, 1972. 11p.
       Cover title. "Reprinted from the Herald of holiness, May
       10, 1972."

1078   Greene, Oliver B., 1915-
          Tongues, by Oliver B. Greene. Greenville, S.C.,
       Gospel Hour, 19--. 29p.

1079   Gromacki, Robert Glenn, 1933-
          The modern tongues movement. Philadelphia, Presby-

terian and Reformed Publishing Co., 1967. 165p. Based
on thesis (Th. D.)--Grace Theological Seminary and College,
1966. DLC, MSohG, TxWaS

1080   Gustafson, Robert R.
            Authors of confusion, by Robert R. Gustafson. Tampa,
        Fla., Grace Publishing Co., c1971. 105p.

1081   Haakonson, R. P.
            Filled with the Holy Spirit, speaking in tongues, healing
        and other phenomenas [!] in religion, by R. P. Haakonson.
        Moorhead, Minn., 19--. 12p.

1082   Haldeman, Isaac Massey, 1845-1933.
            Holy Ghost baptism and speaking with tongues, by I. M.
        Haldeman. New York, 19--. 32p. KyLoS, OMtvM

1083   Harmon, George E.
            The gift of tongues, what it is and what it is not, by
        G. E. Harmon. Glendora, Calif., 19--. 20p. CSdP

1084   Harmon, George E.
            The gift of tongues: what it is and what it is not, by
        George E. Harmon. Guthrie, Okla., Faith Publishing House,
        19--. 20p. Cover title. KyWAT

1085   Harvey, J. F.
            The tongues heresy [by] J. F. Harvey. In Herald of
        Holiness, 23 (Dec. 29, 1934), 10-11.

1086   Hayes, Doremus Almy, 1863-1936.
            The gift of tongues, by D. A. Hayes. Cincinnati, Jen-
        nings and Graham; New York, Eaton and Mains, c1913.
        119p. CSdP, DLC, MBU-T

1087   Hayes, Doremus Almy, 1863-1936.
            The gift of tongues, by D. A. Hayes. New York,
        Methodist Book Concern, 1914, c1913. 119p. OrU

1088   Haynes, Benjamin Franklin, 1851-1923.
            Dangerous fanaticism, by B. F. Haynes. In Herald
        of Holiness, 4 (Apr. 5, 1916), 3-4. Editorial.

1089   Haynes, Benjamin Franklin, 1851-1923.
            Tongues, by B. F. Haynes. In Herald of Holiness, 4
        (June 23, 1915), 1-2. Editorial.

1090   Hefren, H. C.
            From Babel to Pentecost, by H. C. Hefren. Guthrie,
        Okla., Faith Publishing House, 19--. folder (8p.) Caption
        title.

1090a   Hicks, John Mark, 1961-

A teenager speaks on spiritual gifts. Memphis, Tn. ,
Contending for the Faith; Alexandria, Va. , J. M. Hicks,
1977. viii, 95p.

1091   Hills, Aaron Merritt, 1848-1935.
        The tongues movement. Manchester, Star Hall,
        191-. 39p. L

1092   Hinds, J. L.
        The modern gift of tongues exposed, by J. L. Hinds.
        Guthrie, Okla. , Faith Publishing House, 19--. 16p. Caption
        title. "A sermon preached on the public square at Waco,
        Texas, immediately after the tongues people had concluded
        a service--condensed. "

1093   Howard, Richard E. , 1919-
        Tongues speaking in the New Testament, by Dick Howard.
        Norway, Me. , Western Maine Graphics Publications, c1980.
        xii, 126p.

1094   Huckabee, B. W.
        The gift of tongues again, by B. W. Huckabee. In Pente-
        costal Advocate, 10 (Mar. 14, 1907)

1095   Huckabee, B. W.
        The "gift of tongues" and other gifts, by B. W. Huckabee.
        In Pentecostal Advocate, 10 (Feb. 21, 1907).

1095a   Huffman, Jasper Abraham, 1880-1970.
        Speaking in tongues, by J. A. Huffman, Dayton, Oh. ,
        Bethel Publishing Co. , 1910.

1096   Humphreys, Fisher Henry, 1939-
        Speaking in tongues [by] Fisher Humphreys and Malcolm
        Tolbert. Zachary, La. , Printed by Christian Litho, 1973.
        viii, 94p. DLC

1097   Ingler, Arthur F. , 1873-1935.
        The evidence of the baptism with the Holy Ghost, by
        Arthur F. Ingler. In Herald of Holiness, 18 (June 19, 1929),
        5-6.

1098   Irick, Allie, 1878-1949.
        The modern tongues movement indicted. In Herald of
        Holiness, 4 (Aug. 25, 1915), 5.

1099   Ironside, Henry Allan, 1876-1951.
        Apostolic faith missions and the so-called second Pente-
        cost [by] H. A. Ironside. New York, Loizeaux Bros. , 191-.
        15p. Cover title.

1100   Ironside, Henry Allan, 1876-1951.

Holiness: the false and the true, by H. A. Ironside.
Neptune, N. J. , Loizeaux Bros. , 19--. 142p. Reprint of
1912 ed. On Pentecostal churches: p. 38-39.

1101   Irvine, William C.
        The tongues movement: is the present-day tongues move-
        ment scriptural? By Wm. C. Irvine. In Irvine, W. C. ,
        comp. Heresies exposed. 11th ed. Los Angeles, 1940.
        193-199p. "First edition as Timely warnings, 1917; second
        edition as Modern heresies exposed, 1919; third edition as
        Heresies exposed, 1921; ... eighth edition, revised & en-
        larged, 1935. "

1102   James, Maynard G. , 1902-
        I believe in the Holy Ghost, by Maynard James. Fore-
        word by Norman Grubb. Minneapolis, Bethany Fellowship,
        c1965. 167p. "The gifts of the Spirit: prophecy, tongues,
        and interpretation": p. 113-121. DLC, OkTOr

1103   Jividen, Jimmy, 1929-
        Glossolalia, from God or man? A study in the phenom-
        enon of tongue speaking, Fort Worth, Tex. , Star Bible Pub-
        lications, c1971. 196p.

1104   Jolley, Jennie (Arnold), 1882-
        As an angel of light; or, Bible tongues and holiness and
        their counterfeits, by Jennie A. Jolley. New York, Vantage
        Press, c1964. 112p. KyWAT

1105   Jones, Eli Stanley, 1884-1973.
        The divine yes [by] E. Stanley Jones, with the help of
        his daughter, Eunice Jones Mathews. Nashville, Abingdon
        Press, 1975. 160p. "Are there gifts of the Spirit?": p.
        76-82. DLC

1106   Jones, Eli Stanley, 1884-1973.
        The Holy Spirit and the gift of tongues [by] E. Stanley
        Jones. Cleveland, Oh. , Disciplined Order of Christ, 19--.
        folder ([4]p.) (Pamphlet, no. 4.)

1106a   Jones, Eli Stanley, 1884-1973.
        The Holy Spirit and the gift of tongues, by E. Stanley
        Jones. Barrington, R. I. , United Christian Ashrams, 19--.
        folder [8]p.

1107   Jones, Kenneth Effner, 1920-
        What about the gift of tongues? [By] Kenneth E. Jones.
        [Anderson, Ind. , Warner Press, 1962] 32p. Cover title.

1108   Keiper, Ralph L.
        Tongues and the Holy Spirit, by Ralph L. Keiper. In
        Moody Monthly, 64 (Sept. 1963), 61-69.

1109 Keiper, Ralph L.
Tongues and the Holy Spirit, by Ralph L. Keiper.   Chicago, Moody Press, c1963.   23p.   (Acorn booklets.)   Reprinted from Moody Monthly, 64 (Sept. 1963).

1109a King, William Noble
Pentecost and related events, by W. Noble King.   Edited by Charles E. Baldwin.   Colorado Springs, Co., 196-.   10₵.
Mimeographed.

1110 Knox, Lloyd Henry, 1914-
Key Biblical perspectives on tongues, by Lloyd H. Knox.
Winona Lake, Ind., Printed by Light and Life Press, 1974.
26p.   KyWAT

1111 Knudsen, Ralph E.
Speaking in tongues, by Ralph E. Knudsen.   In Foundations [Baptist], 9 (Jan./Mar. 1966), 43-57.

1112 Koch, Kurt Emil Karl
Charismatic gifts, by Karl E. Koch.   Lavel [i.e. Laval],
Que., Association for Christian Evangelism (Quebec), 1975.
175p.   Translation of Die Geistesgaben.   CLamB, LNB

1113 Kornet, A. G., 1922-
De Pinkster Beweging en de Bijbel.   Kampen, Kok, 1963.
192p.   MH-AH

1114 Krajewski, Ekkehard
Geistesgaben; eine Bibelarbeit uber 1. Korinther 12-14.
Kassel, Oncken Verlag, 1963.   64p.   MH-AH

1114a Kühn, Bernhard, 1859-   , ed.
Die Pfingstbewegung im Lichte der Heiligen-Schrift und
ihrer eigenen Geschichte.   Gotha, Missionsbuchhandlung
P. Ott, 19--.   105p.   First ed. has title: In kritlischer
Stunde.

1115 Lang, George Henry, 1874-1958.
The modern gift of tongues: whence is it?   A testimony
and an examination.   London, Marshall Brothers, 1913.   132p.
CLamB

1116 Lightner, Robert Paul, 1931-
Speaking in tongues and divine healing, by Robert P.
Lightner.   Des Plaines, Ill., Regular Baptist Press, 1965.
64p.   DLC, KyWAT, MSohG

1117 Linaweaver, Penrose Grant, 1869-
Nuts for the "tongues movement" to crack [by] P. G.
Linaweaver.   In Herald of Holiness, 22 (Feb. 28, 1934), 15.

1118 [Lindsell, Harold], 1913-

The gift of tongues. In Christianity Today, 13 (Apr. 11, 1969), 27-28. Editorial.

1119   Lindsell, Harold, 1913-
        Spiritual gifts. In Christianity Today, 19 (Apr. 11, 1975), 5-7.

1120   Lindsell, Harold, 1913-
        Tests for the tongues movement. In Christianity Today, 17 (Dec. 8, 1972), 8-12.

1121   Lindsell, Harold, 1913-
        Tests for the tongues movement. In Hillis, D. W. , ed. Is the whole body a tongue? Grand Rapids, Mich. , c1974, 89-99.

1121a   Lohmann, Ernst, 1860-
        Pfingstbewegung und Spiritismus. Frankfurt a. M. , Verlag Orient-Buchhandlung des Deutschen Hülfsbundes fur christliches Liebeswerk im Orient e. V. , 1910. 81p.

1122   Lowry, Oscar, 1872-
        The Pentecostal baptism and the enduement of power. Chicago, Moody Press, 1936. 51p.

1123   Lubahn, Erich, 1923-
        Fromme Verführungen. Information u. Wegweisung. Stuttgart, Christliches Verlagshaus, 1969. 78p. DLC

1123a   McCone, Robert Clyde, 1915-
        Culture and controversy: an investigation of the tongues of Pentecost [by] R. Clyde McCone. Philadelphia, Dorrance, c1978. vii, 136p. CAzPC

1124   McCrossan, Thomas J.
        Speaking with other tongues: sign or gift, which? Seattle, c1927. 52p. CLamB

1125   McCrossan, Thomas J.
        Speaking with other tongues: sign or gift, which? New York, Christian Alliance Publishing Co. , c1927. 53p. KyWAT

1126   McCrossan, Thomas J.
        Speaking with other tongues: sign or gift, which? By T. J. McCrossan. Harrisburg, Pa. , Christian Publications; Beaverlodge, Alta. , Horizon House, 1977. 68p. On spine: Tongues: sign or gift? Reprint of 1927 ed.

1127   McGee, John Vernon, 1904-
        Talking in tongues! By J. Vernon McGee. Whittier, Calif. , W. Smith, 1963. 40p. (The modern tongues movement, 2.)

1128   Mackenzie, Hudson F.
        Natural tongues, by Hudson F. Mackenzie. Hamilton,
N. Z. , Walker Printers, 19--. 70p. MoKN

1129   Mackenzie, Hudson F.
        Your God-given gifts, by Hudson F. Mackenzie. Hamil-
ton, N. Z. , Walker Printers, 19--. 99p. MoKN

1130   Mackintosh, Donald
        La glosolalia: un autnetico don de lenguas?   Buenos
Aires, Asociación Casa Editora Sundamericana, 1976.   34p.
MiBsA

1131   Marine, George W.
        The gift of tongues, by George W. Marine. In Herald
of Holiness, 6 (Sept. 12, 1917), 6; 6 (Jan. 9, 19$\overline{18}$), 7.

1132   Martin, Fay Crendal, 1886-
        The Holy Spirit versus modern tongues, by Fay C. Mar-
tin. Washington, D. C. , c1932. 182p. DLC, OrPWP

1133   Matthews, John
        Satan in the synagogue: the gift of the Spirit vs. the
tricks of the Devil; Jesus on the pinnacle of the Temple [and]
Satan at His side; Satan in the synagogue.   Addresses delivered by Rev. John Matthews. Kansas City, Mo. , 1915.
32p.   CSdP, OkBetC

1134   Matthews, John
        Speaking in tongues. n. p. , c1925. 139p. CLamB,
MWollE

1135   Mauro, Philip, 1859-1952.
        Speaking in tongues. Swengel, Pa. , Reiner Publications,
197-.   22p.

1136   Metz, Donald S. , 1916-
        Speaking in tongues: a Biblical analysis, by Donald S.
Metz.   Kansas City, Mo. , Beacon Hill Press of Kansas City,
1971.   51p.   "Abridged from Speaking in tongues, originally
published in 1964. " IKON

1137   Metz, Donald S. , 1916-
        Speaking in tongues: an analysis, by Donald S. Metz.
Kansas City, Mo. , Nazarene Publishing House, 1964.   115p.
IKON, CPC, MoKN

1138   Metz, Donald S. , 1916-
        Speaking in tongues: an analysis, by Donald S. Metz.
Kansas City, Mo. , Nazarene Publishing House, 1965.   109p.
"Second printing. " CAzPC, CSdP

1139   Miller, Elmer C.

Pentecost examined by a Baptist lawyer [by] Elmer C. Miller. Springfield, Mo. , Gospel Publishing House, c1936. 131p.   MSohG

1140   Molenaar, D. G.
De doop met de Heilige Geest.   Kampen, Kok, 1963. 272p.   MH-AH, OkTOr

1141   Moore, Derman Darrell, 1935-
The gift of the Holy Spirit--literal or representative? By Darrell Moore.   Meridian, Miss. , 19--.   35p.   (Restoration series, 1.)   TMH

1142   Mountain, James
Authority, demons, and tongues.   Have Christians authority over satan?   And may they possess the gift of tongues? Tunbridge Wells, Kent, 1912.   62p.   L

1143   Murray, James Sterling
What we can learn from the Pentecostal churches [by] J. S. Murray.   In Christianity Today, 11 (June 9, 1967) 10-12.

1144   Murrell, Conrad, 1928-
Spiritual baptisms and gifts.   Pineville, La. , Saber Publications, 197-.   215p.

1145   Murrell, Conrad, 1928-
True and false tongues.   Bentley, La. , Saber Publications, 19--.   25p.

1146   Myers, W. L.
Does Paul forbid speaking in tongues?   Evangelist John R. Rice says, "Yes"; Pastor W. L. Myers says, "No. " Rockmart, Ga. , c1948.   68p.

1147   Nash, David Foot
"Tongues" in perspective: what say the scriptures? London, Epworth Press, 1967.   16p.

1148   Nederlandse Hervormde Kerk.   Generale Synode.
De Kerk en de Pinkstergroepen; herderlijk schrijven van de Generale Synode der Nederlandse Hervormde Kerk.   's-Gravenhage, Boekencentrum, 1960.   79p.   MH-AH

1149   Neely, Benjamin Franklin, 1876-1967.
The Bible versus the tongues theory, by B. F. Neely. Kansas City, Mo. , Nazarene Publishing House, 1923.   79p. LNB, MoKN

1150   Neely, Benjamin Franklin, 1876-1967.
The Bible versus the tongues theory [by] B. F. Neely. Rev. ed.   Kansas City, Mo. , Beacon Hill Press, 1946. 72p.   IKON

1151 Neely, Benjamin Franklin, 1876-1967.
The modern tongues movement, by B. F. Neely. In
Herald of Holiness, 12 (Aug. 1, 1923), 4-5; 12 (Aug. 8,
1923), 3-4; 12 (Aug. 15, 1923), 5-6; 12 (Sept. 5, 1923), 4-5;
12 (Sept. 12, 1923), 3.

1152 Neely, Benjamin Franklin, 1876-1967.
Pentecost and consecration, by B. F. Neely. In Pentecostal Advocate, 14 (June 8, 1911).

1153 Neighbour, Ralph Webster, 1929-
This gift is mine [by] Ralph W. Neighbour, Jr. Nashville, Broadman Press, 1974. 122p. DLC

1154 Neighbour, Robert Edward, 1872-1945.
The baptism in the Holy Ghost before and after Pentecost:
an exegesis of Acts 1 and 2, by R. E. Neighbour. Cleveland,
Ohio, Union Gospel Press, 1930. 291p. DLC

1155 Neighbour, Robert Edward, 1872-1945.
Talking in tongues. Elyria, Ohio, Gems of Gold Publishing Co., 19--. 16p.

1156 Nelson, Wade T.
The tongues delusion, by Wade T. Nelson. In Herald
of Holiness, 5 (Feb. 28, 1917), 6-7.

1157 Newell, Arlo F.
Receive the Holy Spirit, by Arlo F. Newell. Anderson,
Ind., Warner Press, c1978. 126p. "Charismata: the gifts
of the Spirit": p. 89-100.

1158 Noorbergen, Rene, 1928-
Charisma of the Spirit; in search of a supernatural experience: a journalist looks at the tongues movement. Mountain View, Calif., Pacific Press Publishing Association,
c1973. 191p. (A Redwood paperback 103.) DLC, IEG,
MSohG

1159 Ockenga, Harold John, 1905-
The Holy Spirit and tongues, by Harold J. Ockenga.
Boston, Park Street Church, 1965. 20p. CCmS, MSohG

1160 Odon, Donald, 1920-
Full gospel, half gospel, quarter gospel. Melbourne,
Scandi Press, 1968. 143p. KyLoS

1161 Oke, Norman R.
Facing the tongues issue, by Norman R. Oke. Kansas
City, Mo., Beacon Hill Press, 1973. 39p.

1161a O'Rear, Arthur T.
The nativity of the Holy Spirit, by Arthur T. O'Rear.

Louisville, Ky. , Pentecostal Publishing Co. , c1929.   188p.
On tongues: p. 116-154.   CAzPC, DLC

1162   Orr, William W.
           If you speak with tongues ... here are the rules, by
        Dr. Orr.   Temple City, Calif. , Grace Gospel Fellowship,
        19--.   35p.

1162a Palmer, Everett Walter, bp. , 1906-1970.
           Statement on the tongues movement, by Everett W. Pal-
        mer.   Seattle, c1961.   folder [4]p.   Caption title.

1163   Pickford, J. H.
           This is not that: what is the baptism of the Holy Spirit?
        By J. H. Pickford.   Port Coquitlam, B.C. , c1953.   43p.
        KyLoS

1164   Pietsch, W. E.
           McPherson-Jeffreys Four Square Gospel heresy: a grave
        warning, by W. E. Pietsch.   Hounslow, Middx. , Bible Wit-
        ness, 1928.   23p.   L

1165   Pollock, Algernon James, 1864-1957.
           Modern Pentecostalism, Foursquare Gospel, "healings"
        and "tongues." Are they of God? London, Central Bible
        Truth Depot, 1929.   84p.   L

1166   Pollock, Algernon James, 1864-1957.
           Modern Pentecostalism, Foursquare Gospel, "healings,"
        and "tongues." Are they of God? 5th ed.   London, Central
        Bible Truth Depot, 1929.   80p.   CLamB

1167   Polovina, Samuel Emil, 1888-
           Light on the tongues movement, by S. E. Polovina.   In
        Herald of Holiness, 5 (Dec. 13, 1916), 8.

1168   Pridie, James Robert
           The spiritual gifts (ta charismata) by J. R. Pridie.
        London, R. Scott, 1921.   160p.   CCSC, DLC, L

1169   Pruitt, Fred
           Baptism of the Holy Ghost.   Guthrie, Okla. , Faith Pub-
        lishing House, 19--.   16p.   Caption title.

1170   Pruitt, Lawrence D.
           Modern Pentecostalism, by L. D. Pruitt.   Guthrie, Okla. ,
        Faith Publishing House, 19--.   folder (8p.) Caption title.

1171   Purkiser, Westlake Taylor, 1910-
           The answer corner.   Conducted by W. T. Purkiser.   In
        Herald of Holiness, 49 (Sept. 14, 1960), 16; 49 (Dec. 21,
        1960), 16.

1172   Purkiser, Westlake Taylor, 1910-
        Conflicting concepts of holiness; some current issues in
        the doctrine of sanctification [by] W. T. Purkiser. Kansas
        City, Mo. , Beacon Hill Press, 1953. 114p. "Sanctification
        and signs": p. 63-81.

1173   Purkiser, Westlake Taylor, 1910-
        The gifts of the Spirit, by W. T. Purkiser. Kansas City,
        Mo. , Beacon Hill Press of Kansas City, 1975. 77p. Expan-
        sion of a chapter in his God's spirit in the world today.

1174   Pyle, Hugh F.
        Truth about tongues [by] Hugh F. Pyle. Denver, Accent
        Books, c1976. 128p.

1175   Radford, William F.
        Apostolic teaching concerning tongues, by Wm. F. Rad-
        ford. Kansas City, Mo. , Pentecostal Nazarene Publishing
        House, 191-. 61p. KyWAT

1176   Ramm, Bernard Lawrence, 1916-
        A study of some special problems in reference to the
        speaking in tongues, by Bernard Ramm. Los Angeles, Bible
        Institute of Los Angeles, 1947. 17p. KyWAT

1177   Ramm, Bernard Lawrence, 1916-
        The witness of the Spirit; an essay on the contemporary
        relevance of the internal witness of the Holy Spirit, by Ber-
        nard Ramm. Grand Rapids, Mich. , Eerdmans, 1960, c1959.
        140p.

1178   Reid, Samuel Joseph, 1874-
        What saith the scriptures: concerning healing of the body,
        "tongues, " baptism of the Holy Spirit. Chicago, 19--. 54p.
        CLamB

1179   Rice, John Richard, 1895-
        Filled with the Spirit; a verse-by-verse commentary on
        Acts of the Apostles, by John R. Rice. Murfreesboro, Tenn. ,
        Sword of the Lord Publishers, c1963. 555p. DLC

1180   Rice, John Richard, 1895-
        The fullness of the Spirit, by John R. Rice. Murfrees-
        boro, Tenn. , Sword of the Lord Publishers, 1946. 29p.

1181   Rice, John Richard, 1895-
        The power of Pentecost; or, The fullness of the Spirit,
        by John R. Rice. Wheaton, Ill. , Sword of the Lord Pub-
        lishers, c1949. 441p. "Speaking with tongues": p. 203-
        276. DLC, TxWaS

1182   Rice, John Richard, 1895-

Speaking with tongues, by John R. Rice.   Murfreesboro,
Tenn. , Sword of the Lord, 1965.   79p.   KyWAT

1183   Ridout, George Whitefield, 1870-1954.
        The deadly fallacy of fanaticism: fanaticism defined,
        the fanatic described, advices and counsels against fanaticism,
        by G. W. Ridout.   Louisville, Ky. , Pentecostal Publishing
        Co. , 19--.   20p.

1184   Ridout, George Whitefield, 1870-1954.
        The deadly fallacy of spurious tongues, by G. W. Ridout.
        Louisville, Ky. , Pentecostal Publishing Co. , 19--.   16p.
        Cover title.   KyWAT

1185   Ridout, George Whitefield, 1870-1954.
        Spiritual gifts, including the gift of tongues: a considera-
        tion of the gifts of the Spirit and particularly the gift of
        tongues, the "pneumatika" and the "charismata" of I. Corinth-
        ians, chapters 12 and 14 closely examined, by G. W. Ridout.
        Kansas City, Mo. , Nazarene Publishing House, 19--.   20p.

1186   Riley, William Bell, 1861-1947.
        Speaking with tongues, by W. B. Riley.   Minneapolis,
        Hall, Black, printer, 19--.   16p.   KyLoS

1187   Robinson, J. S.
        The Holy Ghost His own witness in a soul, by J. S.
        Robinson.   Guthrie, Okla. , Faith Publishing House, 19--.
        4p.   Caption title.

1188   Roddy, Andrew Jackson
        Though I spoke with tongues: a personal testimony.
        Louisville, Ky. , The Harvester, 1952.   45p.   KyLoS

1189   Rubanowitsch, Johannes, 1865-
        Das heutige Zungenreden.   Neumunster, Vereinsbuchhand-
        lung G. Ihloff, 19--.   120p.

1190   Ruth, Christian Wismer, 1865-1941.
        The gift of tongues, by C. W. Ruth.   In Herald of Holi-
        ness, 13 (Dec. 24, 1924), 4-5.

1191   Ruth, Christian Wismer, 1865-1941.
        "Have you received your baptism?" [By] C. W. Ruth.
        In Herald of Holiness, 23 (Oct. 6, 1934), 8-9.

1191a   Saloff-Astakhoff, Nikita Ignatievich, 1893-
        The Holy Spirit, His work, and Pentecostalism, by N. I.
        Saloff-Astakhoff.   Berne, In. , Publishers Printing House,
        1967.

1192   Sanders, John Oswald, 1902-
        The Holy Spirit and His gifts [by] J. Oswald Sanders.

Rev. and enl. ed.   Grand Rapids, Mich. , Zondervan Publishing House, 1970.   155p.   (Contemporary evangelical perspectives)   First published in 1940 under title: The Holy Spirit
of promise.   "The gift of tongues":   p. 123-135.   DLC,
TxWaS

1193   Scroggie, William Graham, 1877-1958.
        The baptism of the Spirit: what is it?   Speaking with
tongues: what saith the scriptures?   [By] W. Graham Scroggie.   London, Pickering & Inglis, 1956.   48p.   CBPac,
CLamB, MoSCS, NjPT, TMH

1194   Scroggie, William Graham, 1877-1958.
        The baptism of the Holy Spirit and speaking with tongues,
by W. Graham Scroggie.   London, Marshall, Morgan & Scott,
19--.   62p.

1195   Seamands, David A.
        Tongues: psychic and authentic; a Biblical study of the
Holy Spirit and the gift of tongues, by David A. Seamands.
Wilmore, Ky. , 1972.   49p.   IGreviC, KyWA, KyWAT

1196   Seitz, Johannes
        Die Selbstentlarvung von "Pfingst"-Geistern, von Johannes
Seitz und Ernst F. Ströter.   Barmen, Montanus u. Ehrenstein,
1911.   29p.

1197   Shelhamer, Elmer Ellsworth, 1869-1947.
        False doctrines and fanaticism exposed, by E. E. Shel-
hamer.   2d and enlarged ed.   Atlanta, Ga. , The Repairer,
19--.   128p.   "The 'Tongues Movement' ":   p. 120-128.
KyWAT

1198   Shelhamer, Elmer Ellsworth, 1869-1947.
        Five reasons I do not seek the gift of tongues, by E. E.
Shelhamer.   5th ed.   Wilmore, Ky. , Mrs. E. E. Shelhamer,
197-.   31p.   Cover title.

1199   Short, John N. , 1841-1922.
        Spiritual lights [by] J. N. Short.   In Herald of Holiness,
1 (May 22, 1912), 16.

1200   Shuler, Robert Pierce, 1880-1965.
        "McPhersonism":   a study of healing cults and modern
day "tongues" movements, by R. P. (Bob) Shuler.   Los
Angeles, 192-.   63p.

1201   Shuler, Robert Pierce, 1880-1965.
        "McPhersonism":   a study of healing cults and modern
day "tongues" movements, by R. P. (Bob) Shuler.   2d ed.
Los Angeles, 192-.   72p.   KyWA

1202   Shuler, Robert Pierce, 1880-1965.

108 Guide to the Pentecostal Movement

"McPhersonism"; a study of healing cults and modern day "tongues" movements, containing a summary of facts as to disappearances and reappearances of Aimee Semple McPherson. 4th ed. Los Angeles, 192-. 128p. DLC, KyWA

1203 Smeltzer, John F.
The tongues movement, by John F. Smeltzer. Boston, 19--. 24p.

1204 Smith, Bertha
How the Spirit filled my life. Nashville, Broadman Press, c1973. 148p. "Speaking in tongues": p. 114-124. DLC

1205 Smith, Charles Russell, 1935-
Tongues in Biblical perspective; a summary of Biblical conclusions concerning tongues, by Charles R. Smith. 2d ed., rev. Winona Lake, Ind., BMH Books, 1973. 141p. Based on thesis (Th.D.)--Grace Theological Seminary and College, 1970. DLC, MSohG, OkBetC

1206 Smith, Frederick George, 1880-1947.
The gift of tongues: what it is, and what it is not, by Frederick G. Smith. Anderson, Ind., Gospel Trumpet Co., 19--. 60p.

1207 Smith, George H.
The unknown tongue, by Geo. H. Smith. 2d ed. Fort Scott, Kan., Church Herald and Holiness Banner, 1928. 62p.

1208 Smith, Timothy Lawrence, 1924-
Speaking the truth in love; some honest questions for Pentecostals, by Timothy L. Smith. Kansas City, Mo., Beacon Hill Press of Kansas City, 1977. 47p. "Presented at the annual meeting of the Society for Pentecostal Studies, Ann Arbor, Mich., December 3, 1975."

1209 Spadafora, Francesco, 1869-
Pentecostali e testimoni di Geova. 3. ed. Rovigo, Ist. padano di arti grafiche, 1968. 298p. DLC, MB

1210 Stanger, Frank Bateman, 1914-
The gifts of the Spirit. Harrisburg, Pa., Christian Publications, 1974. 31p.

1211 Staton, Knofel
Eight lessons on spiritual gifts for Christians today. Joplin, Mo., College Press, 1973. 118p. On cover: Spiritual gifts for Christians today.

1212 Stegall, Carroll
The modern tongues and healing movement, by Carroll Stegall, Jr., and Carl C. Harwood. Denver, Western Bible Institute, 195-. 56p. Cover title. NNUT

1213   Sterner, Russell Eugene, 1912-
        Do all speak in tongues? By R. Eugene Sterner. In
Vital Christianity, 94 (Oct. 6, 1974), 15-17.

1213a   Stokes, Mack Boyd, bp. 1911-
        The Holy Spirit and Christian experience, by Mack B.
Stokes. Nashville, Tn., Graded Press, c1975. 176p. "The
Holy Spirit and speaking in tongues": p. 137-145.

1214   Stolee, Haakon Jacobs, 1882-
        Pentecostalism: the problem of the modern tongues move-
ment, by H. J. Stolee. Minneapolis, Augsburg Publishing
House, c1936. x, 142p. DLC

1215   Stolee, Haakon Jacobs, 1882-
        Speaking in tongues, by H. J. Stolee. Minneapolis,
Augsburg Publishing House, 1963. viii, 142p. First pub-
lished in 1936 under title: Pentecostalism. DLC, KyWAT,
MCE, TxWaS

1216   Taylor, Elwood
        Terrific devil. In Herald of Holiness, 7 (May 29, 1918),
        5-6.

1217   Taylor, Richard Shelley, 1912-
        Tongues: their purpose and meaning, by Richard S. Tay-
lor. Kansas City, Mo., Beacon Hill Press, 1973. 32p.
"First printing." KyWAT

1218   Thieme, Robert Bunger, 1918-
        Tongues [by] R. B. Thieme, Jr. Rev. ed. Houston,
Berachah Tapes and Publications, c1974. 63p. TxLoL

1219   Todd, S. C.
        The tongues that cannot speak, by S. C. Todd. In Holi-
ness Evangel, 2 (Sept. 23, 1908).

1220   The tongues.
        In Pentecostal Advocate, 12 (May 13, 1909).

1221   The tongues movement.
        In Holiness Evangel, 2 (Sept. 16, 1908).

1222   Tongues-speaking: good or bad?
        1   In Good News, 6 (Fall 1972/Winter 1973), 8-10. Edi-
torial.

1223   Torrey, Reuben Archer, 1856-1928.
        The baptism with the Holy Spirit, by R. A. Torrey.
Minneapolis, Bethany Fellowship, 19--. 50p. On tongues:
p. 6.

1224   Torrey, Reuben Archer, 1856-1928.

Is the present "tongues" movement of God? Answered
by R. A. Torrey. Los Angeles, Biola Book Room, 19--.
[11]p. ICMB

1225   Tracy, Leighton Stanley, 1882-1942.
        Counterfeit enduement, by L. S. Tracy. In Herald of
        Holiness, 5 (Sept. 6, 1916), 5.

1226   Unger, Merrill Frederick, 1909-
        The baptism and gifts of the Holy Spirit, by Merrill F.
        Unger. Chicago, Moody Press, 1974. 189p. DLC

1227   Unger, Merrill Frederick, 1909-
        The baptizing work of the Holy Spirit. Wheaton, Ill.,
        Van Kampen Press, 1953. 147p. DLC

1228   Unger, Merrill Frederick, 1909-
        New Testament teaching on tongues [by] Merrill F.
        Unger. Grand Rapids, Mich., Kregel Publications, 1971.
        175p. DLC, KyWAT, IEG, LNB

1229   Unger, Merrill Frederick, 1909-
        New Testament teaching on tongues [by] Merrill F. Unger.
        2d ed. Grand Rapids, Mich., Kregel Publications, 1972.
        175p. RP

1230   Vanzandt, J. C.
        Speaking in tongues; a discussion of speaking in tongues,
        Pentecost, Latter Rain, evidence of the Holy Spirit baptism,
        and a short history of the tongues movement in America and
        some foreign countries, by J. C. Vanzandt. Portland, Ore.,
        1926. 50p. InAndC

1231   Vess, Arthur Lee, 1892-1971.
        The Bible on the tongues doctrine, by Arthur L. Vess.
        Knoxville, Tenn., Evangelist of Truth, 19--. 28p.

1232   Vess, Arthur Lee, 1892-1971.
        The Bible on the tongues doctrine, by Arthur L. Vess.
        Pinellas Park, Fla., Revival Herald, 195-. [37]p. KyWA

1233   Walker, Alan, 1911-
        Breakthrough: rediscovery of the Holy Spirit. London,
        Fontana, 1969. 92p.

1234   Walker, Alan, 1911-
        Breakthrough: rediscovery of the Holy Spirit. Nashville,
        Abingdon Press, 1969. 92p. DLC

1235   Walvoord, John Flipse, 1910-
        The Holy Spirit; a comprehensive study of the person and
        work of the Holy Spirit, by John F. Walvoord. Wheaton, Ill.,
        Van Kampen Press, 1954. 275p. A revision of the author's

The doctrine of the Holy Spirit. DLC

1236   Warfield, Benjamin Breckinridge, 1851-1921.
        Counterfeit miracles, by Benjamin B. Warfield. New
        York, C. Scribner's Sons, 1918. 327p. (The Thomas
        Smyth lectures for 1917-1918.) "Faith-healing": p. 155-
        196. DLC, MSohG

1237   Warfield, Benjamin Breckinridge, 1851-1921.
        Miracles: yesterday and today, true and false, by Ben-
        jamin B. Warfield. Grand Rapids, Mich., Eerdmans, 1953.
        327p. (The Thomas Smyth lectures for 1917-1918.) First
        published in 1918 under title: Counterfeit miracles. "Faith
        healing": p. 155-196. DLC, CSdP

1238   Washington, Cecil Monroe
        Undeniable facts about speaking in tongues. Detroit,
        19--. 27p. InAndC

1239   Washington, Cecil Monroe
        What the Bible teaches about speaking in tongues. De-
        troit, 19--. 40p. InAndC

1240   Webster, Douglas, 1920-
        Pentecostalism and speaking with tongues. London, High-
        way Press, 1964. 47p. IEG

1241   Wells, Bob
        All the Bible says about tongues [by] Bob Wells. Denver,
        Accent Books, c1977. 128p.

1242   What would you like to know about the church? Letter [by]
        Mitchell Blackburn; answer by J. D. Conway.
        In Catholic Digest, 25 (July 1961), 123-131.

1243   White, Alma (Bridwell), bp., 1862-1946.
        Demons and tongues, by Mrs. Alma White. Bound Brook,
        N.J., Pentecostal Union, 1910. 86p. CAzPC

1243a   White, Alma (Bridwell), 1862-1946.
        Demons and tongues, by Alma White. Zarephath, N.J.,
        Pillar of Fire, c1919. 90p. DLC

1244   White, Alma (Bridwell), 1862-1946.
        Demons and tongues, by Alma White. Zarephath, N.J.,
        Pillar of Fire, c1936. 128p. DLC, KyWAT

1245   White, Stephen Solomon, 1890-1971.
        A false versus the true sign. In Herald of Holiness, 39
        (Aug. 14, 1950), 12. (A primer on entire sanctification, 2.)
        Editorial.

1246   White, Stephen Solomon, 1890-1971.

The question box. Conducted by Stephen S. White. In Herald of Holiness, 40 (Mar. 12, 1951), 15-16; 41 (Apr. 2, 1952), 15-16; 42 (May 27, 1953), 15; 43 (Feb. 23, 1955), 15; 45 (June 20, 1956), 17; 48 (Sept. 2, 1959), 17: 49 (July 13, 1960), 17.

1247   Widmeyer, Charles Brenton, 1884-1974.
       Our relation to the tongues' movement, by Charles B. Widmeyer. In Herald of Holiness, 10 (Dec. 7, 1921), 6-7.

1248   Wiley, Henry Orton, 1877-1961.
       The miraculous accompaniment. In Herald of Holiness, 19 (June 11, 1930), 2-3. Editorial.

1249   Wiley, Henry Orton, 1877-1961.
       The tongues question again. In Herald of Holiness, 19 (Oct. 22, 1930), 4. Editorial.

1250   Willett, Herbert Lockwood, 1864-1944.
       The question box [by] H. L. W. In Christian Century, 54 (Mar. 24, 1937), 389.

1251   Wilson, Walter Lewis, 1881-1969.
       Facts or fancies. Grand Rapids, Mich., Zondervan, c1940. 30p. MSohG

1252   Wood, Fern
       The more excellent way. In Herald of Holiness, 24 (July 6, 1935), 8-9. "The personal experience of one converted from the Pentecostal movement."

1253   Woodcock, Eldon Griffith, 1930-
       Discernment and tongues: 1 Corinthians 12:7-11, by Eldon Woodcock. In Alliance Witness, 113 (Dec. 13, 1978), 23-24. (Into the word: studies in First Corinthians, 37.)

1254   Woodrow, O. C.
       The gift of tongues, by O. C. Woodrow. In Pentecostal Advocate, 10 (Jan. 10, 1907).

1255   Woolsey, Warren, comp.
       Speaking in tongues: a Biblical, theological and practical study. Houghton, N.Y., Houghton Wesleyan Church, 1971. [9]ℓ. Mimeographed.

1256   Yocum, Dale Morris
       True and false tongues, by Dale M. Yocum. Salem, Ohio, Schmul Publishers, 1978. 23p. OkBetC

1257   Zeller, George William, 1950-
       God's gift of tongues: the nature, purpose, and duration of tongues as taught in the Bible, by George W. Zeller. Neptune, N.J., Loizeaux Bros., 1978. 126p. DLC

1258   Zepp, Arthur Carroll, 1878-
        The p's of Pentecost contrasted with the Corinthian mani-
        festations, by Arthur C. Zepp. Chicago, Christian Witness
        Co., 1927. 32p. Cover title.

1259   Zōdiatēs, Spyros, 1922-
        Tongues? A study of the Biblical record from the Greek
        text, by Spiros Zodhiates. Ridgefield, N.J., AMG Publishers,
        1975, c1974. 191p. NHou

1260   Zōdiatēs, Spyros, 1922-
        What the Bible says about tongues, by Spiros Zodhiates.
        Ridgefield, N.J., American Mission to Greeks, 1964. 6v.

        --EDUCATION

1261   Christenbury, Eugene Carl, 1923-
        A study of teacher education in sixteen Pentecostal col-
        leges in the United States. Knoxville, 1972. 180ℓ. Thesis
        (Ed. D.)--University of Tennessee. TU

1262   Corvin, Raymond Othel, 1915-
        Religious and educational backgrounds in the founding of
        Oral Roberts University. Norman, 1967. v, 195ℓ. Thesis
        (Ph. D.)--University of Oklahoma. OkU

1263   Fischer, Harold Arthur
        Method in teaching, by H. A. Fischer. Butler, Ind.,
        Higley Press, 195-. 78p. OkTOr

1264   Fischer, Harold Arthur
        Method in teaching, by H. A. Fischer. 2d ed. San
        Diego, Calif., Glenbar Press, 19--. 78p. OkTOr

1265   Kirsch, Elmer Edwin, 1927-
        A study of fringe benefits for full-time faculty in Bible
        colleges. Los Angeles, 1972. 211ℓ. Thesis (Ed. D.)--
        University of Southern California. CLSU

1266   Orsini, Joseph Emmanuel, 1937-
        An educational history of the Pentecostal movement, by
        Joseph E. Orsini. New Brunswick, N.J., 1973. vi, 126ℓ.
        Thesis (Ed. D.)--Rutgers University. NjR

        --EVANGELISTIC WORK

1267   Caldwell, William A.
        Front line evangelism, by William Caldwell. Tulsa,
        Front Line Evangelism, 1968. 53p.

1268   Davis, George Thompson Brown

When the fire fell, by George T. B. Davis. Rev. ed.
Philadelphia, Million Testaments Campaigns, 1945. 104p.
TxWaS

1269   Grant, Walter Vinson, 1913-
        How to win souls and influence sinners. Dallas, Grant's
        Faith Clinic, 19--. 32p. OkTOr

1270   Harris, Leo
        Operation outreach. Blueprint for a New Testament re-
        vival. Secrets of success for every local church. Five
        rules for revival in your church. The New Testament pat-
        tern for preachers and people. Fullarton, S. Austl., Cru-
        sader Publications, 19--. 69p.

1271   Hodges, Melvin Lyle, 1909-
        A guide to church planting, by Melvin L. Hodges. Chi-
        cago, Moody Press, 1973. 95p. DLC

1272   Hollenweger, Walter Jacob, 1927-
        Evangelism and Brazilian Pentecostals, by W. J. Hollen-
        weger. In Ecumenical Review, 20 (Apr. 1968), 163-170.

1273   Jeter, Hugh Preston, 1911-
        Radio in world evangelism. Columbia, S.C., 1963.
        161ℓ. Thesis (M.A.)--Columbia Bible College.

1274   Lindsay, Gordon, 1906-1973.
        World evangelization now by healing and miracles.
        Shreveport, La., 1951. 169p. DLC, TxWaS

1275   Nunn, Davis Oliver
        Worldwide harvest through miracle evangelism, by David
        Nunn. Dallas, 19--. 16p. TxWaS

1276   Osborn, Tommy Lee, 1923-
        The case for soulwinning outside the sanctuary, by T. L.
        Osborn. Tulsa, T. L. Osborn Evangelistic Foundation,
        c1969. 61p.

1277   Osborn, Tommy Lee, 1923-
        Impact, by T. L. Osborn. Tulsa, c1960. 104p.

1278   Osborn, Tommy Lee, 1923-
        Soulwinning out where the sinners are [by] T. L. Osborn.
        Tulsa, c1967. 139p.

1279   Roberts, Oral, 1918-
        How to win your lost loved ones to Christ. Tulsa, c1966.
        vi, 64p.

1280   Roberts, Oral, 1918-
        A master plan for 10 million souls. Tulsa, 195-. 32p.
        MH-AH

1281   Sumrall, Lester Frank, 1913-
            Fishers of men; a handbook for personal workers, by
        Lester F. Sumrall.   Grand Rapids, Mich., Zondervan Pub-
        lishing House, 1946.   54p.

1282   Townsend, Arthur Herbert, 1912-
            How to consider the church evangelist, by Arthur H.
        Townsend.   Tahlequah, Okla., Pan Press, 1969.   53p.   DLC

1283   Wight, Fred Hartley, 1899-
            What every Christian should know about soul winning, by
        Fred H. Wight and Karl G. Sabiers.   Los Angeles, Robert-
        son Publishing Co., c1944.   96p.   (Christian study course
        series, 8.)   DLC

                    --FICTIONAL LITERATURE

1284   Cummings, Gertrude McGovern
            From darkness to light.   Providence, Printed by Snow &
        Farnham Co., 1934.   191p.   DLC

1285   Kirban, Salem
            1000.   Huntingdon Valley, Pa., 1973.   185p.   A novel on
        the millennium years.   Sequel to 666.   DLC

1285a   Slaughter, Frank Gill, 1908-
            Gospel fever; a novel about America's most beloved TV
        evangelist [by] Frank G. Slaughter.   Garden City, N.Y.,
        Doubleday, 1980.   258p.   DLC, Ok

1286   Söderholm, Hilding, 1903-
            Kvarlämnad.   Stockholm, Norman, 1962.   184p.   DLC,
        MnU

1287   Williams, Chancellor
            Have you been to the river?   A novel.   New York, Ex-
        position Press, 1952.   256p.   AU, DLC, InU, IU, NcD, NjR,
        ViU, WaU

                    --FINANCE

1288   Krantz, Patricia Jane, 1941-
            Patterns of giving; a study of contributions to four Pente-
        costal sects, by Patricia J. Krantz.   Madison, 1968.   113ℓ.
        Thesis (M.A.)--University of Wisconsin.   WU

                    --GOVERNMENT

1289   Pethrus, Lewi, 1884-1974.
            Christian church discipline, by Lewi Pethrus.   Translated

from the Swedish by Paul B. Peterson. Chicago, Philadelphia Book Concern, 1944. 103p. Translation of Kristen
församlingstucht. DLC

--HISTORY

1290   Abbott, Joe
        The forgotten church. n. p. , 1962. 1v. (unpaged)

1291   Abrams, Minnie F.
        The baptism of the Holy Spirit at Mukti, by Minnie
        Abrams. In Missionary Review of the World, n. s. 19 (Aug.
        1906), 619-620. Reprinted from the Indian Witness, Apr.
        26, 1906.

1292   Anderson, Robert Mapes, 1929-
        A social history of the early twentieth century Pentecostal
        movement. New York, 1969. 368ℓ. Thesis (Ph. D.)--
        Columbia University. NNC

1293   Anderson, Robert Mapes, 1929-
        Vision of the disinherited: the making of American
        Pentecostalism. New York, Oxford University Press, 1979.
        334p. Based on thesis (Ph. D.)--Columbia University, 1969.
        DLC

1294   Atter, Gordon Francis, 1905-
        "The third force"; a Pentecostal answer to the question
        so often asked by both our own young people and by members
        of other churches: "Who are the Pentecostals ?" Peter-
        borough, Ont. , College Press, 1962. xi, 314p. DLC, TxWaS

1295   Atter, Gordon Francis, 1905-
        "The third force"; a Pentecostal answer to the question
        so often asked by both our own young people and by members
        of other churches: "Who are the Pentecostals ?" 3d ed. ,
        rev. Peterborough, Ont. , College Press, c1970. xi, 314p.
        MSohG

1296   Barratt, Thomas Ball, 1862-1940.
        The truth about the Pentecostal revival, or movement.
        In Ball, T. B. In the days of the latter rain. Rev. ed.
        London, 1928, 143-177.

1297   Bartleman, Frank, 1871-1935.
        Another wave rolls in! Edited by John Walker. Revised
        and enlarged ed. , edited by John G. Myers. Northridge,
        Calif. , Voice Publications, 1970, c1962. 128p. First pub-
        lished in 1962 under title: What really happened at Azusa
        Street. Abridgment of How Pentecost came to Los Angeles.
        TxWaS

1298 Bartleman, Frank, 1871-1935.
      Azusa Street, by Frank Bartleman. With foreword by
      Vinson Synan. Plainfield, N.J., Logos International, c1980.
      xxvi, 184p. First published in 1925 under title: How Pente-
      cost came to Los Angeles. DLC

1299 Bartleman, Frank, 1871-1935.
      How Pentecost came to Los Angeles; as it was in the
      beginning: Old Azusa Mission from my diary. 3d ed. Los
      Angeles, 1925. 167p.

1300 Bartleman, Frank, 1871-1935.
      What really happened at "Azusa Street." Northridge,
      Calif., Voice Christian Publications, 1962. 97p. Abridg-
      ment of How Pentecost came to Los Angeles. KyWAT

1301 Bloch-Hoell, Nils, 1915-
      The Pentecostal movement: its origin, development, and
      distinctive character. Oslo, Universitetforlaget, c1964.
      255p. (Scandinavian university books.) Label on t.p.:
      Humanities Press, New York. Revised translation of Pinse-
      bevegelsen. DLC, MCE, TxWaS

1302 Bloch-Hoell, Nils, 1915-
      The Pentecostal movement: its origin, development, and
      distinctive character. London, Allen & Unwin, c1964. 255p.
      Revised translation of Pinsebevegelsen.

1303 Bloch-Hoell, Nils, 1915-
      Pinsebevegelsen; en undersøkelse av pinsebevegelsens
      tilblivelse, utvikling og saerpreg med saerlig henblikk på
      bevegelsens utforming i Norge. Oslo, Universitetsforlaget,
      1956. viii, 458p. (Norges almenvitenskapelige forskningsråd.
      Gruppe: Språk og historie, A587, 1.) Summary in English.
      DLC, MH

1304 Boddy, Alexander Alfred, 1854-1930.
      "Pentecost" at Sunderland; a vicar's testimony [by] A. A.
      Boddy. Sunderland, Durham, Secretaries, 1908. 20p. "4th
      reprint (with additions)."

1305 Brumback, Carl, 1917-
      A sound from heaven. Springfield, Mo., Gospel Publish-
      ing House, c1977. iii, 153p. First published in 1961 as the
      prologue and part one of the author's Suddenly ... from
      heaven.

1306 Clark, Max A. X.
      Latter rain and holy fire: the beginnings of the Pente-
      costal movement, by Max A. X. Clark. n.p., 19--. 47p.

1307 Conde, Emilio
      O testemunho dos séculos: história e doutrina. 3. ed.

Rio de Janeiro, Livros Evangélicos, 1960.   194p.

1308   Cook, Philip Lee, 1924-
          Zion City, Illinois: twentieth century utopia. Boulder,
       1965.   436ℓ. Thesis (Ph.D.)--University of Colorado. CoU

1309   Crayne, Richard
          Early 20th century Pentecost. Morristown, Tenn., 1960.
       71p. KyWAT

1310   Dallmeyer, Heinrich
          Die Zungenbewegegung: ein Beitrag zu ihrer Geschichte
       und eine Kennzeichnung ihres Geistes. Lindhorst, Adastra-
       Verlag, 1924. 143p. MH-AH

1311   Dallmeyer, Heinrich
          Die Zungenbewegung: ein Beitrag zu ihrer Geschichte
       und eine Kennzeichnung ihres Geistes. 2. Aufl. Lagenthal,
       Swit., 19--. 143p.

1312   Damboriena, Prudencio, 1913-
          Tongues as of fire; Pentecostalism in contemporary
       Christianity. Washington, Corpus Books, 1969. viii, 256p.
       KyLxCB, MBU-T, MH-AH, MSohG, NcD

1313   Du Plessis, David Johannes, 1905-
          Golden jubilees of twentieth-century Pentecostal move-
       ments, by David J. du Plessis. In International Review of
       Missions, 47 (Apr. 1958), 193-201.

1314   Durasoff, Steve
          Bright wind of the Spirit: Pentecostalism today. Engle-
       wood Cliffs, N.J., Prentice-Hall, 1972. 277p. DLC, TxWaS

1315   Durasoff, Steve
          Bright wind of the Spirit: Pentecostalism today. London,
       Hodder and Stoughton, 1973. 277p.

1316   Ewart, Frank J., 1876-
          The phenomenon of Pentecost: a history of the Latter
       Rain. Frank J. Ewart, author; W. E. Kidson, collaborator.
       Houston, Herald Publishing House, c1947. 111p. First pub-
       lished in 1915. OkEG

1317   Fischer, Harold Arthur
          Reviving revivals, by Harold A. Fischer. Introduction
       by Frank M. Boyd. Springfield, Mo., Gospel Publishing
       House, c1950. 229p. "The revival of Pentecostal baptisms
       and gifts": p. 188-194.

1318   Fleisch, Paul, 1878-
          Zur Geschichte der Heiligungsbewegung. Leipzig, H. G.
       Wallmann, 1910- . v. 1- . CtY

1319   Frodsham, Stanley Howard, 1882-1969.
        This Pentecostal revival, by Stanley H. Frodsham.
        Springfield, Mo., Gospel Publishing House, c1941.   32p.
        Reprinted from his With signs following.   TxWaS

1320   Frodsham, Stanley Howard, 1882-1969.
        "With signs following"; the story of the latter-day Pente-
        costal revival, by Stanley H. Frodsham.   Springfield, Mo.,
        Gospel Publishing House, c1926.   254p.   DLC

1321   Frodsham, Stanley Howard, 1882-1969.
        "With signs following"; the story of the latter-day Pente-
        costal revival, by Stanley H. Frodsham.   Springfield, Mo.,
        Gospel Publishing House, 1928.   357p.   NNUT

1322   Frodsham, Stanley Howard, 1882-1969.
        With signs following; the story of the Pentecostal revival
        of the twentieth century.   Rev. ed.   Springfield, Mo., Gos-
        pel Publishing House, 1941.   279p.   DLC, NNUT

1323   Frodsham, Stanley Howard, 1882-1969.
        With signs following; the story of the Pentecostal revival
        of the twentieth century.   Rev. ed.   Springfield, Mo., Gospel
        Publishing House, 1946.   279p.   MSohG, TxWaS

1324   Gee, Donald, 1891-1966.
        Movement without a man.   In Christian Life, 28 (July
        1966), 27-29, 50, 52-53.

1325   Gee, Donald, 1891-1966.
        The Pentecostal movement; a short history and an inter-
        pretation for British readers.   London, Victory Press, 1941.
        vii, 199p.   L

1326   Gee, Donald, 1891-1966.
        The Pentecostal movement; including the story of the war
        years (1940-1947).   Rev. and enlarged ed.   London, Elim
        Publishing Co., 1949.   vii, 236p.   NcD, NjPT, KyLxCB, TxU,
        TxWaS

1327   Gee, Donald, 1891-1966.
        Upon all flesh: a Pentecostal world tour.   Springfield,
        Mo., Gospel Publishing House, 1935.   107p.

1328   Gee, Donald, 1891-1966.
        Upon all flesh: a Pentecostal world tour.   Rev. ed.
        Springfield, Mo., Gospel Publishing House, 1947.   118p.
        MSohG, TxWaS

1329   Gee, Donald, 1891-1966.
        Wind and flame; incorporating the former book The Pente-
        costal movement, with additional chapters.   London, Assem-
        blies of God Publishing House, 1967.   317p.   TxWB

1330   Goss, Howard Archibald, 1883-1964.
        The winds of God; the story of the early Pentecostal days
        (1901-1914) in the life of Howard A. Goss, as told by Ethel
        E. Goss. New York, Comet Press Books, 1958. 178p.
        (A reflection book.) CBBD, IaU, MH-AH, N, NNC, WHi

1331   Goss, Howard Archibald, 1883-1964.
        The winds of God; the story of the early Pentecostal
        movement (1901-1914) in the life of Howard A. Goss, by
        Ethel E. Goss. Rev. ed. Hazelwood, Mo., Word Aflame
        Press, c1977. 286p. KyWAT

1332   Harper, Michael, 1931-
        As at the beginning; the twentieth century Pentecostal re-
        vival. London, Hodder and Stoughton, 1967, c1965. 128p.
        First issued under title: At the beginning; the twentieth cen-
        tury Pentecostal revival. MSohG

1333   Harper, Michael, 1931-
        As at the beginning; the twentieth century Pentecostal
        revival. Plainfield, N.J., Logos International, 1971, c1965.
        122p. British ed. first issued under title: At the beginning;
        the twentieth century Pentecostal revival. TxWaS

1334   Harper, Michael, 1931-
        At the beginning; the twentieth century Pentecostal re-
        vival. London, Hodder and Stoughton, 1965. 128p. CBPac,
        CLgA, ICU, IEG, KyLxCB, NjPT, DLC

1335   Hollenweger, Walter Jacob, 1927-
        Enthusiastisches Christentum. Die Pfingstbewegung in
        Geschichte und Gegenwart. Von Walter J. Hollenweger.
        Wuppertal, Theologischer Verlag Brockhaus; Zürich, Zwingli-
        Verlag, 1969. xxiii, 640p. DLC, MCE

1336   Hollenweger, Walter Jacob, 1927-
        Handbuch der Pfingstbewegung, von Walter J. Hollenweger.
        Zürich, 1966. 3v. in 10. Inaug.-Diss.--Zürich.
        Contents: 1. Hauptt. Sektierer oder Enthusiasten?
        2. Hauptt. Die einzelnen Pfingstgruppen, nach geographis-
        chen Gesichtsspunkten gegliedert: [1] Afrika; [2] Nordamerika;
        [3] Lateinamerika; [4] Asien, Australien und Oceanien; [5]-
        [6] Europa. 3. Hauptt. Kommentierte Bibliographie, Kurz-
        biographien: [1] Einfuhrung in den III. Hauptteil; [2] Selbst-
        darstellungen; [3] Frembddarstellungen, Selbst- und Frembd-
        darstellungen der Heiligungsbewegung. Uebrige Spezialliteratur.
        Microfilm (positive). 3 reels 35mm. Reproduced for
        the American Theological Library Association Microtext Proj-
        ect by Department of Photoduplication, University of Chicago,
        1968. IEG, MH-AH, NjMD

1337   Hollenweger, Walter Jacob, 1927-
        El Pentecostalismo: historia y doctrinas [por] Walter

Hollenweger. Buenos Aires, La Aurora, 1976. 530p.
(Biblioteca de estudios teológicos.) Translation of Enthusiastisches Christentum.

1338   Hollenweger, Walter Jacob, 1927-
       The Pentecostals; the charismatic movement in the
churches. [Translated from the German by R. A. Wilson.]
Minneapolis, Augsburg Publishing House, 1972. xx, 572p.
"First United States edition." Translation of Enthusiastisches
Christentum. DLC, DWT, MBU-T, MH-AH, MNtcA, TxAuE,
TxWaS

1339   Hollenweger, Walter Jacob, 1927-
       The Pentecostals. [Translated from the German by
R. A. Wilson]. London, S. C. M. Press, 1972. xx, 572p.
First British edition. Translation of Enthusiastisches Chris-
tentum. DLC, MH-AH, MSohG

1340   Kendrick, Klaude, 1917-
       The history of the modern Pentecostal Movement. Aus-
tin, 1959. 388ℓ. Thesis (Ph.D.)--University of Texas.
TxU

1341   Kendrick, Klaude, 1917-
       The promise fulfilled; a history of the modern Pentecostal
movement. Springfield, Mo., Gospel Publishing House, 1961.
viii, 237p. "Outgrowth of a dissertation presented ... [at] the
University of Texas ... for the degree of doctor of philosophy
in history." DLC, MSohG, TxWaS

1342   Kenyon, Howard Nelson, 1955-
       An analysis of social separation within the early Pente-
costal movement. Waco, Tex., 1978. ix, 163ℓ. Thesis
(M.A.)--Baylor University. TxWB

1343   Lawrence, Bennett Freeman, 1890-
       The apostolic faith restored, by B. F. Lawrence. St.
Louis, Mo., Gospel Publishing House, c1916. 119p. DLC,
IEG

1344   Lindsay, Gordon, 1906-1973.
       They saw it happen. Dallas, Christ for the Nations,
1972. 47p. KyWAT

1345   Lovett, Leonard
       Black origins of the Pentecostal movement. In Synan,
H. V., ed. Aspects of Pentecostal-Charismatic origins.
Plainfield, N.J., 1975, 123-141.

1346   Lovett, Leonard
       Perspective on the black origins of the contemporary
Pentecostal movement. In Journal of the Interdenominational
Theological Center, 1 (Fall 1973), 36-49.

1347   Murphy, Lyle P.
            Beginning at Topeka; an historical study of the origin of
        the tongues movement, by Lyle P. Murphy. In Calvary Re-
        view, 13 (Spring 1974).

1348   Nichol, John Thomas, 1928-
            Pentecostalism. New York, Harper & Row, 1966.   xvi,
        264p. "Much of this material was originally submitted to
        satisfy the doctoral requirements at the Boston University
        Graduate School." DLC, MCE, MH, MSohG, MH

1349   Nichol, John Thomas, 1928-
            Pentecostalism. Plainfield, N.J., Logos International,
        1971, c1966. xvi, 264p. Cover title: The Pentecostals.
        Reprint of 1966 ed.

1350   Nichol, John Thomas, 1928-
            Pentecostalism; a descriptive history of the origin,
        growth, and message of a twentieth century religious move-
        ment. Boston, 1965. 526ℓ. Thesis (Ph.D.)--Boston Uni-
        versity. MBU

1351   Nickel, Thomas Roy
            In those days, by Thomas R. Nickel. Monterey Park,
        Calif., Great Commission International, c1962. 74p.
        CBPL

1352   Orr, James Edwin, 1912-
            The flaming tongue; the impact of twentieth century re-
        vivals, by J. Edwin Orr. Chicago, Moody Press, 1973.
        xiv, 241p. "The Pentecostal aftermath": p. 178-185, 228-
        229. DLC

1353   Parkes, William
            Pentecostalism: its historical background and recent
        trends. In London Quarterly and Holborn Review, 191 (Apr.
        1966), 147-153.

1354   Riss, Richard Michael, 1952-
            The Latter Rain movement of 1948 and the mid-twentieth
        century evangelical awakening. Vancouver, B.C., 1979.
        viii, 261ℓ. Thesis (M.A.)--Regent College.

1355   Sizelove, Rachel Artamissie (Harper), 1864-1941.
            A sparkling fountain for the whole earth [by] Rachel A.
        Sizelove. Long Beach, Calif., 19--. folder (11p.)

1356   Steiner, Leonhard, 1903-
            Mit folgenden Zeichen; eine Darstallung der Pfingstbewe-
        gung. Basel, Verlag Mission für das volle Evangelium, c1954.
        210p. DLC, MH-AH, MSohG, NNMR

1357   Synan, Harold Vinson, 1934-
            Aspects of Pentecostal-Charismatic origins. Vinson

Synan, editor.   Plainfield, N.J., Logos International, 1975.
iv, 252p.
Papers given at the "third annual meeting of the Society
for Pentecostal Studies at Lee College, Cleveland, Tennessee,
late in 1973" by Thomas F. Zimmerman, Larry Christensen,
Donald W. Dayton, Melvin E. Dieter, William W. Menzies,
Horace S. Ward, Jr., Leonard Lovett, David Reed, Edward
O'Connor, Martin Marty, and Russell P. Spittler.

1358   Tinney, James Stephen
Black origins of the Pentecostal movement [by] James S.
Tinney. In Christianity Today, 16 (Oct. 8, 1971), 4-6.

1359   Turner, William Henry, 1895-1971.
The "Tongues" movement: a brief history with a discussion of its advocates, critics and place in contemporary secular and religious life. Athens, 1948. iii, 106ℓ. Thesis
(M.A.)--University of Georgia. GU

1360   Vanzandt, J. C.
Speaking in tongues; a discussion of speaking in tongues,
Pentecost, Latter Rain, evidence of the Holy Spirit baptism,
and a short history of the tongues movement in America and
some foreign countries, by J. C. Vanzandt. Portland, Ore.,
1926. 50p. InAndC

1361   Warner, Wayne Earl, 1933-
Touched by the fire: eyewitness accounts of the early
twentieth-century Pentecostal revival. Edited by Wayne E.
Warner. Plainfield, N.J., Logos International, c1978. xiv,
163p. DLC

--HISTORY AND STUDY OF DOCTRINES

1362   Alphandéry, Paul
La glossolalie dans le prophétisme mediéval latin. In
Revue de l'Historie des Religions, 104 (Nov. 1931), 417-436.

1363   Arrington, French L., 1931-
Evidence of immortality in this present mortal condition
as reflected in II Corinthians 4:16-5:10, by French L. Arrington. Decatur, Ga., 1969. 87ℓ. Thesis (M.Th.)--Columbia
Theological Seminary. GDC

1364   Arrington, French L., 1931-
Paul's aeon theology in I Corinthians, by French L.
Arrington. St. Louis, 1975. vii, 195ℓ. Thesis (Ph.D.)--
St. Louis University. MoSU

1365   Ashcraft, Jesse Morris, 1922-
Glossolalia in the first epistle to the Corinthians, by J.
Morris Ashcraft. In Dyer, L. B., ed. Tongues. Jefferson
City, Mo., 1971, 60-84.

1366   Ashcraft, Jesse Morris, 1922-
        Speaking in tongues in the book of Acts, by J. Morris
        Ashcraft. In Dyer, L. B., ed. Tongues. Jefferson City,
        Mo., 1971, 85-104.

1367   Associação de Seminários Teológicos Evangélicos.
        O Espírito Santo e o Movimento Pentecostal: Simpósio.
        Sao Paulo, 1966. 93p.

1368   Baillie, Leonard A.
        An exegesis of significant New Testament passages con-
        cerning temporary spiritual gifts, by Leonard A. Baillie.
        Dallas, 1970. 57ℓ. Thesis (Th. M.)--Dallas Theological
        Seminary. TxDaTS

1369   Baker, David L.
        The interpretation of 1 Corinthians 12-14, by David L.
        Baker. In Evangelical Quarterly, 46 (Oct./Dec. 1974), 224-
        234.

1370   Banks, Robert John
        Speaking in tongues; a survey of the New Testament evi-
        dence, by Robert Banks and Geoffrey Moon. In Churchman,
        80 (Winter 1966), 278-294.

1371   Barkheizen, Pieter Erens E. E.
        The charismatic phenomenon. Dunedin, Fla., 1973.
        [69]ℓ. Thesis (B.D.)--Trinity Theological Seminary.

1372   Barnett, Maurice, 1917-
        The gift of the Spirit in the New Testament, with special
        reference to glossolalia. Manchester, 1946. 1v. (pag-
        ing not determined) Thesis (M. A.)--University of Man-
        chester.

1373   Barnett, Maurice, 1917-
        The living flame; being a study of the gift of the Spirit
        in the New Testament, with special reference to prophecy,
        glossolalia, Montanism and perfection. London, Epworth
        Press, 1953. xvi, 152p. NNG

1374   Barrett, Leonard Emanuel, 1920-
        African roots in Jamaican indigenous religion, by Leonard
        E. Barrett. In Journal of Religious Thought, 35 (Spring/
        Summer 1978), 7-26.

1375   Beckmann, David M.
        Trance: from Africa to Pentecostalism [by] David M.
        Beckmann. In CTM, 45 (Jan. 1974), 11-26.

1376   Bellshaw, William G.
        The confusion of tongues [by] William G. Bellshaw. In
        Bibliotheca Sacra, 120 (Apr.-June 1963), 145-153.

1377   Benner, Patterson D.
        The universality of tongues [by] Patterson D. Benner.
        In Japan Christian Quarterly, 39 (Apring 1973), 101-107.
        On Christian and non-Christian glossolalia.

1378   Bergsma, Stuart, 1900-
        Speaking in tongues: some physiological and psychological
        implications of modern glossolalia. Grand Rapids, Mich.,
        Baker Book House, 1965. 26p.

1379   Best, Ernest Edwin, 1919-
        The interpretation of tongues, by Ernest Best. In Scot-
        tish Journal of Theology, 28:1 (1975), 45-62.

1380   Blaney, Harvey Judson Smith, 1905-
        St. Paul's posture on speaking in unknown tongues [by]
        Harvey J. S. Blaney. In Wesleyan Theological Journal, 8
        (Spring, 1973), 52-60.

1381   Boer, Harry R.
        Pentecost and missions, by Harry R. Boer. Grand
        Rapids, Mich., Eerdmans, c1961. 270p. Revision of the
        author's thesis, Free University, Amsterdam, entitled: Pente-
        cost and the missionary witness of the church. DLC, NNMR

1382   Boer, Harry R.
        Pentecost and missions, by Harry R. Boer. London,
        Lutterworth Press, c1961. 270p. Revision of the author's
        thesis, Free University, Amsterdam, entitled: Pentecost and
        the missionary witness of the church. MSohG

1383   Boer, Harry R.
        Pentecost and the missionary witness of the church, by
        Harry R. Boer. Franeker, T. Wever, 1955. 235p. Thesis
        --Free University of Amsterdam. MSohG, NNMR

1384   Brown, Schuyler
        Water-baptism and Spirit-baptism in Luke-Acts. In
        Anglican Theological Review, 59 (Apr. 1977), 135-155.

1385   Brox, Norbert, 1935-
        Charisma veritatis certum (Zu Irenäus adv haer IV 26, 2)
        In Zeitschrift für Kirchengeschichte, 75:3-4 (1964), 327-331.

1386   Bruner, Frederick Dale
        The doctrine and experience of the Holy Spirit in the
        Pentecostal movement and correspondingly in the New Testa-
        ment. Hamburg, 1963. 2v. Thesis (Th.D.)--Hamburg.

1387   Bruner, Frederick Dale
        A theology of the Holy Spirit; the Pentecostal experience
        and the New Testament witness. Grand Rapids, Mich.,
        Eerdmans, 1970. 390p. Based on thesis (Th.D.)--Hamburg,
        1963. DLC

1388   Bruner, Frederick Dale
        A theology of the Holy Spirit; the Pentecostal experience
        and the New Testament witness. London, Hodder and Stough-
        ton, 1971. 390p. Based on thesis (Th. D.)--Hamburg, 1963.
        DLC

1389   Bryant, Christopher
        Psychology and prayer. In Theology, 77 (Apr. 1974),
        181-186.

1390   Bryant, Ernest
        A phonemic analysis of nine samples of glossolalic speech
        [by] Ernest Bryant and Daniel O'Connell. In Psychonomic
        Science, 22 (Jan. 25, 1971), 81-83.

1391   Bunn, John Thomas, 1927-
        Glossolalia in historical perspective [by] John T. Bunn.
        In Mills, W. E. , ed. Speaking in tongues; let's talk about
        it. Waco, Tex. , 1973, 36-47.

1392   Carmen, Calvin C.
        The posture of contemporary Pentecostalism in view of
        the crucial issues of the fundamentalist neo-evangelical debate,
        by Calvin C. Carmen. Springfield, Mo. , 1965. ii, 60ℓ.
        Thesis (M. A.)--Central Bible Institute.

1393   Carter, Charles Webb, 1905-
        A Wesleyan view of the Spirit's gift of tongues in the
        book of Acts, by Charles W. Carter. In Wesleyan Theological
        Journal, 4 (Spring 1969), 39-68.

1394   Carter, Pat Harold, 1926-
        An evangelical critique of the use of the Bible in divine
        healing by representative Protestant groups. Fort Worth,
        Tex. , 1960. 280ℓ. Thesis (Th. D.)--Southwestern Baptist
        Theological Seminary. TxFS

1394a   Chamberlain, Austin Albert
        A comparative study of some modern views of divine
        healing as they relate themselves to the Holy Scriptures.
        Portland, Or. , 1950. 80ℓ. Thesis (B. D.)--Western Evan-
        gelical Seminary. OrPW

1395   Cheshire, C. Linwood
        The doctrine of the Holy Spirit in the Acts, by C. Lin-
        wood Cheshire. Richmond, Va. , 1953. 2v. Thesis (Th. M.)
        --Union Theological Seminary. ViRUT

1396   Christie-Murray, David
        Voices from the gods: speaking with tongues. London,
        R. K. Paul, 1978. 280p. DLC

1397   Chroust, Anton-Hermann, 1907-

Inspiration in ancient Greece. In O'Connor, E. D., ed.
Perspectives on charismatic renewal. Notre Dame, Ind.,
1975, 37-54.

1398   Clements, William Manning, 1945-
         Faith healing narratives from northeast Arkansas [by]
William M. Clements. In Indiana Folklore, 9:1 (1976), 15-
39.

1399   Clow, Harvey Kennedy, 1940-
         Ritual, belief, and the social context: an analysis of a
Southern Pentecostal sect. Durham, N.C., 1976. v, 219ℓ.
Thesis (Ph. D.)--Duke University. NcD

1400   Coulson, Jesse E.
         Glossolalia and internal-external locus of control [by]
Jesse E. Coulson [and] Ray W. Johnson. In Journal of
Psychology and Theology, 5 (Fall 1977), 312-317.

1401   Currie, Stuart Dickson
         Speaking in tongues, by Stuart D. Currie. In Interpreta-
tion, 19 (July 1965), 274-294. Early evidence outside the
New Testament bearing on glossais lalein.

1402   Cutten, George Barton, 1874-1962.
         The psychological phenomena of Christianity. New York,
Scribner, 1909. 497p. Includes analysis of glossolalia. PU

1403   Cutten, George Barton, 1874-1962.
         The psychological phenomena of Christianity. London,
Hodder & Stoughton, 1909. xviii, 497p. Includes analysis of
glossolalia. MB

1404   Cutten, George Barton, 1874-1962.
         Speaking with tongues, historically and psychologically
considered. New Haven, Yale University Press; London,
H. Milford, Oxford University Press, 1927. xii, 193p. DLC

1405   Dalton, Robert Chandler, 1910-
         Glossolalia. Philadelphia, 1940. 65ℓ. Thesis (B. D.)--
Eastern Baptist Theological Seminary. PPEB

1406   Dalton, Robert Chandler, 1910-
         Tongues like as of fire; a critical study of modern tongue
movements in the light of apostolic and patristic times.
Springfield, Mo., Gospel Publishing House, c1945. 127p.
Based on thesis (B. D.)--Eastern Baptist Theological Seminary,
1940. PPEB, ScCoT, TxWaS

1407   Damboriena, Prudencio, 1913-
         Tongues as of fire: Pentecostalism in contemporary Chris-
tianity. Washington, Corpus Books, 1969. viii, 256p. "Speaking with tongues": p. 101-120; "Divine healing": p. 121-139.
KyLxCB, MBU-T, MH-AH, MSohG, NcD

1408   Dautzenberg, Gerhard
           Zum religionsgeschichtlichen Hintergrund der diakriseis
       pneumagon (I Kor. 12:10). In Biblische Zeitschrift, ns 15:1
       (1971); response by Wayne Grudem (1978).

1409   Davies, John Gordon
           Pentecost and glossolalia [by] J. G. Davies. In Journal
       of Theological Studies, ns3 (Oct. 1952), 228-231.

1410   Dayton, Donald Wilber, 1942-
           The doctrine of the baptism of the Holy Spirit: its
       emergence and significance [by] Donald W. Dayton. In
       Wesleyan Theological Journal, 13 (Spring 1978), 114-126.

1411   Dayton, Donald Wilber, 1942-
           The evolution of Pentecostalism [by] Donald W. Dayton.
       In Covenant Quarterly, 32 (Aug. 1974), 28-40.

1412   Dayton, Donald Wilber, 1942-
           From "Christian perfection" to the "baptism of the Holy
       Ghost" [by] Donald W. Dayton. In Synan, H. V., ed. As-
       pects of Pentecostal-Charismatic origins. Plainfield, N. J.,
       1975, 39-54.

1413   Dayton, Donald Wilber, 1942-
           From Christian perfection to the baptism of the Holy
       Ghost; a study in the origin of Pentecostalism, by Donald W.
       Dayton. Chicago, 1973. 16ℓ. NRCR

1414   Decker, Ralph Winfield, 1908-
           The first Christian Pentecost. Boston, 1941. v, 167, ix,
       vii ℓ. Thesis (Ph. D.)--Boston University. MBU

1415   De Vol, Thomas I.
           Ecstatic Pentecostal prayer and meditation [by] Thomas
       I. De Vol. In Journal of Religion and Health, 13 (Oct. 1974),
       285-288.

1416   Dieter, Melvin Easterday, 1924-
           Wesleyan-Holiness aspects of Pentecostal origins: as
       mediated through the nineteenth-century Holiness revival [by]
       Melvin E. Dieter. In Synan, H. V., ed. Aspects of Pente-
       costal-Charismatic origins. Plainfield, N. J., 1975, 55-80.

1417   Dollar, George William, 1917-
           Church history and the tongues movement, by George W.
       Dollar. In Bibliotheca Sacra, 120 (Oct. -Dec. 1963), 316-
       321. A symposium on the tongues movement.

1418   Drummond, Andrew Landale
           Edward Irving and his circle, including some considera-
       tion of the "tongues" movement in the light of modern psy-
       chology. London, J. Clarke, 1937. 305p. DLC

1419   Dubois, Jean Jacques
        En marge des phenomenes charismatiques: bapteme et
        Plenitude du Saint-Esprit selon le Nouveau Testament.
        Geneve, Maison de la Bible, c1975. 64p. DLC, MCW

1420   Dunn, James Douglas Grant, 1939-
        Birth of a metaphor: baptized in the Spirit, by James
        D. G. Dunn. In Expository Times, 89 (Feb. 1978), 134-
        138; 89 (Mar. 1978), 173-175.

1421   Dunn, James Douglas Grant, 1939-
        Spirit-and-fire baptism, by James D. G. Dunn. In
        Novum Testamentum, 14 (Apr. 1972), 81-92.

1422   Dunn, James Douglas Grant, 1939-
        Spirit-baptism and Pentecostalism, by James D. G.
        Dunn. In Scottish Journal of Theology, 23 (Nov. 1970),
        397-407.

1423   Du Plessis, David Johannes, 1905-
        The historic background of Pentecostalism [by] David J.
        Du Plessis. In One in Christ, 10 (1974), 174-179.

1424   Dyer, Luther B., ed.
        Tongues. Edited by Luther B. Dyer. Jefferson City,
        Mo., Le Roi Publishers, 1971. 151p.
        Essays by Wayne E. Ward, Hugh Wamble, J. Morris
        Ashcraft, John Newport, Clark H. Pinnock and John Glover.
        DLC, MCE, MSohG

1425   Eason, Gerald M.
        The significance of tongues, by Gerald M. Eason. Dallas,
        1959. 47ℓ. Thesis (Th. M.)--Dallas Theological Seminary.
        TxDaTS

1426   Elbert, Paul
        The perfect tense in Matthew 16:19 and three charismata.
        In Journal of the Evangelical Theological Society, 17 (Summer
        1974), 149-155.

1427   Ellis, Edward Earle, 1926-
        "Spiritual" gifts in the Pauline community [by] E. Earle
        Ellis. In New Testament Studies, 20 (Jan. 1974), 128-144.

1428   Engelsen, Nils Ivar Johan, 1914-
        Glossolalia and other forms of inspired speech according
        to I Corinthians 12-14. New Haven, 1970. vii, 238ℓ. The-
        sis (Ph. D.)--Yale University. CtY

1429   Epps, Bryan Crandell, 1932-
        Religious healing in the United States, 1940-1960: history
        and theology of selected trends. Boston, 1961. x, 446ℓ.
        Thesis (Ph. D.)--Boston University. MBU

1430   Farrell, Frank
        Outburst of tongues: the new penetration. In Christian-
        ity Today, 7 (Sept. 13, 1963), 3-7; replies (The new penetra-
        tion), 8 (Oct. 25, 1963), 21-23, and (Glossolalia), 8 (Nov. 8,
        1963), 17, 19-20.

1431   Fee, Gordon Donald, 1934-
        Hermeneutics and historical precedent--a major problem
        in Pentecostal hermeneutics [by] Gordon D. Fee. In Spittler,
        R. P., ed. Perspectives on the new Pentecostalism. Grand
        Rapids, Mich., 1976, 118-132.

1432   Flournoy, Théodore, 1854-1920.
        Des Indes à la planète Mars; étude sur un cas de som-
        nambulisme avec glossolalie. 3. éd. Paris, F. Alcan,
        1900. vii, 420p. CLSU, ICU, MB, NN, PU

1433   Flournoy, Théodore, 1854-1920.
        Des Indes à la planète Mars; étude sur un cas de som-
        nambulisme avec glossolalie. 4. ed. conforme aux trois
        premières. Genève, Édition Atar, 1899. xii, 420p. NcD

1434   Flournoy, Théodore, 1854-1920.
        From India to the planet Mars; a study of a case of
        somnambulism, with glossolalia, by Th. Flournoy; tr. by
        Daniel B. Vermilye. New York, Harper, 1900. xix, 446p.
        Translation of Des Indes à la planète Mars. DLC, GU, OCl,
        OClW, MB, NcD, NN, NIC, PU, Wa

1435   Flournoy, Théodore, 1854-1920.
        From India to the planet Mars; a study of a case of som-
        nambulism with glossolalia. Introd. by C. T. K. Chari.
        New Hyde Park, N.Y., University Books, 1963. 457p.
        Translation of Des Indes à la planète Mars. DLC

1436   Forge, James Norman
        The doctrine of miracles in the apostolic church. Dallas,
        1951. iii, 62ℓ. Thesis (Th. M.)--Dallas Theological Seminary.
        TxDaTS

1437   Fowler, Stuart
        Continuance of the charismata. In Evangelical Quarterly,
        45 (July-Sept. 1973), 172-183.

1438   Gerloff, Roswith I. H.
        Theory and practice of the Holy Spirit [by] Roswith Ger-
        loff. In Quaker Religious Thought, 16 (Summer 1975), 2-17.

1439   Gillespie, Thomas William, 1928-
        A pattern of prophetic speech in First Corinthians [by]
        Thomas W. Gillespie. In Journal of Biblical Literature, 97
        (Mar. 1978), 74-95.

1440   Gillespie, Thomas William, 1928-
        Prophecy and tongues: the concept of Christian prophecy
in the Pauline theology, by Thomas W. Gillespie. Claremont, Calif., 1971. ix, 249ℓ. Thesis (Ph.D.)--Claremont
Graduate School and University Center. CCC

1441   Glossolalia: then and now.
        In Christianity Today, 5 (May 22, 1961), 737. Tongues
on the Day of Pentecost and today.

1442   Glynne, William
        Psychology and glossolalia: the book of Acts. In Church
Quarterly Review, 106 (July 1928), 281-300.

1442a   Gonsalvez, Heliodora Emma, 1932-
        The theology and psychology of glossolalia. Evanton,
Il., 1978. iii, 158ℓ. Thesis (Ph.D.)--Northwestern University. IEN

1443   Goodman, Felicitas Daniels, 1914-
        The acquisition of glossolalia behavior [by] Felicitas D.
Goodman. In Semiotica, 3 (1971), 77-82.

1444   Goodman, Felicitas Daniels, 1914-
        Glossolalia and single-limb trance: some parallels [by]
Felicitas D. Goodman. In Psychotherapy and Psychosomatics,
19:1-2 (1971), 92-103.

1445   Goodman, Felicitas Daniels, 1914-
        Glossolalia: speaking in tongues in four cultural settings,
by Felicitas D. Goodman. In Confinia Psychiatrica, 12:2-4
(1969), 113-129.

1446   Goodman, Felicitas Daniels, 1914-
        Phonetic analysis of glossolalia in four cultural settings
[by] Felicitas D. Goodman. In Journal for the Scientific
Study of Religion, 8 (Fall 1969), 227-239. Examines tongue-
speech in Columbus, Ohio, Mexico City, Texas and St. Vincent, W. I.

1447   Goodman, Felicitas Daniels, 1914-
        Speaking in tongues; a cross-cultural study of glossolalia
[by] Felicitas D. Goodman. Chicago, University of Chicago
Press, 1972. xxii, 175p. Based on observation of Pentecostal congregations in the Yucatan, in Mexico City, and in
Hammond, Indiana. DLC, MCE, MH-AH, MSohG

1448   Goodman, Felicitas Daniels, 1914-
        Trance, healing, and hallucination; three field studies in
religious experience, by Felicitas D. Goodman, Jeanette H.
Henney and Esther Pressel. New York, Wiley, 1974. xxiii,
388p. (Contemporary religious movements.) Each field study

was originally presented as a thesis, Ohio State University.
Contents: Henney, J. H. Spirit-possession belief in
two fundamentalist groups in St. Vincent.-Pressel, E. Um-
banda trance and possession in São Paulo, Brazil.-Goodman,
F. D. Disturbances in the Apostolic Church: a trance-based
upheaval in Yucatan.

1449   Graber, John G.
        The temporary gifts of the Holy Spirit, by John B. Graber.
        Dallas, 1947. 82ℓ. Thesis (Th. M.)--Dallas Theological
        Seminary. TxDaTS

1449a   Greet, Kenneth Gerald, 1918-
        When the Spirit moves [by] Kenneth G. Greet. London,
        Epworth Press, 1975. 168p. (The Cato lecture, 1975.)
        "The Pentecostal movement": p. 37-57. DLC, KyWAT,
        MNtcA

1450   Gromacki, Robert Glenn, 1933-
        Scriptural evaluation of the modern tongues movement.
        Winona Lake, Ind., 1966. 280ℓ. Thesis (Th. D.)--Grace
        Theological Seminary and College. InWinG

1451   Gundry, Robert Horton, 1932-
        Ecstatic utterance (N. E. B.)? [By] Robert H. Gundry.
        In Journal of Theological Studies, ns 17 (Oct. 1966), 299-307.

1452   Hahn, Ferdinand
        Charisma und amt: Die Diskussion über das kirchliche
        Amt im Lichte der neutestamentlichen Charismenlehre. In
        Zeitschrift für Theologie und Kirche, 76:4 (1979), 419-449.

1453   Halsema, J. H. van
        Mededeling: de historische betrouwbaarheid van het pink-
        sterhaal [door] J. H. van Halsema. In Nederlands Theologisch
        Tijdschrift, 20 (Feb. 1966), 218.

1454   Harpur, T. W.
        The gift of tongues and interpretation [by] T. W. Harpur.
        In Canadian Journal of Theology, 12 (July 1966), 164-171.

1454a   Harrison, Irvine John, -1972.
        The psychology of the glossolalia, by Irvine J. Harrison.
        Pasadena, Ca., 1946. 110ℓ. Thesis (M. A.)--Pasadena Col-
        lege. CSdP

1455   Harrisville, Roy Alvin, 1922-
        Speaking in tongues: a lexicographical study [by] Roy A.
        Harrisville. In Catholic Biblical Quarterly, 38 (Jan. 1976),
        35-48.

1456   Hart, Larry Douglas, 1947-
        A critique of American Pentecostal theology. Louisville,

1978. iii, 258ℓ. Thesis (Ph.D.)--Southern Baptist Theological Seminary. KyLoS

1457   Hasenhütttl, Gotthold
        Charisma. Ordnungsprinzip d. Kirche. Freiburg (i.
        Br.), Basel, Wien, Herder, 1969. 363p. (Ökumenische
        Forschungen. 1. Ekklesiologische Abteilung, Bd. 5.)
        Habilitationsschrift--Tübingen. DLC, MCE

1458   Hayes, Doremus Almy, 1863-1936.
        The gift of tongues, by D. A. Hayes. Cincinnati, Jen-
        nings and Graham; New York, Eaton and Mains, c1913.
        119p. CSdP, DLC, MBU-T

1459   Hayes, Doremus Almy, 1863-1936.
        The gift of tongues, by D. A. Hayes. New York, Metho-
        dist Book Concern, 1914, c1913. 119p. OrU

1460   Hendricks, William Lawrence, 1929-
        Glossolalia in the New Testament [by] William L. Hen-
        dricks. In Mills, W. E., ed. Speaking in tongues; let's
        talk about it. Waco, Tex., 1973, 48-60.

1461   Henke, Frederick Goodrich, 1876-
        The gift of tongues and related phenomena at the present
        day, by Frederick G. Henke. In American Journal of Theol-
        ogy, 13 (Apr. 1909), 193-206.

1462   Hilgenfeld, Adolf, 1823-1907.
        Die Glossolalie in der alten Kirche, in dem Zusammen-
        hang der Geistesgaben und des Geisteslebens des alten Chris-
        tenthums. Eine exegetisch-historische Untersuchung. Leip-
        zig, Breitkopf und Härtel, 1850. vi, 152p. IEG, MH-AH,
        MCE

1463   Hine, Virginia Haglin, 1920-
        Pentecostal glossolalia: toward a functional interpretation
        [by] Virginia H. Hine. In Journal for the Scientific Study of
        Religion, 8 (Fall 1969), 211-226.

1464   Hinson, Edward Glenn, 1931-
        The significance of glossolalia in the history of Christian-
        ity [by] E. Glenn Hinson. In Mills, W. E., ed. Speaking in
        tongues; let's talk about it. Waco, Tex., 1973, 61-80.

1465   Hocken, Peter
        The significance and potential of Pentecostalism. In Tug-
        well, S. New heaven? New earth? An encounter with Pente-
        costalism. London, 1976, 15-67.

1466   Hodges, Zane C.
        The purpose of tongues [by] Zane C. Hodges. In Biblio-
        theca Sacra, 120 (Oct. 1963), 226-233. A symposium on the
        tongues movement.

1467   Hoffman, R. Joseph
        Meméristai ho Christós? Anti-enthusiast polemic from
        Paul to Augustine, by R. Joseph Hoffman. In Studia Theo-
        logica, 33:2 (1979), 149-164.

1468   Hollenweger, Walter Jacob, 1927-
        Creator spiritus: the challenge of Pentecostal experi-
        ence and Pentecostal theology [by] W. J. Hollenweger. In
        Theology, 81 (Jan. 1978), 32-40.

1469   Holtz, Traugott
        Das Kennzeichen des Geistes (I Kor. XII. 1-3) In
        New Testament Studies, 18 (Apr. 1972), 365-376.

1469a   Hubmer, Fritz
        Zungenreden, Weissagung, umkämpfte Geistesgaben.
        Denkendorf, Gnadauer Verlag, 1972. 173p. DLC

1470   Hurtado, Larry Weir, 1943-
        The function and pattern of signs and wonders in the
        apostolic and sub-apostolic period, by Larry W. Hurtado.
        Deerfield, Ill., 1967. 133ℓ. Thesis (M.A.)--Trinity Evan-
        gelical Divinity School. IDfT

1471   Isbell, Charles David
        Glossolalia and propheteialalia: a study of 1 Corinthians
        14 [by] Charles D. Isbell. In Wesleyan Theological Journal,
        10 (Spring 1975), 15-22.

1472   Isbell, Charles David
        The origins of prophetic frenzy and ecstatic utterance in
        the Old Testament world [by] Charles D. Isbell. In Wesleyan
        Theological Journal, 11 (Spring 1976), 62-80.

1473   Jaquith, James Richard
        Toward a typology of formal communicative behaviors:
        glossolalia [by] James R. Jaquith. In Anthropological Lin-
        guistics, 9 (Nov. 1967), 1-8.

1474   Jaschke, Helmut
        Lalein bei Lukas. In Biblische Zeitschrift, ns 15:1
        (1971), 109-114.

1475   Jennings, George James, 1914-
        An ethnological study of glossolalia [by] George J. Jen-
        nings. In Journal of the American Scientific Affiliation, 20
        (Mar. 1968), 5-16.

1476   Johanson, Bruce C.
        Tongues: a sign for unbelievers? A structural and
        exegetical study of I Corinthians 14:20-25 [by] B. C. Johan-
        son. In New Testament Studies, 25 (Jan. 1979), 180-203.

1477   Johnson, Hugh
       Man's quest for identity. Memphis, World Witness
       Press, c1971. 25p. On Hebraic-Christian concept of his-
       torical meaning.

1478   Johnson, Moody S.
       The phenomenon of speaking with tongues, by Moody S.
       Johnson. Kansas City, Mo., 1949. iii, 91ℓ. Thesis (B.D.)
       --Nazarene Theological Seminary. MoKN

1479   Johnson, S. Lewis
       The gift of tongues and the book of Acts [by] S. Lewis
       Johnson, Jr. In Bibliotheca Sacra, 120 (Oct.-Dec. 1963),
       309-311. A symposium on the tongues movement.

1480   Kaasa, Harris Eugene, 1926-
       An historical evaluation, by Harris Kaasa. In Dialog,
       2 (Spring 1963), 156-158.

1481   Kampmeier, A.
       Recent parallels to the miracle of Pentecost, by A.
       Kampmeier. In Open Court, 22 (Aug. 1908), 492-498.

1482   Kay, Thomas Oliver, 1929-
       Pentecost: its significance in the life of the church.
       Louisville, 1954. vii, 121ℓ. Thesis (Th.M.)--Southern
       Baptist Theological Seminary. KyLoS

1483   Keilbach, W.
       Zungenreden. In Die Religion in Geschichte und Gegen-
       wart. Tübingen, 1962, VI, 1940-1941.

1484   Kelsey, Morton Trippe, 1917-
       Dreams: the dark speech of the spirit; a Christian inter-
       pretation [by] Morton T. Kelsey. Garden City, N.Y., Double-
       day, 1968. viii, 326p. DLC

1485   Kelsey, Morton Trippe, 1917-
       God, dreams, and revelation; a Christian interpretation
       of dreams [by] Morton T. Kelsey. Rev. paperback ed.
       Minneapolis, Augsburg Publishing House, 1973, c1974. x,
       246p. First ed. published in 1968 under title: Dreams:
       the dark speech of the spirit. DLC

1486   Kelsey, Morton Trippe, 1917-
       Healing and Christianity; in ancient thought and modern
       times [by] Morton T. Kelsey. New York, Harper & Row,
       1973. xi, 398p. DLC, MCE, MSohG

1487   Kelsey, Morton Trippe, 1917-
       Speaking with tongues: an experiment in spiritual experi-
       ence, by Morton T. Kelsey. Foreword by Upton Sinclair.

London, Epworth Press, 1965. xii, 252p. American ed.
(Garden City, N.Y., Doubleday) has title: Tongue speaking:
an experiment in spiritual experience. CaOKQ

1488   Kelsey, Morton Trippe, 1917-
Tongue speaking; an experiment in spiritual experience
[by] Morton T. Kelsey. Foreword by Upton Sinclair. Garden City, N.Y., Doubleday, 1964. xii, 252p. DLC, MH-AH,
MCE, MSohG, TxWaS

1489   Kendall, E. Lorna
Speaking with tongues [by] E. Lorna Kendall. In Church
Quarterly Review, 168 (Jan./Mar. 1967), 11-19.

1490   Kirkpatrick, Sherman O.
"Glossolalia"; or, "The gift of tongues," by Sherman O.
Kirkpatrick. Enid, Okla., 1936. 50ℓ. Thesis (M.A.)--
Phillips University. OkEG

1491   Klein, Walter Conrad, 1904-
The church and its prophets, by Walter C. Klein. In
Anglican Theological Review, 44 (Jan. 1962), 1-17.

1492   Knox, Ronald Arbuthnot, 1888-1957.
Enthusiasm: a chapter in the history of religion, with
special reference to the XVII and SVIII centuries [by] R. A.
Knox. Oxford, At the Clarendon Press, 1950. viii, 622p.

1493   Kritzeck, James, 1930-
Holy Spirit in Islam. In O'Connor, E. D., ed. Perspectives on charismatic renewal. Notre Dame, Ind., 1975,
101-111.

1494   Krodel, Gerhard A., 1926-
An exegetical examination, by Gerhard Krodel. In Dialog, 2 (Spring 1963), 154-156.

1495   Kydd, Ronald Alfred Narfi, 1943-
Charismata to 320 A.D.: a study in the overt pneumatic
experience of the early church. Saint Andrews, 1973. 1v.
(paging not determined) Thesis (Ph.D.)--Saint Andrews.

1496   Kydd, Ronald Alfred Narfi, 1943-
Novatian's De Trinitate, 29: evidence of the charismatic?
By Ronald Kydd. In Scottish Journal of Theology, 30:4
(1977), 313-318.

1497   Laffal, Julius, 1920-
Communication of meaning in glossolalia [by] Julius Laf-
fal, James Monahan and Peter Richman. In Journal of Social
Psychology, 92 (Apr. 1974), 277-291.

1498   Laffal, Julius, 1920-

Language, consciousness, and experience. In Psycho-
analytic Quarterly, 36:1 (1967), 61-66. On religious glossolalia: p. 63.

1499   Laporte, Jean, 1924-
        The Holy Spirit, source of life and activity according to
        the early church. In O'Connor, E. D., ed. Perspectives
        on charismatic renewal. Notre Dame, Ind., 1975, 57-99.

1500   Lapsley, James Norvell, 1930-
        Speaking in tongues. I. Token of group acceptance and
        Divine approval. II. Infantile babble or song of the self?
        [By] James N. Lapsley [and] John H. Simpson. In Pastoral
        Psychology, 15 (May 1964), 48-55; 15 (Sept. 1964), 16-24.

1501   Lapsley, James Norvell, 1930-
        Speaking in tongues [by] James N. Lapsley and John H.
        Simpson. In Princeton Seminary Bulletin, 58 (Feb. 1965),
        3-18. Reprint from Pastoral Psychology.

1502   Leuthner, Josef
        Zungenreden? Gnadengaben, Weissagung, Zungenrede.
        Bibelarbeit uber 1. Korinther 14. Wuppertal-Elberfeld, Verl.
        und Schriftenmission d. Evangelischen Ges. f. Deutschland,
        1970. 24p. DLC, MH-AH

1503   Lombard, Émile
        De la glossolalie chez les premiers chrétiens et des
        phénomènes similaires; etude d'exégèse et de psychologie.
        Preface de Th. Flournoy. Lausanne, G. Bridel, 1910.
        xii, 254p. DLC, MH-AH

1504   Loughridge, William H.
        A critical evaluation of the tongues theory, by William
        H. Loughridge. Kansas City, Mo., 1956. xi, 86ℓ. Thesis
        (B.D.)--Nazarene Theological Seminary. MoKN

1505   Lovekin, Arthur Adams, 1928-
        Glossolalia; a critical study of alleged origins, the New
        Testament and the early church. Sewanee, Tenn., 1962. v,
        139ℓ. Thesis (S.T.M.)--University of the South. TSewU

1506   Lowe, Harry William
        Speaking in tongues; a brief history of the phenomenon
        known as glossolalia, or speaking in tongues [by] Harry W.
        Lowe. Mountain View, Calif., Pacific Press Publishing As-
        sociation, 1965. 57p. DLC, KyWA, MH-AH

1507   Lyon, Robert W.
        Baptism and Spirit baptism in the New Testament, by
        Robert W. Lyon. In Wesleyan Theological Journal, 14
        (Spring 1979), 14-26.

1508   Lythgoe, Marianne June Catherine
         The baptism of the Holy Spirit; a study of the meaning
of religious experience. Vancouver, 1969. 151ℓ. Thesis
(M. A.)--University of British Columbia. CaBVaU

1509   McCone, Robert Clyde, 1915-
         The phenomena of Pentecost [by] R. Clyde McCone. In
Journal of the American Scientific Affiliation, 23 (Sept. 1971),
83-88.

1510   MacDonald, William Graham, 1933-
         The concept of anointing in the New Testament. Wenham,
Mass., 1959. 86ℓ. Thesis (B. D.)--Gordon Divinity School.
MSohG

1511   MacDonald, William Graham, 1933-
         The concept of anointing in the Old Testament. Wheaton,
Ill., 1957. 76ℓ. Thesis (M. A.)--Wheaton College.

1512   MacDonald, William Graham, 1933-
         Glossolalia in the New Testament, by William G.
MacDonald. In Bulletin of the Evangelical Theological Society, 7 (Spring 1964), 59-68. Originally presented before
the annual meeting of the Evangelical Theological Society,
December 28, 1963, in Grand Rapids, Michigan.

1513   MacDonald, William Graham, 1933-
         Glossolalia in the New Testament, by William G.
MacDonald. Springfield, Mo., Gospel Publishing House,
1964. 20p. "Originally presented before the annual meeting
of the Evangelical Theological Society, Dec. 28, 1963, in
Grand Rapids, Mich." MnCS, MSohG, NRCR

1514   MacDonald, William Graham, 1933-
         Pentecostal theology: a classical viewpoint [by] William
G. MacDonald. In Spittler, R. P., ed. Perspectives on
the new Pentecostalism. Grand Rapids, Mich., 1976, 58-74.

1515   MacDonald, William Graham, 1933-
         Problems of pneumatology in Christology: the relation-
ship of Christ and the Holy Spirit in Biblical theology.
Louisville, 1970. 327ℓ. Thesis (Th. D.)--Southern Baptist
Theological Seminary. KyLoS

1516   McDonnell, Kilian, 1921-
         Holy Spirit and Pentecostalism. In Commonweal, 89
(Nov. 8, 1968), 198-204.

1517   McDonnell, Kilian, 1921-
         The ideology of Pentecostal conversion. In Journal of
Ecumenical Studies, 5 (Winter 1968), 105-126.

1518   McDonnell, Kilian, 1921-

A sociologist looks at the Catholic charismatic movement. In Worship, 49 (Aug.-Sept. 1975), 378-392. Analyzes Joseph Fichter's criticisms of traditional Pentecostalism.

1519   Mackie, Alexander, 1885-1966.
The gift of tongues; a study in pathological aspects of Christianity. New York, G. H. Doran Co., c1921. 275p. DLC, CPC

1520   Marshall, I. Howard
The significance of Pentecost, by I. Howard Marshall. In Scottish Journal of Theology, 30:4 (1977), 347-369.

1521   Martin, Ira Jay, 1911-
Glossolalia in the Apostolic church. In Journal of Biblical Literature, 63 (June 1944), 123-130.

1522   Martin, Ira Jay, 1911-
Glossolalia in the Apostolic church, a survey of tongue-speech. Berea, Ky., Berea College Press, 1960. 100p. DLC, IEG, KyLxCB, MH-AH, MSohG, RPB

1523   Martin, Ira Jay, 1911-
The place and significance of glossolalia in the New Testament church. Boston, 1942. iv, 142ℓ. Thesis (Th.D.) --Boston University. MBU

1524   May, L. Carlyle
A survey of glossolalia and related phenomena in non-Christian religions [by] L. Carlyle May. In American Anthropologist, 58 (Feb. 1956), 75-96.

1525   Maze, Roger M.
Glossolalia in theological perspective, by Roger M. Maze. Evanston, Ill., 1969. iii, 97ℓ. Thesis (M.A.)--Northwestern University. IEN

1526   Menzies, William Watson, 1931-
The non-Wesleyan origins of the Pentecostal Movement [by] William W. Menzies. In Synan, H. V., ed. Aspects of Pentecostal-Charismatic origins. Plainfield, N.J., 1975, 81-98.

1527   Metz, Donald S., 1916-
The gifts of the Spirit in perspective [by] Donald S. Metz. In Geiger, K. E., comp. The word and the doctrine; studies in contemporary Wesleyan-Arminian theology. Kansas City, Mo., 1965. 317-333.

1528   Millikin, Jimmy Allen, 1936-
The Corinthian glossolalia: the historical setting, an exegetical examination, and a contemporary restatement. Fort Worth, Tex., 1967. 214ℓ. Thesis (Th.D.)--Southwestern

Baptist Theological Seminary.   TxFS

1529   Mills, Watson Early, 1939-
        A theological interpretation of tongues in Acts and First
        Corinthians. Louisville, 1968. 276ℓ. Thesis (Th.D.)--
        Southern Baptist Theological Seminary. KyLoS

1530   Mínguez, Dionisio
        Pentecostés: ensayo de semiótica narrativa en Hch. 2
        Rome, Biblical Institute Press, 1976. 217p. (Analecta
        biblica, 75.) Thesis--Instituto Bíblico de Roma, 1975.
        DLC

1531   Mosiman, Eddison, 1878-
        A dissertation on the gift of tongues in the New Testa-
        ment. Chicago, 1910. ii, 75ℓ. Thesis (M.A.)--University
        of Chicago. ICU

1532   Mosiman, Eddison, 1878-
        Das Zungenreden geschichtlich und psychologisch unter-
        sucht. Leipzig, 1911. xii, 64p. Inaug.-Diss.--Leipzig.   L,
        ICRL, CU, CtY, MH, PPWe, OO

1533   Mosiman, Eddison, 1878-
        Das Zungenreden: geschichtlich und psychologisch unter-
        sucht. Tübingen, Mohr, 1911. xv, 137p. MH-AH, CLSU,
        InU, MH

1534   Motley, Michael Tilden, 1945-
        Glossolalia: analyses of selected aspects of phonology
        and morphology. Austin, 1967. vi, 129ℓ. Thesis (M.A.)--
        University of Texas. TxU

1535   Munro, John Ker
        The New Testament spiritual gifts. Dallas, 1940. 61ℓ.
        Thesis (Th.M.)--Dallas Theological Seminary. TxDaTS

1536   Neff, Harry Richard, 1933-
        The cultural basis for glossolalia in the twentieth century
        [by] H. Richard Neff. In Mills, W. E., ed. Speaking in
        tongues; let's talk about it. Waco, Tex., 1973, 26-35.

1537   Nes, William Hamilton, 1895-
        Glossolalia in the New Testament [by] William H. Nes.
        In Concordia Theological Monthly, 32 (Apr. 1961), 221-223.

1538   Ness, Henry H.
        Demonstration of the Holy Spirit, as revealed by the
        scriptures and confirmed in great revivals of Wesley, Finney,
        Cartwright, Whitefield, Moody, etc. Seattle, Northwest Gos-
        pel Publishing House, 19--. 48p.

1539   Neth, Frederick G., 1931-

Charismatic principles in the church, by Frederick G.
Neth. Chicago, 1961. iii, 51ℓ. Thesis (B.D.)--North Park
Theological Seminary.   ICNPT

1540   Newbigin, James Edward Lesslie, bp., 1909-
The household of God; lectures on the nature of the
church. London, SCM Press, 1953. 155p. (The Kerr lectures, 1952.) "The first attempt at an ecumenical assessment of the Pentecostal movement."--Hollenweger. DLC,
MCE

1541   Newbigin, James Edward Lesslie, bp., 1909-
The household of God; lectures on the nature of the
church. New York, Friendship Press, c1954. 177p. (The
Kerr lectures, 1952.) "The first attempt at an ecumenical
assessment of the Pentecostal movement."--Hollenweger.
DLC

1542   Nilsson, Torsten, 1925-
Andedop och tungotal.   I bibeln, kyrkohistorien och nuti-
den. Bromma, Frontier; Solna Seelig, 1969. 160p. DLC,
MH-AH

1543   Notes on recent exposition. In Expository Times, 77 (May
1966), 225-227.

1544   Oman, John Brady, 1914-
On "speaking in tongues": a psychological analysis [by]
John B. Oman. In Pastoral Psychology, 14 (Dec. 1963), 48-
51.

1545   Oosthuizen, Gerhardus Cornelis, 1922-
The misunderstanding of the Holy Spirit in the independent
movements in Africa [by] G. C. Oosthuizen. n.p., 196-.
172-197p. Cover title. "Reprinted from Christuspredikig
in de wereld." CtY-D

1546   Opsahl, Paul David, 1934- , ed.
The Holy Spirit in the life of the church: from Biblical
times to the present. Edited by Paul D. Opsahl. Minneapolis, Augsburg Publishing House, c1978. 287p. DLC

1547   Palma, Anthony David, 1926-
Glossolalia in the light of the New Testament and subsequent history, by Anthony D. Palma. New York, 1960. iii,
97ℓ. Thesis (S.T.B.)--Biblical Seminary in New York.
NNBS

1547a Palma, Anthony David, 1926-
The Holy Spirit in the corporate life of the Pauline congregation. St. Louis, 1974. 149ℓ. Thesis (Th.D.)--Con-
cordia Seminary.   MoSCS

1547b   Palma, Anthony David, 1926-
        Tongues and prophecy: a comparative study in charis-
        mata. St. Louis, 1966. 94ℓ. Thesis (S. T. M.)--Concordia
        Seminary. MoSCS

1548   Panton, David Morrison, 1870-
        Irvingism, tongues, and the gifts of the Holy Ghost, by
        D. M. Panton. London, Chas. J. Thynne & Jarvis, 19--.

1549   Pattison, Edward Mansell, 1933-
        Faith healing, by E. Mansell Pattison, Nikolajs A.
        Lapins, and Hans A. Doerr. In Journal of Nervous and
        Mental Disease, 157 (Dec. 1973), 397-409. Based on inter-
        views with and testing of "43 Fundamentalist-Pentecostal per-
        sons who experienced 73 faith healings."

1550   Pena, Hilario S.
        A comparison of the distinctive teachings of Holiness and
        Pentecostal groups, by Hilario S. Pena. Pasadena, Calif.,
        1948. 50ℓ. Thesis (M. A.)--Pasadena College. CSdP

1551   Penner, Richard John
        The baptism and filling of the Spirit: is there a differ-
        ence? La Mirada, Calif. , 1974. iii, 61ℓ. Thesis (M. Div.)
        --Talbot Theological Seminary. CLamB

1552   Pfister, Oskar Robert, 1873-1956.
        Die psychologische Enträtselung der religiösen Glossolalie
        und der automatischen Kryptegraphie. Leipzig, F. Deuticke,
        1912. 107p. "Sonderabdruck aus dem Jahrbuch für Psycho-
        analytische und Psychopathologische Forschungen, III. Band."
        NcU, DLC

1553   Piepkorn, Arthur Carl, 1907-1973.
        Charisma in the New Testament and the apostolic fathers.
        In Concordia Theological Monthly, 42 (June 1971), 369-389.

1554   Pierson, Arthur Tappan, 1837-1911.
        Speaking with tongues, by Arthur T. Pierson. In Mis-
        sionary Review of the World, ns 20 (July 1907), 487-492;
        ns 20 (Sept. 1907), 682-684.

1555   Pinnock, Clark Harold, 1937-
        The concept of the Spirit in the epistles of Paul. Man-
        chester, 1963. x, 302, 79ℓ. Thesis (Ph. D.)--University of
        Manchester.

1556   Pitts, John
        Spiritual healing [by] John Pitts, Cyril C. Richardson,
        Don H. Gross [and] Paul E. Johnson. In Religion in Life,
        25 (Spring 1956), 163-204.

1557   Poythress, Vern S.

The nature of Corinthian glossolalia: possible options
[by] Vern S. Poythress. In Westminster Theological Journal,
40 (Fall 1977), 130-135.

1558   Priebe, Duane Allen
        Charismatic gifts and Christian existence in Paul [by]
        Duane A. Priebe. In Agrimson, J. E., ed. Gifts of the
        Spirit and the body of Christ. Minneapolis, 1974, 15-33.

1559   Rasmussen, Marie B.
        De Afrikanske HelligSandskirkers Teologi, av Marie B.
        Rasmussen. In Norsk Teologisk Tidsskrift, 40:2 (1977),
        101-119.

1560   Riedel, Warren C.
        A Biblical approach to the gifts of the Holy Spirit, by
        Warren C. Riedel. Lancaster, Pa., 1971. 137ℓ. Thesis
        (S. T. M.)--Lancaster Theological Seminary. PLT

1561   Righter, James D., 1938-
        A critical study of the charismatic experience of speak-
        ing in tongues, by James D. Righter. Washington, 1974.
        155ℓ. Thesis (D. Min.)--Wesley Theological Seminary. DWT

1562   Ritter, Adolf Martin
        Charisma im Verstandnis des Joannes Chrysostomos und
        seiner Zeit: ein Beitrag zur Erforschung der griechisch-
        orientalischen Ekklesiologie in der Frühzeit der Reichskirche.
        Gottingen, Vandenhoeck & Ruprecht, c1972. 232p. (For-
        schungen zur Kirchen- und Dogmengeschichte, 25.) Habilita-
        tionsschrift--Göttingen. DLC

1563   Robertson, Carl F.
        The nature of New Testament glossolalia, by Carl F.
        Robertson, Jr. Dallas, 1975. iii, 199ℓ. Thesis (Th. D.)--
        Dallas Theological Seminary and Graduate School. TxDaTS

1564   Robertson, O. Palmer
        Tongues: sign of covenantal curse and blessing [by] O.
        Palmer Robertson. In Westminster Theological Journal, 38
        (Fall 1975), 43-53.

1565   Robinson, Donald William Bradley
        Charismata versus pneumatika: Paul's method of discus-
        sion [by] D. W. B. Robinson. In Reformed Theological Re-
        view, 31 (May/Aug. 1972), 49-55.

1566   Robinson, Kenneth Gene, 1931-
        The gifts of the Holy Spirit. Searcy, Ark., 19--. 87ℓ.
        Thesis (M. A.)--Harding College.

1567   Robinson, William Childs, 1922-
        The church in the world: "steward of the mysteries of

God, " by William C. Robinson, Jr. In Interpretation, 19
(Oct. 1965), 412-417.

1568   Roebling, Karl
       Is there healing power? One man's look at America's
       faith healing. New Canaan, Conn., Keats Publishing, c1972.
       112p.

1569   Rofsteucher, Ernst
       Die Gabe der Sprachen in apostolischen Zeitalter. Mar-
       burg, 1850. 125p. MH-AH

1570   Rogers, Cleon Louis
       The gift of tongues in the post-apostolic church (A.D.
       100-400) [by] Cleon L. Rogers, Jr. In Bibliotheca Sacra,
       122 (Apr.-June 1965), 134-143.

1571   Rose, Delbert Roy, 1912-
       Distinguishing things that differ, by Delbert R. Rose.
       In Wesleyan Theological Journal, 9 (Spring 1974), 5-14.

1572   Rossteuscher, Ernst Adolf, -1892.
       Die Gabe der Sprachen im apostolischen Zeitalter; ein
       exegetischer Versuch uber Apostelgesch. II, 1-13, I Kor.
       XIV und die Parallelstellen.... Marburg, Elwert, 1850.
       vi, 125p. MH-AH

1573   Ruble, Richard Lee, 1933-
       A scriptural evaluation of tongues in contemporary theol-
       ogy. Dallas, 1964. vii, 216ℓ. Thesis (Th.D.)--Dallas
       Theological Seminary. TxDaTS

1574   Rückert, Leopold Immanuel, 1797-1871.
       The gifts of prophecy and of speaking with tongues in
       the primitive church, by L. J. Rückert. In Edwards, B. B.,
       ed. Selections from German literature. Andover, Mass.,
       1854.

1575   Rust, Hans, 1879-
       Zungenreden. In Die Religion in Geschichte und Gegen-
       wart. Tübingen, 1927-1932, V, 2142-2143.

1576   Rust, Hans, 1879-
       Das Zungenreden: eine Studie zur kritischen Religions-
       psychologie. München, Verlag von J. F. Bergmann, 1924.
       74p. (Grenzfragen des Nerven- und Seelenlebens, Heft. 118.)
       ODM

1577   Sala, Harold James, 1937-
       An investigation of the baptizing and filling work of the
       Holy Spirit in the New Testament related to the Pentecostal
       doctrine of "initial evidence, " by Harold J. Sala. Greenville,
       S.C., 1966. xiv, 292, 3ℓ. Thesis (Ph.D.)--Bob Jones Uni-
       versity. ScGBJ

1577a Sassaman, Marcus B.
       An investigation of the interpretations of glossolalia, by
       Marcus B. Sassaman. Portland, Or. , 1966. 110ℓ. Thesis
       (B. D.)--Western Evangelical Seminary. OrPW

1578   Satake, Akira
       Apostolat und Gnade bei Paulus. In New Testament Studies,
       15 (Oct. 1968), 96-107.

1579   Schmidt, Karl Ludwig, 1891-
       Die pfingsterzahlung und das pfingstereignis. Leipzig,
       J. C. Hinrichs, 1919. 35p. (On cover: Arbeiten zur
       religionsgeschichte des urchristentums, 1. bd. , 2. hft.)
       CCSC, DLC, OO, CtY-D, TNJ

1580   Scholler, L. W.
       A chapter of church history from south Germany: being
       passages from the life of Johann Evangelist Georg Lutz.
       Translated by W. Wallis. London, Longmans, 1894. ix,
       234p. L, MiD, NN

1581   Schoonenberg, Piet
       Baptism with the Holy Spirit. In Huizing, P. , ed. Ex-
       perience of the Spirit. New York, 1976, 20-37.

1582   Sebree, Herbert T.
       Glossolalia [by] Herbert T. Sebree. In Geiger, K. E. ,
       comp. The word and the doctrine; studies in contemporary
       Wesleyan-Arminian theology. Kansas City, Mo. , 1965, 335-
       351.

1583   Shepard, Darrell Royce, 1941-
       The sensibility of "Holy Spirit. " Lincoln, 1967. xvii,
       247ℓ. Thesis (Ph. D.)--University of Nebraska. NbU

1584   Sheppard, Gerald Thomas
       Wisdom as a hermeneutical construct: a study in the
       sapientializing of the Old Testament, by Gerald T. Sheppard.
       New Haven, Conn. , 1976. 265ℓ. Thesis (Ph. D.)--Yale
       University. CtY

1585   Shilling, Henry, 1902-
       Gifts of the Spirit. Freeport, Pa. , Transylvania Bible
       School, 197-. 43p.

1586   Shumway, Charles William
       A critical history of glossolalia. Boston, 1919. 117 [12]ℓ.
       Thesis (Ph. D.)--Boston University. MBU

1587   Silvers, Kelly Douglas
       Montanism and the charismatic movement in the Spirit-
       structure tension in the history of the church. Dayton, Ohio,
       1973. v, 62ℓ. Thesis (S. T. M.)--United Theological Seminary.
       ODaTS

1588   Sirks, George Johan
        The Cinderella of theology; the doctrine of the Holy Spirit
        [by] G. J. Sirks. In Harvard Theological Review, 50 (Apr.
        1957), 77-89.

1589   Sleeper, Charles Freeman
        Pentecost and resurrection [by] C. Freeman Sleeper. In
        Journal of Biblical Literature, 84 (Dec. 1965), 389-399.

1590   Smalley, Stephen Stewart, 1931-
        Spiritual gifts and I Corinthians 12-16 [by] Stephen S.
        Smalley. In Journal of Biblical Literature, 87 (Dec. 1968),
        427-433.

1591   Smeeton, Donald Dean
        Perfection or Pentecost: a historical comparison of char-
        ismatic and holiness theologies, by Donald D. Smeeton.
        Deerfield, Ill. , 1971.   160ℓ .   Thesis (M. A.)--Trinity Evan-
        gelical Divinity School. IDfT

1592   Smith, Charles Russell, 1935-
        Biblical conclusions concerning tongues. Winona Lake,
        Ind. , 1970.   528ℓ .   Thesis (Th. D.)--Grace Theological
        Seminary and College. InWinG

1593   Smith, Charles Russell, 1935-
        Tongues in Biblical perspective; a summary of Biblical
        conclusions concerning tongues, by Charles R. Smith.   2d ed. ,
        rev.   Winona Lake, Ind. , BMH Books, 1973.   141p. Based
        on thesis (Th. D.)--Grace Theological Seminary and College,
        1970.   DLC, MSohG, OkBetC

1594   Smith, Dwight Moody, 1931-
        Glossolalia and other spiritual gifts in a New Testament
        perspective [by] D. Moody Smith.   In Interpretation, 28
        (July 1974), 307-320.

1595   Smith, Quinton David
        The baptism in the Holy Spirit: subsequence and evidence.
        Springfield, Mo. , 1978.   75, 4ℓ .   Thesis (M. A.)--Assemblies
        of God Graduate School.

1596   Snell, William Robert, 1930-
        Jesus, the servant of God: the origin and evolution of the
        concept as found in Acts 3-4.   Louisville, 1957.   v, 55ℓ .
        Thesis (Th. M.)--Southern Baptist Theological Seminary.
        KyLoS

1597   Sonnack, Paul Gerhardt, 1920-
        A historical perspective on some contemporary religious
        movements [by] Paul G. Sonnack.   In Agrimson, J. E. , ed.
        Gifts of the Spirit and the body of Christ.   Minneapolis,
        1974, 35-53.   On Charles G. Finney as a precursor of the
        Pentecostal movement.

1598   Stanley, Arthur Penrhyn, 1815-1881.
        The gift of tongues and the gift of prophesying. In Noyes,
        G. R. , comp. A collection of theological essays from vari-
        ous authors. Boston, 1856, 453-471.

1599   Steadman, John Marcellus
        Anent "the gift of tongues" and kindred phenomena, by
        J. M. Steadman. In Methodist Quarterly Review, 74 (Oct.
        1925), 688-715.

1600   Sterrett, T. Norton
        New Testament charismata, by T. Norton Sterrett. Dallas,
        1947. vi,256ℓ. Thesis (Th. D.)--Dallas Theological Semi-
        nary. TxDaTS

1601   Stringer, Randy C. , 1949-
        What the Bible teaches about the purpose of tongues speak-
        ing, by Randy C. Stringer. Toccoa Falls, Ga. , 1971. ii,
        40ℓ. Student paper--Toccoa Falls Bible College.

1602   Sweet, John Philip McMurdo, 1927-
        A sign for unbelievers: Paul's attitude to glossolalia [by]
        J. P. M. Sweet. In New Testament Studies, 13 (Apr. 1967),
        240-257.

1603   Synan, Harold Vinson, 1934-
        Los avivamientos pentecostales desde el Pentecostes hasta
        nuestros dias [por] Vinson Synan. Curico, Chile, Imprenta
        Orion, 1967. 12p. Cover title. "Conferencia dictada en el
        Seminario de Pastores en Santiago, Chile, de 25 al 27 de
        Abril, 1967. "

1604   Taylor, James E. , 1933-
        A perspective on Christian glossolalia, by James E. Tay-
        lor. Oklahoma City, 1975. 10ℓ. Caption title. Mimeo-
        graphed. "Presented on April 14, 1975, at the National Con-
        vention of the Christian Association for Psychological Studies
        (CAPS), convened in Oklahoma City, Oklahoma. "

1605   Taylor, Willard Harlan, 1921-1981.
        Baptism with the Holy Spirit: promise of grace or judg-
        ment? By Willard H. Taylor. In Wesleyan Theological
        Journal, 12 (Spring 1977), 16-25.

1606   Thiselton, Anthony C.
        The "interpretation" of tongues: a new suggestion in the
        light of Greek usage in Philo and Josephus, by Anthony C.
        Thiselton. In Journal of Theological Studies, ns 30 (Apr.
        1979), 15-36.

1607   Thomas, Robert L.
        "Tongues ... will cease" [by] Robert L. Thomas. In
        Journal of the Evangelical Theological Society, 17 (Spring
        1974), 81-89.

1607a   Thomas, Thais de Rosa
        Comparison of Charismatic/Pentecostal Christianity and
        Shaktiput yoga.   San Francisco, 1979.   Thesis (Ph. D.)--
        California Institute of Asian Studies.   CSfCI

1608   Todorov, Tzvetan
        L'étrange cas de Mlle.   Hélène Smith (pseudonyme).   In
        Romanic Review, 63 (Apr. 1972), 83-91.

1609   Toussaint, Stanley D.
        First Corinthians thirteen and the tongues question [by]
        Stanley D. Toussaint.   In Bibliotheca Sacra, 120 (Oct. /Dec.
        1963), 311-316.   A symposium on the tongues movement.

1610   Tschiedel, Hans Jürgen
        Ein Pfingstwunder im Apollonhymnos.   In Zeitschrift für
        Religions- und Geistesgeschichte, 27:1 (1975), 22-39.

1611   Tugwell, Simon
        New heaven?   New earth?   An encounter with Pentecostal-
        ism [by] Simon Tugwell, George Every, John Orme Mills and
        Peter Hocken.   Preface by Walter Hollenweger.   London,
        Darton, Longman & Todd, 1976.   205p.

1612   Tugwell, Simon
        Reflections on the Pentecostal doctrine of "baptism in the
        Holy Spirit. "   In Heythrop Journal, 13 (July 1972), 268-281;
        13 (Oct. 1972), 402-404.

1613   Turner, William Henry, 1895-1971.
        Two thousand years of Pentecost, by W. H. Turner.
        Franklin Springs, Ga. , Printed by Publishing House of the
        P. H. Church, c1947.   63p.   TxWaS

1614   Unger, Merrill Frederick, 1909-
        Divine healing [by] Merrill F. Unger.   In Bibliotheca
        Sacra, 128 (July/Sept. 1971), 234-244.

1615   Uzaki, Jundo
        A Biblical and historical study of glossolalia; a survey of
        the gift of tongues from the Wesleyan point of view.   Wilmore,
        Ky. , 1956.   212ℓ .   Thesis (B. D.)--Asbury Theological Semi-
        nary.   KyWAT

1616   Van Elderen, Bastian
        Glossolalia in the New Testament.   In Bulletin of the Evan-
        gelical Theological Society, 7 (Spring 1964), 53-58.

1617   Vivier van Eetveldt, Lincoln Morse
        Glossolalia.   Johannesburg, 1960.   xiv, 439, iiℓ .   Thesis
        (M. D.)--University of Witwatersrand.

1618   Vivier van Eetveldt, Lincoln Morse

The glossolalic and his personality. In Spoerri, T. , ed.
Beiträge zur Ekstase. Basel, New York, 1968, 153-175.

1618a Vix, Henry J.
A comparative study of the doctrine of the Holy Spirit as
taught by the National Holiness Association and by the Pentecostal bodies, by Henry J. Vix. Portland, Or. , 1950. 81ℓ.
Thesis (B. D.)--Western Evangelical Seminary. OrPW

1619   Waldvogel, Edith Lydia, 1950-
The "overcoming life": a study in the reformed evangelical origins of Pentecostalism. Cambridge, Mass. , 1977.
225ℓ. Thesis (Ph. D.)--Harvard University. MH

1620   Walker, Dawson, 1868-
The gift of tongues, and other essays. Edinburgh, T. &
T. Clark, 1906. viii,248p. L, RBaB, IEG

1621   Ward, Horace Singleton, 1939-
The anti-Pentecostal argument [by] Horace S. Ward. In
Synan, H. V. , ed. Aspects of Pentecostal-Charismatic ori-
gins. Plainfield, N. J. , 1975, 99-122.

1622   Wayne, Stanley Milton
These that have turned the world upside down; a history
of charismatic Christians found in church history with emphasis on the patristic period. Fullerton, 1971. ii,92ℓ.
Student project--California State University.

1623   Weatherhead, Benet
Worship at Pentecost. In Life of the Spirit, 16 (June
1962), 519-526.

1624   Welliver, Kenneth Bruce, 1929-
Pentecost and the early church; patristic interpretation of
Acts 2. New Haven, 1961. v,339ℓ. Thesis (Ph. D.)--Yale
University. CtY

1625   Whalley, W. E.
Pentecostal theology, by W. E. Whalley. In Baptist Quarterly (London), 27 (July 1978), 282-289.

1626   Williams, Cyril Glyndwr, 1921-
Ecstaticism in Hebrew prophecy and Christian glossolalia,
by Cyril G. Williams. In Studies in Religion/Sciences Reli-
gieuses, 3:4 (1973-1974), 320-338.

1627   Williams, Cyril Glyndwr, 1921-
Glossolalia as a religious phenomenon: "tongues" at
Corinth and Pentecost [by] Cyril G. Williams. In Religion,
5 (Spring 1975), 16-32.

1627a Williams, Cyril Glyndwr, 1921-

Tongues of the Spirit: a study of Pentecostal glossolalia
and related phenomena [by] Cyril G. Williams. Cardiff,
University of Wales Press, 1981. xiii, 276p. DLC

1628   Williams, George Huntston, 1914-
A history of speaking in tongues and related gifts [by]
George H. Williams and Edith Waldvogel. In Hamilton,
M. P. , ed. The charismatic movement. Grand Rapids,
Mich. , 1975, 61-113.

1629   Williams, Jerry Douglas
The modern Pentecostal movement in America: a brief
sketch of its history and thought. In Lexington Theological
Quarterly, 9 (Apr. 1974), 50-60.

1630   Wilson, Dwight Julian, 1935-
Armageddon now! The premillenarian response to Russia
and Israel since 1917 [by] Dwight Wilson. Santa Cruz, 1975.
iv, 335ℓ. Thesis (Ph. D.)--University of California. CU-SC

1631   Wilson, Dwight Julian, 1935-
Armageddon now! The premillenarian response to Russia
and Israel since 1917 [by] Dwight Wilson. Grand Rapids,
Mich. , Baker Book House, c1977. 258p. Based on thesis
(Ph. D.)--University of California, Santa Cruz. DLC

1632   Womack, David Alfred, 1933-
The wellsprings of the Pentecostal movement, by David A.
Womack. Written in cooperation with the Committee on Ad-
vance for the General Council of the Assemblies of God.
Springfield, Mo. , Gospel Publishing House, 1968. 96p. DLC,
MSohG, TxWaS

1633   Yi, Richard
Spirit baptism and tongues in Acts. La Mirada, Calif. ,
1969. iii, 63ℓ. Thesis (B. D.)--Talbot Theological Seminary.
C LamB

--HYMNS AND SACRED SONGS

1634   Harris, Thoro, 1874-1955.
Blessed hope hymnal. Editor: Thoro Harris. Associate
editors: Orrin R. Jenks [and] Ross L. Fitch. Chicago,
Faith Publishing Co. , 191-. Cover-title, [126]p. With music. ICN

1635   Harris, Thoro, 1874-1955.
Blessed hope hymnal. Revised and enlarged. For the
Bible school, the mid-week meeting, young people's societies
and all services of the sanctuary. Editor: Thoro Harris.
Associate editor: C. B. Widmeyer. Chicago, 191-. Cover-
title, [180]p. With music. ICN

1636   Harris, Thoro, 1874-1955.
            Eternal praise. Editor: Thoro Harris. Special con-
        tributors: Will O. Jones [and] S. L. Flowers. For the
        Bible school, the prayer circle, young people's societies
        and revivals. Chicago, Windsor Music Co. , 191-. Cover-
        title, [94]p. With music. ICN

1637   Harris, Thoro, 1874-1955.
            Revival flame: Bosworth campaign special. Chicago,
        192-. 1v. (unpaged) With music. NNUT

1638   Harris, Thoro, 1874-1955, ed.
            Songs of His coming. Chicago, 191-. [256]p. Cover
        title. With music. ICN

1639   Harris, Thoro, 1874-1955, ed.
            Songs of His coming. Chicago, 192-. 1v. (unpaged)
        Cover title. With music. RPB

1640   Myland, David Wesley, 1858-1943.
            Gospel praise [by] D. Wesley Myland [and] Thoro Harris.
        Columbus, Ohio, Peace Publishing Co. , c1911. 1v. (unpaged)
        Cover title. With music. RPB

1641   Parris, O. A. , ed.
            Banner songs: songs for all religious occasions, by O.
        A. Parris [and others]. Jasper, Ala. , c1944. 128p. With
        music (shape notes).

1642   Parris, O. A. , ed.
            Christian soldier: songs for all religious occasions, by
        O. A. Parris [and others]. Jasper, Ala. , c1945. 127p.
        With music (shape notes) DLC

1643   Pethrus, Lewi, 1884-1974.
            Musik till Segertoner sanger. Utgivna av Lewi Pethrus.
        Stockholm, Rekvireras från Forlaget Filadelfia, 1920. 200p.
        CCmS

1644   Pfingstjubel. Altdorf bei Nürnberg, Missionsbuchhandlung
        und Verlag, 1956. 689p.

1645   Redemption songs; a choice collection of one thousand hymns
        and choruses for evangelistic meetings, soloists, choirs, the
        home. London, Pickering & Inglis, 19--. 223p. With mu-
        sic. RPB

1646   Revivaltime (Radio program)
            Music of the Pentecostal churches. [Phonodisc] Word W
        308 1LP. [196-] 2s. 12 in. 33 1/3 microgroove. Re-
        vivaltime Student Choir, with organ or piano acc. ; Cyril
        McLellan, conductor. Recorded at the Central Bible Institute,
        Springfield, Mo. , Feb. 26-28, 1959. DLC

1646a Shelton, Ruth W.
          Visions of glory. Edited by Ruth W. Shelton. Dayton,
       Tn. , R. E. Winsett Music Co. , c1960. 1v. (unpaged) With
       music (shape notes) OkBetC

1647   Spiers, Phyllis C.
          Spiritual songs by the Spiers; many new Latter Rain
       choruses and hymns, by Phyllis C. Spiers. 46p. Cover
       title. With music.

1648   Squire, Frederick Henry, 1904-1962, comp.
          Full gospel melodies. Burgess Hill, Sussex, Full Gos-
       pel Publishing House, 19--. 132p.

1649   Texas Musical Harts.
          Texas Musical Harts Song book. Detroit, 19--. 1v.
       (unpaged)

1650   Willitts, Ethel R.
          Willitts campaign songs. Chicago, 19--. 1v. (unpaged)

1651   Winsett, Robert Emmet, 1876-1952.
          Celestial echoes: a fine collection of new and old songs
       suitable for revivals, conventions, prayer meetings and all
       religious services. Edited and published by R. E. Winsett.
       Dayton, Tenn. , 1943. 160p. With music (shape notes).

1652   Winsett, Robert Emmet, 1876-1952.
          Favorite radio gems; a choice collection of favorite songs,
       for use over radio, in singing conventions, home singings,
       and all church work where good songs are preferred. Day-
       ton, Tenn. , c1945. 1v. (unpaged) With music (shape notes).
       DLC

1653   Winsett, Robert Emmet, 1876-1952.
          Gospel song messenger: a book of divinely inspired songs
       for all religious services, especially suited to revival work.
       Edited and published by R. E. Winsett. Incomplete ed. Mem-
       phis, Tenn. , 191-. [64]p. Cover title. With music. PPiPT

1654   Winsett, Robert Emmet, 1876-1952.
          Inspired evangel; a book of popular spiritual songs for
       use in revivals, evangelistic work, Sunday schools, prayer
       meetings and all church work, by R. E. Winsett. Dayton,
       Tenn. , c1942. 1v. (unpaged) With music. OrU

1655   Winsett, Robert Emmet, 1876-1952.
          Latter rain revival; spiritual songs with soul appeal,
       especially adapted to revival and evangelistic work and all
       religious endeavor. Edited by R. E. Winsett. Dayton,
       Tenn. , c1931. 1v. (unpaged) At head of title: Named by
       Berl Dodd. With music (shape notes). OkBetC

1656   Winsett, Robert Emmet, 1876-1952.
        New life songs; a book of spiritual songs adapted to all
        religious worship, especially adapted to evangelistic and re-
        vival campaigns. Chattanooga, Tenn. , 192-. 1v. (unpaged)
        With music. NN

1657   Winsett, Robert Emmet, 1876-1952.
        Pentecostal revival songs. Edited and published by R. E.
        Winsett. Chattanooga, Tenn. , 19--. 1v. (unpaged) Cover
        title. With music (shape notes). OkBetC

1658   Winsett, Robert Emmet, 1876-1952.
        Radio and revival special: a book of super specials,
        with soul appeal, for all religious services. Edited by R. E.
        Winsett. Dayton, Tenn. , 1939. 1v. (unpaged) With music
        (shape notes). GU

1659   Winsett, Robert Emmet, 1876-1952.
        Revival joy: a book of spiritual songs for revivals and
        all Christian work, by R. E. Winsett. Dayton, Tenn. , 193-.
        1v. (unpaged) Cover title. With music. GU

1660   Winsett, Robert Emmet, 1876-1952.
        Songs of old-time power; a book of the best spiritual
        songs for evangelistic and all religious purposes. Edited
        and published by R. E. Winsett. Fort Smith, Ark. , c1923.
        1v. (unpaged) Cover title. With music. TxFS

1660a   Winsett, Robert Emmet, 1876-1952.
        Songs of Pentecostal power, complete. Edited by R. E.
        Winsett. Dayton, Tn. , R. E. Winsett Music Co. , c1908.
        1v. (unpaged) Cover title. With music (shape notes) OkBetC

1661   Winsett, Robert Emmet, 1876-1952.
        Songs of spiritual power: songs that win. Dayton, Tenn. ,
        c1936. 1v. (unpaged) With music. NN

1662   Winsett, Robert Emmet, 1876-1952.
        Songs of the kingdom: the camp meeting special. Edited
        and published by R. E. Winsett. Memphis, Tenn. , 191-.
        1v. (unpaged) Cover title. With music. PPiPT

1663   Winsett, Robert Emmet, 1876-1952.
        Soul inspiring songs: a book of the best, selected by
        thousands of God's children. Edited and published by R. E.
        Winsett. Chattanooga, Tenn. , c1929. [192]p. With music.

1664   Winsett, Robert Emmet, 1876-1952.
        Waves of glory. Edited and published by R. E. Winsett.
        Fort Smith, Ark. , 1924. 1v. (unpaged) Cover title. At
        head of title: The best songs for the best people. With mu-
        sic (shape notes) OkBetC

1665   Winsett, Ruth
       Gems of devotion; a book of super specials with soul ap-
       peal for all religious services.   Arranged by R. E. W.
       Dayton, R. E. Winsett, c1940.   1v.   (unpaged)   With music
       (shape notes)   NN

       --JUVENILE LITERATURE

1666   Carey, Floyd D.
       Christian etiquette for teen-agers; a handbook on Chris-
       tian etiquette.   Illustrations by Mrs. Robert Kinsey.   Grand
       Rapids, Mich. , Baker Book House, 1969, c1963.   100p.

1667   Franklin, A. P.
       I tigerskogen, och andra berättelser.   Rockford, Ill. ,
       Författarens Förlag, 1917.   110p.   MnHi

1668   Ski, Sven
       Bålet i urskogen.   Oslo, Filadelfiaforlaget, 1948.   130p.
       DLC

1669   Ski, Sven
       Med tropehjelm i Afrika; en norsk gutt og en norsk jente
       opplever det spennende Afrika.   Oslo, Filadelfia-forlaget,
       1950.   127p.   DLC

1669a Womersley, Harold
       In the glow of the log fire, by Harold Womersley.   Illus-
       trated by W. F. P. Burton.   London, Peniel Press, 1975.
       123p.   OkTOr

       --MISSIONS

1670   Conn, Charles William, 1920-
       A spiritual explosion, by Charles W. Conn.   In Christian
       Life, 28 (July 1966), 30-31, 54.

1671   Damboriena, Prudencio, 1913-
       Tongues as of fire; Pentecostalism in contemporary Chris-
       tianity.   Washington, Corpus Books, 1969.   viii, 256p.
       KyLxCB, MBU-T, MH-AH, MSohG, NcD

1672   Gee, Donald, 1891-1966.
       Upon all flesh: a Pentecostal world tour.   Springfield,
       Mo. , Gospel Publishing House, 1935.   107p.

1673   Gee, Donald, 1891-1966.
       Upon all flesh: a Pentecostal world tour.   Rev. ed.
       Springfield, Mo. , Gospel Publishing House, 1947.   118p.
       MSohG, TxWaS

1674   Hodges, Melvin Lyle, 1909-
        Build my church, by Melvin L. Hodges.   Chicago, Moody
        Press, 1957.   128p.   GDC

1675   Hodges, Melvin Lyle, 1909-
        Growing young churches; how to advance indigenous
        churches today, by Melvin L. Hodges.   Rev. and enlarged ed.
        Chicago, Moody Press, 1970.   127p.   (Christian forum books.)
        Also issued as On the mission field and The indigenous
        church.   NcWfSB, PPiPT

1676   Hodges, Melvin Lyle, 1909-
        On the mission field; the indigenous church, by Melvin
        L. Hodges.   Chicago, Moody Press, 1953.   128p.   Also
        issued under title: The indigenous church.   TxFTC, CMlG,
        KyWAT

1677   Hodges, Melvin Lyle, 1909-
        A Pentecostal's view of mission strategy, by Melvin L.
        Hodges.   In International Review of Missions, 57 (July 1968),
        304-310.

1678   Hollenweger, Walter Jacob, 1927-
        Handbuch der Pfingstbewegung, von Walter J. Hollenweger.
        Zürich, 1966.   3v. in 10.   Inaug.-Diss. --Zürich.
            Contents: 1.   Hauptt.   Sektierer oder Enthusiasten?
        2.   Hauptt.   Die einzelnen Pfingstgruppen, nach geographis-
        chen Gesichtsspunkten gegliedert: [1] Afrika; [2] Nordamerika;
        [3] Lateinamerika; [4] Asien, Australien und Oceanien; [5]-[6]
        Europa; 3.   Hauptt.   Kommentierte Bibliographie, Kurzbio-
        graphien: [1] Einfuhrung in den III.   Hauptteil; [2] Selbstdar-
        stellungen; [3] Frembddarstellungen, Selbst- und Frembddar-
        stellungen der Heiligungsbewegung.   Uebrige Spezialliteratur.
            Microfilm (positive).   3 reels 35mm.   Reproduced for
        the American Theological Library Association Microtext Proj-
        ect by Department of Photoduplication, University of Chicago,
        1968.   IEG, MH-AH, NjMD

1679   Magnusson, John
        Under Guds ledning: Örebro Missionsförenings fram-
        trädande och verksamhet.   Örebro, Omis Förlag, 1957.   97p.

1680   Sumrall, Lester Frank, 1913-
        Sumrall's Short stories, by Lester F. Sumrall.   Grand
        Rapids, Mich. , Zondervan Publishing House, 1946.   97p.
        True stories collected during world travels.   cf. Pref.   DLC

        --MUSIC

1681   Alford, Delton Lynol
        Music in the Pentecostal church [by] Delton L. Alford.

Cleveland, Tenn. , Pathway Press, 1967. 120p. (Church training course series, 703) DLC

1682   Alford, Delton Lynol
        Music in worship [by] Delton L. Alford. In Knight, C. B. , ed. Pentecostal worship. Cleveland, Tenn. , 1974, 63-75.

1683   Boeckman, Charles, 1920-
        And the beat goes on; a survey of pop music in America. Washington, Luce, 1972. 224p. "That old-time religion": p. 67-74. DLC

1684   Conn, Philip Wesley, 1942-
        The relationship between congregational hymn preference and socioeconomic status: a study in congregational variation in religious orientation. Knoxville, 1972. ix, 132ℓ . Thesis (M. A.)--University of Tennessee. TU

1685   Heilbut, Anthony Otto, 1941-
        The gospel sound: good news and bad times [by] Tony Heilbut. New York, Simon and Schuster, 1971. 350p. "The Holiness church": p. 199-278. DLC

1686   Heilbut, Anthony Otto, 1941-
        The gospel sound: good news and bad times [by] Tony Heilbut. Garden City, N. Y. , Anchor Press /Doubleday, 1975, c1971. xxxv, 364p. (Anchor books). "The Holiness church": p. 171-251.

1687   Hollenweger, Walter Jacob, 1927-
        Spirituals [by] W. J. Hollenweger. In Davies, J. G. , ed. A dictionary of liturgy and worship. New York, 1972, 349-350.

1688   Hopkin, John Barton
        Music in the Jamaican Pentecostal churches. Cambridge, Mass. , 1974. 76ℓ . Thesis (B. A.)--Harvard University. MH

1689   Marks, Morton, 1918-
        Uncovering ritual structures in Afro-American music. In Zaretsky, I. I. , ed. Religious movements in contemporary America. Princeton, N. J. , c1974, 60-134. Comments on glossolalia.

1689a   Smeeton, Donald Dean
        Holiness hymns and Pentecostal power: a theologian looks at Pentecostal hymnody. In Hymn, 31 (July 1980), 183-185, 193.

1690   Walker, William, 1809-1875.
        The Christian harmony in the seven-syllable character

note system of music; hymn and psalm tunes, odes and an-
thems, selected from the best authors in Europe and America, adapted to the use of singing schools, choirs, social
and private singing societies. Rev. 1958 by John Deason
and O. A. Parris. n. p. , Christian Harmony Publishing Co. ,
1958. 381p.

1691   Whalum, Wendell
          The folk stream. In Smyth, M. M. , ed.   The Black
       American reference book.   Englewood Cliffs, N. J. , c1976,
       791-808.   "Gospel music": p. 805-808.

1692   Winsett, Robert Emmet, 1876-1952.
          Standard rudiments, a self instructor; a complete course
       in all departments of the rudiments of music, melodics,
       rhythmics, dynamics and voice culture, by R. E. Winsett.
       Cincinnati, Printed by Cincinnati Music Printing Co. , c1908.
       25p.   Cover title.   DLC

                    --PASTORAL LITERATURE

1693   Adams, Leonard P.
          Our life in Christ, by Leonard P. Adams.   Memphis,
       Tenn. , 19--.   160p.   TxWaS

1694   Armstrong, Hart Reid, 1912-
          How do I pray?   By Hart R. Armstrong.   Wichita, Kan. ,
       Defenders of the Christian Faith, c1968.   97p.

1695   Booth-Clibborn, Catherine, 1859-1955.
          Love and courtship, by the Maréchale, Catherine Booth-
       Clibborn.   New York, G. H. Doran Co. , 192-.   88p.   DLC,
       NcD, NN

1696   Booth-Clibborn, Catherine, 1859-1955.
          Our children, by the Maréchale: Catherine Booth-Clibborn.
       New York, G. H. Doran Co. , c1925.   148p.   DLC, ICJ, NN

1697   Caldwell, Louis Oliver, 1935-
          The adventure of becoming one [by] Louis O. Caldwell.
       Grand Rapids, Mich. , Baker Book House, 1969.   80p.   DLC

1698   Caldwell, Louis Oliver, 1935-
          After the tassel is moved; guidelines for high school
       graduates [by] Louis O. Caldwell.   Grand Rapids, Mich. ,
       Baker Book House, 1968.   80p.   DLC

1699   Caldwell, Louis Oliver, 1935-
          Another tassel is moved; guidelines for college graduates
       [by] Louis O. Caldwell.   Grand Rapids, Mich. , Baker Book
       House, 1970.   95p.   DLC

1700   Caldwell, Louis Oliver, 1935-
        If you talk to teens; a source book for youth leaders, by
        Louis O. Caldwell. Grand Rapids, Mich. , Baker Book House,
        1966. 149p. DLC

1701   Caldwell, Louis Oliver, 1935-
        When partners become parents [by] Louis O. Caldwell.
        Grand Rapids, Mich. , Baker Book House, 1971. 80p. DLC

1702   Hagin, Kenneth E. , 1917-
        Demons and how to deal with them, by Kenneth E. Hagin.
        Tulsa, 19--. 27p.

1703   Hagin, Kenneth E. , 1917-
        How to turn your faith loose. Tulsa, Kenneth E. Hagin
        Evangelistic Association, 1975. 31p. "Sixth printing. "

1704   Hagin, Kenneth E. , 1917-
        How you can know the will of God, by Kenneth E. Hagin.
        Tulsa, Kenneth Hagin Evangelistic Association, 1976. 32p.
        "Fifth printing. "

1705   Hagin, Kenneth E. , 1917-
        The interceding Christian, by Kenneth Hagin. Tulsa,
        Kenneth E. Hagin Evangelistic Association, 1976. 32p.
        "Fifth printing. "

1706   Hagin, Kenneth E. , 1917-
        The key to scriptural healing, by Kenneth Hagin. Tulsa,
        Kenneth Hagin Evangelistic Association, 1975. 31p. "Seventh
        printing. "

1707   Hagin, Kenneth E. , 1917-
        Ministering to the oppressed. Tulsa, Kenneth Hagin
        Evangelistic Association, 1975. 29p. "Sixth printing. "

1708   Hagin, Kenneth E. , 1917-
        The ministry of a prophet, by Kenneth Hagin. 5th ed.
        Tulsa, Kenneth E. Hagin Evangelistic Association, 1974.
        30p.

1709   Hagin, Kenneth E. , 1917-
        Prayer secrets, by Kenneth E. Hagin. Tulsa, Kenneth
        E. Hagin Evangelistic Association, 1976. 30p. "Eighth
        printing. "

1710   Hagin, Kenneth E. , 1917-
        Right and wrong thinking for Christians, by Kenneth E.
        Hagin. Tulsa, Kenneth Hagin Evangelistic Association, 1976.
        32p.

1711   Hagin, Kenneth E. , 1917-
        What faith is, by Kenneth E. Hagin. Tulsa, Kenneth

Hagin Evangelistic Association, 1976.   30p.   "Eighth printing. "

1712   Hagin, Kenneth E. , 1917-
The woman question [by] Kenneth E. Hagin.   Tulsa,
Kenneth E. Hagin Evangelistic Association, c1975.   93p.

1713   Harris, Leo
Five keys of authority.   Fullarton, S. Austl. , Crusader
Publications, 196-.   44p.   OkTOr

1714   Hodges, Melvin Lyle, 1909-
Grow toward leadership, by Melvin L. Hodges.   Rev. ed.
Chicago, Moody Press, 1969.   63p.   (Christian forum books)
PPiPT

1715   Kirban, Salem
Health guide for survival.   Huntingdon Valley, Pa. ,
c1976.   180p.   DLC

1716   Kirban, Salem
How to eat your way back to vibrant health.   Huntingdon
Valley, Pa. , c1977.   92p.   DLC

1717   Kirban, Salem
How to keep healthy and happy by fasting.   Huntingdon
Valley, Pa. , c1976.   173p.   DLC

1718   Kirban, Salem
How to live above & beyond your circumstances.   Huntingdon Valley, Pa. , c1974.   218p.   DLC

1719   Marlow, John David, 1919-
Beyond Pentecost [by] John D. Marlow.   Silsbee, Tex. ,
Deeper Life Ministry, 19--.   13p.   OkTOr

1720   Montgomery, Granville Harrison, 1903-1966.
Why people like you; a Christian approach to human rela-
tions.   New York, Taplinger Publishing Co. , 1963.   277p.
DLC

1721   Osborn, Tommy Lee, 1923-
Join this chariot [by] T. L. Osborn.   Tulsa, Osborn
Foundation, c1974.   131p.   KyWAT

1722   Pethrus, Lewi, 1884-1974.
Play today, pay tomorrow [by] Lewi Pethrus.   Translated
by J. O. Backlund.   Chicago, Philadelphia Book Concern,
c1949.   141p.

1723   Pethrus, Lewi, 1884-1974.
Ungdom kärlek, äktenskap.   Stockholm, Norman, 1962.
62p.

1724   Spence, Inez
         Coping with loneliness.   Grand Rapids, Mi. , Baker Book
         House, 1975.   111p.   (Directions books.)   First published
         under title: When the heart is lonely.

1724a Spence, Inez
         When the heart is lonely.   Grand Rapids, Mich. , Baker
         Book House, 1970.   111p.   DLC

1725   Squire, Frederick Henry, 1904-1962.
         Salvation and helps to converts, by Frederick H. Squire.
         Southend-on-Sea, Essex, Full Gospel Publishing House, 194-.
         15p.   L

                          --PASTORAL THEOLOGY

1726   Beall, James Lee, 1924-
         Your pastor, your shepherd [by] James Lee Beall.   Edited
         by Marjorie Barber.   Plainfield, N. J. , Logos International,
         c1977.   xii, 208p.

1727   Coe, Juanita (Scott)
         Women preachers, by Juanita Coe.   Dallas, Loftin-
         Shepherd Ptg. & Litho. , 19--.   29p.   OkTOr

1728   Fiorentino, Joseph, 1912-
         Pulpit ethics and procedures.   n. p. , 1972.   8p.   Caption
         title.

1729   Fitch, Theodore
         How to be a successful minister: one hundred mistakes
         of ministers.   3d ed.   Dallas, 19--.   245p.

1730   Gee, Donald, 1891-1966.
         Os dons do ministério de Cristo; continuacão de "Acêra
         dos dons espirituais. "   Rio de Janeiro, Libros Evangélicos,
         1961.   99p.   Translation of The ministry-gifts of Christ.

1731   Gee, Donald, 1891-1966.
         Die Gaben Christi für den geistlichen Dienst.   Übers.
         von Johan Justus Meier.   Vaihingen-Enz, K. Fix, 19--.   63p.
         Translation of The ministry-gifts of Christ.

1732   Gee, Donald, 1891-1966.
         The ministry-gifts of Christ.   Springfield, Mo. , Gospel
         Publishing House, c1930.   110p.   Sequel to Concerning spirit-
         ual gifts.   DLC, MSohG

1733   Grant, Walter Vinson, 1913-
         Deliverance ministry.   Dallas, Grant's Faith Clinic, 19--.
         32p.   "Taken from How you may receive this ministry. "
         OkTOr

1734   Hembree, Charles Ron, 1938-
        Effective illustrations from everyday life [by] Charles R.
        Hembree. Grand Rapids, Mich., Baker Book House, c1973.
        143p.

1735   Lindsay, Gordon, 1906-1973.
        The Pentecostal ministry. Dallas, Christ for the Nations
        Publishing Co., 1968. 2v.

1736   Macpherson, Ian, 1912-
        The art of illustrating sermons. New York, Abingdon
        Press, 1964. 219p. DLC

1737   Macpherson, Ian, 1912-
        The art of illustrating sermons. Grand Rapids, Mich.,
        Baker Book House, 1976, c1964. 219p.

1738   Macpherson, Ian, 1912-
        The burden of the Lord; lectures on preaching. London,
        Epworth Press, 1955. 147p. DLC, L

1739   Macpherson, Ian, 1912-
        The burden of the Lord. New York, Abingdon Press,
        1955. 157p. DLC

1740   O'Guin, Carl M., 1896-
        Special occasion helps, by C. M. O'Guin. Grand Rapids,
        Mich., Baker Book House, 1965. 87p. [Minister's handbook
        series.] DLC

                    --PERIODICALS

1741   Abundant life. 1- 1947-
        Tulsa. 1947-Aug. 1953 as Healing waters; Sept. 1953-
        1955 as America's healing magazine; Jan.-June 1956 as
        Healing.

1742   Abundant life and healing. 1- 1951-
        Amprior, Ont.

1743   Apostolic banner. 1- 1908-
        San Marcial, N.M.

1744   Apostolic herald. 1- 1909-
        Seattle.

1745   Apostolic herald. 1- 1907-191-.
        Winnipeg, Man. 1907-1910 as Apostolic messenger.

1746   Apostolic light. 1- 190 -
        Salem, Ore.

1747   Apostolic rivers of living waters. 1- 19 -
        New Haven, Conn.

1748   Apostolic truth. 1- 190 -
        Los Angeles.

1749   Apostolic witness and missionary advocate. 1- 1908-
        Dallas, Ore.

1750   Back to God. 1- 195 -
        East London, S. Afr.

1751   Beams of light. 1- 1942-
        Tulsa.

1752   Bible friend. 1- Dec. 1912-
        Robbinsdale, Minn.

1753   Bread of life. 1- Dec. 1951-
        Brooklyn.

1754   Buletinul cultuli penticostal. 1- 1952-
        Bucuresti. MH-AH

1755   Byposten. 1- 1905-1909.
        Christiania (Oslo).

1756   Call to faith. 1- 1910-
        Wardensville, W. Va.

1757   Christian challenge. 1- July 1947-
        Waxahachie, Tx. Dallas. 1947-1954 as Herald of
        healing; 1955-May 1962 as International healing magazine.

1758   Christian vanguard. 1- 1949-
        Oakland, Ca.

1759   Christian world news. 1- 1948-
        Houston.

1760   Church. 1- May 1, 1922-
        Houston.

1761   Confidence. 1- Apr. 1908-1923.
        Sunderland, Durham.

1762   Dagen. 1- 1945-
        Stockholm.

1763   Daily blessing. 1- 1959-
        Tulsa.

1764   Deeper life. 1- 1965-
        San Diego.

1765   Elbethel.   1-28, no. 3, 1914-July/Sept. 1965; 28, no. 4-
       Oct. 1967-
           Chicago; Asheville, N.C.

1766   Eleven fifty seven.   1- 195-
           Miami, Fla.

1767   Eleventh hour.   1- 19 -
           Tukkudal, Tinnevelly (now Tirunelveli) dist., India.

1768   Euroflame.   1- 1953-
           Slough, Bucks.; Nottingham.   1-22, no. 5, 1953-Aug.
       1973 as European herald.

1769   Evangelii Härold.   1- 1916-
           Stockholm.

1770   Evangelist.   1- 1970-
           Baton Rouge, La.

1771   Evangelist.   1- 1962-1966.
           Beirut.

1772   Evangelist.   1- 1937-
           Dallas.

1773   Evangelist.   1- 1926-1930.
           Odessa.

1774   Evangelistic times.   1- 1961-
           Milwaukee.

1775   Ewangelskij Holos.   1- 19 -
           Ketrzyn.

1776   Faith digest.   1- 1956-
           Tulsa.

1777   First-fruit harvester.   1- 1897-
           Rumney Depot, N.H.

1778   Flames of fire.   1- Oct. 1911-Jan. 1925.
           Bedford.

1779   Fragments of flame.   1- 1910-
           London.

1780   Full gospel advocate.   1-24, no. 6, 1917-Aug. 1941.
           Houston.   Merged into Gospel call.   IEG, TxH

1781   Full gospel echoes.   1- 1946-
           St. Clair, Mich.

1782   Full gospel herald.   1- Aug. 1925-
       Dallas, Bethel Church.

1783   Full gospel missionary herald.   1- 1916-
       Newark, N.J.

1784   Full gospel monthly.   1- 1928-
       Orlando, Fla.

1785   Full gospel testimony.   Revival news.   1-18, no. 2, Apr./
       June 1935-Apr./June 1952.
       Southend-on-Sea, Essex.   L

1786   Glad tidings herald.   1-27, 1918-1948.
       New York.

1787   Glaubens Zeuge.   1- 196-
       Düsseldorf.   OkTOr

1788   Glos Ewangelii.   1- 19 -
       Ketrzyn.

1789   Glos Prawdy.   1- 1920-
       Warszawa.

1790   God's messenger of truth.   1- 1945-
       Ashland, Ore.

1791   God's searchlight.   1- Dec. 1927-
       Des Moines.

1792   Golden grain.   1- Mar. 1926-May 1957.
       Seattle, Wa.; Pasadena, Ca.

1793   Good report.   1- 1912-
       Ottawa, Ont.

1794   Good tidings.   1- 1908-
       Dayton, Ohio.

1795   Gospel call.   1- 1927-
       Chicago, Ill.; Pasadena, Calif.   1927-19-- as Gospel
       call of Russia.   "Incorporating the Latter Rain Evangel,
       Word and Work [and] the Full Gospel Advocate."   DLC

1796   Gospel call.   1- 1934-
       Fort Worth, Tex.

1797   Gospel defender.   1-17, 1953-1971.
       Ottumwa, Ia.

1797a Gospel faith messenger.   1- 1964-
       Palmerston, N.Z.

1798   Gospel front.   1-   1947-1949.
        Basel.

1799   Gospel light.   1-   191 -
        West Plains, Mo.

1800   Gospel messenger.   1-   Oct. 1927-
        Sherburn, Minn.

1801   Gospel of the kingdom.   1-   190 -
        ----, Tex.

1802   Gospel witness.   1-   July 1915-
        Los Angeles.

1803   Grace and glory.   1-   1916-
        Kansas City, Mo.   To 19-- as Pentecost.

1804   Grace and truth.   1-   191 -
        Memphis.

1805   Healing messenger.   1-   1949-1956.
        Chicago.

1806   Healing messenger.   1-   1963-
        Dallas.

1807   Healing today.   1-   19 -
        Cleveland, Tenn.

1808   Hearts for Jesus.   1-   19 -
        [Place unknown]

1809   Heilszeugnisse.   1-   1930-1941, 1946-
        Altdorf bei Nürnberg.

1810   Herald of healing.   1-   1947-
        Santa Ana, Calif.

1811   Herald of hope.   1-   1937-
        Los Angeles.

1812   Herald of Pentecost.   1-   1956-
        Chicago.

1813   Herald of Pentecost.   1-   1953-1956.
        Duluth.

1814   Highway messenger.   1-   19 -
        Chicago.

1815   Impact.   1-   194 -
        Fullarton, S. Austl., Adelaide, S. Austl.   To 197- as
        Revivalist.

1816   Intercessory missionary.   1- 1907-
        Fort Wayne, Ind.

1817   Journal of Pentecostal literature.   1- 1975-
        Fort Pierce, Fla.

1818   Der König kommt! 1- 1947-
        Saarbrucken.

1819   Korsets Seier.   1- 1904-
        Oslo.

1820   Latter rain evangel.   1-30, no. 8, Oct. 1908-June 1939.
        Chicago.   Merged into Gospel call. DLC

1821   Latter rain evangel.   1- July 1951-
        Detroit.

1822   Latter rain evangel.   1- Oct. 1949-
        Los Angeles.

1823   Der Leuchter.   1- 1932-
        Erzhausen.   1922-1950 as Der feste Grund.

1824   Life in the Spirit.   1- 1963-
        Dallas.

1824a   Link. [1]- 197 -
        Spartanburg, S.C.

1825   Living truth.   1- 1907-
        Los Angeles.

1826   Living word.   1- 191 -
        St. Paul, Minn.

1827   Manney revival news.   1- Oct. 22, 1937-
        Weatherford, Tex.

1828   Maranatha.   1- 1929-
        Kopenhagen.   1929-1931 as Korsets Evangelium.

1829   March of faith.   1- 1945-
        Portland, Ore.; Los Angeles, Calif.

1830   Messenger.   1- 1927-1928, Feb. 1935-1937, June 1949-
        July/Aug. 1964.
        Sharon, Pa.; San Jose, Calif.

1831   Midnight cry.   1-8, 1911-1918.
        New York.

1832   Midnight cry.   1- 1908-
        Seattle.

1833   Miracle.   1- 1954-
         Dallas, Tex.; Miracle Valley, Ariz.; Phoenix, Ariz.

1834   Miracle word.   1- 1966-
         Phoenix.

1835   Miracles and missions digest.   1- 1956-
         Dallas.

1836   New acts.   1- 1907-
         Alliance, Oh.

1837   New day.   1- 1954-
         Daytona Beach, Fla.; Indiana, Pa.   1954-1970 as Missions through faith.

1838   Old camp meeting news.   1- 1931-
         Dallas.

1839   Omega.   1- 190 -
         Surrey.

1840   PFNA news.   1- 1960-
         Springfield, Mo.

1841   Page.   1- 19 -
         Battleford, Sask.   To 19-- as Rose of Sharon.

1842   Pentecost.   1-77, Sept. 1947-Sept./Nov. 1966.
         Louth, Lincs.; Bedford, Beds.; Kenley, Surrey; London.
         CtY-D

1843   Pentecost in the Twin Cities.   1- 1908-
         Minneapolis.

1844   Pentecostal Alliance crescendo.   1- Feb./Mar. 1952-
         Chicago.   DLC

1845   Pentecostal Christian.   1- 1919-
         East Moline, Ill.

1846   Pentecostal Friend.   1- 19 -
         Detroit.

1847   Pentecostal herald.   1- 1913-1927.
         Chicago.

1848   Pentecostal journal.   1- 1906-
         Oakland, Calif.

1849   Pentecostal latter rain.   1- July 1928-
         Amarillo, Tex.

168 Guide to the Pentecostal Movement

1850 Pentecostal missionary neighbors messenger. 1- 19 -
Detroit.

1851 Pentecostal power. 1- 1941-
Seattle.

1852 Pentecostal record. 1- 1908-
Spokane, Wash.

1853 Pentecostal rescue journal. 1- 1911-
Columbia, S. C.

1854 Pentecostal trumpet. 1- 1908-
Denver, Colo.

1855 Pentecostal visitor. 1- July 1937-
Washington, D. C.

1856 Pentecostal wonders. 1- 19 -
Akron, Ohio.

1857 Pentecostal world. 1- 1926-
Long Island City, N. Y.

1858 Pentecostal world. 1- 1970-
Philadelphia.

1859 Pfingstgrüsse. 1- Feb. 1909-1919.
Breslau.

1860 Philadelphia Briefe. 1- 1948-1963.
Leonberg, Württ. Merged into Der König kommt!

1861 De Pinksterboodschap. 1- 1961-
Groningen, Neth.; Huizen, Neth.

1862 Pinksterklanken. 1- 191 -1960.
Amsterdam. To 1948 as De Spade Regen. Merged into
De Pinksterboodschap.

1863 Pisgah. 1- 1909-1972.
Los Angeles; Summit, Ca.; Pikeville, Tn.

1864 Present truth. 1- 191 -
Indianapolis.

1865 Priidet Primiritel. 1- 193 -
Danzig (Gdansk).

1866 Promise. 1- 1909-
Toronto.

1867 Prophetic news. 1- 1935-
Fairmont, Minn.

1868   Prophetic reporter. 1- 1954-
        Kansas City, Mo.

1869   Przystep. 1- 19 -
        Ketrzyn.

1870   Radio evangel. 1- Nov. 1930-
        Portland, Ore. 1930 as Radio broadcast.

1871   Record of faith. 1- 192 -
        Pittsburgh; Gibsonia, Pa.

1872   Restoration. 1- 19 -
        Nelson, N. Z. 19 -1966 as Revival news.

1873   Revival herald. 1- 1948-
        Seattle.

1874   Revival news. 1- 19 -
        New Bern, N. C.

1875   Revival of America. 1- 1960-
        Tampa, Fla.; Delaware, Ohio. 1960-Mar. 1967 as
        Revival; Apr. -Aug. 1967 as Today with Leroy Jenkins.

1876   Revival time. 1- 19 -
        Portland, Ore.

1877   Ristin Voitto. 1- 1911-
        Helsinki.

1878   Sharon star. 1- 1947-19--.
        North Battleford, B. C.

1879   Shield of faith. 1- 1929-
        Amarillo, Tx.; Fort Worth, Tx.; St. Louis.

1880   Shield of truth. 1- 1922-
        Newcastle, Tx.

1881   Sieg des Kreuzes. 1- 1950-
        Hamburg. 1950-19-- as Licht und Leben

1882   Spirit. 1- 1977-
        Washington, D. C. "A journal of issues incident to Black
        Pentecostalism. " DLC

1883   Spirit of truth. 1- 190 -
        ----, Hants.

1884   Standard bearer. 1- 19 -
        Dayton, Ohio.

1884a   Star of hope.   1-   19 -
        El Monte, Ca.

1885   Stromen van Kracht.   1-   1954-
        Baarn.

1886   Student statesman.   1-   196 -
        Los Angeles.

1887   Things old and new.   1-   192 -
        London.

1888   Tried by fire.   1-   Dec. 1910-191-.
        Topeka, Kan.

1889   Triumphs of faith.   1-   1881-19--.
        Buffalo, N.Y.; Oakland, Calif.   NBu, OO

1890   Trooster/Comforter.   1-   1933-
        Johannesburg.

1891   Trust.   1-   1902-
        Rochester, N.Y.

1892   Truth and glorious hope.   1-   19 -
        Chicago.

1893   Twilight tidings.   1-   Nov. 1950-195-.
        Long Beach, Calif.

1894   Upper room.   1-   1909-
        Los Angeles.

1895   Victorious gospel.   1-   191 -
        Los Angeles.

1896   Victory.   1-15, 1909-1916.
        Bournemouth, Hants.

1897   Victory.   1-   Apr. 1951-
        Houston.

1898   Victory Emmanuel evangel.   1-   19 -
        Toledo, Ohio.

1899   Viens et vois.   1-   1932-
        Paris, Rouen, Louviers.

1900   Voice of deliverance.   1-   1962-
        Dallas.   Aug. 1965-Dec. 1966 as Evangelize.

1901   Voice of deliverance.   1-   195 -
        Port Arthur, Tex.

1902   Voice of faith. 1- 195 -
        Memphis.

1903   La Voix Chrétienne. 1- 1954-
        Bruxelles.

1904   Wings of healing. 1- 19 -
        Portland, Ore.

1905   Word and witness. 1- 191 -1913.
        Nashville. Merged into Apostolic faith as Word and
        witness.

1906   Word and witness. 1- 1907-1916.
        Houston, Tex.; Malvern, Ark.; Findlay, Ohio; St. Louis,
        Mo. 1907-1913 as Apostolic faith.

1907   Word and work. 1-61, 1879-1939.
        Springfield, Ma.; Russell, Ma.; Framingham, Ma. IEG,
        IU, NN, NNUT

1908   Word of faith. 1- 1967-
        Tulsa.

1909   World evangelism. 1- 1959-
        Dallas.

1910   World Pentecost. 1- 1971-
        Cardiff. Supersedes Pentecost. DLC

1911   World revival. 1- 1957-
        Cleveland, Tenn. 1957-Sept. 1963 as Herald of deliver-
        ance.

1912   World-wide revival reports. 1- 1961-1970.
        Dallas.

1913   Wort und Zeugnis. 1- 19 -
        Berlin.

-- --BIBLIOGRAPHY

1914   Oral Roberts University. Pentecostal Collection.
        A bibliography of the Pentecostal periodical holdings in
        the Oral Roberts University Pentecostal Collection. S. Juan-
        ita Walker, comp. Tulsa, Okla., 1971. 27ℓ. DLC

--QUOTATIONS, MAXIMS, ANECDOTES, ETC.

1915   Grant, Walter Vinson, 1913-
        Nuggets in a nutshell, by W. V. Grant. Dallas, Faith
        Clinic, 19--. 29p. OkTOr

1916   Grant, Walter Vinson, 1913-
       Our treasure chest of poems and proverbs. Compiled by
       W. V. Grant. Dallas, Faith Clinic, 19--. 32p. OkTOr

1917   Grant, Walter Vinson, 1913- , comp.
       Recitations, readings and snappy sayings for Sunday
       schools, bulletin boards, speakers, preachers, teachers [and]
       business. Compiled by W. V. Grant. Dallas, Faith Clinic,
       19--. 32p. OkTOr

1918   Pentz, Croft Miner
       1001 sentence sermons for every need. Grand Rapids,
       Mich., Zondervan Publishing House, 1962. 61p. TxDaTS

1919   Pentz, Croft Miner, comp.
       Preaching poems for sermons and addresses. Grand
       Rapids, Mich., Baker Book House, 1966. 79p. (Preaching
       helps series.)

1920   Pentz, Croft Miner, comp.
       Speaker's treasury of 400 quotable poems. Grand Rapids,
       Mich., Zondervan Publishing House, c1963. 159p. DLC, NN

1921   Ramsay, Charles L.
       101 Christian cartoons, by Charles L. Ramsay. With a
       foreword by Vaughn Shoemaker and text by Hart R. Armstrong.
       Springfield, Mo., Independent Printing Co., 1949. 112p.

1922   Shaffer, Robert
       20th century proverbs. Canyonville, Ore., 1965. 227p.

1923   Waldvogel, Hans R.,   -1969.
       Daily manna: gleanings from the sermons of Hans R.
       Waldvogel. Compiled by Gordon P. Gardiner. n. p., 19--.
       1v. (unpaged)

1924   Warner, Wayne Earl, 1933-
       1, 000 stories and quotations of famous people. Compiled
       by Wayne E. Warner. Grand Rapids, Baker Book House,
       1972. 362p. DLC

                   --RELATIONS WITH OTHER CHURCHES

1925   Canty, George
       Pentecostalist hesitations. In Frontier, 11 (Winter 1968/
       1969), 264-266.

1926   Courtney, Howard Perry, 1911-
       Classical Pentecostals: a miraculous demonstration, by
       Howard P. Courtney. In Christian Life, 39 (June 1977), 45-
       46. Will renewal come out of Kansas City ? pt. 1.

1927   Du Plessis, David Johannes, 1905-
        Pentecost outside "Pentecost"; the astounding move of
        God in the denominational churches. Dallas, 1960. 28p.
        NNMR

1928   Du Plessis, David Johannes, 1905-
        The Spirit bade me go: an astounding move of God in
        the denominational churches; a survey of the work of the
        Holy Spirit in the ecumenical movements during the decade,
        1951-61; a report on the Pentecostal ministry of the writer
        in Protestant institutions and churches; a record of the ex-
        periences, lectures and messages of the writer. Dallas,
        1961. 96p. CBPac, CSaT, NNUT

1929   Du Plessis, David Johannes, 1905-
        The Spirit bade me go; the astounding move of God in
        the denominational churches, by David J. du Plessis. Rev.
        and enl. ed. Oakland, Calif., 1963. 122p. IEG, MSohG

1930   Du Plessis, David Johannes, 1905-
        The Spirit bade me go; the astounding move of God in
        the denominational churches, by David J. du Plessis. Oak-
        land, Calif., 1964. 122p. TxWaS

1931   Du Plessis, David Johannes, 1905-
        The Spirit bade me go; the astounding move of God in
        the denominational churches, by David J. du Plessis. Rev.
        ed. Plainfield, N.J., Logos International, 1970. 119p.
        MoSCS, NHou

1932   Krust, Christian Hugo
        Pentecostal churches and the ecumenical movement by
        Christian Krust. In Goodall, N., ed. The Uppsala report
        1968; official report of the Fourth Assembly of the World
        Council of Churches, Uppsala, July 4-20, 1968. Geneva,
        1968, 340-343.

1933   McDonnell, Kilian, 1921-
        The ecumenical significance of the Pentecostal Movement.
        In Worship, 40 (Dec. 1966), 608-629.

1934   Synan, Harold Vinson, 1934-
        Pentecostal Holiness: demonstration of dynamic growth,
        by Vinson Synan. In Christian Life, 39 (July 1977), 56, 58.
        Will renewal come out of Kansas City? pt. 2.

-- --CATHOLIC CHURCH

1935   Bittlinger, Arnold, 1928-
        Papst und Pfingstler: d. röm.-kath.-pfingstl. Dialog u.
        seine ökumen. Relevanz. Frankfurt am Main, Bern, Las
        Vegas, Lang, 1978. 498p. (Studien zur interkulturellen
        Geschichte des Christentums, 16.) Includes text in English.
        DLC

1936   Canty, George
            Pentecostalist hesitations. In Frontier, 11 (Winter 1968/
        1969), 264-266.

1937   Le dialogue avec les pentecotistes.
            In La Documentation Catholique, 71 (June 16, 1974),
        583-586.

1938   McDonnell, Kilian, 1921-
            Classical Pentecostal/Roman Catholic dialogue: hopes
        and possibilities. In Spittler, R. P., ed. Perspectives on
        the new Pentecostalism. Grand Rapids, Mich., 1976, 246-
        268.

1939   McDonnell, Kilian, 1921-
            The distinguishing characteristics of the charismatic-
        Pentecostal spirituality. In One in Christ, 10 (1974), 117-
        128; reply (Water baptism [by] John McTernan), 10 (1974),
        203-205.

1940   McDonnell, Kilian, 1921-
            The international Roman Catholic-Pentecostal dialogue:
        the meeting of a structural church and a movement. In One
        in Christ, 10 (1974), 4-6.

1941   Moura, Abdalaziz de
            Importância das Igrejas Pentecostais para a Igreja Cató-
        lica. Recife, 1969. 44p. Processed.

1942   Pentecostals and Roman Catholics dialogue in Rome.
            In Journal of Ecumenical Studies, 10 (Fall 1973), 858-
        859. On meeting at the Convent of the Sisters of the Sacred
        Heart, June 18-22, 1973.

1943   The Roman Catholic/Pentecostal dialogue.
            In One in Christ, 10 (1974), 106-116; includes editorials
        by Basil Meeking and John McTernan, lists of participants
        and papers presented, and reports of the meetings: a "dia-
        logue between the Secretariat for Promoting Christian Unity
        of the Roman Catholic Church and leaders of some Pentecostal
        churches and participants in the charismatic movement within
        Protestant, Anglican and Orthodox churches." Meeting at
        Zurich-Horgen, 1972; at Rome, 1973.

1944   Roman Catholic/Pentecostal dialogue.
            In One in Christ, 10 (1974), 419-420. Report of the
        "third meeting of the dialogue between the Roman Catholic
        Church and some Pentecostal churches and members of char-
        ismatic renewal movements from Anglican, Lutheran, Re-
        formed and Baptist churches."

1945   Tinney, James Stephen
            Pentecostals to Rome [by] James S. Tinney. In Chris-

tianity Today, 16 (Dec. 3, 1971), 45. On Pentecostal-Roman
Catholic dialogue in Rome in December.

-- --DISCIPLES OF CHRIST

1946   Rivera, Juan Marcos
        An experiment in sharing personnel: from historical
church to Pentecostal movement. In International Review of
Mission, 62 (Oct. 1973), 446-456.

-- --NEDERLANDSE HERVORMDE KERK

1947   Broederschap van Pinkstergemeenten in Nederland.
        De Pinkstergemeente en de Kerk. De Broederschap van
Pinkstergemeenten in Nederland geeft antwoord op het Herderlijk schrijven van de Generale Synode der Nederlandse Hervormde Kerk over: De Kerk en de Pinkstergroepen. Rotterdam, Stichting Volle Evangelie Lectuur, 1962. 21p.

--SERMONS, TRACTS, ADDRESSES, ESSAYS

1948   Allen, Asa Alonso, 1911-1970.
        How to have power over the devil, and other best loved
revival sermons, by A. A. Allen. Dallas, 1954. 67p.

1949   Allen, Asa Alonso, 1911-1970.
        How to renew your youth, by A. A. Allen. Dallas,
c1954. 59p. TxWaS

1950   Allen, Asa Alonso, 1911-1970.
        Invasion from hell, by A. A. Allen. Dallas, c1953.
59p. TxWaS

1951   Allen, Asa Alonso, 1911-1970.
        Seven women take hold of one man, by A. A. Allen.
Dallas, c1954. 69p. TxWaS

1952   Beall, Myrtle D. (Monville)
        The plumb line, by M. D. Beall. Detroit, Latter Rain
Evangel, 1951. 77p.

1953   Behold, the lamb of God!
        Bournemouth, Hants., Victory Press, 1909. 12p.
(Messages given in prophecy, 4.)

1954   Bosworth, Fred Francis, 1877-1958.
        Christ, the healer; sermons on divine healing, by F. F.
Bosworth. Racine, Wis., c1924. 172p. DLC

1955   Bosworth, Fred Francis, 1877-1958.
        Christ, the healer; sermons on divine healing, by F. F.
Bosworth. River Forest, Ill., c1924. 172p.

1956   Bosworth, Fred Francis, 1877-1958.
            Christ, the healer; messages on divine healing, by F. F.
        Bosworth. 7th ed. Miami Beach, Fla., 1947. 249p. DLC

1957   Bosworth, Fred Francis, 1877-1958.
            Christ, the healer; messages on divine healing, by F. F.
        Bosworth. 8th ed. Dallas, R. V. Bosworth, 19--. 241p.

1958   Bosworth, Fred Francis, 1877-1958.
            Christ, the healer [by] F. F. Bosworth. Old Tappan,
        N.J., F. H. Revell Co., 1974, c1973. 241p. Reprint of
        the 8th ed., with a new introd. DLC

1959   Britton, Bill
            Cleansing the temple. Springfield, Mo., 19--. 11p.
        Cover title.

1960   Britton, Bill
            Eagle saints arise. Springfield, Mo., Voice of the
        Overcomer, 1967. 84p.

1961   Britton, Bill
            The foundations, the controversial, the glory. Spring-
        field, Mo., 19--. 15p. Cover title.

1962   Britton, Bill
            Garden of God. Springfield, Mo., 19--. 7p. Cover
        title.

1963   Britton, Bill
            God's two armies. Springfield, Mo., 19--. 13p. Cover
        title.

1964   Britton, Bill
            The golden altar of incense. Springfield, Mo., 19--.
        12p. Cover title.

1965   Britton, Bill
            The greater glory. Springfield, Mo., 19--. 10p.
        Cover title.

1966   Britton, Bill
            The harness of the Lord. Salisbury Center, N.Y.,
        Pinecrest Publications, 19--. 8p. Cover title.

1967   Britton, Bill
            Have you arrived? Springfield, Mo., 1965. 4p.

1968   Britton, Bill
            The hidden manna. Springfield, Mo., 19--. 12p.
        Cover title.

1969   Britton, Bill

Hold fast to that which is good. Springfield, Mo., 19--.
6p. Cover title.

1970 Britton, Bill
The horns of the altar. Springfield, Mo., 19--. 4p.
Cover title.

1971 Britton, Bill
Look to the hills. Springfield, Mo., 19--. [8]p. Cover
title.

1972 Britton, Bill
Peter's shadow. Springfield, Mo., 19--. 10p. Cover
title.

1973 Britton, Bill
The rapture of the church: "what is it?" Springfield,
Mo., 19--. 15p. Cover title.

1974 Britton, Bill
Reach for the stars. Springfield, Mo., Voice of the
Overcomer, 1970. 108p.

1975 Britton, Bill
Sons of God, awake. Springfield, Mo., Voice of the
Overcomer, 1967. 84p.

1976 Britton, Bill
Ten dangerous possessions. Springfield, Mo., 19--.
14p. Cover title.

1977 Britton, Bill
The two kingdoms. Springfield, Mo., 19--. 7p. Cover
title.

1978 Britton, Bill
The year of jubilee. Springfield, Mo., 19--. 8p.
Cover title.

1979 Burton, William Frederick Padwick, 1886-1971.
Christ's millennial reign on earth. Johannesburg, D.
Fischer, 196-. folder.

1980 Burton, William Frederick Padwick, 1886-1971.
Preaching power. Johannesburg, D. Fischer, 196-.
folder.

1981 Burton, William Frederick Padwick, 1886-1971.
The promise. Johannesburg, D. Fischer, 196-. folder.

1982 Burton, William Frederick Padwick, 1886-1971.
Should Christians smoke? Johannesburg, D. Fischer,
196-. folder.

1983   Burton, William Frederick Padwick, 1886-1971.
        Three in one--Trinity. Johannesburg, D. Fischer,
        196-. folder.

1984   Cho, Yong-gi, 1936-
        Mokhoe saenghwal tansang. Seoul, Yungsan Chul Pan
        Sa, 1977- . v. 1- . DLC

1985   Cho, Yong-gi, 1936-
        Successful living. La Canada, Calif., Mountain Press,
        19--. viii, 192p.

1986   Cho, Yong-gi, 1936-
        To God be the glory! A compilation of God's messages
        delivered by Dr. Yonggi Cho to the congregation at the Full
        Gospel Church in Seoul, Korea. Seoul, c1973. 208p. "This
        edition (sermons condensed and translated into English) pre-
        pared especially for the tenth World Pentecostal Conference
        in Seoul, Korea, September 18-23, 1973."

1987   Collins, Arch P.,   -1921.
        Sign of the Son of Man; sermons on the second coming of
        Christ, by Arch P. Collins. Houston, United Prayer and
        Workers League, 19--. 133p.

1988   Copley, A. S.
        The race course of the sons of God; sermons on Philip-
        pians, by A. S. Copley. Kansas City, Mo., Grace and Glory,
        1954. 54p.

1989   Culpepper, Richard Weston
        The magnetic power of believing, by R. W. Culpepper.
        Dallas, 19--. 28p.

1990   Dangerfield, Dorothea
        Homely talks on divine healing. London, Victory Press,
        1931. x, 129p. L, TxWaS

1991   Daoud, Jane (Collins)
        An unforgettable Easter in Martinique, by Mrs. M. A.
        Daoud. Dallas, Voice of Miracles and Missions, 19--.
        folder (5p.) (Tract no. 26.)

1992   Duncan, Susan A.
        What is it? By S. A. Duncan. n.p., 19--. 31p.

1993   Ekeroth, George
        The Ramat Aviv affair. With a special prophetic message
        by Morris Cerullo. San Diego, Morris Cerullo World Evan-
        gelism, c1974. 32p.

1994   Erickson, E. C.
        Together with God, by E. C. Erickson. n.p., 19--. 23p.

1995   Fox, Lorne Franklin
        The last weapon. Naselle, Wash., 19--. 15p.

1996   Fox, Lorne Franklin
        Visions of heaven, hell and the cross. Naselle, Wash.,
        19--. 30p.

1997   Garr, Alfred Goodrich, 1874-1944.
        Gems from the pulpit; choice sermons on salvation,
        healing, Holy Spirit, and second coming of our Lord Jesus
        Christ, by A. G. Garr. Los Angeles, F. A. Sharp, c1927.
        191p. DLC

1998   Girded with gladness; the testimony of one healed, redeemed,
        crowned and satisfied by the Lord. Bournemouth, Hants.,
        Victory Press, 191-. 16p.

1999   Grant, Walter Vinson, 1913-
        Just before the healing service read these seven sermons.
        Dallas, Grant's Faith Clinic, 19--. 31p.

2000   Grant, Walter Vinson, 1913-
        Sins which are unpardonable, and other sermons. Dallas,
        Grant's Faith Clinic, 19--. 31p. OkTOr

2001   Grant, Walter Vinson, 1913-
        The whole armour of God: eleven get-free sermons [by]
        W. V. Grant. Dallas, Grant's Faith Clinic, 19--. 34p.
        OkTOr

2002   Hall, Franklin
        Atlantic Ocean storms destroying many cities; building the
        new stormproof ark of protection, also other special writings.
        Phoenix, c1973. 79p.

2003   Harris, Leo
        Divine deliverance; a message of encouragement and coun-
        sel. Fullarton, S. Austl., Commonwealth Revival Crusade,
        19--. 8p.

2004   Harris, Leo
        The gift of the Holy Spirit and how to receive it. Fullar-
        ton, S. Austl., Commonwealth Revival Crusade, 19--. 8p.

2005   Harris, Leo
        How to receive healing. Fullarton, S. Austl., Common-
        wealth Revival Crusade, 19--. 8p.

2006   Harris, Leo
        The power of positive believing; a message that can revo-
        lutionize your life. Fullarton, S. Austl., Commonwealth Re-
        vival Crusade, 19--. 8p.

2007   Harris, Leo
             The second coming of Christ: seven wonderful features
         of that glorious event. Fullarton, S. Austl., Commonwealth
         Revival Crusade, 19--. 10p.

2008   Harris, Leo
             What salvation really means. Fullarton, S. Austl.,
         Commonwealth Revival Crusade, 19--. 6p.

2009   Harris, Leo
             Your faith is power. Fullarton, S. Austl., Crusader
         Publications, 196-. 83p. OkTOr

2010   Jenkins, Leroy, 1935-
             Man shall not live by bread alone. Compiled and edited
         by June Buckingham. Tampa, Leroy Jenkins Evangelistic
         Association, 1974. 113p.

2011   Karol, Stanley W.
             Whys and wherefores, by S. W. Karol. Philadelphia,
         Karol Evangelistic Association, c1953. 52p. TxWaS

2012   Karol, Stanley W.
             Yours for the asking, by S. W. Karol. Philadelphia,
         Karol Evangelistic Association, 19--. 52p. TxWaS

2013   Lake, John Graham, 1870-1935.
             The John G. Lake sermons on dominion over demons,
         disease and death. Dallas, Voice of Healing Publishing Co.,
         1949. 144p.

2014   Lake, John Graham, 1870-1935.
             The John G. Lake sermons on dominion over demons,
         disease and death. Edited by Gordon Lindsay. 8th ed.
         Dallas, Christ for the Nations, 1978, c1949. 138p.

2015   Lake, John Graham, 1870-1935.
             The new John G. Lake sermons. [Edited] by Gordon
         Lindsay. Dallas, Christ for the Nations, 1974. 61p. Re-
         print of 1971 ed.

2016   Lake, John Graham, 1870-1935.
             Die sichere Grundlage für die Heilung der Kranken und
         Gebrechlichen. Zürich, E. Weber, 1959. 24p.

2017   Lake, John Graham, 1870-1935.
             Spiritual hunger, the God-men, and other sermons, by
         John G. Lake. Edited by Gordon Lindsay. Dallas, Christ
         for the Nations, 1976. 103p. KyWAT

2018   Lindsay, Gordon, 1906-1973.
             A citizen of two worlds. Dallas, Christ for the Nations,
         1970. 28p.

2019   Lindsay, Gordon, 1906-1973.
        Dramatic gospel sketches of life and death. Shreveport,
La., Voice of Healing Publishing Co., 195-. 137p.

2020   Lindsay, Gordon, 1906-1973.
        Messages of hope given by the gift of prophecy during
the months of July to October 1955. Dallas, Voice of Healing Publishing Co., 1957. 48p.

2021   Lowery, Thomas Lanier
        Delivering power. Cleveland, Tenn., T. L. Lowery
Evangelistic Association, 19--. 44p.

2022   Lowery, Thomas Lanier
        The next world dictator, by T. L. Lowery. Cleveland,
Tenn., Lowery Publications, 1966. 107p.

2023   Lowery, Thomas Lanier
        Power plus. T. L. Lowery's faith building sermons,
compiled and edited by Donald D. Rowe. Cleveland, Tenn.,
T. L. Lowery Evangelistic Association, 19--. 108p.

2024   Macpherson, Ian, 1912-
        God's middleman. London, Epworth Press, 1965. 161p.
DLC, L, NcD

2025   Macpherson, Ian, 1912-
        God's middleman. Westwood, N.J., F. H. Revell Co.,
c1964. 161p.

2026   Macpherson, Ian, 1912-
        More sermons I should like to have preached. London,
Epworth Press, 1967. 178p. L

2027   Macpherson, Ian, ed., 1912-
        More sermons I should like to have preached. Westwood,
N.J., F. H. Revell Co., 1967. 178p. DLC

2028   Macpherson, Ian, 1912-
        None other name. London, Epworth Press, 1946. 148p.
L, TxFTC

2029   Macpherson, Ian, ed., 1912-
        Sermons I should like to have preached. London, Ep-
worth Press, 1964. 131p. L, NcD

2030   Macpherson, Ian, ed., 1912-
        Sermons I should like to have preached. Westwood, N.J.,
Revell, 1964. 131p. DLC

2031   Macpherson, Ian, 1912-
        This man loved me, and other addresses. London, Ep-
worth Press, 1942. 108p. L, PPiPT

2032   Montgomery, Carrie (Judd), 1858-
        Jesus Christ, our covenant of healing. Oakland, Calif.,
        Office of Triumphs of Faith, 19--. 8p.

2033   Montgomery, Carrie (Judd), 1858-
        The promise of the Father. Oakland, Calif., Office of
        "Triumphs of Faith, " 19--. 14p.

2034   Noble, John
        The ministry of the apostle. Springfield, Mo., Bill
        Britton, 19--. 8p. Cover title.

2035   Nunn, David Oliver
        Mission accomplished; From Calvary to the resurrection;
        and two other short sermons: Faithful to the end, Mountain
        top experiences. Dallas, Bible Revival Evangelistic Associa-
        tion, 19--. 31p.

2036   Nunn, David Oliver
        When America fights Russia. Dallas, Bible Revival
        Evangelistic Association, 19--. 63p.

2037   Osborn, Tommy Lee, 1923-
        Jesucristo el sanador. Tulsa, Officina General Hispana,
        195-. 246p. DLC

2038   Parker, Charles A.
        Concerning the Holy Spirit, by Charles A. Parker.
        Columbia, Mo., 19--. 46p. Sermons given over Station
        KFRU, Columbia, Missouri.

2039   Pethrus, Lewi, 1884-1974.
        Gud med oss; predikosamling. Stockholm, Filadelfia,
        1931. 722p. WaE

2040   Pethrus, Lewi, 1884-1974.
        Jesu kommer; sju predikningar om Kristi tilkommelse.
        Stenografiskt upptecknade. 10. uppl. Stockholm, Filadelfia,
        1940. 112p. CLU

2041   Powell, Don
        Footprints of Jesus. Tampa, Fla., Missions through
        Faith, 1956. 79p. OkTOr

2042   The preparation of the bride.
        Kansas City, Mo., Grace and Glory, 19--. 12p.

2043   Price, Charles Sydney, 1887-1947.
        And signs followed; the life story of Charles S. Price.
        Rev. ed. Plainfield, N.J., Logos International, 1972. 145p.
        Autobiography and sermons.

2044   Price, Charles Sydney, 1887-1947.

Creative word, by Charles S. Price. Pasadena, Calif., 1941. 111p.

2045   Price, Charles Sydney, 1887-1947.
        Divine intervention. Pasadena, Calif., C. S. Price Publishing Co., 1944. 128p.

2046   Price, Charles Sydney, 1887-1947.
        Made alive, by Charles S. Price. Pasadena, Calif., C. S. Price Publishing Co., c1945. 127p. TxWaS

2047   Price, Charles Sydney, 1887-1947.
        Made alive, by Charles S. Price. Plainfield, N. J., Logos International, 1972. 127p. Reprint of 1945 ed.

2048   Price, Charles Sydney, 1887-1947.
        The potter and the clay, by Charles S. Price. Pasadena, Calif., C. S. Price Publishing Co., 1943. 52p.

2049   Price, Charles Sydney, 1887-1947.
        The real faith, by Charles S. Price. Pasadena, Calif., C. S. Price Publishing Co., 1940. 111p.

2050   Price, Charles Sydney, 1887-1947.
        The real faith, by Charles S. Price. Plainfield, N. J., Logos International, 1972. 125p. Reprint of 1968 ed.

2051   Price, Charles Sydney, 1887-1947.
        The real faith, by Charles S. Price. Plainfield, N. J., Logos International, 1972. 125p. Reprint of 1968 ed.

2052   Price, Charles Sydney, 1887-1947.
        See God, by Charles S. Price. Pasadena, Calif., C. S. Price Publishing Co., 1943. 110p.

2053   Price, Charles Sydney, 1887-1947.
        Two worlds, by Charles S. Price. Pasadena, Calif., c1946. 173p. TxWaS

2054   Price, Charles Sydney, 1887-1947.
        Two worlds, by Charles S. Price. Plainfield, N. J., Logos International, 1972. 172p. Reprint of 1946 ed.

2055   Price, Charles Sydney, 1887-1947.
        You can know God here and now, by Charles S. Price. Pasadena, Calif., 1956. 47p.

2056   Price, Charles Sydney, 1887-1947.
        You can know God here and now, by Charles S. Price. Plainfield, N. J., Logos International, 1972. 47p. Reprint of 1956 ed.

2057   The promise of the Father: the baptism in the Holy Spirit.

Chicago, Evangel Publishing House, 19--. 16p.

2058 Rader, Paul, 1879-1938.
      Life's greatest adventure. 2d ed. London, Victory
      Press, 1939. 163p. L

2059 Roberts, Oral, 1918-
      Oral Roberts' best sermons and stories, as presented in
      his great evangelistic campaigns around the world. Tulsa,
      1956. 124p. DLC

2060 Roberts, Oral, 1918-
      The 4th man, and other famous sermons exactly as Oral
      Roberts preached them from the revival platform. Tulsa,
      Healing Waters, Inc., 1951. 139p. DLC, CPC

2061 Roberts, Oral, 1918-
      The 4th man, and other famous sermons exactly as Oral
      Roberts preached them from the revival platform. 4th ed.
      Tulsa, 1958, c1951. 139p. NjPT

2062 Roberts, Oral, 1918-
      The fourth man. Rev. ed. Tulsa, Summit Book Co.,
      1960. 124p. First ed. published in 1951 under title: The
      4th man, and other famous sermons. DLC, MSohG

2063 Roberts, Oral, 1918-
      The Oral Roberts reader. Rockville Centre, N.Y.,
      Zenith Books, 1958. 191p. (Zenith books, ZB-6.) DLC

2064 Roberts, Oral, 1918-
      The second coming of Christ, and other sermons. Tulsa,
      c1967. 1v. (various pagings)

2065 Roberts, Oral, 1918-
      Who are you? Tulsa, 19--. folder.

2066 Solbrekken, Max
      Alt er mulig. Oslo, Filadelfiaforlaget, 1968. 77p. DLC

2067 Squire, Frederick Henry, 1904-1962.
      Signposts to safety, by Frederick H. Squire. London,
      Edinburgh, Marshall, Morgan & Scott, 1938. 121p. L

2068 Steil, Harry J., 1901-
      God's diamonds [by] Harry J. Steil. Springfield, Mo.,
      Printed by Midwest Litho and Publishing Co., 1965. 30p.

2069 Stemme, Harry A.
      Pentecost today, by Harry A. Stemme. Chicago, 1939.
      30p. "A series of radio broadcasts devoted to the exposition
      of scriptures regarding the Pentecostal baptism and sign gifts
      for the body of Christ."

2070   Törnberg, Allan, 1907-1956.
         Bilder och budskap. Stockholm, Filadelfia; Solna, Seelig,
       1969. 166p. DLC

2071   Törnberg, Allan, 1907-1956.
         Herrn tänker på Dig; efterlämnade presikninger för ut-
       givning redigerade av Göran Strömbeck. Stockholm, Förlaget
       Filadelfia, 1958. 156p. MH-AH

2072   Törnberg, Allan, 1907-1956.
         En mann, et budskap; om og av Allan Törnberg. Oslo,
       Filadelfiaforlaget, 1959. 191p. DLC

2073   Ward, Charles Morse, 1909-
         What happens to sinners? [By] C. M. Ward. Westwood,
       N.J., Fleming H. Revell Co., 1967. 127p. DLC

2074   Wigglesworth, Smith, 1859-1947.
         Ever-increasing faith. South Pasadena, Calif., c1924.
       160p. DLC

2075   Willitts, Ethel R.
         Healing in Jesus' name, by Ethel R. Willitts. Fifteen
       sermons and addresses on salvation and healing. Crawfords-
       ville, Ind., c1931. 251p. DLC

2076   Willitts, Ethel R.
         Healing in Jesus' name, by Ethel R. Willitts. Fifteen
       sermons and addresses on salvation and healing. 11th ed.
       Chicago, c1931. 251p.

2077   Woodworth-Etter, Maria Beulah (Underwood), 1844-1924.
         Acts of the Holy Ghost; or, The life, work, and experi-
       ence of Mrs. M. B. Woodworth-Etter, evangelist. Written
       by herself. Complete, including sermons. Dallas, John F.
       Worley Printing Co., 1912. 581p. L, TxU

2078   Woodworth-Etter, Maria Beulah (Underwood), 1844-1924.
         Holy Ghost sermons preached by Mrs. M. B. Woodworth-
       Etter, evangelist. Compiled and chronologically arranged by
       herself. Indianapolis, 1918. 190p.

2079   Woodworth-Etter, Maria Beulah (Underwood), 1844-1924.
         Signs and wonders God wrought in the ministry for forty
       years, by Mrs. M. B. Woodworth-Etter, evangelist. Compiled
       and written by herself. Complete, including sermons. Indian-
       apolis, 1916. 584p. DLC

2080   Woodworth-Etter, Maria Beulah (Underwood), 1844-1924.
         Spirit-filled sermons preached by Mrs. M. B. Woodworth-
       Etter, evangelist. Compiled and arranged by herself. With a
       brief account of her early life and particulars regarding the
       new tabernacle. Indianapolis, 1921. 208p.

2081   Wyatt, Thomas, -1964.
        The flaming sword. Portland, Ore., c1948. 75p.

2082   Wyatt, Thomas, -1964.
        Then Jesus came. 2d ed. Portland, Ore., c1946. 168p.

2083   Wyatt, Thomas, -1964.
        Wings of healing. 6th ed. Portland, Ore., c1944. 144p.

2084   Wyatt, Thomas, -1964.
        The work of demons. 5th ed. Portland, Ore., c1946.
        32p.

-- --OUTLINES

2085   Horrell, Benjamin C.
        150 topical sermon outlines on Christ [by] Benjamin
        Horrell. Grand Rapids, Mich., Baker Book House, 1973.
        54p. (Dollar sermon library.)

2086   Horrell, Benjamin C.
        150 topical sermon outlines on God, by Benjamin Horrell.
        Grand Rapids, Mich., Baker Book House, 1972. 54p. (Dol-
        lar sermon library.)

2087   Horrell, Benjamin C.
        150 topical sermon outlines on Romans [by] Benjamin C.
        Horrell. Grand Rapids, Mich., Baker Book House, 1974.
        58p. (Dollar sermon library.)

2088   Macpherson, Ian, 1912-
        Bible sermon outlines. Nashville, Abingdon Press, 1966.
        191p. DLC

2089   Macpherson, Ian, 1912-
        Bible sermon outlines. Grand Rapids, Mich., Baker Book
        House, 1976. 191p.

2090   Macpherson, Ian, 1912-
        Kindlings: outlines and sermon starters. Old Tappan,
        N.J., Revell, 1969. 159p. DLC

2091   Macpherson, Ian, 1912-
        Live sermon outlines. Grand Rapids, Mich., Baker Book
        House, 1974. 64p.

2092   Macpherson, Ian, 1912-
        Sermon outlines from sermon masters. New York, Abing-
        don Press, 1960-1962. 2v. DLC, CMIG, IEG, ODW, KyLxCB

2093   Macpherson, Ian, 1912-
        Usable outlines and illustrations. Grand Rapids, Mich.,
        Baker Book House, 1976. 62p.

2094 Pentz, Croft Miner
Evangelistic sermon outlines. Grand Rapids, Mich.,
Baker Book House, 1970. 70p. (Dollar sermon library.)

2095 Pentz, Croft Miner
52 simple sermon outlines. Grand Rapids, Mich., Baker
Book House, 1968. 82p. (Dollar sermon library.)

2096 Pentz, Croft Miner
48 simple sermon outlines. Grand Rapids, Mich., Baker
Book House, 1965. 82p. (Dollar sermon library.)

2097 Pentz, Croft Miner
150 expository sermon outlines. Grand Rapids, Mich.,
Baker Book House, 1972. 82p.

2098 Pentz, Croft Miner
175 simple sermon outlines. Grand Rapids, Mich.,
Baker Book House, 1963. 87p. (Dollar sermon library.)

2099 Pentz, Croft Miner
Prayer meeting outlines. Grand Rapids, Mich., Baker
Book House, 1970. 80p. (Dollar sermon library.)

2100 Pentz, Croft Miner
Preaching: outlines, poems, and illustrations. Grand
Rapids, Mich., Baker Book House, 1968. 85p. (Dollar
sermon library.)

2101 Pentz, Croft Miner
Sermon outlines from the Psalms. Grand Rapids, Mich.,
Baker Book House, 1974. 63p. (Dollar sermon library.)

2102 Pentz, Croft Miner
Sermon outlines on the epistles: Galatians-II Timothy.
Grand Rapids, Mich., Baker Book House, 1971. 60p. (Dollar sermon library.)

2103 Pentz, Croft Miner
Sunday morning sermon outlines. Grand Rapids, Mich.,
Baker Book House, 1972. 64p. (Dollar sermon library.)

--STATISTICS

2104 Du Plessis, David Johannes, 1905-
Golden jubilees of twentieth-century Pentecostal movements,
by David J. du Plessis. In International Review of Missions,
47 (Apr. 1958), 193-201. "Pentecostal adherents in various
countries": p. 201.

2105 Kantzer, Kenneth Sealer, 1917-
The charismatics among us [by] Kenneth S. Kantzer.

In Christianity Today, 24 (Feb. 22, 1980), 25-29.

--WORK WITH SPECIAL GROUPS

2106   Bair, Bill
        Love is an open door, by Bill Bair with Glenn D. Kittler.
New York, Chosen Books, 1974. 222p. On home for troubled
children in New Wilmington, Pennsylvania. DLC

2107   Bartlett, Robert Lee, 1942-
        The soul patrol: "Here comes the God squad," by Bob
Bartlett with Jorunn Oftedal. Plainfield, N.J., Logos Inter-
national, c1970. 170p. On Teen Challenge in Philadelphia.
DLC

2108   Favorite recipes from Pentecostal church ladies: desserts,
including party beverages.
        Montgomery, Ala., Favorite Recipes Press, c1969. 382p.
DLC

2109   Hobe, Laura
        Try God, by Laura Hobe. Forewood by David Wilkerson.
Garden City, N.Y., Doubleday, 1977. 191p. On the Walter
Hoving Home, Garrison, New York, affiliated with Teen Chal-
lenge. DLC

2110   Homan, Roger
        Pentecostal youth organizations and the Bulgarian kom-
somol. In Comparative Education, 13 (Oct. 1977), 243-248.

2111   McDonnell, Kilian, 1921-
        The Pentecostals and drug addiction. In America, 118
(Mar. 30, 1968), 402-406; discussion (Pentecostalism), 118
(May 11, 1968), 626.

2112   Manuel, David
        The Jesus factor, by David Manuel, Jr., Donald Wilker-
son and Reginald Yake. Plainfield, N.J., Logos International,
c1977. vii, 183p.

2113   Morse, Tom
        When the music stops [by] Tom Morse, with Bobbie
Lauster. Old Tappan, N.J., Revell, 1971. 125p. DLC

2114   Palmquist, Al
        Miracle at city hall, by Al Palmquist, with Kay Nelson.
Minneapolis, Bethany Fellowship, 1974. 173p. DLC

2115   Pellén, Siv, comp., 1917-
        Vakuum i tonarsvarlden. Sammanställd av Siv och Robert
Pellén. [Utg. av] Affarsman i andlig aktion (A.A.A.) 2.,
utokade uppl. Solna, 1966. 23p. DLC

2116   Steele, James E.
        I have a ghetto in my heart; a portrait of the Chicago
        challenge--youth action reaching the lost of a large city, by
        James E. Steele with Neigel and Peggy Scarborough.   Cleve-
        land, Tenn., Pathway Press, 1973.   121p.   DLC

2117   Stultz, Bob
        White Black man, by Bob Stultz and Phil Landrum.
        Carol Stream, Ill., Creation House, c1972.   172p.

2118   Taylor, Julia Maria
        God's kids and Mom, by Julia Maria Taylor [with Cliff
        Dudley].   Harrison, Ark., New Leaf Press, c1975.   127p.
        DLC

2118a   Tinney, James Stephen
        In the tradition of William J. Seymour; essays commemo-
        rating the dedication of Seymour House at Howard University,
        by James S. Tinney [and] Stephen N. Short, editors.   Wash-
        ington, Spirit Press, 1978.   81p.

2119   Torres, Victor
        Son of evil street, by Victor Torres, with Don Wilkerson.
        Minneapolis, Bethany Fellowship, 1973.   160p.   DLC

2120   Torres, Victor
        Son of evil street [by] Victor Torres, with Don Wilkerson.
        2d ed.   Minneapolis, Bethany Fellowship, 1977.   166p.   (Di-
        mension books.)   DLC

2121   Walker, John Herbert, 1928-
        God's living room, by John Herbert Walker, Jr., with
        Lucille Walker and Irene Burk Harrell.   Plainfield, N.J.,
        Logos International, 197-.   141p.   DLC

2122   Wilkerson, David Ray, 1931-
        Beyond the cross and the switchblade [by] David Wilkerson.
        Special introd. by John and Elizabeth Sherrill.   Old Tappan,
        N.J., Chosen Books; distributed by F. H. Revell, 1974.   191p.

2123   Wilkerson, David Ray, 1931-
        Born old [by] David Wilkerson, with Phyllis Murphy.
        London, Oliphants, 1966.   159p.   American ed.   (Westwood,
        N.J., F. H. Revell Co.) has title: The little people.   L

2124   Wilkerson, David Ray, 1931-
        The cross and the switchblade, by David Wilkerson, with
        John & Elizabeth Sherrill.   New York, B. Geis Associates;
        distributed by Random House, 1963.   217p.   DLC, KyLxCB,
        MH-AH, MCE, MoU, NjPT, NN, OCl, PPULC

2125   Wilkerson, David Ray, 1931-
        The cross and the switchblade, by David Wilkerson with

John & Elizabeth Sherrill.   London, Hodder & Stoughton,
1967.   217p.   DLC

2126   Wilkerson, David Ray, 1931-
        The cross and the switchblade [by] the Reverend David
Wilkerson, with John and Elizabeth Sherrill.   New York,
Published for Teen Challenge by Pyramid Publications, c1963.
174p.   FTaSU

2127   Wilkerson, David Ray, 1931-
        The cross and the switchblade, by David Wilkerson, with
John & Elizabeth Sherrill.   Westwood, N.J., F. H. Revell
Co., 1968.   174p.   (Spire books.)   OkU

2128   Wilkerson, David Ray, 1931-
        Gang war.   In Harrell, I. B., comp.   God ventures:
true accounts of God in the lives of men.   Waco, Tex.,
1970, 23-33.

2129   Wilkerson, David Ray, 1931-
        Get your hands off my throat, by David Wilkerson.   Grand
Rapids, Mich., Zondervan Publishing House, 1971.   124p.
DLC

2130   Wilkerson, David Ray, 1931-
        Hey, Preach--you're comin' through!   Westwood, N.J.,
Revell, 1968.   160p.   DLC, ICU

2131   Wilkerson, David Ray, 1931-
        Hey, Preach--you're comin' through!   By David Wilkerson.
Old Tappan, N.J., Revell, 1971, c1968.   144p.   (Spire books.)

2132   Wilkerson, David Ray, 1931-
        I've given up on parents, by David Wilkerson with Claire
Cox.   London, Hodder & Stoughton, 1967.   157p.   L

2133   Wilkerson, David Ray, 1931-
        I've given up on parents, by David Wilkerson with Claire
Cox.   London, Hodder & Stoughton, 1969.   157p.   A reduced
photographic reprint of the edition of 1967.   L

2134   Wilkerson, David Ray, 1931-
        The little people [by] David Wilkerson, with Phyllis Mur-
phy.   Westwood, N.J., F. H. Revell Co., 1966.   159p.   London ed.   (Oliphants) has title: Born old.   DLC, ICU

2135   Wilkerson, David Ray, 1931-
        The little people [by] David Wilkerson, with Phyllis Mur-
phy.   Old Tappan, N.J., F. H. Revell Co., 1969, c1966.
126p.   (Spire books.)   London ed.   (Oliphants) has title: Born
old.

2136   Wilkerson, David Ray, 1931-

Man, have I got problems [by] David Wilkerson. Old
Tappan, N.J., F. H. Revell Co., 1969. 128p. DLC

2137   Wilkerson, David Ray, 1931-
       Purple violet squish [by] David Wilkerson. Grand Rapids,
       Mich., Zondervan Publishing House, 1969. 152p. DLC

2138   Wilkerson, David Ray, 1931-
       Purple violet squish [by] David Wilkerson. Grand Rapids,
       Mich., Zondervan Books, 1970, c1969. 139p.

2139   Wilkerson, David Ray, 1931-
       Twelve angels from hell [by] David Wilkerson, with Leon-
       ard Ravenhill. New York, Pyramid Books, 1965. 157p.
       CaBVaU

2140   Wilkerson, David Ray, 1931-
       Twelve angels from hell [by] David Wilkerson, with Leon-
       ard Ravenhill. Westwood, N.J., F. H. Revell Co., 1965.
       152p. DLC

2141   Wilkerson, David Ray, 1931-
       Twelve angels from hell [by] David Wilkerson with Leon-
       ard Ravenhill. London, Oliphants, 1965. 152p. L

2142   Wilkerson, David Ray, 1931-
       Twelve angels from hell, by David Wilkerson. Old Tap-
       pan, N.J., F. H. Revell Co., 1966, c1965. 157p. (Spire
       books.) "Published by Pyramid Publications for the Fleming
       H. Revell Company." MB

2143   Wilkerson, David Ray, 1931-
       The untapped generation, by David & Don Wilkerson.
       Grand Rapids, Mich., Zondervan Publishing House, 1971.
       256p. DLC

2144   Wilkerson, Don
       Fast track to nowhere [by] Don Wilkerson. Old Tappan,
       N.J., F. H. Revell Co., c1979. 190p. DLC

2145   Wilkerson, Don
       The gutter and the ghetto, by Don Wilkerson with Herm
       Weiskopf. Waco, Tex., Word Books, 1969. 179p. DLC

2146   Wilkerson, Don
       Hell-bound [by] Don Wilkerson with David Manuel. Or-
       leans, Mass., Rock Harbor Press, c1978. 199p. A fictional
       account of the street ministry of Teen Challenge. DLC

2147   Wilson, R. Marshall
       God's guerillas: the true story of Youth with a Mission,
       by R. Marshall Wilson. Illus. by Jim Howard. Plainfield,
       N.J., Logos International, 1971. 166p. DLC

2148   Wilson, R. Marshall
            Youth with a Mission, by R. Marshall Wilson. Illus. by
        Jim Howard. Plainfield, N.J., Logos International, 1974,
        c1971. 166p. First issued under title: God's guerillas.

            --WORSHIP

2149   Bishop, David S.
            The sacraments in worship [by] David S. Bishop. In
        Knight, C. B., ed. Pentecostal worship. Cleveland, Tenn.,
        1974, 101-120.

2150   Bois, Jules, 1871-
            The holy rollers: the American dervishes. In Forum,
        73 (Feb. 1925), 145-155. The new religions of America, 1.

2151   Clements, William Manning, 1945-
            The rhetoric of the radio ministry [by] William M. Clem-
        ents. In Journal of American Folklore, 87 (Oct./Dec. 1974),
        318-327. On Pentecostal preachers in northeastern Arkansas.

2152   Daniel, Vattel Elbert, 1890-
            Ritual in Chicago's South Side churches for Negroes.
        Chicago, 1940. iv, 155ℓ. Thesis (Ph.D.)--University of
        Chicago. Includes Pentecostal churches. CtY-D, DLC, ICU,
        NBuU

2153   Daniel, Vattel Elbert, 1890-
            Ritual stratification in Chicago Negro churches. In
        American Sociological Review, 7 (June 1942), 352-361. In-
        cludes Pentecostal churches.

2154   Fisher, Robert Elwood, 1931-
            Preparation for worship [by] Robert E. Fisher. In
        Knight, C. B., ed. Pentecostal worship. Cleveland, Tenn.,
        1974, 17-31.

2155   Hollenweger, Walter Jacob, 1927-
            "Blumen und Lieder"; ein mexikanischer Beitrag zum
        theologischen Verstehensprozess [von] Walter J. Hollenweger.
        In Evangelische Theologie, 31 (Aug. 1971), 437-448.

2156   Hollenweger, Walter Jacob, 1927-
            Flowers and songs; a Mexican contribution to theological
        hermeneutics, by Walter J. Hollenweger. In International
        Review of Mission, 60 (Apr. 1971), 232-244.

2157   Hollenweger, Walter Jacob, 1927-
            Liturgies: Pentecostal [by] W. J. Hollenweger. In
        Davies, J. G., ed. A dictionary of liturgy and worship.
        New York, 1972, 241.

2158   Hollenweger, Walter Jacob, 1927-
        Pentecostal worship [by] W. J. Hollenweger. In Davies,
        J. G., ed. A dictionary of liturgy and worship. New York,
        1972, 311-312.

2159   Hollenweger, Walter Jacob, 1927-
        The social and ecumenical significance of Pentecostal
        liturgy, by W. J. Hollenweger. In Studia Liturgica, 8:4
        (1971-1972), 207-215.

2160   Homan, Roger
        Interpersonal communication in Pentecostal meetings. In
        Social Research, ns 26 (Aug. 1978), 499-518.

2161   Jules-Rosette, Benneta
        Ceremonial trance behavior in an African church: private
        experience and public expression. In Journal for the Scientific
        Study of Religion, 19 (Mar. 1980), 1-16.

2162   Knight, Cecil Brigham, ed., 1926-
        Pentecostal worship. Edited by Cecil B. Knight. Cleve-
        land, Tenn., Pathway Press, 1974. 140p. Essays by Cecil
        B. Knight, Robert E. Fisher, Lucille Walker, Robert White,
        Delton L. Alford, David S. Bishop, Bob E. Lyons and M. G.
        McLuhan. DLC, MSohG

2163   Knight, Cecil Brigham, 1926-
        The wonder of worship. In Knight, C. B., ed. Pente-
        costal worship. Cleveland, Tenn., 1974, 7-15.

2164   Lyons, Bobby Elton, 1939-
        The Word in worship [by] Bob E. Lyons. In Knight,
        C. B., ed. Pentecostal worship. Cleveland, Tenn., 1974,
        77-99.

2165   McLuhan, Mervyn G.
        Spiritual gifts in worship [by] M. G. McLuhan. In
        Knight, C. B., ed. Pentecostal worship. Cleveland, Tenn.,
        1974, 121-140.

2166   Mello, Manoel de, 1929-
        Participation is everything; evangelism from the point of
        view of a Brazilian Pentecostal. In International Review of
        Mission, 60 (Apr. 1971), 245-248.

2167   Ranaghan, Kevin Mathers, 1940-
        Conversion and baptism; personal experience and ritual
        celebration in Pentecostal churches, by Kevin M. Ranaghan.
        In Studia Liturgica, 10:1 (1974), 65-76.

2168   Rosenberg, Bruce Alan, 1934-
        The art of the American folk preacher [by] Bruce A.

Rosenberg. New York, Oxford University Press, 1970. x, 265p. DLC, FTaSU, KyLxCB

2169   Rosenberg, Bruce Alan, 1934-
        The psychology of the spiritual sermon [by] Bruce A. Rosenberg. In Zaretsky, I. I., ed. Religious movements in contemporary America. Princeton, N.J., c1974, 135-149.

2170   Walker, Lucille (Settle)
        Prayer in worship [by] Lucille Walker. In Knight, C. B., ed. Pentecostal worship. Cleveland, Tenn., 1974, 33-47.

2171   White, Robert
        Praise in worship. In Knight, C. B., ed. Pentecostal worship. Cleveland, Tenn., 1974, 49-61.

                        --AFRICA

2172   Barrett, David B.
        Schism and renewal in Africa; an analysis of six thousand contemporary religious movements [by] David B. Barrett. Nairobi, Oxford University Press, 1968. xx, 363p. DLC

2173   Beckmann, David M.
        Trance: from Africa to Pentecostalism [by] David M. Beckmann. In CTM, 45 (Jan. 1974), 11-26.

2174   Benz, Ernst, 1907- , ed.
        Messianische Kirchen, Sekten und Bewegungen in heutigen Afrika. Leiden, E. J. Brill, 1965. 127p.

2175   Bhengu, Nicholas Bhekinkosi Hepworth, 1909-
        Evangelism in Africa [by] Nicholas B. H. Bhengu. In Henry, C. F. H., ed. One race, one gospel, one task. World Congress on Evangelism, Berlin, 1966; official reference volumes: papers and reports. Minneapolis, 1967, I, 178-181. DLC, KyWAT

2176   Culpepper, Richard Weston
        The sweat and tears of Africa, by R. W. Culpepper. Dallas, 19--. 65p. OkTOr

2177   Lewis, W. G.
        Missionary trails, by W. G. Lewis. Lincoln, Neb., 1937. 123p.

2178   Oosthuizen, Gerhardus Cornelis, 1922-
        The misunderstanding of the Holy Spirit in the independent movements in Africa [by] G. C. Oosthuizen. n.p., 196-. 172-197p. Cover title. "Reprinted from Christusprediking in de wereld." CtY-D

2179 Rasmussen, Marie B.
De Afrikanske HelligSandskirkers Teologi, av Marie B.
Rasmussen. In Norsk Teologisk Tidsskrift, 40:2 (1977),
101-119.

2180 Strøm, Erling
Blant svarte og hvite i Afrika. Oslo, Filadelfiaforlaget,
1952. 152p. DLC

2181 Westgarth, J. W.
The Holy Spirit and the primitive mind; a remarkable
account of a spiritual awakening in darkest Africa. London,
Victory Press, 1946. 64p. L

-- --ETHIOPIA

2182 Rayner, DeCourcy H.
Persecution in Ethiopia [by] DeCourcy H. Rayner. In
Christianity Today, 17 (Nov. 10, 1972), 54-55.

-- --GHANA

2183 Beckmann, David M.
Eden revival: spiritual churches in Ghana [by] David M.
Beckmann. Foreword by William J. Dunker. St. Louis,
Concordia Publishing House, 1975. 144p. DLC

2183a Breidenbach, Paul S.
Sunsum edwuma: the limits of classification and the significance of event, by Paul S. Breidenbach. In Social Research, 46 (Spring 1979), 63-87.

2184 Wyllie, Robert W.
Pioneers of Ghanian Pentecostalism: Peter Anim and
James McKeown, by Robert W. Wyllie. In Journal of Reli-
gion in Africa, 6:2 (1974), 109-122.

-- --KENYA

2185 Charsley, S. R.
Dreams in an independent African church [by] S. R.
Charsley. In Africa, 43 (July 1971), 244-257.

2186 Raatikainen, Alma, 1916-
Itkevä musta kukka. Pohjois-Kenian karua arkipäivää.
Tikkurila, Ristin Voitto, c1972. 219p. DLC, NNUT

2187 Welbourn, Frederick Burkewood
A place to feel at home: a study of two independent
churches in western Kenya [by] F. B. Welbourn [and] B. A.
Ogot. London, Nairobi, Oxford University Press, 1966. xv,
157p. DLC

-- --NIGERIA

2188   Mbagwu, John R.
        A living testimony, by John R. Mbagwu. Dayton, Ohio,
        c1978. 98p. DLC

2189   Turner, Harold Walter, 1911-
        History of an African independent church, by H. W. Tur-
        ner. Oxford, Clarendon Press, 1967. 2v. DLC

2190   Turner, Harold Walter, 1911-
        Profile through preaching; a study of the sermon texts
        used in a West African independent church [by] Harold W.
        Turner. London, Published for the World Council of Churches,
        Commission on World Mission and Evangelism by Edinburgh
        House Press, 1965. 86p. (C. W. M. E. research pamphlets,
        13.) On label: Distributed by Friendship Press, New York,
        N. Y. DLC

-- --SOUTH AFRICA

2191   Kiernan, J. P.
        Old wine in new wineskins: a critical appreciation of
        Sundkler's leadership types in the light of further research
        [by] J. P. Kiernan. In African Studies, 34:3 (1975), 193-
        201.

2192   Kiernan, J. P.
        Where Zionists draw the line: a study of religious ex-
        clusiveness in an African township [by] J. P. Kiernan. In
        African Studies, 33:2 (1974), 79-90.

2193   Orr, James Edwin, 1912-
        Evangelical awakenings in Africa [by] J. Edwin Orr.
        Minneapolis, Bethany Fellowship, 1975. x, 245p. Published
        in 1970 under title: Evangelical awakenings in South Africa.
        Includes Pentecostal churches. DLC

2194   Sundkler, Bengt Gustaf Malcolm, 1909-
        Bantu prophets in South Africa. 2d ed. New York, Pub-
        lished for the International African Institute by the Oxford Uni-
        versity Press, c1961. 381p.

2195   Sundkler, Bengt Gustaf Malcolm, 1909-
        Zulu Zion and some Swazi Zionists [by] Bengt Sundkler.
        London, New York, Oxford University Press, 1976. 337p.
        (Oxford studies in African affairs.) DLC, MH-AH, KyWAT

        (Cape Province, East London)

2196   Dubb, Allie A.
        Community of the saved: an African revivalist church in
        the East Cape [by] Allie A. Dubb. Johannesburg, Witwaters-

rand University Press for African Studies Institute, 1976.
xvii, 175p. DLC, MH-AH

2197   Moennich, Martha
           God at work in South Africa. In Evangelical Christian,
       54 (Aug. 1958), 368.

                   (Natal Province, Durban)

2198   Oosthuizen, Gerhardus Cornelis, 1922-
           Pentecostal penetration into the Indian community in
       Metropolitan Durban, South Africa [by] G. C. Osthuizen.
       Durban, Human Sciences Research Council, 1975. xi, 256p.
       (Human Sciences Research Council. Publication series, 52.)
       MH-AH, KyWAT

                   (Transvaal Province)

2199   Tyler, Philip
           Pattern of Christian belief in Sekhukuniland. In Church
       Quarterly Review, 167 (Apr. /June 1966), 225-236; 167 (July/
       Sept. 1966), 335-347. Includes Pentecostal churches: p. 338-
       346.

               -- --TUNISIA

2200   Planter, Josephine
           Book of remembrance; or, Led by the Spirit. Experi-
       ences of Josephine Planter, missionary to Tunis, North Africa.
       Chicago, Herald Publishing Co., c1925. 109p. DLC

2201   Planter, Josephine
           Book of remembrance; or, Led by the Spirit. Experi-
       ences of Josephine Planter, missionary to Tunis, North Africa.
       3d ed. Los Angeles, D. C. Welty, printer, 1936. 144p.
       DLC

               -- --UPPER VOLTA

2202   Dean, Curtis L.
           A survey of the missionary work in French West Africa
       by Curtis L. Dean, Columbia, S.C., 1956. v, 177ℓ. Thesis
       (M.A.)--Columbia Bible College.

               -- --ZAIRE

2203   Burton, William Frederick Padwick, 1886-1971.
           Congo sketches. Illustrated by the author. London, Vic-
       tory Press, 1950. v, 177p. DLC, L

2204   Burton, William Frederick Padwick, 1886-1971.
           God working with them; being eighteen years of Congo
       Evangelistic Mission history, by W. F. P. Burton. London,

Victory Press, 1933. xiv, 264p. L, MH-AH, NcD, NNMR,
WU

2205   Burton, William Frederick Padwick, 1886-1971.
        How they live in Congoland; an account of the character
and customs of this most interesting race and efforts to win
them for Christ, by William F. P. Burton. London, Pickering & Inglis, 1938. 159p. CtY, DHU, IEN, L

2206   Burton, William Frederick Padwick, 1886-1971.
        How they live in Congoland; an account of the character
and customs of this most interesting race and efforts to win
them for Christ, by William F. P. Burton. London, Victory
Press, 1938. 159p.

2207   Burton, William Frederick Padwick, 1888-1971.
        Missionary pioneering in Congo forests; a narrative of
the labours of William F. P. Burton and his companions in
the native villages of Luba-land. Compiled from letters,
diaries and articles by Max W. Moorhead. Preston, Lancs. ,
R. Seed, 1922. 216p. CtY, InU

2208   Burton, William Frederick Padwick, 1886-1971.
        When God changes a village. London, Victory Press,
1933. x, 162p. L

2209   Doering, Alma Emma, 1878-
        Leopard spots or God's masterpiece, which? ... Attempt-
ing the answer after 18 years of service among races of three
colors: white, black and copper. By Alma E. Doering,
Malembe (Bantu name) ... Cleveland, "Malembe"; Chicago,
Evangel Publishing House, c1916. 203p. DLC

2210   Hodgson, Edmund, 1898-1960.
        Fishing for Congo fisher folk, by E. Hodgson. Illustrated
with 80 pen and ink sketches by W. F. P. Burton. London,
Assemblies of God in Great Britain and Ireland, 1934. 182p.
CtY, CtY-D, IEN, L, NNMR, OrU

2211   Hodgson, Edmund, 1898-1960.
        Out of the darkness; the story of an indigenous church
in the Belgian Congo, by E. Hodgson. London, Victory Press,
1946. 186p.

2212   Hodgson, Edmund, 1898-1960.
        Out of the darkness; the story of an indigenous church in
the Belgian Congo, by E. Hodgson. Luton, Beds. , Assemblies of God Publishing House, 1946. 186p.

2213   Jacobsson, Per-Olof, 1931-
        Hemma hos oss i Kongo. Stockholm, Filadelfia; Solna,
Seelig, 1968. 47p. DLC

2214   Muchoku, Stephano
        Stephano Muchoku blant opprørere i Kongo. Pastor
        Stephano Muchoku og hans jungelmenighets opplevelser under
        opprørere in Kongo. Nedtegnet og gjenfortalt av Frank M.
        Matre. Oslo, Filadelfiaforlaget, 1966. 92p. DLC

2215   Womersley, Harold
        Congo miracle: fifty years of God's working in Congo
        (Zaire). Eastbourne, Sussex, Victory Press, 1974. 160p.
        DLC

            -- --ZAMBIA

2216   Bellman, Beryl Larry, 1941-
        A paradigm for looking: cross-cultural research with
        visual media [by] Beryl L. Bellman [and] Bennetta Jules-
        Rosette. Norwood, N.J., Ablex Publishing Corp., 1977.
        vii, 211p. DLC

2217   Jules-Rosette, Bennetta
        African apostles: ritual and conversion in the Church of
        John Maranke. Ithaca, N.Y., Cornell University Press, 1975.
        302p. (Symbol, myth, and ritual series)

2218   Jules-Rosette, Bennetta
        Ceremonial trance behavior in an African church: private
        experience and public expression. In Journal for the Scien-
        tific Study of Religion, 19 (Mar. 1980), 1-16.

            -- --ZIMBABWE

2219   Daneel, M. L.
        Zionism and faith-healing in Rhodesia; aspects of African
        independent churches. [By] M. L. Daneel. Translated from
        the Dutch by V. A. February. Afrika-Studiecentrum, Leiden.
        's-Gravenhage, Mouton, 1970. 64p., 8p. of photos (Communi-
        cations, 2.) DLC, MCE

            --NORTH AND CENTRAL AMERICA

            -- --BELIZE

2219a   Birdwell-Pheasant, Donna B.
        Cycles of power: social organization in a Belizean vil-
        lage, by Donna B. Birdwell. Dallas, 1979. vii, 383ℓ. The-
        sis (Ph.D.)--Southern Methodist University. TxDaM

2219b   Birdwell-Pheasant, Donna B.
        The power of Pentecostalism in a Belizean village [by]
        Donna Birdwell-Pheasant. In Glazier, S. D. Perspectives
        on Pentecostalism: case studies from the Caribbean and
        Latin America. Washington, c1980, 95-109.

-- --CANADA

2220   Ferry, Anthony
        Oh, sing it, you precious Pentecostal people. In
        Maclean's Magazine, 75 (Nov. 3, 1962), 20-23, 63-68.

        (Alberta)

2221   Mann, William Edward, 1918-
            Sect, cult and church in Alberta, by W. E. Mann.
        Toronto, University of Toronto Press, c1955. xiii, 166p.
        (Social credit in Alberta: its background and development,
        6.) Includes comment on Pentecostal churches: p. 18, 19-
        20, 21, 23, 24, 30, 32, 33, 34, 55, 66, 68, 71, 74, 82,
        83, 84, 87, 99, 113, 122, 128, 132, 134-135, 136, 144,
        145, 148, 150, 154. RPB

        (Ontario, Toronto)

2222   Gardiner, Gordon P. , 1916-
            Radiant glory: the life of Martha Wing Robinson, by
        Gordon P. Gardiner. 2d ed. Brooklyn, N. Y. , Bread of
        Life, 1970, c1962. xxii, 346p. On the East End Mission,
        Toronto: p. 126-171.

2223   Cressman, Salome M.
            Pentecost in Quebec, by Salome Cressman. Toronto,
        Pentecostal Assemblies of Canada, 19--.

                        -- --GUATEMALA

                        (Guatemala City)

2224   Roberts, Bryan R. , 1939-
            Protestant groups and coping with urban life in Guatemala
        City [by] Bryan R. Roberts. In American Journal of Sociol-
        ogy, 74 (May 1968), 753-767. Pentecostals constituted a ma-
        jority of the sample, and the findings most closely apply to
        them as a group.

                        -- --MEXICO

2225   Hollenweger, Walter Jacob, 1927-
            "Blumen und Lieder"; ein mexikanischer Beitrag zum
        theologischen Verstehenspozess [von] Walter J. Hollenweger.
        In Evangelische Theologie, 31 (Aug. 1971), 437-448.

2226   Hollenweger, Walter Jacob, 1927-
            Flowers and songs; a Mexican contribution to theological
        hermeneutics, by Walter J. Hollenweger. In International
        Review of Mission, 60 (Apr. 1971), 232-244.

2227   McGavran, Donald Anderson, 1897-
        Church growth in Mexico, by Donald McGavran, John
Huegel [and] Jack Taylor. Grand Rapids, Mi., W. B. Eerdmans Co., c1963. 136p. "The Pentecostal contribution":
p. 113-124. CtY-D, DLC, MH-AH, NcD, NjPT, OkBetC

        (Hidalgo, Pachuca)

2228   Crouch, Archie R.
        A shoot out of dry ground: the most rapidly growing
church in Mexico, by Archie R. Crouch. In New World
Outlook, ns 30 (Apr. 1970), 33-36.

        (D. F., Mexico City)

2229   Goodman, Felicitas Daniels, 1914-
        Phonetic analysis of glossolalia in four cultural settings
[by] Felicitas D. Goodman. In Journal for the Scientific
Study of Religion, 8 (Fall 1969), 227-239. Based in part on
observation in Mexico City.

2230   Goodman, Felicitas Daniels, 1914-
        Speaking in tongues; a cross-cultural study of glossolalia
[by] Felicitas D. Goodman. Chicago, University of Chicago
Press, 1972. xxii, 175p. Based in part on observation in
Mexico City.

        (Yucatan)

2231   Goodman, Felicitas Daniels, 1914-
        Apostolics of Yucatán: a case study of a religious move-
ment [by] Felicitas D. Goodman. In Bourguinon, E., ed.
Religion, altered states of consciousness, and social change.
Columbus, 1973, 178-218.

2232   Goodman, Felicitas Daniels, 1914-
        Disturbances in the Apostolic Church; case study of a
trance-based upheaval in Yucatan. Columbus, 1971. viii,
244ℓ. Thesis (Ph. D.)--Ohio State University. OU

2233   Goodman, Felicitas Daniels, 1914-
        Disturbances in the Apostolic church: a trance-based
upheaval in Yucatan, by Felicitas D. Goodman. In Goodman,
F. D. Trance, healing, and hallucination: three field studies
in religious experience. New York, 1974. DLC, RPRC

2234   Goodman, Felicitas Daniels, 1914-
        Speaking in tongues; a cross-cultural study of glossolalia
[by] Felicitas D. Goodman. Chicago, University of Chicago
Press, 1972. xxii, 175p. Based in part on observation in
the Yucatan.

-- --NICARAGUA

2235   Robeson, Gerald B.
        Faith in eruption, by Gerald B. Robeson.   Monroeville,
        Pa. , Banner Publications, c1973.   125p.

-- --UNITED STATES

2236   Aikman, Duncan, 1889-1955.
        The holy rollers.   In American Mercury, 15 (Oct. 1928),
        180-191.   An unsympathetic account of Pentecostal and Holi-
        ness churches.

2237   Anderson, Robert Mapes, 1929-
        A social history of the early twentieth century Pentecostal
        movement.   New York, 1969.   368ℓ.   Thesis (Ph. D.)--
        Columbia University.   NNC

2238   Anderson, Robert Mapes, 1929-
        Vision of the disinherited: the making of American
        Pentecostalism.   New York, Oxford University Press, 1979.
        334p.   Based on thesis (Ph. D.)--Columbia University, 1969.
        DLC

2239   Armstrong, O. K.
        Beware the commercialized faith healers, by O. K.
        Armstrong.   In Reader's Digest, 98 (June 1971), 179-180,
        182-184, 186.

2240   Bach, Marcus, 1906-
        Some emerging religious groups.   An elective unit for
        adults.   New York, Abingdon Press, 1959.   40p.   "Reprinted
        from Adult Student, copyright 1956. "   Includes Pentecostal
        churches.   NBuU

2241   Benz, Ernst, 1907-
        Der heilige Geist in Amerika.   Düsseldorf, Köln, Dieder-
        ichs, 1970.   229p.   DLC

2242   Bianchi, Eugene Carl, 1930-
        Ecumenism and the Spirit-filled communities [by] Eugene
        C. Bianchi.   In Thought, 41 (Fall 1966), 390-412.

2243   Biersdorf, John Edgar, 1930-
        New wine in old skins, and vice versa [by] John E.
        Biersdorf.   In Journal of Applied Behavioral Science, 9
        (Mar. 1973), 305-320.

2244   Brumback, Carl, 1917-
        A sound from heaven.   Springfield, Mo. , Gospel Publish-
        ing House, c1977.   iii, 153p.   First published in 1961 as the
        prologue and part one of the author's Suddenly ... from
        heaven.

2245   Cintron, Pedro
        American denominational revivalism and the Pentecostal
        movement: a comparative study. New York, 1963. 125ℓ.
        Thesis (S. T. M.)--Union Theological Seminary. NNUT

2246   Clark, Elmer Talmage, 1886-1966.
        The small sects in America, by Elmer T. Clark. Nash-
        ville, Tenn., Cokesbury Press, 1937. 311p. "Charismatic
        sects": p. 107-161. DLC

2247   Clark, Elmer Talmage, 1886-1966.
        The small sects in America, by Elmer T. Clark. Rev.
        ed. New York, Abingdon-Cokesbury Press, 1949. 256p.
        "Charismatic or Pentecostal sects": p. 85-132. DLC, RPB

2247a   De Leon, Victor, 1927-
        The silent Pentecostals: a biographical history of the
        Pentecostal movement among the Hispanics in the twentieth
        century. La Habra, Ca., c1979. ix, 206p. Originally pre-
        sented as the author's thesis (M. Div.), Melodyland School of
        Theology. DLC

2248   Demidov, Vasilii
        Apologelicheskie ocherki sektantstva; novaia amerikanskaia
        sekta Piatidesiatnikov (Pentikostolov). New York, Izd. Pro-
        tivosektantskango fonda Russko-Amerikanskago Pravoslavnogo
        vestnika, 1944. 70p. Cover title. MH

2249   Douglass, Harlan Paul, 1871-1953.
        Cultural differences and recent religious divisions. In
        Christendom, 10 (Winter 1945), 89-105.

2250   Elinson, Howard
        The implications of Pentecostal religion for intellectualism,
        politics, and race relations. In American Journal of Sociology,
        70 (Jan. 1965), 403-415.

2251   Epps, Bryan Crandell, 1932-
        Religious healing in the United States, 1940-1960: history
        and theology of selected trends. Boston, 1961. x, 446ℓ.
        Thesis (Ph. D.)--Boston University. MBU

2252   Fastest-growing church in the hemisphere.
        In Time, 80 (Nov. 2, 1962), 56.

2253   Faupel, David William, 1944-
        The American Pentecostal movement; a bibliographical
        essay, by David W. Faupel. Wilmore, Ky., B. L. Fisher
        Library, Asbury Theological Seminary, 1972. 56p. (Occa-
        sional bibliographical papers of the B. L. Fisher Library, 2.)
        "Revised version of the text published originally in the 1972
        Proceedings of the American Theological Library Association."
        KyLxCB, KyWAT, MNtcA, TxWaS

2254   Fiorentino, Joseph, 1912-
            In the power of His Spirit: "a summary of the Italian
        Pentecostal movement in the U.S.A. and abroad." Niagara
        Falls, N.Y., Christian Church of North America; distributed
        by Niagara Religious Supply Center, 1968. 17p.

2255   Garrison, Winfred Ernest, 1874-
            The march of faith; the story of religion in America
        since 1865. New York, Harper & Brothers, 1933. viii,
        332p. "Not less than twenty-five Pentecostal and Holiness
        organizations have been formed since 1880. Their members
        are, for the most part, rural, poor, ignorant, and emotional.
        The cultural advance of Methodism has been facilitated by the
        sloughing off of this element among which a fiery religion is
        compensatory for the consciousness of financial, social, and
        intellectual inferiority. p. 181. DLC, RPB

2256   Garvin, Philip, 1947-
            Religious America. Photographs by Philip Garvin. Text
        by Philip Garvin and Julia Welch. New York, McGraw-Hill
        Book Co., 1974. 189p. "Gifts of the Spirit": p. 141-169.
        DLC

2257   Gerlach, Luther Paul, 1930-
            Pentecostalism: revolution or counter-revolution? [By]
        Luther P. Gerlach. In Zaretsky, I. I., ed. Religious move-
        ments in contemporary America. Princeton, N.J., c1974.

2258   Götestam, K. Gunnar
            Personlighet hos Pingstvanner i U.S.A. In Svensk Mis-
        sionstidskrift, 55:1 (1967), 53-63.

2259   Hardon, John Anthony, 1914-
            The Protestant churches of America, by John A. Hardon.
        Westminster, Md., Newman Press, 1956. xxiii, 365p. "Pente-
        costal churches": p. 305-310. DLC, MH-AH, NN, TxDaM

2260   Harrell, David Edwin, 1930-
            All things are possible; the healing & charismatic revivals
        in modern America. Bloomington, Indiana University Press,
        1975. xi, 304p. DLC

2261   Hart, Larry Douglas, 1947-
            A critique of American Pentecostal theology. Louisville,
        1978. iii, 258ℓ. Thesis (Ph.D.)--Southern Baptist Theolog-
        ical Seminary. KyLoS

2262   Jones, Lawrence Neale, 1921-
            The Black Pentecostals. In Hamilton, M.P., ed. The
        charismatic movement. Grand Rapids, Mich., 1975, 145-158.

2263   Kantzer, Kenneth Sealer, 1917-
            The charismatics among us [by] Kenneth S. Kantzer. In

Christianity Today, 24 (Feb. 22, 1980), 25-29.

2264   Kenyon, Howard Nelson, 1955-
        An analysis of social separation within the early Pente-
        costal movement. Waco, Tex., 1978.   ix, 163ℓ.   Thesis
        (M. A.)--Baylor University.   TxWB

2265   Knight, Cecil Brigham, 1926-
        An historical study of distinctions among the divergent
        groupings of American Pentecostalism, by Cecil B. Knight.
        Indianapolis, 1968.   114ℓ.   Thesis (M. A.)--Butler Univer-
        sity.   InIB

2266   Kobler, John, 1910-
        The truth about faith healers.   In McCall's, 84 (Feb.
        1957), 39, 74, 77, 80, 82.

2267   Martin, Robert Francis
        The early years of American Pentecostalism, 1900-1940.
        Chapel Hill, 1975.   238ℓ.   Thesis (Ph. D.)--University of
        North Carolina.   NcU

2268   Marty, Martin Emil, 1928-
        A nation of behavers [by] Martin E. Marty.   Chicago,
        University of Chicago Press, 1976.   xi, 239p.   "Pentecostal-
        Charismatic religion": p. 106-125.   DLC

2269   Marty, Martin Emil, 1928-
        Pentecostalism in the context of American piety and prac-
        tice [by] Martin Marty.   In Synan, H. V., ed.   Aspects of
        Pentecostal-Charismatic origins.   Plainfield, N. J., 1975,
        193-233.

2270   Mathison, Richard Randolph, 1919-
        Faiths, cults and sects of America: from atheism to
        Zen, by Richard R. Mathison.   Indianapolis, Bobbs-Merrill
        Co., 1960.   384p.   "The street preachers": p. 327-333.

2271   Mayer, Frederick Emanuel, 1892-1954.
        The religious bodies of America, by F. E. Mayer.   2d
        ed.   St. Louis, Concordia Publishing House, 1956.   xiii, 591p.
        Revised by Arthur Carl Piepkorn.   "The Holiness bodies":
        p. 315-341; includes Pentecostal churches.   DLC, RPB

2272   Melton, John Gordon, 1942-
        The encyclopedia of American religions [by] J. Gordon
        Melton.   Wilmington, N. C., McGrath Publishing Co., c1978.
        2v.   Vol. 1, chapter 8:   The Pentecostal family.

2273   Moore, Everett Leroy, 1918-
        Handbook of Pentecostal denominations in the United States.
        Pasadena, Calif., 1954.   vii, 346ℓ.   Thesis (M. A.)--Pasadena
        College.   CSdP

2274   Nichol, John Thomas, 1928-
       The role of the Pentecostal movement in American church
       history [by] John T. Nichol. In Gordon Review, 2 (Dec. 1956),
       127-135. "Originally read before the Evangelical Theological
       Society, Eastern Division, at Gordon Divinity School, April
       13, 1956. "

2274a Nietmann, Carol Hutchins
       Pentecostalism: a case for world view. Washington,
       1978. 108ℓ. Thesis (M.A.)--Catholic University of Amer-
       ica. DCU

2275   Padberg, Jean Adele, 1938-
       The falling of the latter rain: a study of the rise and
       development of the Pentecostal movement in the United States.
       Madison, N.J., 1959. 259ℓ. Thesis (B.A.)--Drew Univer-
       sity. NjMD

2276   Pethrus, Lewi, 1884-1974.
       Västerut; en resenära erfarenheter. 2. uppl. Stockholm,
       Förlaget Filadelfia, 1937. 301p. MnU

2277   Piepkorn, Arthur Carl, 1907-1973.
       Profiles in belief: the religious bodies of the United
       States of America. New York, Harper & Row, c1979. 4v.
       in 3. Vol. 3, pt. 2: Pentecostal churches.

2278   Ranaghan, Kevin Mathers, 1940-
       Conversion and baptism; personal experience and ritual
       celebration in Pentecostal churches, by Kevin M. Ranaghan.
       In Studia Liturgica, 10:1 (1974), 65-76.

2279   Ranaghan, Kevin Mathers, 1940-
       Rites of initiation in representative Pentecostal churches
       in the United States, 1901-1972. Notre Dame, Ind., 1974.
       xiv, 787ℓ. Thesis (Ph.D.)--University of Notre Dame. InNd

2280   Shopshire, James Maynard, 1942-
       A socio-historical characterization of the Black Pente-
       costal movement in America. Evanston, Ill., 1975. v, 238ℓ.
       Thesis (Ph.D.)--Northwestern University. IEN

2281   Simpson, George Eaton, 1904-
       Black Pentecostalism in the United States. In Pylon, 35
       (June 1974), 203-211.

2282   Simson, Eve (Tammisoo)
       The faith healer: a study of deliverance evangelism in
       the United States. Columbus, 1969. vii, 124ℓ. Thesis
       (Ph.D.)--Ohio State University. OU

2283   Simson, Eve (Tammisoo)
       The faith healer: deliverance evangelism in North America

[by] Eve Simson. New York, Pyramid Books, 1977. 223p.
Based on thesis (Ph. D.)--Ohio State University, 1969. DLC

2284 Smylie, James Hutchinson, 1925-
Testing the spirits in the American context: great awak-
enings, Pentecostalism, and the charismatic movement [by]
James H. Smylie. In Interpretation, 33 (Jan. 1979), 32-46.

2285 Synan, Harold Vinson, 1934-
The Pentecostal movement in the United States. Athens,
1967. vi, 296ℓ. Thesis (Ph. D.)--University of Georgia. GU

2286 Thurston, Floyd H.
History and growth of Pentecostal churches in the United
States, by Floyd H. Thurston. Kansas City, Mo. , 1954.
iii, 103ℓ . Thesis (B. D.)--Nazarene Theological Seminary.
MoKN

2287 Tinney, James Stephen
Pentecostals refurbish the Upper Room [by] James S.
Tinney. In Christianity Today, 10 (Apr. 1, 1966), 47-48.

2288 Van Dusen, Henry Pitney, 1897-1975.
The challenge of the "sects. " In Christianity and Crisis,
18 (July 21, 1958), 103-106. "Excerpts from this longer
article appeared in the June 9 issue of Life" under title:
The third force in Christendom. On dynamic Pentecostal,
Holiness, Adventist, and Church of Christ groups.

2289 Van Dusen, Henry Pitney, 1897-1975.
The third force in Christendom. In Life, 44 (June 9,
1958), 113-122, 124; includes commentary by Henry P. Van
Dusen (Force's lessons for others), 122, 124. On dynamic
Pentecostal, Holiness, Adventist, and Church of Christ groups.

2290 Washington, Joseph Reed, 1930-
Black religion; the Negro and Christianity in the United
States [by] Joseph R. Washington, Jr. With a new preface
by the author and a review by Martin E. Marty. Boston,
Beacon Press, 1966, c1964. xvii, 308p. On Holiness and
Pentecostal churches: p. 114-122.

2291 Washington, Joseph Reed, 1930-
Black sects and cults, by Joseph R. Washington, Jr.
Garden City, N. Y. , Doubleday, 1972. xii, 176p. "Holiness
and Pentecostal Blacks: the permanent sects": p. 58-82.

2292 Whalen, William Joseph, 1926-
Minority religions in America [by] William J. Whalen.
Staten Island, N. Y. , Alba House, c1972. vi, 302p. "The
Pentecostals": p. 179-193.

2293 Williams, Jerry Douglas

The modern Pentecostal movement in America: a brief
sketch of its history and thought. In Lexington Theological
Quarterly, 9 (Apr. 1974), 50-60.

2294   Young, Pauline (Vislick), 1896-
        The pilgrims of Russian-town. Obshchestvo dukhovnykh
khrpstian prygunov v Amerikie. The community of spiritual
Christian jumpers in America; the struggle of a primitive
religious society to maintain itself in an urban environment,
by Pauline V. Young. With an introd. by Robert E. Park.
Chicago, University of Chicago Press, c1932. 296p. (University of Chicago sociological series.) Text in English.
DLC

2295   Young, Pauline (Vislick), 1896-
        The pilgrims of Russian-town. Obshchestvo dukhovnykh
khrpstian prygunov v Amerikie. The community of spiritual
Christian jumpers in America, by Pauline V. Young. With
an introd. by Robert E. Park. New York, Russell & Russell, 1967. 296p. (University of Chicago sociological series.)
"The struggle of a primitive religious society to maintain itself in an urban environment. " Text in English. Reprint of
1932 ed. DLC

-- --EASTERN STATES

(Massachusetts)

2296   Gow, Haven Bradford
        As the Spirit leads us. In Christian Century, 89 (Sept.
27, 1972), 957-958.

(Massachusetts, Boston)

2297   Eddy, George Norman, 1906-
        Store-front religion [by] G. Norman Eddy. In Religion
in Life, 28 (Winter 1958/1959), 68-85 [Pentecostal churches:
p. 68-74]; abridged in Lee, R. , ed. Cities and churches;
readings on the urban church. Philadelphia, c1962, 177-194
[Pentecostal churches: p. 178-182].

2298   Paris, Arthur Ernest, 1945-
        Black Pentecostalism: world view, society and politics.
Evanston, Ill. , 1974. vi, 183[31]ℓ . Thesis (Ph. D.)--North-
western University. On three congregations in Boston. IEN

2299   Parsons, Anne, 1930-1964.
        Pentecostal immigrants; a study of an ethnic central city
church. In Journal for the Scientific Study of Religion, 4
(Apr. 1965), 183-197; reprinted in Practical Anthropology, 14
(Nov. /Dec. 1967), 249-266.

(New Jersey, Plainfield)

2300   Schneider, Dick
           A modern-day New Testament church. In West, A. , ed.
       The New Testament church book. Plainfield, N. J. , 1973,
       25-29. On First Christian Assembly, Plainfield, New Jersey.

           (New York, New York City)

2301   Baldwin, James, 1924-
           Go tell it on the mountain. New York, Knopf, 1953.
       303p. A novel about a day in the life of several members
       of a Pentecostal church in Harlem. DLC

2302   Bois, Jules, 1871-
           The holy rollers: the American dervishes. In Forum,
       73 (Feb. 1925), 145-155. The new religions of America, 1.

2303   Brooklyn. Ridgewood Pentecostal Church.
           Commemorating fifty years of God's blessing and faithful-
       ness to the Ridgewood Pentecostal Church, Brooklyn, N. Y.
       Brooklyn, 1975. ix,95p. Cover title: Ridgewood Pentecostal
       Church, 1925-1975.

2304   Gardiner, Gordon P. , 1916-
           The origin of Glad Tidings Tabernacle, by Gordon P.
       Gardiner; and, The altar of incense, a sermon by Marie E.
       Brown. New York, 1955. vii,47p.

2305   Garrison, Vivian Eva, 1933-
           Sectarianism and psychosocial adjustment: a controlled
       comparison of Puerto Rican Pentecostals and Catholics [by]
       Vivian Garrison. In Zaretsky, I. I. , ed. Religious move-
       ments in contemporary America. Princeton, N. J. , c1974,
       298-329.

2306   Gustaitis, Rasa
           The Pentecostals. In Jubilee, 15 (May 1967), 8-15. On
       Iglesia de la Trinidad, New York.

2307   Jones, Raymond Julius, 1910-
           A comparative study of religious cult behavior among
       Negroes, with special reference to emotional group condition-
       ing factors. Washington, Published by the Graduate School
       for the Division of the Social Studies, Howard University,
       1939. v, 125p. (Howard University studies in the social sci-
       ences, vol. 2, no. 2.) Cover title. Thesis (M. A.)--Howard
       University, 1939. On eleven churches in Washington, D. C. ,
       and three in New York, all but three of which are Pentecostal.
       DLC, OrU, ScU

2308   Poblete Barth, Renato
           Anomie and the quest for community: the formation of
       sects among Puerto Ricans of New York, by Renato Poblete
       and Thomas F. O'Dea. In American Catholic Sociological

Review, 21 (Spring 1960), 18-36; abridgment (Sectarianism as a response to anomie) in Lee, R., ed. Cities and churches; readings on the urban church. Philadelphia, c1962, 195-206.

2309-   Poblete Barth, Renato
  10   Secretarismo portorriqueno; búsqueda de comunidad y ex-
         pansión pentecostal [por] Renato Poblete. Cuernavaca, Centro
         Intercultural de Codumentación, 1969. 1v. (various pagings)
         (Sondeos, no. 55.) DLC

2311   Smith, Malcolm, 1938-
          An inner city New Testament church. In West, A., ed.
        The New Testament church book. Plainfield, N.J., c1973,
        31-36. On Salem Gospel Tabernacle, Brooklyn, New York.

                    (Pennsylvania, Pittsburgh)

2312   Williams, Melvin Donald, 1933-
          Community in a Black Pentecostal church; an anthropolog-
        ical study [by] Melvin D. Williams. Pittsburgh, University
        of Pittsburgh Press, 1974. xii, 202p. Based on thesis, Uni-
        versity of Pittsburgh, 1973. DLC, MSohG

2313   Williams, Melvin Donald, 1933-
          Food and animals: behavioral metaphors in a Black Penta-
        costal [sic] church in Pittsburgh [by] Melvin D. Williams. In
        Urban Anthropology, 2 (Spring 1973), 74-79.

2314   Williams, Melvin Donald, 1933-
          A Pentecostal congregation in Pittsburgh; a religious com-
        munity in a Black ghetto. Pittsburgh, 1973. 328ℓ. Thesis
        (Ph.D.)--University of Pittsburgh. PPiU

                    (Rhode Island, Providence)

2315   Splain, Michael
          "They called us Holy Rollers." In Grass-Roots (Provi-
        dence), 1 (Dec. 14-20, 1977), 5. On store-front churches in
        Providence, Rhode Island. Comments on the shift from rural
        newcomers to Spanish and Portuguese-speaking constituents.

                    -- --MIDDLE WEST

2316   Whitbeck, Leslie B.
          Charismata and status in two charismatic groups, by
        Leslie B. Whitbeck. Richmond, Ind., 1973. 72ℓ. Thesis
        (M.A.)--Earlham College. On a small poor Pentecostal
        church and a Neo-Pentecostal upper-middle class college
        group in the Middle West. InRE

                    (Illinois, Chicago)

2317   Brazier, Arthur M.

Black self-determination; the story of the Woodlawn Organization, by Arthur M. Brazier. Grand Rapids, Mich., Eerdmans, 1969. 148p. Self-help neighborhood organization in Chicago led by the author, a Black Pentecostal pastor. DLC, RPB

2318   Daniel, Vattel Elbert, 1890-
Ritual in Chicago's South Side churches for Negroes. Chicago, 1940. iv, 155ℓ. Thesis (Ph. D.)--University of Chicago. Includes Pentecostal churches. CtY-D, DLC, ICU, NBuU

2319   Daniel, Vattel Elbert, 1890-
Ritual stratification in Chicago Negro churches. In American Sociological Review, 7 (June 1942), 352-361. Includes Pentecostal churches.

2320   Fastest-growing church in the hemisphere. In Time, 80 (Nov. 2, 1962), 56.

2321   Von Hoffman, Nicholas, 1929-
Interviewing Negro Pentecostals [by] Nicholas von Hoffman and Sally W. Cassidy. In American Journal of Sociology, 62 (Sept. 1956), 195-197. On participant-observer research in a Negro Pentecostal church in Chicago.

2322   Boisen, Anton Theophilus, 1876-1965.
Divided Protestantism in a midwest county: a study in the natural history of organized religion, by Anton T. Boisen. In Journal of Religion, 20 (Oct. 1940), 359-381; reprinted in Schuler, E. A., ed. Readings in sociology. 3d ed. New York, 1967, 487-496. On Monroe County, including Bloomington, Indiana.

2323   Boisen, Anton Theophilus, 1876-1965.
The Holy Rollers come to town, by Anton T. Boisen. In Chicago Theological Seminary Register, 29 (Jan. 1939), 5-8.

2324   Boisen, Anton Theophilus, 1876-1965.
Religion in crisis and custom; a sociological and psychological study, by Anton T. Boisen. New York, Harper & Brothers, 1955. xv, 271p. "Holy rollers and churches of custom": p. 8-20. RPB

(Indiana, Hammond)

2325   Goodman, Felicitas Daniels, 1914-
Speaking in tongues; a cross-cultural study of glossolalia [by] Felicitas D. Goodman. Chicago, University of Chicago Press, 1972. xxii, 175p. Based in part on observation in Hammond, Indiana.

(Kansas, Fairfield)

2326   Bach, Marcus, 1906-
        Report to Protestants; a personal investigation of the
        weakness, need, vision, and great potential of Protestants
        today. 277p. Includes account of the revival which led to
        organization of a Pentecostal church in Fairfield, Kansas.

                    (Minnesota, Minneapolis)

2327   Gerlach, Luther Paul, 1930-
        Five factors crucial to the growth and spread of a modern
        religious movement [by] Luther P. Gerlach and Virginia H.
        Hine. In Journal for the Scientific Study of Religion, 7
        (Spring 1968), 23-40. Based in part on study of Pentecostals
        in Minneapolis.

2328   Hine, Virginia (Haglin), 1921-
        Bridge-burners: commitment and participation in a reli-
        gious movement [by] Virginia H. Hine. In Sociological Analy-
        sis, 31 (Summer 1970), 61-66. Based on questionnaires ad-
        ministered to 239 neo- and traditional Pentecostals in Minne-
        sota.

2329   Hine, Virginia (Haglin), 1921-
        Personal transformation and social change: the role of
        commitment in a modern religious movement. Minneapolis,
        1969. 248, 9ℓ. Thesis (M. A.)--University of Minnesota.
        Based on questionnaires administered to 239 neo- and tradi-
        tional Pentecostals in Minnesota. MnU

                    (Minnesota, St. Paul)

2330   Gerlach, Luther Paul, 1930-
        Five factors crucial to the growth and spread of a modern
        religious movement [by] Luther P. Gerlach and Virginia H.
        Hine. In Journal for the Scientific Study of Religion, 7
        (Spring 1968), 23-40. Based in part on study of Pentecostals
        in St. Paul.

2331   Hine, Virginia (Haglin), 1921-
        Bridge-burners: commitment and participation in a reli-
        gious movement [by] Virginia H. Hine. In Sociological Analy-
        sis, 31 (Summer 1970), 61-66. Based on questionnaires ad-
        ministered to 239 neo- and traditional Pentecostals in Minne-
        sota.

2332   Hine, Virginia (Haglin), 1921-
        Personal transformation and social change: the role of
        commitment in a modern religious movement. Minneapolis,
        1969. 248, 9ℓ. Thesis (M. A.)--University of Minnesota.
        Based on questionnaires administered to 239 neo- and tradi-
        tional Pentecostals in Minnesota. MnU

2333   Holsteen, Melbourne Edward

Controlled resistance to change in a Pentecostal church.
Minneapolis, 1968.   iii, 181ℓ.   Thesis (M. A.)--University of
Minnesota. MnU

(Missouri, Kansas City)

2334   Lunn, Harry
       A midwestern New Testament church. In West, A. , ed.
       The New Testament church book. Plainfield, N. J. , 1973, 39-
       44.

(Missouri, St. Louis)

2335   Douglass, Harlan Paul, 1871-1953.
       The St. Louis church survey; a religious investigation
       with a social background, by H. Paul Douglass. New York,
       Doran, c1924. xxi, 27-327p. On Holiness and Pentecostal
       churches: p. 119-120. RPB

2336   Harris, John William, 1870-
       Tears and triumphs; the life story of a pastor-evangelist,
       by John W. Harris. Louisville, Ky. , Pentecostal Publishing
       Co. , c1948. 445p. Account of 1907 take-over of the Marvin
       Camp Meeting near St. Louis by Pentecostals: p. 333-340.
       The camp meeting was sponsored by the Vanguard Mission of
       St. Louis, a Holiness group. WHi

(Missouri, Springfield)

2337   Sizelove, Rachel Artamissie (Harper), 1864-1941.
       A sparkling fountain for the whole earth [by] Rachel A.
       Sizelove. Long Beach, Calif. , 19--. folder (11p.) Includes
       account of the introduction of Pentecostalism in Springfield,
       Missouri.

(Ohio, Columbus)

2338   Dynes, Russell Rowe, 1923-
       Rurality, migration, and sectarianism, by Russell R.
       Dynes. In Rural Sociology, 21 (Mar. 1956), 25-28.

2339   Goodman, Felicitas Daniels, 1914-
       Phonetic analysis of glossolalia in four cultural settings
       [by] Felicitas D. Goodman. In Journal for the Scientific Study
       of Religion, 8 (Fall 1969), 227-239. Based in part on obser-
       vation in Columbus, Ohio.

(Wisconsin, Milwaukee)

2340   Bach, Marcus, 1906-
       Report to Protestants; a personal investigation of the
       weakness, need, vision, and great potential of Protestants
       today. Indianapolis, Bobbs-Merrill, 1948. 277p. Includes

account of participation in a Pentecostal church in Milwaukee
in the 1930s. DLC, RPB

-- --SOUTHERN STATES

2341   Boeckman, Charles, 1920-
          And the beat goes on; a survey of pop music in America.
       Washington, Luce, 1972. 224p. "That old-time religion":
       p. 67-74. DLC

2342   Clow, Harvey Kennedy, 1940-
          Ritual, belief, and the social context: an analysis of a
       Southern Pentecostal sect. Durham, N.C., 1976. v, 219ℓ.
       Thesis (Ph.D.)--Duke University. NcD

2343   Cobb, Alice Luch, 1909-
          Sect religion and social change in an isolated rural com-
       munity of southern Appalachia, by Alice Cobb. Boston, 1965.
       viii, 236, 4, 241ℓ. Thesis (Ph.D.)--Boston University. In-
       cludes case story: Fruit of the land. MBU

2344   Dickinson, Eleanor (Creekmore), 1931-
          Revival. Text: Barbara Benziger. Introd. by Walter
       Hopps. New York, Harper & Row, 1974. xi, 180p. DLC

2345   Dorough, Charles Dwight, 1912-
          The Bible belt mystique, by C. Dwight Dorough. Phila-
       delphia, Westminster Press, 1974. 217p. "Sensationalism
       and excesses": p. 144-173. DLC, OkTOr

2346   Gerrard, Nathan Lewis
          Churches of the stationary poor in southern Appalachia,
       by Nathan L. Gerrard. In Photiadis, J.D., ed. Change in
       rural Appalachia; implications for action programs. Philadel-
       phia, 1970, 99-114.

2347   Harrell, David Edwin, 1930-
          White sects and black men in the recent South. Foreword
       by Edwin S. Gaustad. Nashville, Vanderbilt University Press,
       1971. xix, 161p. DLC

2348   Preece, Harold, 1906-
          Dew on Jordan, by Harold Preece and Celia Kraft. New
       York, Dutton, 1946. 221p. "Sanctified folks": p. 15-102.
       RP, RPB

2349   Sargant, William Walters, 1907-
          The mind possessed; a physiology of possession, mysticism
       and faith healing [by] William Sargant. Philadelphia, Lippin-
       cott, 1974, c1973. xii, 212p. "Revivals in the United States
       of America": p. 182-193. DLC

2350   Sargant, William Walters, 1907-

The mind possessed; a physiology of possession, mysticism and faith healing [by] William Sargent. London, Pan Books, 1976. 256p.

2351   Weatherford, Willis Duke, 1875-1970, ed.
        Religion in the Appalachian Mountains; a symposium.
        W. D. Weatherford, editor. Berea, Ky., Berea College,
        1955. 132p. "Pentecostal sects": p. 100-102. KyU, RPB

        (Arkansas)

2352   Clements, William Manning, 1945-
        The American folk church: a characterization of American folk religion based on field research among white Protestants in a community in the south central United States.
        Bloomington, 1974. 451ℓ. Thesis (Ph.D.)--Indiana University. On Pentecostal and Baptist churches. InU

2353   Clements, William Manning, 1945-
        Faith healing narratives from northeast Arkansas [by]
        William M. Clements. In Indiana Folklore, 9:1 (1976), 15-39.

2354   Clements, William Manning, 1945-
        The rhetoric of the radio ministry [by] William M. Clements. In Journal of American Folklore, 87 (Oct./Dec. 1974), 318-327. On Pentecostal preachers in northeastern Arkansas.

        (District of Columbia)

2355   Davis, Arnor S., 1919-
        The Pentecostal movement in Black Christianity, by Arnor S. Davis. In Black Church, 2:1 (1972), 65-88.

2356   Jones, Raymond Julius, 1910-
        A comparative study of religious cult behavior among Negroes, with special reference to emotional group conditioning factors. Washington, Published by the Graduate School for the Division of the Social Sciences, Howard University, 1939. v, 125p. (Howard University studies in the social sciences, vol. 2, no. 2.) Cover title. DLC, OrU, ScU

        (Florida, Tallahassee)

2357   Benz, Ernst, 1907-
        Der heilige Geist in Amerika. Düsseldorf, Köln, Diederichs, 1970. 229p. DLC

        (Georgia, Atlanta)

2358   Hedgepeth, William
        Brother A. A. Allen on the gospel trail: he feels he heals & he turns you on with God. In Look, 33 (Oct. 7, 1969), 23-31.

(Georgia, Patterson)

2359   Davis, Arnor S., 1919-
        The Pentecostal movement in Black Christianity, by
        Arnor S. Davis. In Black Church, 2:1 (1972), 65-88.

(Kentucky)

2360   Brown, James Stephen, 1916-
        Social class, intermarriage, and church membership in
        a Kentucky community. In American Journal of Sociology,
        57 (Nov. 1951), 232-242.

2361   Cobb, Alice Luch, 1909-
        Sect religion and social change in an isolated rural com-
        munity in southern Appalachia, by Alice Cobb. Boston, 1965.
        viii, 236, 4, 241ℓ. Thesis (Ph.D.)--Boston University. In-
        cludes case story: Fruit of the land. MBU

(Mississippi, Aberdeen)

2362   Hamilton, Charles Granville, 1905-
        Seven hundred a year. In Christian Century, 58 (Jan.
        29, 1941), 150-151. Account of growth of a Pentecostal
        church in Aberdeen, Mississippi, by the rector of a neigh-
        boring Episcopal congregation.

(North Carolina)

2363   Wise, James Edgar
        The "Sons of God" in the North Carolina mountains; an
        exercise in "thick description." Chapel Hill, 1977. 78ℓ.
        Thesis (M.A.)--University of North Carolina. On a Pente-
        costal congregation in Wilkes County, North Carolina. NcU

(North Carolina, Gastonia)

2364   Earle, John Rochester, 1935-
        Spindles and spires; a re-study of religion and social
        change in Gastonia, by John R. Earle, Dean D. Knudsen and
        Donald W. Shriver, Jr. Atlanta, John Knox Press, c1976.
        382p. Includes Pentecostal churches. DLC

2365   Pope, Liston, 1909-1974.
        Churches and mills in a Southern county, 1880-1939.
        New Haven, Conn., 1939. 211ℓ. Thesis (Ph.D.)--Yale
        University. CtY

2366   Pope, Liston, 1909-1974.
        Millhands & preachers; a study of Gastonia. New Haven,
        Conn., Yale University Press; London, H. Milford, Oxford
        University Press, 1942. xvi, 369p. (Yale studies in religious
        education, 15.) DLC

(Oklahoma City, Oklahoma)

2367   Shewmaker, Kenneth Lee, 1931-
        Authoritarianism in a religious sect. Norman, 1956. v,
43ℓ . Thesis (M. S.)--University of Oklahoma. Psychological
study of sixty Pentecostal adherents in Oklahoma City. OkU

(Tennessee, Dayton)

2368   Mencken, Henry Louis, 1880-1956.
        The hills of Zion. In Mencken, H. L. A Mencken
chrestomathy. New York, 1949, 392-398. "From Preju-
dices: Fifth Series, 1926, pp. 75-86. In its first form this
was a dispatch to the Baltimore Evening Sun." Includes description of a Pentecostal meeting in 1925 at Morgantown,
near Dayton, Tennessee.

2369   Sumner, Allene M.
        The holy rollers on Shin Bone Ridge, by Allene M. Sum-
ner. In Nation, 121 (July 29, 1925), 137-138. On group
near Dayton, Tennessee.

(Texas)

2370   Goodman, Felicitas Daniels, 1914-
        Phonetic analysis of glossolalia in four cultural settings
[by] Felicitas D. Goodman. In Journal for the Scientific
Study of Religion, 8 (Fall 1969), 227-239. Based in part on
observation in Texas.

(Texas, Blossom)

2371   Owens, William A., 1905-
        This stubborn soil [by] William A. Owens. New York,
Scribner, c1966. 307p. Description of "holy roller" meetings at the Pin Hook Schoolhouse near Blossom, Texas, in
the 1920's: p. 254-255, 261-262. DLC

(Texas, El Paso)

2372   Weigert, Andrew Joseph, 1934-
        Protestant and assimilation among the Mexican Americans;
an exploratory study of ministers' reports [by] Andrew J.
Weigert, William V. D'Antonio [and] Arthur J. Rubel. In
Journal for the Scientific Study of Religion, 10 (Fall 1971),
219-232. On ministers of predominantly Mexican-American congregations in El Paso, Tx. Pentecostal ministers: p. 225-227.

(Virginia)

2373   Forbes, James Alexander, 1935-
        Ministry of hope from a double minority [by] James A.
Forbes, Jr. In Theological Education, 9 (Summer 1973 suppl.),
305-316.

-- --WESTERN STATES

2374   Gilmore, Susan Kay
        Personality differences between high and low dogmatism
        groups of Pentecostal believers [by] Susan K. Gilmore. In
        Journal for the Scientific Study of Religion, 8 (Spring 1969),
        161-164. Study of a group drawn from three Pentecostal
        congregations in a city in northwestern United States.

2375   Walker, Deward Edgar
        Schismatic factionalism and the development of Nez Percé
        Pentecostalism. Eugene, 1964. 215ℓ. Thesis (Ph. D.)--
        University of Oregon. OrU

                    (California)

2376   Muelder, Walter George, 1907-
        From sect to church, by Walter G. Muelder. In Chris-
        tendom, 10 (Autumn 1945), 450-462; abridged in Yinger, J. M.
        Religion, society and the individual. New York, c1957, 480-
        488. Compares the institutional development of rural Pente-
        costal sects with that of the Church of the Nazarene in Cali-
        fornia.

2377   Stein, Walter Joseph
        California and the Dust Bowl migration [by] Walter J.
        Stein. Westport, Conn., Greenwood Press, c1973. xiv,
        302p. On Pentecostal churches: p. 52. 169-170, 268-269.

2378   Young, Frank Wilbur, 1928-
                Adaptation and pattern integration of a California sect
        [by] Frank W. Young. In Review of Religious Research, 1
        (Spring 1960), 137-150; reprinted in Knudten, R. D., ed. The
        sociology of religion: an anthology. New York, c1967, 136-
        146.

2379   Young, Frank Wilbur, 1928-
        Sociocultural analysis of a California Pentecostal church,
        by Frank W. Young. Ithaca, N. Y., 1954. vii, 163ℓ. The-
        sis (M. A.)--Cornell University. NIC

                (California, Live Oak)

2380   Jamieson, Stuart Marshall, 1914-
        A settlement of rural migrant families in the Sacramento
        Valley, California, by Stuart M. Jamieson. In Rural Sociol-
        ogy, 7 (Mar. 1942), 49-61. Discussion on religious life
        (p. 57-58).

                (California, Los Angeles)

2381   Bartleman, Frank, 1871-1935.
        Another wave rolls in! Edited by John Walker. Revised

and enlarged ed., edited by John G. Myers. Northridge, Calif., Voice Publications, 1970, c1962. 128p. First published in 1962 under title: What really happened at Azusa Street. Abridgment of How Pentecost came to Los Angeles. TxWaS

2382 Bartleman, Frank, 1871-1935.
      Azusa Street, by Frank Bartleman. With foreword by Vinson Synan. Plainfield, N.J., Logos International, c1980. xxvi, 184p. First published in 1925 under title: How Pentecost came to Los Angeles. DLC

2383 Bartleman, Frank, 1871-1935.
      How Pentecost came to Los Angeles; as it was in the beginning: Old Azusa Mission from my diary. 3d ed. Los Angeles, 1925. 167p.

2384 Bartleman, Frank, 1871-1935.
      What really happened at "Azusa Street." Northridge, Calif., Voice Christian Publications, 1962. 97p. Abridgment of How Pentecost came to Los Angeles. KyWAT

2385 Getting back double from God.
      In Time, 93 (Mar. 7, 1969), 64, 67.

2386 Getting the power.
      In Nazarene Messenger, 10 (June 7, 1906), 12.

2387 The gift of tongues.
      In Nazarene Messenger, 11 (Dec. 13, 1906), 6.

2388 Lovett, Leonard
      Black origins of the Pentecostal movement. In Synan, H. V., ed. Aspects of Pentecostal-Charismatic origins. Plainfield, N.J., 1975, 123-141. On the Azusa Street revival.

2389 Lovett, Leonard
      Perspective on the black origins of the contemporary Pentecostal movement. In Journal of the Interdenominational Theological Center, 1 (Fall 1973), 36-49. On the Azusa Street revival.

2390 Richardson, Robert Porterfield, 1876-
      Pentecostal prophets, by Robert P. Richardson. In Open Court, 42 (Nov. 1928), 673-680. On a service at Victoria Hall, Los Angeles.

2391 Shuler, Robert Pierce, 1880-1965.
      "McPhersonism": a study of healing cults and modern day "tongues" movements, by R. P. (Bob) Shuler. Los Angeles, 192-. 63p.

2392   Shuler, Robert Pierce, 1880-1965.
       "McPhersonism": a study of healing cults and modern
       day "tongues" movements, by R. P. (Bob) Shuler. 2d ed.
       Los Angeles, 192-. 72p. KyWA

2393   Shuler, Robert Pierce, 1880-1965.
       "McPhersonism"; a study of healing cults and modern day
       "tongues" movements, containing a summary of facts as to
       disappearances and reappearances of Aimee Semple McPher-
       son. 4th ed. Los Angeles, 192-. 128p. DLC, KyWA

2394   Sizelove, Rachel Artamissie (Harper), 1864-1941.
       A sparkling fountain for the whole earth [by] Rachel A.
       Sizelove. Long Beach, Calif., 19--. folder (11p.)

                        (California, Riverside)

2395   Garvin, Philip, 1947-
       Religious America. Photographs by Philip Garvin. Text
       by Philip Garvin and Julia Welch. New York, McGraw-Hill
       Book Co., 1974. 189p. "Gifts of the Spirit": p. 141-169;
       includes description of the worship of Faith Tabernacle, River-
       side, California.

                        (California, Santa Ana)

2396   Garvin, Philip, 1947-
       Religious America. Photographs by Philip Garvin. Text
       by Philip Garvin and Julia Welch. New York, McGraw-Hill
       Book Co., 1974. 189p. "Gifts of the Spirit": p. 141-169;
       includes description of the worship of Calvary Chapel, Santa
       Ana, California.

                        (California, Wasco)

2397   Goldschmidt, Walter Rochs, 1913-
       Class denominationalism in rural California churches [by]
       Walter R. Goldschmidt. In American Journal of Sociology,
       49 (Jan. 1944), 348-355. On Wasco, Kern County, California.

2398   Goldschmidt, Walter Rochs, 1913-
       Social structure of a California rural community. Berke-
       ley, 1942. 271ℓ. Thesis (Ph.D.)--University of California.
       On Wasco, Kern County, California. "Religious life": ℓ. 133-
       161. CU

                        (Montana)

2399   Dusenberry, Verne, 1906-
       Montana Indians and the Pentecostals. In Christian Cen-
       tury, 75 (July 23, 1958), 850-851.

                        (New Mexico, Albuquerque)

2400   Ellis, Florence (Hawley), 1906-
        The Keresan Holy Rollers: an adaptation to American in-
        dividualism [by] Florence Hawley. In Social Forces, 26 (1948),
        272-280. On conversion of some Indians in Albuquerque by
        Black Pentecostals.

2401   Hodge, William Howard, 1932-
        Navaho Pentecostalism [by] William H. Hodge. In Anthro-
        pological Quarterly, 37 (July 1964), 73-93.

        (Washington)

2402   Garvin, Philip, 1947-
        Religious America. Photographs by Philip Garvin. Text
        by Philip Garvin and Julia Welch. New York, McGraw-Hill
        Book Co. , 1974. 189p. "Gifts of the Spirit": p. 141-169.
        Includes account of King's Temple, Seattle.

        --WEST INDIES

        -- --CUBA

2403   Osborn, Tommy Lee, 1923-
        Revival fires sweep Cuba; miracles of healing, by T. L.
        Osborn. Tulsa, 19--. 46p.

        -- --HAITI

2404   Conway, Frederick James, 1946-
        Pentecostalism in Haiti: healing and hierarchy [by]
        Frederick J. Conway. In Glazier, S. D. Perspectives on
        Pentecostalism: case studies from the Caribbean and Latin
        America. Washington, c1980, 7-26.

2404a   Conway, Frederick James, 1946-
        Pentecostalism in the context of Haitian religion and
        health practice, by Frederick J. Conway. Washington, 1978.
        vii, 284ℓ. Thesis (Ph. D.)--American University. DAU

2405   Gerlach, Luther Paul, 1930-
        Five factors crucial to the growth and spread of a modern
        religious movement [by] Luther P. Gerlach and Virginia H.
        Hine. In Journal for the Scientific Study of Religion, 7
        (Spring 1968), 23-40. Based in part on study of Pentecostal
        churches in Haiti.

2405a   Gerlach, Luther Paul, 1930-
        Pentecostalism: revolution or counter-revolution? [By]
        Luther P. Gerlach. In Zaretsky, I. I., ed. Religious move-
        ments in contemporary America. Princeton, N. J. , c1974.
        Based in part on study of Pentecostal churches in Haiti.

-- --JAMAICA

2406   Barrett, Leonard Emanuel, 1920-
        African roots in Jamaican indigenous religion, by Leonard
        E. Barrett. In Journal of Religious Thought, 35 (Spring/
        Summer 1978), 7-26.

2407   Dreher, M. C.
        Getting high: ganja man and his socio-economic milieu
        [by] M. C. Dreher and C. M. Rogers. In Caribbean Studies,
        16 (July 1976), 219-231.

2408   Gerlach, Luther Paul, 1930-
        Five factors crucial to the growth and spread of a mod-
        ern religious movement [by] Luther P. Gerlach and Virginia
        H. Hine. In Journal for the Scientific Study of Religion, 7
        (Spring 1968), 23-40. Based in part on study of Pentecostal
        churches in Jamaica.

2409   Hopkin, John Barton
        Music in the Jamaican Pentecostal churches. Cambridge,
        Mass. , 1974. 76ℓ. Thesis (B. A.)--Harvard University.
        MH

2409a   Wedenoja, William Andrew, 1948-
        Modernization and the Pentecostal movement in Jamaica
        [by] William Wedenoja. In Glazier, S. D. Perspectives on
        Pentecostalism: case studies from the Caribbean and Latin
        America. Washington, c1980, 27-48.

2409b   Wedenoja, William Andrew, 1948-
        Religion and adaptation in rural Jamaica. San Diego,
        1978. xx, 515ℓ. Thesis (Ph. D.)--University of California,
        San Diego. CU-S

-- --PUERTO RICO

2410   Benz, Ernst, 1907-
        Der heilige Geist in Amerika. Düsseldorf, Köln, Die-
        derichs, 1970. 229p. Includes Puerto Rico. DLC

2411   Mintz, Sidney Wilfred, 1922-
        Worker in the cane; a Puerto Rican life history. New
        Haven, Conn. , Yale University Press, 1960. ix, 288p.
        (Caribbean series, 2.) CU, DLC, KU, MB, NN, OCU, OkU,
        OO: OrU, OU, RPB

2412   Mintz, Sidney Wilfred, 1922-
        Worker in the cane; a Puerto Rican life history by Sidney
        W. Mintz. Westport, Conn. , Greenwood Press, 1974, c1960.
        ix, 288p. Reprint of the ed. published by Yale University
        Press, New Haven, which was issued as no. 2 of Caribbean
        series. DLC

2413   Osborn, Tommy Lee, 1923-
        Revival harvest with miracles of healing: Puerto Rico,
        by T. L. Osborn.   Tulsa, 19--.   46p.

        (San Cipriano)

2414   La Ruffa, Anthony Louis, 1933-
        Culture change and Pentecostalism in Puerto Rico.   In
        Social and Economic Studies, 18 (Sept. 1969), 273-281.

2414a   La Ruffa, Anthony Louis, 1933-
        Pentecostalism in a Puerto Rican community.   New York,
        1966, c1967.   vii, 283ℓ.   Thesis (Ph. D.)--Columbia Univer-
        sity.   On San Cipriano, Puerto Rico.   NNC

2414b   La Ruffa, Anthony Louis, 1933-
        Pentecostalism in Puerto Rican society [by] Anthony L.
        La Ruffa.   In Glazier, S. D.   Perspectives on Pentecostalism:
        case studies from the Caribbean and Latin America.   Wash-
        ington, c1980, 49-65.

2414c   La Ruffa, Anthony Louis, 1933-
        San Cipriano: life in a Puerto Rican community [by]
        Anthony L. La Ruffa.   New York, Gordon and Breach, 1971.
        xiii, 149p.   (Library of anthropology, [1].)   DLC

        (San Juan)

2415   Rivera, Juan Marcos
        The church in Puerto Rico: a public nuisance?   In
        Christian Century, 91 (Apr. 17, 1974), 413-414.   On deci-
        sion by the Supreme Court of Puerto Rico concerning the
        Pentecostal Church of Old San Juan.

                    -- --ST. VINCENT

2416   Goodman, Felicitas Daniels, 1914-
        Phonetic analysis of glossolalia in four cultural settings
        [by] Felicitas D. Goodman.   In Journal for the Scientific
        Study of Religion, 8 (Fall 1969), 227-239.   Includes tongue-
        speech in St. Vincent, West Indies.

2417   Henney, Jeannette Hillman, 1918-
        Spirit possession belief and trance behavior in a religious
        group in St. Vincent, British West Indies.   Columbus, 1968.
        x, 216ℓ.   Thesis (Ph. D.)--Ohio State University.   OU

2418   Henney, Jeanette Hillman, 1918-
        Spirit-possession belief in two fundamentalist groups in
        St. Vincent, by Jeannette H. Henney.   In Goodman, F. D.
        Trance, healing, and hallucination; three field studies in
        religious experience.   New York, 1974.

-- --TRINIDAD

2418a   Glazier, Stephen D.
Pentecostal exorcism and modernization in Trinidad,
West Indies [by] Stephen D. Glazier. In Glazier, S. D.
Perspectives on Pentecostalism: case studies from the
Caribbean and Latin America. Washington, c1980, 67-80.

--SOUTH AMERICA (including Latin America)

2419   Amerson, Philip
Latin American Pentecostals: urbanization and migrant
resocialization. Atlanta, 1972. 24ℓ. Student paper--Emory
University. KyWAT

2420   Bena-Silu.
The message of expectation from indigenous Christian
movements: a reaction by Bena-Silu. In International Review
of Mission, 66 (Jan. 1977), 71-74; discussion, 66 (Jan. 1977),
75-80.

2421   Bianchi, Eugene Carl, 1930-
Ecumenism and the Spirit-filled communities [by] Eugene
C. Bianchi. In Thought, 41 (Fall 1966), 390-412.

2422   Castro, Emilio
Pentecostalism and ecumenism in Latin America. In
Christian Century, 89 (Sept. 27, 1972), 955-957.

2423   César, Waldo A.
The condition of Protestantism in Latin America, by
Waldo A. César. In Cutler, D. R. , ed. The religious
situation: 1969. Boston, c1969, 146-163. "Pentecostalism":
p. 157-162.

2423a   Domínguez, Roberto
Pioneros de Pentecostes en el mundo de habla Hispana.
Miami, Fl. , 1971. v. 1- . NR

2424   Fastest-growing church in the hemisphere.
In Time, 80 (Nov. 2, 1962), 56.

2425   Franklin, A. P.
Bland pingstvänner och övergivan helgonbilder i Sydamer-
ika. Chicago, Filadelfia Förlaget, 192-. 314p. OrU

2426   Gaxiola, Manuel Jesús, 1927-
The Pentecostal ministry [by] Manuel J. Gaxiola. In
International Review of Mission, 66 (Jan. 1977), 57-63. On
Latin America.

2426a   Glazier, Stephen D.

Perspectives on Pentecostalism: case studies from the
Caribbean and Latin America [by] Stephen D. Glazier. Washington, University Press of America, c1980. viii, 197p. DLC

2427   Hayward, Victor
       Latin America--an ecumenical bird's eye view. In Inter-
national Review of Mission, 60 (Apr. 1971), 161-185.
"Strengths and weaknesses of Pentecostalism": p. 167-169.

2428   Hollenweger, Walter Jacob, 1927-
       Pfingstler, Katholiken und Politik in Lateinamerica. In
Reformatio, 22 (June 1973), 334-341.

2429   Hollenweger, Walter Jacob, 1927-
       Pfingstvanner, Katoliker och politik in Latinamerika. In
Svensk Missionstidskrift, 60:2 (1972), 90-98.

2430   Hollenweger, Walter Jacob, 1927-
       The religion of the poor is not a poor religion, by W. J.
Hollenweger. In Expository Times, 87 (May 1976), 228-232.
Theology of the new world, 3.

2431   Klaiber, Jeffrey L.
       Pentecostal breakthrough [by] Jeffrey L. Klaiber. In
America, 122 (Jan. 31, 1970), 99-102. On the impact of
Protestant missions on the Catholic Church in Latin America.

2432   Kliewer, Gerd Uwe, 1939-
       Das neue Volk der Pfingstler: Religion, Unterentwicklung
und sozialer Wandel in Lateinamerika. Bern, Herbert Lang;
Frankfurt /M. , Peter Lang, 1975. 229p. (Studien zur inter-
kulturellen Geschichte des Christentum, 3.) Originally presented as thesis--Marburg, 1974. DLC, NN

2433   Kloppenburg, Boaventura
       O problema das seitas no contexto ecumênico. In Re-
vista Eclesiástica Brasileira, 33 (Dec. 1973), 928-941. Includes Pentecostal groups.

2434   Lalive d'Epinay, Christian, 1938-
       Latin American Protestantism in a revolutionary context.
In Lutheran Quarterly, 22 (Feb. 1970), 29-39.

2435   Lalive d'Epinay, Christian, 1938-
       Toward a typology of Latin American Protestantism. In
Review of Religious Research, 10 (Fall 1968), 4-11.

2436   Lindell, Paul J.
       Why Pentecostals are popular in Latin America, by Paul
J. Lindell. In Lutheran Standard, 10 (Jan. 20, 1970), 9-10.

2437   Mackay, John Alexander, 1889-
       Latin America and revolution II: the new mood in the

churches [by] John A. Mackay. In Christian Century, 82
(Nov. 24, 1965), 1439-1443. Includes comments on Pentecostal churches.

2437a Manning, Frank Edward, 1944-
         Pentecostalism: Christianity and reputation [by] Frank E.
Manning. In Glazier, S. D. Perspectives on Pentecostalism:
case studies from the Caribbean and Latin America. Washington, c1980, 177-187.

2437b Margolies, Luise, 1945-
         The paradoxical growth of Pentecostalism. In Glazier,
S. D. Perspectives on Pentecostalism: case studies from
the Caribbean and Latin America. Washington, c1980, 1-5.

2438   Nida, Eugene Albert, 1914-
         The indigenous churches in Latin America. New York,
National Council of the Churches of Christ in the U. S. A.,
1960. 14p. Address presented at the Study Conference of
the Committee on Cooperation in Latin America, Buck Hill
Falls, Pennsylvania, November 20-22, 1960. OSW

2439   Nida, Eugene Albert, 1914-
         The indigenous churches in Latin America [by] Eugene A.
Nida. In Practical Anthropology, 8 (May/June 1961), 97-
105, 110.

2440   Read, William Richard, 1923-
         Latin American church growth, by William R. Read,
Victor M. Monterroso [and] Herman A. Johnson. Grand
Rapids, Mich., Eerdmans, 1969. xxiv, 421p. (Church
growth series.) Includes Pentecostal churches. DLC, MCE

2441   Roberts, W. Dayton
         Latin American Protestants: which way will they go?
[By] W. Dayton Roberts. In Christianity Today, 14 (Oct. 10,
1969), 14-16. Includes comment on Pentecostals.

2442   Roberts, W. Dayton
         Pentecost south of the border [by] W. D. R. In Chris-
tianity Today, 7 (July 19, 1963), 32.

2443   Robertson, Edwin Hanton
         Tomorrow is a holiday; record of a South American jour-
ney. London, SCM Press, 1959. 128p. Includes comment
on Pentecostals. CtY-D, DLC, CMlG, IEG, MH-AH, KyLxCB,
NNUT, ViU

2444   Sapsezian, Aharon
         Ministry with the poor: an introduction. In International
Review of Mission, 66 (Jan. 1977), 3-13.

2445   Saracco, J. Norberto

The type of ministry adopted by the Pentecostal churches in Latin America [by] J. Norberto Saracco. In International Review of Mission, 66 (Jan. 1977), 64-70.

2446   Schuurman, Lambert
Some observations on the relevance of Luther's theory of the two realms for the theological task in Latin America. In Lutheran Quarterly, 22 (Feb. 1970), 77-91.

2447   Sumrall, Lester Frank, 1913-
Through blood and fire in Latin America, by Lester F. Sumrall. Grand Rapids, Mich., Zondervan Publishing House, 1944. 246p. DLC

2448   Tschuy, Théo
The World Council of Churches and Latin America. In Christian Century, 87 (Mar. 18, 1970), 320-323. Discussion on the potential impact of membership of Latin American Pentecostal churches on the World Council of Churches.

2449   Wagner, Charles Peter, 1930-
Look out! The Pentecostals are coming [by] C. Peter Wagner. Carol Stream, Ill., Creation House, 1973. 196p. DLC, MSohG, TxWaS

2450   Wagner, Charles Peter, 1930-
Look out! The Pentecostals are coming [by] C. Peter Wagner. London, Coverdale House, 1974. 196p.

2450a   Wagner, Charles Peter, 1930-
What are we missing? [By] C. Peter Wagner. Carol Stream, Il., Creation House, 1978. 196p. "Formerly titled: Look out! The Pentecostals are coming." "Third printing." CAzPC

2451   Wagner, Charles Peter, 1930-
Why does revival come only to some? By C. Peter Wagner. In Christian Life, 34 (Dec. 1972), 28-29, 34, 38.

2452   Walker, Alan, 1911-
Where Pentecostalism is mushrooming. In Christian Century, 85 (Jan. 17, 1968), 81-82.

-- --ARGENTINA

2453   Miller, Elmer S.
Pentecostalism among the Argentine Toba. Pittsburgh, 1967. 283ℓ. Thesis (Ph.D.)--University of Pittsburgh. PPiU

2454   Miller, R. Edward
Thy God reigneth; the story of revival in Argentina, by R. Edward Miller. Santa Fe, Argentina, El Mensajero Evangélico, c1964. 32p.

2455   Miller, R. Edward
       Thy God reigneth; the story of revival in Argentina
       [by] R. Edward Miller. Burbank, Ca. , World Missionary
       Assistance Plan, 1968, c1964. 56p. "Fourth printing. "

2456   Reyburn, William David, 1922-
       The Toba Indians of the Argentina Chaco: an interpretive
       report. Elkhart, In. , Mennonite Board of Missions & Chari-
       ties, 1954. 84p. ViHarEM, WaU

2457   Stokes, Louie W.
       Historia del Movimiento Pentecostal en la Argentina [por]
       Louie W. Stokes. Buenos Aires, 1968. 67p.

2458   Wilson, Bryan Ronald, 1926-
       Magic and the millennium; a sociological study of reli-
       gious movements of protest among tribal and third-world peo-
       ples [by] Bryan R. Wilson. New York, Harper & Row, 1973.
       xi, 547p. "Pentecostalism reinterpreted": p. 121-123. DLC,
       RPB

                    -- --BOLIVIA

2459   Wagner, Charles Peter, 1930-
       The Protestant movement in Bolivia [by] C. Peter Wagner.
       South Pasadena, Calif. , William Carey Library, c1970. xxii,
       240p.

                    -- --BRAZIL

2460   Bonnevier, Jan
       Pingstvackelsen i Brasilien. In Svensk Missionstidskrift,
       59:1 (1971), 65-70.

2461   Carvalho, José Soares de, 1942-
       Nas selvas do Xingú. São Bernardo do Campo, Brazil,
       Imprensa Metodista, 1969 or 70. 73p. DLC

2462   Edwards, Fred E.
       The role of the faith mission; a Brazilian case study, by
       Fred E. Edwards. South Pasadena, Ca. , William Carey Li-
       brary, 1971. xxiii, 139p.

2463   Endruveit, Wilson Harle, 1937-
       Pentecostalism in Brazil: a historical and theological
       study of its characteristics, by Wilson H. Endruveit. Evan-
       ston, Il. , 1975. iv, 216ℓ . Thesis (Ph. D.)--Northwestern
       University. IEN

2464   Hoffnagel, Judith (Chambliss)
       Pentecostalism: a revolutionary or conservative move-
       ment? In Glazier, S. D. Perspectives on Pentecostalism:
       case studies from the Caribbean and Latin America. Wash-

ington, c1980, 111-123.

2465   Hollenweger, Walter Jacob, 1927-
        Enthusiastisches Christentum in Brasilien.   In Reformatio,
        13 (Aug. /Oct. 1964), 623-631.

2466   Hollenweger, Walter Jacob, 1927-
        Evangelism and Brazilian Pentecostals, by W. J. Hollen-
        weger. In Ecumenical Review, 20 (Apr. 1968), 163-170.

2466a   Howe, Gary Nigel
        Capitalism and religion at the periphery: Pentecostalism
        and Umbanda in Brazil. In Glazier, S. D.   Perspectives on
        Pentecostalism: case studies from the Caribbean and Latin
        America. Washington, c1980, 125-141.

2467   Kloppenburg, Boaventura
        O problema das seitas no contexto ecumênico.   In Re-
        vista Eclesiástica Brasileira, 33 (Dec. 1973), 928-941. In-
        cludes Pentecostal groups.

2468   Kostyu, Frank A.
        Will Brazil stay Christian? By Frank A. Kostyu. In
        Lamp, 68 (Mar. 1970), 14-19, 27-28.

2469   Leonard, Emile G. , 1891-
        O Protestantismo brasileiro; estudo de eclesiologia e
        história social.   Traducão do manuscrito original em francês
        por Linneu de Camargo Schützer. Sao Paulo, ASTE, 1963.
        354p. Also published in Revista de historia, 1951-52, nos.
        5-12. Includes Pentecostal groups. CtY-D, NjPT

2470   Mello, Manoel de, 1929-
        Participation is everything; evangelism from the point of
        view of a Brazilian Pentecostal. In International Review of
        Mission, 60 (Apr. 1971), 245-248.

2471   Meyer, Harding
        "Die Pfingstbewegung in Brasilien," die evangelische
        Diaspora. In Jahrbuch des Gustav-Adolf-Vereins, 39 (1968),
        9-50.

2472   Moura, Abdalaziz de
        O Pentecostalismo como fenomeno religioso popular no
        Brasil. In Revista Eclesiastica Brasileira, 31 (Mar. 1971),
        78-94; abridged (Pentecostalism and Brazilian religion) in
        Theology Digest, 20 (Spring 1972), 44-48.

2473   Pentecostals make marked gains in Brazil. In Christian
        Century, 88 (Jan. 6, 1971), 7.

2474   Read, William Richard, 1923-
        New patterns of church growth in Brazil, by William R.

Read. Grand Rapids, Mi., Eerdmans, 1965. 240p. (Church growth series.) On Pentecostal churches: p. 117-179. DLC, OkBetC

2475 Säwe, Willis
      Brasiliansk pingstvackelse. In Svensk Missionsridskrift, 59:1 (1971), 54-64.

2476 Törnberg, Allan, 1907-1956.
      Från Amazonas till La Plata; med svenska pingstmissionärer i Sydamerika. Stockholm, Forlaget Filadelfia, 1956. 135p. DLC

2477 Turner, Frederick Clair, 1938-
      Protestantism and politics in Chile and Brazil; review article, by Frederick C. Turner. In Comparative Studies in Society and History, 12 (Apr. 1970), 213-229.

2478 Willems, Emilio, 1905-
      Followers of the new faith; culture change and the rise of Protestantism in Brazil and Chile. Nashville, Vanderbilt University Press, 1967. x, 290p.

2479 Willems, Emilio, 1905-
      Validation of authority in Pentecostal sects of Chile and Brazil. In Journal for the Scientific Study of Religion, 6 (Fall 1967), 253-258.

2480 Yuasa, Key
      A study of the Pentecostal movement in Brazil: its importance. In Reformed and Presbyterian World, 29 (June 1966), 63-72.

(Bahia)

2481 Harper, Gordon Peacock
      The children of Hipólito; a study in Brazilian Pentecostalism [by] Gordon P. Harper. Cambridge, Mass., 1963. 94ℓ. Student paper--Harvard University. "Based on field work done in ... 1963 in Bahia, Brazil." MH

(Nova Iguacú)

2482 Cartaxo Rolim, Francisco
      Pentecostalismo. In Revista Eclesiástica Brasileira, 33 (Dec. 1973), 950-964. On the Diocese of Nova Iguacú.

(Recife)

2482a Hoffnagel, Judith (Chambliss)
      The believers: Pentecostalism in a Brazilian city. Bloomington, 1978. x, 285ℓ. Thesis (Ph. D.)--Indiana University. InU

(São Paulo)

2483   Souza, Beatriz Muniz de
        A experiência da salvacão pentacostais em São Paulo.
        São Paulo, Duas Cidades, 1969. 181p. (Colecao Religião
        e sociedade, 1.) DLC, MB

        -- --CHILE

2484   Chacón, Arturo
        The Pentecostal movement in Chile. In Student World,
        57:1 (1964), 85-88.

2485   Fernández Arlt, Augusto E.
        The significance of the Chilean Pentecostals' admission
        to the World Council of Churches [by] Augusto E. Fernández
        Arlt. In International Review of Missions, 51 (Oct. 1962),
        480-482.

2486   Hoover, Willis C. , -1936.
        Historia del avivamiento pentecostal en Chile [por] W. C.
        Hoover. Valparaiso, Impr. Excelsior, 1948. 128p. "Tra-
        ducido del ingles en 1909. " CtY-D, CPFT

2487   Hoover, Willis C. , -1936.
        Pentecost in Chile [by] W. C. Hoover. In World Domin-
        ion, 10 (Apr. 1932), 155-162.

2488   Housley, John B.
        Protestant failure in Chile [by] John B. Housley. In
        Christianity and Crisis, 26 (Oct. 31, 1966), 244-246; replies
        by Théo Tschuy, 26 (Dec. 12, 1966), 287; and James
        McCracken, 26 (Dec. 12, 1966), 287-288.

2489   Johnson, Norbert Edwin, 1925-
        The history, dynamic, and problems of the Pentecostal
        movement in Chile, by Norbert E. Johnson. Richmond,
        1970. 132ℓ . Thesis (Th. M.)--Union Theological Seminary.
        ViRUT

2490   Kessler, Jean Baptiste August, 1925-
        A study of the older Protestant missions and churches
        in Peru and Chile. With special reference to the problems
        of division, nationalism and native ministry, by J. B. A.
        Kessler. Goes, Oosterbaan & Le Cointre, 1967. xii, 372p.
        Thesis--Utrecht. DLC

2491   Lalive d'Epinay, Christian, 1938-
        Haven of the masses; a study of the Pentecostal Move-
        ment in Chile. Translated from the French ms. by Marjorie
        Sandle. London, Lutterworth Press, 1969. xxxiii, 263p.
        (World studies of churches in mission.) DLC, MH-AH

2492   Lalive d'Epinay, Christian, 1938-
        The Pentecostal "conquista" in Chile. In Ecumenical
Review, 20 (Jan. 1968), 16-32.

2493   Lalive d'Epinay, Christian, 1938-
        The Pentecostal "conquest" of Chile: rudiments of a
better understanding. In Cutler, D. R. , ed. The religious
situation: 1969. Boston, c1969, 179-194.

2494   Lalive d'Epinay, Christian, 1938-
        El refugio de las Masas; estudio sociolgoico del Protes-
tantismo chileno. Traduccion de Narciso Zamanillo. Santiago de Chile, Editorial del Pacifico, 1968. 287p. "Esta
obra se publica bajo los auspicios de la Comunidad Teólogica
Evangélica de Chile. " WU

2495   Lalive d'Epinay, Christian, 1938-
        O refugio dos massas; estudo sociológico do protestantismo
chileno. Traducão de Waldo A. Cesar. Rio de Janeiro, Paz
e Terra, 1970. 353p. (Estudos sobre o Brasil e a America
Latina, v. 14.) Translation of El refugio de las Massas.
WU

2496   Lalive d'Epinay, Christian, 1938-
        Training of pastors and theological education; the case of
Chile. In International Review of Missions, 56 (Apr. 1967),
185-192.

2497   Rajana, Eimi Watanabe
        A sociological study of new religious movements: Chilean
Pentecostalism and Japanese new religions. London, 1974.
288ℓ . Thesis (Ph. D.)--University of London.

2498   Tennekes, Johannes, 1936-
        Le mouvement pentecotiste chilean et la politique. In
Social Compass, 25:1 (1978), 55-80; comment by Christian
Lalive d'Epinay (Conformisme passif, conformisme actif et
solidarité de classe), 25:1 (1978), 81-84.

2499   Tennekes, Johannes, 1936-
        De Pinksterbeweging in Chili: een Uiting van Sociaal
Protest. In Sociologische Gids, 17 (Nov. /Dec. 1970), 480-
487.

2500   Tschuy, Théo
        Shock troops in Chile. In Christian Century, 77 (Sept.
28, 1960), 1118-1119; reply (Postscript on Chile [by] J.
Tremayne Copplestone.), 77 (Nov. 9, 1960), 1314.

2501   Turner, Frederick Clair, 1938-
        Protestantism and politics in Chile and Brazil; review
article, by Frederick C. Turner. In Comparative Studies in
Society and History, 12 (Apr. 1970), 213-229.

2502   Vergara, Ignacio
        El protestantismo en Chile.   Santiago de Chile, Editorial
        del Pacífico, 1962.   256p.   Includes Pentecostal churches.
        DLC

2503   Wagner, Charles Peter, 1930-
        The street "seminaries" of Chile [by] C. Peter Wagner.
        In Christianity Today, 15 (Aug. 6, 1971), 5-8.

2504   Willems, Emilio, 1905-
        Followers of the new faith; culture change and the rise
        of Protestantism in Brazil and Chile.   Nashville, Vanderbilt
        University Press, 1967.   x, 290p.

2505   Willems, Emilio, 1905-
        Validation of authority in Pentecostal sects of Chile and
        Brazil.   In Journal for the Scientific Study of Religion, 6
        (Fall 1967), 253-258.

                (Santiago)

2506   Synan, Harold Vinson, 1934-
        World's largest congregation: a cathedral in Chile [by]
        Vinson Synan.   In Christianity Today, 19 (Jan. 17, 1975),
        33-34.   On the dedication of the new "temple-cathedral" of
        the Jotabeche Church in Santiago, Chile.

2507   Walker, Alan, 1911-
        Where Pentecostalism is mushrooming.   In Christian
        Century, 85 (Jan. 17, 1968), 81-82.

                -- --COLOMBIA

2508   Flora, Cornelia (Butler), 1943-
        Mobilizing the masses; the sacred and the secular in
        Colombia.   Ithaca, N. Y. , 1970.   xiii, 285p.   (Cornell Uni-
        versity.   Latin American Studies Program.   Dissertation
        series, 25.)   Thesis (Ph. D.)--Cornell University.   MH, NIC

2509   Flora, Cornelia (Butler), 1943-
        Pentecostal women in Colombia; religious change and the
        status of working-class women [by] Cornelia B. Flora.   In
        Journal of Interamerican Studies, 17 (Nov. 1975), 411-425.

2509a   Flora, Cornelia (Butler), 1943-
        Pentecostalism and development: the Colombian case.
        In Glazier, S. D.   Perspectives on Pentecostalism: case
        studies from the Caribbean and Latin America.   Washington,
        c1980, 81-93.

2510   Flora, Cornelia (Butler), 1943-
        Pentecostalism in Colombia; baptism by fire and Spirit.
        Rutherford, N. J. , Fairleigh Dickinson University Press,

1976.   288p.   Based on thesis (Ph. D.)--Cornell University,
1970.   DLC

2511   Flora, Cornelia (Butler), 1943-
            Social dislocation and Pentecostalism; a multivariate
       analysis. In Sociological Analysis, 34 (Winter 1973), 296-
       304.

2512   Gerlach, Luther Paul, 1930-
            Five factors crucial to the growth and spread of a mod-
       ern religious movement [by] Luther P. Gerlach and Virginia
       H. Hine. In Journal for the Scientific Study of Religion, 7
       (Spring 1968), 23-40. Based in part on study of Pentecostal
       churches in Colombia.

2513   Palmer, Donald C. , 1934-
            Explosion of people evangelism, by Donald C. Palmer.
       Chicago, Moody Press, 1974. 191p. Based on thesis (M. A.)
       --Trinity Evangelical Divinity School. "An analysis of Pente-
       costal church growth in Colombia. " DLC, MSohG

2514   Palmer, Donald C. , 1934-
            The growth of the Pentecostal churches in Colombia, by
       Donald C. Palmer. Deerfield, Ill. , 1972. vi, 196ℓ . Thesis,
       (M. A.)--Trinity Evangelical Divinity School.

                    (César)

2514a Adamoli, Ambrosio
            La reclidad sagrada en una communidad pentecostal del
       César. Bogata, Comité de Publicaciones, Universidad de
       los Andes, 1973. 133p. (Cuadernos de anthropologia, 2.)
       Originally presented as the author's thesis (licenciado), Uni-
       versidad de los Andes, 1973. DLC

                    -- --PERU

2515   Kessler, Jean Baptiste August, 1925-
            A study of the older Protestant missions and churches
       in Peru and Chile. With special reference to the problems
       of division, nationalism and native ministry, by J. B. A.
       Kessler. Goes, Neth. , Oosterbaan & Le Cointre, 1967. xii,
       372p. Thesis--Utrecht. DLC

                    -- --VENEZUELA

2516   Rivera, Juan Marcos
            An experiment in sharing personnel: from historical
       church to Pentecostal movement. In International Review of
       Mission, 62 (Oct. 1973), 446-456.

                    --ASIA

2517   Orr, James Edwin, 1912-
        Evangelical awakenings in Eastern Asia [by] J. Edwin
        Orr. Minneapolis, Bethany Fellowship, 1975. x, 180p. In-
        cludes Pentecostal churches. DLC

                -- --AFGHANISTAN

2518   Daoud, Mounir Aziz
        The shooting frontier: revival, by M. A. Daoud. Dallas,
        Voice of Miracles and Missions, 1960. 36p.

                -- --CHINA

2519   Baker, H. A.
        God in Ka Do land, by H. A. Baker. Yunnanfu, Adullan
        Mission, 19--. 95p. ICU

2520   Baker, H. A.
        God in Ka Do land, by H. A. Baker. Mokiang, Yunnan,
        Ch. , Adullan Reading Campaign, 1937. 118p. CtY

2521   Baker, H. A.
        God in Ka Do land, by H. A. Baker. 3d ed. n. p. ,
        195-. 184p. CLamB

2522   Baker, H. A.
        Visiones mas alla del velo. Callaom Peru, W. L. Hunter,
        1952. 120p. Translation of Visions beyond the veil.

2523   Baker, H. A.
        Visions beyond the veil, by H. A. Baker. Minneapolis,
        Osterhus Publishing House, 19--. 122p. CLamB

2524   Baker, H. A.
        Visions beyond the veil, by H. A. Baker. Monroeville,
        Pa. , Whitaker Books, 1973. 144p. DLC

                -- --HONG KONG

2525   The "Tongue" movement.
        In Independent, 66 (June 10, 1909), 1286-1289. By an
        unnamed contributor in Hong Kong.

                -- --INDIA

2526   Abrams, Minnie F.
        The baptism of the Holy Spirit at Mukti, by Minnie Abrams.
        In Missionary Review of the World, n. s. 19 (Aug. 1906), 619-
        620. Reprinted from the Indian Witness, Apr. 26, 1906.

2527   Barratt, Thomas Ball, 1862-1940.
        Sussie's homegoing. Madras, Printed at the Lawrence
        Asylum Press, 1908. 22p. NN

2528   Culpepper, Richard Weston
        The travail of India, by R. W. Culpepper.   Dallas,
        19--.   66p.

2529   Engbretsen, Rolf
        India og misjonen idag; inspeksjonsreise i India.   Oslo,
        Filadelfiaforlaget, 1952.   1v. (unpaged) DLC

2530   Franklin, A. P.
        Bhilmissionen.   Ny tillökad uppl.   Rockford, Ill. , För-
        fattarens Förlag, 1918.   137p.   MnHi

2531   Kim, Taek-Yong
        A socio-historic study of the development of the charis-
        matic movement in India.   Washington, 1973.   1v. (paging
        not determined)   Project (D. Min.)--Howard University.

2532   Wead, Douglas, 1946-
        The compassionate touch.   Carol Stream, Ill. , Creation
        House, c1977.   163p.   DLC

        -- --KOREA

2533   Choi, Ja Shil.
        Korean miracles.   La Canada, Ca. , Mountain Press,
        197-.   xii, 108p.   MnMNC

        (Seoul)

2534   The Spirit in Asia.
        In Time, 102 (Oct. 8, 1973), 102.

        -- --PHILIPPINES

2535   Sturgeon, Inez
        Give me this mountain.   Oakland, Calif. , Hunter Adver-
        tising Co. , 1960.   175p.   OkTOr

        (Manila)

2536   Sumrall, Lester Frank, 1913-
        Modern Manila miracles.   Springfield, Mo. , C. O.
        Erickson, 1954.   110p.

        -- --SIBERIA

2537   Pollock, John Charles
        The Siberian seven, by John Pollock.   London, Hodder
        and Stoughton, 1979.   252p.   DLC

        -- --TAIWAN

2538   Bolton, Robert Joseph, 1929-

Treasure island: church growth among Taiwan's urban
Minnan Chinese. Pasadena, Calif., 1974. xvii, 389ℓ. Thesis (M. A.)--Fuller Theological Seminary. Includes Pentecostals. CPFT

--EUROPE

2539   Durasoff, Steve
        Pentecost behind the Iron Curtain. Plainfield, N. J.,
        Logos International, 1972. x, 128p. DLC, IEG

2540   Handspicker, Meredith B.
        An ecumenical exercise: the Southern Baptist Convention,
        the Seventh Day Adventist Church, the Kimbanguist Church
        in the Congo, the Pentecostal movement in Europe. Edited
        by M. B. Handspicker and Lukas Vischer. Geneva, World
        Council of Churches, 1967. 46p. (Faith and order paper,
        49.) MBU-T, OkEG

2541   Hollenweger, Walter Jacob, 1927-
        "Touching" and "thinking" the Spirit: some aspects of
        European charismatics [by] Walter J. Hollenweger. In Spit-
        tler, R. P., ed. Perspectives on the new Pentecostalism.
        Grand Rapids, Mich., 1976, 44-56.

2542   The Pentecostal movement in Europe. In Ecumenical Review,
        19 (Jan. 1967), 37-47. Ecumenical exercise.

        -- --BELGIUM

2543   Hollenweger, Walter Jacob, 1927-
        Literatur von und über die Pfingstbewegung (Weltkonferen-
        zen, Holland, Belgien), von Walter J. Hollenweger. In Neder-
        lands Theologisch Tijdschrift, 18 (Apr. 1964), 289-306.

2544   Sundstedt, Arthur
        Med Nordexpressen till Belgien. Stockholm, Förlaget Fila-
        delfia, 1947. 111p. DLC

        -- --BULGARIA

2545   Durasoff, Steve
        Pentecost behind the Iron Curtain. Plainfield, N. J.,
        Logos International, 1972. x, 128p. "Bulgarian burden-
        bearers": p. 89-99. DLC, IEG

2546   Homan, Roger
        Pentecostal youth organizations and the Bulgarian kom-
        somol. In Comparative Education, 13 (Oct. 1977), 243-248.

        -- --CZECHOSLOVAKIA

2547 Durasoff, Steve
      Pentecost behind the Iron Curtain.   Plainfield, N. J.,
      Logos International, 1972.   x, 128p.   "Czechoslovakia--gearing
      for growth": 111-117.   DLC, IEG

                  -- --DENMARK

2548 Prince, Lydia (Christensen), 1890-
      Appointment in Jerusalem, by Lydia Prince, as told to
      her husband Derek Prince.   Chappaqua, N. Y., Chosen Books;
      distributed by F. H. Revell Co., Old Tappan, N. J., 1975.
      189p.   Includes comment on Pentecostal churches in Denmark
      in the 1920s.

2549 Prince, Lydia (Christensen), 1890-
      Appointment in Jerusalem, by Lydia Prince, as told to
      her husband Derek Prince.   Eastbourne, Sussex, Victory
      Press, 1976.   189p.   Includes comment on Pentecostal
      churches in Denmark in the 1920s.

                  -- --ESTONIA

2550 Gobert, Maria
      Bland ryska ortodoxa; mia upplevelser som evangelist i
      Estlands ryska distrikt.   Stockholm, Förlaget Filadelfia, 1946.
      112p.   DLC

                  -- --FINLAND

2551 Holm, Nils G., 1943-
      Pingströrelsen: en religionsvetenskaplig studie av ping-
      strörelsen i Svensfinland, av Nils G. Holm.   Åbo, Stifteisens
      för Abo adademi forskningsinstitut, 1978.   228p.   (Meddeian-
      dern fran Stifeisens för Åbo akademi forskningsinstitut, 31.)
      DLC

2552 Holm, Nils G., 1943-
      Pingströrelsen i Svenskfinland, 1908-1935.   Från overkon-
      fessionell pingstväckelse till autonom pingströrelse.   Åbo,
      1970.   133p.   (Kyrkohistoriska arkivet vid Åbo akademi, med-
      delander nr 1.)   MH-AH

2553 Holm, Nils G., 1943-
      Tungotal och andedop: en religionspsykologisk under-
      sökning av glossolali hos finlandssvenska pingstvänner [av]
      Nils G. Holm.   Uppsala, Univ.; Stockholm, Almqvist & Wik-
      sell International, distr., 1976.   255p.   (Psychologia reli-
      gionum, 5)   (Acta Universitatis Upsallensis.)   Thesis--Uppsala.
      DLC

2554 Schmidt, Wolfgang Amadeus, 1904-
      Die Pfingstbewegung in Finnland.   Helsingfors, 1935.
      256p.   (Suomen Kirkkohistoriallisen Seuran toimituksia, no.
      27.)   L, MH-AH

(Helsinki)

2555 Seila, Taito
Mitä todella tapahtui. Helsinki, Ristin Sanoma, 1970.
91p. DLC

-- --FRANCE

2556 Säwe, Willis
När Frankrike besegrades; intryck Fran Kampen Samman-
brottet och ockupationen. Stockholm, Filadelfia, 1942. 157p.
MH, NN, WaE

2556a Stotts, George Raymond, 1929-
The history of the modern Pentecostal movement in
France. Lubbock, 1973. ix, 340ℓ. Thesis (Ph.D.)--Texas
Tech University. TxLT

-- --GERMANY

2557 Dallmeyer, Heinrich
Die Zungenbewegung: ein Beitrag zu ihrer Geschichte
und eine Kennzeichnung ihres Geistes. Lindhorst, Adastra-
Verlag, 1924. 143p. MH-AH

2558 Durasoff, Steve
Pentecost behind the Iron Curtain. Plainfield, N.J.,
Logos International, 1972. x, 128p. "East Germany":
p. 123-124. DLC, IEG

2559 Eicken, Erich von
Heiliger Geist--Menschengeist--Schwarmgeist; ein Beitrag
zur Geschichte der Pfingstbewegung in Deutschland. Wupper-
tal, R. Brockhaus, 1964. 92p. MCW

2560 Fleisch, Paul, 1878-
Die Pfingstbewegung in Deutschland; ihr Wesen und ihre
Geschichte in funfzig Jahren. Hannover, Heinr. Feesche
Verlag, c1957. 399p. (Die moderne Gemeinschaftsbewegung
in Deutschland, II:2.) PPWe

2561 Krust, Christian Hugo
50 Jahre Deutsche Pfingstbewegung; Mülheimer Richtung,
nach ihrem geschichtlichen Ablauf dargestellt. Altdorf bei
Nürnberg, Missionsbuchhandlung und Verlag, 1958. 253p.
PPWe, PPULC

(Kassel)

2562 Kampmeier, A.
Recent parallels to the miracle of Pentecost, by A. Kampmeier. In Open Court, 22 (Aug. 1908), 492-498.

(Leonberg)

2563   Philadelphia-Verein e. V.
        20 [Zwanzigste] Philadelphia-Konferenz in Leonberg vom
        26. Juli bis 1. August 1965. Konferenz-Reden. Leonberg/
        Württ, Philadelphia-Verlag, 1965. 239p. DLC, IEG

        -- --GREAT BRITAIN

2564   Gee, Donald, 1891-1966.
        The Pentecostal movement: a short history and an inter-
        pretation for British readers. London, Victory Press, 1941.
        vii, 199p. L

2565   Gee, Donald, 1891-1966.
        The Pentecostal movement; including the story of the war
        years (1940-1947). Rev. and enl. ed. London, Elim Publish-
        ing Co., 1949. vii, 236p. KyLxCB, NcD, NjPT, TxU, TxWaS

2566   Gee, Donald, 1891-1966.
        Wind and flame; incorporating the former book The Pente-
        costal movement, with additional chapters. London, Assem-
        blies of God Publishing House, 1967. 317p. TxWB

2567   Hill, Clifford S., 1927-
        Black churches: West Indian & African sects in Britain,
        by Clifford Hill. London, British Council of Churches, Com-
        munity and Race Relations Unit, 1971. 23p. (Its Booklets,
        1.)

2568   Hill, Clifford S., 1927-
        From church to sect; West Indian religious sect develop-
        ment in Britain [by] Clifford Hill. In Journal for the Scien-
        tific Study of Religion, 10 (Summer 1971), 114-123.

2569   Hill, Clifford S., 1927-
        Immigrant sect development in Britain; a case study of
        status deprivation? [By] Clifford Hill. In Social Compass,
        18:2 (1971), 231-236.

2570   Pearson, David G.
        Race, religiosity and political activism: some observa-
        tions on West Indian participation in Britain. In British
        Journal of Sociology, 29 (Sept. 1978), 340-357.

2571   Warburton, Thomas Rennie, 1937-
        A comparative study of minority religious groups, with
        special reference to Holiness and related movements in Bri-
        tain in the last 50 years. London, 1966. 1v. (paging not
        determined) Thesis (Ph. D.)--London School of Economics.
        LE

        -- --ENGLAND

2572   Calley, Malcolm John Chalmers
        God's people; West Indian Pentecostal sects in England,
        by Malcolm J. C. Calley. London, New York, Oxford Uni-
        versity Press, 1965. xiv, 182p. "Issued under the auspices
        of the Institute of Race Relations, London." DLC

2573   Calley, Malcolm John Chalmers
        Pentecostal sects among West Indian migrants [by] Mal-
        colm J. C. Calley. In Race, 3 (May 1962), 55-64.

2574   Kiev, Ari, 1933-
        Psychotherapeutic aspects of Pentecostal sects among
        West Indian immigrants to England. In British Journal of
        Sociology, 15 (June 1964), 129-138.

2575   Lewis, Myrddin
        Are we missing something? In Christian Life, 26 (Jan.
        1965), 44-45, 83, 85.

2576   Ottosson, Krister
        The Pentecostal churches. Exeter, Devon., Religious
        Education Press, 1977. 55p. (Christian denominations
        series.) OkEG

2577   Pearson, David G.
        West Indians in Easton: a study of their social organiza-
        tion with particular reference to participation in formal and
        informal associations. Leicester, 1975. 1v. (paging not
        determined) Thesis (Ph.D.)--Leicester University.

2577a   Root, John
        Encountering West Indian Pentecostalism: its ministry
        and worship. Bramcote, Grove Books, 1979. 24p. (Grove
        booklet on ministry and worship, 66.)

2578   Walker, Andrew G.
        An Easter Pentecostal convention: the successful manage-
        ment of a "time of blessing" [by] Andrew G. Walker and James
        S. Atherton. In Sociological Review, ns 19 (Aug. 1971), 367-
        387.

            (London)

2579   Hill, Clifford S., 1927-
        West Indian migrants and the London churches [by] Clif-
        ford S. Hill. London, New York, Oxford University Press,
        1963. 89p. "Issued under the auspices of the Institute of
        Race Relations, London." "Pentecostals": p. 72-74.

            (Sunderland)

2580   Boddy, Alexander Alfred, 1854-1930.
        "Pentecost" at Sunderland; a vicar's testimony [by] A. A.

Boddy. Sunderland, Durham, Secretaries, 1908. 20p. "4th reprint (with additions)."

-- --SCOTLAND

2581   Allen, Gillian
       Pentecostalists as a medical minority [by] Gillian Allen
       and Roy Wallis. In Wallis, R., ed. Marginal medicine.
       New York, c1976, 110-137. Based on study of a small Scot-
       tish congregation.

-- --HUNGARY

2582   Durasoff, Steve
       Pentecost behind the Iron Curtain. Plainfield, N.J.,
       Logos International, 1972. x, 128p. "Hungary and East
       Germany--quiet progress": p. 119-124. DLC, IEG

-- --ICELAND

2583   Ericson, Eric, 1899-1959.
       Från Jökelön med de varma källorna; erfarenheter från
       det andliga arbetet på Island. Stockholm, Förlaget Filadelfia,
       1946. 183p. DLC

-- --ITALY

2584   Fiorentino, Joseph, 1912-
       In the power of His Spirit: "a summary of the Italian
       Pentecostal movement in the U.S.A. and abroad." Niagara
       Falls, N.Y., Christian Church of North America; distributed
       by Niagara Religious Supply Center, 1968. 17p. "The Pente-
       costal revival in Italy": p. 14-17.

2585   Hedlund, Roger E.
       Why Pentecostal churches are growing faster in Italy [by]
       Roger E. Hedlund. In Evangelical Missions Quarterly, 8
       (Spring 1972), 129-136.

2586   Peyrot, Giorgio
       La circolare Buffarini-Guidi e i pentecostali. Roma, As-
       sociazione italiana per libertà della cultura, 1955. 62p. (As-
       sociazione italiana per la libertà della cultura. Opuscoli, 26.
       Serie: Attuare la Costituzione.) DLC

2587   Spadafora, Francesco, 1869-
       Pentecostali e testimoni di Geova. 3. ed. Rovigo, Ist.
       padano di arti grafiche, 1968. 298p. DLC, MB

-- --NETHERLANDS

2588   Boerwinkel, Feitse, 1906-
       De Pinkstergroepen. Den Haag, Plein, 1963. 15p.
       (Oekumenische Leergang, 5.)

2589   Broderschap van Pinkstergemeenten in Nederland.
       De Pinkstergemeente en de Kerk. De Broederschap van
Pinkstergemeenten in Nederland geeft antwoord op het Herderlijk schrijven van de Generale Synode der Nederlandse Hervormde Kerk over: De Kerk en de Pinkstergroepen.
Rotter-
dam, Stichting Volle Evangelie Lectuur, 1962. 21p.

2590   Endedijk, H. C.
       Het werk van de Heilige Geest in de gemeente. Voor-
lichtend geschrift over de Pinkstergroepen, uitg. in opdracht
van de Generale Synode van de Gereformeerde Kerken. [Door
H. C. Endedijk, A. G. Kornet en G. Y. Vellenga] Kampen,
J. H. Kok, 1968. 80p. DLC, MH-AH

2591   Hollenweger, Walter Jacob, 1927-
       Literatur von und über die Pfingstbewegung (Weltkonferen-
zen, Holland, Belgien), von Walter J. Hollenweger. In Neder-
lands Theologisch Tijdschrift, 18 (Apr. 1964), 289-306.

2592   Nederlandse Hervormde Kerk. Generale Synode.
       De Kerk en de Pinkstergroepen; herderlijk schrijven van
de Generale Synode der Nederlandse Hervormde Kerk. 's-
Gravenhage, Boekencentrum, 1960. 79p. MH-AH

2593   Stilma, Lize
       Strohalm of staf. Wat bewegt de gebedsgenezer [door]
Lize Stilma, A. Klamer [en] M. Zeegers. Apeldoorn, Semper
Agendo, 1972. 93p. (Tijd-boek.) DLC, MH-AH

2594   Vellenga, G. Y.
       Stromen van kracht, de nieuwe opwekkingsbeweging, door
G. Y. Vellenga en A. J. Kret. Kampen, J. H. Kok, 1957.
91p. DLC

2595   Wumkes, G. A.
       De Pinksterbeweging voornamelijk in Nederland. Amster-
dam, G. R. Polman, 1917. 23p.

-- --NORWAY

2596   Bloch-Hoell, Nils, 1915-
       The Pentecostal movement: its origin, development, and
distinctive character. Oslo, Universitetforlaget, c1964. 255p.
(Scandinavian university books.) Label on t. p.: Humanities
Press, New York. Revised translation of Pinsebevegelsen.
DLC, MCE, TxWaS

2597   Bloch-Hoell, Nils, 1915-
       The Pentecostal movement: its origin, development, and
distinctive character. London, Allen & Unwin, c1964. 255p.
Revised translation of Pinsebevegelsen.

2598   Bloch-Hoell, Nils, 1915-

Pinsebevegelsen; en undersøkelse av pinsebevegelsens til-
blivelse, utvikling og saerpreg med saerlig henblikk på be-
vegelsens utforming i Norge.   Oslo, Universitetsforlaget,
1956.   viii, 458p.   (Norges almenvitenskapelige forskningsråd.
Gruppe: Språk og historie, A587, 1.) Summary in English.
DLC, MH

2599   Eritsland, Lars
       Sva er sunn charismatisk vekkelse?   Oslo, Lutherstiftel-
       sen, Credo, 1971.   22p.   DLC

2600   Ski, Martin, 1912-
       Fram til urkristendommen; Pinsevekkelsen gjennom 50 år.
       Redaksjon: E. Strand, E. Strøm, M. Ski.   Skrevet av M.
       Ski.   Oslo, Filadelfiaforlaget, 1955-1957.   2v.   MH

2601   Ski, Martin, 1912- , ed.
       Norges fem krigsår; upplevda av pingstvänner och pingst-
       församlingar.   Minnen och intryck.   Stockholm, Norske pinse-
       venners gjenreisningskomité for Finnmark i distribution genom
       Förlaget Filadelfia, 1945.   151p.   MH

2602   Söderberg, Gustav
       Sex år norr om Poleirkeln, pionjarminnen från Nord-
       Norge.   Stockholm, Filadelfia, 1947.   174p.   DLC

       -- --POLAND

2603   Durasoff, Steve
       Pentecost behind the Iron Curtain.   Plainfield, N. J. ,
       Logos International, 1972.   x, 128p.   "Poland--preparing for
       Pentecost": p. 75-87.   DLC, IEG

       -- --ROMANIA

2604   Durasoff, Steve
       Pentecost behind the Iron Curtain.   Plainfield, N. J. ,
       Logos International, 1972.   x, 128p.   "Romania's perpetual
       revival": p. 65-73.   DLC, IEG

       -- --RUSSIA

2605   Durasoff, Steve
       The All-Union Council of Evangelical Christians-Baptists
       in the Soviet Union: 1944-1964.   New York, 1968.   361ℓ.
       Thesis (Ph. D.)--New York University.   NNU

2606   Durasoff, Steve
       Pentecost behind the Iron Curtain.   Plainfield, N. J. ,
       Logos International, 1972.   x, 128p.   DLC, IEG

2607   Durasoff, Steve
       The Russian Protestants: evangelicals in the Soviet Union,

1944-1964. Rutherford, N.J., Fairleigh Dickinson University
Press, 1969. 312p. Based on thesis (Ph.D.)--New York
University. DLC, TxWaS

2608 Fletcher, William C.
American influence on Russian religion: the case of the
Pentecostals, by William C. Fletcher. In Journal of Church
and State, 20 (Spring 1978), 215-232.

2608a Fritz, Esther
New hope for the Siberian seven. In Christian Century,
97 (Nov. 5, 1980), 1064-1066.

2609 Gardner, D. Joseph
The Russian evangelical church, by D. Joseph Gardner.
Wollaston, Ma., 1972. ix, 175ℓ. Thesis (M.A.)--Eastern
Nazarene College. On Pentecostalism: ℓ. 45-47, 98-105.
MWollE

2610 Grazhdan, Valeriĭ Dmitrievich
Kto takie piatidesiatniki. Alma-Ata, Kazakhstan, 1965.
110p. DLC

2611 Klibanov, Aleksandr Il'ich
In the world of religious sectarianism: at a meeting of
Prygun Molokans [by] A. I. Klibanov. In Soviet Review, 16
(Summer 1975), 11-24.

2612 Klibanov, Alexsandr Il'ich
Istoriia religloznogo sektanstva v Rossii, 60-e godi xix
v.-1917 r. Moskva, Nauka, 1965. 345p. At head of title:
Akademīia Nauk S.S.S.R. Institut istorii. A. I. Klibanov.
Includes Pentecostal groups. DLC

2613 Kol'tŝov, Nikolaĭ Vasil'evich
Kto takie piatidesiatniki; otvety na voprosy. Moskva,
Znanie, 1965. 435p. (V pomoshch' lektoru.) DLC

2614 Mĩachin, Fedor Nikolaevich
Moi razryv s sektantami-triasunami; rasskaz byvshego
propovednika. Vladivostok, Primorskoye knizhnoye izd-vo,
1958. 57p. DLC

2615 Moskalenko, Alekseĭ Trofimovich
Piatidesiatniki. Moskva, Izd-vo polit. lit-ry, 1966. 223p.
(Biblioteka "Sovremennye religii.") At head of title: A. T.
Moskalenko. DLC

2616 Moskalenko, Alekseĭ Trofimovich
Pĩatidesĩatniki. Izd. 2-e. Moskva, Politizdat, 1973.
199p. (Biblioteka "Sovremennye religii.") At head of title:
A. T. Moskalenko. DLC, NN

2617   Musatova, V. M.
        V mire koshmara; dokumental'nyi fotoocherk o sektantakh-
        piatidesiatnikakh.   V. M. Musatova i V. P. Troshkin.   Khu-
        dozhnik A. F. Kokhov.   Moskva, Gospolitizdat, 1962.   [36]p.
        DLC

2618   Pentecostals appeal.
        In Religion in Communist Lands, 2 (May/June 1974), 25-
        26.   Appeal of Pentecostals in Nakhodka and Chernogorsk to
        emigrate.

2619   Pollock, John Charles
        The Siberian seven, by John Pollock.   London, Hodder
        and Stoughton, 1979.   252p.   DLC

2620   Pollock, John Charles
        The Siberian seven [by] John Pollock.   Waco, Tx. , Word
        Books, c1980.   267p.   DLC

2621   Rowe, Michael
        Pentecostal documents from the USSR.   In Religion in
        Communist Lands, 3 (Jan. /June 1975), 16-18; documents
        (Harassment of Pentecostals), 25-28, and (Arrest of Ivan
        Fedotov), 29-30.

2622   Rowe, Michael
        Soviet Pentecostals: movement for emigration.   In Reli-
        gion in Communist Lands, 5 (Autumn, 1977), 170-174; docu-
        ments and biographies, 5 (Autumn 1977), 174-179.

2623   Soldatenko, Vladimir Emel'ianovich
        Pi͡atides͡i͡atniki.   Donetsk, "Donbas, " 1972.   67p.   At
        head of title: V. E. Soldatenko.   DLC

2624   Verkholomov, Mykola Semenovych
        Chomu i͡a porvav z religii͡ei͡u.   Kiïv, Derkh. vid-vo polit.
        lit-ri ChRSR, 1960.   25p.   DLC

2625   Voevodin, I.
        During the trial intermission.   In Wurmbrand, R. , ed.
        The Soviet saints.   London, 1968,   77-80.   From Komsomol-
        skaia Pravda, Sept. 25, 1962.

2626   Voevodin, I.
        During the trial intermission.   In Wurmbrand, R. , ed.
        Underground saints.   Plainfield, N.J., 1969.   From Kom-
        somolskaia Pravda, Sept. 25, 1962.

2627   Waiting for the promised land.
        In Economist, 268 (July 29, 1978), 43.

                (Moscow)

2628   Guzanov, Vitalii Grigorévich
       Izuvery; iz zapisnol knizhki zhurnalista.   Moskva, Znanie,
       1962.   87p.   (Prochti tovarishch.)   DLC

2629   Heaven help the Moscow seven.
       In Economist, 270 (Jan. 20, 1979), 46.

2630   Moscow pray-in.
       In Time, 113 (Apr. 23, 1979), 44.   On Pentecostalists
       seeking to emigrate from the Soviet Union.

       -- --SWEDEN

2631   Alenius, Gottfried
       Bland katornas folk; minnen och intryck från missionsresor
       i låpplandska fjalltrakter.   Stockholm, Förlaget Filadelfia,
       1946.   142p.   DLC

2632   Andreén, Birger, 1908-
       Gyllne stad med parleportar.   Orebro, Evangeliipress,
       1968.   93p.   DLC

2633   Björkquist, Curt
       Den svenska pingstväckelsen.   Stockholm, Förlaget Fila-
       delfia, 1959.   121p.   DLC, MH

2634   Blomquist, Axel, ed.
       Svenska pingstväckelsen femtio år, en krönika i ord och
       bild.   Stockholm, Forlaget Filadelfia, 1957.   295p.   CtY, NN

2635   Carlén, Erik, 1906-
       Gud behover inga kryckor.   Hallabrottet, Författaren,
       1966.   48p.   DLC

2635a Carlsson, Bertil
       Organizations and decision procedures with the Swedish
       Pentecostal movement.   [Härnösand, 1974] 131p.   Cover title.
       Translation of Organisationer och Beslutsprocesser inom
       Pingströrelsen, the author's thesis at the University of Stock-
       holm.   MoSpA

2636   Forsberg, Carl, 1899-
       Okänd soldat.   Örebro, Evangeliipress, 1969.   208p.
       DLC

2637   Lidman, Sam, 1921-
       Vildaasnor och paadrivare; en arbetsbok.   Stockholm,
       Almqvist & Wiksell, c1968.   260p.   Sub-title on cover:
       Beraettelser om Sven Lidman och Lewi Pehtrus.   MH-AH

2638   Lidman, Sven, 1882-1960.
       Resan till domen.   3. uppl.   Stockholm, Natur och kultur,
       1949.   210p.   NcU, NNUT, WaU

2639 Linderholm, Emanuel, 1872-1937.
Pingströrelsen i Sverige. Ekstas, under och apokalyptik
i nutida Svensk folkreligiositet. Stockholm, A. Bonnier, 1925.
351p. MH-AH, NN

2640 Pethrus, Lewi, 1884-1974.
Den anständiga sanningen; en början på historien om vallpojken som blev herde. Stockholm, C. E. Fritzes bokförlag,
1953. 296p. DLC, MnU, NN, WaE

2641 Pethrus, Lewi, 1884-1974.
Ett sagolikt liv: memoarer. Stockholm, Bonnier, 1976.
232p. DLC

2642 Pethrus, Lewi, 1884-1974.
Hänryckningens tid; vallpojken som herde. Stockholm,
C. E. Fritze, 1954. 297p. MnU, NN, WaE

2643 Pethrus, Lewi, 1884-1974.
Hos Herren är makten. Herren är min herde. Stockholm, C. E. Fritzes bokförlag, 1955. 302p. MnU, WaE

2644 Pethrus, Lewi, 1884-1974.
Lewi Pethrus som ledarskribent; ett urval ledante artiklar
ur Dagens tio forsta årgångar, sammanstallt av Dagens redak-
tion. Stockholm, Förlaget Filadelfia, 1954. 383p. DLC,
MnU, NN

2645 Pethrus, Lewi, 1884-1974.
Medan du stjärnorna räknar; vallpojken och Vår Herre.
Stockholm, C. E. Fritzes bokförlag, 1953. 294p. Sequel to
Den anständiga sanningen. DLC, MnU, NN, WaE

2646 Pethrus, Lewi, 1884-1974.
En såningsman gick ut; eftertankar och utblickar. Stockholm, C. E. Fritzes bokförlag, 1956. 166p. MnU

2647 Söderholm, Gustav Emil, 1871-1943.
Den svenska pingstväckelsens historia, 1907-33, av G. E.
Söderholm. Stockholm, Filadelfia, 1929-1933.

2648 Stafberger, Ellis, 1900-
Dagar mörka och ijusa: en pingstväns memoarer. Stockholm, Gummesson, 1978. 139p. DLC

2649 Sundstedt, Arthur
Pingstväckelsen. Stockholm, Norman; Solna, Seelig, 1969-
1973. 5v. Title from spine. DLC

2650 Svanell, Elon, 1930-
För facklan vidare. Av Elon Svanell, Olof Djurfeldt,
Samuel Halldorf [och] Sven Ahdrian. Stockholm, Filadelfia
[Seelig] 1967. 109p. DLC

2651   Tägt, Nils, 1913-
        Vi tror på den Helige ande. Stockholm, Gummesson
        [Solna, Seelig] 1971. 164p. DLC

2652   Wiström, Rolf
        Från skolkatedern till pingstestraden. Stockholm, För-
        laget Filadelfia, 1956. 134p. DLC

2653   Zettersten, Birger, 1887-1957.
        Allt av nåd; minnen och upplevelser sammanställda av
        Paul Zettersten. Med avslutande bidrag av Lisa Zettersten,
        Anna Nyquist [och] Pef Zettersten. Stockholm, Filadelfia,
        1958. 120p.

        (Katrineholm)

2654   Katrineholm. Filadelfiaforsämlingen.
        Jubileumsskrift, 1916-1966. Katrineholm, 1966. 49p.
        DLC

        (Stockholm)

2655   Holmberg, Adrian, 1894-
        Utstött. Minnen från Söders slum och Pethrus' estrader.
        Stockholm, Bok o. bild (Seelig), 1966. 239p. DLC

2656   Söderholm, Hilding, 1903-
        Filadelfiaförsamlingen i Stockholm: 50 aar, 1910-1960.
        Stockholm, Förlaget Filadelfia, 1960. 39p. MH-AH

        -- --SWITZERLAND

2657   Eggenberger, Oswald, 1923-
        Evangelischer Glaube und Pfingstbewegung, mit besonderer
        Beruecksichtigung der Verhaeltnisse in der Schweiz. Zollikon,
        Evangelischer Verlag, 1956. 61p. (Schriftenreihe zur Sekten-
        kunde, 1.) MH-AH

        -- --YUGOSLAVIA

2658   Durasoff, Steve
        Pentecost behind the Iron Curtain. Plainfield, N. J.,
        Logos International, 1972. x, 128p. "Yugoslavia--abundant
        opportunities": p. 101-109. DLC, IEG

        --OCEANIA

        -- --AUSTRALIA

2659   Calley, Malcolm John Chalmers
        Aboriginal Pentecostalism; a study of changes in religion,
        North Coast, N.S.W., by Malcolm J. C. Calley. Sydney,

1955. 1v. (various pagings)

2660   Chant, Barry, 1938-
       Heart of fire: the story of Australian Pentecostalism.
       Fullarton, S. Austl. , 212p. DLC, KyWAT, NNUT

2661   Duncan, Philip B.
       Pentecost in Australia, by Philip B. Duncan,   n. p.,
       19--. 93p.

2662   Enticknap, C. G.
       Pentecost in Australia and New Zealand.   In Atter, G. F.
       The third force.   Peterborough, Ont. , c1962, 114-116.

2663   Travail of the healer.
       In Newsweek, 47 (Mar. 19, 1956), 82.   On trouble in
       Oral Roberts' meetings in Australia.

                   -- --NEW ZEALAND

2664   Enticknap, C. G.
       Pentecost in Australia and New Zealand.   In Atter, G. F.
       The third force.   Peterborough, Ont. , c1962, 114-116.

2665   Waldegrave, Charles
       Social and personality correlates of Pentecostalism: a
       review of the literature and a comparison of Pentecostal
       Christian students with non-Pentecostal Christian students.
       Hamilton, N. Z. , 1972. 1v. (paging not determined) Thesis
       (Ph. D.)--University of Waikato.

2666   Worsfold, James Evans
       A history of the charismatic movements in New Zealand;
       including a Pentecostal perspective and a breviate of the
       Catholic Apostolic Church in Great Britain, by J. E. Wors-
       fold. Bradford, Yorks. , Julian Literature Trust, c1974.   xx,
       368p. DLC

PART II: DOCTRINAL TRADITIONS

Section A:

WESLEYAN-ARMINIAN TRADITION

In the background of charismatic manifestations that appeared
in various parts of Protestant Christendom in the first decade of the
twentieth century lay two great nineteenth-century movements for the
deepening of the Christian life. The first of these, the Holiness
movement, sprang from American Methodist sources, and took tang-
ible form in 1867 in the National Camp Meeting Association for the
Promotion of Holiness. It taught that sanctification, which began in
repentance for sins at conversion, might be made complete in a second crisis experience following total personal consecration. This experience, known variously as "perfect love," "entire sanctification,"
"personal holiness," and "the baptism of the Holy Spirit," was held
to be that for which Christ prayed for His disciples in His high-
priestly prayer recorded in John 17. It was believed that the entirely sanctified Christian enjoyed release from the natural "bent
toward sinning," since the carnal nature was eradicated and since
through grace he was free to love God perfectly. In Methodist Holiness terms the key result was purity of heart. In the last decades
of the century, National Camp Meeting Association evangelists and
key Methodist leaders, such as Bishop William Taylor, succeeded in
spreading the Holiness message throughout global Methodism, and
made notable impact on Christians of other denominations, chiefly,
Baptists, Presbyterians, Anglicans, Friends, and Mennonites.

The second of these movements for the deepening of the Christian life, the Keswick movement, takes its name from the Keswick
Convention for the Promotion of Scriptural Holiness. Founded by
Anglicans, Friends, Presbyterians, and Methodists deeply influenced
by the American Holiness movement, the Keswick Convention has been
held every year since 1875 at Keswick in the Lake District in north-
western England. The Keswick movement also taught a second crisis
experience identical in many respects to that of the American
Methodist-inspired movement. Both movements taught that purity
and power are the twin results of sanctification. The Methodist
Holiness leaders saw power as a natural result of the purified heart
and stressed purity as a pre-condition to empowerment. Keswick
teachers concentrated on the infilling of the Holy Spirit, or, as A. B.
Simpson later said, the "habitation" of the Spirit. Unlike the American Methodist Holiness leaders, Keswick spokesmen were reluctant

to attribute removal of the carnal nature to sanctification, and taught instead that ungodlike characteristics remaining the sanctified personality must simply be suppressed. The conflict between purity and power in the emphases of the two movements remained, and influenced crucial doctrinal decisions in the earliest days of the Pentecostal movement.

Other aspects of the inheritance of Pentecostalism from the Holiness and Keswick movements are the expectation of additional crisis experiences subsequent to regeneration, and reliance on Spirit-guidance and subjective experience as illuminators of Scripture. The thorough-going Arminianism of most traditional Pentecostalism is the product of Methodist Holiness antecedents, as are puritanical standards of personal conduct. Stress on physical healing and speculation about last things, frowned on by early Methodist Holiness leaders, are the indirect legacy of Keswick.

1. HOLINESS-PENTECOSTAL BODIES

Although it is certainly true that the original Pentecostal or Apostolic Faith movement was a child of the Methodist Holiness movement, there are legitimate questions concerning the quality of its pedigree. The leaders of the Topeka revival of 1901 and the Los Angeles revival of 1906, Charles F. Parham and William J. Seymour, had virtually no standing in established Holiness circles, and tolerated, even experimented with teachings that were either frowned upon or forbidden by National Holiness leaders. Faith healing and speculation about prophecy had been declared divisive; unknown tongues and third crisis experiences (such as the "fire") had been ruled heretical. Experimentation with these ideas by the Fire-Baptized people and others had made them suspect in the eyes of their conventional Holiness brethren years before they embraced Pentecostal teachings. Wesleyan Holiness people taught two crisis experiences, regeneration and entire sanctification, and held that entire sanctification and the baptism with the Holy Spirit are one and the same experience, purifying the believer and empowering him for Christian service. Those who accepted the new Pentecostal or Apostolic Faith teachings modified the Holiness doctrinal schema significantly. They substituted three crises for two (distinguishing between entire sanctification which purifies the heart and the baptism with the Holy Spirit which empowers for service) and added the initial-evidence theory: speaking with tongues is the essential first indication of baptism with the Holy Spirit. Acceptance of these new teachings finally cut the umbilical cord between Holiness Pentecostals and their spiritual mother, the Wesleyan Holiness movement. Ostracism notwithstanding, the new teachings proved attractive enough to sweep almost the entire independent Holiness movement of the southeastern United States into the Pentecostal camp. They provided a theological consensus strong enough to unify the entire movement during its first decade.

This consensus remains in denominations descended from the south-eastern Holiness independents, and in large segments of the movement in Chile and South Africa.

2667   Holt, John Bradshaw
       Holiness religion: cultural shock and social reorganization [by] John B. Holt. In American Sociological Review, 5 (Oct. 1940), 740-747; abridged in Yinger, J. M. Religion, society and the individual. New York, c1957, 463-470.

2668   Johnson, Guy Benton, 1928-
       Do holiness sects socialize in dominant values? [By] Benton Johnson. In Social Forces, 39 (May 1961), 309-316. On both Holiness and Pentecostal churches.

2669   Johnson, Guy Benton, 1928-
       A framework for the analysis of religious action, with special reference to holiness and non-holiness groups. Cambridge, Mass., 1953 [i.e. 1954] iii, 307ℓ. Thesis (Ph.D.)-- Harvard University.   MH

2670   Kroll-Smith, J. Stephen
       The testimony as performance: the relationship of an expressive event to the belief system of a Holiness sect [by] J. Stephen Kroll-Smith. In Journal for the Scientific Study of Religion, 19 (Mar. 1980), 16-25.

2671   Synan, Harold Vinson, 1934-
       The relationship of the Holiness movement to the Pentecostal movement, by Vinson Synan. Wilmore, Ky., 1972. 8ℓ. Lecture presented at Asbury Theological Seminary, May 2, 1972.   KyWAT

2672   Warburton, Thomas Rennie, 1937-
       Holiness religion: an anomaly of sectarian typologies [by] T. Rennie Warburton. In Journal for the Scientific Study of Religion, 8 (Spring 1969), 130-139.

2673   Wood, William Woodhull
       Culture and personality aspects of the Pentecostal Holiness religion. Chapel Hill, 1961. 184ℓ. Thesis (Ph.D.)-- University of North Carolina. Based on Rorschach tests administered to members of two Southern rural Pentecostal churches and a control group. Indicates that the persons attracted by Pentecostal religion tend to live in conditions of deprivation or disruption.   NcU

2674   Wood, William Woodhull
       Culture and personality aspects of the Pentecostal Holiness religion, by William W. Wood. The Hague, Mouton, 1965. 125p. Thesis (Ph.D.)--University of North Carolina.

2675   Wood, William Woodhull
          Culture and personality aspects of the Pentecostal Holi-
        ness religion, by William W. Wood. The Hague, Mouton,
        1965. 125p. Imprint covered by label: New York, Humani-
        ties Press. Thesis (Ph. D.)--University of North Carolina.
        DLC

          --BIBLIOGRAPHY

2676   Jones, Charles Edwin, 1932-
          A guide to the study of the Holiness Movement. Metuchen,
        N. J., Scarecrow Press and the American Theological Library
        Association, 1974. xxviii, 918p. (ATLA bibliography series,
        1.) On spine: The Holiness Movement. "Holiness-Pentecostal
        movement": p. 513-536. DLC

          --DOCTRINAL AND CONTROVERSIAL WORKS

2677   Abrams, Minnie F.
          The baptism of the Holy Ghost and fire. Kegdaon, India,
        1905. 80p.

2677a   Goins, J. E.
          Pearl of prophecy, by J. L. Goins. Chattanooga, Tn.,
        19--. 94p.

2678   Holmes, Nickels John, 1847-1919.
          The baptism by the Spirit, the baptism by Christ, and
        other topics, by N. J. Holmes. Greenville, S. C., Holmes
        Bible College, 1952. 68p. First published in 1915.

2679   Holmes, Nickels John, 1847-1919.
          The baptism by the Spirit, the baptism by Christ and
        other topics, by N. J. Holmes. Greenville, S. C., Holmes
        Theological Seminary, 1971. 68p. "Third printing. "

2680   Holmes, Nickels John, 1847-1919.
          God's provision for holiness, by N. J. Holmes. Nash-
        ville, Pentecostal Mission Publishing Co., 190-. 138p.

2681   Holmes, Nickels John, 1847-1919.
          God's provision for holiness, by N. J. Holmes. Green-
        ville, S. C., Holmes Bible College, 1952. 131p. "Revised. "

2682   Holmes, Nickels John, 1847-1919.
          God's provision for holiness, by Rev. N. J. Holmes.
        3d ed. Greenville, S. C., Holmes Theological Seminary,
        1969. 131p.

2683   Lemons, Frank W., 1901-
          Our Pentecostal heritage, by Frank W. Lemons. Cleve-

land, Tenn., Pathway Press, c1963. 173p. TxWaS

2684   Simpson, Alvin B.
        The beast, false prophet and satan: "the end of time"
        [by] A. B. Simpson. Fresno, Calif., 19--. 32p. Cover
        title.

2685   Sisk, L. W.
        Entire sanctification, by L. W. Sisk. n. p., 19--. 60p.

2686   Spence, Othniel Talmadge, 1926-
        Flutauviel, by O. Talmadge Spence. Benson, N. C.,
        Printed by Heritage Tribute Press, c1972. 107p. An epic
        poem dealing with the fall of man and historical and contem-
        porary theological issues.

2687   Spence, Othniel Talmadge, 1926-
        Foundations Bible commentary [by] O. Talmadge Spence.
        Dunn, N. C., Foundry Press, Foundations Bible College,
        c1977- . v. 1- . (5v. projected) DLC

2688   Spence, Othniel Talmadge, 1926-
        Sanctification--God's cure for sin and self, by O. Tal-
        madge Spence. Dunn, N. C., Heritage Tribute Press, 197-.
        folder (4p.)

2688a   Stroup, John, 1853-1929.
        What God can do. South Solon, Oh., 1913. 136p.

        --HISTORY AND STUDY OF DOCTRINES

2689   Synan, Harold Vinson, 1934-
        Los avivamientos pentecostales desde el Pentecostes hasta
        nuestros dias [por] Vinson Synan. Curico, Chile, Imprenta
        Orion, 1967. 12p. Cover title. "Conferencia dictada en el
        Seminario de Pastores en Santiago, Chile, de 25 al 27 de
        Abril, 1967. "

2690   Synan, Harold Vinson, 1934-
        Theological boundaries: the Arminian tradition [by] Vin-
        son Synan. In Wells, D. F., ed. The Evangelicals: what
        they believe, who they are, where they are changing. Rev.
        ed. Grand Rapids, Mich., 1977, 38-57.

        --HYMNS AND SACRED SONGS

2691   Alewine, Orion L.
        Chimes of glory, no. 2, for all religious works. [Com-
        piled by] Mr. and Mrs. Orion L. Alewine. Cleveland, Tenn.,
        c1935. 1v. (unpaged)

2692   Alford, Delton Lynol
          Gospel choir arrangements, by Delton L. Alford. Cleve-
        land, Tenn., Tennessee Music and Printing Co., c1966.   3v.

2693   Alford, Delton Lynol
          Magnify the Lord; choral arrangements, by Delton L.
        Alford. Editorial assistant: Jimi Hall. Cleveland, Tenn.,
        Tennessee Music and Printing Co., c1963.   32p.

2694   Burroughs, Lonnie
          Billows of love. Lonnie Burroughs, music editor. V. B.
        (Vep) Ellis, associate editor. Cleveland, Tenn., Tennessee
        Music and Printing Co., c1957.   160p.

2695   Burroughs, Lonnie
          Echoes of Calvary. Lonnie Burroughs, music editor.
        V. B. (Vep) Ellis, associate editor. Cleveland, Tenn., Ten-
        nessee Music and Printing Co., c1958.   160p.

2696   Choruses of Calvary. Cleveland, Tn., Tennessee Music and
        Printing Co., c1952.   64p.

2697   Church hymnal. Cleveland, Tn., Tennessee Music and Print-
        ing Co., c1951.   410[6]p. With music (shape notes).

2698   Ellis, V. B.
          Christian joy: a combination of new and favorite revival
        songs for church services, singing conventions, and revivals.
        V. B. (Vep) Ellis, music editor. Cleveland, Tenn., Tennes-
        see Music and Printing Co., c1946.   160p.

2699   Ellis, V. B.
          Encore; a collection of tried and proven songs. Compiled
        by V. B. (Vep) Ellis. Cleveland, Tenn., Tennessee Music
        and Printing Co., c1946.   284p.

2700   Ellis, V. B.
          Forward in faith. Compiled by Vep Ellis [and others].
        Cleveland, Tenn., Tennessee Music and Printing Co., c1959.
        160p.

2701   Ellis, V. B.
          Golden notes. V. B. (Vep) Ellis, ed. Cleveland, Tenn.,
        Tennessee Music and Printing Co., c1953.   1v. (unpaged)

2702   Ellis, V. B.
          Gospel praise. Edited by V. B. (Vep) Ellis, Whit Den-
        son and Otis L. McCoy. Cleveland, Tenn., Tennessee Mu-
        sic and Printing Co., c1951.   160p.

2703   Ellis, V. B.
          Lasting covenant, prayerfully dedicated to the cause of
        Christ. [Edited by] V. B. (Vep) Ellis [and others]. Cleve-

land, Tenn., Tennessee Music and Printing Co., c1969.
160p.

2704 Ellis, V. B.
Sing of Calvary. Edited by V. B. (Vep) Ellis. Cleveland, Tenn., Tennessee Music and Printing Co., c1947.
159p.

2705 Ellis, V. B.
Songs of the redeemed [no. 1]. V. B. (Vep) Ellis,
music ed. Cleveland, Tenn., Tennessee Music and Printing
Co., c1955. 159p.

2706 Ellis, V. B.
Songs of the redeemed, no. 2. V. B. (Vep) Ellis,
music ed. Cleveland, Tenn., Tennessee Music and Printing
Co., c1956. 160p.

2707 Greene, Sammy Newell, 1907-1982.
His hands. Edited and published by S. N. Greene.
Oklahoma City, c1959. 1v. (unpaged) With music (shape
notes).

2708 Greene, Sammy Newell, 1907-1982.
Songs we love. Edited and published by S. N. Greene.
Oklahoma City, c1969. 1v. (unpaged) With music (shape
notes).

2709 [Hall, Connor B.]
Evangelistic revival; favorite gospel songs and hymns
compiled from nation-wide survey for camp meetings, revivals, prayer meetings. [Edited by Connor B. Hall] Cleveland, Tenn., Tennessee Music and Printing Co., c1962. 1v.
(unpaged) Cover title: Songs of worship and praise. With
music (shape notes).

2710 Hall, Connor B.
God's glory. Connor B. Hall, ed. Cleveland, Tenn.,
Tennessee Music and Printing Co., c1970. 160p.

2711 Hall, Connor B.
Hallowed faith. Connor B. Hall, music ed. Jimi Hall,
assistant ed. Cleveland, Tenn., Tennessee Music and Printing Co., c1966. 160p.

2712 Hall, Connor B.
Joy in the camp. Connor B. Hall, ed. Cleveland, Tenn.,
Tennessee Music and Printing Co., c1972. 160p.

2713 Hall, Connor B.
Living hope. Connor B. Hall, ed. Jimi Hall, assistant
ed. Cleveland, Tenn., Tennessee Music and Printing Co.,
c1969. 160p. With music (shape notes). OkBetC

2713a   Hall, Connor B.
            Love supreme.   Connor B. Hall, ed.   F. W. Goff,
        publisher.   Cleveland, Tn., Tennessee Music and Printing
        Co., c1974.   160p.   With music (shape notes).   OkBetC

2714   Hall, Connor B.
            New songs.   Connor B. Hall, music ed.   Jimi Hall,
        editor's assistant.   Cleveland, Tenn., Tennessee Music and
        Printing Co., c1963.   160p.

2715   Hall, Connor B.
            Sacred chimes.   Connor B. Hall, ed.   Jimi Hall, assist-
        ant ed.   Cleveland, Tenn., Tennessee Music and Printing Co.,
        c1968.   160p.

2716   Hall, Connor B.
            Sing glory.   Connor B. Hall, music ed.   Jimi Hall, as-
        sistant ed.   Cleveland, Tenn., Tennessee Music and Printing
        Co., c1965.   160p.

2717   Hall, Connor B.
            Songs for today.   Connor B. Hall, music ed.   Jimi Hall,
        assistant ed.   Cleveland, Tenn., Tennessee Music and Print-
        ing Co., c1964.   160p.

2718   Hall, Connor B.
            Songs of life; a choice selection of hymns and gospel
        songs for every occasion.   Compiled by Connor B. Hall [and]
        Jimi Hall.   Cleveland, Tenn., Tennessee Music and Printing
        Co., c1962.   288,[32]p.

2719   Hall, Connor B.
            Sounds of victory.   Connor B. Hall, ed.   Jimi Hall, as-
        sistant ed.   Cleveland, Tenn., Tennessee Music and Printing
        Co., c1969.   160p.

2720   Hall, Connor B.
            Voice of love.   Connor B. Hall, ed.   Jimi Hall, assist-
        ant ed.   Cleveland, Tenn., Tennessee Music and Printing
        Co., c1967.   160p.

2721   Jernigan, John C., 1900-
            Kentucky favorites.   Compiled by John C. Jernigan.
        Somerset, Ky., 19--.   28p.

2722   Jernigan, John C., 1900-
            Soul stirring songs, with ancient proverbs and beatitudes
        for church members.   Compiled and arranged by J. C. Jer-
        nigan and J. R. West.   Stone, Ky., 19--.   24p.

2723   McCoy, Otis L.
            Eternal joy, by Otis L. McCoy [and others].   Cleveland,
        Tenn., Tennessee Music and Printing Co., c1939.   141p.

2724   McCoy, Otis L.
        Forever song. Otis L. McCoy, music editor. Cleveland, Tenn., Tennessee Music and Printing Co., c1962. 160p.

2725   McCoy, Otis L.
        Heart beats of heaven [by] Otis L. McCoy [and others]. Cleveland, Tenn., Tennessee Music and Printing Co., c1935. 1v. (unpaged)

2726   McCoy, Otis L.
        Homeland harmony [by] Otis L. McCoy [and others]. Cleveland, Tenn., Tennessee Music and Printing Co., c1936. 142p.

2727   McCoy, Otis L.
        Living jewels: songs for all occasions. [Edited by] Otis L. McCoy [and others]. Cleveland, Tenn., Tennessee Music and Printing Co., c1949. 160p.

2728   McCoy, Otis L.
        Living presents. Edited by Otis L. McCoy. Cleveland, Tenn., Tennessee Music and Printing Co., c1938. 1v. (unpaged)

2729   McCoy, Otis L.
        Pathway of praise. Otis L. McCoy, music ed. Cleveland, Tenn., Tennessee Music and Printing Co., c1960. 160p.

2730   McCoy, Otis L.
        Peaks of paradise [by] Otis L. McCoy [and others]. Cleveland, Tenn., Tennessee Music and Printing Co., c1948. 159p.

2731   McCoy, Otis L.
        Pearls of the cross [by] Otis L. McCoy [and others]. Cleveland, Tenn., Tennessee Music and Printing Co., c1934. 1v. (unpaged)

2732   McCoy, Otis L.
        Rays of hope. Otis L. McCoy, music ed. Cleveland, Tenn., Tennessee Music and Printing Co., c1942. 1v. (unpaged) With music (shape notes). OkBetC

2733   McCoy, Otis L.
        Singing for Jesus, by Otis L. McCoy, music ed. [and] Owel Denson, field manager. Cleveland, Tenn., Tennessee Music and Printing Co., c1940. 1v. (unpaged)

2734   McCoy, Otis L.
        Songs divine. Edited by Otis L. McCoy. Cleveland, Tenn., Tennessee Music and Printing Co., c1945. 128p.

2735   McCoy, Otis L.
            Songs forever. Otis L. McCoy, music ed. Cleveland,
        Tenn., Tennessee Music and Printing Co., c1944. 128p.

2736   McCoy, Otis L.
            Songs of prayer and praise [no. 1]; the complete church
        hymnal for all worship. Edited by Otis L. McCoy. Rev.
        ed. Cleveland, Tenn., Tennessee Music and Printing Co.,
        c1945. 222p.

2737   McCoy, Otis L.
            Songs of prayer and praise, no. 2; a complete church
        hymnal for all worship. Edited by Otis L. McCoy. Cleve-
        land, Tenn., Tennessee Music and Printing Co., c1944.
        222p. With music (shape notes).

2738   McCoy, Otis L.
            Songs of rapture. Otis L. McCoy, music ed. Cleve-
        land, Tenn., Tennessee Music and Printing Co.; Fort Worth,
        Tex., National Music Co., c1943. 1v. (unpaged)

2739   McCoy, Otis L.
            Victory specials. Edited by Otis L. McCoy. Cleveland,
        Tenn., Tennessee Music and Printing Co., c1942. 1v. (un-
        paged)

2740   Parks, Joe
            Sing of Him [by] Joe Parks [and others]. Cleveland,
        Tenn., Tennessee Music and Printing Co., c1950. 160p.

2741   Roberts, Oral, 1918-
            Official song book of Oral Roberts healing campaigns.
        Tulsa, 1954, c1949. 1v. (unpaged) OkBetC

2741a   Sisk, J. L.
            Good songs for everybody for all religious work and wor-
        ship, especially revival work. Compiled by J. L. Sisk [and
        others]. Toccoa, Ga., Sisk Music Co., 194-. 1v. (unpaged)
        With music. GU

                    --PERIODICALS

2742   Altamont witness. 1- Oct. 1911-May 1918.
            Greenville, S.C.

2743   Apostolic evangel. 1- Mar. 13, 1907-1928.
            Royston, Ga., Falcon, N.C.

2744   Apostolic faith. 1-15, Sept. 1906-Oct./Nov. 1908.
            Los Angeles. Nos. 1-13, Sept. 1906-May 1908, collected
        by Fred T. Corum and issued as Like as of fire (Wilmington,
        Ma., 1981).

2745   Bridegroom's messenger. 1-60, Oct. 1, 1907-Oct. 1974;
        61- Oct. 1976-
            Atlanta, Detroit, Atlanta. Dec. 1974-Aug. 1976 replaced
        by Bridegroom's messenger and Pentecostal witness, continu-
        ing the numbering of the Pentecostal witness and issued from
        Canton, Oh. Original title and numbering resumed with vol.
        61, no. 1, Oct. 1976. OkTOr

2746   Gospel visitor. 1- -May 1963.
            Anderson, Mo. OkTOr

2746a   Herald of truth. 1- Dec. 1927-1928.
            Greenville, S.C.

2747   Household of God. 1- 1908-
            Dayton, Oh.

            --SERMONS, TRACTS, ADDRESSES, ESSAYS

2748   Compton, W. H.,
            Compton's 50 new sermon outlines; 35 contributors.
        Compiled by W. H. Compton. Grand Rapids, Mich., Baker
        Book House, 197-. 64p. (Dollar sermon library.)

2749   Compton, W. H.
            Compton's 50 select sermon outlines. Grand Rapids,
        Mich., Baker Book House, 197-. 64p. (Dollar sermon
        library.)

2750   Compton, W. H.
            Funeral sermon outlines [by] W. H. Compton. Grand
        Rapids, Mich., Baker Book House, 1976, c1965. 64p.
        (Dollar sermon library.) "Sixth printing."

2751   Compton, W. H.
            Salvation sermon outlines. Compiled by W. H. Compton.
        Westwood, N.J., F. H. Revell Co., 1961. 64p. (Revell's
        sermon outline series.) DLC

2752   Compton, W. H.
            Sermons from God's word [by] W. H. Compton. West-
        wood, N.J., Revell, 1961. 64p. (Revell's sermon outline
        series.) DLC

2753   Compton, W. H.
            Vital sermon outlines. Grand Rapids, Mich., Baker Book
        House, 197-. 64p. (Dollar sermon library.)

2754   Holmes, Nickels John, 1847-1919.
            Life sketches and sermons, by N. J. Holmes and wife.
        Royston, Ga., Press of the Pentecostal Holiness Church,
        c1920. 310p. DLC

2755   Jernigan, John C., 1900-
        The preachers' gold mine; three volumes of sermon out-
        lines by eminent ministers. Compiled by John C. Jernigan.
        Chattanooga, Tn., Gospel Book House, 19--. 3v.   OkBetC

2756   Wicks, Mildred
        Dawn of a better day; expository sermons on divine heal-
        ing. Tulsa, Standard Printing Co., 19--. 109p.   TxWaS

2757   Wicks, Mildred
        There is healing for you. Dallas, c1950. 171p.   TxWaS

        --WORSHIP

2758   Burns, Thomas A.
        Symbolism of becoming in the Sunday service of an urban
        black Holiness church [by] Thomas A. Burns and J. Stephen
        Smith. In Anthropological Quarterly, 51 (July 1978), 185-204.

2759   Clark, William A., 1891-
        Sanctification in Negro religion [by] William A. Clark.
        In Social Forces, 15 (May 1937), 544-551.   On worship in
        Pentecostal churches.

2760   Knight, Cecil Brigham, ed., 1926-
        Pentecostal worship. Edited by Cecil B. Knight.   Cleve-
        land, Tenn., Pathway Press, 1974. 140p.   Essays by Cecil
        B. Knight, Robert E. Fisher, Lucille Walker, Robert White,
        Delton L. Alford, David S. Bishop, Bob E. Lyons and M. G.
        McLuhan. DLC, MSohG

        --UNITED STATES

2761   Abell, Troy Dale
        The holiness-Pentecostal experience in southern Appala-
        chia. Lafayette, Ind., 1974. 487ℓ. Thesis (Ph.D.)--
        Purdue University. InLP

2762   Backman, Milton Vaughn, 1927-
        Christian churches of America: origins and beliefs [by]
        Milton V. Backman, Jr. Provo, Utah, Brigham Young Uni-
        versity Press, 1976. xvii, 230p. "The Holiness-Pentecostal
        movement": p. 194-198, 214. DLC

2763   Bentley, William H.
        Bible believers in the Black community [by] William H.
        Bentley. In Wells, D. F., ed. The Evangelicals: what they
        believe, who they are, where they are changing. Nashville,
        c1975, 108-121. "Black Holiness and Pentecostals": p. 115-
        116.

2764   Gaddis, Merrill Elmer, 1891-
            Christian perfectionism in America. Chicago, 1929.
        viii, 589ℓ. Thesis (Ph.D.)--University of Chicago. On
        Pentecostal churches: ℓ. 460-462, 465-482, 531-539, 561-
        562, 563-564, 573. ICU

2764a   Lovett, Leonard
            Black Holiness-Pentecostalism: implications for ethics
        and social transformation. Atlanta, 1978. 3, viii, 183ℓ.
        Thesis (Ph.D.)--Emory University. GEU

2765   Synan, Harold Vinson, 1934-
            The Holiness-Pentecostal movement in the United States,
        by Vinson Synan. Grand Rapids, Mich., Eerdmans, 1971.
        248p. Based on thesis (Ph.D.)--University of Georgia, 1967.
        DLC, MBU-T, MH-AH, MSohG, TxWaS

2766   Synan, Harold Vinson, 1934-
            The Pentecostal movement in the United States. Athens,
        1967. vi, 296ℓ. Thesis (Ph.D.)--University of Georgia. GU

ALPHA AND OMEGA CHRISTIAN CHURCH (1962-   )

        In 1962 a group of Filipino immigrants affiliated with the
Pearl City Full Gospel Mission in Hawaii withdrew and formed the
Alpha and Omega Christian Church. Alejandro B. Fagaragan, who
led the separation, became pastor. By 1966 members returning to
the Philippines had established a second congregation at Dingras in
the province of Ilocos Norte on the northwest tip of Luzon. Following a disastrous flood in 1968 which destroyed the Pearl City building,
the bulk of the membership in Hawaii fell away, leaving the combined
membership at fewer than two hundred. The headquarters remain,
however, in Pearl City.

2767   Elwood, Douglas J.
            Churches and sects in the Philippines; a descriptive study
        of contemporary religious movements [by] Douglas J. Elwood.
        Dumaguete City, Phil., Silliman University, 1968. xi, 213p.
        (Silliman University monograph. Series A: Religious studies,
        1.) On Alpha and Omega Christian Church: p. 78, 180.
        DLC

ALPHA AND OMEGA PENTECOSTAL CHURCH OF AMERICA
    (1945-   )
[Mar.-Apr. 1945 as Alpha and Omega Church of God Tabernacle;
    Apr. 1945-19-- as Alpha and Omega Pentecostal Church.]

        On March 12, 1945, Magdelene Mabe Phillips and eight other

former members of a Baltimore Holiness church established the
Alpha and Omega Church of God Tabernacle.   The next month they
changed the name to Alpha and Omega Pentecostal Church, "of
America" being added upon incorporation sometime later.   After
Phillips' successor, Charles E. Waters, Sr., left to found the True
Fellowship Pentecostal Church of America in 1964, John Mabe,
brother of Mrs. Phillips, became overseer.   The body consists of
two churches and a mission, all in Baltimore, with a combined membership of about 400.

ASSOCIATION OF INTERNATIONAL GOSPEL ASSEMBLIES (19 -   )

     Closely tied to the International Bible Institute of St. Louis,
the Association of Gospel Assemblies is a loose federation of
churches.   Led by Granville M. Rayl, who is also president of the
school, the Association meets annually.   Tithing is enjoined, footwashing is observed as an ordinance, and women and men are treated
as equals in the ministry.   The Association, which claimed 5,200
members in 62 churches in 1970, sponsors missions in India and the
Philippines.

2768   Association of International Gospel Assemblies.
            Constitution and by-laws.   St. Louis, 1970.

ASSOCIATION OF PENTECOSTAL ASSEMBLIES (1921-1936)

     The Association of Pentecostal Assemblies was organized in
1921 by Mrs. Elizabeth A. Sexton and her daughter and son-in-law,
Dr. Hattie M. Barth and Paul T. Barth.   The membership was
drawn from subscribers to the Bridegroom's Messenger, founded by
Mrs. Sexton in 1907, and from supporters of the Beulah Heights
Bible Institute, founded in 1918.   Headquarters were in Atlanta,
where both paper and school were located.   The Association of
Pentecostal Assemblies merged with the International Pentecostal
Church (formerly known as the National and International Pentecostal
Missionary Union) to form the International Pentecostal Assemblies
on August 25, 1936.   The joint council which effected the merger
met at the Radio Church, Lombard and Parkin streets, Baltimore.

                    --PERIODICALS

2769   Bridgeroom's messenger.   1- Oct. 1, 1907-
            Atlanta

BAPTISTS:

EVANGELICAL BAPTIST CHURCH, GENERAL CONFERENCE (1935-   )
[1935-194- as Church of the Full Gospel; 194 -present as General Conference of the Evangelical Baptist Church.]

Organized in January 1935, the Church of the Full Gospel at first consisted of a single congregation in Goldsboro, North Carolina, the result of the preaching of R. H. Askew in the local Free Will Baptist Church during the previous year. Two years later under the leadership of William H. Carter of Dunn, North Carolina, the group reorganized, at which time congregations in Rocky Mount, Elm City, and Snow Hill joined the movement. Cooperative relations were soon established with the Pentecostal Full Gospel Church of Baltimore, Maryland, and for a time the two groups jointly published the Full Gospel Herald. Headquarters remained in Goldsboro. After it changed its name to the General Conference of the Evangelical Baptist Church, the group began its own paper, the Evangelical Baptist. In 1952 the denomination, which fifteen years earlier had claimed only 300 members in four congregations, reported 2,200 members in 31 churches.

2770   Evangelical Baptist Church, General Conference.
          Discipline of the General Conference of the Evangelical Baptist Church. n.p., 19--.

--PERIODICALS

2771   Evangelical Baptist. 1-   194 -
          Goldsboro, N.C.

2772   Full Gospel Herald. 1-   193 -
          Baltimore

FREE WILL BAPTIST CHURCH OF THE PENTECOSTAL FAITH (1959-   )

During the first decades of the twentieth century, a large number of Free Will Baptists in South Carolina adopted Pentecostal doctrines. In 1923 they formed a statewide conference, thus providing a vehicle for cooperation among otherwise autonomous congregations. Twenty years later the South Carolina Conference joined with three like-minded conferences in North Carolina--Cape Fear, Wilmington, and New River--in a general conference. Cooperative efforts, at first limited to production of educational materials, led the North Carolina conferences to desire organic union. In 1958 the South Carolina Conference responded by withdrawing from the general conference. The next year, while the North Carolina churches were forming the Pentecostal Free-Will Baptist Church, the South Carolina

Conference incorporated itself as the Free Will Baptist Church of the
Pentecostal Faith. In 1961 it ratified a discipline, and four years
later adopted a new constitution. The Free Will Baptist Church of
the Pentecostal Faith combines an amalgam of doctrinal and behavioral standards derived from Baptist, Wesleyan-Arminian, and Pentecostal sources. Recent merger talks with Pentecostal Free Will
Baptist and Pentecostal Holiness churches have been impeded by non-
theological issues, such as clergy pensions. By the mid-1970s the
denomination claimed 38 congregations (including two in North Carolina and one in Georgia) and 1,300 members. It also sponsors mission work in Mexico, Costa Rica, and Argentina. Headquarters offices are in Elgin, South Carolina.

2773   Free Will Baptist Church of the Pentecostal Faith.
            Faith and government of the Free Will Baptist Church
        of the Pentecostal Faith. n. p. , 1961. 48p.

                    --CATECHISMS AND CREEDS

2774   Rumsey, Ray
            Fundamentals of the faith.   Florence, S. C. , Free Will
        Baptist Church Conference--Pentecostal Faith, 19--.   2v.

                    --PERIODICALS

2775   Free Will Baptist advance.   1-   1958-
            Camden, S. C.

        HOLINESS BAPTIST ASSOCIATION (1894-   )

        In 1893 because of their teaching on "sinless perfection, "
two congregations and several ministers were expelled from the
Little River Baptist Association.   The next year these, together
with two additional newly-organized churches, met at the Pine City
Church in Wilcox County, Georgia and formed the Holiness Baptist
Association.   Adding a Wesleyan understanding of sanctification, the
new Association retained Missionary Baptist standards of faith and
decorum.   Tongues-speech, while permitted by the group, is not
regarded as evidence of the baptism of the Holy Spirit.   By
the mid-1970s there were 46 member congregations in Georgia and
Florida with a combined baptized membership of about 2,000.   The
Association operates a campground on the Alma Highway seven miles
east of Douglas, Georgia.   Association business is transacted there
annually during camp meeting.

2775a Holiness Baptist Association.
            Minutes of the annual session of the Holiness Baptist As-
        sociation.   1st-   1894-   Cordele, Ga. , 19 - v. [1]-   OkTOr

HOLINESS BAPTIST CHURCHES OF SOUTHWESTERN
ARKANSAS (1903-1914)

Organized in 1903 at Sutton, Arkansas, the Holiness Baptist
Churches of Southwestern Arkansas drew together former Baptists
who had been excluded from church fellowship because of their profession of entire sanctification. Consisting of a few congregations
in Nevada County, Arkansas, Holiness Baptists participated in merger-
talks in 1904 with the Independent Holiness Church and the New Testament Church of Christ, but withdrew when other participants failed
to accept immersion as the only valid mode of baptism. W. Jethro
Walthall, the founder, had had a number of tongues-speaking experiences. As a consequence, he welcomed workers who taught that
tongues-speech was the initial evidence of the baptism of the Holy
Spirit. This emphasis led to absorption into the General Council of
the Assemblies of God, a non-Wesleyan body, soon after it was
formed in 1914. Walthall served as chairman of the Assemblies'
of God Arkansas District Council during its formative years.

2776   Holiness Baptist Churches of Southwestern Arkansas.
        Minutes of the first annual convocation of the Holiness
        Baptist Churches of Southwestern Arkansas, held with the
        church at Sutton, Arkansas, Nov. 6, 7, 8, 1903. n. p.,
        1903. 7p. DLC

2777   Jernigan, Charles Brougher, 1863-1930.
        Pioneer days of the Holiness movement in the southwest,
        by C. B. Jernigan. Kansas City, Mo., Pentecostal Nazarene
        Publishing House, c1919. 157p. On the Holiness Baptist
        Churches of Southwestern Arkansas: p. 122-123. OkBetC, WiH

PENTECOSTAL FREE WILL BAPTIST CHURCH (1916-1919)

On November 21, 1919, the North Carolina Annual Conference of
the Pentecostal Free-Will Baptist Church united with the Pentecostal
Fire-Baptized Church at Toccoa, Georgia. The Pentecostal Free-Will
Baptist group had been created on October 21, 1916, at Pembroke, North
Carolina, by former Fire-Baptized adherents dissatisfied with the re-
sults of union with the Pentecostal Holiness Church five years earlier.

PENTECOSTAL FREE WILL BAPTIST CHURCH (1959-   )

Organized in 1855, the Cape Fear Conference of the Free
Will Baptist Church, which from its founding taught free grace and
instantaneous sanctification, also accepted the Pentecostal interpretation of the baptism with the Holy Spirit in the years following the
Dunn, North Carolina revival of 1907. So rapid was its growth that
in 1908 the conference was divided and the Wilmington Conference
was established. Three years later the infant conference itself was
divided and the New River Conference was formed. In 1912, a mi-

nority who did not believe in either sanctification or baptism with
the Holy Spirit subsequent to regeneration, separated from the Cape
Fear Conference, leaving the Holiness Pentecostal majority clearly
in control. In 1943 the three Pentecostal-dominated conferences in
North Carolina joined with the like-minded South Carolina Conference
to form a general conference for cooperative ventures, such as production of educational materials. Concern for local control remained
strong. Consequently, when in 1958 the three North Carolina conferences pressed for organic union, the South Carolina Conference
withdrew. The next year the North Carolina brethren formed the
Pentecostal Free Will Baptist Church. Its headquarters offices are
in Dunn, North Carolina. In 1978 there were 12,272 members in
128 churches in North Carolina, Virginia and Hawaii, and official
missionary work in India, the Philippines, Mexico, Nicaragua and
Venezuela. By the mid-1970s there were 34 United States workers
under denominational appointment and more than $100,000 was being
given annually for missionary work. Merger talks continued with
the Free Will Baptist Church of the Pentecostal Faith, denominational
successor to the South Carolina Conference which had spurned union
in the late 1950s.

2778   Pentecostal Free Will Baptist Church.
            Discipline of the Pentecostal Free Will Baptist Church,
        Inc. [Dunn, N.C.], 1962. 109p.

2778a   Pentecostal Free Will Baptist Church.
            Minutes of the Pentecostal Free Will Baptist Church,
        Inc. Dunn, N.C., 1959- v.[1]- Annual.

                        --CATECHISMS AND CREEDS

2778b   Pentecostal Free Will Baptist Church.
            Faith and practices of the Pentecostal Free Will Baptist
        Church. [Dunn, N.C., Printed by] Advocate Press, Franklin
        Springs, Ga., 1971. 123p.

                    --DOCTRINAL AND CONTROVERSIAL WORKS

2779   Pentecostal Free Will Baptist Church.
            Discipline of the Pentecostal Free Will Baptist Church.
        Dunn, N.C., 19--.

2780   Carter, Herbert Franklin, 1933-
            The effects of entire sanctification on the human nature,
        by Herbert Carter and Ned Sauls. [Dunn, N.C., Pentecostal
        Free Will Baptist Messenger, 1977] [70]p. OkTOr

2780a   Carter, Herbert Franklin, 1933-
            The spectacular gifts: prophecy, tongues, interpretations,
        by Herbert Carter. n.p., 19--. 44p.

2780b   Sauls, Ned Douglas, 1932-
          Pentecostal doctrines: a Wesleyan approach [by] Ned D.
        Sauls.   Dunn, N. C. , Heritage Bible College, c1979-   v. 1-
        DLC

        --HISTORY

2780c   Carter, Herbert Franklin, 1933-
          History of the Pentecostal Free Will Baptist Church,
        Inc.   Written by Herbert F. Carter and Mrs. Ruth K. Moore.
        In Discipline of the Pentecostal Free Will Baptist Church,
        Inc.   [Dunn, N. C.], 1962, 5-16.

        --PERIODICALS

2781   Pentecostal Free Will Baptist messenger.   1-   194 -
        Dunn, N. C.

CALVARY HOLINESS CHURCH (1934-1955)

          An outgrowth of itinerant evangelism, called "trekking," the
Calvary Holiness Church was founded in 1934 to conserve converts
made by four young British evangelists: Maynard James, Jack Ford,
Leonard Ravenhill, and Clifford Filer.   The four had worked under
the auspices of the International Holiness Mission until tension over
their willingness to permit tongues-speaking in their services led to
separation.   They stopped short of regarding glossolalia as the initial evidence of the baptism of the Holy Spirit, however, and remained in all essentials in the Wesleyan Holiness camp.   Guided by
the founders who occupied permanent seats on the Executive Council,
the Calvary Holiness Church proved to be extremely evangelistic,
concentrating its efforts in industrial areas of northern England and
Wales.   Cooperative projects followed close after organization.   In
1936, the Flame, a paper started by Maynard James the previous
year, became the official organ.   The next year the group sent its
first missionaries to Colombia.   In 1947 it established the Beech
Lawn Bible College.   First located at Uppermill, the school moved
to Stalybridge, near Manchester, in 1948.   Support of these projects
taxed the financial resources of the movement, leading the Executive
Council into talks with officials of the Church of the Nazarene.   At
Manchester on June 11, 1955, the merger was effected.   At that
time the Calvary Holiness Church consisted of 22 congregations and
about 600 members in England and Wales, and was supporting missionary efforts in Colombia and Pakistan.   Largely because of a
pledge not to countenance tongues-speaking in public services of the
merged body, a half dozen Calvary Holiness ministers refused to
unite.   Missionary constituencies were released to other agencies,
and the Flame again became independent, serving a unique readership drawn from both Holiness and Pentecostal churches.

2782   Calvary Holiness Church.
        The Calvary Holiness Church: what it is, and what it
        stands for. Nelson, Lancs., Coulton & Co., 194-.

2783   Calvary Holiness Church.
        Rules and regulations of the Calvary Holiness Church.
        Manchester, 1943.

                    --DOCTRINAL AND CONTROVERSIAL WORKS

2784   James, Maynard G., 1902-
        Facing the issue, by Maynard G. James. Burnley,
        Lancs., Pilgrim Publishing House, 194-. vii, 132p. KyWAT

                    --EVANGELISTIC WORK

2785   James, Maynard G., 1902-
        Evangelize, by Maynard G. James. Colchester, Essex,
        Evangelical Pub., 1945. 80p. KyWAT

                    --HISTORY

2786   Ford, Jack, 1908-1980.
        The Church of the Nazarene in Britain, the International
        Holiness Mission and the Calvary Holiness Church. London,
        1967. 1v. (paging not determined) Thesis (Ph.D.)--Univer-
        sity of London.

2787   Ford, Jack, 1908-1980.
        In the steps of John Wesley: the Church of the Nazarene
        in Britain. Kansas City, Mo., Printed by Nazarene Publish-
        ing House, 1968. 300p. Based on thesis (Ph.D.)--University
        of London. "The Calvary Holiness Church": p. 139-181.
        DLC, KyWAT, OkBetC

2788   Mitchell, T. Crichton
        To serve the present age: the Church of the Nazarene
        in the British Isles, by T. Crichton Mitchell. Kansas City,
        Mo., Nazarene Publishing House, 1980. 79p. On Calvary
        Holiness Church: p. 24, 40-44. OkBetC

                    --HISTORY AND STUDY OF DOCTRINES

2789   Ford, Jack, 1908-1980.
        What the Holiness people believe; a mid-century review
        of holiness teaching. Birkenhead, Cheshire, Emmanuel Bible
        College and Missions, 1955. 70p. (J. D. Drysdale memor-
        ial lecture.) Cover sub-title: A mid-century review of holi-
        ness teaching among Holiness groups of Britain. "The baptism

of the Spirit": p. 42-51; particularly "The initial evidence":
p. 48-51. KyWAT, OkBetC

--PERIODICALS

2790   Flame. 1- 1935-
        Southport, Lancs. , Grimsby, Lincs.

--COLOMBIA

2791   Hall, Trella Belle
        A historical sketch of the progress of Protestantism in
        Colombia, South America. Pittsburgh, 1959. vii,125ℓ .
        Thesis (M. S.)--Kansas State College. Includes Calvary Holi-
        ness Church: ℓ . 74-75. KPT

CHURCH OF GOD (Cleveland, Tennessee) (1886-   )
[1886-1902 as Christian Union; 1902-1907 as Holiness Church.]

On August 19, 1886, eight persons met in the Barney Creek
Meetinghouse near the confluence of the Barney and Coker creeks in
Monroe County, Tennessee and organized the Christian Union.   Led
by Richard G. Spurling and his son, former Baptist ministers, the
new organization proposed to revive primitive Christianity, a goal
it felt could not be realized in existing churches.   Although by 1896
membership reached nearly 130, dramatic losses during the next
few years nearly dissipated the membership.   Reorganized as the
Holiness Church in 1902 and re-named the Church of God five years
later, the group experienced phenomenal growth under the inspired
leadership of A. J. Tomlinson, a former Quaker, who served as its
general overseer from 1909 to 1923 and who led it into the Pentecostal movement.   Numbering only 25 in 1903, the year Tomlinson
joined, the group increased to 1,005 by the end of the decade, and
to 22,394 by the end of his term in office.   Except for a ten-year
lull during a controversy over Tomlinson's alleged mismanagement,
numerical gains continued.   In 1976 at the end of ninety years of
existence as a church, the Cleveland, Tennessee headquarters reported 828,643 members, of whom 361,099 were in 4,615 churches
in the United States and Canada.   That year the Church of God was
at work in eighty world areas and had 48 North American workers
under appointment.   Expenditures outside North America were in excess of $2,000,000.   The denomination sponsors the Church of God
Graduate School of Christian Ministries and Lee College in Cleveland,
Tennessee; Bible colleges in Estevan, Saskatchewan; Minot, North
Dakota; Fresno, California; and Charlotte, North Carolina; and the
Indian Bible Institute in Gallup, New Mexico. The Church of God
Evangel, begun in 1910, is the official organ.   Pathway Press and
Tennessee Music and Printing Company are trade imprints for Church
of God publications.

2792   Church of God (Cleveland, Tn.)
           The book of doctrines; issued in the interest of the Church
       of God. Cleveland, Tn., Church of God Publishing House,
       c1922. 147p. DLC, MH-AH

2793   Church of God (Cleveland, Tn.)
           Manual de ensenanzas, disciplina, y gobierno. 3. éd.
       San Antonio, Tx., Editorial Evangélica, 1971. 95p.

2794   Church of God (Cleveland, Tn.)
           Presenting the Church of God, America's oldest Pente-
       costal church, 1886-1961. Cleveland, Tn., Church of God
       Publishing House, 1961. 31p.

2795   Church of God (Cleveland, Tn.)
           Presenting the Church of God, America's oldest Pente-
       costal church. Rev. ed. Cleveland, Tn., Church of God
       Publishing House, 1964. 40p.

2796   Church of God (Cleveland, Tn.). General Assembly.
           Minutes, 1906- . Cleveland, Tn., Church of God Pub-
       lishing House, 1922- v.[1]- . 1906-1958 as Book of minutes.
       1906-1917 issued in 1922 under title: Book of minutes; a com-
       piled history of the General Assemblies of the Church of God.

2797   Church of God: growing.
           In Christianity Today, 20 (Sept. 24, 1976), 56, 58. On
       the General Assembly of the Church of God (Cleveland, Tn.)
       in Dallas.

2798   Conn, Charles William, 1920-
           The Evangel reader; selections from the Church of God
       Evangel, 1910-1958, comp. and ed. with an introd. and notes
       by Charles W. Conn. Cleveland, Tn., Pathway Press, 1958.
       256p. DLC, TxWaS

2799   Diversifying the outreach.
           In Christianity Today, 22 (Sept. 8, 1978), 54, 46. On
       General Assembly of the Church of God (Cleveland, Tn.) in
       Kansas City, Missouri, in August.

2800   For such a time.
           In Christianity Today, 8 (Sept. 11, 1964), 52. On the
       fiftieth General Assembly of the Church of God (Cleveland,
       Tn.), held in Dallas in August.

2801   Gaddis, Merrill Elmer, 1891-
           Christian perfectionism in America. Chicago, 1929.
       viii, 589ℓ. Thesis (Ph.D.)--University of Chicago. On
       Church of God (Cleveland, Tn.): ℓ. 468-473. ICU

2802   Gaustad, Edwin Scott, 1923-
           Historical atlas of religion in America. New York,

Harper & Row, 1962. xii, 179p. On Church of God (Cleveland, Tn.): p. 124-125.

2803   Green, Hollis Lynn, 1933-
        The degree to which the Church of God remains Pentecostal in experience. Jacksonville, Fla., 1968. viii, 197ℓ.
        Thesis (Th. D.)--Luther Rice Seminary.

2804   Hughes, Ray Harrison, 1924-
        Church of God distinctives, by Ray H. Hughes. Cleveland, Tn., Pathway Press, 1968. 135p. (Church study course, 302.) MnCS, TxWaS

2805   Hughes, Ray Harrison, 1924-
        Distintivos de la Iglesia de Dios, por Ray H. Hughes.
        Traducido al español por Hiram Almirudis; revisado por Rafael González. Héctor Camacho, ed. Cleveland, Tn.,
        Pathway Press, c1968. 116p. "Primera edición en español autorizada por el Comité de Misiones de la Iglesia de Dios y por el autor. " Edición en español: San Antonio, Editorial Evangélica, 1970.

2806   Johnson, Guy Benton, 1928-
        A framework for the analysis of religious action, with special reference to holiness and non-holiness groups. Cambridge, Mass., 1953 [i. e. 1954] iii, 307ℓ. Thesis (Ph. D.)--Harvard University. Based in part on research in Robeson County, North Carolina in 1948, 1949 and 1951 including responses from ten non-Pentecostal and ten Pentecostal religionists (ministers from Pentecostal Holiness (5), Church of God (Cleveland, Tn.) (4), and Assemblies of God (1) denominations.
        MH

2807   Lane, G. W.
        Program and purpose: what we do and why we do it.
        n. p., 19--. 35p.

2808   Moore, Everett Leroy, 1918-
        Handbook of Pentecostal denominations in the United States.
        Pasadena, Ca., 1954. vii, 346ℓ. Thesis (M. A.)--Pasadena College. "Church of God": ℓ. 138-154, 333, 340. CSdP

2809   Tinney, James Stephen
        A right to be heard on tongues [by] James S. Tinney.
        In Christianity Today, 10 (Sept. 16, 1966), 46-47. On the biennial General Assembly of the Church of God in Memphis, August 10-15.

2810   Tinney, James Stephen
        Then there were 700, 000 [by] James S. Tinney. In Christianity Today, 12 (Sept. 27, 1968), 28. On the General Assembly of the Church of God (Cleveland, Tennessee) held in Dallas in August.

2811   U.S. Bureau of the Census.
           Census of religious bodies: 1926. Church of God. Sta-
       tistics, denominational history, doctrine, and organization.
       Washington, Government Printing Office, 1928. 10p.
       DLC

2812   U.S. Bureau of the Census.
           Census of religious bodies: 1936. Churches of God.
       Statistics, denominational history, doctrine, and organization.
       Washington, Government Printing Office, 1941. iv, 33p.
       NNUT

                      --BIOGRAPHY

2813   Church of God (Cleveland, Tn.). World Missions Board.
           Meet your missionaries; a manual for those who pray.
       Cleveland, Tn., 197-. 152p.

                      --BUILDINGS

2814   Shoemaker, Lowell T.
           Church of God building program guide, by Lowell T.
       Shoemaker. Cleveland, Tn., 1964. 34p. "Prepared under
       the direction of the Church of God Architectural Department."

                 --CATECHISMS AND CREEDS

2815   Church of God (Cleveland, Tn.)
           The book of doctrines; issued in the interest of the Church
       of God. Cleveland, Tn., Church of God Publishing House,
       c1922. 147p. DLC, MH-AH

2816   Church of God (Cleveland, Tn.)
           Teachings of the Church of God. In Hardon, J. A. The
       spirit and origins of American Protestantism: a source book
       in its creeds. Dayton, Ohio, 1968, 254-256.

2817   Day, Ralph E.
           Manual de instrucción en la fe de la Iglesia; para jóvenes
       (de 12 hasta 24 años de edad). Redactor: Antonino Bonilla.
       Traductor: Juan M. Vergara. San Antonio, Tex., Editorial
       Evangelica, 19--. 71p. "Preparado bajo los auspicios del
       Comite Nacional de Escuela Dominical y Esfuerzo Juvenil de
       la Iglesia de Dios."

2818   Day, Ralph E.
           Manual of instruction in the faith of the church; for young
       people (ages 12 years through 24 years), by Ralph E. Day.
       Cleveland, Tn., Pathway Press, c1959. 95p. Cover title:
       Our Church of God faith; a manual of instruction for young

people. "Prepared under the auspices of the Church of God National Sunday School and Youth Board."

2819   Day, Ralph E.
        Our faith: a manual of instruction in the faith of the Church of God; for children (ages 4 through 11 years). Cleveland, Tn., Pathway Press, 19--. 64p. Cover title: Our Church of God faith. "Prepared under the auspices of the Church of God National Sunday School and Youth Board."

2820   Leroy, Douglas, 1943-
        We believe: a book for children on the Church of God declaration of faith. Written by Douglas Leroy. Illustrated by Julius Miller. Cleveland, Tn., Pathway Press, 1974. 52p.

2821   Slay, James Linwood
        Esto creemos, por James L. Slay. [Traducido al español por] Leopoldo Domínguez; [revisado por] Hiram Almirudiz. Héctor Camacho H., ed. San Antonio, Tex., Editorial Evangelica, 1969, c1963. 156p. "Primera edición hispaña autorizada por el Comité de Misiones de la Iglesia de Dios y por el autor."

2822   Slay, James Linwood
        This we believe, by James L. Slay. Cleveland, Tn., Pathway Press, 1963. 139p. (Workers' training course 301.) "Prepared under the auspices of the Church of God National Sunday School and Youth Board." TxWaS

                    --CHARITIES

2823   [Church of God (Cleveland, Tn.). Orphanage Board]
        The Church of God orphans; a historiette and code of rules for the Church of God orphan homes. Cleveland, Church of God Publishing House, 194-. 15p.

2824   Cleveland, Tn. Church of God Orphanage.
        Pictorial review of the Church of God Orphanage, 1940. 20th anniversary. Cleveland, Tn., 1940. 19p.

                    --DEVOTIONAL LITERATURE

2825   Byrd, James Franklin, 1939-
        Manna: table devotions; a guide for family worship and inspiration. Compiled by James F. Byrd and Floyd D. Carey. Cleveland, Tn., Pathway Press, c1973. 204p. "Prepared under the auspices of the Church of God General Youth and Christian Education Department."

2826   Conn, Charles William, 1920-

A certain journey, by Charles W. Conn. Cleveland, Tn.,
Pathway Press, c1965.   152p.

2827   Hargrave, Vessie Dee, 1915-
Moved by the Spirit, by Vessie D. Hargrave.   San Antonio, Evangelical Publishing House, c1957.   23p.

2828   Heil, L. E.
But I must decrease, by L. E. Heil.   Cleveland, Tn.,
Pathway Press, c1963.   173p.

--DIRECTORIES

2829   Church of God (Cleveland, Tn.)
Church directory, 1972-74- . Cleveland, Tn.   v.[1]- .

--DOCTRINAL AND CONTROVERSIAL WORKS

2830   Church of God (Cleveland, Tn.).   World Missions Board.
Curso Biblico por correspondencia.   San Antonio, c1946.
1v. (various pagings)

2831   Alton, William D.
El discipulado.   El don de profecia y El mundo post
cristiano que ha de enfrentar la iglesia.   n. p., 19--.   11,
64, 78p.

2832   Batts, Albert H.
Debate on instrumental music in worship, by Albert Batts
and Gus Nichols.   Anniston, Al., 1967.   53p.

2833   Batts, Albert H.
Here a little, there a little, by Albert H. Batts.   Decatur, Al., 19--.   47p.

2834   Batts, Albert H.
The power of faith; deliverance for soul, body, mind and
spirit, by Albert H. Batts.   Decatur, Al., 19--.   60p.

2835   Batts, Albert H.
Sabbath day doctrine, by Albert H. Batts.   Chattanooga,
Tn., 19--.   [35]p.

2836   Batts, Albert H.
A threefold sanctification for a threefold man, by Albert
H. Batts.   n. p., 19--.   76p.

2837   Batts, Albert H.
Water and Spirit baptism; Batts-Sain debate, held at
Morrison, Tennessee, February 15-18, 1965, between Albert
Batts, representing the Church of God, and Harold Sain,

representing the Church of Christ. Cleveland, Tn., Church
of God Publishing House, 1966. 148p.

2838   Benton, Clarence L.
        Ontology of the baptism into the Holy Ghost, by Clarence
        L. Benton. n.p., 19--. 28p.

2839   Bible. N.T. John. English.
        The Gospel of John. Cleveland, Tn., Church of God,
        Evangelism and Home Missions Department, 19--. 60p.

2840   Bowdle, Donald Nelson
        Redemption accomplished and applied, by Donald N.
        Bowdle. Cleveland, Tn., Pathway Press, c1972. 120p.
        (Church training course series, 304.)

2841   Bowen, C. E.
        The Lord's Supper and feet washing, by C. E. Bowen.
        Cleveland, Tn., Church of God Publishing House, 1955.
        134p. TxWaS

2842   Bright, Jonathan D.
        The baptism of the Holy Ghost, by Jonathan D. Bright.
        Cleveland, Tn., Church of God Publishing House, 19--. 32p.

2843   Britt, George L.
        The hour has come, by George L. Britt. Cleveland,
        Tn., Pathway Press, c1966. 96p.

2844   Britt, George L.
        Was wartet auf Europa? Und andere prophetische Be-
        trachtungen. 2. erweiterte Aufl. Stuttgart, W. Greiner &
        W. Schmidt, 1969. 80p. "Copyright: Pathway Press, 1958."

2845   Britt, George L.
        When dust shall sing; the world crisis in the light of
        Bible prophecy, by George L. Britt. Cleveland, Tn., Path-
        way Press, 1958. 203p.

2846   Brumback, Carl, 1917-
        God in three Persons; a Trinitarian answer to the one-
        ness or "Jesus only" doctrine concerning the Godhead and
        water baptism. Cleveland, Tn., Pathway Press, 1959. 192p.
        DLC

2847   Buxton, Clyne W.
        What about tomorrow? [By] Clyne W. Buxton. Cleve-
        land, Tn., Pathway Press, 1974. 144p. DLC

2848   Carey, Floyd D.
        Insight for Christian young people, by Floyd D. Carey.
        Cleveland, Tn., Youth Evangelism, c1964. 32p.

2849   Carey, Floyd D.
           Involved, by Floyd D. Carey. Cleveland, Tn., Pathway
        Press, c1969. 107p.

2850   Carroll, Ramon Leonard, 1920-1972.
           Stewardship: total-life commitment. Cleveland, Tn.,
        Pathway Press, 1967. 144p. (Church training course series,
        403.)

2851   Catoe, Harold
           Why I preach divine healing. n. p., 19--. [11]p.

2852   Clark, Elijah Columbus
           The baptism of the Holy Ghost "and more," by Elijah C.
        Clark. Cleveland, Tn., c1928. 128p. DLC

2853   Clark, Elijah Columbus
           The baptism of the Holy Ghost "and more," by Elijah C.
        Clark. 2d ed. Cleveland, Tn., Church of God Publishing
        House, c1931. 129p. DLC, NNUT

2854   Clark, Elijah Columbus
           Eloheim; or, The manifestation of the Godhead, by Elijah
        C. Clark. Cleveland, Tn., Church of God Publishing House,
        c1929. 134p. DLC, NNUT

2855   Clark, Elijah Columbus
           Marvelous healings God wrought among us, ed. by E. C.
        Clark. Cleveland, Tn., Church of God Publishing House,
        194-. 160p.

2856   Coleman, E. E.
           The Bible's greatest secret, by E. E. Coleman. n. p.,
        19--. 41p.

2857   Coleman, E. E.
           Jesus Christ the same yesterday, today, and tomorrow,
        by E. E. Coleman. Greenville, Oh., 19--. 58p.

2858   Compton, W. H.
           As the Spirit gave, by W. H. Compton. Cleveland, Tn.,
        Church of God Publishing House, c1970. 72p. TxWaS

2859   Conn, Charles William, 1920-
           Acts of the Apostles, by Charles W. Conn. Cleveland,
        Tn., Pathway Press, c1965. 127p. (Church training course
        series, 206.)

2860   Conn, Charles William, 1920-
           A balanced church, by Charles W. Conn. Introd. by Ray
        H. Hughes. Cleveland, Tn., Pathway Press, c1975. 183p.

2861   Conn, Charles William, 1920-

The Bible: book of books, by Charles W. Conn. Cleveland, Tn., Pathway Press, c1961. 111p. (Church training course, 201.) "Prepared under the auspices of the Church of God National Sunday School and Youth Board." DLC

2862 Conn, Charles William, 1920-
Christ and the gospels. Cleveland, Tn., Pathway Press, c1964. 119p. (Church training course, 205.)

2863 Conn, Charles William, 1920-
A guide to the Pentateuch. Cleveland, Tn., Pathway Press, c1963. 109p. (Workers' training course, 202.)

2864 Conn, Charles William, 1920-
Highlights of Hebrew history, by Charles W. Conn. Cleveland, Tn., Pathway Press, c1975. 112p. (Church training course, 203.) "Prepared under the auspices of the Church of God General Youth and Christian Education Board."

2865 Conn, Charles William, 1920-
Pillars of Pentecost, by Charles W. Conn. Cleveland, Tn., Pathway Press, 1956. 141p. DLC, NNUT, TxWaS

2866 Conn, Charles William, 1920-
A survey of the Epistles, by Charles W. Conn. Cleveland, Tn., Pathway Press, c1969. 112p. (Church training course, 207.) "Prepared under the auspices of the Church of God General Sunday School and Youth Board."

2867 Conn, Charles William, 1920-
Why men go back; studies in defection and devotion, by Charles W. Conn. Foreword by Wade H. Horton. Cleveland, Tn., Pathway Press, 1966. 136p. DLC

2868 Coward, Parnell C.
Revelation systematically studied; a study with the layman in mind, by Parnell C. Coward. Cleveland, Tn., Pathway Press, 1974. 300p. DLC

2869 Cox, Clyde C., 1905-
Evangelical precepts of the Revelation; with a verse-by-verse interpretation, by Clyde C. Cox. Cleveland, Tn., Pathway Press, c1971. 167p. DLC

2870 Cox, Clyde C., 1905-
Footprints of the great tribulation; the book of Revelation reverently narrated, by Clyde C. Cox. Cleveland, Tn., Pathway Press, c1961. 128p.

2871 Cox, Clyde C., 1905-
Prophetical events and the great tribulation; a study of prophecy in Revelation, by Clyde C. Cox. New York, Exposition Press, 1957. 126p.

2872   Cross, James Adam, 1911-
            Answers from the word, by James A. Cross. Cleveland,
        Tn., Pathway Press, c1974. 160p.

2873   Cross, James Adam, 1911-
            Healing in the church, comp. and ed. by James A. Cross.
        Cleveland, Tn., Pathway Press, 1962. 141p. DLC, TxWaS

2874   Cross, James Adam, 1911-
            A study of the Holy Ghost, by James A. Cross. Cleve-
        land, Tn., Pathway Press, c1973. 164p.

2875   Donahue, C. B.
            Questions and answers on once in grace, always in grace,
        by C. B. Donahue. Rev. ed. n.p., 19--. 24p.

2876   Geren, Gilbert L.
            Divine healing: how to receive and keep, by Gilbert L.
        Geren. Cleveland, Tn., 19--. 75[8]p.

2877   Goins, J. L.
            Pearl of prophecy, by J. L. Goins. Chattanooga, Tn.,
        19--. 94p.

2878   Green, Hollis Lynn, 1933-
            Dynamics of Christian discipleship; an adventure in Chris-
        tian living, by Hollis L. Green. Cleveland, Tn., Pathway
        Press, c1962. 112p. (Workers' training course, 401.)

2879   Green, Hollis Lynn, 1933-
            Hitching your star to a wagon; a guide for those in
        search of a vocational direction, by Hollis L. Green. n.p.,
        19--. 30p.

2880   Green, Hollis Lynn, 1933-
            Understanding Pentecostalism. Cleveland, Tn., Pathway
        Press, c1970. 26p.

2881   Hammel, W. W., 1900-
            How shall we escape if we neglect so great salvation; a
        scriptural study with poems and chart [by] W. W. Hammel.
        Cleveland, Tn., Pathway Press, 1972. 95p.

2882   Hargrave, Vessie Dee, 1915-
            Glossolalia interpreted by theological works and commen-
        taries, by Vessie D. Hargrave. n.p., 1966. 52ℓ.

2883   Hawk, Monte Ray, 1936-
            Debate notes on Holy Ghost baptism, for Church of God
        and United Pentecostal arguments. Gadsden, Al., Hawk's
        Publications, 1974. 51p. Notes on a debate with E. J.
        Reynolds of the Church of God, October 15-16, 1973. TMH

2884   Horton, Wade Henry, 1908-
        Fifty undeniable facts that prove the trinitarian concept
        of God, by Wade H. Norton. Cleveland, Tn., Pathway Press,
        1964. 55p.

2885   Horton, Wade Henry, ed., 1908-
        The glossolalia phenomenon. General editor: Wade H.
        Horton. Contributing editors: Charles W. Conn [and others].
        Cleveland, Tn., Pathway Press, 1966. 304p. DLC, MH-AH,
        TxWaS

2886   Horton, Wade Henry, 1908-
        The seven golden candlesticks [by] Wade H. Horton.
        Cleveland, Tn., Pathway Press, 1974. 216p. DLC

2887   Hughes, J. P.
        The twofold aspect and final consummation of the church.
        Cleveland, Tn., Church of God Publishing House, 19--. 57p.

2888   Hughes, Ray Harrison, 1924-
        Church of God distinctives, by Ray H. Hughes. Cleve-
        land, Tn., Pathway Press, 1968. 135p. (Church study
        course, 302.) MnCS, TxWaS

2889   Hughes, Ray Harrison, 1924-
        Distintivos de la Iglesia de Dios, por Ray H. Hughes.
        Traducido al español por Hiram Almirudis; revisado por
        Rafael González. Héctor Camacho, ed. Cleveland, Tn.,
        Pathway Press, c1968. 116p. "Primera edición en español
        autorizada por el Comité de Misiones de la Iglesia de Dios
        y por el autor." Edición en español: San Antonio, Editorial
        Evangélica, 1970.

2890   Hughes, Ray Harrison, 1924-
        The order of future events, by Ray H. Hughes. Cleve-
        land, Tn., 1962. 80p. DLC

2891   Hughes, Ray Harrison, 1924-
        Qué es Pentecostés? Por Ray H. Hughes. Editor-
        traductor, Héctor Camacho. Cleveland, Tn., Pathway Press,
        c1963. 98p. "Primera edición en español autorizada por el
        Comité de Misiones de la Iglesia de Dios y por el autor.
        San Antonio, Editorial Evangélica, 1971."

2892   Hughes, Ray Harrison, 1924-
        What is Pentecost? Cleveland, Tenn., Pathway Press,
        1963. 108p. DLC, TxWaS

2893   Hurst, Ruby Wright
        That I may know Him. n. p., 19--. 15p.

2894   Kee, Jack H.

Before the world's foundation, by Jack H. Kee. Powderly, Tx., 1973. 54p.

2895   Kee, Jack H.
        The end of the world, by Jack H. Kee. Powderly, Tx., 19--. 48p.

2896   Kee, Jack H.
        This life and the life to come, by Jack H. Kee. Powderly, Tx., 19--. 30p.

2897   Kee, Jack H.
        Tongues like fire: the evidence of Pentecost, by Jack H. Kee. Powderly, Tx., 19--. 32p.

2898   Keyser, Leander Sylvester, 1856-1937.
        Un Sistema de evidencias cristianas [por] Leander S. Keyser. Raúl del Piero, traductor. Héctor Camacho, ed. 2. ed. San Antonio, Editorial Evangélica, 1971, c1956. viii, 172p. Translation of A system of Christian evidence. "Décima edición revisada en inglés, the Lutheran Literary Board, Burlington, Iowa, [1950]."

2899   Lane, G. W.
        Doctrine of the New Testament in ten great subjects: sin and sins; atonement; justification; sanctification; baptism of the Holy Ghost; New Testament church; controversy of water baptism; financial system; divine healing; answer to eternal security. Cincinnati, Church of God, 19--. 127p. MnCS

2900   Lee, Flavius Josephus, 1875-1928.
        Book of prophecy; questions and answers on the entire book of Revelation, edited by F. J. Lee. 2d ed. Cleveland, Tn., Church of God Publishing House, 1931. 170p.

2901   Lee, Flavius Josephus, 1875-1928.
        Demonology. n.p., 19--. 110p.

2902   Lee, Flavius Josephus, 1875-1928.
        Divine healing: series one. Cleveland, Tn., Church of God Publishing House, c1925. 29p.

2903   Lemons, Frank W., 1901-
        Looking beyond; Christian outlook at time of bereavement, by Frank W. Lemons. Cleveland, Tn., Pathway Press, 19--. 78p.

2904   Lemons, Frank W., 1901-
        Our Pentecostal heritage, by Frank W. Lemons. Cleveland, Tn., Pathway Press, c1963. 173p. TxWaS

2905   Lemons, Frank W., 1901-

Profiles of faith [by] Frank W. Lemons. Cleveland, Tn., Pathway Press, 1971. 103p. DLC

2906   Lemons, M. S.
Advice to girls, by M. S. Lemons. Atlanta, Printed by Church of God Publishing House, Cleveland, Tn., 1919. 44p.

2907   Lemons, M. S.
Questions answered on regeneration, sanctification, baptism with the Holy Ghost, the Church of God and speaking with tongues, etc., by M. S. Lemons. n. p., 19--. 30p.

2908   Leroy, Douglas, 1943-
I didn't know that! Cleveland, Tn., Pathway Press, 1973. 144p. DLC

2909   Llewellyn, Joseph Steele
The Bible church. Cleveland, Tn., Church of God Publishing House, 1924. 95p.

2910   Llewellyn, Joseph Steele
Bible training for Christian workers, by J. S. Llewellyn. Cleveland, Tn., Church of God Publishing House, c1925. 214p.

2911   Llewellyn, Joseph Steele
Summarized Bible study, by J. S. Llewellyn. Cleveland, Tn., Church of God Publishing House, c1925. 121p. DLC

2912   Maxwell, John
God's eternal glory; an introduction to apostolic acts, with some sacred songs and scriptural writings. Coimbatore, India, 19--. 28p.

2913   [Maxwell, John]
The nature and name of the church. Coimbatore, India, 19--. 8p.

2914   [Maxwell, John]
Prophetic writings. Coimbatore, India, 19--. 32p.

2915   Moore, E. L.
Law and sabbath keepers on trial. Cleveland, Tn., Church of God Publishing House, 19--. 22p.

2916   Newton, C. M.
My visit with the angels. Memphis, C. M. Newton Revivals, 19--. 20p.

2917   Paulk, Earl Pearly, 1927-
Your Pentecostal neighbor, by Earl P. Paulk. Cleveland, Tn., Pathway Press, 1958. 237p. DLC, TxWaS

2918   Polen, Olly Wayne, 1920-
        Editorially speaking; a selection of twelve choice editor-
        ials on subjects of special interest [by] O. W. Polen. Cleve-
        land, Tenn. , Pathway Press, 1975. 80p. First published
        in Church of God Evangel. DLC

2919   Pospisil, William
        Scriptural divine healing. Mulakuzha, Chengannur, India,
        C. G. I. Press, 1959. 16p.

2920   Pospisil, William
        Water baptism: its importance, meaning and method.
        Mulakuzha, Chengannur, India, C. G. I. Press, 1960. 20p.

2921   Reesor, James B.
        The fall, restoration and manifestation of the sons of
        God. n. p. , 19--. 77p.

2922   Remarkable incident: the story of Walter.
        Cleveland, Tn. , Church of God Publishing House, 19--.
        29p.

2923   Richardson, Carl Herbert, 1939-
        Exorcism: New Testament style! [By] Carl Richardson.
        Old Tappan, N. J. , F. H. Revell Co. , 1974. 128p. (Spire
        books.) DLC

2924   Richardson, Carl Herbert, 1939-
        Forecasts for the future, by Carl H. Richardson. Cleve-
        land, Tn. , Pathway Press, c1973. 41p.

2925   Roberts, Philemon
        God's will for God's people; a treatise on sanctification.
        Cleveland, Tn. , Pathway Press, 1958. 122p. CMlG

2926   Roberts, Philemon
        The Holy Spirit and you. Tampa, Fl. , 19--. 87p.

2927   Rouse, L. G.
        Marvels and miracles of healing, by L. G. Rouse. Knox-
        ville, Tn. , 19--. 92p.

2928   Simmons, Ernest Lesley, 1893-
        The mystery of the Trinity, by E. L. Simmons. n. p. ,
        c1928. 31p.

2929   Slay, James Linwood
        Rescue the perishing, by James L. Slay. Cleveland,
        Tn. , Pathway Press, 1961. 166p. DLC

2930   Smith, Horace C.
        Agape: truth, life, love. Birmingham, Al. , Action
        Printing Co. , c1975. 152p.

2931   Sullivan, William F. , 1924-
             God still does the "impossible. " Charlotte, N. C. , 19--.
       85p.

2932   Swiger, Avis (Randolph)
             Old Testament narrative, by Avis Swiger. Cleveland,
       Tn. , Lee College, 1954-1959. 2v.

2933   Tomlinson, Ambrose Jessup, bp. , 1865-1943.
             The last great conflict. Cleveland, Tn. , Press of Walter
       E. Rodgers, 1913. 213p.

2934   Tomlinson, Homer Aubrey, bp. , 1892-1968.
             Home study Bible lessons. Cleveland, Tn. , Church of
       God Publishing House, 1919. 20v.

2935   Triplett, Bennie Stevens, 1929-
             A contemporary study of the Holy Spirit, by Bennie S.
       Triplett. Cleveland, Tn. , Pathway Press, c1970. 144p.
       (Church training course series, 305.) "Prepared under the
       auspices of the Church of God General Sunday School and
       Youth Board. " TMH, TxWaS

2936   Vest, Lamar
             What a life--the Jesus way. Cleveland, Tn. , Pathway
       Press, 1973. 144p. DLC

2937   Voorhis, George D. , 1930-
             Revelation, by G. D. Voorhis. n. p. , 19--. 78p.

2938   Voorhis, George D. , 1930-
             Satan exposed: a study of the occult, by George D.
       Voorhis. n. p. , c1973. 105p.

2939   Voorhis, George D. , 1930-
             The truth about Catholicism, by George D. Voorhis.
       n. p. , 19--. 23p.

2940   Voorhis, George D. , 1930-
             Waiting to see the Lord: Simeon, by George D. Voorhis.
       n. p. , 19--. 33p.

2941   Walker, Paul Haven, 1901-
             The baptism with the Holy Ghost and the evidence, by
       Paul H. Walker. Cleveland, Tn. , Church of God Publishing
       House, 19--. 32p.

2942   Walker, Paul Haven, 1901-
             The baptism with the Holy Ghost and the evidence, by
       Paul H. Walker. 4th ed. Cleveland, Tn. , Church of God
       Publishing House, 1972. 34p. Cover title.

2943   Walker, Paul Haven, 1901-

The Lord's Supper and feet washing, by Paul H. Walker. Cleveland, Tn. , Church of God Publishing House, 19--.   31p.

2944   Walker, Paul Haven, 1901-
        The manifestation of the Godhead, by Paul H. Walker. Beckley, W. Va. , 19--.   42p.

--EDUCATION

2945   Church of God (Cleveland, Tn.)
        Continuing education program.   Cleveland, Tn. , 1976- v. [1]-

2946   [Church of God (Cleveland, Tn.).   National Sunday School and Youth Board]
        A constitution for the Sunday school.   Cleveland, Tn. , 19--.   1v. (unpaged)

2947   Church of God (Cleveland, Tn.).   National Sunday School and Youth Board.
        Workers training course.   Cleveland, Tn. , Pathway Press, 19 - . v. 1- . DLC

2948   Church of God (Cleveland, Tn.).   Youth and Christian Educa-tion Board.
        Christian education standard.   Cleveland, Tn. , c1966. 32p.

2949   Aultman, Donald Sarrell, 1930-
        Contemporary Christian education, by Donald S. Aultman. Cleveland, Tn. , Pathway Press, 1967.   122p.

2950   Aultman, Donald Sarrell, 1930-
        A guide to family training hour.   3d ed.   Cleveland, Tn. , Pathway Press, 1968.   44p.   "Published under the auspices of the Church of God Sunday School and Youth Department. "

2951   Aultman, Donald Sarrell, 1930-
        The ministry of Christian teaching, by Donald S. Aultman. Cleveland, Tn. , Pathway Press, 1966.   111p.   (Church train-ing course series.)

2952   Baldree, J. Martin, 1927-
        How to enlarge your Sunday school, by J. Martin Baldree. Cleveland, Tn. , Church of God National Sunday School and Youth Department, 1962.   55p.

2953   Baldree, J. Martin, 1927-
        Sunday school growth, by J. Martin Baldree.   Cleveland, Tn. , Pathway Press, c1971.   142p.   (Church training course series, 127.)

2954   Buxton, Clyne W.
       This way to better teaching, by Clyne W. Buxton. Cleveland, Tn. , Pathway Press, c1974. 112p. (Church training course, 129.)

2955   Carey, Floyd D.
       Building Sunday school power, by Floyd D. Carey. Cleveland, Tn. , Pathway Press, c1971. 40p.

2956   Carey, Floyd D.
       Fuel for Sunday school growth, by Floyd D. Carey. Cleveland, Tn. , Pathway Press, 1971. 88p.

2957   Carey, Floyd D.
       Respond to the Sunday school challenge, by Floyd D. Carey. n. p. , c1973. 32p.

2958   Carey, Floyd D.
       Salty Sunday schools, by Floyd D. Carey. Cleveland, Tn. , Pathway Press, c1970. 32p.

2959   Carey, Floyd D.
       Stand up for the Sunday school. Compiled by Floyd D. Carey. Cleveland, Tn. , Pathway Press, 19--. 32p.

2960   Carey, Floyd D.
       Sunday school basics. Edited by Floyd D. Carey. Cleveland, Tn. , Pathway Press, c1976. 142p. (Church training course, 130.) DLC

2961   Carey, Floyd D.
       Sunday school bus evangelism, by Floyd D. Carey. n. p. , c1973. 41p.

2962   Carey, Floyd D.
       Sunday school visitation [by] Floyd D. Carey. Cleveland, Tn. , Pathway Press, c1980. 88p. DLC

2963   Carroll, Geneva
       Learning God's word. Cleveland, Tn. , Pathway Press, c1970. 3v. in 1.

2964   Carroll, Willie Mae
       Daily vacation Bible school. Cleveland, Tn. , Church of God Publishing House, 19--. 4v.

2965   Carroll, Willie Mae
       Train up a child in the way he should go. Cleveland, Tn. , Church of God Publishing House, 19--. 116p.

2966   Green, Hollis Lynn, 1933-
       Christian education cyclopedia. Edited by Hollis L.

Green. Cleveland, Tn. , Pathway Press, c1965. 184p.
"Compiled under the auspices of the Church of God Sunday
School and Youth Board. "

2967   Green, Hollis Lynn, 1933-
       Promotion plus ... Compiled and ed. by Hollis L. Green.
Cleveland, Tn. , Church of God Sunday School and Youth,
19--. 1v. (unpaged)

2968   Harrison, Alda B.
       How to conduct a daily vacation Bible school, by Alda B.
Harrison. Cleveland, Tn. , Church of God Publishing House,
19--. 132p.

2969   Henson, Paul F.
       Teach the word [by] Paul F. Henson. Cleveland, Tn. ,
Pathway Press, c1972. 96p. (Church training course series,
128.)

2970   Hughes, Ray Harrison, 1924-
       Planning for Sunday school progress. Prepared under
the auspices of the Church of God National Sunday School and
Youth Board. Cleveland, Tn. , Pathway Press, c1955. 128p.
(Workers' training course series, 101.)

2971   Hunt, Sonjia Lee
       Shaping faith through involvement. Cleveland, Tn. , Path-
way Press, c1981. 72p. "Prepared under the auspices of
the Church of God General Department of Youth and Christian
Education. " DLC

2972   Knight, Cecil Brigham, 1926-
       Keeping the Sunday school alive, by Cecil B. Knight.
Cleveland, Tn. , Pathway Press, c1959. 134p. (Workers'
training course series, 105.) "Prepared under the auspices
of the Church of God National Sunday School and Youth Board."

2973   Paulk, Earl Pearly, 1927-
       Sunday school evangelism, by Earl P. Paulk. Cleveland,
Tn. , Pathway Press, c1958. 125p. (Workers' training
course, 104.) "Prepared under the auspices of the Church
of God Sunday School and Youth Board. "

2974   Polen, Olly Wayne, 1920-
       The Sunday school teacher, by O. W. Polen. Cleveland,
Tn. , Pathway Press, c1956. 112p. (Workers' training
course, 102.) "Prepared under the auspices of the Church
of God Sunday School and Youth Board. "

2975   Scherz, Heinrich C.
       Initiating a long-range Christian education program in an
evangelical denominational church in west Germany, by Heinrich C. Scherz. Wheaton, Il. , 1969. iv, 97ℓ . Thesis
(M. A.)--Wheaton College. IWW

2976   Stanley, W. Perdue
            The student, by W. Perdue Stanley. Cleveland, Tn.,
        Pathway Press, c1957. 114p. (Workers' training course
        series, 103.) "Prepared under the auspices of the Church
        of God National Sunday School and Youth Board."

2977   Walker, Paul Laverne, 1932-
            Reaching with records. Cleveland, Tn., Pathway Press,
        c1961. 203p. (Workers' training course, 701.) "Prepared
        under the auspices of the Church of God National Sunday
        School and Youth Board."

                    --EVANGELISTIC WORK

2978   [Church of God (Cleveland, Tn.)]
            Encyclopedia on evangelism. Cleveland, Tn., Church
        of God Publishing House, 19--. 154p.

2979   Church of God (Cleveland, Tn.). International Evangelism
        Congress, Mexico City, 1973.
            Total evangelism: "until all have heard." Cleveland,
        Tn., Church of God Publishing House, c1973. 156p.

2980   Albert, Leonard C.
            Reaching for results; a lecture manual for lay-witnessing
        seminars on outreach evangelism, by Leonard C. Albert.
        Cleveland, Tn., Church of God Evangelism and Home Mis-
        sions Department, 19--. 56p.

2981   Maye, Aubrey D.
            Pentecostal witnessing; a training manual on personal
        soulwinning, by Aubrey D. Maye. Cleveland, Tn., Pathway
        Press, 19--. 76p.

2982   Pettit, Walter Raymond, 1921-
            The evangelism ministry of the local church, by Walter
        R. Pettitt. Cleveland, Tn., Pathway Press, c1969. 124p.
        (Church training course series, 502.) "Prepared under the
        auspices of the Church of God National Sunday School and
        Youth Board."

2983   Richardson, Carl Herbert, 1939-
            Down at the altar, by Carl H. Richardson. Tampa, Fl.,
        Nebraska Press, c1971. 34p.

2984   Richardson, Carl Herbert, 1939-
            Let's have revival, by Carl H. Richardson and Luchen
        A. Bailey. Marietta, Oh., State Committee on Evangelism
        of the Churches of God in Ohio, 1966. 24[5]p.

2985   Richardson, Carl Herbert, 1939-
            Let's have revival; a complete manual for the local

church revival crusade, by Carl H. Richardson. Cleveland,
Tn., Pathway Press, c1969. 48p. "Prepared under the aus-
pices of the Church of God National Evangelism and Home
Missions Department."

2986   Winters, William E.
        Convert conservation, by William E. Winters. Cleveland,
Tn., Pathway Press, c1970. 119p. (Church training course
series, 503.) "Prepared under the auspices of the Church
of God Evangelism and Home Missions Board."

                    --FICTIONAL LITERATURE

2987   Angley, Ernest W.
        Raptured, by Ernest W. Angley. 6th ed. Akron, Oh.,
Winston Press, 1964. 247p.

                    --GOVERNMENT

2988   Gause, Rufus Hollis, 1925-
        Church of God polity, by R. H. Gause. Cleveland, Tn.,
Pathway Press, 1958. 208p. DLC, TxWaS

2989   Gause, Rufus Hollis, 1925-
        Church of God polity, by R. H. Gause. Rev. ed.
Cleveland, Tn., Pathway Press, 1973. 285p.

2990   Pospisil, William
        Scriptural church government. Mulakuzha, Chengannur,
India, C. G. I. Press, 1960. 32p.

                    --HISTORY

2991   Church of God (Cleveland, Tn.)
        Presenting the Church of God, America's oldest Pente-
costal church, 1886-1961. Cleveland, Tn., Church of God
Publishing House, 1961. 31p.

2992   Church of God (Cleveland, Tn.)
        Presenting the Church of God, America's oldest Pente-
costal church. Rev. ed. Cleveland, Tn., Church of God
Publishing House, 1964. 40p.

2993   Church of God (Cleveland, Tn.). General Assembly.
        Book of minutes; a compiled history of the work of the
General Assemblies of the Church of God. Cleveland, Tn.,
Church of God Publishing House, 1922. 302p. Compiled by
L. Howard Juillerat and Mrs. Minnie E. Haynes. Includes
1st-13th annual assembly, 1906-1917.

2994   Conn, Charles William, 1920-
        The Evangel reader; selections from the Church of God
        Evangel, 1910-1958.   Compiled and ed. with introd. and
        notes by Charles W. Conn.   Cleveland, Tn. , Pathway Press,
        1958.   256p.   DLC, TxWaS

2995   Conn, Charles William, 1920-
        Like a mighty army moves the Church of God, 1886-
        1955.   Cleveland, Tn. , Church of God Publishing House,
        1955.   xxiv, 380p.   DLC, OkBetC, TxWaS

2996   Conn, Charles William, 1920-
        Like a mighty army: a history of the Church of God,
        1886-1976 [by] Charles W. Conn.   Rev. ed.   Cleveland, Tn. ,
        Pathway Press, 1977.   xxxi, 477p.   DLC

2997   Green, Hollis Lynn, 1933-
        Marching as to war; a survey of Church of God history.
        n. p. , 19--.   [13]p.   Based on Like a mighty army, by
        Charles W. Conn.

2998   History of the Church of God (local & general) and business
        directory of Cleveland, Tenn.
        Cleveland, Tn. , Church of God Publishing House, 1933.
        1v. (unpaged)

2999   Simmons, Ernest Lesley, 1893-
        History of the Church of God, by E. L. Simmons.   Cleve-
        land, Tn. , Church of God Publishing House, 1938.   156p.
        DLC

3000   Spurling, Richard G. , 1858-1935.
        The lost link, by R. G. Spurling.   Turtletown, Tn. ,
        Farner Church of God, 1920, c1971.   52p.

3001   Stanley, W. Perdue
        Outline study course on Church of God history, by W.
        Perdue Stanley.   Cleveland, Tn. , 19--.   40p.   "Based on
        Like a mighty army, by Charles W. Conn. "

3002   Tomlinson, Ambrose Jessup, bp. , 1865-1943.
        Historical annual addresses [by] A. J. Tomlinson.   Com-
        piled by Perry E. Gillum.   Cleveland, Tn. , White Wing Pub-
        lishing House and Press, 1970-1972.   3v.   Includes addresses
        before the separation of 1923.   KyWAT

                    --HYMNS AND SACRED SONGS

3003   Church of God (Cleveland, Tn.)
        Church hymnal.   Cleveland, Tn. , Tennessee Music and
        Printing Co. , c1951.   410p.   With music (shape notes).

3004   Church of God (Cleveland, Tn.)
        Diamond jubilee.   Otis L. McCoy, ed.   Cleveland, Tn. ,
        Tennessee Music and Printing Co. , c1961.   160p.

3005   Church of God (Cleveland, Tn.)
        Hymns of the Spirit.   Connor B. Hall, ed.; Jimi Hall,
        assistant ed.   Cleveland, Tn. , Pathway Press, c1969.   viii,
        511p.   With music (shape notes).   KyLxCB

        --JUVENILE LITERATURE

3006   Carey, Floyd D.
        Teen tonic, by Floyd D. Carey.   Cleveland, Tn. , Path-
        way Press, c1968.   87p.

3007   Carey, Floyd D.
        Teen-agers' pocket companion, by Floyd D. Carey.
        Cleveland, Tn. , Pathway Press, c1962.   3v.

3008   Carey, Floyd D.
        The teen-agers' ten commandments on missions, by
        Floyd D. Carey.   Cleveland, Tn. , Pathway Press, c1961.
        31p.

3009   Carey, Floyd D.
        Teen-agers' trail guide, by Floyd D. Carey, Jr.   Cleve-
        land, Tn. , Pathway Press, c1960.   76p.

3010   Carey, Floyd D.
        Teenlife, by Floyd D. Carey.   Cleveland, Tn. , Pathway
        Press, c1970.   32p.

3011   Carey, Floyd D.
        Trials that trip teen-agers; a conduct and courage manual,
        by Floyd D. Carey.   Cleveland, Tn. , Pathway Press, c1960.
        32p.

3012   Green, Peggy (Lane)
        The way to teen-age charm.   Cleveland, Tn. , Pathway
        Press, c1970.   84p.   "Prepared under the auspices of the
        Women's Auxiliary (LWWB) of the Church of God for use in
        the Young Ladies' Auxiliary program. "

3013   Leroy, Douglas, 1943-
        We believe: a book for children on the Church of God
        declaration of faith.   Written by Douglas Leroy.   Illustrated
        by Julius Miller.   Cleveland, Tn. , Pathway Press, 1974.   52p.

        --LITURGY AND RITUAL

3014   Clark, Elijah Columbus

The practical handbook for ministers, by Elijah C. Clark.
Cleveland, Tn., Church of God Publishing House, c1933.
165p.   DLC

3015   Llewellyn, Joseph Steele
Ministers guide book for marriage and funeral occasions.
Cleveland, Tn., Church of God Publishing House, 19--.
131p.

3016   Tharp, Zeno Chandler, 1896-
The ministers' guide for special occasions.   Cleveland,
Tn., Church of God Publishing House, c1952.   241p.

--MISSIONS

3017   Church of God (Cleveland, Tn.).   World Missions Board.
Foreign missionary policy of the Church of God.   Rev.
ed.   Cleveland, Tn., Church of God Foreign Missions Board,
1955.   56p.   NNMR

3018   Church of God (Cleveland, Tn.).   World Missions Board.
Foreign missionary policy of the Church of God.   Rev.
ed.   Cleveland, Tn., Church of God Foreign Missions Board,
1959.   46p.   NNMR

3019   Church of God (Cleveland, Tn.).   World Missions Board.
Manual for missionaries.   Cleveland, Tn., Pathway
Press, 19--.   57p.

3020   Church of God (Cleveland, Tn.).   World Missions Board.
Meet your missionaries; a manual for those who pray.
Cleveland, Tn., 197-.   152p.

3021   Conn, Charles William, 1920-
Where the saints have trod; a history of Church of God
missions [by] Charles W. Conn.   Cleveland, Tn., Pathway
Press, 1959.   312p.   DLC

3022   Hargrave, Vessie Dee, 1915-
The church and world missions [by] Vessie D. Hargrave.
Cleveland, Tn., Pathway Press, 1970.   128p.   (Church training course, 702.)   "Prepared under the auspices of the Church
of God General Sunday School and Youth Board."

3023   Horton, Wade Henry, 1908-
Unto the uttermost, by Wade H. Horton.   Cleveland, Tn.,
Pathway Press, c1973.   279p.

3024   Hughes, Ray Harrison, 1924-
The influence of Lee College on the development of the
world missions program of the Church of God.   Knoxville,
1964.   vi, 77ℓ.   Thesis (M. S.)--University of Tennessee.
TU

3025 McCracken, Horace
      History of Church of God missions.   Cleveland, Tn. ,
      Church of God Missions Department, 1943.   173p.

      --MUSIC

3026 Alford, Delton Lynol
      Music in the Pentecostal church [by] Delton L. Alford.
      Cleveland, Tn. , Pathway Press, 1967.   120p.   (Church train-
      ing course series, 703.)   DLC

3027 Alford, Delton Lynol
      Music in worship [by] Delton L. Alford.   In Knight,
      C. B. , ed.   Pentecostal worship.   Cleveland, Tn. , 1974,
      63-75.

3028 Batts, Albert H.
      Debate on instrumental music in worship, by Albert Batts
      and Gus Nichols.   Anniston, Al. , 1967.   53p.

3028a Conn, Philip Wesley, 1942-
      The relationship between congregational hymn preference
      and socioeconomic status: a study of congregational variation
      in religious orientation.   Knoxville, 1972.   172ℓ .   Thesis
      (M. A.)--University of Tennessee.   TU

3029 McCoy, Otis L.
      Tenmuco music course for beginners in music.   Ar-
      ranged by Otis L. McCoy.   Cleveland, Tn. , Tennessee Mu-
      sic and Printing Co. , 19--.   96p.

3030 Showalter, Anthony Johnson, 1858-1924.
      Showalter's Practical harmony, by A. J. Showalter.
      Cleveland, Tn. , Tennessee Music and Printing Co. , c1907.
      188p.   On cover: The A. J. Showalter Company.

3031 Showalter, Anthony Johnson, 1858-1924.
      Showalter's Practical rudiments and music reader, by
      A. J. Showalter.   Rev. ed.   Cleveland, Tn. , Tennessee
      Music and Printing Co. , 1926.   64p.   At head of title:
      Shape notes.

3032 Showalter, Anthony Johnson, 1858-1924.
      Rudiments of music, with a few choice selections for
      the singing school, by A. J. Showalter.   Cleveland, Tn. ,
      Tennessee Music and Printing Co. , 19--.   32p.   Cover title.
      At head of title: Shape notes.

      --PASTORAL LITERATURE

3033 Aultman, Donald Sarrell, 1930-

Learning Christian leadership, by Donald S. Aultman.
Cleveland, Tn. , Pathway Press, c1960. 108p. (Workers'
training course series, 106.) "Prepared under the auspices
of the Church of God National Sunday School and Youth Board."

3034   Conn, Charles Paul, 1945-
        The meaning of marriage. Cleveland, Tn. , Pathway
        Press, c1977. 138p. (Making life count: new life series.)
        DLC

3035   Conn, Charles William, 1920-
        The rudder and the rock, by Charles W. Conn. Cleve-
        land, Tenn. , Pathway Press, 1960. 151p. DLC

3036   Harrison, Alda B.
        Consolation for the tempted and tried. Compiled by Alda
        B. Harrison. Cleveland, Tn. , Church of God Publishing
        House, 19--. 52p.

3037   Harrison, Alda B.
        Home scenes; a dramatic service in the interest of the
        homes of our land. Prepared by Alda B. Harrison. Cleve-
        land, Tn. , Church of God Publishing House, 19--. 15p.

3038   Harrison, Alda B.
        Silver lining. Compiled by Alda B. Harrison. Jones-
        boro, Tn. , 19--. 52p.

3039   Polen, Olly Wayne, 1920-
        Editorially speaking; a selection of twelve choice editor-
        ials on subjects of special interest [by] O. W. Polen. Cleve-
        land, Tn. , Pathway Press, 1975. 80p. First published in
        Church of God Evangel. DLC

3040   Pospisil, William
        Now that I have accepted Christ; helpful suggestions to
        new Christians. Mulakuzha, Chengannur, India, C. G. I.
        Press, 19--. 18p.

3041   Stone, Hoyt Edward, 1935-
        Of course you can! [By] Hoyt E. Stone. Cleveland,
        Tn. , Pathway Press, c1973. 144p. DLC

3042   Truesdell, Cecil M.
        The eye opener, by C. M. Truesdell and Dana North,
        artist. Cleveland, Tn. , c1944. 80p.

3043   Vaught, Laud Oswald, 1925-
        Focus on the Christian family. Cleveland, Tn. , Pathway
        Press, 1976. 143p. DLC

--PASTORAL THEOLOGY

3044   Bava, John, 1912-
        Scrapbook of radiant gems, no. 1; gems for ministers
        [and] Christian workers; ideal helps for young people's ser-
        vice, radio ministry. Davis, W. Va., John Bava's Music,
        c1966. 1v. (unpaged)

3045   Bright, Jonathan D.
        Chin lifters for ministers and laymen, by Jonathan D.
        Bright. Cleveland, Tn., Church of God Publishing House,
        c1943. 168p.

3046   Clark, Elijah Columbus
        The practical handbook for ministers, by Elijah C. Clark.
        Cleveland, Tn., Church of God Publishing House, c1933.
        165p. DLC

3047   Clark, Elijah Columbus
        The victory; practical handbook for ministers, by Elijah
        C. Clark. Cleveland, Tn., Church of God Publishing House,
        c1944. 230p.

3048   Fisher, Robert Elwood, 1931-
        The challenge of the ministry. Edited by Robert E.
        Fisher. Cleveland, Tn., Pathway Press, c1977. 155p.
        DLC

3049   Hargrave, Vessie Dee, 1915-
        Sermones. ----, 19--. 5v.
        Contents: 1. Sermones de Caracter General. -2. Manual
        ministerial. -3. Sermones para Ocasiones especiales. -4. Ser-
        mones evangelisticos. -5. Sermones doctrinales.

3050   Jenkins, Robert J.
        O yes you can, by Robert J. Jenkins. n.p., 19--. 22p.

3051   Jernigan, John C., 1900-
        Advice to ministers. Cleveland, Tn., c1948. 143p.

3052   Polen, Olly Wayne, ed., 1920-
        Pastoral pointers. O. W. Polen, editor-in-chief. Cleve-
        land, Tn., Pathway Press, 1976, c1975. 92p. DLC

3053   Tharp, Zeno Chandler, 1896-
        Favorite stories and illustrations, by Zeno C. Tharp.
        Cleveland, Tn., Church of God Publishing House, 1956. 144p.
        DLC

3054   Walker, Paul Laverne, 1932-
        The ministry of church and pastor, by Paul L. Walker.
        Cleveland, Tenn., Pathway Press, 1965. 107p. (Church
        training course, 320.) "Prepared under the auspices of the

Church of God National Sunday School and Youth Board. "
CMlG

--PERIODICALS

3055   Adult teacher. 1- 1933-
       Cleveland, Tn.

3056   Bote de Gemeinde Gottes. 1- 1948-1957.
       Krehwinkel bei Schorndorf, Württ.

3057   Campus call. 1- 1963-
       Cleveland, Tn.

3058   Church of God evangel. 1- Mar. 1, 1910-
       Cleveland, Tn. 1910-1911 as Evening light and Church
       of God evangel. DLC, KyLxCB

3059   Church of God gospel herald. 1- 19 -Nov. 1965.
       Cleveland, Tn.

3060   El Evangelio de la Iglesia de Dios. 1- Dec. 1945-
       San Antonio

3061   L'Evangile. 1- Mar. 1949-
       Port-au-Prince

3062   Lighted pathway. 1- Aug. 1929-
       Cleveland, Tn.

3063   Macedonian call. 1- 1946-1950.
       Cleveland, Tn., Church of God Missions Board.

3064   On guard: Pentecostal servicemen's magazine. 1- 1961-
       Cleveland, Tn.

3065   Our junior jewels. 1- 1941-
       Cleveland, Tn.

3065a Pentecostal minister. 1- 1981-
       Cleveland, Tn.

3066   Pilot. 1- 1953-
       Cleveland, Tn.

3067   Sow. 1- 1962-
       Cleveland, Tn., Church of God World Missions.

3068   Die Wahrheit. 1- 1957-
       Krehwinkel bei Schorndorf, Württ.

3068a Willing worker. 1- 1967-
       Cleveland, Tn.

3069   Youth teacher.   1-   July 1948-
        Cleveland, Tn., Church of God Publishing House.   1-17,
        1948-1965 as Church of God Pentecostal teacher for youth
        classes.

                --PUBLISHERS AND PUBLISHING

3070   Church of God Publishing House.
        Style manual for editors and writers.   Cleveland, Tn.,
        197-.   121p.

                --SERMONS, TRACTS, ADDRESSES, ESSAYS

3071   Bridges, Jackie G.
        Heartbeats of Calvary, by ministers of Tennessee.   Spon-
        sored by the Tennessee Chapter of the Lee College Alumni
        Association.   Cleveland, Tn., 19--.   39p.

3072   Campbell, Manuel F.
        One minute please; one-minute sermons, by Manuel F.
        Campbell.   Cleveland, Tn., Church of God Publishing House,
        19--.   31p.

3073   Catoe, Harold
        Fear hath torment.   n.p., 19--.   8p.

3074   Catoe, Harold
        Reach out and touch the Lord.   n.p., 1968.   23p.

3075   Clark, Elijah Columbus
        Ever-ready all occasion sermon outlines, comp. by E. C.
        Clark.   Cleveland, Tn., Church of God Publishing House,
        194-.   101p.

3076   Compton, W. H.
        Selected sermon subjects.   Compiled by W. H. Compton.
        Cleveland, Tn., Pathway Press, c1963.   111p.   MnCS

3077   Compton, W. H.
        Compton's 75 sermon outlines by 38 different ministers.
        Compiled by W. H. Compton.   Cleveland, Tn., Pathway
        Press, 1954.   147p.

3078   Compton, W. H.
        Special day sermons [by] W. H. Compton.   Contributors:
        Donald B. Gibson [and others].   Cleveland, Tn., Pathway
        Press, c1971.   121p.   DLC

3079   Conn, Charles William, 1920-
        Twelve men and their message, by Charles W. Conn.
        n.p., 197-.   19ℓ.   1973 Church of God Florida State Camp-

meeting lectures. On the twelve apostles.

3080   Crenshaw, G. E.
            Three sermons: depravity, hell, entire sanctification.
        Central, S. C. , 19--. 20p.

3081   Cross, James Adam, 1911-
            The glorious gospel, by James A. Cross. Cleveland,
        Tn. , Church of God Publishing House, 1956. 135p. DLC

3082   Cross, James Adam, 1911-
            Healing in the church, comp. and ed. by James A. Cross.
        Cleveland, Tn. , Pathway Press, 1962. 141p. DLC, TxWaS

3083   Free, J. D.
            Camp meeting sermons, by J. D. Free. n. p. , 19--.
        93p.

3084   Heil, L. E.
            The double portion, by L. E. Heil. Cleveland, Tn. ,
        Pathway Press, c1961. 141p.

3085   Hinkley, Emmett B.
            The unseen worlds, by Emmett B. Hinkley. Radford,
        Va. , c1956. 30p. (Doctrinal series.)

3086   Horton, Wade Henry, 1908-
            Evangel sermons [by] Wade H. Horton. Cleveland, Tn. ,
        Pathway Press, c1977. 127p. Sermons printed in the Church
        of God evangel, 1974-1976. DLC

3087   Horton, Wade Henry, 1908-
            Pentecost yesterday and today, by Wade H. Horton.
        Cleveland, Tn. , Pathway Press, 1964. 176p. CMlG, TxWaS

3088   Horton, Wade Henry, 1908-
            Pentecost yesterday and today, by Wade H. Horton. Rev.
        ed. Cleveland, Tn. , Pathway Press, 1972. 235p.

3089   Horton, Wade Henry, 1908-
            Sound scriptural sermon outlines, no. 2, by Wade H.
        Horton. Cleveland, Tn. , Pathway Press, 1974. 220p.

3090   Horton, Wade Henry, 1908-
            Sound scriptural sermons, by Wade H. Horton. Fore-
        word by Ray H. Hughes. Cleveland, Tn. , Lee College
        Alumni Association, c1973. 176p.

3091   Hughes, Ray Harrison, 1924-
            The order of future events, by Ray H. Hughes. Cleve-
        land, Tn. , 1962. 80p. DLC

3092   Hughes, Ray Harrison, 1924-

Religion on fire, by Ray H. Hughes. Cleveland, Tn.,
Pathway Press, 1956. 159p. DLC

3093   Jernigan, John C., 1900-
Doctrinal sermon outlines. Cleveland, Tn., Church of
God Publishing House, 1946. 200p.

3094   Jernigan, John C., 1900-
Evangelistic sermon outlines. Cleveland, Tn., Church
of God Publishing House, 1946. 200p.

3095   Jernigan, John C., 1900- , comp.
Homiletic treasure. Atlanta, Jernigan Press, 19--. 3v.

3096   Jernigan, John C., 1900-
Sermon outlines with helps. Chattanooga, Gospel Book
House, 19--. 3v.

3097   Jernigan, John C., 1900-
Sermon outlines with helps. Atlanta, Jernigan Press,
19--. 3v.

3098   Jernigan, John C., 1900-
Sermon outlines with helps, for ministers and Christian
workers, by Jno. C. Jernigan. Cleveland, Tn., c1929.
400p. DLC

3099   Juillerat, L. Howard, 1886-1918.
Gems of religious truth from the pen of L. Howard Juil-
lerat. Compiled by Mrs. L. Howard Juillerat. Cleveland,
Tn., Church of God Evangel Press, 1919. 223p.

3100   Lane, G. W.
Bring the book. Cleveland, Tn., Pathway Press, c1968.
158p.

3101   Lane, G. W.
But his man. Cleveland, Tn., Pathway Press, c1960.
105p.

3102   Lane, G. W.
Material for ministers; fifty-two sermons in outline. 2d
ed. Cleveland, Tn., Pathway Press, 1961. 101p.

3103   Lane, G. W.
Sermon nuggets: fifty-two sermons in outline. Cleveland,
Tn., Pathway Press, 19--. 111p.

3104   Lane, G. W.
The voice of Calvary. Cleveland, Tn., Printed by Pathway Press, 1958. 112p. PPT, PPULC

3105   Lemons, Frank W., 1901-

       Perennial Pentecost. Cleveland, Tn., Pathway Press, 1971. 126p. DLC

3106   Lemons, Frank W., 1901-
       Profiles of faith [by] Frank W. Lemons. Cleveland, Tn., Pathway Press, 1971. 103p. DLC

3107   McLuhan, Mervyn G.
       Youth and the Bible, by M. G. McLuhan. n. p., 195-.
30p. From a sermon preached at the Florida State Camp Meeting, Wimauma, Florida, on June 13, 1953.

3108   Milligan, Joseph Lacey, 1921-
       The blushing bride, and other sermons, by Joseph L. Milligan. Cleveland, Tn., Pathway Press, c1968. 190p.

3109   Milligan, Joseph Lacey, 1921-
       Divinely guarded, and other sermons. Birmingham, Al., c1953. v. 1- DLC

3110   Paulk, Earl Pearly, 1927-
       Forward in faith sermons; sermons preached on the national radio broadcast "Forward in Faith," by Earl P. Paulk. Cleveland, Tn., Pathway Press, 1960. 275p. DLC

3111   Pettyjohn, Glenn C.
       Hearthrobs of Calvary, by Glenn C. Pettyjohn. n. p., 19--. 99p.

3112   Polen, Olly Wayne, 1920-
       Editorially speaking; a selection of twelve choice editorials on subjects of special interest [by] O. W. Polen. Cleveland, Tn., Pathway Press, 1975. 80p. First published in Church of God Evangel. DLC

3113   Reesor, James B.
       Gospel sermons for saint and sinner. Cleveland, Tn., Pathway Press, c1968. 107p.

3114   Tharp, Zeno Chandler, 1896-
       Inspirational short sermons. Cleveland, Tn., Church of God Publishing House, 1956. 150p. DLC

3115   Timmerman, Floyd J.
       Changing times with a changeless Christ, by Floyd J. Timmerman. Cleveland, Tn., Forward in Faith, 19--. 30p.

3116   Timmerman, Floyd J.
       Life's greatest discovery, by Floyd J. Timmerman. Cleveland, Tn., c1972. 80p.

3117   Timmerman, Floyd J.
       The pathway of promise, by Floyd J. Timmerman.

Cleveland, Tn., Pathway Press, c1968.   80p.

3118   Timmerman, Floyd J.
        The second coming of Christ, by Floyd J. Timmerman.
        Cleveland, Tn., Forward in Faith, 19--.   34p.

3119   Walker, Paul Haven, 1901-
        50 bosquejos para sermones, con ilustraciones y abun-
        dante material biblico, por Paul H. Walker.   Version es-
        panola de Rafael González G.   San Antonio, Editorial Evan-
        gelica, 1962.   108p.

3120   Walker, Paul Haven, 1901-
        Fifty sermon outlines from the scriptures; with illustra-
        tions and material for Bible studies and lectures, by Paul H.
        Walker.   n. p., 19--.   139p.

                    --WORK WITH CHILDREN

3121   Harrison, Alda B.
        Child training and social evangelism, by Alda B. Harri-
        son.   Cleveland, Tn., Church of God Publishing House, 19--.
        63p.

3122   Llewellyn, Joseph Steele
        Bible training for children.   Cleveland, Tn., Church of
        God Publishing House, c1924.   31p.

                    --WORK WITH PRISONERS

3123   Paulk, Earl Pearly, 1926-
        Execution of six men, by Earl P. Paulk.   3d ed.   n. p.,
        c1952.   40p.

                    --WORK WITH WOMEN

3124   Favorite recipes of Church of God homemakers: desserts,
        including party beverages.
        Montgomery, Al., 1969.   382p.   DLC

3125   Favorite recipes of Church of God homemakers: meats, in-
        cluding seafood and poultry.
        Montgomery, Al., Favorite Recipes Press, 1968.   382p.
        On cover: 1, 000 favorite recipes.   DLC

3126   Favorite recipes of Church of God homemakers: salads, in-
        cluding appetizers.
        Montgomery, Al., Favorite Recipes Press, 1970.   382p.
        DLC

3127   Favorite recipes from Church of God ladies: casseroles,
        including breads.
            Montgomery, Al., Favorite Recipes Press, 1970.   382p.
        DLC

3128   Favorite recipes from Church of God ladies: desserts, in-
        cluding party beverages.
            Montgomery, Al., Favorite Recipes Press, 1968.   382p.
        DLC

3129   Morrow, Helen L.
            Medical lectures for women only, by Helen L. Morrow.
        n. p. , 19--.   43p.

                --WORK WITH YOUTH

3130   [Church of God (Cleveland, Tn.).   National Sunday School
        and Youth Board]
            Scouting in the Church of God. Cleveland, Tn. , 19--.
        12p.

3131   Church of God (Cleveland, Tn.).   Youth and Christian Educa-
        tion Board.
            It matters to Him. Cleveland, Tn., Pathway Press,
        c1974.   48p.   At head of title: Church of God national youth
        emphasis.

3132   Aultman, Donald Sarrell, 1930-
            Guiding youth, by Donald S. Aultman. Cleveland, Tn.,
        Pathway Press, 1965.   109p.   (Church training course, 601.)
        CLamB

3133   Aultman, Donald Sarrell, 1930-
            Saved to serve; a guide to PFC International, by Donald
        S. Aultman. Cleveland, Tn., Church of God Sunday School
        and Youth Department, 19--.   48p.

3134   Carey, Floyd D.
            Campus champion; Pioneers for Christ daily devotions:
        a journey in daily devotions, by Floyd D. Carey and Marie
        Johnston. Cleveland, Tn., Youth Evangelism, c1964.   32p.

3135   Carey, Floyd D.
            Campus champion for Christ; a P. F. C. promotion, by
        Floyd D. Carey. Cleveland, Tn., Pathway Press, c1963.
        32p.

3136   Carey, Floyd D.
            Teen-age convention flames; commitment and conflict.
        Compiled by Floyd D. Carey. Cleveland, Tn., Pathway
        Press, c1960.   31p.

3137   Carey, Floyd D.
          Trials that trip teen-agers: conduct and courage manual,
       by Floyd D. Carey. Cleveland, Tn., Pathway Press, 1960.
       32p. OkTOr

3138   Guiles, Cecil R.
          Ministering to youth, by Cecil R. Guiles. Cleveland,
       Tn., Pathway Press, c1973. 107p. (Church training course,
       603.)

3139   Harrison, Alda B.
          Youth at the crossroads, by Alda B. Harrison. n.p.,
       19--. 276p. OkTOr

3140   Walker, Paul Laverne, 1932-
          Counseling youth [by] Paul L. Walker. Cleveland, Tn.,
       Pathway Press, 1967. 111p. (Church training course, 602.)
       "Prepared under the auspices of the Church of God National
       Sunday School and Youth Board."

          --WORSHIP

3141   Batts, Albert H.
          Debate on instrumental music in worship, by Albert Batts
       and Gus Nichols. Anniston, Al., 1967. 53p.

3142   Bishop, David S.
          The sacraments in worship [by] David S. Bishop. In
       Knight, C. B., ed. Pentecostal worship. Cleveland, Tn.,
       1974, 101-120.

3143   Fisher, Robert Elwood, 1931-
          Preparation for worship [by] Robert E. Fisher. In
       Knight, C. B., ed. Pentecostal worship. Cleveland, Tn.,
       1974, 17-31.

3144   Knight, Cecil Brigham, ed., 1926-
          Pentecostal worship. Edited by Cecil B. Knight. Cleve-
       land, Tn., Pathway Press, 1974. 140p. Essays by Cecil B.
       Knight, Robert E. Fisher, Lucille Walker, Robert White,
       Delton L. Alford, David S. Bishop, Bob E. Lyons and M. G.
       McLuhan. DLC, MSohG

3145   Knight, Cecil Brigham, 1926-
          The wonder of worship. In Knight, C. B., ed. Pente-
       costal worship. Cleveland, Tn., 1974, 7-15.

3146   McLuhan, Mervyn G.
          Spiritual gifts in worship [by] M. G. McLuhan. In Knight,
       C. B., ed. Pentecostal worship. Cleveland, Tn., 1974, 121-
       140.

3147   Walker, Lucille (Settle)
        Prayer in worship [by] Lucille Walker. In Knight, C. B.,
        ed. Pentecostal worship. Cleveland, Tn. , 1974, 33-47.

3148   White, Robert
        Praise in worship. In Knight, C. B. , ed. Pentecostal
        worship. Cleveland, Tn. , 1974, 49-61.

        --NORTH AND CENTRAL AMERICA

        -- --GUATEMALA

3149   Furman, Charles Truman, -1947.
        Guatemala and the story of Chuce, by Charles T. Fur-
        man. Cleveland, Tn. , Church of God Publishing House,
        c1940. 46p.

3150   Pullin, Alice
        In the morning sow. Cleveland, Tn. , Church of God
        Foreign Missions, 19--. 64p.

        -- --MEXICO

3151   Iglesia de Dios (Cleveland, Tn.)
        Enseñanzas, disciplina, y gobierno de la Iglesia de Dios.
        Tacubaya, C. F. , Imprenta Popular, 1945. 47p.

3152   Archer, James Willis
        Miracles in Mexico. n. p. , 194-. 64p. TxWaS

3153   Hargrave, O. T. , 1936-
        A history of the Church of God in Mexico, by O. T.
        Hargrave. San Antonio, 1958. vii, 159ℓ. Thesis (M. A.)--
        Trinity University. TxSaT

3154   Hargrave, Vessie Dee, 1915-
        South of the Rio Bravo, by Vessie D. Hargrave. Cleve-
        land, Tn. , Church of God Missions Department, 1952. 53p.

3155   Hargrave, Vessie Dee, 1915-
        South of the Rio Bravo, by Vessie D. Hargrave. Rev.
        ed. Cleveland, Tn. , Church of God Missions Department,
        1954. 56p.

        (Sonora)

3156   Elliott, William Winston, 1927-
        Sociocultural change in a Pentecostal group: a case study
        in education and culture of the Church of God in Sonora, Mex-
        ico. Knoxville, 1971. x, 260ℓ. Thesis (Ed. D.)--University
        of Tennessee. TU

-- --UNITED STATES

-- --MIDDLE WEST

(Illinois)

3157   The Church of God of Illinois: a history, 1916-1981.
        Charlotte, N.C., Delmar Co., 1981.   104p.   Caption
        title.   Cover title: Church of God of Illinois, 65th anniver-
        sary, 1916-1981.   DLC

(Michigan)

3158   Historical Records Survey.   Michigan.
        Inventory of the church archives of Michigan.   Churches
        of God, Michigan assemblies.   Prepared by the Michigan
        Historical Records Survey Project, Division of Community
        Service Programs, Work Projects Administration.   Detroit,
        Michigan Historical Records Survey Project, 1941.   62ℓ.
        On Church of God (Cleveland, Tenn.): ℓ. 2-5, 27-31, 42,
        51-53.   MiU-H, NNUT

(North Dakota)

3159   Daffe, Jerald J.
        The Church of God in the Dakotas during the depression
        of the 1930s, by Jerald J. Daffe.   Wheaton, Il., 1973.   iv,
        73ℓ.   Thesis (M.A.)--Wheaton College.   IWW

(Ohio, Cincinnati)

3160   Bock, Paul R.
        The Pentecostals: the story of Cincinnati's Central Park-
        way Church of God, by Paul R. Bock.   Cincinnati, c1973.
        77p.

(South Dakota)

3161   Daffe, Jerald J.
        The Church of God in the Dakotas during the depression
        of the 1930s, by Jerald J. Daffe.   Wheaton, Il., 1973.   iv,
        73ℓ.   Thesis (M.A.)--Wheaton College.   IWW

-- --SOUTHERN STATES

(Alabama)

3162   Ellis, James Benton, 1870-1946.
        Blazing the gospel trail, by James B. Ellis.   Plainfield,
        N.J., Logos International, c1976.   127p.   DLC

(Florida, Deerfield Beach)

3163   Deerfield Beach, Fl.   Church of God.
           50th anniversary souvenir program: November 15, 16 &
        17, 1974.   Joan Poitier Jerkins, chairman.   Deerfield Beach,
        Fl., 1974.   1v. (unpaged)

(Maryland)

3164   Church of God (Cleveland, Tn.).   State offices.   Maryland.
           Peninsular Pentecost, 1919-1969.   Simpsonville, Md.,
        1969.   1v. (unpaged)

(Maryland, Princess Anne)

3165   Morris, Philip Crockett, 1941-
           The unending chapter, by Philip Morris.   In Walker,
        P. H.   Paths of a pioneer.   Cleveland, Tn., c1970, 369-371.

(North Carolina)

3166   Johnson, Guy Benton, 1928-
           A framework for the analysis of religious action, with
        special reference to holiness and non-holiness groups.   Cam-
        bridge, Ma., 1953 [i. e. 1954] iii, 307ℓ.   Thesis (Ph. D.)--
        Harvard University.   Based in part on research in Robeson
        County, North Carolina, in 1948, 1949 and 1951, including
        responses from ten non-Pentecostal and ten Pentecostal reli-
        gionists (ministers from Pentecostal Holiness (5), Church of
        God (Cleveland, Tenn.) (4), and Assemblies of God (1) de-
        nominations).   MH

3167   Slocumb, Douglas W.
           Church of God of North Carolina: a history of the Church
        of God of North Carolina, 1886-1978.   Charlotte, N.C., H.
        Eaton, c1978.   103p.   Prepared by Douglas W. Slocumb in
        collaboration with Lawrence Ownby and Bobby Smith.   DLC

(Tennessee)

3168   Bridges, Jackie G.
           Heartbeats of Calvary, by ministers of Tennessee.   Spon-
        sored by the Tennessee Chapter of the Lee College Alumni
        Association.   Cleveland, Tn., 19--.   39p.

3169   History of the Church of God (local & general) and business
        directory of Cleveland, Tenn.
           Cleveland, Tn., Church of God Publishing House, 1933.
        1v. (unpaged)

(Texas)

3170   Porter, Travis

He shall direct thy paths: beginning of the Church of God in Texas, 1917. n.p., 1972. 1v. (unpaged)

(West Virginia, Gorman)

3171   Bava, John, 1912-
My life story and beginning of the Gorman Church of God. Davis, W. Va., 19--. 24p.

-- --WESTERN STATES

(California)

3172   Church of God (Cleveland, Tn.). State offices. Southern California-Nevada.
A challenging new frontier; presenting the Church of God in Southern California-Nevada. Upland, Ca., 1970. 27p.

(Nevada)

3173   Church of God (Cleveland, Tn.). State offices. Southern California-Nevada.
A challenging new frontier; presenting the Church of God in Southern California-Nevada. Upland, Ca., 1970. 27p.

-- --WEST INDIES

-- --BAHAMA ISLANDS

3174   Woodside, Kenneth L.
The great awakening, by Kenneth L. Woodside. n.p., 19--. 32p.

-- --HAITI

3175   Eglise de Dieu (Cleveland, Tn.)
L'Eglise de Dieu: enseignments & organisations. Port-au-Prince, 1949. 69p. Compiled by John Herbert Walker. "Histoire de l'Eglise de Dieu en Haiti, 1929-1949": p. 30-57.

3176   Walker, John Herbert, 1928-
Haiti, by Rev. and Mrs. John Herbert Walker, Jr. Cleveland, Tn., Church of God Publishing House, 1950. 67p.

-- --PUERTO RICO

3177   La Ruffa, Anthony Louis, 1933-
Pentecostalism in a Puerto Rican community. New York, 1966, c1967. 2, vii, 283ℓ. Thesis (Ph.D.)--Columbia University. NNC

3177a La Ruffa, Anthony Louis, 1933-
       Pentecostalism in Puerto Rican society [by] Anthony L.
       La Ruffa. In Glazier, S. D. Perspectives on Pentecostalism:
       case studies from the Caribbean and Latin America. Wash-
       ington, c1980, 49-65.

3177b La Ruffa, Anthony Louis, 1933-
       San Cipriano: life in a Puerto Rican community [by]
       Anthony L. La Ruffa. New York, Gordon and Breach, 1971.
       xiii, 149p. (Library of anthropology, [1].) DLC

                   --SOUTH AMERICA

3178   Hargrave, Vessie Dee, 1915-
       South of the Rio Bravo, by Vessie D. Hargrave. Cleve-
       land, Tn., Church of God Missions Department, 1952.   53p.

3179   Hargrave, Vessie Dee, 1915-
       South of the Rio Bravo, by Vessie D. Hargrave. Rev.
       ed. Cleveland, Tn., Church of God Missions Department,
       1954. 56p. At head of title: The Church of God in the
       Americas.

                   --ASIA

              -- --INDIA

3180   Cook, Robert F.
       A quarter century of divine leading in India, by Robert
       F. Cook. Ootacamund, Printed by Ootacamund & Nilgiri
       Press, 1938. 72p.

3181   Cook, Robert F.
       Half a century of divine leading and 37 years of apostolic
       achievements in South India, by Robert F. Cook. Cleveland,
       Tn., Church of God Foreign Missions Department, 1955.
       257p. MH-AH, NNMR, TxWaS

3182   [Maxwell, John]
       The Christian scriptures for India. Coimbatore, India,
       19--. leaflet

3183   Turner, Harold L.
       16th anniversary declaring Great is Thy faithfulness; for
       Christ and India [by] Harold L. [and] Lucille M. Turner.
       Andhra Pradesh, India, 19--. 13p.

--EUROPE

-- --GERMANY

3184   Gemeinde Gottes (Cleveland, Tn.)
       Lehren und Aufbau der Gemeinde Gottes.   Basel, 19--.
       76p.

3185   Scherz, Heinrich C.
       Initiating a long-range Christian education program in an
       evangelical denominational church in West Germany, by Hein-
       rich C. Scherz.   Wheaton, Il., 1969.   iv, 97ℓ.   Thesis
       (M.A.)--Wheaton College.   IWW

-- --ITALY

3186   Chiesa di Dio (Cleveland, Tn.)
       Gli insegnamenti della Chiesa di Dio.   Cleveland, Tn.,
       19--.   120p.

       CHURCH OF GOD (Huntsville, Alabama) (1943-   )
       [Also as Church of God, World Headquarters.]

       After the death of A. J. Tomlinson in 1943, a dispute erupted
between his two sons over control of the Tomlinson Church of God.
Convinced that he was the rightful successor, Homer, the older son,
observed a thirty-day mourning period, then called an assembly of
the whole church to meet in December in New York.   The resulting
body, the Church of God, World Headquarters, with Homer as general overseer or bishop, consisted of a single congregation in New
York and scattered elements of the former Tomlinson Church of God
who felt that Homer was the legitimate successor.   Starting with
teachings identical to those of the two Church of God bodies his
father had led, Homer Tomlinson gradually modified the received
teachings.   By 1953 he had announced the beginning of an era of
peace when by the intercontinental transfer of 280 million people an
end of war could be achieved, poverty be abolished, and the church
"holy and without blemish" be established.   Persuaded that he had
been divinely chosen as king of the world, he visited 101 nations between 1954 and 1966.   In each capital he enthroned himself in some
public place and in each proclaimed an end to war.   In 1952, 1960,
1964, and 1968, he ran as the Theocratic Party candidate for president of the United States.   Bishop Voy M. Bullen, who became general overseer upon Homer Tomlinson's death in 1968, moved the
headquarters from Queens Village, New York to Huntsville, Alabama
where the Church of God, the official organ, is now published.   In
1974, the Church of God claimed 2,035 churches and 75,890 members in the United States, and missionary activity in Panama, Nigeria, and the United Kingdom.   Annually the church holds two general meetings, a national assembly in the United States and a world
assembly in Israel.   The latter is convened in Jerusalem each October in connection with a tour of the Holy Land.

3187   Church of God (Huntsville, Al.). General Assembly.
       Minutes. 42d [i.e. 1st]- . 1944- . Queens Village,
       N.Y.; Huntsville, Al. v. 42- . Annual.

3188   As Moses did.
       In Life, 35 (Dec. 14, 1953), 67-68.

3189   Bishop misbehaves.
       In Newsweek, 42 (Nov. 9, 1953), 92.

3190   Chips on the mountain.
       In Time, 62 (Nov. 9, 1953), 55.

3191   Mathison, Richard Randolph, 1919-
       Faiths, cults and sects of America: from atheism to
       Zen, by Richard R. Mathison. Indianapolis, Bobbs-Merrill
       Co., 1960. 384p. "The street preachers": p. 327-333.
       DLC, RPB

3192   Piepkorn, Arthur Carl, 1907-1973.
       Church of God, World Headquarters. In Concordia Theo-
       logical Monthly, 40 (Oct. 1969), 622-625.

                --CATECHISMS AND CREEDS

3193   Church of God (Huntsville, Al.)
       The book of doctrines, 1903-1970; issued in the interest
       of the Church of God. Huntsville, Al., Church of God Pub-
       lishing House, c1970. 196p.

             --DOCTRINAL AND CONTROVERSIAL WORKS

3194   Tomlinson, Homer Aubrey, bp., 1892-1968.
       The blessings of newspapers, radio, television for the
       Church of God, by Homer A. Tomlinson. New York, c1940.
       16ℓ. Cover title. DLC

3195   Tomlinson, Homer Aubrey, bp., 1892-1968.
       The great vision of the church of God. Queens Village,
       N.Y., Church of God Publishing House, 19--. 26p.

3196   Tomlinson, Homer Aubrey, bp., 1892-1968.
       Kingdom of God on earth, by Homer A. Tomlinson. New
       York, Church of God Publishing Co., 195-. 32p. Cover
       title. CMlG, ICMcC, MH-AH, MCE

3197   Tomlinson, Homer Aubrey, bp., 1892-1968.
       Theocracy: Bible government for the nation; handbook of
       the Theocratic Party. New York, Church of God, World
       Headquarters, 196-. 72p. MH-AH

--PERIODICALS

3198   Church of God.   1-   1944-
        Queens Village, N.Y., Huntsville, Al.

        CHURCH OF GOD (Jerusalem Acres) (1957-   )
        [1957-1962 as Church of God of All Nations.]

        According to Grady Kent, Milton A. Tomlinson abdicated his
seat as the divinely anointed leader of the Church of God of Prophecy
in 1956 when he accepted the jurisdiction of the annual assembly.
The next year, after Kent himself was excommunicated for claiming
a divine commission as leader and prophet, he, together with
three hundred followers, proceeded to make good his claims by organizing the Church of God of All Nations.   The church, which dropped "of All Nations" from its name in 1962, is governed on the theocratic principles of its founding (the so-called reformation of 1957),
but adheres for the most part to doctrines inherited from its parent.
In addition it replaces the Roman calendar with the Jewish one, rejects as pagan the observance of Christmas, Easter and Halloween,
and celebrates several days significant in its own history and teachings: Reformation Day (the founding of the church by Bishop Kent);
Arise, Shine Day (the founding of the Church of God by A. J. Tomlinson); Passover; Pentecost; and Lights, or Hanukkah (celebrated
not by lighting candles, but by making an offering for the evangelization of the Jews).   The work of about thirty churches in the United
States and missionary activity in the Caribbean, Mexico, Nigeria,
England, Finland and Israel is directed from Jerusalem Acres,
Cleveland, Tennessee.   The Vision Speaks, the official periodical,
is also published there.

3199   Church of God (Jerusalem Acres)
        The Church of God business guide and spiritual manual.
        [Compiled] by Grady R. Kent and Marion W. Hall. Cleve-
        land, Tn., 1966. 42ℓ. Mimeographed.

3200   Church of God (Jerusalem Acres)
        Manual of apostles' doctrine and business procedure [of]
        the Church of God; a manual outlining the history, govern-
        mental organization, and principle doctrines of the Church of
        God. Compiled and edited at the general offices. Published
        with the advice and consent of the Council of Apostles and
        Elders. Cleveland, Tn., Church Publishing Co. and Press,
        19--. 1v. (unpaged) OkTOr

                    --DOCTRINAL AND CONTROVERSIAL WORKS

3201   Church of God (Jerusalem Acres)
        Basic Bible teachings. Cleveland, Tn., Church Publish-
        ing Co., 19--. 32p.

3202   Kent, Grady R., 1909-1964.
        Treatise of the 1957 reformation stand, by Grady R.
        Kent. Cleveland, Tn., Church Publishing Co., 19--. 20p.

        --PERIODICALS

3202   Vision speaks. 1- 19 -
        Cleveland, Tn.

        CHURCH OF GOD (Pulaski, Va.) (1942-)

        Formed at Alldreds, North Carolina in November 1942, by
members of various branches of the Tomlinson movement, the new
body was augmented on March 5, 1944, by dissatisfied adherents of
the (Original) Church of God, who complained that "double married"
people had been received into membership and had been allowed even
to serve as bishops. The overseer, they said, had married a woman
with four living husbands. After W. B. Davis, a member of this
group, was chosen overseer, headquarters were moved to Pulaski,
Virginia. In 1947 the group reported ten congregations and 500
members. It expected soon to absorb additional small groups.

3203a   Church of God (Pulaski, Va.)
        Declaration of Bible order of the Church of God. Pula-
ski, Va., 19--.

        CHURCH OF GOD (Rodgers) (1909-1912)

        Formed during a three-day council called by H. G. Rodgers
at Dothan, Alabama, in the fall of 1909, the Church of God consisted
of workers in southeastern Alabama and northern Florida. In February 1911, a second conference was held at Slocomb, Alabama during
which four were ordained and seven licensed to preach. At first
Rodgers was unaware of any other body named the Church of God.
By the time he learned of other groups with the same name, the
founder had come into contact with other whites, who under the leadership of Howard A. Goss, had accepted ministerial credentials from
the previously all-black Church of God in Christ. Soon an arrangement was worked out which allowed the white brethren under Rodgers
virtual autonomy, and in late 1911 or early 1912 a merger was effected under the Church of God in Christ designation.

        CHURCH OF GOD BY FAITH (1919-)

        The Church of God by Faith was founded by Elder John Bright
at Jacksonville Heights, Florida in 1919, and chartered at Alachua,
Florida in 1923. Led by a bishop, an executive secretary, and three
ruling elders, the group has headquarters offices in Jacksonville,

Florida where the Spiritual Guide, the official organ, also is published.   A general assembly meets three times a year.   The Church
of God by Faith sponsors the Matthews-Scippio Academy in Ocala,
Florida.   In 1970 the denomination reported 5,000 members in 135
congregations in Florida, Georgia, Alabama, South Carolina, Maryland, New Jersey, and New York.   A determined effort is made to
exclude willful sinners from the church body.

--PERIODICALS

3204   Spiritual guide.   1- 19 -
           Jacksonville, Fl.

CHURCH OF GOD FOUNDED BY JESUS CHRIST (19 -)

The editorial offices of the Holy Crier Inspirational Magazine,
official organ of this small black denomination, are in Lexington,
Kentucky.   The paper is published in Baltimore.

--PERIODICALS

3205   Holy crier inspirational magazine.   1- 19 -
           Lexington, Ky.

CHURCH OF GOD HOUSE OF PRAYER (1939-)

As overseer of Maine (and eventually five other northeastern
states), Harrison W. Poteat was for over twenty years a key figure
in the expansion of the Church of God (Cleveland, Tennessee) into
New England and eastern Canada.   Only three years after establishing the denomination on Prince Edward Island, however, he was appointed overseer of the church in Montana.   Cut off from his Eastern
following, Poteat decided to break with the Cleveland headquarters,
and in 1939 he founded the Church of God House of Prayer.   Taking
with him many congregations he had previously supervised, Poteat
continued for thirteen years after the separation to woo additional
Cleveland-affiliated congregations into the Church of God House of
Prayer and desisted only after the parent body won legal suits for
recovering church properties.   Other congregations which at some
point had joined Poteat's group withdrew and chose independency instead.   In 1967 the founder reported 24 churches in eastern United
States and two in eastern Canada, with a combined membership of
1,200.   Headquarters are in Markleysburg, Pennsylvania, where the
general superintendent also resides.   Legal incorporation was finally
completed in 1966.

3206   Church of God House of Prayer.
           Declaration of Bible order of the Church of God House

of Prayer.   Edited by Howard Carr.   Rev. ed.   Markleysburg, Pa. , 1964.   16p.

CHURCH OF GOD IN CHRIST (1897-   )

Rejected by black Baptists in Arkansas because of their emphasis on holiness, C. H. Mason and C. P. Jones in 1897 established the Church of God in Christ in a cotton gin house at Lexington, Mississippi.   Both leaders stressed entire sanctification as a
distinct work of grace subsequent to regeneration.   When Mason received the gift of tongues and declared it to be evidence of a third
work of grace, the baptism with the Holy Spirit, the group split,
the holiness faction following Jones in 1907 into a reorganized body
called the Church of Christ (Holiness).   Mason, who assumed the
title and role of senior bishop, established headquarters at Memphis,
Tennessee, and led the group until his death in 1961.   At that time
the Church of God in Christ claimed 382, 679 members in 4, 500 congregations.   Following Mason's death, extended dispute and litigation
over church polity racked the denomination, leading in 1969 to the
defection of fourteen bishops and the formation of a new body, the
Church of God in Christ, International.

For a few years before 1914 several hundred white workers
in transit from the Wesleyan holiness to the "Finished Work of Calvary" position on sanctification, held ministerial credentials with the
Church of God in Christ.   With their departure following organization
of the General Council of the Assemblies of God, the group again became entirely black.   Until recently, segregation and racial prejudice
largely isolated the Church of God in Christ from fraternal fellowship.   In 1948-1949, for instance, it was not invited to participate
in the formation of the Pentecostal Fellowship of North America.
Under the leadership of Mason's son-in-law and successor, Bishop
J. O. Patterson, increased participation in both ecumenical and educational activity has been achieved.   The denomination is represented
in the triennial Pentecostal World conferences.   Since 1954 it has
sponsored the Saints Junior College in Lexington, Mississippi and in
1970 it established the Charles H. Mason Theological Seminary as a
unit of the Interdenominational Theological Center in Atlanta.   The
Whole Truth, the official organ, is published in Memphis.   The
Church of God in Christ sponsors missionary work in Jamaica, Haiti,
and west Africa.

3207   Church of God in Christ.
         Manual of the Church of God in Christ.   7th ed.   Mem-
      phis, 1957.

3208   Church of God in Christ.
         Official manual with the doctrines and discipline of the
      Church of God in Christ, 1973.   Written by the authorization
      and approval of the General Assembly.   Memphis, Church of
      God in Christ Publishing House, 1973.   xl, 256p.   DLC

3209   Church of God in Christ.
            Yearbook of the Church of God in Christ.   Memphis,
        19 - .   v.[1]- .

3210   Jones, Lawrence Neale, 1921-
            The Black Pentecostals.   In Hamilton, M. P. , ed.   The
        charismatic movement.   Grand Rapids, Mi. , 1975, 145-158.
        Includes the Church of God in Christ.

3211   Kroll-Smith, J. Stephen
            The testimony as performance: the relationship of an
        expressive event to the belief system of a Holiness sect [by]
        J. Stephen Kroll-Smith.   In Journal for the Scientific Study
        of Religion, 19 (Mar. 1980), 16-25.

3212   Tinney, James Stephen
            Black Pentecostals convene [by] James S. Tinney.   In
        Christianity Today, 15 (Dec. 4, 1970), 36.   On the annual
        convocation of the Church of God in Christ in Memphis in
        November.

3213   Tinney, James Stephen
            Black Pentecostals: setting up the kingdom [by] James
        S. Tinney.   In Christianity Today, 20 (Dec. 5, 1975), 42-43.
        On the Church of God in Christ.

3214   U.S. Bureau of the Census.
            Census of religious bodies: 1926.   Church of God in
        Christ.   Statistics, denominational history, doctrine, and or-
        ganization.   Washington, U.S. Government Printing Office,
        1929.   10p.   DLC, NNUT

3215   U.S. Bureau of the Census.
            Census of religious bodies: 1936.   Church of God in
        Christ.   Statistics, denominational history, doctrine, and or-
        ganization.   Washington, U.S. Government Printing Office,
        1940.   iv, 8p.   NNUT

                --DOCTRINAL AND CONTROVERSIAL WORKS

3216   Goodwin, Bennie Eugene
            Pray and grow rich, by Bennie Goodwin.   Jersey City,
        N.J. , Goodpatrick Publishers, 1974.   66p.

3217   Patterson, William Archie, bp. , 1898-
            From the pen of Bishop W. A. Patterson.   Memphis,
        Deakins Typesetting Service, 1970.   xx, 122p.   DLC

                --HISTORY

3218   Mason, Charles Harrison, bp. , 1866-1961.

The history and life of Elder C. H. Mason, chief apostle, and his co-laborers. Memphis, Howe Printing Dept., 1920. 97p. Compiled by Prof. Jas. Courts. DLC

3219   Mason, Charles Harrison, bp. , 1866-1961.
The history and life work of Elder C. H. Mason, chief apostle, and his co-laborers from 1893 to 1924. Introduction by J. Courts. San Francisco, T. L. Delaney, c1977. 89p. "Recompiled in 1924."

3220   Mason, Mary
The history and life work of Bishop C. H. Mason, chief apostle and his co-laborers. Memphis, 1934. 103p.

3221   Ross, German R.
History and formative years of the Church of God in Christ, with excerpts from the life and works of its founder: Bishop C. H. Mason. Reproduced by J. O. Patterson, German R. Ross [and] Mrs. Julia Mason Atkins. Memphis, Church of God in Christ Publishing House, 1969. 143p. On cover: Reproduced by Rev. German R. Ross & associates.

--MUSIC

3222   Heilbut, Anthony Otto, 1941-
The gospel sound: good news and bad times [by] Tony Heilbut. New York, Simon and Schuster, 1971. 350p. "The holiness church": p. 201-214. DLC

3223   Heilbut, Anthony Otto, 1941-
The gospel sound: good news and bad times [by] Tony Heilbut. Garden City, N. Y., Anchor Press/Doubleday, 1975, c1971. xxxv, 364p. (Anchor books.) "The holiness church": p. 173-186.

--PERIODICALS

3224   Evangelist speaks. 1- 19 -
Memphis

3225   Pentecostal Alliance crescendo. 1- Feb. /Mar. 1952-
Chicago, Pentecostal Singers and Musicians Alliance.
DLC

3226   Whole truth. 1- 1907-
Argenta, Ar., Memphis, Tn.

--WORK WITH WOMEN

3227   Calhoun, Lillian S.

Woman on the go for God, by Lillian S. Calhoun. In Ebony, 18 (May 1963), 78-81, 84, 86, 88.

--WORSHIP

3228   Clark, William A., 1891-
Sanctification in Negro religion [by] William A. Clark. In Social Forces, 15 (May 1937), 544-551. On the doctrine and worship of the Church of God in Christ.

--UNITED STATES

-- --EASTERN STATES

(Pennsylvania, Pittsburgh)

3229   Williams, Melvin Donald, 1933-
Community in a Black Pentecostal church; an anthropological study [by] Melvin D. Williams. Pittsburgh, University of Pittsburgh Press, 1974. xii, 202p. Based on thesis, University of Pittsburgh, 1973. On a congregation of the Church of God in Christ in Pittsburgh. DLC, MSohG

3230   Williams, Melvin Donald, 1933-
Food and animals: behavioral metaphors in a Black Pentacostal [sic] church in Pittsburgh [by] Melvin D. Williams. In Urban Anthropology, 2 (Spring 1973), 74-79. On a congregation of the Church of God in Christ.

3231   Williams, Melvin Donald, 1933-
A Pentecostal congregation in Pittsburgh; a religious community in a Black ghetto. Pittsburgh, 1973. 328ℓ. Thesis (Ph.D.)--University of Pittsburgh. On a congregation of the Church of God in Christ. PPiU

-- --MIDDLE WEST

(Illinois)

3232   Church of God in Christ. Convocations. Southeast Missouri and Western Illinois.
50th golden convocation of the Churches of God in Christ in session, May 15th through May 25th, 1959, Bishop D. Bostick presiding. St. Louis, 1959. 1v. (unpaged) MoS

(Kansas, Wichita)

3233   Disorderly conduct.
In Christianity Today, 20 (Apr. 9, 1976), 45. On disruption of the services of a Church of God in Christ congregation by four of its members.

(Missouri)

3234   Church of God in Christ.   Convocations.   Southeast Missouri
        and Western Illinois.
            50th golden convocation of the Churches of God in Christ
        in session, May 15th through May 25th, 1959, Bishop D. Bos-
        tick presiding.   St. Louis, 1959.   1v. (unpaged) MoS

        (Ohio)

3235   Church of God in Christ.   Convocations.   Ohio Northwest.
            50th year jubilee; 6th annual holy convocation, Ohio North-
        west Diocese.   Cleveland, 1967.   28p.   Cover title.   OCl

            -- --SOUTHERN STATES

        (Arkansas, Stamps)

3236   Angelou, Maya, 1928-
            I know why the caged bird sings.   New York, Random
        House, 1970, c1969.   281p.   Autobiography.   Account of tent
        meeting in Stamps, Arkansas, sponsored by the Church of
        God in Christ: p. 118-128.   DLC, OkEG

        (District of Columbia, Washington)

3237   Davis, Arnor S., 1919-
            The Pentecostal movement in Black Christianity, by Ar-
        nor S. Davis.   In Black Church, 2:1 (1972), 65-88.   Includes
        comment on Church of God in Christ congregations in Wash-
        ington, D.C.

        (Mississippi, Drew)

3238   Garvin, Philip, 1947-
            Religious America.   Photographs by Philip Garvin.   Text
        by Philip Garvin and Julia Welch.   New York, McGraw-Hill
        Book Co., 1974.   189p.   "Gifts of the Spirit":   p. 141-169.
        Includes description of worship of the Church of God in Christ
        in Drew, Mississippi.

        (Mississippi, Itta Benna)

3239   Garvin, Philip, 1947-
            Religious America.   Photographs by Philip Garvin.   Text
        by Philip Garvin and Julia Welch.   New York, McGraw-Hill
        Book Co., 1974.   189p.   "Gifts of the Spirit":   p. 141-169.
        Includes description of worship of the Church of God in Christ
        in Itta Benna, Mississippi.

        (Mississippi, Sunflower)

3240   Garvin, Philip, 1947-

Religious America.   Photographs by Philip Garvin.   Text
by Philip Garvin and Julia Welch.   New York, McGraw-Hill
Book Co., 1974.   189p.   "Gifts of the Spirit":   p. 141-169.
Includes description of worship of the Church of God in Christ
in Sunflower, Mississippi.

(Tennessee, Memphis)

3241   Battle, Allen Overton, 1927-
Status personality in a Negro holiness sect.   Washington,
1961.   v, 114ℓ.   Thesis (Ph.D.)--Catholic University.   On
Church of God in Christ in Memphis, Tennessee.   DCU

-- --WESTERN STATES

(California, Los Angeles)

3242   Soapbox sermons.
In Human Behavior, 7 (Apr. 1978), 38.   On street
preachers of the Church of God in Christ in Los Angeles in
study by sociologists Lawrence K. Hong and Marion V. Dearman.

CHURCH OF GOD IN CHRIST, CONGREGATIONAL (1932-   )

In 1932 the belief that the proper form of church government
is congregational, not episcopal, forced Bishop J. Bowe out of the
Church of God in Christ.   He then founded the Church of God in
Christ, Congregational.   Two years later, Bowe was joined by George
Slack, who had been excommunicated by the parent body for failing
to teach that paying tithes is an essential response to salvation.
(Slack held that tithing is not a New Testament doctrine.)   The new
group also espoused conscientious objection to war.   Except for these
emphases, however, the teachings of the Church of God in Christ,
Congregational, remain identical to those of the parent body, to which
Bowe returned in 1945.   Headquarters are in East St. Louis, Illinois.
In 1971 there were 43 affiliates of this predominantly black denomination in the United States, Mexico, and Great Britain.

3243   Church of God in Christ, Congregational.
Manual of the Church of God in Christ, Congregational.
East St. Louis, Ill., 1948.

CHURCH OF GOD IN CHRIST, INTERNATIONAL (1969-   )

In 1969 fourteen bishops dissatisfied with changes in the
Church of God in Christ following the death of Bishop C. H. Mason,
met in Kansas City, Missouri and formed the Church of God in
Christ, International.   Disagreement over policy, not doctrine, led
to separation.   In 1971 the new denomination reported 1,041 congre-

gations and 501, 000 members, the latter figure larger than that claimed by the parent body before separation. A general assembly meets annually. The headquarters of the church are in Kansas City, Kansas and the official organs, Message and Holiness Call, are published in Hartford, Connecticut and Memphis, Tennessee respectively.

--PERIODICALS

3244   Holiness call. 1- 19 -
        Memphis, Tn.

3245   Message. 1- 19 -
        Hartford, Ct.

CHURCH OF GOD OF PROPHECY (1923-   )
[1923-1952 as Church of God (Tomlinson).]

        Seeing itself as the true successor of the Church of God over which A. J. Tomlinson became overseer in 1903, the Church of God of Prophecy is the product of reorganization by Tomlinson loyalists following the "disruption" of the parent body in 1923. The successful challenge the following year to continued use of the name "Church of God" by the Tomlinson group, led to a twenty-eight year appeal process, which sustained the original decision in favor of the Church of God (Cleveland, Tennessee). Following the founder's death in 1943, the General Assembly confirmed Milton, his younger son, as general overseer, an action which Homer, the older son, refused to accept since it contravened the theocratic policy of the church. Thereupon, the presbytery, consisting of the general overseer and state overseers, expelled Homer from the church. This is turn resulted in the exodus of Homer's followers (which included most of the urban membership) and formation of the Church of God, World Headquarters. Except for veneration of A. J. Tomlinson and strong emphasis on eschatology, the teaching of the Church of God of Prophecy is almost identical to that of the Church of God (Cleveland, Tennessee). The headquarters offices are in Cleveland, Tennessee where the official organ, White Wing Messenger, is published, and the denominational training school, Tomlinson College, is located. In 1975 the Church of God of Prophecy had 65, 801 members in 1, 791 congregations in the United States and Canada. At that time it was sponsoring missionary efforts on 45 fields in all six continents.

3246   Church of God of Prophecy.
        Cyclopedic index of assembly minutes and important acts,
        1906-1974. Cleveland, Tn., White Wing Publishing House,
        1975. 557p.

3247   Church of God of Prophecy. General Assembly.
        Minutes. 18th [i. e. 1st]- . 1923- . Cleveland, Tn.
        Annual.

3248   Church of God of Prophecy.   General Properties Committee.
            The all nations flag of the Church of God of Prophecy.
        Prepared by Perry E. Gillum and C. T. Davidson.   Cleve-
        land, Tn., White Wing Publishing House, 19--.   40p.

3249   Church of God of Prophecy.   Public Relations Department.
            These truths about the Church of God of Prophecy.
        Cleveland, Tn., 19--.   18p.

3250   As Moses did.
            In Life, 35 (Dec. 14, 1953), 67-68.

3251   Bishop misbehaves.
            In Newsweek, 42 (Nov. 9, 1953), 92.

3252   Chips on the mountain.
            In Time, 62 (Nov. 9, 1953), 55.

3253   Flying churchmen.
            In Newsweek, 40 (Sept. 1, 1952), 58.

3254   Holy hoopla.
            In Newsweek, 22 (Dec. 13, 1943), 108, 110.

3255   Moore, Everett Leroy, 1918-
            Handbook of Pentecostal denominations in the United
        States.   Pasadena, Ca., 1954.   vii, 346ℓ.   Thesis (M.A.)--
        Pasadena College.   "Church of God of Prophecy":   ℓ. 155-
        165.   CSdP

3256   Rollers at Cleveland.
            In Time, 28 (Sept. 28, 1936), 42, 44.

3257   U.S. Bureau of the Census.
            Census of religious bodies: 1936.   Churches of God.
        Statistics, denominational history, doctrine, and organiza-
        tion.   Washington, Government Printing Office, 1941.   iv,
        33p.   Includes (Tomlinson) Church of God.   NNUT

                        --BIOGRAPHY

3258   Church of God of Prophecy.
            Memoirs of our ministry: nineteen hundred seventy-five.
        Edited by Harry Lee Moore.   Cleveland, Tn., White Wing
        Publishing House and Press, 1975.   390p.

                    --CATECHISMS AND CREEDS

3259   Church of God of Prophecy.
            Catechism of the Church of God of Prophecy teachings.
        This is a manual of instructions in the form of questions and

answers.   Recommended for the new convert and young people.   Cleveland, Tn., White Wing Publishing House, 1969.
50p.

3260   Church of God of Prophecy.   General Assembly.
        These things necessary; the doctrine and practices of the
Church of God of Prophecy as set forth by the General As-
sembly.   3d ed.   Cleveland, Tn., White Wing Publishing
House, 1968.   79p.

                --DEVOTIONAL LITERATURE

3261   Johnson, Buford M., 1921-
        This is the day; a sentence sermon approach to daily de-
votions: a guide for family worship, Bible study, private
meditations, by Buford M. Johnson.   Cleveland, Tn., White
Wing Publishing House, 197-.   189p.

            --DOCTRINAL AND CONTROVERSIAL WORKS

3262   Church of God of Prophecy.
        Twenty-nine important Bible truths.   Cleveland, Tn.,
19--.   12p.   Cover title.

3263   Church of God of Prophecy.   Bible Training Institute.
        The body of Christ; a searching analysis in lesson form
of the divine church as it is outlined in holy scripture.   A
correspondence course of the Bible Training Institute of the
Church of God of Prophecy.   Cleveland, Tn., 19--.   99p.

3264   Church of God of Prophecy.   Bible Training Institute.
        General Bible study by correspondence, prepared espe-
cially for those desiring a comprehensive knowledge of God's
word through the auspices of the official institution of the
Church of God of Prophecy.   Cleveland, Tn., 1970, c1950.
195p.

3265   Church of God of Prophecy.   Bible Training Institute.
        Lessons in Bible training, prepared especially for first
term students of Bible Training Institute, the official institution of Bible training in the Church of God of Prophecy.
Written and compiled by the faculty.   Cleveland, Tn., White
Wing Publishing House and Press, c1968.   3v.

3266   Davidson, Charles Theodore, bp., 1905-
        Light in our dwellings.   Cleveland, Tn., White Wing
Publishing House & Press, 1952.   250p.   DLC

3267   Moxley, Luther Altamont, 1893-
        Teachings of the Church of God of Prophecy explained,
by L. A. Moxley.   Cleveland, Tn., Church of God of Prophecy, 1952.   8p.

3268   Preston, Daniel D.
            The church triumphant, by Daniel D. Preston. Cleve-
        land, Tn., White Wing Publishing House, c1969. 240p.

3268a   Pruitt, Raymond McRay, 1922-
            Fundamentals of the faith, by Raymond M. Pruitt.
        Cleveland, Tn., White Wing Publishing House and Press,
        c1981. 457p.

3269   Pruitt, Robert Jennings, 1926-
            The death of the third nature, by Robert J. Pruitt.
        Cleveland, Tn., White Wing Publishing House, 1975. 57p.

3270   Stubbs, John A., 1914-
            Christ and Him crucified, by John A. Stubbs. n.p.,
        19--. 57p.

3271   Tomlinson, Ambrose Jessup, bp., 1865-1943.
            The Church of God marches on. Cleveland, Tn., White
        Wing Publishing House, 1939. 127p.

3272   Tomlinson, Milton Ambrose, 1906-
            Basic Bible beliefs of the Church of God of Prophecy;
        29 sermons delivered on the Voice of Salvation radio pro-
        gram, by Milton A. Tomlinson. Cleveland, Tn., White Wing
        Publishing House, c1961. 128p.

3273   Tomlinson, Milton Ambrose, 1906-
            The glorious Church of God, by M. A. Tomlinson.
        Cleveland, Tn., White Wing Publishing House and Press,
        c1968. 133p. KyWAT

3274   Tomlinson, Milton Ambrose, 1906-
            God's church in the plan of the ages [by] Milton A. Tom-
        linson. Cleveland, Tn., White Wing Publishing House, c1974.
        100p. KyWAT

                    --EDUCATION

3275   Murray, Billy, 1930-
            Called to teach. Cleveland, Tn., White Wing Publishing
        House, c1968. 112p.

3276   Murray, Oma Lee (Hensley)
            Leading little lambs. Written and illustrated by Oma
        Lee Murray. Cleveland, Tn., White Wing Publishing House,
        19--. 48p.

3277   Stone, James, 1940-
            God's age: the juniors, ages 9-12. Cleveland, Tn.,
        White Wing Publishing House, c1972. 71p.

--FICTIONAL LITERATURE

3278   Covey, Rudolph Orval, 1911-
       The night shineth, by Rudolph O. Covey. Cleveland, Tn.,
       White Wing Publishing House and Press, 1952. 168p. OkTOr

3279   Covey, Rudolph Orvall, 1911-
       Refuge at last; a story of struggle with a hard, cruel
       world, physically and spiritually, by R. O. Covey. Cleve-
       land, Tn., White Wing Publishing House, 1972. 160p.

3280   Davidson, Charles Theodore, bp., 1905-
       There will be peace: a story of the Civil War days.
       Cleveland, Tn., White Wing Publishing House & Press, 1951.
       152p. DLC

3281   Steward, James Jean, 1921-
       Misty mountains. Cleveland, Tn., White Wing Publishing
       House and Press, 1952. 157p. DLC

3282   Steward, James Jean, 1921-
       So high the wall, a book-length story. Cleveland, Tn.,
       White Wing Publishing House and Press, 1955, c1954. 152p.
       DLC

3283   Steward, James Jean, 1921-
       Sunrise on Guam. Cleveland, Tn., White Wing Publishing
       House and Press, 1950. 136p. DLC

--FINANCE

3284   Wagar, Ashel T., 1909-
       Church business guide: for all ministers and members
       of the Church of God of Prophecy, by A. T. Wagar. 3d ed.
       Cleveland, Tn., White Wing Publishing House, 1969. 1v.
       (unpaged)

--GOVERNMENT

3285   Gillum, Perry Eugene, 1933-
       The Church of God deacon, by Perry E. Gillum. Cleve-
       land, Tn., White Wing Publishing House and Press, c1971.
       73p.

3286   Stone, James, 1940-
       The Church of God of Prophecy: history & polity.
       Cleveland, Tn., White Wing Publishing House, c1977. 310p.
       DLC

--HISTORY

3287   Church of God of Prophecy.   Church of Prophecy Marker
       Association.
            Biblical wonder of the twentieth century: souvenir.
       Cleveland, Tn., Church of Prophecy Marker Association;
       printed by White Wing Publishing House and Press, c1964.
       40p.

3288   Church of God of Prophecy.   Church of Prophecy Marker
       Association.
            The C. P. M. A. department: its origin, organization, and
       purpose.   Compiled by John A. Stubbs.   Cleveland, Tn.,
       19--.   74p.

3289   [Church of God of Prophecy.   Church of Prophecy Marker
       Association]
            The written vision; the pictorial story of Christ and the
       church, presented from tables of stone as given by the proph-
       ets.   Compiled by John A. Stubbs.   Cleveland, Tn., 1969.
       1v. (unpaged)

3290   Davidson, Charles Theodore, bp., 1905-
            America's unusual spot; an authentic history of Fields
       of the Wood, Biblical wonder of the twentieth century, in-
       cluding an explanation of some of the other activities of the
       Church of Prophecy Marker Association.   Cleveland, Tn.,
       White Wing Publishing House & Press, 1954.   176p.   DLC

3291   Davidson, Charles Theodore, bp., 1905-
            Fields of the Wood, Biblical wonder of the twentieth cen-
       tury.   Cleveland, Tn., Church of Prophecy Marker Associa-
       tion, 1948.   144p.   DLC

3292   Davidson, Charles Theodore, bp., 1905-
            Upon this rock, by C. T. Davidson.   Cleveland, Tn.,
       White Wing Publishing House and Press, 1973-1976.   3v.
       Vol. 2, 1923-1943; v. 3, 1943-1953.   DLC

3293   Gillum, Perry Eugene, 1933-
            These stones speak, by Perry Gillum.   Cleveland, Tn.,
       White Wing Publishing House and Press, 1974.   121p.   DLC

3294   Johnson, Buford M., 1921-
            Written in heaven, by Buford M. Johnson.   Cleveland,
       Tn., White Wing Publishing House and Press, c1971.   138p.

3295   Stone, James, 1940-
            The Church of God of Prophecy: history & polity.
       Cleveland, Tn., White Wing Publishing House, c1977.   310p.
       DLC

3296   Tomlinson, Ambrose Jessup, bp., 1865-1943.

A. J. Tomlinson: God's anointed, prophet of wisdom.
Choice writings of A. J. Tomlinson in times of his greatest
anointings. 2d ed. Cleveland, Tn. , White Wing Publishing
House, 1970, c1943. 104p. Cover title: Historical notes.

3297   Tomlinson, Ambrose Jessup, bp. , 1865-1943.
Historical annual addresses [by] A. J. Tomlinson. Compiled by Perry E. Gillum. Cleveland, Tn. , White Wing Publishing House, 1970-1972. 3v. KyWAT

--HYMNS AND SACRED SONGS

3298   [Church of God of Prophecy]
Banner hymns. Cleveland, Tn. , White Wing Publishing
House, c1957. 378[5]p. With music (shape notes).

3299   [Church of God of Prophecy]
Gleams of glory. Cleveland, Tn. , White Wing Publishing
House, c1937. 1v. (unpaged) With music.

3300   Church of God of Prophecy.
Hymns of glorious praise. Cleveland, Tn. , c1969.
537p. With music. "Church section": p. 528-537.

--MISSIONS

3301   Church of God of Prophecy. Women's Missionary Band.
Libro anual misionero de programas, ayudas y planes.
Compilado por el departamento de la B. M. F. Cleveland,
Tn. , 19 - . v. [1]- .

3302   Church of God of Prophecy. Women's Missionary Band.
The mission yearbook of programs, aids, and plans.
Compiled by the W. M. B. Department. Cleveland, Tn. ,
1968- . v. [1]- .

3303   Mixon, Roy D. , 1922-
The connections: missionary journeys of 1974-1975, by
Roy D. Mixon. n. p. , 197-. 93p. Cover title.

--PASTORAL THEOLOGY

3304   Davidson, Charles Theodore, bp. , 1905-
Minister's manual; some helps for the busy minister:
funerals, dedications [and] weddings. Cleveland, Tn. , White
Wing Publishing House & Press, 1952. 91p. DLC

3305   Preston, Daniel D.
The life and work of the minister, a glimpse of the ministerial office [by] Daniel D. Preston. Cleveland, Tn. , White

Wing Publishing House, c1968.   193[4]p.

3306   Tomlinson, Homer Aubrey, bp., 1892-1968.
       The blessings of newspapers, radio, television for the
       Church of God. New York, 1940. 16ℓ. Cover title. DLC

       --PERIODICALS

3307   Church of God preacher. 1- 19 -
       Bedford, Beds.

3308   Happy harvester. 1- 194 -
       Cleveland, Tn. Published "in the interest of men and
       women behind bars and for all those restricted for any rea-
       son from public liberties." OkTOr

3309   White wing messenger. 1- 1923-
       Cleveland, Tn.

3310   Wings of truth. 1- 19 -
       South Covington, Va., Roanoke, Va.

3311   Youth life magazine. 1- 1964-1968.
       Cleveland, Tn.

       --SERMONS, TRACTS, ADDRESSES, ESSAYS

3312   Fisher, Fred S., 1934-
       You can't get blood out of a turnip, by Fred S. Fisher.
       Cleveland, Tn., White Wing Publishing House, 197-. 97p.

3313   Johnson, Buford M., 1921-
       79 sermon outlines, by Buford Johnson. Cleveland, Tn.,
       White Wing Publishing House, 197-. 144p.

3314   Moore, Harry Lee, bp., 1930-
       The church Christ established is the Church of Prophecy,
       by H. L. Moore. Cleveland, Tn., Church of God of Proph-
       ecy, 19--. leaflet.

3315   Moore, Harry Lee, bp., 1930-
       The promise of His coming, by H. L. Moore. Cleve-
       land, Tn., Bethel Book Publishers, 1965. 98p. DLC

3316   Tomlinson, Ambrose Jessup, bp., 1865-1943.
       The all nations flag. Cleveland, Tn., White Wing Pub-
       lishing House and Press, 1952. 8p.

3317   Tomlinson, Ambrose Jessup, bp., 1865-1943.
       The covering removed, the church we honor. Cleveland,
       Tn., White Wing Publishing House, 19--. 12p.

3318   Tomlinson, Ambrose Jessup, bp., 1865-1943.
        Feet washing. Cleveland, Tn., White Wing Publishing
House, 19--.   4p.

3319   Tomlinson, Ambrose Jessup, bp., 1865-1943.
        He has shed forth this which you now see and hear.
Cleveland, Tn., White Wing Publishing House, 19--.   4p.

3320   Tomlinson, Ambrose Jessup, bp., 1865-1943.
        The Holy Ghost and fire. Cleveland, Tn., White Wing
Publishing House, 19--.   4p.

3321   Tomlinson, Ambrose Jessup, bp., 1865-1943.
        How many churches does the Bible recognize, and what
are their names? Cleveland, Tn., White Wing Publishing
House, 19--.   8p.

3322   Tomlinson, Ambrose Jessup, bp., 1865-1943.
        The last days Church of God, by A. J. Tomlinson.
Cleveland, Tn., White Wing Publishing House, 19--.   12p.
Cover title.

3323   Tomlinson, Ambrose Jessup, bp., 1865-1943.
        Sanctification: a peculiar treasure, by A. J. Tomlinson.
Setting forth the glorious teaching of the second work of grace.
Cleveland, Tn., [White Wing Publishing House, 19--]   18p.
Cover title.   Caption title: A peculiar treasure.

3324   Tomlinson, Ambrose Jessup, bp., 1865-1943.
        Sanctification, a second work of grace. Cleveland, Tn.,
White Wing Publishing House, 19--.   folder (4p.)   Caption
title.

3325   Tomlinson, Ambrose Jessup, bp., 1865-1943.
        The signs that follow. Cleveland, Tn., White Wing Pub-
lishing House, 19--.   8p.

3326   Tomlinson, Ambrose Jessup, bp., 1865-1943.
        Speaking in tongues. Cleveland, Tn., White Wing Pub-
lishing House, 19--.   8p.

3327   Tomlinson, Homer Aubrey, bp., 1892-1968.
        There shall be wings. Queens Village, N.Y., Churches
of God of Greater New York, c1941.   21p.   Cover title.
Mimeographed.   NcU

        --WORK WITH CHILDREN

3328   Murray, Oma Lee (Hensley)
        Leading little lambs. Written and illustrated by Oma
Lee Murray. Cleveland, Tn., White Wing Publishing House,
19--.   48p.

3329   Stone, James, 1940-
          God's age: the juniors, ages 9-12.   Cleveland, Tn.,
        White Wing Publishing House, c1972.   71p.

            --WORK WITH YOUTH

3330   Gillum, Perry Eugene, 1933-
          Youth aflame, by Perry E. Gillum.   Cleveland, Tn.,
        White Wing Publishing House, 197-.   83p.

            --UNITED STATES

            -- --MIDDLE WEST

            (Michigan)

3331   Historical Records Survey.   Michigan.
          Inventory of the church archives of Michigan.   Churches
        of God, Michigan assemblies.   Prepared by the Michigan
        Historical Records Survey Project, Division of Community
        Service Programs, Work Projects Administration.   Detroit,
        Michigan Historical Records Survey Project, 1941.   62ℓ.
        On Church of God (A. J. Tomlinson, General Overseer):
        ℓ. 5-6, 32-34, 42, 54-56.   MiU-H, NNUT

            -- --SOUTHERN STATES

            (Virginia)

3332   Davidson, Charles Theodore, bp., 1905-
          W. M. Lowman, Bishop of Virginia.   South Covington,
        Va., Wings of Truth, 1944.   128p.   DLC

      CHURCH OF GOD OF THE APOSTOLIC FAITH (1914-   )

        Organized in 1914 at the Cross Roads Mission near Ozark,
Arkansas, the Church of God of the Apostolic Faith traces its roots
to the Parham-led revivals of the first decade of the century.   Its
doctrinal teachings resemble those of the Portland-based Apostolic
Faith.   The general conference, which meets annually in mid-winter,
elects a general superintendent and a presbytery of twelve elders
(ordained ministers) who oversee the work in the interim between
its sessions.   Local congregations elect their own pastors and ar-
range for their support, and are free to keep rosters of members
if they so choose.   Although there are churches in Texas, New Mexico, and California, the group is concentrated in the eastern parts
of Oklahoma and Kansas, and the western parts of Arkansas and Missouri.   From headquarters in Tulsa, two periodicals--the Church of
God Herald and Christian Youth--are issued.   A camp meeting is
held annually near Stilwell in Adair County, Oklahoma and missionary

work is sponsored in northern Mexico under the name Iglesia Cristiana Evangelica Mexicana. Support for general church activities is derived from an assessment of three fourths of the tithes of ministers. In the early 1970s the Church of God of the Apostolic Faith had more than 1, 400 members in 27 churches.

3333   Church of God of the Apostolic Faith.
        The articles of faith of the General Conference of the
        Church of God of the Apostolic Faith, Incorporated. Rev. ed.
        Tulsa, 1966. 27p.

--DOCTRINAL AND CONTROVERSIAL WORKS

3334   Buckles, Edwin Alvie, 1877-1938.
        God's plan of salvation, by E. A. Buckles. Ozark, Ar.,
        19--. 14p.

3335   Buckles, Edwin Alvie, 1877-1938.
        The sabbath question, by E. A. Buckles. Guthrie, Ok. ,
        Press of the Full Gospel Message, 1923. 30p.

--HISTORY

3336   Bond, Oscar Harrison, 1890-1957.
        Life story of the Rev. O. H. Bond. Oak Grove, Ar.,
        1957. 186p. Completed posthumously by his wife, Mrs.
        Georgia Bond.

3337   Buckles, Edwin Alvie, 1877-1938.
        A brief history: the Church of God of the Apostolic Faith,
        by E. A. Buckles. Drumright, Ok. , 1935. 20p.

3338   Buckles, Edwin Alvie, 1877-1938.
        A brief history of the Church of God of the Apostolic
        Faith, by E. A. Buckles. n. p., 19--. 3p. Mimeographed.

--PERIODICALS

3339   Apostolic Faith messenger. 1- Sept. 1930-1957.
        Tahlequah, Ok. , Bixby, Ok. , Oak Grove, Ar.

3340   Christian youth. 1- 19 -
        Tulsa

3341   Church of God herald. 1- 19 -
        Tulsa

CHURCH OF GOD OF THE MOUNTAIN ASSEMBLY (1906-   )
[1906-1911 as Church of God.]

Similar in origin and belief to the Church of God (Cleveland,
Tennessee), the Church of God of the Mountain Assembly is a direct
result of Wesleyan holiness teaching in the South Union Association
of the United Baptist Church in Kentucky.   Beginning in 1895, a number of United Baptist ministers, including J. H. Parks and Steve
Bryant, began preaching the necessity of a sanctified life free from
sin and the possibility that one, even after genuine conversion, might,
because of sin, be lost.   In 1903 opponents of these teachings within
the South Union Association secured the adoption of a resolution calling for expulsion of any minister who taught that a regenerated Christian might be lost.   The ruling led in 1906 to organization of the
Church of God at Jellico Creek Church, Whitley County, Kentucky,
under the leadership of Parks and Bryant.   In 1911, after it became
aware of other groups calling themselves "Church of God," the new
organization added "of the Mountain Assembly" to its name.   Legal
incorporation followed in 1917.

Distinctive teachings of the Church of God of the Mountain Assembly include baptism by immersion, mandatory use of the King
James version of the Bible, and pacificism.   The denomination has
experienced several schisms.   In 1920 a small group left to found
the Church of God of the Union Assembly.   In 1923 and 1924 a number of ministers left to join the Church of God (Cleveland, Tennessee), and after reorganization in 1944, nearly a fourth of the body
separated to form the Church of God of the Original Mountain Assembly.   Merger negotiations with the Pentecostal Church of Christ in
1950 failed.

With migration of adherents from the mountain region, the
movement spread to other areas.   The church is now in thirteen
states.   In 1977 it reported 3,125 members in 105 congregations.
Headquarters are in Jellico, Tennessee where the General Assembly
meets annually and where the Gospel Herald, the official organ, is
published.   The church maintains a foreign missionary outreach in
Jamaica and Haiti.

3342   Church of God of the Mountain Assembly.
            The C.G.M.A. file: inside information about the Church
        of God of the Mountain Assembly, Inc.   Jellico, Tn., 19--.
        [20]p.   Cover title.

3343   Church of God of the Mountain Assembly.
            Minutes.   1st- 1906- .   Jellico, Tn.   v.[1]- .   Annual.

--DOCTRINAL AND CONTROVERSIAL WORKS

3343a   Goins, J. L.
            Pearl of prophecy, by J. L. Goins.   Chattanooga, Tn.,
        19--.   94p.

--HISTORY

3344   Gibson, Luther
       History of the Church of God, Mountain Assembly:
       founded, Jellico Creek, Kentucky, 1906. n. p., 1954. 53p.

--PERIODICALS

3345   Gospel herald. 1- 1942-
       Jellico, Tn.

3345a Old path. 1- 191 -
       ----, Tn.

CHURCH OF GOD OF THE UNION ASSEMBLY (1920-   )
[1920-1950 as Union Assembly of the Church of God.]

Dissatisfied with the tithing system of the Church of God of
the Mountain Assembly, the congregation at Center, Jackson County,
Georgia, withdrew. The movement spread to other Georgia communities and in 1920 was chartered by the superior court of Bartow
County as the Union Assembly of the Church of God. It was incorporated in Georgia the next year. Beliefs are similar to those of
the parent body, with the exception that tithing is held to have no
New Testament sanction and the Millennium is spiritual rather than
literal. Christ's kingdom is already here.

An assembly meets annually at the headquarters in Dalton,
Georgia. Superior to it is the fifteen-member Supreme Council, the
"official and only ruling and governing body." And at the head is
the general overseer, to whom in recent years has been given un-
checked discretionary power in financial and administrative matters.
All ministers must notify the state or general overseer of their
whereabouts each month. The Church of God of the Union Assembly
is at work in seventeen states.

3346   Church of God of the Union Assembly.
       Minutes. 1st- 1920- . Dalton, Ga., 19 - . v.[1]- .
       Annual.

--DOCTRINAL AND CONTROVERSIAL WORKS

3347   Pratt, Jesse F.
       The first resurrection--the key to the Bible, by Jesse F.
       Pratt. Dalton, Ga., The Southerner, 19--. 15p.

3348   Pratt, Jesse F.
       The throne of David, by Jesse F. Pratt. Dalton, Ga.,
       19--. folder (5p.)

3349   Pratt, Jesse F.
             The tithing system fully explained, by Jesse F. Pratt.
        Dalton, Ga., The Southerner, 19--.   16p.

3350   Pratt, Jesse F.
             When shall we look for the kingdom? Fully explained,
        by Jesse L. Pratt. Dalton, Ga., 19--.   11p.

               --PERIODICALS

3351   Quarterly news.   1-   1968-
             Salome, Az.

           CHURCHES OF GOD OF THE ORIGINAL MOUNTAIN
              ASSEMBLY (1946-   )

        Upon the death of Steve N. Bryant in 1939, A. J. Long was
elected to succeed the founder as moderator of the Church of God
of the Mountain Assembly.   In 1944 Long led the body through a reorganization, only to fail of reelection two years later.   As a result he, along with fourteen other preachers, eight deacons, and
about 200 lay members, left the denomination and organized the
Churches of God of the Original Mountain Assembly at Williamsburg,
Kentucky later that year.   Reaffirming the covenant originally adopted
in 1917, the new group added articles on the necessity of harmony
between pastors and deacons, the subordinate status of women, and
the unlawfulness of snake-handling.   Headquarters are in Williamsburg, Kentucky where the General Assembly meets annually.   Government is in the hands of the general overseer and a council of
twelve elders.   In 1967 there were eleven congregations in Kentucky,
Tennessee, and Ohio.

3352   Churches of God of the Original Mountain Assembly.
             Minutes.   40th [i.e. 1st]- .   1946- .   Williamsburg,
        Ky., 1946- .   v.[1]- .   Annual.

           EVANGELISTIC CHURCH OF GOD (1949-   )

        Incorporated at Denver, Colorado in 1949, the Evangelistic
Church of God grew out of the work of Norman L. Chase, former
minister of the Church of God (Cleveland, Tennessee) and the (Original) Church of God.   By 1955 the group claimed 774 members in
twelve churches.   The Church of God Final Warning, the official
organ, was then published in Soddy, Tennessee where the general
assembly also met annually.

--PERIODICALS

3353   Church of God final warning.   1- 195 -
       Soddy, Tn.

       FIRE BAPTIZED HOLINESS CHURCH OF GOD OF THE
         AMERICAS (1908-   )
       [1908-1922 as Colored Fire Baptized Holiness Church; 1922-
       1926 as Fire Baptized Holiness Church of God.]

       Organized on May 1, 1908, the Colored Fire Baptized Holiness
Church at first consisted entirely of black members of the earlier bi-
racial third-blessing movement. W. E. Fuller, the only black among
the 140 founding members of the Fire Baptized Holiness Association of
America in 1898, developed a black membership in the parent
body, which ultimately numbered 925. Difficulty in obtaining facilities for bi-racial meetings steadily increased, causing the black
brethren to request a separate convention. Release, including the
division of property, was achieved amicably. Fuller became bishop
of the new body, which during his tenure experienced two name
changes. In 1922 Colored Fire Baptized Holiness Church was changed
to Fire Baptized Holiness Church of God, with "of the Americas" being added four years later, when the General Council met with the
Mount Moriah Fire Baptized Church of Knoxville, Tennessee. The
True Witness, the official organ, is published by the Fuller Press
in Atlanta. In 1966 the organization reported 570 churches and
9,012 members. The work of the Fire Baptized Church of God is
concentrated in South Carolina. In addition, there are scattered
congregations in a ten-state area bounded by Connecticut, New
York, and Ohio on the north, and by Florida and Alabama on
the south.

3354   Fire Baptized Holiness Church of God of the Americas.
           Discipline of the Fire Baptized Holiness Church of God
       of the Americas. Atlanta, Fuller Press, 1966. 162p.

       --HYMNS AND SACRED SONGS

3354a Fire Baptized Holiness Church of God of the Americas.
           Discipline of the Fire Baptized Holiness Church of God
       of the Americas. Atlanta, Fuller Press, 1966. 162p.
       "Hymnal of the F. B. H. Church of God": p. 100-162.

       --PERIODICALS

3355   True witness. 1- 19 -
       Atlanta.

FREE CHURCH OF GOD IN CHRIST (1915-1921, 1925-   )
[1915-1921 as Church of God in Christ.]

In 1915 sixteen black Baptists of Enid, Oklahoma experienced
what they believed was the baptism of the Holy Spirit. The group,
which consisted mostly of the family of the Rev. J. H. Morris,
rallied around E. J. Morris, the patriarch's son, who "felt he was
selected" to lead. Calling itself the Church of God in Christ, the
Enid-based group merged in 1921 with the Memphis-based denomination of the same name. The union lasted only four years, however,
and upon separation, the Oklahoma body added "Free" to its name.
Except for greater emphasis on divine healing, its doctrine remained
identical to that of the merged group. In the late 1940s, the Free
Church of God in Christ claimed 40 churches and 900 members.

3356   U.S. Bureau of the Census.
           Census of religious bodies: 1926. Free Church of God
in Christ. Statistics, denominational history, doctrine, and
organization. Washington, U.S. Government Printing Office,
1929. 8p. DLC

FULL GOSPEL CHURCH OF GOD IN SOUTHERN AFRICA
(1921-   )
[1921-1951 as Full Gospel Church.]

Formed in 1921 by the merger of the Pentecostal Mission and
the Churches of God, the Full Gospel Church of God in Southern
Africa (known in Afrikaans as Die Volle Evangelie Kerk van God in
Suidelike Afrika) traces its origin to 1910. That year followers of
Archibald H. Cooper, who had been in fellowship with the work of
John G. Lake, separated over differences relating to church policy
and the administration of the sacraments. In 1921 these white and
East Indian believers came together as the Full Gospel Church. The
first constitution was formally adopted on April 19, 1922. Growth
was phenomenal: from about 100 in 1910 to 56,839 in 1954. Through
David du Plessis contact was made with the Church of God (Cleveland,
Tennessee), and in 1951 amalgamation of the Full Gospel Church and
the North American body was achieved under the name Full Gospel
Church of God in Southern Africa. At its headquarters in Irene,
Transvaal, the group publishes the Full Gospel Herald. It sponsors
the Berea Bible College in Kroonstad, Orange Free State, and with
significant support from the United States conducts missionary work
in Zambia, Rhodesia, Swaziland, Botswana, Angola, Lesotho, South-
West Africa, and Japan. In 1968 the church had 1,200 congregations
and 79,000 members in South Africa.

--PERIODICALS

3357   Full gospel herald. 1-   19 -
           Irene, Tvl.

HOLINESS CHURCH OF GOD (1920-   )

In 1917 under the leadership of Elder James A. Foust, a revival (the so-called Big May Meeting) broke out in Madison, North Carolina. Continuing for the next three years, this meeting was responsible for sweeping several Wesleyan Holiness congregations, including the Kimberley Park Holiness Church of Winston-Salem, into the tongues-speaking camp. As a result, in 1920 supporters of the revival organized the Holiness Church of God at Madison. Eight years later at Winston-Salem legal incorporation was secured. In 1968 the Holiness Church of God reported 28 congregations and 927 members. Although there are churches in Virginia, West Virginia, and New York, work is concentrated in North Carolina. Headquarters are in Winston-Salem.

NEW TESTAMENT CHURCH OF GOD (1953-   )

A by-product of missionary efforts of the Church of God (Cleveland, Tennessee) in the West Indies, the New Testament Church of God is composed of West Indian immigrants in Great Britain. Organized in 1953, the denomination proposed to provide a church home for West Indians faced with racial prejudice and cultural isolation in England. From the rented YMCA hall in Wolverhampton, near Birmingham, in which it was born, the New Testament Church of God had expanded by 1975 to include 85 ministers and 20,230 adherents. In a period of declining attendance in the established denominations and the white Pentecostal bodies of England, the New Testament Church of God is almost unique in reporting substantial gains. Headquarters are in Birmingham.

3358   Hill, Clifford S., 1927-
        From church to sect; West Indian religious sect development in Britain [by] Clifford Hill. In Journal for the Scientific Study of Religion, 10 (Summer 1971), 114-123.

3359   Hill, Clifford S., 1927-
        Immigrant sect development in Britain; a case study of status deprivation? [By] Clifford Hill. In Social Compass, 18:2 (1971), 231-236.

(ORIGINAL) CHURCH OF GOD (1917-   )

Although like the Church of God (Cleveland, Tennessee) in that it claims 1886 as its founding date, the (Original) Church of God has existed as a separate body only since 1917. That year J. L. Scott, Church of God pastor in Chattanooga, Tennessee led his congregation out of the Cleveland, Tennessee-based group. Ostensibly a continuation of the original group, the new body challenged the denomination's teaching on tithing and divorce. Incorporated in 1922, the (Original) Church of God follows a congregational form of

church government. In 1971 it reported 70 churches (including one
in Trinidad) and 20,000 members. Headquarters are in Chattanooga,
where the Messenger, the official periodical, is also published.

3360   (Original) Church of God.
            Manual or discipline of the (Original) Church of God,
        Incorporated. Chattanooga, Tn., 1966.

3361   (Original) Church of God. General Convention.
            Minutes. 31st [i.e. 1st]- . 1917- . v.[1]- .
        Annual.

3362   Gaddis, Merrill Elmer, 1891-
            Christian perfectionism in America. Chicago, 1929.
        viii, 589ℓ. Thesis (Ph.D.)--University of Chicago. On
        (Original) Church of God: ℓ. 465-467. ICU

3363   Moore, Everett Leroy, 1918-
            Handbook of Pentecostal denominations in the United
        States. Pasadena, Ca., 1954. vii, 346ℓ. Thesis (M.A.)--
        Pasadena College. "The (Original) Church of God": ℓ. 169-
        172. CSdP

3364   U.S. Bureau of the Census.
            Census of religious bodies: 1926. The (Original) Church
        of God. Statistics, denominational history, doctrine, and or-
        ganization. Washington, Government Printing Office, 1928.
        8p. NNUT, DLC

3365   U.S. Bureau of the Census.
            Census of religious bodies: 1936. Churches of God.
        Statistics, denominational history, doctrine, and organization.
        Washington, Government Printing Office, 1941. iv, 33p. In-
        cludes the (Original) Church of God. NNUT, DLC

                    --PERIODICALS

3366   Messenger. 1- 1919-
            Chattanooga, Tn.

3367   Youth messenger. 1- 19 -
            Chattanooga, Tn.

                    --NORTH CAROLINA

                    -- --RALEIGH

3368   Jericho on Saunders Street.
            In Time, 63 (June 28, 1954), 65. On brush arbor re-
        vival conducted by an (Original) Church of God evangelist in
        Raleigh, North Carolina.

SOUGHT OUT CHURCH OF GOD IN CHRIST AND SPIRITUAL
HOUSE OF PRAYER (1947-)

A black group, the Sought Out Church of God in Christ and
Spiritual House of Prayer, was founded early in 1947 by "Mother"
Mozella Cook at Brunswick, Georgia. The founder's mother, who
was "often absent from this world while she talked with God" and
who once was examined in court on a lunacy charge, was instrumental in her daughter's conversion during a "yard service." Mozella then joined the Baptist church in Brunswick. Later, however,
she moved to Pittsburgh, Pennsylvania where she affiliated with the
Church of God in Christ. While there, she believed that she received instructions to found a new church.

Following organization of the first congregation in a garage
in the back yard of her home in Brunswick, Mother Cook organized
three other groups. In 1949, membership of the four congregations
totaled about sixty persons.

CHURCH OF THE LIVING GOD, CHRISTIAN WORKERS FOR
FELLOWSHIP (1889-)
[1889-1915 as Church of the Living God, Christian Workers for
Friendship.]

Formed in 1889 by William Christian and his followers of
Wrightsville, Arkansas, the Church of the Living God, Christian
Workers for Fellowship, in many respects resembles the Church of
God in Christ. Christian, a former Baptist minister who had been
born in slavery, was in fact an early associate of C. H. Mason.
The Church of the Living God differs from Mason's group, however,
in permitting tongues-speech in recognizable languages only. It dis-
countenances "unintelligible utterance" and the initial evidence theory
as well. It affirms the racial pride of its membership by the as-
sertion that all Biblical saints were black. Fellowship Echoes, the
official periodical, is published in St. Louis. In 1964 the denomination reported 276 churches and 45,320 members.

3369   U.S. Bureau of the Census.
            Census of religious bodies: 1926. Churches of the Liv-
        ing God. Statistics, denominational history, doctrine, and or-
        ganization. Consolidated report: Church of the Living God,
        Christian Workers for Fellowship; Church of the Living God,
        "The Pillar and Ground of Truth." Washington, Government
        Printing Office, 1928. 15p. DLC, NNUT

3370   U.S. Bureau of the Census.
            Census of religious bodies: 1936. Churches of the Liv-
        ing God. Statistics, denominational history, doctrine, and or-
        ganization. Consolidated report: Church of the Living God,
        Christian Workers for Fellowship; Church of the Living God,

"The Pillar and Ground of Truth." Washington, Government Printing Office, 1940. iv, 12p. (Bulletin, 41.) NNUT

3371   Wilmore, Gayraud S.
        Black religion and Black radicalism, by Gayraud S. Wilmore. Garden City, N. Y., Doubleday, 1972. xiii, 344p. (The C. Eric Lincoln series on Black religion.) On Church of the Living God, Christian Workers for Fellowship: p. 211-212.

--PERIODICALS

3372   Fellowship echoes. 1- 19 -
        St. Louis

CHURCH OF THE LIVING GOD, THE PILLAR AND GROUND OF THE TRUTH (1903-)

        Akin to the Church of the Living God, Christian Workers for Fellowship, the Church of the Living God, the Pillar and Ground of the Truth, is the outgrowth of the work of a black evangelist, "Mother" M. L. Ester Tate. Together with her two sons, W. C. Lewis and F. C. Lewis, "Saint Mary Magdalena Tate" organized the group in 1903. The first General Assembly, which met five years later at Greenville, Alabama, elected Mother Tate as the first overseer. Although her sons had become bishops in 1914, they were unable to stem the tide of dissatisfaction and schism which accompanied the founder's death in 1930. As a result the next year the church was reorganized into three dominions, which hold their respective conferences in May, June, and July each year. By 1970s the combined group had approximately 20,000 members in 500 churches located in forty states, and was supporting missionary efforts in Jamaica, Nassau, and Spain. Headquarters offices are in Nashville, Tennessee.

3372a   Church of the Living God, the Pillar and Ground of the Truth.
        The constitution, government, and general decree book of the Church of the Living God, the Pillar and Ground of the Truth (Incorporated): St. Mary Magdalena, first chief overseer. 2d and rev. ed. Nashville, 1924. 84p. Publication date stamped on t. p. DLC

--HISTORY

3372b   Church of the Living God, the Pillar and Ground of the Truth.
        Seventy-fifth anniversary yearbook of the Church of the Living God, the Pillar and Ground of the Truth, Inc., 1903-1978: Mary Magdalena Tate, revivor and first chief overseer, Felix Early Lewis, co-revivor and bishop. [Helen M. Lewis and Meharry H. Lewis, editors]. Nashville, c1978. 65p. DLC

COLONIAL VILLAGE PENTECOSTAL CHURCH OF THE NAZARENE
  (1968-   )
[1968-19-- as Colonial Village Church.]

    In 1968 Bernard Gill, who for thirteen years had been a min-
ister in the Church of the Nazarene, established the Colonial Village
Church, an independent congregation, on the southside of Flint, Michigan.   An attempt to form the true church composed solely of "wholly
sanctified holy people with the gifts of the Spirit operating among
them, " the new congregation accepted as its mission the reformation
of the parent denomination.   Considering himself "God's Prophet of
the Latter Rain, " the pastor received numerous revelations directly
from God, which, together with those received by Mescal McIntosh,
one of the members, were published in the Macedonian Call in the
first half of 1974.   In the July 3rd issue, a resurrection was pre-
dicted, only to be followed two weeks later by the pastor's death.
On August 11 a letter to readers of the Macedonian Call announced
the belief of Gill's faithful followers that the prophecy obviously applied to their pastor, and that they were waiting in faith.

3373   Waiting for Gill.
          In Time, 105 (Apr. 14, 1975), 47, 53.

          --PERIODICALS

3374   Macedonian call.   1, no. 1-14, Jan. -July 3, 1974.
          Flint, Mi.   MiU-H

CONGREGATIONAL HOLINESS CHURCH (1921-   )

    The result of a schism within the Georgia Conference of the
Pentecostal Holiness Church, the Congregational Holiness Church
was organized January 29, 1921, at High Shoals, Georgia.   The previous year, a prominent evangelist and the Georgia Conference superintendent, Watson Sorrow and Hugh Bowling, had been expelled without a proper, legal hearing for liberal views on the use of medicine.
Twenty-eight ministers and mission workers and twelve congregations
followed Sorrow and Bowling into the new organization.

    Although the government of the Congregational Holiness Church
is less centralized and more democratic than that of the Pentecostal
Holiness Church, many connectional features remain.   Publication of
the Gospel Messenger, the official organ, begun in 1924, was followed by inauguration of a denomination-wide annual camp meeting
on church-owned grounds near Cleveland, Georgia the next year.   In
1935 regional associations distinct from the General Association were
instituted, and in 1947 a church-owned publishing house was established.   Following organization of a foreign missionary board in 1949,
missionary work in six Latin American countries and Spain was

started.   In 1966 the Congregational Holiness Church reported 147 congregations and 4,859 members.

Present relations between the Congregational Holiness Church and the Pentecostal Holiness Church are amicable.   Negotiations in 1944 looking forward to reunion produced an official apology by the parent body for the circumstances which occasioned the rift.   On March 12, 1980, an Agreement of Affiliation providing for significant enlargement of cooperation between the two groups was signed in Oklahoma City.

3375   Congregational Holiness Church.
        Discipline.   Griffin, Ga., 1979.   55p.   Cover title.

        --HISTORY

3376   Campbell, Joseph Enoch, 1903-
        The Pentecostal Holiness Church, 1898-1948: its back-
        ground and history; presenting complete background material
        which adequately explains the existence of this organization,
        also the existence of other kindred Pentecostal and Holiness
        groups, as an essential and integral part of the total church
        set-up, by Joseph E. Campbell.   Franklin Springs, Ga.,
        Publishing House of the Pentecostal Holiness Church, c1951.
        573p.   "Congregational Holiness Church organized, 1920":
        p. 277.

3377   Cox, B. L., 1899-
        History and doctrine of the Congregational Holiness
        Church, by B. L. Cox.   Greenwood, S. C., Publishing House
        of the Congregational Holiness Church, 1958.   94p.

3378   Cox, B. L., 1899-
        History and doctrine of the Congregational Holiness
        Church, by B. L. Cox.   2d ed.   Greenwood, S. C., Publish-
        ing House of the Congregational Holiness Church, 1959.   94p.

3379   Moore, Everett Leroy, 1918-
        Handbook of Pentecostal denominations in the United
        States.   Pasadena, Ca., 1954.   vii, 346ℓ.   Thesis (M. A.)--
        Pasadena College.   "Congregational Holiness Church": ℓ. 211-
        217.   CSdP

3380   Sorrow, Watson, 1884-
        Some of my experiences.   Atlanta, [Printed by] Publish-
        ing House [of the] Pentecostal Holiness Church, Franklin
        Springs, Ga., 1954.   94p.   "Some divisions": p. 65-67.

3381   U. S. Bureau of the Census.
        Census of religious bodies: 1926.   Congregational Holi-
        ness Church.   Statistics, denominational history, doctrine,

and organization. Washington, U.S. Government Printing
Office, 1929. 8p. DLC

--PERIODICALS

3382   Gospel messenger. 1- 1924-
       Greenwood, S.C., Griffin, Ga.

3383   Harvest call. 1- 19 -
       Griffin, Ga.

CORPORACIÓN EVANGÉLICA DE VITACURA (1933-)

The Corporación Evangélica de Vitacura separated from the
Iglesia Metodista Pentecostal de Chile in 1933. In 1962 its more
than 8,000 members were concentrated in the area between Santiago
and Puerto Montt.

DOOR OF FAITH CHURCHES OF HAWAII (1940-)

Chartered by the Territory of Hawaii in 1940, the Door of
Faith Churches is the outgrowth of the missionary efforts of
Mildred Johnson Brostek. She was sent to the islands in 1936 by
the Pentecostal Holiness Church, where, in addition to ministry in
a leper camp, she opened the Door of Faith Mission in Honolulu.
Unfortunate complications following her marriage to a United States
Army officer in 1938 resulted in withdrawal of denominational support, making it necessary to establish the work on an independent
basis. Under Mrs. Brostek's direction, the Door of Faith Churches
has become an international denomination. In 1979 it reported 40
churches and more than 3,000 members in Hawaii. In addition it
had affiliates in Indonesia, Okinawa, and the Philippines. Headquarters are in Honolulu, where its Bible training school also is located.

EJÉRCITO EVANGÉLICO NACIONAL DE CHILE (1942-)

The Ejército Evangélico Nacional separated from the Iglesia
Metodista Pentecostal de Chile in 1942. Churches are located in the
area between Santiago and Llanquihue.

EMMANUEL HOLINESS CHURCH (1953-)

Organized March 19, 1953, at Columbus County Camp Grounds,
Whiteville, North Carolina, the Emmanuel Holiness Church was composed initially of former members of the Pentecostal Fire Baptized

Holiness Church who objected to recent rulings of the General Conference of that body. Of particular significance was legislation out-
lawing the wearing of neckties. Doctrinally in substantial agreement
with the parent body, the new church opposed racial integration, the
ordination of "double" married persons, and the taking up of arms
in war. The Emmanuel Holiness Messenger, the official organ, is
published in Anderson, South Carolina. Beginning in 1959, this was
replaced for a few years by the Witness and Messenger, a periodical
issued jcintly by the Pentecostal Church of Christ and the Emmanuel
Holiness Church. In 1975 the Emmanuel Holiness Church reported
56 congregations and 1,200 members. Churches are located in North
Carolina, South Carolina, Georgia, Alabama, Florida, Indiana, and
Michigan.

3384   Emmanuel Holiness Church.
            Discipline of the Emmanuel Holiness Church; and, Minutes
        of the 1959 assemblies of the Alabama, Georgia, North Caro-
        lina, and South Carolina conferences of the Emmanuel Holi-
        ness Church. n. p. , 1959. iv, 65p. Cover title.

3385   Emmanuel Holiness Church.
            Discipline of the Emmanuel Holiness Church. n. p.,
        1963. 24p.

3385a   Emmanuel Holiness Church.
            Discipline of the Emmanuel Holiness Church, 1973.
        n. p. , 1972. 27p. "Printed following General Assembly,
        1972. "

3386   Emmanuel Holiness Church.
            Minutes of the first session of the Emmanuel Holiness
        Church. Laurel Hill, N. C. , 1953. 20p.

3386a   Emmanuel Holiness Church.
            1965 minutes of Emmanuel Holiness Church annual state
        assemblies of Alabama, Florida, Georgia, North Carolina,
        and South Carolina, held in each of the five states; also min-
        utes of the 1965 session of the General Assembly, Emmanuel
        Holiness Church, [convening at Tabor City, North Carolina,
        October 13-15, 1965]. n. p. , 1965. 36p. Cover title.

3387   Moore, Evevett Leroy, 1918-
            Handbook of Pentecostal denominations in the United States.
        Pasadena, Ca. , 1954. vii, 346ℓ. Thesis (M. A.)--Pasadena
        College. "Emmanuel Holiness Church": ℓ. 217-220. CSdP

                    --PERIODICALS

3388   Emmanuel Holiness messenger. 1- 1967-
            Anderson, S. C.

3388a   Emmanuel messenger.   1-   195 -
            Anderson, S. C.

3389   Witness and messenger.   1-8, Mar. 1959-1966.
            London, Oh.   Issued jointly by the Emmanuel Holiness
            Church and the Pentecostal Church of Christ.

EVANGELISTIC AGENCIES:

APOSTOLIC FAITH MISSION (1907-   )

        Legally incorporated as the Apostolic Faith Mission of Port-
land, Oregon, U.S.A., this body is most commonly known simply
as the Apostolic Faith.   Dating from 1907, it was organized by
Florence L. Crawford, one of the original leaders of the Azusa
Street revival in Los Angeles, who during an evangelistic campaign
in Minneapolis became convinced that Portland should be the center
of her work.   As editor of the Apostolic Faith, official organ of the
Azusa Street Mission, Mrs. Crawford took the non-Los Angeles
mailing lists of the periodical, and without the knowledge of William
J. Seymour, moved the publication to Portland.   There, in addition
to publishing the paper (re-named Light of Hope in 1966), she took
over and greatly enlarged a small mission, pursuing every night
evangelistic work there in the winter months, and in a suburban
camp meeting during the summer.   Conducted on the faith principle
(that is, without advance pledges, but simply in trust that God would
supply material needs), the movement soon spread to Minneapolis
and other American cities, and to foreign countries.   Adhering to
the three-crisis doctrine taught by Parham and Seymour, the Apostolic Faith Mission remained under Crawford family leadership until
the death of the founder's son, Robert, in 1965.   The present general overseer is Loyce C. Carver.   In 1978 there were 45 churches
and 4,100 members in the United States.   Dedicated missionary effort together with the production of printed materials in at least
seventy languages, has resulted in establishment of more than 200
affiliated churches in Africa, the Caribbean, Europe, and Japan.
Branches are under the direction of nationals of the countries in
which they are located.

        The Portland-based movement has suffered two major schisms.
In 1915 the Minneapolis branch under Jackson White withdrew to form
a rival organization also known as the Apostolic Faith Mission.   Four
years later, the Eugene, Oregon branch under Fred Hornshuh also
withdrew in protest against the requirement that divorced and remarried couples separate.   It became the mother congregation of
the Bible Standard Churches.

3390   Apostolic Faith Mission.
            The Apostolic Faith, an international evangelistic organi-
        zation, Trinitarian, fundamental: its origin, functions and

doctrines.   Portland, Or. , Apostolic Faith, 19--.   12p.
OrU

3391   Camp meeting.
       In Time, 26 (Aug. 19, 1935), 34-35.   On Apostolic Faith
       camp meeting near Portland, Oregon.

3392   Moore, Everett Leroy, 1918-
       Handbook of Pentecostal denominations in the United
       States.   Pasadena, Ca. , 1954.   vii, 346ℓ .   Thesis (M. A.)--
       Pasadena College.   "The Apostolic Faith Mission of Portland,
       Oregon":   ℓ . 200-210.   CSdP

3393   U. S. Bureau of the Census.
       Census of religious bodies: 1926.   Apostolic Faith Mis-
       sion.   Statistics, denominational history, doctrine, and or-
       ganization.   Washington, U. S. Government Printing Office,
       1928.   8p.   DLC

                    --DOCTRINAL AND CONTROVERSIAL WORKS

3394   Apostolic Faith Mission.
       Apostolic faith doctrine.   Portland, Or. , Apostolic Faith,
       1939.   673p.   TxWaS

3395   Apostolic Faith Mission.
       The baptism of the Holy Ghost.   Portland, Or. , Apostolic
       Faith, 19--.   folder (6p.)

3396   Apostolic Faith Mission.
       Entire sanctification, the second work of grace.   Port-
       land, Or. , Apostolic Faith, 19--.   16p.

3397   Apostolic Faith Mission.
       The series of Bible studies; a course of brief outlines
       and notes on Biblical teachings, formulated and compiled with
       the intention of aiding all who are earnestly desiring the truth.
       Portland, Or. , Apostolic Faith, 19 - .   v. 1- .   CLSU

3398   Apostolic Faith Mission.
       Studies in the scriptures, as given at the Apostolic Faith
       Camp Ground, 1940.   Portland, Or. , Apostolic Faith, 1940.
       98p.   OrU

3399   Apostolic Faith Mission.
       Studies in the scriptures, as given at the Apostolic Faith
       camp ground, 1958-1959.   Portland, Or. , Apostolic Faith,
       1959.   68p.

3400   Apostolic Faith Mission.
       Studies in the scriptures, as given at the Apostolic Faith
       Camp Ground, 1970-71.   Portland, Or. , Apostolic Faith,
       1971.   96p.

--NON-PENTECOSTAL AUTHORS

3401   Ironside, Henry Allen, 1876-1951.
         Apostolic Faith missions and the so-called second Pente-
cost [by] H. A. Ironside.   New York, Loizeaux Bros. , 191-.
15p.   Cover title.

--HISTORY

3402   Apostolic Faith Mission.
         A historical account of the Apostolic Faith, a Trinitarian-
fundamental evangelistic organization: its origin, functions,
doctrinal heritage, and departmental activities of evangelism.
Portland, Or. , Apostolic Faith Publishing House, 1965.   315p.
DLC, MH-AH

--PASTORAL THEOLOGY

3403   Apostolic Faith Mission.
         Minister's manual.   Portland, Or. , 1950.   400p.   DLC

--PERIODICALS

3404   Armour bearer.   1-   19 -
         Portland, Or.

3405   Light of hope.   1-   Sept. 1906-
         Los Angeles, Portland, Or.   1906-1965 as Apostolic
Faith.   Vol. 2, no. 15, July-Aug. 1908 [no. 1 of Portland];
numbering corrected with no. 7 [of Portland], May-June 1909.

3406   Lower light.   1-   19 -
         Portland, Or.

3407   Morning star.   1-   19 -
         Portland, Or.

--SERMONS, TRACTS, ADDRESSES, ESSAYS

3408   Crawford, Florence Louise, 1872-1936.
         Sermons and scriptural studies.   Portlane, Or. , Apos-
tolic Faith, 19--.   2v.   OrU

3409   Crawford, Raymond Robert, 1891-1965.
         Sermons and scriptural studies, by Raymond R. Craw-
ford.   Book one.   Portland, Or. , Apostolic Faith, 19--.
90p.   No more published.

--ALASKA

3410   Crawford, Raymond Robert, 1891-1965.
        A gleam across the wave; a brief account of the purpose
        and travels of the missionary motor vessel Lower Light.
        Portland, Or., Apostolic Faith Publishing House, 195-.   32p.
        OrU

APOSTOLIC FAITH MISSION (1915-   )

        About 1915 Jackson White, who six years earlier had become
leader of the Minneapolis branch of the Apostolic Faith Mission,
broke with the Portland-based group.   Following his death, the work
was continued by his widow, Mrs. Martha White, and Miss Minnie
Hanson.   Apparently it did not survive them.   The official organ,
Eventide, was published in Minneapolis.

3411   Gaddis, Merrill Elmer, 1891-
            Christian perfectionism in America.   Chicago, 1929.
        viii, 589ℓ.   Thesis (Ph. D.)--University of Chicago.   On Apos-
        tolic Faith Mission: ℓ. 474-479.   ICU

        --PERIODICALS

3412   Eventide.   [1]- [19]-
        Minneapolis

APOSTOLIC FAITH MOVEMENT (1901-   )

        An association of workers in fellowship with the Apostolic
Faith Bible College of Baxter Springs, Kansas, the Apostolic Faith
Movement is the continuation of the work of Charles Fox Parham,
founder of the modern Pentecostal Movement.   Originating in Parham's Bible school at Topeka, Kansas where on December 31, 1900,
was born the belief that tongues-speech is evidence of the baptism
with the Holy Spirit, the movement soon spread to other communities in Kansas and Missouri.   By 1904 Parham had begun organizing
Apostolic Faith assemblies.   With converts garnered in the Kansas
meetings, in 1905 he took the message to Galveston and Houston,
Texas.   Out of the short-term Bible school which Parham conducted
in connection with the Houston campaign came William J. Seymour,
a black evangelist who, in the next year, became leader of the famous Azusa Street revival in Los Angeles.   Personal indiscretions,
together with his espousal of Anglo-Israelism and the annihilation of
the wicked doctrine, soon cost Parham his leadership in the larger
movement.   His family and a few others who remained loyal returned
to Kansas.   Although Parham continued as an itinerant evangelist,
the establishment of his home, an annual camp meeting, and the publication office of the Apostolic Faith made Baxter Springs the permanent center of the Apostolic Faith Movement.

Although the founder died in 1929, the Parham family has continued to occupy a dominant position in the movement. Its rigidity may account in part for the expulsion in 1952 of clergy participating in the reform-minded Ministerial and Missionary Alliance of the Original Apostolic Faith. Lack of significant growth is certainly related in large part to this loss. In 1951, 136 ministers and 83 churches scattered throughout a thirteen-state area were affiliated with the Apostolic Faith Movement. The 2,800 subscribers to the paper in 1951 had increased to only 3,000 in 1967.

--DOCTRINAL AND CONTROVERSIAL WORKS

3413   Apostolic Faith Movement.
        Doctrinal teachings of the Apostolic Faith Movement.
        Baxter Springs, Ks., Apostolic Faith Bible School, 19--. 6p.

3414   Barker, Raymond B.
        Signs of His coming, by Raymond B. Barker. n.p.,
        19--. 59p.

3415   Carothers, W. F.
        The baptism with the Holy Ghost and speaking in tongues,
        by W. F. Carothers. Houston, 1906. 31p. Cover title.
        Date on title page: 1906-7.

3416   Parham, Charles Fox, 1873-1929.
        Baptism with the Holy Ghost: the gift of tongues and
        sealing of the church and bride, by Chas. F. Parham. In
        Carothers, W. F. The baptism with the Holy Ghost and
        speaking in tongues. Houston, 1906, 5-18.

3417   Parham, Charles Fox, 1873-1929.
        A voice crying in the wilderness, by Chas. F. Parham,
        4th ed. Baxter Springs, Ks., R. L. Parham, 1944. 138p.
        On cover: Kol kare bomidbar. First published in 1902.

3418   Regier, Jacob C.
        Bible doctrine. n.p., 1963. 171p.

--NON-PENTECOSTAL AUTHORS

3419   Averill, R. L.
        The Apostolic Faith Movement, by R. L. Averill. In
        Holiness Evangel, 1 (Jan. 1, 1907).

3420   Kauffman, Abram Huber, 1852-1929.
        Fanaticism explained: symptoms, cause and cure, by A. H.
        Kauffman. 3d ed. Grand Rapids, Mi., 1904, i.e. 1906. 140p.
        On cover: "Third edition, published by A. H. Kauffman, Grand
        Rapids, Mich., 1906." Includes "The gift of tongues," supplement to Fanaticism explained.

--HISTORY

3421   Anderson, Robert Mapes, 1929-
            Vision of the disinherited: the making of American Pente-
        costalism. New York, Oxford, Oxford University Press,
        1979. 334p. Based on thesis (Ph. D.)--Columbia University.
        "The Apostolic Faith Movement": p. 47-61.

3422   Parham, Lula Ann, 1898-1972.
            Movement history, by Lula A. Parham. Baxter Springs,
        Ks. , Apostolic Faith Bible School, 1966. 12p. Mimeographed.

--PERIODICALS

3423   Apostolic faith. 1-28, Mar. 15, 1899-1901, 1905-1907,
        1911-1918, 1925-1953.
            Topeka, Ks. , Melrose, Ks. , Zion City, Il. , Baxter
        Springs, Ks.

3424   Apostolic faith report. 1- 1954-
            Baxter Springs, Ks.

--SERMONS, TRACTS, ADDRESSES, ESSAYS

3425   Parham, Charles Fox, 1873-1929.
            The everlasting gospel, by Charles Parham. Baxter
        Springs, Ks. , Apostolic Faith Church, 1911. 123p.

3426   Parham, Charles Fox, 1873-1929.
            The everlasting gospel, by Charles F. Parham. [Baxter
        Springs, Ks.] R. L. Parham, 1942. 123p. Reprint of 1911
        ed.

3427   Parham, Charles Fox, 1873-1929.
            Selected sermons of the late Charles F. Parham and
        Sarah E. Parham. Compiled by Robert L. Parham. n. p. ,
        R. L. Parham, 1941. 135p.

3428   Parham, Charles Fox, 1873-1929.
            Sermons of the late Charles F. Parham [and] Sarah E.
        Parham. Compiled by Robert L. Parham. Baxter Springs,
        Ks. , Apostolic Faith Church, 1941. 135p.

APOSTOLIC FAITH MOVEMENT (1907-1914)

In late 1906 or early 1907 allegations that Charles Fox Parham had committed sins named in the first chapter of Romans dis-
credited the "projector" of the Apostolic Faith Movement in the eyes
of most of his followers. Determined to preserve the "old" movement, W. F. Carothers and Howard A. Goss (who during the Houston

camp meeting in August 1906 had been appointed "general field director" and Texas "state field director" respectively) used their offices to maintain unity. The next year, A. G. Canada replaced Goss as state director. In addition to camp meetings held annually in connection with the Bruner Tabernacle at Orchard, near Houston, the constituency was held together by short-term Bible schools conducted in many places by Daniel C. O. Opperman, former school superintendent of Zion, Illinois, and by the Apostolic Faith, a paper started iin Houston in 1907. At first led by converts of Parham with Wesleyan views on sanctification, the group steadily gained adherents from other traditions and moved rapidly toward the Finished Work of Calvary position. After debate, the group also adopted belief in tongues as the initial evidence of the baptism with the Holy Ghost. Particularly influential in these changes were E. N. Bell and A. P. Collins, former Baptists, who with W. T. Gaston, Goss, and Opperman signed ministerial credentials. Like the Rodgers-led Church of God in the southeastern states, the Apostolic Faith Movement secured the backing of the Church of God in Christ, a black body led by C. H. Mason, in issuing ministerial credentials. Ordination certificates for 1912 were issued by the "Church of God in Christ in unity with the Apostolic Faith movement." The 1913 merger of the Apostolic Faith paper with Word and Witness, the Rodgers-group organ, was followed the next year by absorption of the constituencies of both in the newly formed General Council of the Assemblies of God.

--DOCTRINAL AND CONTROVERSIAL WORKS

3429   Carothers, W. F.
       Church government, by W. F. Carothers of the "old"
       Apostolic Faith Movement. Houston, J. V. Dealy Co. , 1909.
       72p. TxDaM

--PERIODICALS

3430   Apostolic faith. 1- Sept. 1907-1913.
       Houston, Tx. , Malvern, Ar. Merged into Word and witness.

CHRISTIAN PURITIES FELLOWSHIP (1973-   )

Established in 1973 by O. Talmadge Spence, a former Pentecostal Holiness minister, the Christian Purities Fellowship aims at re-establishing doctrinal fundamentals in the churches. In its role as the "witness outreach" of the Foundations Bible College of Dunn, North Carolina, the Fellowship serves as an information and coordinating agency for independent churches and missionary societies served by alumni of the school. It accepts recent statements issued by the World Congress of Fundamentalists and seeks to further traditional standards of personal sanctity. A close relationship also is maintained with Bob Jones University. Straightway, the official newsletter, is issued from Dunn.

--PERIODICALS

3431   Straightway. 1- 1973-
        Dunn, N. C.

        FIRST INTERDENOMINATIONAL CHRISTIAN ASSOCIATION
        (1946-)

        In 1946 Watson Sorrow, who twenty-six years earlier had
left the Pentecostal Holiness Church to found the Congregational
Holiness Church, became dissatisfied with the centralization of authority in that body and established the First Interdenominational
Christian Association.   The new organization carries congregationalism to its ultimate conclusion.   Under Association rules, local
churches owe no obligation beyond Christian fellowship to the General Association.   Although other local congregations have been organized according to Association guidelines, the jurisdiction of the
First Interdenominational Christian Association extends no further
in fact than to Sorrow's own hundred-member congregation, the Calvary Temple Church of Atlanta.

3432   First Interdenominational Christian Association.
            Our rules and faith.   Atlanta, Calvary Temple, 19--.
        4p.

        FULL GOSPEL EVANGELISTIC ASSOCIATION (1951-)
        [1951-1952 as Ministerial and Missionary Alliance of the
            Original Trinity Apostolic Faith.]

        During the late 1940s, leaders of the Apostolic Faith Move-
ment frowned increasingly upon use of scientific medical services,
attendance at non-affiliated churches, and pursuit of foreign missionary activity.   To counteract this tendency, in 1951 foreign missions
devotees formed the Ministerial and Missionary Alliance of the Original Trinity Apostolic Faith.   They in turn were disfellowshipped by
the Apostolic Faith Bible School of Baxter Springs, Kansas, the
agency responsible for ministerial credentials.   Cut loose, the next
year the Alliance transformed itself into the Full Gospel Evangelistic
Association.   Headquarters were established.   By the mid-1970s
there were thirty affiliated churches in seven states.   At that time
the approximately 4,000 members in the United States were supporting twenty missionaries in Mexico, Guatemala, Peru, and Taiwan.
The Full Gospel Evangelistic Association operates the Midwest Bible
Institute in Houston.   Its official organ is Full Gospel News.

3433   Full Gospel Evangelistic Association.
            Full Gospel Evangelistic Association.   Katy, Tx., 19--.
        4p.

--PERIODICALS

3434   Full gospel news.   1-   1972-
        Katy, Tx. , Houston, Tx.

INTERNATIONAL APOSTOLIC EVANGELISTIC AND MISSION-
    ARY ASSOCIATION (1935-   )

Founded in 1935, the International Apostolic Evangelistic and
Missionary Association exists to spread the "apostolic gospel as il-
luminated to Rev. C. G. Meyers. " Basic teachings include "salvation, divine healing, the power of the ministry, the gifts of the Holy
Spirit, and perfect love. " Headquarters offices are on the campus
of the Apostolic Bible School in Lakeland, Florida. After the founder's death in 1965, the Rev. Novella Meyers became Association
president.

--DOCTRINAL AND CONTROVERSIAL WORKS

3435   Meyers, Charles G. , 1878-1965.
            The divine attributes of the perfect love of God [by] C. G.
        Meyers. Lakeland, Fl. , Printed by I. A. E. & M. Assn. ,
        19--.   264p.

3436   Meyers, Charles G. , 1878-1965.
            Divine power, by Charles G. Meyers. Lakeland, Fl. ,
        Printed by I. A. E. & M. Assn. , 19--.   174p.

3437   Meyers, Charles G. , 1878-1965.
            Personal work, by C. G. Meyers. Lakeland, Fl. ,
        I. A. E. and M. Assn. , 19--.   145p.

--PERIODICALS

3438   Apostolic evangel.   1-   1938-1961.
            Lakeland, Fl.

--SERMONS, TRACTS, ADDRESSES, ESSAYS

3439   Meyers, Charles G. , 1878-1965.
            Evangelistic sermons autographed. Lakeland, Fl. ,
        I. A. E. & M. Assn. , 19--.   118p. OkTOr

PACIFIC APOSTOLIC FAITH MOVEMENT (1906-1922)

In the fall of 1906, Charles F. Parham, "projector" of the
Apostolic Faith Movement, visited Los Angeles. Arriving at the

height of the Azusa Street revival, Parham came at the invitation
of William J. Seymour, the one-eyed black pastor of the Apostolic
Faith Gospel Mission. Although Parham had assisted the Los Angeles pastor in moving from Houston a few months earlier, the visit
was an unfriendly one, to be followed shortly by disclosure of an un-
named indiscretion by the original leader and his resignation as projector. The October issue of the Apostolic Faith, the official publication, listed Parham as projector. By November the mission
letter-head had been revised. Omitting mention of Parham, the
heading read:

THE PACIFIC APOSTOLIC FAITH MOVEMENT
W. J. Seymour, Pastor and Manager. Clara Lum, Secretary
Headquarters: 312 Azusa Street
Hiram Smith, Deacon   G. Cook, Ass't State Manager
Jenny Moore, City Missionary   Florence Crawford, State Director
Phoebe Sargent, City Missionary G. W. Evans, Field Director

Including among its staff Seymour's future wife, Jenny Moore, and
his future rival, Florence Crawford, the organization represented a
transparent attempt by Seymour to wrest control of the movement from
Parham. Despite his personal charisma, Seymour's failure as an or-
ganizer and diplomat cost him dearly. In 1907 Mrs. Crawford (without Seymour's knowledge) took the non-Los Angeles mailing lists of
the paper and moved the publication to Portland, Oregon. Two years
later a rift between Seymour and William H. Durham, pioneer proponent of the "Finished Work of Calvary" teaching among Pentecostals, resulted in a dampened spiritual atmosphere and in departure
of most whites from the mission. Although the Apostolic Faith Gospel Mission survived until the pastor's death in 1922, the glory of
the exciting revival days of 1906 and 1907 had departed.

--HISTORY

3440   Bartleman, Frank, 1871-1935.
          Another wave rolls in! By Frank Bartleman. Edited by
       John Walker. Revised and enlarged ed. , edited by John G.
       Myers. Northridge, Ca. , Voice Publications, 1970, c1962.
       128p. First published in 1962 under title: What really hap-
       pened at "Azusa Street?" Abridgment of How Pentecost came
       to Los Angeles. TxWaS

3441   Bartleman, Frank, 1871-1935.
          Azusa Street, by Frank Bartleman. With foreword by
       Vinson Synan. Plainfield, N. J. , Logos International, c1980.
       xxvi, 184p. First published in 1925 under title: How Pente-
       cost came to Los Angeles.

3442   Bartleman, Frank, 1871-1935.
          How Pentecost came to Los Angeles; as it was in the be-
       ginning: old Azusa mission from my diary. 3d ed. Los
       Angeles, 1925. 166p.

3443   Bartleman, Frank, 1871-1935.
        What really happened at "Azusa Street?" Northridge,
        Ca. , Voice Christian Publications, 1962. 97p. Abridgment
        of How Pentecost came to Los Angeles. Edited by John
        Walker. KyWAT

3444   Nelson, Douglas J. , 1931-
        For such a time as this: the story of Bishop William
        J. Seymour and the Azusa Street revival; a search for Pente-
        costal/Charismatic roots, by Douglas J. Nelson. Birming-
        ham, 1981. 363ℓ . Thesis (Ph. D.)--University of Birming-
        ham.

3445   Nickel, Thomas Roy
        Azusa Street outpouring, as told to me by those who were
        there, by Thomas R. Nickel. Hanford, Ca. , Great Commis-
        sion International, 1956. 28[14]p.

3445a   Parham, Sarah E. (Thistlewaite), 1877-1937.
        The life of Charles F. Parham, founder of the Apostolic
        Faith Movement. Joplin, Mo. , Tri-State Printing Co. , 1930.
        452p. "Try the spirits": p. 161-170. CoD, MnHi

3446   Synan, Harold Vinson, 1934-
        The Holiness-Pentecostal movement in the United States,
        by Vinson Synan. Grand Rapids, Mi. , Eerdmans, c1971.
        248p. Based on thesis (Ph. D.)--University of Georgia, 1967.
        "The American Jerusalem--Azusa Street": p. 95-116.

3447   Synan, Harold Vinson, 1934-
        The Pentecostal movement in the United States. Athens,
        1967. vi,296ℓ . Thesis (Ph. D.)--University of Georgia.
        "The American Jerusalem": ℓ . 113-143. GU

3448   Valdez, Arthur Clarence, 1896-
        Fire on Azusa Street, by A. C. Valdez, Sr. , with James
        F. Scheer. Costa Mesa, Ca. , Gift Publications, c1980.
        139p.

        --PERIODICALS

3449   Apostolic faith. 1-15, Sept. 1906-Oct. /Nov. 1908.
        Los Angeles. Nos. 1-13, Sept. 1906-May 1908, collected
        by Fred T. Corum and issued as Like as of fire (Wilmington,
        Ma. , 1981).

SOUTHERN PENTECOSTAL ASSOCIATION (1905-1913)
[1905-1908 as Alabama Pentecostal Association.]

The "Third Annual Meeting of the Alabama Pentecostal

Association" was held in Birmingham, September 17-19, 1908.
Deeply influenced by the preaching by G. B. Cashwell, who a year
earlier had returned from Los Angeles with the new teaching concerning the Holy Spirit baptism, the group assembled included M. M.
Pinson, H. G. Rodgers, Anna M. Deane, O. N. Todd, Sr., N. J.
Holmes, and R. E. Massey, individuals influential in the later development of the General Council of the Assemblies of God and the
Pentecostal Holiness Church. At this meeting Rodgers successfully
led a move to enlarge the scope and change the name of the organization to include the whole Southern region. Tentative plans to meet
again in Atlanta the first Tuesday of June the next year were also
made. Designed to provide a base of support for foreign missionary
work (Miss Deane later was to serve many years in China), the Association disintegrated after Cashwell lost interest and other members got caught up in other organizational efforts.

THEA JONES EVANGELISTIC ASSOCIATION (1949-   )

Incorporated at Cleveland, Tennessee in 1949, the Thea Jones
Evangelistic Association is devoted to promoting the activities of its
founder. In 1954 Jones moved to Philadelphia where, under the auspices of the Association, he acquired the old Philadelphia Metropolitan Opera House and established a church. By the mid-1970s the
congregation claimed an active membership of 6,000, and an inclusive membership of over 22,000.

FIRE BAPTIZED HOLINESS CHURCH (1898-1911)
[1898-1902 as Fire Baptized Holiness Association of America.]

The result of the third blessing teaching, which troubled
Methodist Holiness circles in the last decade of the nineteenth century, the Fire Baptized Holiness Church owed its existence to the
evangelistic ministry of Benjamin Hardin Irwin. The exponent of a
third experience, the so-called baptism of fire, Irwin ranged widely
in his evangelistic endeavors, first in the Middle West, soon also
in the South. Although strict dietary and dress standards were
stressed and emotional displays were common, the meetings were
popular. As a result, starting in 1895 with Iowa, Kansas, Oklahoma, and Texas, Irwin organized state Fire Baptized Holiness associations. These, in turn, were followed by formation of the Fire
Baptized Holiness Association of America at Anderson, South Carolina with the founder himself as general overseer. The next year
marked the beginning of Live Coals of Fire, the official periodical,
in Lincoln, Nebraska. Although Irwin was soon removed for "open
and gross sin" and the baptism-of-fire was likewise abandoned as
fanatical, the movement survived under the leadership of J. H. King,
former minister of the Methodist Episcopal Church, South, who rather reluctantly led the group into the Pentecostal movement in 1907.
Four years later the Fire Baptized Holiness Church and the Pentecostal Holiness Church united, taking the name of the latter.

3450   Fire-Baptized Holiness Church.
        Constitution and general rules of the Fire-Baptized Holiness Church. Royston, Ga., 1905-1910. 2v.

        --HISTORY

3451   Campbell, Joseph Enoch, 1903-
        The Pentecostal Holiness Church, 1898-1948: its background and history, by Joseph E. Campbell. Franklin Springs, Ga., Publishing House of the Pentecostal Holiness Church, c1951. 573p. Thesis (Th.D.)--Union Theological Seminary (Virginia), 1948. "The Fire-Baptized Holiness Church": p. 192-215.

3452   Jernigan, Charles Brougher, 1863-1930.
        Pioneer days of the Holiness Movement in the Southwest, by C. B. Jernigan. Kansas City, Mo., Pentecostal Nazarene Publishing House, 1919. 157p. On "The Fire": p. 152-154. OkBetC

3453   Paul, George Harold, 1910-
        The religious frontier in Oklahoma: Dan T. Muse and the Pentecostal Holiness Church. Norman, 1965. 302ℓ. Thesis (Ph.D.)--University of Oklahoma. "Joseph H. King and the Fire-Baptized Holiness Church": ℓ. 22-34. OkU

3454   Synan, Harold Vinson, 1934-
        The Holiness-Pentecostal movement in the United States, by Vinson Synan. Grand Rapids, Mi., Eerdmans, c1971. 248p. Based on thesis (Ph.D.)--University of Georgia, 1967. "The Fire-Baptized way": p. 55-76.

3455   Synan, Harold Vinson, 1934-
        The old-time power, by Vinson Synan. Franklin Springs, Ga., Advocate Press, c1973. 296p. "The Fire-Baptized Holiness Church": p. 81-101.

3456   Synan, Harold Vinson, 1934-
        The Pentecostal movement in the United States. Athens, 1967. vi,296ℓ. Thesis (Ph.D.)--University of Georgia. "The Fire-Baptized way": ℓ. 59-89. GU

        --PERIODICALS

3457   Apostolic evangel. 1-20, Mar. 13, 1907-1929.
        Royston, Ga., Falcon, N.C.

3458   Live coals. 1- Oct. 6, 1899-June 15, 1900, 1902-1907.
        Lincoln, Ne., Mercer, Mo., Royston, Ga. 1899-1900 as Live coals of fire.

FREE WILL HOLINESS CHURCH (-1930)

In 1930 C. B. Till and S. D. Page received the Free Will Holiness Church, consisting of three churches and five ministers, into the Pentecostal Holiness Church. From this nucleus sprang the Pentecostal Holiness work in southern Alabama and the Florida panhandle.

FULL GOSPEL CHURCH ASSOCIATION (1952-)

Organized in 1952 at Amarillo, Texas by the Rev. Dennis W. Thorn, the Full Gospel Church Association sought to bring together as many independent Pentecostal churches and missions as possible in the southern and western United States. Headquarters are in Amarillo. The general board of directors meets four times a year; the general convention, at the call of the board of directors. By the mid-1970s, 72 churches, with a combined membership of 2,010, held charters with the Association. The group sponsors foreign missionary efforts in Mexico, the Philippines, and Africa.

3459   Full Gospel Church Association.
        Constitution, faith, and teaching. [Compiled by] Dennis
        W. Thorn. Amarillo, Tx., 1958. 33p.

FULL GOSPEL CONFERENCE OF THE WORLD (1927-)

Incorporated in 1927 at Calgary, Alberta, the Full Gospel Conference of the World soon spread to the United States. It also sponsored missionary efforts in Africa, China, and the Hawaiian Islands. The central organization was weak and kept no records. Commenting on the movement in a letter written at Niles, California, May 20, 1953, Fred Hahn said, "Our motive is a clean work, rather than a great work. "

3460   Moore, Everett Leroy, 1918-
        Handbook of Pentecostal denominations in the United
        States. Pasadena, Ca., 1954. vii, 346ℓ. Thesis (M. A.)--
        Pasadena College. "Full Gospel Conference of the World":
        ℓ. 223-224. CSdP

GEREDJA BETHEL INDJIL SEPENUH (1950-)

The result of an organizational dispute within the Geredja Pentekosta di Indonesia in 1950, the Geredja Bethel Indjil Sepenuh is, like its parent, the end-product of work begun in 1921 by repre-

sentatives of the Bethel Temple of Seattle.   Unlike the Geredja Pentekosta, member congregations of the Geredja Bethel enjoy a great
deal of local autonomy.   An unusual drift toward Wesleyanism resulted in 1967 in amalgamation with the Church of God (Cleveland,
Tennessee).   Numbering more than 50,000 members in 200 congregations that year, the Geredja Bethel retained its national autonomy
while reaping the benefits of participation in the worldwide program
of the American-based body.   Headquarters are in Djakarta.

HOLINESS ASSEMBLIES OF THE CHURCH OF THE FIRST-BORN WHICH ARE WRITTEN IN HEAVEN (1921-)

Beginning in 1921, the Holiness Assemblies of the Church of
the First-born which are Written in Heaven issued its official periodical, the Iowa Latter Rain, from Des Moines.

--PERIODICALS

3461   Iowa latter rain. 1- 1921-
       Des Moines, Ia.

HOUSE OF GOD, WHICH IS THE CHURCH OF THE LIVING GOD, THE PILLAR AND GROUND OF THE TRUTH (1919-)

Formed in 1919 as a result of a division in the Nashville-
based Church of the Living God, the Pillar and Ground of the Truth,
the House of God, which is the Church of the Living God, the Pillar
and Ground of the Truth, shares with its parent a common ancestor,
the Church of the Living God, Christian Workers for Fellowship.
Personalities, rather than doctrinal differences, appear to be behind
the separations.   Headquarters and the editorial offices of the Spirit
of Truth Magazine are in Philadelphia.   In 1956 the House of God
reported 107 churches, 120 clergy, and 2,350 members.

--PERIODICALS

3462   Spirit of truth magazine. 1- 19 -
       Philadelphia

IGLESIA CRISTIANA EVANGÉLICA MEXICANA (19 -)

The result of missionary efforts of the Church of God of the
Apostolic Faith, the Iglesia Cristiana Evangélica Mexicana took a
distinctive name to avoid confusion with Oneness groups, which often
use "Apostolic" in their names.   Although the Iglesia Cristiana

Evangélica is committed to the Wesleyan Holiness position on sanctification, its doctrinal statement bears a striking resemblance to the
one developed by Aimee Semple McPherson, a Finished Work of Calvary advocate.

3463   Iglesia Cristiana Evangélica Mexicana.
              Articulos de Fe. Reynosa, Tamaulipas, 19--. 8p.

IGLESIA DEL SEÑOR (19 -)

        In 1969 the Chilean Iglesia del Señor appeared to have fewer
than ten congregations.

IGLESIA EVANGÉLICA CONGREGACIONAL, INCORPORADA, DE
    PUERTO RICO (1948-)

        In 1937 some members of the Iglesia Evangélica Unida in the
Barrio Aguacate de Yabucoa, Puerto Rico, who had received the
baptism of the Holy Ghost and fire, withdrew and organized as the
Hermanos Unidos en Cristo.   Eleven years later after additional
congregations had been formed, they dissolved this fellowship and
organized the Iglesia Evangélica Congregacional, Incorporada, de
Puerto Rico.   Members pledge to keep the Lord's Day, to abstain
from attendance at services of other denominations, and to refrain
from wearing expensive or ostentatious clothing and jewelry, even
wristwatches.   By the mid-1970s, there were seven congregations
in Puerto Rico, two in Chicago, and one in Gary, Indiana, with a
combined membership of 575.   Headquarters are in Humacao, Puerto
Rico.

3464   Iglesia Evangélica Congregacional, Incorporada, de Puerto
              Rico.
                    La Constitución de la Iglesia Evangélica Congregacional,
              Incorporada, de Puerto Rico. Humacao, P.R., 19--.   8p.
              Typewritten.

IGLESIA EVANGÉLICA PENTECOSTAL DE CHILE (1909-)
[1909-1932 as Iglesia Metodista Nacional de Chile.]

        Established in 1932 by supporters of W. C. Hoover, the
Iglesia Evangélica Pentecostal is the second largest Pentecostal and
the second largest Protestant group in Chile.   Although Hoover had
founded the Iglesia Metodista Nacional, mounting nationalist sentiment in the old group made the American's continued leadership in
that body impossible.   Since the founder's death in 1936, Chilean

nationals have headed the Iglesia Evangélica Pentecostal, also. Despite a series of successions beginning in the year of its formation, the Iglesia Evangélica Pentecostal has, like its sister denominations, enjoyed numerical prosperity. By 1968 it claimed 538 congregations and 100,000 communicant members. Like the Iglesia Metodista Pentecostal, the Iglesia Evangélica Pentecostal de Chile claims 1909 as its founding date. Headquarters are in Curico.

3465   Tschuy, Théo
        Shock troops in Chile. In Christian Century, 77 (Sept. 28, 1960), 1118-1119; reply (Postscript on Chile [by] J. Tremayne Copplestone), 77 (Nov. 9, 1960), 1314.

--HISTORY

3466   Hoover, Willis C. , -1936.
        Historia del avivamiento pentecostal en Chile [por] W. C. Hoover. Valparaiso, Impr. Excelsior, 1948. 128p. "Traducido del ingles en 1909. " CtY-D, CPFT

3467   Hoover, Willis C. , -1936.
        Pentecost in Chile [by] W. C. Hoover. In World Dominion, 10 (Apr. 1932), 155-162.

--PERIODICALS

3468   Fuego de pentecostés. 1- 1933-
        Santiago

IGLESIA PENTECOSTAL APOSTÓLICA DE CHILE (1938-)

        Led initially by Francisco Anabalón, the Iglesia Pentecostal Apostólica de Chile separated from the Iglesia Metodista Pentecostal in 1938. Membership is concentrated in Santiago and Antofagasta.

IGLESIA PENTECOSTAL DE CHILE (1946-)

        In 1946 Enrique Chávez, a pastor despairing of further advancement in the Iglesia Metodista Pentecostal, left that body to found the Iglesia Pentecostal de Chile. Starting with a single congregation composed of followers from the older group, Chávez during the next decade organized 26 other congregations, and established 136 additional preaching points. In 1961, together with the Misión Iglesia Pentecostal, the Iglesia Pentecostal de Chile took for Pentecostals the unprecedented and unpopular step of joining the World Council of Churches. Following the Berlin Congress of Evangelism

in 1967, the Iglesia Pentecostal de Chile and the Iglesia Metodista
Pentecostal affilated with the Pentecostal Holiness Church, in the
World Council.   Learning of it, the North American group unilater-
ally severed its connection with the Iglesia Pentecostal de Chile in
March 1968.   Accurate estimates of membership are hard to establish.   In 1961 the combined membership of the two churches joining
the World Council of Churches was said to be 20,000.   It would be
reasonable to guess, therefore, that the Iglesia Pentecostal de Chile
may have consisted of half that number.   In 1967 the church claimed
58,000, and four years later, the founder himself claimed 60,000.
In 1969, however, an outside observer estimated only 13,500.

3469   Iglesia Pentecostal de Chile.
             Manual del Ministro.   Curico, 1963.   142p.

3470   Lalive d'Epinay, Christian, 1938-
             The Pentecostal "conquest" of Chile: rudiments of a
        better understanding.   In Cutler, D. R. , ed.   The religious
        situation: 1969.   Boston, c1969, 179-194.

3471   Lalive d'Epinay, Christian, 1938-
             The Pentecostal "conquista" in Chile.   In Ecumenical Re-
        view, 20 (Jan. 1968), 16-32.

3472   Wagner, Charles Peter, 1930-
             The street "seminaries" of Chile [by] C. Peter Wagner.
        In Christianity Today, 15 (Aug. 6, 1971), 5-8.

3473   Willems, Emilio, 1905-
             Validation of authority in Pentecostal sects of Chile and
        Brazil.   In Journal for the Scientific Study of Religion, 6
        (Fall 1967), 253-258.

             --HYMNS AND SACRED SONGS

3474   Iglesia Pentecostal de Chile.
             Himnos y Alabanzas, para uso de la Iglesia Pentecostal
        de Chile.   Temuco, Imprenta y Editorial Alianza, 19--.
        284p.

             --PERIODICALS

3475   La voz pentecostal.   1-   Apr. 1947-
             Curico.

IGLESIA WESLEYANA NACIONAL DE CHILE (1928-   )

        Formed in 1928 by followers of Victor Manuel Mora, a

Methodist pastor, the Iglesia Wesleyana Nacional regards itself as a return to primitive Methodism. Before attending seminary, Mora worked as a miner and trade union leader, a background with deep significance to the development of the movement. The church, which incorporates tongues-speaking and faith healing into its worship, requires active participation by its members in the Socialist Party. Centered in a coal-mining area of south central Chile, the Iglesia Wesleyana Nacional has experienced near stagnation in recent years. Headquarters are in Lota.

INTERNATIONAL PENTECOSTAL ASSEMBLIES (1936-1976)

The product of the union, August 25, 1936, of the Association of Pentecostal Assemblies and the International Pentecostal Church, the International Pentecostal Assemblies on August 10, 1976, merged with the Pentecostal Church of Christ to form the International Pentecostal Church of Christ. During its forty-year existence, the International Pentecostal Assemblies vigorously pursued foreign missions. In 1971 it reported 55 churches and 10,000 members in the United States, had more than thirty missionaries under appointment, and was supporting work in ten world areas. At its headquarters in Atlanta were the editorial offices of the Bridegroom's Messenger, the official organ, and the Beulah Heights Bible College.

3476   International Pentecostal Assemblies.
        General principles of the International Pentecostal Assemblies. Atlanta, 19--. 8p.

3477   International Pentecostal Assemblies.
        Introducing the International Pentecostal Assemblies. Atlanta, 19--. folder (3p.)

3478   International Pentecostal Assemblies.
        Statement of policy. Atlanta, 1966. 10p.

3479   Moore, Everett Leroy, 1918-
        Handbook of Pentecostal denominations in the United States. Pasadena, Ca., 1954. vii, 346ℓ. Thesis (M.A.)--Pasadena College. "International Pentecostal Assemblies": ℓ. 224-229. CSdP

3480   U.S. Bureau of the Census.
        Census of religious bodies: 1936. Pentecostal assemblies. Statistics, denominational history, doctrine, and organization. Consolidated report. Washington, Government Printing Office, 1940. iv, 49p. Includes International Pentecostal Assemblies. NNUT

--PERIODICALS

3481   Bridegroom's messenger. 1- Oct. 1, 1907-
           Atlanta, Detroit, Atlanta.   Suspended with v. 60, no. 4,
        Oct. 1974.   Resumed with v. 61, no. 1, Oct. 1976.

3481a   Bridegroom's messenger and Pentecostal witness. 15, no.
        12-17, no. 8, Dec. 1974-Aug. 1976.   Canton, Oh. Continues
        numbering of Pentecostal witness.   Issued jointly by Interna-
        tional Pentecostal Assemblies and Pentecostal Church of
        Christ.   OkTOr

3482   I. P. A. messenger. 1-3, 1942-1944.
           Detroit.

INTERNATIONAL PENTECOSTAL CHURCH (1914-1936)
[1914-19-- as National and International Pentecostal Missionary
   Union.]

        Organized in 1914 by Philip Wittich, the National and Inter-
national Pentecostal Missionary Union merged with the Association
of Pentecostal Assemblies on August 25, 1936, to form the International Pentecostal Assemblies.   The joint council which effected the
merger met at the Radio Church, Lombard and Parkin streets in
Baltimore.   At the time of the union the group was known as the
International Pentecostal Church.

INTERNATIONAL PENTECOSTAL CHURCH OF CHRIST (1976-   )

        Formed on August 10, 1976, at London, Ohio, the Interna-
tional Pentecostal Church of Christ is the product of the union of
the International Pentecostal Assemblies and the Pentecostal Church
of Christ.   Committed to premillennialism, it denounces war as in-
compatible with the gospel.   The Lord's Supper and baptism by immersion are observed as ordinances; foot washing is optional.   The
headquarters are in London, Ohio, site of the former Pentecostal
Church of Christ general offices.   The Bridegroom's Messenger, the
former International Pentecostal Assemblies organ, is the official
publication.   In 1977 the united body reported 11,659 members and
105 churches in the United States, and missionary activity in nine
fields: Hong Kong, Japan, India, Uganda, South Africa, Nigeria,
Puerto Rico, Mexico, and Brazil.   Membership in Brazil is about
one-fourth that claimed in the United States.

3483   International Pentecostal Church of Christ.
           Constitution and bylaws of International Pentecostal Church
        of Christ. [London, Oh. , 1976] 64p.   Cover title.

--PERIODICALS

3483a Bridegroom's messenger.   61-   Oct. 1976-
       Atlanta.

KINGSTON CITY MISSION (1925-   )
[Also as City Mission.]

The Kingston City Mission is the result of the evangelistic efforts of W. Raglan Phillips, an Englishman. Born in Bristol in 1854, Phillips at age seventeen migrated to Jamaica, where for a time he worked as an estate bookkeeper. Turned down for the Baptist ministry, in 1887 he joined the Salvation Army and applied to General Booth to send officers to the island. He commenced work as an evangelist under Salvation Army auspices, pursuing, however, a rather independent course. His independency, plus his tolerance of charismatic manifestations in his meetings, caused repeated rifts with the Army headquarters in London, yet he remained an officer until his death in 1930.

As early as 1925 Phillips' work had been known as the City Mission, and with his death separation from the Salvation Army became final. Charismatic manifestations, periodic during the founder's lifetime, now characterized worship, and the group became, in fact, a Pentecostal sect, very similar to the Church of God (Cleveland, Tennessee). Unlike the latter, the City Mission does not practice foot washing. Like the Salvation Army, the City Mission employs a system of rank and members wear uniforms. Migration of members to England, the United States (New York and California), British Honduras, and the Bahamas has made the movement international. Yet Jamaica, with over fifty congregations, remains the center.

3483b Calley, Malcolm John Chalmers
       God's people: West Indian sects in England [by] Malcolm
       J. C. Calley. London, Oxford University Press, 1965. xiv,
       182p. "History of the City Mission": p. 159-160.

METHODISTS:

IGLESIA METODISTA PENTECOSTAL DE CHILE (1909-   )
[1909-1932 as Iglesia Metodista Nacional de Chile.]

The largest Protestant body in Chile, the group now known as the Iglesia Metodista Pentecostal, was founded in 1909 by W. C.

Hoover, an American missionary. Going to Chile as a teacher in
1889, Hoover worked as a self-supporting missionary under Bishop
William Taylor. Four years later he was listed as a probationer
at the formation of the South America Annual Conference of the
Methodist Episcopal Church. In 1907 a revival of tongues-speaking
broke out in Hoover's church in Valparaiso, splitting the large congregation two years later. Although in February 1910, the Methodist conference decided to send Hoover back to the states, it acted
too late. Several months earlier about 400 of Hoover's supporters
in Valparaiso had left the Methodist Episcopal Church. Additional
defections in Santiago followed, and in April 1910 the Iglesia Metodista Nacional, consisting of three congregations, was formed.
Hoover was chosen superintendent, and early growth was phenomenal.
In 1932, however, nationalist feeling split the movement, and a substantial minority who supported the founder formed the Iglesia Evangélica Pentecostal. The majority under Manuel Umaña, who they
designated as bishop, then adopted the present name. Though troubled by a series of secessions which had begun even before the 1932
crisis, the Iglesia Metodista Pentecostal far outstripped its American-
sponsored parent. By 1962 it claimed 800 congregations and 400,000
communicant members whereas the Iglesia Metodista had only 96 congregations and 4,900 members. In 1967 an agreement of affiliation
linked the Iglesia Metodista Pentecostal and the Pentecostal Holiness
Church, a North American group with roots in Methodism.

3484   Iglesia Metodista Pentecostal de Chile.
            Disciplina y Ritual de la Iglesia Metodista Pentecostal de
        Chile. Santiago, Imprenta Vidal, 1962. 131p. Cover title:
        Rituales de la Iglesia Metodista Pentecostal de Chile. Date
        on cover: 1963.

3485   Lalive d'Epinay, Christian, 1938-
            The Pentecostal "conquest" of Chile: rudiments of a bet-
        ter understanding. In Cutler, D. R., ed. The religious
        situation: 1969. Boston, c1969, 179-194.

3485a   Lalive d'Epinay, Christian, 1938-
            The Pentecostal "conquista" in Chile. In Ecumenical
        Review, 20 (Jan. 1968), 16-32.

3486   Wagner, Charles Peter, 1930-
            The street "seminaries" of Chile [by] C. Peter Wagner.
        In Christianity Today, 15 (Aug. 6, 1971), 5-8.

3487   Willems, Emilio, 1905-
            Validation of authority in Pentecostal sects of Chile and
        Brazil. In Journal for the Scientific Study of Religion, 6
        (Fall 1967), 253-258.

                --HISTORY

3488   Hoover, Willis C., -1936.

Historia del avivamiento pentecostal en Chile [por] W. C. Hoover. Valparaiso, Impr. Excelsior, 1948. 128p. "Traducido del ingles en 1909." CtY-D, CPFT

3489 Hoover, Willis C., -1936.
      Pentecost in Chile [by] W. C. Hoover. In World Dominion, 10 (Apr. 1932), 155-162.

--PERIODICALS

3490 Chile pentecostal. 1- 1911-
      Santiago

IGREJA METODISTA WESLEYANA (1967-)

Founded on January 5, 1967, at Nova Friburgo, by clergy and laity who had separated from the Igreja Metodista do Brasil during its "XI Concilio Regional," the Igreja Metodista Wesleyana sees itself as a continuation of historic Methodism. Intent on creating an organism in which spiritual gifts might be freely exercised, temporary officers chosen at Nova Friburgo called a "Concilio Constituinte" which met at Petrópolis from the 16th to 19th of February that year. The permanent organization was set forth in the Manual, the first edition of which was issued in 1968. Headquarters are in Rio de Janeiro, where apparently the offices of the Voz Wesleyana and the Seminário e Instituto Biblico Wesleyana also are located.

3491 Igreja Metodista Wesleyana.
      Manual da Igreja Metodista Wesleyana. [Rio de Janeiro],
      1978. 208[4]p. Cover title.

--PERIODICALS

3492 Voz Wesleyana. 1- 1967-
      [Rio de Janeiro]

MIEMBROS DEL CUERPO DE CRISTO (1968-)

In 1968 the pastor of one of the Misión Panamericana congregations in Bogota was charged by Panamericana leaders with immorality. He, in turn, charged them with dictatorial tactics and withdrew, taking with him half the Panamericana members in the city. Calling themselves simply Members of the Body of Christ, the new group grew rapidly and by 1974 claimed a larger membership in Bogota than did the Misión Panamericana.

MISIÓN IGLESIA PENTECOSTAL (1952-   )

In 1952 Victor Pavez, Jr. and 120 other members were dismissed from the Chilean Iglesia Evangélica Pentecostal following several efforts to reform it.   This action proved a turning point for Pavez, whose father had followed W. C. Hoover into the Iglesia Metodista Nacional when Victor was a small child.   In 1954 the new group built a church on the Avenida Pedro Montt in Santiago.   Also that year, Pavez entered the ministry and left to do missionary work in Buenos Aires.   By 1956, however, he had returned to Santiago as denominational superintendent.   Missionary outposts had been established in both Argentina and Uruguay, and work was spreading rapidly in the Santiago area.   Early in its existence, the Misión Iglesia Pentecostal adopted a pattern of agressive evangelism and thoroughgoing ecumenism.   Lay evangelists, who are forbidden to make derogatory statements about Catholicism, spend Sundays and holidays calling in homes and holding open-air services.   Contacts are referred to the nearest evangelical church.   In 1961 the Misión Iglesia Pentecostal and the Iglesia Pentecostal de Chile took what for Pentecostals was an unprecedented and unpopular step when they joined the World Council of Churches.   The combined membership of the two groups was said to be 20,000.   It would be reasonable to assume, therefore, that the Misión Iglesia Pentecostal at that time may have consisted of half that number.

--PERIODICALS

3493   Sembrado.   1-   195 -
         Santiago

MISIÓN PANAMERICANA (1956-   )

In 1956 Ignacio Guevara, having accepted Pentecostal beliefs, left the indigenous holiness Iglesia Evangélica Interamericana and founded the mother congregation of what was to become the Misión Panamericana.   More than half of his former Interamericana congregation in Bogota followed Pastor Guevara into independency, and additional congregations of the new group were organized in rapid succession.   The 105 members in 1962 had grown to 862 by 1968. Continued growth appeared to be assured.   In the latter year, however, the pastor of the second church in Bogota was accused of immorality.   When confronted by Guevara, the accused pastor charged the founder with being a dictator, and withdrew from the Misión Panamericana.   He took half of the Panamericana members in Bogota with him into a new group, called simply Miembros del Cuerpo de Cristo.   By 1974 the new organization claimed more members in the city of Bogota than did the Misión Panamericana.

3494   Palmer, Donald C. , 1934-
         Explosion of people evangelism, by Donald C. Palmer.

Chicago, Moody Press, 1974.   191p.   Based on thesis (M. A.)
--Trinity Evangelical Divinity School.   On Misión Panamericana: p. 50-51.

MISSIONARY AGENCIES:

BETHANY MISSION (1928-1943)

The personal project of Paul C. Pitt in north China, the
Bethany Mission took its name from an independent church in Vancouver, British Columbia, which was the founder's original sponsor.
Pitt's conversion from Catholicism and the formation of the Bethany
Mission in Vancouver both had resulted from the 1923 campaign of
Evangelist Charles Price in the city.   Arriving in China in the late
fall of 1928, the missionary immersed himself in study of the language and culture.   By 1932 he was in Shantung.   During the next
five years, he established the work.   In 1936 he first made contact
with the Church of God (Cleveland, Tennessee), a movement he was
to join in absentia at its Assembly the following year.   At that time,
Pitt reported organized churches at Lang Shan and Yeh Tau with a
combined membership of 600.   In addition there were five outstations,
he said.   Although he desired the Tennessee-based group to take
over the work, war prevented church officials from even visiting
the field.   After Pearl Harbor, Pitt remained in Shantung, where
he died in September 22, 1943.   He is buried in the churchyard at
Wang Tsun.

3495   Conn, Charles William, 1920-
         Like a mighty army: a history of the Church of God,
       1886-1976 [by] Charles W. Conn.   Rev. ed.   Cleveland,
       Tn. , Pathway Press, 1977.   xxxi, 477p.   "China": p. 238-
       241.   DLC

3496   Conn, Charles William, 1920-
         Where the saints have trod: a history of Church of God
       missions [by] Charles W. Conn.   Cleveland, Tn. , Pathway
       Press, 1959.   312p.   "The land of more sorrow": p. 31-36.
       DLC

3497   Humphrey, Peggy
         Paul C. Pitt: beloved of the Chinese.   Cleveland, Tn. ,
       Pathway Press, c1968.   124p.   (Missionary series.)   Cover
       title: Beloved of the Chinese.   "Published under the auspices
       of Church of God World Missions. "

MISIÓN EVANGÉLICA PENTECOSTAL (19 -   )

From headquarters in Santiago, Chile, the Misión Evangélica
Pentecostal directs missionary activities in Argentina and Uruguay.

PACIFIC COAST MISSIONARY SOCIETY (1909-1945)

In 1909 an independent church in Vancouver, British Columbia
headed by G. S. Paul sent its first missionary couple, the Rev. and
Mrs. Harwood, to China. Consisting eventually of more than a half-
dozen Canadian missionaries, the China work resulted in organization
of the Pacific Coast Missionary Society, composed of the original
Vancouver congregation and its satellite congregations which supported
the overseas project. On March 23, 1942, the Canadian churches
under the leadership of the founder's son, Harold, united with the
Pentecostal Holiness Church, becoming the British Columbia Conference of that body. At the time of the merger there were four congregations and 25 ministers in Canada affiliated with the Pacific
Coast Missionary Society. In 1945 the China work followed its sponsor into the Pentecostal Holiness Church.

MOUNT CALVARY HOLY CHURCH OF AMERICA (19 -   )

In 1929 Bishop Bromfield Johnson and 200 followers left the
United Holy Church of America and chartered the Mount Calvary Church.
At the founder's death in 1972, the group claimed eighty churches in thir-
teen states. Headquarters moved from Buffalo to Boston in the 1960s.

3498   Paris, Arthur Ernest, 1945-
        Black Pentecostalism: world view, society and politics.
        Evanston, Il. , 1974. vi, 183[31]ℓ . Thesis (Ph. D.)--North-
        western University. On three Boston congregations of the
        Mount Calvary Holy Church of America. IEN

3499   Paris, Arthur Ernest, 1945-
        Black Pentecostalsim: Southern religion in an urban world
        [by] Arthur E. Paris. Amherst, University of Massachusetts
        Press, 1982. vii, 183p. Based on thesis (Ph. D.)--Northwestern
        University. DLC, OkU

MOUNT SINAI HOLY CHURCH OF AMERICA (1924-   )

As youthful pastor of the Mount Olive Holy Church in Philadelphia, Elder Ida Robinson had a series of dreams and visions in
which she was the head of a large ministry. In these dreams people from the north, the south, the east, and the west flocked to her
Philadelphia church in search of help. Following a ten-day fast in
1924, she believed the Holy Spirit commanded her to "Come out on
Mount Sinai. " As a result, she left the United Holy Church of
America and founded the Mount Sinai Holy Church of America later
that year. Women have been prominent in this church from the beginning. It embraces a strict code of personal behavior, eschewing
remarriage after divorce in every case and condemning by name

many alleged evidences of worldliness. Belief in a specific sequence of last things and in baptism as essential to salvation is accepted as dogma. Under Mother Robinson and her successor, Bishop Elmira Jeffries, the Mount Sinai movement spread along the Atlantic coast from Massachusetts to Florida, and leaped across the continent to California. In 1968 there were 92 congregations in the United States with an estimated membership of 7,000. Headquarters are in Philadelphia.

3500 Mount Sinai Holy Church of America.
          Manual of Mount Sinai Holy Church of America. Rev.
      ed. Philadelphia, 1947. 48p.

ORIGINAL UNITED HOLY CHURCH INTERNATIONAL (1977-   )
[1977-1980 as Original United Holy Church of the World.]

Organized June 29, 1977, during a meeting called for the purpose in the Memorial Auditorium, Raleigh, North Carolina, the Original United Holy Church owes its existence to a struggle within the United Holy Church of America between Bishop W. N. Strobhar, denominational president, and Bishop J. A. Forbes, president of the Southern District Convocation. The final rift came during a meeting in Cleveland, Ohio in May 1977 in which the Southern District Convocation, though itself parent to the general organization, was ousted from the denomination. The new body remains in essential doctrinal agreement with the continuing one, and while protesting its adherence to congregationalism, remains committed to the polity of the parent body as well.

Consisting of more than 200 congregations and 15,000 members, the Original United Holy Church is concentrated on the Atlantic coast from South Carolina to Connecticut. Additional churches are located in Kentucky, Texas, and California. Bishop Forbes, its general president, serves also as pastor and administrator of the Greater Forbes Temple of Hollis, New York, and as president of the Southern District Convocation. Headquarters are in Goldsboro, North Carolina, site of the United Christian College, which the church sponsors. The church supports missionary work in Liberia. Voice of the World, the official periodical, is printed by Advocate Press, the publishing house of the Pentecostal Holiness Church. On January 24, 1979, in Wilmington, North Carolina, an agreement of affiliation between the Original United Holy Church and the Pentecostal Holiness Church was signed, which envisions a close cooperative relationship between the two denominations.

3501 Original United Holy Church of the World.
          State of the church address, delievered [!] by General
      President Bishop J. A. Forbes to the First General Convo-
      cation of the Original United Holy Church of the World, Inc.

May 16, 1979. n.p. , 1979. 8ℓ . Cover title. Mimeographed.

3502   Original United Holy Church of the World.
        1980 minutes [of the] quadrennial session [of the] Origi-
nal United Holy Church of the World, Inc. Goldsboro, N.C. ,
1980. 20ℓ . Cover title. Mimeographed.

            --CATECHISMS AND CREEDS

3503   Original United Holy Church of the World. Young People
Holy Association.
        Quarterly. Clifton E. Buckrham, writer and editor.
n.p. , 197-. 24p. Cover title.

            --PERIODICALS

3504   Voice of the world. 1- July 1978-
        [Goldsboro, N.C.]

PENTECOSTAL CHURCH OF CHRIST (1917-1976)

        In 1907 John Stroup, an evangelist of South Solon, Ohio,
started preaching extensively in the area where Ohio, West Virginia,
and Kentucky join. He won the allegiance of several ministers in
the area. On May 10, 1917, at Flatwoods (Advance), Kentucky,
Stroup joined with them to form the Pentecostal Church of Christ.
The conference chose Stroup as bishop. Although at first the group
was composed solely of ministers, the need for organized churches
soon became apparent. The Pentecostal Church of Christ was incorporated at Portsmouth, Ohio in 1927. Headquarters were established in London, Ohio. Missionary efforts begun in Brazil in 1935
had garnered 125 members by 1941, when the work there was formally organized. By 1965, the thirtieth anniversary of the Brazilian
mission, the number had grown to 3,500, about three times the
United States membership. Openness to union with other groups is
a pervasive theme in Pentecostal Church of Christ history. Short-
lived mergers in 1928 with the Pentecostal Full Gospel Church and
the United Pentecostal Association were followed by unsuccessful negotiations with the Church of God of the Mountain Assembly, the Emmanuel Holiness Church, and the Pentecostal Holiness Church in the
1950s and 1960s. The Pentecostal Witness, official Pentecostal
Church of Christ organ, was issued jointly with the Emmanuel Holiness Church as Witness and Messenger for a few years following
1959. Similarly, in 1975 and 1976 prior to union with the International Pentecostal Assemblies, it was issued jointly with that body
as the Bridegroom's Messenger and Pentecostal Witness. On August
10, 1976, at London, Ohio, the merger was consummated under a
composite of the two names, the International Pentecostal Church of

Christ. At that time the Pentecostal Church of Christ had 50 churches, 1,659 members, and 58 ministers in the United States.

3505   Pentecostal Church of Christ.
            Manual of the Pentecostal Church of Christ. London, Oh., 1966. 83p. Cover title.

--DOCTRINAL AND CONTROVERSIAL WORKS

3506   Stroup, John, 1853-1929.
            The New Testament church. South Solon, Oh., 192-. 19p.

--PERIODICALS

3507   Bridegroom's messenger and Pentecostal witness. 1-17, no. 8, Dec. 1923-May 1935, June 1942-Feb. 1959, 1967-Aug. 1976.
            Kenova, W. Va., Conneaut, Oh., Portsmouth, Oh., Akron, Oh., Ashland, Ky., London, Oh., Canton, Oh. Vols. 1-15, no. 11, Dec. 1923-Nov. 1974 as Pentecostal witness. Vols. 15, no. 12-17, no. 8, issued jointly by Pentecostal Church of Christ and International Pentecostal Assemblies. Merged into Bridegroom's messenger.

3508   Good tidings. 1-3, no. 20, Nov. 1919-Jan. 1922.
            Ironton, Oh.

3509   Gospel messenger. 1, July-Dec. 1922.
            Ironton, Oh., Jackson, Oh.

PENTECOSTAL CHURCH OF CHRIST (1930-   )

Apparently a splinter of the London, Ohio-based group of the same name, the Pentecostal Church of Christ was formed June 17, 1930, at Toledo, Ohio. The expressed purpose of the founders was to free the ministry of unnecessary restrictions. Headquarters later moved to Los Angeles, where the group reorganized. On July 27, 1935, it incorporated under California law. By 1954 there were about forty churches in the United States, twenty of them in California, the others in New Mexico, Colorado, Oklahoma, and Ohio. At that time there were approximately 1,000 members. The church teaches that "all regenerated persons may be sanctified through the blood." Foot-washing is always administered following observance of the Lord's Supper. Members are committed to non-combatant service during war.

3510   Pentecostal Church of Christ.
        By-laws. Bell, Ca. , 1942. 35p.

3511   Moore, Everett Leroy, 1918-
        Handbook of Pentecostal denominations in the United
        States. Pasadena, Ca. , 1954. vii, 346ℓ. Thesis (M. A.)--
        Pasadena College. "Pentecostal Church of Christ": ℓ. 230-
        236. CSdP

PENTECOSTAL FIRE-BAPTIZED HOLINESS CHURCH (1918-   )

        Following the union of the Fire-Baptized Holiness Church and
the Pentecostal Holiness Church in 1911, a minority of former Fire-
Baptized members became increasingly dissatisfied over laxity in the
merged body in relation to the wearing of ornaments and extravagance
in dress. Of particular concern was the wearing of neckties. As a
result on August 9, 1918, at Nicholson, Georgia, three clergy and
four laymen withdrew and reorganized as the Pentecostal Fire-
Baptized Holiness Church. On November 21st of the next year at
Toccoa, Georgia, the infant church united with the North Carolina
Annual Conference of the Pentecostal Free-Will Baptist Church,
which had been formed three years earlier by other former Fire-
Baptized adherents. Growth was slow. A high point was reached
in 1952 when the denomination consisted of 1, 929 members in 85
churches. Formation the next year of the Emmanuel Holiness
Church by "liberals" desirous of relaxing the stricture against wearing ties cost the Pentecostal Fire-Baptized group more than half its
members. Decline continued and in 1981 the church reported only
298 members. Churches in Alabama, Georgia, North Carolina,
South Carolina, and Virginia support independent missionary efforts
in Mexico and Haiti. While the church condemns many pleasures
and vanities, including the drinking of "cola" beverages and the cut-
ting and waving of women's hair, its worship is characterized by
joyous expression, shouting, hand-clapping, and other emotional
demonstrations.

3512   Fire-Baptized Holiness Church.
        Discipline of the Fire-Baptized Holiness Church. Pem-
broke, N. C. , 1916.

3512a   Wood, Dillard L.
        Baptized with fire: a history of the Pentecostal Fire-
Baptized Holiness Church, by Dillard L. Wood and William
H. Preskitt, Jr. Colbert, Ga. , [Printed by] Advocate Press,
Franklin Springs, Ga. , 1983, c1982. 172p. DLC

--HYMNS AND SACRED SONGS

3513   Pentecostal Fire-Baptized Holiness Church.
        Celestial songs. Montgomery, Al. , 1941.

3513a   Pentecostal Fire-Baptized Holiness Church.
        Celestial songs, no. 2. Montgomery, Al. , 1942.

--PERIODICALS

3514   Echoes of faith. 1- June 1955-May 1957.
        Nicholson, Ga. Merged into Faith and truth.

3515   Faith and truth. 1- Feb. 1919-
        Toccoa, Ga. , Montgomery, Al. , Lula, Ga. , Nicholson,
        Ga.

PENTECOSTAL FULL GOSPEL CHURCH (192 -   )

        Centered in Baltimore, the Pentecostal Full Gospel Church
is known chiefly for its attempts at cooperation with other groups.
Union from 1928 to 1934 with the Pentecostal Church of Christ was
followed by a joint periodical-publishing effort with the Church of
the Full Gospel in the 1930s. This journal, the Full Gospel Herald,
was published in Baltimore.

--PERIODICALS

3516   Full gospel herald. 1- 193 -
        Baltimore.

PENTECOSTAL HOLINESS CHURCH (1899-1911)
[1899-1909 as Holiness Church.]

        Organized during a convention held at Goldsboro, North Caro-
lina, October 26-28, 1899, the Holiness Church of North Carolina
was to a large extent composed of followers of A. B. Crumpler,
former minister in the Methodist Episcopal Church, South. From
its inception, the body adhered to second-crisis sanctification, premillennialism, and faith healing. It stood in opposition to "worldliness, " "needless ornamentation, " "tobacco, " and entertainments,
such as "oyster stews, " for the support of the church. During the
famous revival which began at Dunn, North Carolina on December
31, 1906, a majority of the Holiness Church clergy (but not the
founder) had tongues-speaking experiences. Although Crumpler's
leadership was at no time challenged, tension resulting from the

new experiences so marred the 1908 convention at Dunn that he
walked out, taking two churches and five or six preachers with him.
Representatives of the remaining thirteen churches then revised the
articles of faith, making a distinction between entire sanctification
and the baptism with the Holy Ghost and witnessing to the belief that
tongues-speech is the initial evidence of the latter.   Meeting in November the next year in Falcon, North Carolina, the convention completed transition to the new movement and changed the name to
Pentecostal Holiness Church.   Remarkable growth followed.   When
it merged with the Fire-Baptized Holiness Church in 1911, the Pentecostal Holiness Church reported 49 churches, more than three times
its 1908 total.

3517   Holiness Church.
            Constitution and by-laws, and minutes of the first ses-
       sion, held October 26-28, in Goldsboro, 1899.   Goldsboro,
       N. C. , Nash Brothers, 1899.   8p.   NcU

3518   Holiness Church.
            The discipline of the Holiness Church.   Goldsboro, N. C. ,
       Nash Brothers, 1902.

               --DOCTRINAL AND CONTROVERSIAL WORKS

3519   Taylor, George Floyd, 1881-1934.
            The devil, by G. F. Taylor.   Dunn, N. C. , 1906.   76p.

               --HISTORY

3520   Synan, Harold Vinson, 1934-
            The old-time power, by Vinson Synan.   Franklin Springs,
       Ga. , Advocate Press, c1973.   296p.   "The Pentecostal Holi-
       ness Church of North Carolina": p. 55-79.

               --PERIODICALS

3521   Holiness advocate.   1-   1900-1908.
       Clinton, N. C.

PENTECOSTAL HOLINESS CHURCH (1911-   )
[1975 to present also as International Pentecostal Holiness Church.]

       Organized January 31, 1911, at Falcon, North Carolina, the
Pentecostal Holiness Church is the result of the union of an earlier
body of the same name and the Fire-Baptized Holiness Church.
Composed initially of about 2,000 members scattered along the Atlantic seaboard from Virginia to Florida and westward to Tennessee

and Oklahoma, the new denomination took on many features of the Fire-Baptized Holiness Church, the larger of the merging groups. Led from 1917 until his death in 1946 by J. H. King, the Pentecostal Holiness Church combines features of both congregationalism and episcopacy. Centralization has increased steadily. Beginning in 1937 the general superintendents were also given the honorary title of bishop. By 1945 the process of installation in this office was being called "ordination. "

Educational institutions are supported in Greenville, South Carolina; Franklin Springs, Georgia; Oklahoma City, Oklahoma; McAllen, Texas; and Sacramento, California. Although membership continues to be concentrated in rural areas in the southeastern United States, the church has made a determined effort to expand into other sections. Particular attention has been given to ministry to rural newcomers in the cities. The 1974 decision to move the denominational offices from Franklin Springs, Georgia, a hamlet where they had been located for fifty-five years, to Oklahoma City was influenced by both of these factors. In 1981, with a United States membership of 125,702, the denomination had 95 missionaries under appointment in sixteen world areas, and was spending more than $2,000,000 annually overseas. That year membership in world mission conferences stood at 68,922. Still commonly known as the Pentecostal Holiness Church, the legal designation of the denomination was changed to International Pentecostal Holiness Church in December 1975. Although the Advocate Press remains in Franklin Springs, the editorial offices of the International Pentecostal Holiness Advocate are at the new headquarters in Oklahoma City.

In an effort to strengthen its missionary outreach, to augment its witness to racial minorities, and to restore its fellowship with once estranged brethren, the Pentecostal Holiness Church has during the past fifteen years entered into agreements of affiliation with six like-minded denominations: Iglesia Metodista de Chile (1967), Iglesia Pentecostal de Chile (1967), Soul Saving Station for Every Nation (1973), Original United Holy Church International (1978), Congregational Holiness Church (1980), and Pentecostal Fire-Baptized Holiness Church (1981). The agreement with the Iglesia Pentecostal de Chile was terminated in 1968 because of the membership of that body in the World Council of Churches. The other agreements remain intact.

3522   Pentecostal Holiness Church.
              Manual, 1911- . Falcon, N. C. , Royston, Ga. , Franklin Springs, Ga. v. [1]- . 1911 as Constitution and general rules; 1913-1957 as Discipline. Quadrennial, 1913- .

3523   Pentecostal Holiness Church.
              Manual. International ed. Franklin Springs, Ga. , 19--.
        29p.

3524   Pentecostal Holiness Church.

Welcome to the Pentecostal Holiness Church. Let's get acquainted! Oklahoma City, 197-. 35p. Cover title.

3525   Pentecostal Holiness Church.
            Yearbook, 1929-1972. Franklin Springs, Ga. v. [1]-[40].

3526   Pentecostal Holiness Church. General Conference.
            Minutes. 1st- . 1911- . Falcon, N.C., Franklin
        Springs, Ga. Meeting called General Convention, 1911-1917.
        Quadrennial, 1913- .

3527   Pentecostal Holiness Church. General Department of Evan-
        gelism.
            Introducing the Pentecostal Holiness Church. Franklin
        Springs, Ga., Advocate Press, 197-. 48p.

3528   Pentecostal Holiness Church. Loyalty Committee.
            Loyalty manual of the Pentecostal Holiness Church.
        Franklin Springs, Ga., Advocate Press, 1974. 24p. "The
        final draft of the [Loyalty] committee's report was adopted by
        the General Board of Administration in Memphis, Tennessee,
        on December 13, 1973."

3529   Gaddis, Merrill Elmer, 1891-
            Christian perfectionism in America. Chicago, 1929.
        viii, 589ℓ. Thesis (Ph.D.)--University of Chicago. On
        Pentecostal Holiness Church: ℓ. 561-562. ICU

3530   Johnson, Guy Benton, 1928-
            A framework for the analysis of religious action, with
        special reference to holiness and non-holiness groups. Cam-
        bridge, Ma., 1953 [i.e. 1954] iii, 307ℓ. Thesis (Ph.D.)--
        Harvard University. Based in part on responses from ten
        non-Pentecostal and ten Pentecostal religionists, including
        five Pentecostal Holiness ministers. MH

3531   Moore, Everett Leroy, 1918-
            Handbook of Pentecostal denominations in the United States.
        Pasadena, Ca., 1954. vii, 346ℓ. Thesis (M.A.)--Pasadena
        College. "Pentecostal Holiness Church": ℓ. 185-199. CSdP

3532   U.S. Bureau of the Census.
            Census of religious bodies: 1926. Pentecostal Holiness
        Church. Statistics, denominational history, doctrine, and or-
        ganization. Washington, U.S. Government Printing Office,
        1928. 11p. DLC, NNUT

3533   U.S. Bureau of the Census.
            Census of religious bodies: 1936. Pentecostal assemblies.
        Statistics, denominational history, doctrine, and organization.
        Consolidated report. Washington, Government Printing Office,
        1940. iv, 49p. Includes Pentecostal Holiness Church. NNUT

3534   Urging expansion.
       In Christianity Today, 6 (Dec. 8, 1961) 30.   On General
       Conference of the Pentecostal Holiness Church, meeting in
       Richmond, Virginia.

3535   Wood, William Woodhull
       Culture and personality aspects of the Pentecostal Holi-
       ness religion.   Chapel Hill, 1961.   184ℓ.   Thesis (Ph.D.)--
       University of North Carolina.   NcU

3536   Wood, William Woodhull
       Culture and personality aspects of the Pentecostal Holi-
       ness religion, by William W. Wood.   The Hague, Mouton,
       1965.   125p.   Thesis (Ph.D.)--University of North Carolina.

3537   Wood, William Woodhull
       Culture and personality aspects of the Pentecostal Holi-
       ness religion, by William W. Wood.   The Hague, Mouton,
       1965.   125p.   Imprint covered by label: New York, Humani-
       ties Press.   Thesis (Ph.D.)--University of North Carolina.
       DLC

--BUILDINGS

3538   Pentecostal Holiness Church.   General Department of Evan-
       gelism.
       Church plans.   Franklin Springs, Ga., 19--.   [16]p.

--CATECHISMS AND CREEDS

3539   Pentecostal Holiness Church.
       Enfocando la doctrina.   Corpus Christi, Tx., Victory
       Press, 196-.   94p.   Cover sub-title: Un estudio detallado
       de la doctrina de la Iglesia Pentecostal de Santidad.   Trans-
       lation of Focus on doctrine.

3540   Pentecostal Holiness Church.
       Focus on doctrine; a detailed study of the major tenets
       of the Pentecostal Holiness Church.   Franklin Springs, Ga.,
       Advocate Press, 1965.   80p.   TxWaS

3541   Pentecostal Holiness Church.   General Lifeliners Department.
       A Bible memory program for young people of the Pente-
       costal Holiness Church.   Prepared by C. L. Turpin.   Frank-
       lin Springs, Ga., 197-.   48p.   Cover title: The Bible mem-
       ory program for juniors and youth.   "Revised by Advocate
       Press and General Lifeliners Department."

3542   Beacham, Paul Franklin, bp., 1888-1978.
       Advanced catechism for the home, Sunday school, and

Bible classes, by Paul F. Beacham.   Franklin Springs, Ga.,
Publishing House [of the] Pentecostal Holiness Church, 19--.
31[1]p. "Published by Board of Publication of the Pentecostal
Holiness Church." NcC

3543   Beacham, Paul Franklin, bp., 1888-1978.
       Primary catechism for the home, Sunday school, and
Bible classes, by Paul F. Beacham.   Franklin Springs, Ga.,
Board of Publication of the Pentecostal Holiness Church; dis-
tributed by Advocate Press, 1971.   31p.   Reprint of 193- ed.

3544   Brooks, Noel, 1914-
       Studies in Christian doctrine.   Franklin Springs, Ga.,
Advocate Press, 19--.   3v.   "On the Articles of Faith of the
Pentecostal Holiness Church."

3545   Smith, Susan L.
       Come alive in the word! A detailed study for teenagers
of the major tenets of the Pentecostal Holiness Church, by
Susan L Smith.   Franklin Springs, Ga., Advocate Press,
c1975.   39p.

3546   Taylor, George Floyd, 1881-1934.
       A primary catechism, by G. F. Taylor.   Chapel Hill,
N.C., 1927.   40p.

                    --CONTROVERSIAL LITERATURE

3547   Robinson, Wayne Austin, 1937-
       I once spoke in tongues, by Wayne A. Robinson.   Atlanta,
Forum House, 1973.   144p.   DLC

3548   Spence, Othniel Talmadge, 1926-
       Charismatism: awakening or apostasy? By O. Talmadge
Spence.   Greenville, S.C., Bob Jones University Press, 1978.
xi, 266p.

                    --DEVOTIONAL LITERATURE

3549   Jones, Harold E.
       A moment a day, by Harold E. Jones.   Norfolk, Va.;
printed by Advocate Press, Franklin Springs, Ga., c1966.
64p.

                    --DIRECTORIES

3550   Pentecostal Holiness Church.
       Church directory of the Pentecostal Holiness Church.
Franklin Springs, Ga., 19 - .   v.[1]- .

--DOCTRINAL AND CONTROVERSIAL WORKS

3551   Anderson, Mary Mabbette
         Lights and shadows of the life in Canaan, by Mrs. Mary
Mabbette Anderson.   Toronto, Pentecostal Holiness Church,
1929.   94p.   First published in 1906.   "There is no reference
to the recent outpouring of the Holy Spirit in the latter rain
and the writing is lacking the added illumination on the baptism
of the Holy Ghost as revealed in this great visitation"--Ed-
ward D. Reeves.

3552   Andrews, Henry Elmo, 1909-1972.
         Qualifications for the bride, by H. E. Andrews.   Bethany,
Ok., Printed by Religious Press, Independence, Ks., c1956.
viii, 143p.

3553   Beacham, Paul Franklin, bp., 1888-1978.
         Questions and answers on the scriptures and related sub-
jects, by Paul F. Beacham.   Franklin Springs, Ga., Publishing House of the P. H. Church, 1950.   577p.

3554   Beacham, Paul Franklin, bp., 1888-1978.
         Scriptural sanctification, by Paul F. Beacham.   9th ed.
Franklin Springs, Ga., [Advocate Press, 19--] 15[1]p.   Cover
title.

3555   Britton, Francis Marion, 1870-1937.
         Pentecostal Holiness Bible readings or text book.   Falcon,
N.C., Falcon Publishing Co., 1915.   470p.

3556   Britton, Francis Marion, 1870-1937.
         Pentecostal truth; or, Sermons on regeneration, sanctifi-
cation, the baptism of the Holy Spirit, divine healing, the
second coming of Jesus, etc., together with a chapter on the
life of the author, by F. M. Britton.   Royston, Ga., Publishing House of the Pentecostal Holiness Church, 1919.   255p.

3557   Brooks, Noel, 1914-
         Bible validation for sanctification.   Franklin Springs,
Ga., Advocate Press, 1975.   37p.

3558   Brooks, Noel, 1914-
         Biblical basis for missions.   Franklin Springs, Ga.,
Advocate Press, 1976.   116p.

3559   Brooks, Noel, 1914-
         Fingertip holiness: studies in practical holiness.   [Frank-
lin Springs, Ga., 197-] 70p.   Delivered as the Muse Memorial Lectures, Southwestern College, Oklahoma City, 1975.

3560   Brooks, Noel, 1914-
         Let there be life!   Franklin Springs, Ga., Advocate

Press, c1975.   117p.   Delivered as the King Memorial Lectures, Emmanuel College, 197-.

3561   Brooks, Noel, 1914-
          Pardon, purity and power: the threefold ministry of the
       Holy Spirit.   Bristol, 1959.   28p.   Cover title.

3562   Brooks, Noel, 1914-
          Pardon, purity and power: the threefold ministry of the
       Holy Spirit.   Franklin Springs, Ga., Advocate Press, 1969.
       30p.
       _____   A programmed study guide, by Harold Dalton.
       Franklin Springs, Ga., Overseas Literature Committee by
       Advocate Press, 1973.   56p.   Cover title.

3563   Brooks, Noel, 1914-
          Scriptural holiness.   Franklin Springs, Ga., Advocate
       Press, 1967.   70p.   Delivered as the King Memorial Lec-
       tures, Emmanuel College, 1965.   GU

3564   Brooks, Noel, 1914-
          Sickness, health and God.   Franklin Springs, Ga., Ad-
       vocate Press, 1965.   87p.

3565   Brooks, Noel, 1914-
          Studies in Christian doctrine.   Franklin Springs, Ga.,
       Advocate Press, 19--.   3v.

3566   Bullard, Rayford
          Glimpses into the Revelation.   Franklin Springs, Ga.,
       Advocate Press, c1975.   275p.

3567   Campbell, Joseph Enoch, 1903-
          Can a man live above sin?   By Joe E. Campbell.   Frank-
       lin Springs, Ga., Publishing House [of the Pentecostal Holi-
       ness Church], 1942.   79p.

3568   Campbell, Joseph Enoch, 1903-
          Can a man live above sin?   [By] Joe E. Campbell.
       Raleigh, N.C., World Outlook Publications, 1974.   79p.
       "Fourth printing."

3569   Campbell, Joseph Enoch, 1903-
          See you in heaven [by] Joe E. Campbell.   Raleigh, N.C.,
       World Outlook Publications, 1974.   xi, 146p.   "Bible facts
       about eternal security."

3570   Campbell, Joseph Enoch, 1903-
          Warning! Do not seek for tongues; a sound scriptural
       appraisal of a present-day trend in the church [by] Joe E.
       Campbell.   Raleigh, N.C., World Outlook Publications, 1970.
       166p.

3571   Campbell, Joseph Enoch, 1903-
            What to believe and why? By Evangelist Joe E. Camp-
        bell. Greenville, S.C., 19--.   97p.

3572   Campbell, Joseph Enoch, 1903-
            What to believe and why about sanctification, by Joe E.
        Campbell. Franklin Springs, Ga., Publishing House [of the
        Pentecostal Holiness Church] 1941.   102p.

3573   Campbell, Joseph Enoch, 1903-
            What to believe & why about sanctification [by] Joe E.
        Campbell. Raleigh, N.C., World Outlook Publications, 1974.
        102p. "Fourth printing."

3574   Campbell, Joseph Enoch, 1903-
            A whole gospel for the whole man. Franklin Springs,
        Ga., Publishing House [of the Pentecostal Holiness Church],
        1952. 28p. Originally published in Healing waters.   OkTOr

3575   Campbell, Joseph Enoch, 1903-
            The whole gospel for the whole man; information about
        healing [by] Joe E. Campbell. Raleigh, N.C., World Outlook
        Publications, 1974. 28p. "Second printing."

3576   Correll, Harry B.
            The gift and the gifts, by Harry B. Correll. Franklin
        Springs, Ga., Publishing House of the Pentecostal Holiness
        Church, 19--.   24p.

3577   Corvin, Raymond Othel, 1915-1981.
            Crusaders Bible studies. Salem, Or., Crusaders Bible
        Studies, 1958.   5v.

3578   Corvin, Raymond Othel, 1915-1981.
            David and his mighty men, by R. O. Corvin.   Grand
        Rapids, Mi., Eerdmans, 1950. 175p.   DLC

3579   Corvin, Raymond Othel, 1915-1981.
            David and his mighty men, by R. O. Corvin.   Freeport,
        N.Y., Books for Libraries Press, 1970, c1950. 175p.
        (Biography index reprint series.) DLC, GU, PPULC

3580   Corvin, Raymond Othel, 1915-1981.
            Looking at the future through the eyes of Daniel; a syl-
        labus, by R. O. Dorvin. Franklin Springs, Ga., Advocate
        Press, c1973. 127p. (Studies in prophecy, v. 1.)

3581   Dalton, Harold
            Behold He cometh. Franklin Springs, Ga., Advocate
        Press, 19--. 159p. A "programmed text."

3582   Evans, Dan Webster, 1885-1963.

The Revelation message. Franklin Springs, Ga., Publishing House, Pentecostal Holiness Church, 1951. 356p. DLC

3583   Hall, Burton Allen, 1879-1938.
       The promise of the Father; or, This is that, by Burton A. Hall. McKinney, Tex., Printed by Publishing House, P. H. Church, Franklin Springs, Ga., c1926. 169p. DLC

3584   Hatfield, Jesse L., 1910-
       Bible answers to vital questions in 31, 804 words. 3d ed. Franklin Springs, Ga., Publishing House [of the Pentecostal Holiness Church], 1953. 119p.

3585   Kelley, J. W., -1955.
       Spirit leadership in the wilderness temptations, by J. W. Kelley. Franklin Springs, Ga., 19--. 30p.

3586   King, Joseph Hillery, bp., 1869-1946.
       Christ--God's love gift, by Joseph Hillery King. Compiled and ed. by B. E. Underwood. Franklin Springs, Ga., Advocate Press, 1969. 165p. (Selected writings, 1.)

3587   King, Joseph Hillery, bp., 1869-1946.
       From Passover to Pentecost, by J. H. King. Senath, Mo., F. E. Short, 1914. 182p.

3588   King, Joseph Hillery, bp., 1869-1946.
       From Passover to Pentecost. Memphis, Press of the H. W. Dixon Co., 1914. 182p. OkTOr

3589   King, Joseph Hillery, bp., 1869-1946.
       From Passover to Pentecost, by Rev. J. H. King. 2d ed., rev. and enl. Franklin Springs, Ga., Publishing House of the Pentecostal Holiness Church, c1934. 219p. DLC

3590   King, Joseph Hillery, bp., 1869-1946.
       From Passover to Pentecost. 3d ed., rev. and enl. Franklin Springs, Ga., Publishing House of the Pentecostal Holiness Church, 1955. 208p. DLC

3591   Montgomery, Granville Harrison, 1903-1966.
       After Armageddon--what? By Granville H. Montgomery. 2d ed. Franklin Springs, Ga., Published by Board of Publication of the Pentecostal Holiness Church; order from Publishing House, P. H. Church, Franklin Springs, Ga., 19--. 64p.

3592   Montgomery, Granville Harrison, 1903-1966.
       Bible holiness as exemplified by the heroes of faith, by Granville H. Montgomery. Franklin Springs, Ga., 1945. 20p.

3593 Montgomery, Granville Harrison, 1903-1966.
         Practical holiness. Franklin Springs, Ga., Publishing
      House of the Pentecostal Holiness Church, 19--. 64p.

3594 Moore, H. L., 1928-
         The battle of Armageddon and the millennial reign, by
      H. L. Moore. Franklin Springs, Ga., Advocate Press, 1974.
      52p.

3595 Moore, H. L., 1928-
         The first hippie, by H. L. Moore. Toccoa, Ga., Printed
      by Advocate Press, Franklin Springs, Ga., 1971. 43p.

3596 Moore, H. L., 1928-
         The mark of the beast, by H. L. Moore, Toccoa, Ga.,
      Printed by Advocate Press, Franklin Springs, Ga., 1969.
      64p. "Sixth printing."

3597 Moore, H. L., 1928-
         The mark of the beast, by H. L. Moore. Toccoa, Ga.,
      Printed by Advocate Press, Franklin Springs, Ga., 1975.
      90p. "Eighth printing."

3598 Moore, H. L., 1928-
         The rapture, by H. L. Moore. Rev. ed. Franklin
      Springs, Ga., Advocate Press, 1969. 59p.

3599 Moore, H. L., 1928-
         The rapture, by H. L. Moore. Franklin Springs, Ga.,
      Advocate Press, 1974. 60p. "Third printing."

3600 Muse, Dan Thomas, bp., 1882-1950.
         The Song of Songs. Franklin Springs, Ga., Pentecostal
      Holiness Publishing House, 1947. 231p. DLC

3601 Muse, Dan Thomas, bp., 1882-1950.
         The Song of Songs, by Dan T. Muse. Franklin Springs,
      Ga., Advocate Press, 1975, c1947. 231p. "Second printing."

3602 Oliver, Luther James
         Oliver's observations, by L. J. Oliver. Franklin Springs,
      Ga., Publishing House [of the Pentecostal Holiness Church],
      1948. 74p.

3603 Roberts, Oral, 1918-
         The drama of the end-time. Franklin Springs, Ga.,
      Publishing House [of the] P. H. Church, c1941. 79p. DLC

3604 Roberts, Oral, 1918-
         Salvation by the blood. Franklin Springs, Ga., Pente-
      costal Holiness Publishing House, c1938. 29p.

3605 Robinson, Albert Ernest, 1877-1950.

A layman and the Book, by A. E. Robinson. Takoma Park, Md., c1936. 192p. DLC

3606   Robinson, Albert Ernest, 1877-1950.
A layman and the Book, by A. E. Robinson. Washington, 1950, c1936. 153p. "Fourth printing."

3607   Robinson, Hugh Padgett,   -1965.
Redemption conceived and revealed, by H. Padgett Robinson. Franklin Springs, Ga., Advocate Press, c1965. 78p. Delivered as the King Memorial Lectures, Emmanuel College, 1965. GU

3608   Robinson, Ralph, 1893-
The promise of the Father, by Ralph Robinson. Introduction by Joseph A. Synan. Franklin Springs, Ga., 1976. 110p.

3609   Sorrow, Watson, 1884-
The plain gospel. Franklin Springs, Ga., Publishing House of the Pentecostal Holiness Church, c1950. 244p.

3610   Sorrow, Watson, 1884-
Through the Bible. Hapeville, Ga., [Printed by] Publishing House [of the] Pentecostal Holiness Church, Franklin Springs, Ga., c1952. 352p.

3611   Spence, Hubert Talmadge, bp., 1898-1969.
Pentecost is not a tangent, by Hubert T. Spence. 3d ed. Franklin Springs, Ga., Pentecostal Holiness Church, 19--. 11p.

3612   Spence, Hubert Talmadge, bp., 1898-1969.
The person, work and witness of the Holy Spirit, by Hubert T. Spence. Franklin Springs, Ga., Pentecostal Holiness Church, 1940. 59p.

3613   Spence, Hubert Talmadge, bp., 1898-1969.
The person, work and witness of the Holy Spirit, by Hubert T. Spence. 2d ed. Franklin Springs, Ga., Board of Publication, P. H. Church, 1945. 61p.

3614   Spence, Hubert Talmadge, bp., 1898-1969.
Suffering and healing, by Hubert T. Spence. Greenville, Pa., Tribute Press, c1956. 84p.

3615   Spence, Hubert Talmadge, bp., 1898-1969.
The work and ministry of the Holy Spirit, by Hubert T. Spence. Memphis, Fundamental Book Shop, c1952. 39p. ViRUT

3616   Spence, Othniel Talmadge, 1926-
The lexi-chord of the New Testament. Franklin Springs,

Ga., Advocate Press, c1967. x, 100p. "Greek word index [and] English word index [to] The quest for Christian purity": p. 98-100.

3617   Spence, Othniel Talmadge, 1926-
       The lexi-chord of the New Testament [by] O. Talmadge Spence. 2d ed., revised. Dunn, N.C., Printed by Advocate Press, 1976, c1967. x, 129p.

3618   Spence, Othniel Talmadge, 1926-
       The quest for Christian purity, by O. Talmadge Spence. Richmond? 1964. xxxiv, 286p. DLC

3619   Swails, John Washington
       The Holy Spirit and the messianic age, by John W. Swails. Franklin Springs, Ga., Advocate Press, c1975. 163p. Delivered as the King Memorial Lectures, Emmanuel College. OkTOr

3620   Synan, Joseph Alexander, bp., 1905-
       Christian life in depth, by J. A. Synan. [Franklin Springs, Ga., Advocate Press, 1964] 87p. Delivered as the King Memorial Lectures, Emmanuel College, 1960.

3621   Synan, Joseph Alexander, bp., 1905-
       The shape of things to come, by J. A. Synan. Franklin Springs, Ga., Advocate Press, 1969. 107p. Delivered as the King Memorial Lectures, Emmanuel College.

3622   Synan, Joseph Alexander, bp., 1905-
       Three elements of sanctification, by J. A. Synan. Franklin Springs, Ga., Advocate Press, 19--. folder (7p.)

3623   Synan, Joseph Alexander, bp., 1905-
       The trinity--or the tri-personal being of God, by J. A. Synan. Franklin Springs, Ga., Advocate Press, 1980. 81p. (King memorial lectures, 1975.)

3624   Taylor, George Floyd, 1881-1934.
       The rainbow, by G. F. Taylor. Franklin Springs, Ga., Publishing House of the Pentecostal Holiness Church, c1924. 223p. DLC

3625   Taylor, George Floyd, 1881-1934.
       The second coming of Jesus, by G. F. Taylor. Falcon, N.C., Press of the Falcon Publishing Co., c1916. viii, 264p. DLC, NcU, ViU

3626   Taylor, George Floyd, 1881-1934.
       The second coming of Jesus, by G. F. Taylor. Franklin Springs, Ga., Publishing House [of the] Pentecostal Holiness Church, 1950. 225p.

3627   Taylor, George Floyd, 1881-1934.
        The Spirit and the bride, by G. F. Taylor.   Falcon,
        N. C. , Falcon Printing Co. , 1911.   175p.

3628   Turner, William Henry, 1895-1971.
        Are we baptized with the Holy Ghost when converted?
        [Franklin Springs, Ga.] c1947.   39p.

3629   Turner, William Henry, 1895-1971.
        Christ, the great physician.   Franklin Springs, Ga. ,
        Publishing House of the P. H. Church, 1941.   179p.

3630   Turner, William Henry, 1895-1971.
        The difference between regeneration, sanctification, and
        the Pentecostal baptism, by W. H. Turner.   Franklin Springs,
        Ga. , Printed by Publishing House of the P. H. Church, c1947.
        40p.

3631   Turner, William Henry, 1895-1971.
        The finished work of Calvary, or the second blessing--
        which? By W. H. Turner.   Franklin Springs, Ga. , Printed
        by the Publishing House of the P. H. Church, c1947.   62p.

3632   Turner, William Henry, 1895-1971.
        Five thousand years of healing, by W. H. Turner.
        Franklin Springs, Ga. , Printed by the Publishing House of
        the P. H. Church, c1947.   43p.   TxWaS

3633   Turner, William Henry, 1895-1971.
        How may the experience of sanctification be obtained?
        By W. H. Turner.   Franklin Springs, Ga. , Publishing House
        of the P. H. Church, 1947.   40p.

3634   Turner, William Henry, 1895-1971.
        I am the Lord that healeth thee, by W. H. Turner.
        Franklin Springs, Ga. , Printed by Publishing House of the
        Pentecostal Holiness Church, 1947.   48p.   TxWaS

3635   Turner, William Henry, 1895-1971.
        Is it the will of God to heal all who are sick? By W. H.
        Turner.   Franklin Springs, Ga. , Printed by the Publishing
        House of the P. H. Church, c1947.   38p.   TxWaS

3636   Turner, William Henry, 1895-1971.
        Is Pentecost scriptural? By W. H. Turner.   Franklin
        Springs, Ga. , Printed by the Publishing House of the Pente-
        costal Holiness Church, 1947.   48p.

3637   Turner, William Henry, 1895-1971.
        Pentecost and tongues: the doctrine and history, by
        W. H. Turner.   Shanghai, Shanghai Modern Publishing House,
        1939.   ii, 182, ivp.

3638   Turner, William Henry, 1895-1971.
        Pentecost and tongues, by W. H. Turner. 2d ed. Flor-
ence, S.C., Printed by Advocate Press, Franklin Springs,
Ga., c1968. 208p. TxWaS

3639   Turner, William Henry, 1895-1971.
        Pentecostal manifestations, by W. H. Turner. Franklin
Springs, Ga., Publishing House of the P. H. Printed by the
Church, c1947. 51p. TxWaS

3640   Turner, William Henry, 1895-1971.
        The sanctified way of life. Franklin Springs, Ga., Pub-
lishing House of the Pentecostal Holiness Church, 1948. 40p.

3641   Turner, William Henry, 1895-1971.
        Shall God's people take medicine? Franklin Springs, Ga.,
Publishing House of the P. H. Church, c1947. 37p.

3642   Turner, William Henry, 1895-1971.
        Six thousand years of tithing, by W. H. Turner. Frank-
lin Springs, Ga., Printed by the Publishing House of the P. H.
Church, 1945. 138p.

3643   Turner, William Henry, 1895-1971.
        Two thousand years of Pentecost, by W. H. Turner.
Franklin Springs, Ga., Printed by Publishing House of the
P. H. Church, c1947. 63p. TxWaS

3644   Turner, William Henry, 1895-1971.
        What must I do to be healed? By W. H. Turner. Frank-
lin Springs, Ga., Printed by Publishing House of the P. H.
Church, c1947. 43p.

3645   Turner, William Henry, 1895-1971.
        What the churches say about sanctification as a second
blessing, by W. H. Turner. Franklin Springs, Ga., Printed
by Publishing House of the P. H. Church, c1947. 46p.

3646   Turner, William Henry, 1895-1971.
        What's next? Andrews, S.C., c1963. 40p.

3647   Turner, William Henry, 1895-1971.
        Why are not all healed? By W. H. Turner. Franklin
Springs, Ga., Printed by Publishing House of the P. H.
Church, 1947. 42p. TxWaS

3648   Underwood, Bernard Edward, 1925-
        The gifts of the Spirit: supernatural equipment for Chris-
tian service, by B. E. Underwood. Franklin Springs, Ga.,
Advocate Press, 1967. 79p. Delivered as the King Memorial
Lectures, Emmanuel College, 1964.
        _____ A programmed study, by Harold Dalton. Frank-
lin Springs, Ga., Overseas Literature Committee at Advocate
Press, 1974. 58p.

3649   Underwood, Bernard Edward, 1925-
        The Spirit's sword: God's infallible word, by B. E.
Underwood.   Franklin Springs, Ga., Printed by Advocate
Press, 1969.   104p.   Delivered as the King Memorial Lectures, Emmanuel College, 1967.
                        Why I believe the Bible: a programmed study,
by Harold Dalton.   Franklin Springs, Ga., Overseas Literature Committee at Advocate Press, 1973.   24p.

3650   West, Charlene
        Close out of the ages.   Franklin Springs, Ga., Advocate
Press, c1975.   118p.   "A correlation between Daniel's Seven-
tieth Week and the book of Revelation."

3651   Williams, Julius Floyd, bp., 1924-
        Christ Jesus--the god-man, by J. Floyd Williams.
Franklin Springs, Ga., Advocate Press, c1975.   112p.

3652   Williams, Julius Floyd, bp., 1924-
        The church, by J. Floyd Williams.   Franklin Springs,
Ga., Printed by Advocate Press, 1973.   133p.   Delivered
as the Muse Memorial Lectures, Southwestern College,
Oklahoma City, 1972.

                        --EDUCATION

3653   Callahan, Victor Warren
        The model Sunday school, by V. W. Callahan.   Franklin
Springs, Ga., Publishing House of the Pentecostal Holiness
Church, 1952.   30p.

3654   Corvin, Raymond Othel, 1915-1981.
        History of education by the Pentecostal Holiness Church
in South Carolina and Georgia.   Columbia, 1942.   63ℓ.
Thesis (M.A.)--University of South Carolina.   ScU

3655   Corvin, Raymond Othel, 1915-1981.
        History of the educational institutions of the Pentecostal
Holiness Church.   Fort Worth, 1957.   329ℓ.   Thesis (D.R.E.)
--Southwestern Baptist Theological Seminary.   TxFS

3656   Tarkenton, Dallas Matthew, 1912-1975.
        The history and development of the Sunday school as an
educational unit in the Pentecostal Holiness Church since
1911.   Athens, 1952.   iii, 103ℓ.   Thesis (M.S. in Ed.)--
University of Georgia.   GU

3657   Tarkenton, Dallas Matthew, 1912-1975.
        The model Sunday school workshop outlines, by Dallas M.
Tarkenton.   Franklin Springs, Ga., Advocate Press, 1952.
30p.

3658   Tarkenton, Dallas Matthew, 1912-1975.
        The Sunday school guide, by Dallas M. Tarkenton.
Franklin Springs, Ga., Publishing House [of the Pentecostal
Holiness Church], 1952. 109p.

3659   Taylor, George Floyd, 1881-1934.
        Christian education. n. p., 1928. 6p.

        --EVANGELISTIC WORK

3660   Pentecostal Holiness Church. Department of Evangelism.
        Successful methods of evangelism. Franklin Springs,
Ga., 1969. 31p. "Delivered as the King Memorial Lectures in October 1968, at Franklin Springs, Georgia."
        Contents: Preparing for a revival, by R. L. Rex.-
Personal soul winning, by Zeb D. Smith.-Planning and con-
ducting a district revival, by J. D. Simmons.-Mother church
evangelism, by E. L. Boyce.

        --FICTIONAL LITERATURE

3661   Stewart, Leon Otto, 1929-
        Too late! A stimulating religious novel, by Leon O.
Stewart. Franklin Springs, Ga., Advocate Press, 1958.
207p.

        --FINANCE

3662   Pentecostal Holiness Church. Development Department.
        Financing the kingdom: developing the church budget.
Oklahoma City, 1977. 23[1]p. Cover title.

        --GOVERNMENT

3663   Pentecostal Holiness Church. Department of Church Ministries.
        Job description manual. Franklin Springs, Ga., Advo-
cate Press, 1976. 47p.

        --HISTORY

3664   Campbell, Joseph Enoch, 1903-
        The Pentecostal Holiness Church, 1898-1948: its back-
ground and history; presenting complete background material
which adequately explains the existence of this organization,
also the existence of other kindred Pentecostal and Holiness
groups, as an essential and integral part of the total church

set-up, by Joseph E. Campbell. Franklin Springs, Ga.,
Publishing House of the Pentecostal Holiness Church, c1951.
573p. Thesis (Th. D.)--Union Theological Seminary, Richmond, Va., 1948. TxU, TxWaS

3665   Synan, Harold Vinson, 1934-
       The old-time power, by Vinson Synan. Franklin Springs,
Ga., Advocate Press, 1973. 296p. "Official history of the
Pentecostal Holiness Church." IEG

3666   Synan, Harold Vinson, 1934-
       The Pentecostal Holiness Church, 1948-1958. Richmond,
1958. i, 39, iiiℓ. Thesis (B. A.)--University of Richmond.
ViRU

       --HISTORY AND STUDY OF DOCTRINES

3667   Goodrum, Claude Lee
       Some studies in the life and times of John Wesley, by
Claude L. Goodrum. Athens, 1939. iv, 77ℓ. Thesis (M. A.)
--University of Georgia. GU

3668   Synan, Harold Vinson, 1934-
       Christian initiation in the Pentecostal Holiness Church,
by Vinson Synan. In Studia Liturgica, 10:1 (1974), 56-64.

       --HYMNS AND SACRED SONGS

3669   Pentecostal Holiness Church.
       The gospel hymnal. Hymnal Committee: O. N. Todd,
Jr., Charles Presley, Madeline S. Atkins, Lonnie Rex, Jr.
Franklin Springs, Ga., Advocate Press, c1973. 1v. (un-
paged) With music (shape notes). OkBetC

3670   Pentecostal Holiness Church.
       Gospel melodies for use in all services of the church.
Compiled and ed. by I. H. Presley. Franklin Springs, Ga.,
Publishing House [of the] Pentecostal Holiness Church, c1939.
1v. (unpaged) With music (shape notes). NN

3671   Pentecostal Holiness Church.
       Pentecostal Holiness hymnal, for use in all services of
the church, comp. and ed. by Rev. I. H. Presley. Published
by Board of Education and Publication of the Pentecostal Holiness Church. Franklin Springs, Ga., Publishing House P. H.
Church, 1938. [192]p. DLC

3672   Pentecostal Holiness Church.
       Pentecostal Holiness hymnal, no. 2, comp. and ed. by
Rev. I. H. Presley. Published by Board of Publication of
the Pentecostal Holiness Church.... Franklin Springs, Ga.,

Publishing House P. H. Church, c1941. [240], 12[4]p. With music (shape notes). DLC

--JUVENILE LITERATURE

3673 Johnson, May Gould (Jones)
      Stories to tell, by May Gould Johnson. ----, 1948. 71p.

3674 Jones, Byon A., 1896-1977.
      Story time, by Byon A. Jones. Franklin Springs, Ga.,
      Advocate Press, 1956. 24p.

--MISSIONS

3675 Beacham, Sara (Lane), -1947.
      Men and missions. Greenville, S.C., c1938. 146p.
      "Missionaries of the Pentecostal Holiness Church": p. 132-
      140.

3676 Brooks, Noel, 1914-
      Biblical basis for missions. Franklin Springs, Ga.,
      Advocate Press, 1976. 116p.

3677 Muse, Dan Thomas, bp., 1882-1950.
      Missionary program material. Edited by Dan T. Muse.
      Franklin Springs, Ga., Board of Publication, Pentecostal Holi-
      ness Church; distributed by Publishing House, P. H. Church,
      19--. 64p.

3678 Turner, William Henry, 1895-1971.
      The relationship of the pastor to foreign missions. With
      an introd. by Paul F. Beacham. Franklin Springs, Ga.,
      Publishing House of the P. H. Church, c1929. 76p.

--PASTORAL LITERATURE

3679 Pentecostal Holiness Church. General Department of Evan-
      gelism.
      Adventures in Christian living. Oklahoma City, Witness
      Ministries, c1974. 15p. Cover title.

3680 Pentecostal Holiness Church. General Department of Evan-
      gelism.
      Your guide to a deeper spiritual life. Franklin Springs,
      Ga., 197-. 56p. Includes essays by E. L. Boyce, Gilbert
      Dean, Frank Tunstall, James Pennington, Joel S. McGraw,
      and R. L. Rex.

3681 Oden, Margaret (Muse), 1916-
      God's recipes for my life. Franklin Springs, Ga.,

Advocate Press, 197-.   29p.   Cover title: Not bread alone, but by every word.

3682   Tunstall, Frank Gee, 1943-
        Dinah went out on the town: a Pentecostal looks at the new morality, by Frank G. Tunstall.   Franklin Springs, Ga., Advocate Press, 1976.   71p.   Delivered as the King Memorial Lectures, Emmanuel College, 1975.

3683   Turner, William Henry, 1895-1971.
        The sanctified way of life.   Franklin Springs, Ga., Publishing House of the Pentecostal Holiness Church, 1948.   40p.

                    --PASTORAL THEOLOGY

3684   Beller, Dan, 1932-
        Progress through pioneer evangelism, by Dan Beller. Franklin Springs, Ga., Advocate Press, 1973.   128p.   Delivered as the Muse Memorial Lectures, Southwestern College, Oklahoma City, 1973.

3685   Moore, Oscar, bp., 1909-
        Preachers: you asked for it.   Franklin Springs, Ga., Advocate Press, c1975.   82p.   Delivered as the Muse Memorial Lectures, Southwestern College, Oklahoma City, 1974.

3686   Smith, Laverne
        The dynamics of spiritual leadership.   n. p., 197-.   54p.

3687   Synan, Joseph Alexander, bp., 1905-
        Four lectures on the good minister of Jesus Christ, by Joseph A. Synan.   Franklin Springs, Ga., Publishing House, Pentecostal Holiness Church, 1950.   59p.   Cover title: The good minister of Jesus Christ.

3688   Synan, Joseph Alexander, bp., 1905-
        The good minister of Jesus Christ, by Joseph A. Synan. 2d ed.   Franklin Springs, Ga., Advocate Press, 1975.   59p.

3689   Turner, William Henry, 1895-1971.
        The relationship of the pastor to foreign missions.   With an introd. by Paul F. Beacham.   Franklin Springs, Ga., Publishing House of the P. H. Church, c1929.   76p.

3690   Whichard, Sam L.
        500+ bright ideas, comp. by Sam L. Whichard.   Franklin Springs, Ga., Advocate Press, 197-.   271p.   Cover title.

                    --PERIODICALS

3691   Apologist.   1- 19 -1950.
        Washington.

3692   Gospel news review.   1-   1943-1945.
        Hogansville, Ga.

3693   Helping hand.   1-   195 -
        Franklin Springs, Ga., Oklahoma City, Ok., Woman's
        Auxiliary of the Pentecostal Holiness Church.

3694   Hong Kong harbor lights.   1-   July 1957-
        Hong Kong.   L

3695   International Pentecostal Holiness advocate.   1-   May 3, 1917-
        Falcon, N.C., Royston, Ga., Franklin Springs, Ga.,
        Oklahoma City, Ok.   1-59, no. 19, May 3, 1917-
        Jan. 25, 1976 as Pentecostal Holiness advocate.   DLC

3696   Navajoland news flasher.   1-   1964-
        Ganado, Az., P. H. Navajo Mission.

3697   P. Y. P. S. Quarterly.   1-   July 1929-193-.
        Franklin Springs, Ga., Pentecostal Young People's Society
        of the Pentecostal Holiness Church.

3698   Pentecostal Holiness faith.   1-   1920-1931.
        Oklahoma City.

3699   Pentecostal pulpit.   1-6, 1946-1954.
        Franklin Springs, Ga.

3700   Proclaimer.   1-   1966-
        Halifax, Yorks., Bristol, Glos.

3701   Reach.   1-   19 -
        Oklahoma City, Lifeliners International [of the] Pentecostal
        Holiness Church.

3702   Southwestern Pentecostal Holiness news.   1-   1947-1953.
        Oklahoma City.

3703   Tips on the lesson.   1-   1965-
        Franklin Springs, Ga.   1965-1967 as Tips on teaching.

3704   Witness.   1-   1973-
        Franklin Springs, Ga., Oklahoma City, Ok., Evangelism
        Department of the Pentecostal Holiness Church.

3705   Worldorama.   1-   Fall 1966-
        Franklin Springs, Ga., Oklahoma City, Ok., Pentecostal
        Holiness Church, World Missions Department.

3706   Youth's leader.   1-5, 1936-1939.
        Franklin Springs, Ga.   Supersedes P. Y. P. S. quarterly.
        DLC

--SERMONS, TRACTS, ADDRESSES, ESSAYS

3707   Pentecostal Holiness Church.
       The Pentecostal message.   Franklin Springs, Ga. , Pub-
lishing House [of the] Pentecostal Holiness Church, 1950-1953.
2v.   Sermons by J. H. King, J. A. Synan, T. A. Melton,
Dan T. Muse, Edward D. Reeves, J. Vinson Ellenberg,
W. H. Turner, W. J. Nash, Oral Roberts, R. O. Corvin,
Paul F. Beacham, Hubert T. Spence, Harold Paul, Blanche
L. King, A. H. Butler, R. L. Rex, Ruth Moore, S. J. Todd,
Virgil Gaither, H. Padgett Robinson, G. A. Byus, T. T.
Lindsey, L. J. Oliver, G. F. Taylor, L. R. Graham, Leo
Edwards, George R. Harris, F. A. Dail, W. Eddie Morris,
W. J. Anderson, E. E. Howard, Colbert B. Bigby, Rayford
Bullard, Harold A. Probst, Mary Ford, R. J. Wells, Paul
Hopkins, J. [i. e. F.] Vernon Ellenberg.

3708   Aaron, Thomas Lee, 1897-1951.
       Sermon notes and outlines.   Franklin Springs, Ga. , Ad-
vocate Press, 1964.   126p.   GU

3709   Beacham, Arthur Douglas, 1921-
       All power is given unto me, by A. D. Beacham.   In
Williams, J. F. , comp.   The great commission.   Washington,
1969, 7-20.

3710   Beacham, Paul Franklin, bp. , 1888-1978.
       Meat in due season, by Paul F. Beacham.   Franklin
Springs, Ga. , Publishing House of the P. H. Church, 1954.
185p.

3711   Beacham, Paul Franklin, bp. , 1888-1978.
       Scriptural sanctification, by Paul F. Beacham.   9th ed.
Franklin Springs, Ga. , [Advocate Press, 19--] 15[1]p.
(Advocate tracts.)   Cover title.

3712   Britton, Francis Marion, 1870-1937.
       Pentecostal truth; or, Sermons on regeneration, sanctifica-
tion, the baptism of the Holy Spirit, divine healing, the second coming of Jesus, etc. , together with a chapter on the life
of the author, by F. M. Britton.   Royston, Ga. , Publishing
House of the Pentecostal Holiness Church, 1919.   255p.

3713   Case, James Daniel, 1926-
       The beginning of the end, and other messages, by James
D. Case.   Franklin Springs, Ga. , Advocate Press, 1973.
82p.

3714   Case, James Daniel, 1926-
       Pressing into the kingdom, and other messages [by] James
D. Case.   Franklin Springs, Ga. , Printed by Advocate Press,
c1966.   85p.

3715   Corvin, Raymond Othel, 1915-1981.
         Teach all things, by R. O. Corvin. In Williams, J. F. ,
       comp. The great commission. Washington, 1969, 41-50.

3716   Ellenberg, Frank Vernon, 1906-
         Bearing precious seed, by F. Vernon Ellenberg.   Frank-
       lin Springs, Ga. , Printed by Advocate Press, 1976.   95p.

3717   Montgomery, Granville Harrison, 1903-1966.
         Steps to the upper room; eight gospel messages pointing
       the way to full salvation, by Granville H. Montgomery.   2d
       ed.   Frederick, Md. , 1938.   60p.

3718   Montgomery, Granville Harrison, 1903-1966.
         Steps to the upper room; eight gospel messages pointing
       the way to full salvation, by G. H. Montgomery.   3d ed.
       Franklin Springs, Ga. , Board of Publication of the Pente-
       costal Holiness Church; distributed by Publishing House of
       the Pentecostal Holiness Church, 19--.   64p.   NcC

3719   Morris, William Eddie, 1907-
         New Testament Pentecost.   Franklin Springs, Ga. , Ad-
       vocate Press, 19--.   8p.

3720   Oliver, Omar Clarence, 1893-1970.
         Walking with God, by O. C. Oliver.   Royston, Ga. ,
       c1968.   78p.

3721   Powers, Richard Elleby
         "God's eagles" and twenty-four other sermons by a Pente-
       costal Holiness pioneer.   Rev. R. E. Powers.   Franklin
       Springs, Ga. , Advocate Press, c1974.   72p.   Cover-title:
       Twenty five sermons by a Pentecostal Holiness pioneer.

3722   Reeves, Edward Dulaney, 1874-1936.
         Edward D. Reeves: his life and message.   Edited and
       arranged by R. H. Lee and G. H. Montgomery.   Franklin
       Springs, Ga. , Publishing House of the Pentecostal Holiness
       Church, c1940.   268p.   "Published by Mrs. E. D. Reeves. "
       Includes life sketch, sermons, poems, and Bible lessons.
       KyWAT

3723   Robinson, Hugh Padgett, -1965.
         Heaven's quest for a man like God; twenty sermons, by
       H. P. Robinson.   Compiled and edited by Agnes Robinson.
       Franklin Springs, Ga. , Advocate Press, 1969.   181p.   "This
       volume of sermons has been approved by the General Board
       of Publication of the Pentecostal Holiness Church as a mem-
       orial to the author. "

3724   Spence, Hubert Talmadge, bp. , 1898-1969.
         Twelve radio sermons as preached over station WINX,

Washington, D. C. , by Hubert T. Spence. Washington, 1945.
72p.

3725   Synan, Joseph Alexander, bp. , 1905-
            The abiding presence, by J. A. Synan. In Williams,
        J. F. , comp. The great commission. Washington, 1969,
        51-66.

3726   Tunstall, Frank Gee, 1943-
            Pentecost: God's practical answer for the occultic, and
        other sermons, by Frank G. Tunstall. Franklin Springs,
        Ga. , Advocate Press, 1973. 76p. Cover title: Pentecost:
        God's answer for the occultic.

3727   Underwood, Bernard Edward, 1925-
            The crux of the great commission, by B. E. Underwood.
        In Williams, J. F. , comp. The great commission. Wash-
        ington, 1969, 21-40.

3728   Underwood, Bernard Edward, 1925-
            True freedom, by B. E. Underwood. Franklin Springs,
        Ga. , Advocate Press, 1969. 13p.

3729   Wicks, Mildred
            Dawn of a better day; expository sermons on divine heal-
        ing. Tulsa, Standard Printing Co. , 19--. 109p. TxWaS

3730   Wicks, Mildred
            There is healing for you. Dallas, c1950. 171p. TxWaS

3731   Williams, Julius Floyd, comp. , bp. , 1924-
            The great commission. Compiled by J. Floyd Williams.
        Washington, North Washington Press, 1969. 83p. Sermons
        delivered at the sixteenth General Conference of the Pente-
        costal Holiness Church, Memphis, Tennessee, August 21-26,
        1969, by A. D. Beacham, B. E. Underwood, R. O. Corvin,
        J. A. Synan and J. Floyd Williams.

3732   Williams, Julius Floyd, bp. , 1924-
            They went forth and preached everywhere, by J. Floyd
        Williams. In Williams, J. F. , comp. The great commis-
        sion. Washington, 1969, 67-83.

                    --WORK WITH YOUTH

3733   Robinson, Albert Ernest, 1877-1950.
            Problem helps for young people, by A. E. Robinson.
        Franklin Springs, Ga. , Board of Publication of the Pente-
        costal Holiness Church, 1940. 64p.

3734   Smith, Susan I.
            Help! I'm a teenager, by Susan I. Smith. Franklin

Springs, Ga. , Advocate Press, c1976.   97p.

3735   Tunstall, Frank Gee, 1943-
       Dinah went out on the town: a Pentecostal looks at the
new morality, by Frank G. Tunstall. Franklin Springs, Ga. ,
Advocate Press, 1976.   71p.   Delivered as the King Memorial Lectures, Emmanuel College, 1975.

       --AFRICA

       -- --NIGERIA

3736   Pentecostal Holiness Church.   Department of Foreign Mis-
       sions.
       Africa: Nigeria. Franklin Springs, Ga. , 1969.   15p.
Cover title.   On cover: Pentecostal Holiness Church Missions Department.

       -- --SOUTH AFRICA

3737   Pentecostal Holiness Church.   Department of Foreign Mis-
       sions.
       South Africa: Transvaal and Orange Free State Confer-
ence.   Franklin Springs, Ga. , 196-.   14p.   Cover title.
On cover: Pentecostal Holiness Church, Missions Department.

3738   Case, James D.
       The beginning of the end, and other messages, by James
D. Case.   Franklin Springs, Ga. , Advocate Press, 1973.
82p.   "Facts and figures on missionary activity in Africa by
the Pentecostal Holiness Church": p. 51-70.

3739   Duncan, Florine (Freeman), 1925-
       You gave, yet Africa calls, by Florine and Montgomery
Duncan.   Franklin Springs, Ga. , Advocate Press, 1959.
106p.

3740   Freeman, Dallas Dolphus, 1900-
       Customs, observations and missionary addresses, by
D. D. Freeman.   Falcon, N. C. , 1940.   53p.

3741   Freeman, Dallas Dolphus. 1900-
       A missionary, heart and soul: an autobiographical sketch
of Dallas Dolphus (Ned) Freeman, pioneer missionary to South
Africa, by D. D. Freeman.   Franklin Springs, Ga. , Advocate
Press, c1980.   62p.

3742   Freeman, Dallas Dolphus, 1900-
       Missions on the march; Pentecostal Holiness Church in
southern Africa, by Rev. and Mrs. D. D. Freeman.   Franklin Springs, Ga. , Advocate Press, 1961.   52p.

3743   Freeman, Dallas Dolphus, 1900-
       Observe the African, by D. D. Freeman.   Franklin
Springs, Ga. , Printed by Publishing House P. H. Church,
1937.   121p.   CtY-D, DLC

3744   Spooner, Geraldine M.
       Sketches of the life of K. E. M. Spooner, missionary,
South Africa.   Material collected and arranged by Mrs.
K. E. M. Spooner, A. E. Robinson [and] P. F. Beacham.
[Franklin Springs, Ga. , 1945] 108p.

       --NORTH AMERICA

       -- --MEXICO

3745   [Pentecostal Holiness Church.   Department of Foreign Missions.]
       Mexican conferences: Mexico.   [Franklin Springs, Ga. ,
196-] 15p.   Cover title.

       -- --UNITED STATES

       -- --SOUTHERN STATES

       (Georgia)

3746   Corvin, Raymond Othel, 1915-1981.
       History of education by the Pentecostal Holiness Church
in South Carolina and Georgia.   Columbia, 1942.   63ℓ .   Thesis (M. A.)--University of South Carolina.   ScU

       (North Carolina)

3747   Johnson, Guy Benton, 1928-
       A framework for the analysis of religious action, with
special reference to holiness and non-holiness groups.   Cambridge, Mass. , 1953 [i. e. 1954] iii, 307ℓ .   Thesis (Ph. D.)--
Harvard University.   Based in part on research in Robeson
County, North Carolina, in 1948, 1949 and 1951, including
responses from ten non-Pentecostal and ten Pentecostal religionists (ministers from Pentecostal Holiness (5), Church
of God (Cleveland, Tenn.) (4), and Assemblies of God (1)
denominations.)   MH

       (Oklahoma)

3748   Paul, George Harold, 1910-
       The religious frontier in Oklahoma: Dan T. Muse and
the Pentecostal Holiness Church.   Norman, 1965.   302ℓ .
Thesis (Ph. D.)--University of Oklahoma.   OkU

(South Carolina)

3749   Corvin, Raymond Othel, 1915-1981.
       History of education by the Pentecostal Holiness Church
in South Carolina and Georgia.   Columbia, 1942.   63ℓ.   Thesis (M. A.)--University of South Carolina.   ScU

(Virginia)

3750   Underwood, Bernard Edward, 1925-
       Fiftieth anniversary history of the Virginia Conference
of the Pentecostal Holiness Church; a sketch, by B. E. Underwood.   [Dublin, Va.], Virginia Conference of the Pentecostal Holiness Church, 1960.   [10]p.

-- --WESTERN STATES

(Alaska)

3751   Pentecostal Holiness Church.   Department of Foreign Missions.
       Alaska.   Franklin Springs, Ga. , 196-.   15p.   Cover
title.   At head of title: Pentecostal Holiness Church, Missions Department.

--ASIA

-- --CHINA

3752   Turner, William Henry, 1895-1971.
       Pioneering in China, by W. H. Turner.   Introduction by
J. H. King.   Franklin Springs, Ga. , Printed by the Publishing House of the P. H. Church, c1928.   312p.   DLC

-- --HONG KONG

3753   King, Blanche Leon (Moore)
       I saw the highest mountain and stood beside the lowest
sea, by Blanche Leon King.   Franklin Springs, Ga. , Advocate
Press, 1957.   159p.   DLC

3754   Turner, William Henry, 1895-1971.
       "Rain" over Hong Kong.   Franklin Springs, Ga. , Ad-
vocate Press, c1965.   47p.

-- --INDIA

3755   King, Blanche Leon (Moore)
       I saw the highest mountain and stood beside the lowest
sea, by Blanche Leon King.   Franklin Springs, Ga. , Advocate
Press, 1957.   159p.   DLC

PENTECOSTAL HOLINESS CHURCH OF CANADA (1971-)

On April 27, 1971, Canadian congregations affiliated with the Pentecostal Holiness Church were granted a dominion charter. Despite legal autonomy thus attained, close ties to the American body remain. When, for instance, the first General Conference of the Pentecostal Holiness Church of Canada convened in Toronto in May 1971, the general superintendent of the parent body was in the chair. Uniformity of doctrinal teachings and disciplinary practices of the two bodies is maintained. Clustered near three centers--Halifax, Nova Scotia; Toronto, Ontario; and Vancouver, British Columbia-- the group consists of 600 members in about 22 churches. It supports the Christianview Bible College at Ailsa Craig, Ontario. The general superintendent resides in Willowdale, Ontario, a suburb of Toronto. Impact, the official organ, is issued from Willowdale.

--PERIODICALS

3756   Impact. 1- 1976-
        Willowdale, Ont.

3757   Lamplighter. 1- 19 -
        Halifax, N. S.

SOUL SAVING STATION FOR EVERY NATION CHRIST CRUSADERS
    OF AMERICA (1940-)

Soul Saving Station is an 11,000-member black denomination, the outgrowth of a single congregation in Harlem. In 1932 Billy Roberts, a gangster and drug addict, was converted in Seattle. Moving to New York, he first evangelized in various city churches. There in 1940, with the help of nine young people who had supported his evangelistic work, Roberts founded the first Soul Saving Station. Branches developed in Buffalo and other eastern cities. In 1957, when what proved to be a terminal illness forced Roberts to step down, Jesse F. Winley, the Buffalo pastor and one of the founder's converts, became pastor of the New York congregation and general overseer of the movement, positions he continued to occupy after Billy Roberts' death in 1962. In 1973 the Soul Saving Station entered into an Agreement of Affiliation with the Pentecostal Holiness Church. At Bishop Winley's funeral in June 1980, twenty pastors of Soul Saving affiliates were given opportunity to speak.

3758   Roberts, Billy, 1900-1962.
            Out of crime into Christ. Saratoga Springs, N. Y. , 196-.
        32p.

3759   Winley, Jesse, 1920-1980.
            Jesse, by Jesse Winley with Robert Paul Lamb. Springdale, Pa. , Whitaker House, c1976. 223p.

TABERNACLE PENTECOSTAL CHURCH (1910-1915)
[1910-191- as Tabernacle Presbyterian Church.]

Organized July 10, 1910, at Greenville, South Carolina, the
Tabernacle Presbyterian Church was the outgrowth of the Brewerton
Independent Presbyterian Church, a holiness congregation which years
earlier had accepted belief in tongues-speech as the initial evidence
of the baptism of the Holy Spirit.   Led by N. J. Holmes, former
pastor of the Brewerton church and founder of the Altamont Bible
and Missionary Institute, the Tabernacle Presbyterian Church (soon
re-named Tabernacle Pentecostal Church) used an amended version
of the Presbyterian larger and shorter catechisms as its creedal
statement.   Drawing together converts of G. B. Cashwell, G. F.
Taylor, and N. J. Holmes, the organization consisted of a half-
dozen churches in such South Carolinian towns as Greenville, Gum
Springs, Brewerton, and Easley.   From the beginning, Holmes'
group enjoyed warm fellowship and shared evangelistic ministries
with the newly-formed Pentecostal Holiness Church.   In 1915 it
elected to merge with that body, the union being consummated during the meeting of the Georgia-Upper South Carolina Convention of
the Pentecostal Holiness Church at Canon, Georgia, that year.   Fearing loss of the interdenominational character of his ministry, neither
Holmes nor his church and school in Greenville, joined in the merger.   The founder remained, however, in warm sympathy with the
Pentecostal Holiness Church, and nearly thirty years following his
death under the leadership of Paul F. Beacham, both church and
school came under the control of the Pentecostal Holiness Church.

3760   Campbell, Joseph Enoch, 1903-
        The Pentecostal Holiness Church, 1898-1948: its back-
        ground and history; presenting complete background material
        which adequately explains the existence of this organization,
        also the existence of other kindred Pentecostal and Holiness
        groups, as an essential and integral part of the total church
        set-up, by Joseph E. Campbell.   Franklin Springs, Ga.,
        Publishing House of the Pentecostal Holiness Church, c1951.
        573p.   "Tabernacle Presbyterian Church," p. 263-266.

TRUE FELLOWSHIP PENTECOSTAL CHURCH OF AMERICA (1964-   )

In 1964 Charles E. Waters, Sr., overseer of the Alpha and
Omega Pentecostal Church of America, left that body and formed
the True Fellowship Pentecostal Church of America.   It consists of
two congregations, both in Baltimore.   The combined membership is
about 25.

UNITED HOLY CHURCH OF AMERICA (1894-   ).
[1894-1900 as Holy Church of North Carolina; 1900-1910 as Holy
    Church of North Carolina and Virginia; 1910-1916 as Holy Church
    in America.]

In May 1886, a holiness revival broke out among blacks in
Method, a suburb of Raleigh, North Carolina, which during the next
decade and a half spread to Durham, Wilmington, and other places
in the piedmont and tidewater sections of North Carolina and Virginia.
This revival resulted in formation of the United Holy Church of America in several stages over the next three decades. Although the first
convocation of the Holy Church of North Carolina met in Durham,
October 13, 1894, completion of a manual for the government of the
churches lay sixteen years in the future. An organizational convention which met in Durham, October 15, 1900, drew together under
one "banner" the constituencies of the Union Holiness Convention and
the Big Kahara [i. e. Coharie] Holiness Association, the principal
agencies of the revival. Calling itself the Holy Church in America,
the group adopted its first discipline, H. L. Fisher's Standard Manual for Holy Churches, in 1910. It took its present name in 1916
and obtained legal incorporation two years later. With the organization of the Northern District Convocation in 1920, the "parent" body
became the Southern District Convocation, an action of key importance in the dispute that produced the Original United Holy Church
fifty-seven years later. Headquarters are in Durham. The official
publication is the Holiness Union. In 1960 the United Holy Church
of America reported 470 churches and 28,980 members. Formation
of the Original United Holy Church in 1977 cost the Durham-based
group its missionary work in Liberia, and perhaps one-half of its
membership in the United States.

3761   United Holy Church of America.
           Standard manual, and constitution and by-laws of the
        United Holy Church of America, Incorporated. Revised 1966
        [ed.]. [Philadelphia], Printed by Christian Printing Co.,
        Durham, N.C., 1966. 124p.

3762   United Holy Church of America.
           Yearbook. [1]- 19 - . Philadelphia. v.[1]- .

3763   Fisher, Henry Lee, bp., -1947.
           Standard manual for Holy churches, by H. L. Fisher.
        [Durham, N.C.], 1910; Eden, N.C., Printed by Dalcoe Print-
        ing Co., 1975. 45p. "Adopted September 1910, by 'The Holy
        Church in America'." Reprint has introduction by James
        Alexander Forbes.

           --HISTORY

3764   Fisher, Henry Lee, bp., -1947.
           The history of the United Holy Church of America, Inc.,
        by H. L. Fisher. [Durham, N.C., 194-] 55p.

--PERIODICALS

3765   Holiness union. 1- 19 -
       Durham, N.C.

--VIRGINIA

-- --RICHMOND

3766   Forbes, James Alexander, 1935-
          Ministry of hope from a double minority [by] James A.
       Forbes, Jr. In Theological Education, 9 (Summer 1973
       suppl.), 305-3$\overline{16}$.   On St. John's United Holy Church of
       America, Richmond, Virginia.

UNITED PENTECOSTAL FAITH, GENERAL COUNCIL CHURCHES
    (1915-1924, 1927-   )
[1915-1924 as United Pentecostal Association.]

       In 1915 R. E. Erdman, pastor of an independent church in
Buffalo, New York and an evangelist of some distinction, organized
his own and nearby churches into the United Pentecostal Association.
Having been in attendance the previous year at the formation of the
General Council of the Assemblies of God in Hot Springs, Arkansas,
Erdman apparently had not chosen to ally himself with that movement on account of his belief in second-crisis sanctification, a tenet
the Assemblies did not endorse. In his work as an evangelist, Erdman came into contact with the Pentecostal Holiness Church.   As a
result, in 1924 he led the United Pentecostal Association into union
with it.   Many of Erdman's people were not committed to his doctrinal views, however, and following the founder's death in 1927, all
of the former United Pentecostal Association churches except those
in Greenville, Pennsylvania and Conneaut, Ohio withdrew from the
union.   The United Pentecostal congregations, which were concentrated in southwestern New York, western Pennsylvania, and northeastern Ohio, maintained a loose federation with the Pentecostal
Church of Christ from 1928 to 1934, when this affiliation also was
severed.   Expanding southward, the group established a center at
Knoxville, Maryland from which by the 1950s it had begun issuing
the Gospel Trumpeter, its official publication.

--HISTORY

3767   Campbell, Joseph Enoch, 1903-
          The Pentecostal Holiness Church, 1898-1948: its back-
       ground and history; presenting complete background material
       which adequately explains the existence of this organization,
       also the existence of other kindred Pentecostal and Holiness
       groups, as an essential and integral part of the total church
       set-up, by Joseph E. Campbell.   Franklin Springs, Ga.,

Publishing House of the Pentecostal Holiness Church, c1951.
573p. "United Pentecostal Association": p. 282-284.

--PERIODICALS

3768   Gospel trumpeter. 1- 195 -
          Knoxville, Md.

2. SIGNS-FOLLOWING BODIES

In 1909 George Went Hensley, a twenty-four-year-old resident
of the Grasshopper Valley in eastern Tennessee, became convinced
that statements in Mark 16:17-18, concerning speaking in other
tongues, taking up serpents, and drinking poison were indeed com-
mands.   (The passage is not in fact in the earliest extant Biblical
manuscripts.) A few days after making this discovery, Hensley cap-
tured a rattlesnake and, during a service at the Sale Creek meetinghouse nearby, induced worshippers to handle it as a test of faith.
From the Grasshopper Valley, belief that these "signs" would follow
true faith spread throughout the southern Appalachian region and beyond.   Worship incorporated familiar elements such as testimonies,
tongues-speaking, baptism, footwashing, and prayers for the sick,
with novel practices such as the kiss of peace (either between men
and women, or between members of the same sex), the drinking of
poison, and the handling of snakes.   When participants were bitten
and died, as in the case of Lewis Ford in 1945, spokesmen for the
believers traced the cause to a failure of faith.   Ostracized by other
religionists, both Pentecostal and non-Pentecostal, the "signs" people established independent congregations.   Located in remote places
such as Dolley Pond, Tennessee and Scrabble Creek, West Virginia
and calling themselves Church of All Nations, Church of God with
Signs Following After, Holiness Church of God in Jesus' Name, and
Original Pentecostal Church of God, they have met harassment every-
where.   In the wake of the breaking-up of an interstate convention at
Durham, North Carolina in 1947, Tennessee and several other states
outlawed snake-handling as a religious rite.   Although adherents in
West Virginia continue to be free to worship openly, the movement
in other states has been driven underground.   In the 1970s, the total
membership was estimated at 1, 000.

3769   Carden, Karen (Wilson), 1946-
          The persecuted prophets [by] Karen W. Carden [and]
          Robert W. Pelton.   South Brunswick, N.J., A. S. Barnes;
          London, T. Yoseloff, c1976.   188p.   DLC

3770   Crapps, Robert W.
        Religion of the plain folk in the Southern United States,
        by Robert W. Crapps. In Perspectives in Religious Studies,
        4 (Spring 1977), 37-53.

3771   Daugherty, Mary L.
        Serpent-handling as sacrament, by Mary L. Daugherty.
        In Theology Today, 33 (Oct. 1976), 232-243.

3772   Gerrard, Nathan Lewis
        The holiness movement in southern Appalachia [by] Nathan
        L. Gerrard. In Hamilton, M. P., ed. The charismatic
        movement. Grand Rapids, Mich., 1975, 159-171.

3773   Gerrard, Nathan Lewis
        The serpent-handling religions of West Virginia [by]
        Nathan L. Gerrard. In Trans-action, 5 (May 1968), 22-28.
        On churches in Scrabble Creek and Jolo, West Virginia.

3774   Gerrard, Nathan Lewis
        The serpent-handling religions of West Virginia [by]
        Nathan L. Gerrard. In Henslin, J. M., ed. Deviant life-
        styles. New Brunswick, N.J., c1977, 79-86.

3775   Holiness faith healers.
        In Life, 17 (July 3, 1944), 59-62.   "Virginia mountaineers
        handle snakes to prove their piety."

3776   Holliday, Robert Kelvin, 1933-
        Tests of faith. Oak Hill, W. Va., Fayette Tribune, 1966.
        104p. DLC

3777   The Holy Ghost people (Motion picture)
        Blair Boyd. Released by Contemporary Films/McGraw-
        Hill, 1968. 53 min. sd. b&w. 16mm. Credits: Consul-
        tant, Nathan Gerrard; photographer, Peter Adair.

3778   Kane, Steven M.
        Aspects of Holy Ghost religion; the snake-handling sect
        of the American southeast, by Steven Kane. Chapel Hill,
        1973.   45ℓ.   Thesis (M.A.)--University of North Carolina.
        NcU

3779   Kane, Steven M.
        Holy Ghost people: the snake-handlers of southern Ap-
        palachia, by Steven M. Kane. In Appalachian Journal, 1
        (Spring 1974), 255-262.

3780   Kane, Steven M.
        Ritual possession in a southern Appalachian religious sect
        [by] Steven M. Kane. In Journal of American Folklore, 87
        (Oct./Dec. 1974), 293-302.

3781   Kane, Steven M.
        Snake handlers of southern Appalachia [by] Steven M.
        Kane. Princeton, N.J., 1979. vi, 291ℓ. Thesis (Ph.D.)--
        Princeton University. NjP

3782   Kobler, John, 1910-
        America's strangest religion. In Saturday Evening Post,
        230 (Sept. 28, 1957), 26-27, 153-154, 156.

3783   La Barre, Weston, 1911-
        They shall take up serpents; psychology of the southern
        snake-handling cult. Minneapolis, University of Minnesota
        Press, 1962. 208p. DLC

3784   La Barre, Weston, 1911-
        They shall take up serpents; psychology of the southern
        snake-handling cult. New York, Schocken, 1969. ix, 208p.
        Reprint of the 1962 ed., with a new introd. by the author.

3785   Larsen, Egon, 1904-
        Strange sects and cults: a study of their origins and in-
        fluence. London, Burker, 1971. 202p. On the Holiness
        Church of God in Jesus' Name, Big Stone Gap, Virginia:
        p. 171-172. DLC

3786   Larsen, Egon, 1904-
        Strange sects and cults: a study of their origins and in-
        fluence. New York, Hart Publishing Co., 1972, c1971. 245p.
        "The snake cult": p. 205-206. DLC, OkEG

3787   Maguire, Marsha
        Confirming the word: snake-handling sects in southern
        Appalachia. In Quarterly Journal of the Library of Congress,
        38 (Summer 1981), 166-179.

3788   Pelton, Robert Wayne, 1937-
        Snake handlers: God-fearers? Or, fanatics? [By]
        Robert W. Pelton and Karen W. Carden. Nashville, T. Nel-
        son, 1974. 110, [49]p. DLC

3789   Religion in transit.
        In Christianity Today, 17 (June 8, 1973), 45. On Holi-
        ness Church of God in Jesus' Name, Carson Springs, Tennessee.

3790   Robertson, Archibald Thomas
        That old-time religion, by Archie Robertson. Boston,
        Houghton Mifflin, 1950. 282p. "Tongues and snakes": p. 156-
        181. DLC, RPB

3791   Schwarz, Berthold Eric, 1924-
        Ordeal by serpents, fire and strychnine: a study of some
        provocative psychosomatic phenomena, by Berthold E. Schwarz.
        In Psychiatric Quarterly, 34 (1960), 405-429.

3792   Snake power.
        In Time, 92 (Nov. 1, 1968), 86. On the trial of Roscoe
        Mullins, member of the Holiness Church of God in Jesus'
        Name at Big Stone Gap, Virginia.

3793   Snakes and strychnine.
        In Christianity Today, 17 (May 11, 1973), 28. Editorial.

3794   Stekert, Ellen Jane, 1935-
        The snake-handling sect of Harlan County, Kentucky: its
        influence on folk tradition, by Ellen Stekert. In Southern
        Folklore Quarterly, 27 (Dec. 1963), 316-322.

3795   Taylor, Alva W.
        Snake handling cults flourish [by] Alva W. Taylor. In
        Christian Century, 64 (Oct. 29, 1947), 1308. On groups in
        Kentucky, Virginia, Tennessee and Alabama.

3796   Test of faith--or sanity?
        In Christianity Today, 17 (May 11, 1973), 44. On Holi-
        ness Church of God in Jesus' Name in Carson Springs, Ten-
        nessee.

3797   They shall take up serpents.
        In Newsweek, 24 (Aug. 21, 1944), 88-89. On Stone
        Creek, Virginia.

3798   Wigginton, B. Eliot
        Unto the Church of God [etc., etc.] In Foxfire, 7:1
        (Spring 1973), 2-75.

3799   Womeldorf, John A.
        Rattlesnake religion, by John A. Womeldorf. In Christian
        Century, 64 (Dec. 10, 1947), 1517-1518.

PART II: DOCTRINAL TRADITIONS

Section B:

FINISHED WORK OF CALVARY OR
BAPTISTIC TRADITION

Although Parham and Seymour hewed to the line of Methodist Holiness orthodoxy as far as the doctrine of entire sanctification was concerned, converts from the non-Wesleyan backgrounds soon challenged the original Pentecostal consensus. Questions were raised both as to the nature and purpose of sanctification. Some (particularly former Anglicans, Congregationalists, Presbyterians, Disciples of Christ, and Baptists) regarded sanctification as a gradual process, the natural development of gifts and graces necessary for mature Christian living, not a second crisis subsequent to regeneration. Others, former members of the aforementioned groups who had come into the Pentecostal movement by way of the Keswick movement or the Christian and Missionary Alliance, recognized the need for a second crisis experience, but believed that its primary function was the enduement of power for Christian service. The eradication of the carnal nature or bent toward sinning and the resulting purity of desire which Methodist Holiness advocates declared to be the consequence of the second crisis were simply not taught in the Bible, they said. All that was purchased for us by Christ's death on Calvary was made a free gift to us by faith, in conversion. This was the finished work of Calvary, Christ's complete saving work. The result of Pentecost, called in these latter days the baptism of the Holy Ghost, was power for Christian service, and the initial physical evidence of having received this power was speaking in other tongues as the Spirit gave "utterance."

A significant shift also occurred in thinking about baptism. Whatever their former tradition, Finished Work advocates with few exceptions became immersionists, holding that baptism is the sign or testimony of salvation. In this view neither the baptism of infants nor the baptism of adults by any other mode than immersion is any baptism at all.

1. TRINITARIAN BODIES

The pioneer proponent of the Finished Work teaching was

William H. Durham, an independent Baptist who as pastor of the North Avenue Mission of Chicago, led his flock into the new movement. Himself a convert of the Azusa Street meeting, Durham was a key figure in establishing the Pentecostal movement in Chicago. Led into the movement through Durham's influence were William Hammer Piper, pastor of the Stone Church; Andrew Urshan, Persian immigrant and student at Moody Bible Institute; Eudorus N. Bell, former Baptist pastor and student at the University of Chicago; and A. H. Argue, Holiness preacher from Winnipeg. Also deeply influenced was Aimee Semple McPherson who, during a stop in Chicago, claimed special healing at the North Avenue Mission. For several years before Durham returned to California in 1911, his Pentecostal Testimony and Piper's Latter Rain Evangel, both published in Chicago, had been spreading the new doctrine. Although Pastor Durham died in 1912, his teaching swept over the northeastern, midwestern, and far western United States, and engulfed the Canadian provinces and Great Britain. Within a few years, it became a cardinal belief of the majority of Pentecostal adherents in these areas, and a part of the doctrinal shibboleth of the soon-to-be-formed General Council of the Assemblies of God, Pentecostal Assemblies of Canada, and Assemblies of God in Great Britain and Ireland.

--DOCTRINAL AND CONTROVERSIAL WORKS

3800   Baptême de l'Esprit et dons spirituels.
        Paris, Viens et Vois, 19--.   40p.

3801   Blossom, Willis W.
        The gift (dorea) of the Holy Spirit; what is the gift of the Holy Spirit and how obtained? [By] Willis W. Blossom. Rev. ed.   Madison, Wi., 1925.   230p.   CAzPC

3802   Brandt, Robert L.
        Spiritual gifts, by Robert L. Brandt.   Brussels, International Correspondence Institute, 1978.   176p.

3802a   Brewster, Percy S.
        Pentecostal doctrine.   Editor: P. S. Brewster. [Cheltenham, Glos., Grenehurst Press], c1976.   400p.   KyWAT

3803   Burton, William Frederick Padwick, 1886-1971.
        Gospel nuggets.   Collected and illustrated by W. F. P. Burton.   Preston, Lancs., Congo Evangelistic Mission, 196-.   96p.   OkTOr

3803a   Burton, William Frederick Padwick, 1886-1971.
        Mafundijyo a ku mukanda wa Leza.   Elisabethville, 1948.   100p.   L

3803b   Burton, William Frederick Padwick, 1886-1971.
        Teachings from the word of God, by W. F. P. Burton. Translated by Arie and Alice Blomerus.   Johannesburg,

W. F. Burton's Publications, 196-.   65p.   Translation of
Mafundijyo a ku mukanda wa Leza.   OkTOr

3804   Courtney, Howard Perry, 1911-
       The baptism in the Holy Spirit, by Howard P. Courtney
       and Vaneda H. Courtney.   Los Angeles, 1963.   40p.   OkTOr,
       TxWaS

3805   Gee, Donald, 1891-1966.
       Os dons do ministério de Cristo; continuacão de "Acêrca
       dos dons espirituals. "   Rio de Janeiro, Livros Evangélicos,
       1961.   99p.   Translation of The ministry-gifts of Christ.

3806   Gee, Donald, 1891-1966.
       Die Gaben Christi für den geistlichen Dienst.   Übers.
       von Johann Justus Meier.   Vaihingen-Enz, K. Fix, 19--.
       63p.   Translation of The ministry-gifts of Christ.

3807   Gee, Donald, 1891-1966.
       Gottes grosse gabe; sieben betrachtungen uber den heiligen
       geist, von Donald Gee.   Ubersetst von Leonhard Steiner.
       Bamberg, Christlicher schristenvertrieb J. Maar, 194-.   32p.
       Translation of God's great gift.   NN, NNUT, TNJ

3808   Gee, Donald, 1891-1966.
       Hengen hedelmä; raamatuntutkisteluja.   Suomentanut
       Lauri Ohrnberg.   Helsinki, Kustantaja: Ristin voitto, 1948.
       96p.   MH

3809   Gee, Donald, 1891-1966.
       The ministry gifts of Christ.   Springfield, Mo. , Gospel
       Publishing House, c1930.   110p.   Sequel to Concerning spirit-
       ual gifts.   DLC, MSohG

3810   Gee, Donald, 1891-1966.
       Need believers die.   In Scruby, J. J.   Need believers
       die? A reply to Rev. Donald Gee of London, England.   Day-
       ton, Oh. , 194-, 9-13.   Reprinted from Redemption tidings.

3811   Gee, Donald, 1891-1966.
       Pfingsten.   Übersetzt von Johan Justus Meier.   Reisach,
       Württ. , K. Fix, 1948.   51p.   Translation of Pentecost.   DLC,
       MH, NN

3812   Gee, Donald, 1891-1966.
       Pfingsten.   Übersetzt von Johan Justus Meier.   Schorn-
       dorf, Württ. , K. Fix, 1964.   64p.   Translation of Pentecost.

3813   Gee, Donald, 1891-1966.
       Studies in guidance.   Rev. ed.   London, Elim Publishing
       Co. , 1941.   vi, 74p.   L

3814   Gee, Donald, 1891-1966.

"This is the will of God----"; the Bible and sexual problems, an exposition of the scriptures. London, Victory
Press, 1940. 53p. L

3815   Gee, Donald, 1891-1966.
        Trophimus I left sick: our problems of divine healing.
London, Elim Publishing Co. , 1952. 30p. L, OkTOr,
TxWaS

3816   Gee, Donald, 1891-1966.
        Über die geistlichen Gaben; eine Reihe von Bibelstudien.
Übersetzt von Leonhard Steiner. 2 Aufl. ----, Württ. , K.
Fix, 194-. 78p. Translation of Concerning spiritual gifts.
DLC

3817   Glover, Kelso R.
        God is in Pentecost, by Kelso R. Glover. Los Angeles,
1946. 35p.

3818   Gortner, John Narver, 1874-
        Water baptism and the Trinity. Studies by J. Narver
Gortner, Donald Gee [and] Hy Pickering. Springfield, Mo. ,
Gospel Publishing House, 19--. 62p.

3818a   Hoekstra, Raymond G.
        The ascension gift ministries: apostles, prophets, evan-
gelists, pastors, teachers, by Raymond G. Hoekstra. Portland, Or. , Wings of Healing, 1950. 63p.

3818b   Hoekstra, Raymond G.
        The "latter rain," by Raymond G. Hoekstra. Portland,
Or. , Wings of Healing, 1950. 62p.

3819   Holdcroft, Leslie Thomas
        The Holy Spirit from a Pentecostal viewpoint. Santa
Cruz, Ca. , Bethany Books, c1962. 119p.

3820   Horton, Harold Lawrence Cuthbert, 1880-1968.
        The gifts of the Spirit, by Harold Horton. Shreveport,
La. , Voice of Healing, 19--. 222p. TxWaS

3821   Horton, Harold Lawrence Cuthbert, 1880-1968.
        Recevez sans attendre; ce que, les écritures, enseignent,
an sujet de la réception du Saint-Esprit, par Harold Horton.
Paris, Viens et Vois, 196-. 29p.

3822   Kinne, Seeley D. , 1858-1950.
        The prophetic state. The mystery church. The body of
Christ. By Seeley D. Kinne. St. Louis, Glad Tidings Book
Concern, 1950. 2v. (208p.)

3823   Kinne, Seeley D. , 1858-1950.
        Spirituals: gifts, graces, operations, ministries, demon-

strations, and various phases of the Spirit kingdom, by Seeley
D. Kinne. St. Louis, 1911. 128p.

3824   McAlister, Robert Edward, 1880-1953.
        A Plenitude do Espírito Santo. Rio de Janeiro, Em-
        prevan Editôra, 1969. 61p.

3825   MacIlravy, Cora Harris, 1860-1952.
        Christ and His bride; an exposition of the Song of Solo-
        mon. Chicago, Elbethel Publishing House, c1916. 554p.
        DLC

3826   McPherson, Aimee Semple, 1890-1944.
        Lost and restored; or, The dispensation of the Holy
        Spirit from the ascension of the Lord Jesus to His coming
        descension. Framingham, Ma., 191-. 32p. CLamB

3827   McPherson, Aimee Semple, 1890-1944.
        The second coming of Christ. Is He coming? When is
        He coming? For whom is he coming? Los Angeles, c1921.
        120p. DLC, TxU

3828   Myland, David Wesley, 1858-1943.
        The latter rain covenant and Pentecostal power, with
        testimony of healings and baptism, by D. Wesley Myland.
        Chicago, Evangel Publishing House, 1910. 215p. "These
        lectures, with the exception of 'The Pentecostal psalm' were
        delivered in 'the Stone Church' (undenominational) ... Chicago
        ... at a Pentecostal convention called in the spring of 1909."
        DLC

3829   Myland, David Wesley, 1858-1943.
        The latter rain covenant and Pentecostal power; with
        testimony of healings and baptism, by D. Wesley Myland.
        2d ed. Chicago, Evangel Publishing House, 1910, i.e. 1911.
        184p. Cover title: The latter rain Pentecost.

3830   Myland, David Wesley, 1858-1943.
        The latter rain covenant, by D. Wesley Myland. Billings,
        Mo., A. N. Trotter; printed by Temple Press, Springfield,
        Mo., 1973. 177p. Reprint of 1910 ed. with prefatory, ap-
        pended material and advertisements omitted.

3831   Myland, David Wesley, 1858-1943.
        The Revelation of Jesus Christ; a comprehensive har-
        monic outline and perspective view of the book, by D. Wesley
        Myland. Chicago, Evangel Publishing House, 1911. 255p.
        DLC

3832   Nelson, Peter Christopher, 1868-1942.
        Les doctrines de la Bible. 2. éd. Paris, Viens et
        Vois, 1969. 109p. Translation of Bible doctrines.

3833   Ness, Henry H.
       The baptism with the Holy Spirit, by Henry H. Ness.
       Springfield, Mo. , Bill Britton, 197-.   23p.

3834   Ness, Henry H.
       The baptism with the Holy Spirit, what is it?   Haywood,
       Ca. , Evangelism Crusaders, 196-.   28p.   OkTOr

3835   Perkins, Jonathan Elsworth, 1889-
       The brooding presence and Pentecostalism.   Springfield,
       Mo. , Gospel Publishing House, 1924.   124p.

3836   Perkins, Jonathan Elsworth, 1889-
       What the Bible says about the laying on of hands; or,
       Pentecostal truth defended.   Seattle, 19--.   145p.   TxWaS

3837   Schell, William Gallio
       Sanctification and holiness, the false and the true, by
       Wm. G. Schell.   Chicago, Herald Publishing Co. , c1922.
       208p.   DLC

3838   Stemme, Harry A.
       Pentecost today, by Harry A. Stemme.   Chicago, 1939.
       30p.   "A series of radio broadcasts devoted to the exposition
       of scriptures regarding the Pentecostal baptism and sign gifts
       for the body of Christ. "

3839   Stemme, Harry A.
       Speaking with other tongues, sign and gift, by Harry A.
       Stemme.   Minneapolis, Northern Gospel Publishing House,
       1946.   56p.   "A reply to Speaking with other tongues, sign
       or gift, which?"   By T. J. McCrossan.   TxWaS

3840   Stiles, John Edwin
       The gift of the Holy Spirit, by J. E. Stiles.   Burbank,
       Ca. , 1963.   156p.

3841   Thom, Robert, 1915-
       The Holy Spirit and the authority of the name.   n. p. ,
       c1977.   236p.

       --HYMNS AND SACRED SONGS

3842   Boulton, Ernest Charles William, -1960.
       Songs of the sanctuary: a selection of hymns and chor-
       uses written by E. C. W. Boulton.   [Musical settings by M.
       Helyer ... et al.]   London, Victory Press, 193-.   [32]p.
       Cover title.   With music.

3843   Buffum, Herbert, 1879-1939.
       Above the shadows (4): featuring the songs of Herbert

Buffum, and other favorites.   Edited and compiled by Herbert
Buffum, Jr.   Stockton, Ca. , Herbert Buffum's Songs, c1951.
64p.   With music.   OkBetC

3844   Follette, John Wright, 1883-1966.
       Psalms, hymns, and spiritual songs.   Asheville, N. C. ,
       Follette Books, 1968.   31p.

3845   Munger, Oren E. , 1920-1945.
       Songs of the saviour.   Malverne, N. Y. , Gospel Songs,
       1950.   31p.

3845a Olsen, J. O.
       Heavenly praises.   Compiled by J. O. Olsen [and] Thoro
       Harris for Evangelist John Goben.   Chicago, T. Harris,
       192-.   [292]p.   KyLoS

                    --PERIODICALS

3845b Apostolic faith.   1- 1908-1913.
       Houston, Tx. , Malvern, Ar.   Merged into Word and wit-
       ness.

3846   Bridal call.   1-6, no. 7, June 1917-1922.
       Framingham, Ma.; Los Angeles

3847   Evangelii Härold.   1- Dec. 1915-
       Stockholm

3848   Faith.   1- June 1, 1915-
       East Providence, R. I.

3849   Folke Vennen.   1- 190 -
       Chicago

3850   Full gospel advocate.   1- 1917-
       Houston.   Merged into Gospel call.

3851   Full gospel monthly.   1- 1928-
       Orlando, Fl.

3852   Gospel call.   1- 1927-
       Chicago; Pasadena, Ca.   1927-19-- as Gospel call of
       Russia.   DLC

3853   Latter rain evangel.   1-30, no. 8, Oct. 1908-June 1939.
       Chicago.   Merged into Gospel call.   DLC

3853a Pentecostal herald.   1- 1913-1927.
       Chicago

3854   Pentecostal testimony.   1- Mar. 27, 1907-Feb. 1912.
       Chicago; Los Angeles.

3855   Pfingstgrüsse.   1-   1909-1919.
       Breslau

3856   Ristin Voitto.   1-   1912-
       Helsinki

3857   Die Verheissung des Vaters.   1-   1909-
       Zürich

3858   Word and work.   1-54, 1879-1932.
       Springfield, Ma.; Framingham, Ma.   IEG

--SERMONS, TRACTS, ADDRESSES, ESSAYS

3859   McPherson, Aimee Semple, 1890-1944.
       Divine healing sermons.   Los Angeles, Printed by Biola
       Press, 1921.   146p.   CLU, CU-S, DLC, DNLM, InU, Or,
       TxWaS

3860   McPherson, Aimee Semple, 1890-1944.
       The last days.   Los Angeles, Bridal Call, 192-.
       folder ([4]p.)

3861   McPherson, Aimee Semple, 1890-1944.
       This is that; personal experiences, sermons and writings
       of Aimee Semple McPherson, evangelist.   Los Angeles,
       Bridal Call Publishing House, c1919.   685p.   CU, DLC, IAU,
       InU, WaSp

APOSTOLIC CHURCH (1916-   )

       In 1916, charging gross misuse of the prophetic gift and doc-
trinal errors, a largely Welsh contingent within the Apostolic Faith
Church withdrew and formed the Apostolic Church.   Like its Winton,
Bournemouth-based parent, the new body continued to rely on Spirit-
guidance in making governmental decisions.   In keeping with this
tradition, the headquarters church at Penygroes, South Wales, called
W. J. Williams, a miner, to the office of apostle and his brother,
Dan P. Williams, to the office of prophet.   The Apostolic Church
spread rapidly both in Britain and abroad.   In 1918 the large Burning Bush Assembly in Glasgow joined the movement.   This action
created a bridgehead in Scotland, the first of more than forty congregations established there during the next half century.   Expansion
into continental Europe and North America was accompanied by evangelistic efforts in India, China, Nigeria, Ghana, the West Indies,
Australia, and New Zealand.   Autonomous bodies have developed in
Canada, Nigeria, Australia, and New Zealand.

       Although Apostolic Church headquarters remain in Penygroes,
missionary and publishing headquarters are in Bradford, Yorkshire.

In 1975 the group reported 191 congregations and about 4,000 members in Britain.

3862   Apostolic Church.
         The Apostolic Church: its principles and practices.
         Penygroes, 1937. xxv,414p. L

         --CATECHISMS AND CREEDS

3863   Apostolic Church.
         Fundamentals: a brief statement of fundamental truths
         contained in the scriptures, and believed and taught by the
         Apostolic Church. Bradford, Apostolic Church Publishing
         House, 19--. 31p.

         --DOCTRINAL AND CONTROVERSIAL WORKS

3864   Apostolic Church.
         Bible readings given at Penygroes Convention, 1958.
         Bradford, Puritan Press, 195-. 36p. OkTOr

3865   Ireson, Cecil Charles
         The nine gifts of the Holy Ghost. n.p., 19--. 31p.
         (Teachings of the Apostolic Church, 6.)

3866   Ireson, Cecil Charles
         The nine gifts of the Holy Spirit. Bradford, Puritan
         Press, 1957. 31p. (Tenets of the Apostolic Church, 6/1.)

3867   Macpherson, Ian, 1912-
         Dial the future; a book about the second coming of Christ.
         Eastbourne, Sussex, Prophetic Witness, 1975. 69p. DLC

3868   Macpherson, Ian, 1912-
         News of the world to come; panorama of Biblical proph-
         ecy. Eastbourne, Sussex, Prophetic Witness, 1973. 299p.
         DLC

3869   Macpherson, Ian, 1912-
         Paired parables; companion pictures from Jesus portrait
         gallery. Bradford, Puritan Press, 1946. 65p.

3870   Purnell, Jacob
         Twelve studies of the Epistle of St. Paul to the Gala-
         tians.... Bradford, Apostolic Church, 1937. 43p. L

3871   Turnbull, Thomas Napier
         The full gospel. Bradford, Yorks., Puritan Press, 1949.
         76p. OkTOr

3871a Turnbull, Thomas Napier
       The second coming of Christ and His millennial reign
       upon earth. Bradford, Puritan Press, 1954. 19p. (Tenets
       of the Apostolic Church, 3/3.)

3872   Williams, Daniel Powell, 1882-1947.
       And they shall prophesy, by D. P. Williams. Bradford,
       Puritan Press, 1959. 35p. First published in 1931 under
       title: The prophetical ministry in the church. OkTOr

--HISTORY

3873   Turnbull, Thomas Napier
       What God hath wrought; a short history of the Apostolic
       Church. Bradford, Yorks., Puritan Press, 1959. 186p.
       MnCS, OkTOr

--HYMNS AND SACRED SONGS

3874   Apostolic Church.
       New songs before the throne. Bradford, Puritan Press,
       19--. 28p.

--MISSIONS

3875   Apostolic Church. Missionary Movement.
       The vision glorious: an account of the Apostolic Church
       Missionary Movement since its inception in 1922. Issued in
       celebration of the jubilee commemoration services held to
       celebrate the twenty-fifth anniversary of its foundation by
       Hugh Mitchell, secretary. Bradford, 1949. 40p. MoSCS

--PASTORAL THEOLOGY

3876   Williams, W. Jones
       The good minister of Jesus Christ, by W. Jones Williams.
       Bradford, Puritan Press, 19--. 34p.

--PERIODICALS

3877   Apostolic herald. 1- 1922-1973.
       Bradford. OkTOr

3878   Apostolic messenger. 1- 1930-
       Glasgow

3879   Herald of grace. 1-3, no. 1, 1974-1976.
       Penygroes. OkTOr

3880   Riches of grace. 1- 1916-1973; 1- 1977-
            Penygroes. OkTOr

                --SERMONS, TRACTS, ADDRESSES, ESSAYS

3881   Macpherson, Ian, 1912-
            The cross in war-time. London, A. H. Stockwell, 1941.
        32p. L

3882   Macpherson, Ian, 1912-
            On the wings of the wind; Bradford addresses. Bradford,
        Puritan Press, 1958. 87p.

3883   Macpherson, Ian, 1912-
            The punctuality of God. Bradford, Puritan Press, 1946.
        144p.

APOSTOLIC CHURCH, AUSTRALIAN COUNCIL (1930-)

        The result of missionary efforts begun in 1927 by representa-
tives of the Apostolic Church with headquarters in Penygroes, Wales,
the Apostolic Church in Australia, though an autonomous body, is
identical to its parent in doctrine and practice. Consisting of forty
congregations, the body supports missionary work among the aborigines, as well as in India, New Guinea, and the New Hebrides. Aus-
tralians were also active in early Apostolic Church activity in New
Zealand. Headquarters are in Richmond, Victoria where the Bible
college also is located.

3884   Herald of grace. 1- 1941-
            Richmond, Vict. NNMR

3885   Revival echoes. 1- June 1933-
            Melbourne

APOSTOLIC CHURCH IN CANADA (1924-)

        A product of the evangelistic outreach of the Apostolic Church
based in Penygroes, Wales, the Apostolic Church in Canada is at
work in Nova Scotia, Quebec, Ontario, and Alberta. In the mid-
1970s the Apostolic Church in Canada reported thirteen congregations,
seven of them in Ontario. With a domestic membership of about
700, the group supports missionary work in Jamaica, Barbados, and
Brazil. Headquarters are in Toronto.

APOSTOLIC CHURCH, NEW ZEALAND COUNCIL (1934-   )

Although as early as 1925 individual adherents were reported in the government census, and although as early as 1929 a Wellington congregation gained recognition by the Penygroes convention, it was not until 1934 that a dominion-wide fellowship of Apostolic churches was established in New Zealand. Aggressively evangelistic, Apostolic Church work spread from Wellington, its original center and headquarters, to other areas of the islands. Early work among the Maoris coincided with the sending of workers to Nigeria, New Guinea, the New Hebrides, and to the aborigines of Australia. The Apostolic Church in New Zealand has experienced rapid growth, reporting an increase in its total constituency from 1,399 to 2,361 in the 1961-1971 decade.

--HISTORY

3886   Worsfold, James Evans
        A history of the charismatic movements in New Zealand, including a Pentecostal perspective and a breviate of the Catholic Apostolic Church in Great Britain, by J. E. Worsfold. Bradford, Yorks., Julian Literature Trust; printed by Purtian Press, c1974. xx, 368p. "The Apostolic Church": p. 237-291. DLC

--PERIODICALS

3887   Apostolic life. 1-   1956-
        Wellington. 1956-May 1968 as Treasures of grace.
        OkTOr

3888   World and New Zealand. 1-   1941-1956.
        Wellington. 1941-1946 as Witness newsletter; 1946-1947 as Witness news.

DIE APOSTOLIESE GELOOF SENDING VAN SUID-AFRIKA (1913-   )
[Also as Apostolic Faith Mission of South Africa.]

Organized in 1913, the Apostoliese Geloof Sending van Suid-Afrika is the outgrowth of the evangelistic work of John G. Lake and Tom Hezmalhalch, both of whom had been deeply influenced by John Alexander Dowie. Arriving in South Africa in 1908, the evangelists first held meetings in Doornfontein, but soon moved on to Johannesburg, where they secured an abandoned Presbyterian Church in Bree Street for their services. From this center the work spread among the European population. Their mission completed, the evangelists returned to the United States. (Lake was present at the formation of the General Council of the Assemblies of God in 1914).

The Apostoliese Geloof Sending is among the largest and most
influential bodies in white South Africa. Although its leaders defend
aparteid, it has been from its earliest years mission-minded, spawn-
ing daughter churches in the Bantu, Colored, and Indian communities,
each under its own government. Headquarters are in Johannesburg.
In 1962 the denomination reported 535 churches and 70,000 members.
It has approximately 200 full-time ordained European workers, and
120 Bantu, Colored and Indian workers. In addition to an orphanage,
a home for the aged, and a Bible college for its white constituents,
the organization operates Bible school for its Bantu and Colored affiliates in Pretoria and Cape Town, respectively.

--DOCTRINAL AND CONTROVERSIAL WORKS

3889   Möller, F. P.
        Die apostoliese leer.   Johannesburg, Evangelie Uitgewers,
        1961. 73p.

3890   Möller, F. P.
        Die volle gestalte.   Johannesburg, Evangelie Uitgewers,
        1956. 79p.

--PERIODICALS

3891   Trooster/Comforter.   1-   1933-
        Johannesburg

ARBEITSGEMEINSCHAFT DER CHRISTEN-GEMEINDEN IN DEUTSCHLAND (1954-)

The Arbeitsgemeinschaft der Christen-Gemeinden, formed in
1954, is a fellowship of formerly independent congregations.   It is
similar in structure to the General Council of the Assemblies of
God, with which it works in close cooperation.   Headquarters are
in Erzhausen bei Darmstadt, where the Bibelschule "Beröa" is also
located, and where Der Leuchter, the official organ, is published.
By the mid-1960s the Arbeitsgemeinschaft had 80 congregations and
10,000 members.   It sends out foreign missionaries under the auspices of the Velberter Mission.   In 1967 it had workers under appointment in South Africa, Zambia, Nigeria, and India.

--DOCTRINAL AND CONTROVERSIAL WORKS

3892   Eisenlöffel, Ludwig, 1928-
        Ein Feuer auf Erden.   Einführung in Lehre und Leben
        der Pfingstbewegung.   Erzhausen bei Darmstadt, Leuchter-
        Verlag, 1965. 147p. MnCS

--PERIODICALS

3893   Der Leuchter. 1- 1950-
        Erzhausen bei Darmstadt

ASAMBLEAS DE DIOS EN EL PERU (1919-)

The outgrowth of missionary activity begun in 1919, the Asambleas de Dios en el Peru maintains close ties to its parent, the General Council of the Assemblies of God. Scattered from the coastal plain to the Amazon jungles, there were by 1959 more than 290 churches and outstations with a combined membership of 7,000. Although North American workers continued to assist, churches were led by Peruvian pastors of whom 186 were either ordained or licensed, and 119 were laymen. Headquarters are in Lima, where a Bible institute for the training of national workers has been in operation since 1936.

--HYMNS AND SACRED SONGS

3894   Asambleas de Dios en el Peru.
        Evangelyu cantucuna: himnos evangélicos en quechua de Ancash, Peru. Lima, Casa de Publicaciones, 1963. 74p. Without music. MnU

ASAMBLEAS DE DIOS EN MEXICO (1931-)

The product of evangelistic activity dating from 1915, the Asambleas de Dios en Mexico has been entirely under the direction of Mexican nationals since 1931, when it registered with the government and gained official recognition. In 1975, after forty-four years of independent existence, the body reported 1,070 organized churches and missions. Headquarters are in Mexico City, where the Instituto Biblico Elim also is located. Fourteen additional Bible training schools serve various regions.

ASSEMBLEE DI DIO IN ITALIA (1947-)

In 1908 Giacomo Lombardi, an Italian immigrant who had espoused Pentecostalism in Chicago, returned to Italy to spread his new-found faith. Under the leadership of Lombardi and other Italian-American and national workers, scores of independent churches were established. When suppressed by the Fascist regime in 1934, the movement went underground. Following the war, the ban lifted, and in 1947 all but five percent of the churches united in forming the

Assemblee di Dio in Italia. Although persecution continued and government recognition was still another seven years in coming, growth was phenomenal. In 1967 the Assemblee reported 650 congregations and 80,000 members. With material aid and some workers from the Italian Branch of the General Council of the Assemblies of God, the Christian Church of North America, and the Italian Pentecostal Church of Canada, the Assemblee di Dio in Italia continues an aggressive evangelistic program. In 1958 a permanent site for the Bible training school was secured in Rome.

3895   Assemblee di Dio in Italia.
                Statuto delle Assemblee di Dio in Italia. Roma, Tipografia Ferraiolo, 1957. 30p.

                --HISTORY

3896   Fiorentino, Joseph, 1912-
                In the power of His Spirit: "a summary of the Italian Pentecostal movement in the U.S.A. and abroad." Niagara Falls, N.Y., Christian Church of North America; distributed by Niagara Religious Supply Center, 1968. 17p. "The Pentecostal revival in Italy": p. 14-17.

                --PERIODICALS

3897   Il risveglio pentecostale. 1- 1946-
                Roma

ASSEMBLÉES DE DIEU EN FRANCE (1932-   )

        Built on the foundation of the successful ministry of Douglas R. Scott, a semi-literate British evangelist and musician, the Assemblées de Dieu en France is a fellowship of autonomous congregations. With a handful of affiliates in 1932, the group experienced phenomenal growth, reporting 650 churches and 29,000 members thirty-five years later. Headquarters and the editorial offices of Viens et Vois, the official organ, are in Rouen.

                --PERIODICALS

3898   Viens et Vois. 1- 1932-
                Rouen

ASSEMBLÉES DE DIEU EN HAITI (1957-   )

        Although missionaries of the General Council of the Assemblies of God first entered Haiti in 1945, they withdrew in favor of another mission. In 1957 upon the invitation of Haitian nationals, representatives of the American body returned. Soon a thriving work was established. Headquarters are at Petionville, near Port-au-Prince, where the Institut Biblique Louis F. Turnbull, established in 1960, also is located. In 1967 the Assemblées de Dieu en Haiti reported 57 churches and 1,143 members.

--GOVERNMENT

3899 Assemblées de Dieu en Haiti.
Réglement local des Assémblees de Dieu en Haiti. 2. ed. Port-au-Prince, Thèodore, 1957. 28p. "Réglement local des Assemblées de Dieu en Amérique Centrale. Accepté par les Assemblées de Dieu en Haiti." Translated from Spanish by W. Lawrence Perrault in 1948. FU

ASSEMBLÉES DE DIEU EN HAUTE VOLTA (1955-)

An indigenous church since 1955, the Assemblées de Dieu en Haute Volta is the outgrowth of missionary efforts begun by the General Council of the Assemblies of God in 1921, and by the Asemblées de Dieu en France in 1948. In 1967 the group, which ministers to Mossi, Gourounsi, Kasina, Bussansi, and related tribes, reported 199 churches and 16,000 members. A Bible training school, and boarding and day schools have been established, and an ambitious publishing program in French and the tribal languages has been undertaken. Headquarters offices and a printshop are located in Ouagadougou.

--HISTORY

3900 Assembléss de Dieu en Haute Volta.
Les Assemblées de Dieu, Haute Volta, 50eme Anniversaire, 1921-1971. n.p., 1971. 40p. TxWaS

--HYMNS AND SACRED SONGS

3900a Protestant Mission, Ouagadougou, Upper Volta.
Yili sebere; cantiques en Moore et Francais. Tamale, Chana, 1957. 116p. IEN

--MISCELLANEA

3900b Protestant Mission, Ouagadougou, Upper Volta.
More, language of the Mossi tribe; phrase book. Ouagadougou, 19--. 36ℓ. DLC

--PERIODICALS

3901   Mossi land news.   1-   1934-
        Ouagadougou

ASSEMBLÉIAS DE DEUS DO BRASIL (1911-   )

        With 1,400,000 members in 1967, the Assembléias de Deus
is by far the largest evangelical denomination in Brazil.   Built on
the foundation of work begun in 1911 in Para, the movement spread
from northeastern Brazil to other regions of the country in the
1920s and 1930s.   Daniel Berg and Gunnar Vingren, the founders,
were Swedish Baptists who had espoused Pentecostalism in Chicago
in 1910.   Determined to minister to the Brazilian people on their
own terms, they recruited national workers.   In 1930 this group
was augmented by a number of preachers from the Igreja de Cristo.
As a result of the type of workers attracted and the determination
to minister to people where they live, the distribution of the Assembléias membership resembles that of the Brazilian population as a
whole.   Eighty percent of the members live in urban areas, where
93 percent of the people live.   Work is directed from Rio de Janeiro,
where a publishing house and several schools are located, and from
which the Voz Evangélica das Assembléias de Deus, a radio program, is broadcast.

3902   Hoffnagel, Judith (Chambliss)
        Pentecostalism: a revolutionary of conservative move-
        ment?   In Glazier, S. D.   Perspectives on Pentecostalism:
        case studies from the Caribbean and Latin America.   Wash-
        ington, c1980, 111-123.

3903   Read, William Richard, 1923-
        New patterns of church growth in Brazil, by William R.
        Read.   Grand Rapids, Mi., Eerdmans, 1965.   240p.   "The
        Assemblies of God": p. 117-143.   DLC, OkBetC

        --DOCTRINAL AND CONTROVERSIAL WORKS

3904   Ballenger, Albion Fox
        Poder para testemunhar, por A. F. Ballenger.   Belo
        Horizonte, Editora Betania, 1966.   199p.   Translation of
        Power for witnessing.

3905   Brumback, Carl, 1917-
        "Que quer isto dizer?"   Uma reposta Pentecostal a uma
        pergunta Pentecostal.   Rio de Janeiro, Livros Evangélicos,
        1960.   313p.   Translation of What meaneth this?   Translated
        by O. S. Boyer and Joaquim Luiz Dos Santos.

3906   Conde, Emilio

Etapas da vida espiritual. Rio de Janeiro, Casa Publicadora das Assembléias de Deus, 1951. 110p.

3907   Conde, Emilio
Etapas da vida espiritual. 3. ed. Rio de Janeiro, Casa Publicadora das Assembléias de Deus, 1962. 126p.

3908   Conde, Emilio
Igrejas sem brilho. Rio de Janeiro, Casa Publicadora das Assembléias de Deus, 1951. 82p.

3909   Conde, Emilio
Nos domínios da fe. 2. ed. Rio de Janeiro, Casa Publicadora das Assembléias de Deus, 1962. 141p.

3910   Conde, Emilio
Pentecoste para todos; doutrina do Espírito Santo. Rio de Janeiro, Casa Publicadora da Assembléias de Deus, 1951. 109p.

3911   Conde, Emilio
Pentecoste para todos; doutrina do Espírito Santo. 5. ed. Rio de Janeiro, Casa Publicadora da Assembléias de Deus, 19--. 109p.

3912   Conde, Emilio
Tesouro de conhecimentos Bíblicos. Destinado aos ministros de evangelho, professôres da escola dominical e aos amigos da palavra de Deus. Rio de Janeiro, Casa Publicadora das Assembleias de Deus, 19--. 2v.

3913   Conde, Emilio
O testemunho dos séculos: história e doutrina. 3. ed. Rio de Janeiro, Livros Evangélicos, 1960. 194p.

3914   Gee, Donald, 1891-1966.
Acêrca dos dons espirituais; uma série de estudos Biblicos. Traducão de Orlando Boyer. 4. ed. Rio de Janeiro, O. S. Boyer, 1966. 135p. Translation of Concerning spiritual gifts.

3915   Gee, Donald, 1891-1966.
Os dons do ministério de Cristo; continuacão de "Acêrca dos dons espirituais." Rio de Janeiro, Livros Evangélicos, 1961. 99p. Translation of The ministry-gifts of Christ.

3916   Gomes, Francisco Assis, 1909-
O Despertar da aurora. Rio de Janeiro, Casa Publicadora da Assembléia de Deus, 1961. 104p.

3917   Grant, Walter Vinson, 1913-
O Batismo no Espírito Santo; como recebê-lo. Para os que ensinam e os que buscam, por W. V. Grant. 2. ed.

Rio de Janeiro, O. S. Boyer, 1964. 133p.   Translation of
How to receive the Holy Spirit baptism.   Translated by An-
tônio Gilberto de Souza.

3918   Nelson, Peter Christopher, 1868-1942.
         Doutrinas Bíblicas; a exposicão de uma declaracão de
verdades fundamentais.   Traducão de E. Adiens.   Sao Paulo,
Livraria dos Evangélicos, 19--.   99p.   Translation of Bible
doctrines.

3919   Olson, N. Lawrence
         O plano divino através dos séculos; estudo das dispensa-
cões.   Rio de Janeiro, Casa Publicadora das Assembléias de
Deus, 19--.   124p.

3920   Smith, Oswald Jeffrey, 1889-
         Revestidos de poder [por] Oswald J. Smith.   Prefácio
[por] Gipsy Smith.   Traducão [por] Jõao Marques Bentes.
Rio de Janeiro, O. S. Boyer, 1969.   94p.   Translation of
Enduement of power.

3921   Vasconcélos, A. P.
         Paracletologia; uma palavra aos novos convertidos.   Rio
de Janeiro, Casa publicadora da Assembléias de Deus, 1957.
141p.   On cover: Doutrina do Espirito Santo.

--EVANGELISTIC WORK

3922   Boyer, Orla S.
         Esforca-te para ganhar almas; uma série de licoes sobre
a obra de ganhar almas, individualmente, para Cristo, por
Orlando S. Boyer.   8. ed.   Rio de Janeiro, Emprevan Edi-
tôra, 1970.   120p.

--HISTORY

3923   Conde, Emilio
         Historia das Assembleias de Deus no Brasil.   Rio de
Janeiro, Casa Publicadora das Assembleias de Deus, 1960.
355p.   NjPT, WU

--PERIODICALS

3924   O Mensageiro da Paz.   1-   1930-
         Rio de Janeiro.

--NOVA IGUACÚ

3925   Cartaxo Rolim, Francisco

Pentecostalismo. In Revista Eclesiástica Brasileira, 33
(Dec. 1973), 950-964.

--RECIFE

3926   Hoffnagel, Judith (Chambliss)
        The believers: Pentecostalism in a Brazilian city.
        Bloomington, 1978.   x, 285ℓ.   Thesis (Ph. D.)--Indiana Uni-
        versity.   InU

ASSEMBLIES OF GOD, GENERAL COUNCIL (1914-   )
[Also as General Council of the Assemblies of God.]

In November 1914, in an effort to draw together all "Finished
Work" forces of the United States and Canada, an ad hoc committee
consisting of M. M. Pinson, A. P. Collins, H. A. Goss, D. C. O.
Opperman, and E. N. Bell, issued a call in the Word and Witness
for a "General Convention of Pentecostal Saints and Churches of God
in Christ" to meet April 2-12, 1914, in Hot Springs, Arkansas.
The General Council of the Assemblies of God, which was organized
as a result of this meeting, was, the founders said, a fellowship of
independent churches rather than a donomination.   The new organization set up machinery for granting ministerial credentials, but stopped
short of adopting a creedal statement.   Two previously independent
publications, the Word and Witness and the Christian Evangel, then
published respectively at Malvern, Arkansas, and Plainfield, Indiana,
gained official endorsement and re-located jointly in Findlay, Ohio.
The next year the publishing operation again moved, this time to St.
Louis, where it remained until 1918, when Springfield, Missouri, became the headquarters site.

The movement toward tighter central control, as symbolized
by the development of headquarters, had a parallel in the adoption
of a "Statement of Fundamental Truths" in 1916.   Designed to counteract the "new" teaching concerning baptism in Jesus' name, the
Statement also put forth guidelines on the significance of tongues-
speech and sanctification, thereby defining Assemblies teaching on
these subjects.   Eleven years later a similar action occurred in the
government of the General Council when the title of the principal officer was changed from "Chairman" to "General Superintendent."

The General Council of the Assemblies of God has proved an
organizational and doctrinal model for like-minded bodies in Canada,
Australia, New Zealand, Great Britain, and continental Europe, as
well as those growing out of missionary efforts in Asia, Africa, and
Latin America.   The largest white denomination in North America,
it increased from 6,703 members in 118 congregations in 1916, to
932,365 members in 9,410 congregations in 1978.   By the mid-1970s
it was supporting 1,001 American workers in 95 world areas.   The
Pentecostal Evangel has been the official organ since 1919.

3927   Assemblies of God, General Council.
        Assemblies of God. Springfield, Mo. , 1958. 18p. MH-
        AH, PPLT, TxDaM

3928   Assemblies of God, General Council.
        Departmental reports and financial statements. Spring-
        field, Mo. , 1945- . v. [1]- . Biennial. Period covered
        by reports ends Mar. 31. DLC

3929   Assemblies of God, General Council.
        Introducing the Assemblies of God, one of the fastest
        growing churches. Springfield, Mo. , Gospel Publishing House,
        1960. 32p. Cover-title. MH-AH

3930   Assemblies of God, General Council.
        Many members, one body: ministries of the Assemblies
        of God. Springfield, Mo. , 1962. 29p. IEG

3931   Assemblies of God, General Council.
        Minutes. [1st]-31st, 1914-1965. In Library of American
        Church Records, ser. 1, [pt. 1], reel 1-2, microfilm. NN

3932   Assemblies of God, General Council.
        Who we are and what we believe; presenting the Assem-
        blies of God. Springfield, Mo. , 19--. 23p.

3933   Assemblies assemble.
        In Christianity Today, 17 (Sept. 14, 1973), 45-46. On
        the General Council meeting of the Assemblies of God in
        Miami in August.

3934   Assemblies of God: record growth.
        In Christianity Today, 19 (Sept. 12, 1975), 62. On thirty-
        sixth General Council meeting in Denver in August.

3935   Bufkin, Robert Lee
        The Assembly of God: movement along the continuum
        from cult to church. Fayetteville, 1968. 108ℓ . Thesis
        (M. A.)--University of Arkansas. ArU

3936   Carlson, Guy Raymond, 1918-
        Our faith and fellowship, by G. Raymond Carlson. Spring-
        field, Mo. , Gospel Publishing House, 1977. 128p. (Radiant
        books.) Adapted from Our faith and fellowship, by Ralph W.
        Harris. TxWB

3937   Daane, James, 1914-
        Making non-pacifism official. In Christianity Today, 11
        (Sept. 15, 1967), 46. On the action of the biennial General
        Council of the Assemblies of God, meeting in Long Beach,
        California, regarding military service.

3938   Daane, James, 1914-

Taking stock [by] J. D. In Christianity Today, 7 (Sept. 13, 1963), 36. On the thirtieth biennial General Council of the Assemblies of God in Memphis in August.

3939   Faupel, Charles Edward, 1951-
Bridge-burning: a factor contributing to religiosity, by Charles E. Faupel. Mount Pleasant, 1978. viii,106ℓ. Thesis (M. A.)--Central Michigan University. MiMtpT

3940   Friedrich, Robert E.
Assemblies of God: fair skies in Dallas [by] Robert E. Friedrich, Jr. In Christianity Today, 13 (Sept. 26, 1969), 41. On General Council meeting in Dallas.

3941   Frodsham, Stanley Howard, 1882-1969.
Assemblies of God [by] Stanley H. Frodsham. In New Republic, 104 (June 16, 1941), 827. Letter to the editor disavowing anti-Semitism.

3942   Gaddis, Merrill Elmer, 1891-
Christian perfectionism in America. Chicago, 1929. viii,589ℓ. Thesis (Ph. D.)--University of Chicago. On Assemblies of God: ℓ. 480-482. ICU

3943   Gaustad, Edwin Scott, 1923-
Historical atlas of religion in America. New York, Harper & Row, 1962. xii,179p. "Assemblies of God": p. 122-123.

3944   The General Council of the Assemblies of God.
In Sunday: the Magazine for the Lord's Day, 60 (July-Aug. 1974), 4, 14.

3945   Gross, Donald George, 1926-
A study of norms of conduct in the Assemblies of God, by D. George Gross. Springfield, Mo., 1963. v,67ℓ. Thesis (M. A.)--Central Bible Institute.

3946   How to submit.
In Christianity Today, 20 (Sept. 24, 1976), 59. On annual meeting of the General Presbytery of the Assemblies of God where criticism of the "discipleship and submission" movement was made.

3947   Moore, Everett Leroy, 1918-
Handbook of Pentecostal denominations in the United States. Pasadena, Ca., 1954. vii,346ℓ. Thesis (M. A.)--Pasadena College. "Assemblies of God": ℓ. 23-56. CSdP

3948   Pentecost revisited.
In Christianity Today, 12 (Nov. 24, 1967), 39. On proposed evaluation of the Pentecostal movement being endorsed by the General Council of the Assemblies of God.

3949   Pentecostal landmark.
            In Christianity Today, 8 (June 19, 1964), 34.   On fiftieth
        anniversary convention of the Assemblies of God, held in
        Springfield, Missouri in April.

3950   Pentecostal social credo.
            In Christianity Today, 12 (Sept. 13, 1968), 55.   State-
        ment by the General Presbytery of the General Council of
        the Assemblies of God on Christian social action.

3951   A "plan" for Assemblies.
            In Christianity Today, 12 (Sept. 27, 1968), 28.   On Coun-
        cil on Evangelism, held in St. Louis.

3952   Plowman, Edward Earl, 1931-
            Assemblies of God: a leader upheld [by] Edward E.
        Plowman.   In Christianity Today, 21 (Sept. 9, 1977), 64-69.

3953   Shewmaker, Kenneth Lee, 1931-
            Authoritarianism in a religious sect.   Norman, 1956.
        v, 43ℓ.   Thesis (M. S.)--University of Oklahoma.   OkU

3954   Sizelove, Rachel A.
            A sparkling fountain for the whole earth [by] Rachel A.
        Sizelove.   Long Beach, Ca. , 19--.   folder (11p.) Includes
        prophecy concerning the importance of Springfield, Missouri,
        in the Pentecostal movement.

3955   Stemme, Harry A.
            The faith of a Pentecostal Christian: a personal testi-
        mony, by Harry A. Stemme.   Milwaukee, Word & Witness
        Publishing Co. , c1938.   46p.   "The Assemblies of God":
        p. 35-46.   TxWaS

3956   Thorkelson, Willmar L. , 1918-
            Charismatic sweep in Minneapolis [by] Willmar L. Thor-
        kelson.   In Christianity Today, 16 (Sept. 15, 1972), 50-51.
        On the Assemblies of God Council on Spiritual Life, Aug. 14-
        18, and the First International Lutheran Conference on the
        Holy Spirit, Aug. 8-12.

3957   Tinney, James Stephen
            The Assemblies' line [by] James S. Tinney.   In Chris-
        tianity Today, 15 (Sept. 10, 1971), 45-46.   On the General
        Council of the Assemblies of God meeting in Kansas City in
        August.

3958   Tinney, James Stephen
            Establishmentarianism [by] James S. Tinney.   In Chris-
        tianity Today, 23 (Sept. 21, 1979), 53.   On General Council
        of the Assemblies of God, held in Baltimore in August.

3959   U. S. Bureau of the Census.

Census of religious bodies: 1926. Assemblies of God, General Council. Statistics, denominational history, doctrine, and organization. Washington, Government Printing Office, 1928. 11p. DLC, NNUT

3960 U.S. Bureau of the Census.
Census of religious bodies: 1936. Assemblies of God, General Council. Statistics, denominational history, doctrine, and organization. Washington, Government Printing Office, 1939. iv, 10p. NNUT

3961 Ward, Charles Morse, 1909-
Assemblies of God, by C. M. Ward. Springfield, Mo., c1956. 20p.

3962 Winehouse, Irwin, 1922-
The Assemblies of God: a popular survey, by Irwin Winehouse. With an introduction by J. Roswell Flower. New York, Vantage Press, 1959. 224p. DLC, NNUT, TxWaS

--BIOGRAPHY

3963 Assemblies of God, General Council.
The prayer fellowship. Springfield, Mo., Gospel Publishing House, 19--. 128p.

--CATECHISMS AND CREEDS

3964 Assemblies of God, General Council.
Statement of fundamental truths, Assemblies of God. In Hardon, J. A. The spirit and origins of American Protestantism: a source book in its creeds. Dayton, Oh., 1968, 250-254.

3965 Lane, Mrs. A. C.
Bible truths: a scripture course for boys and girls. Prepared by Mrs. A. C. Lane. Springfield, Mo., Gospel Publishing House, 19--. 47p.

--CHARITIES

3967 Baar, Anne
The Hillcrest story. Springfield, Mo., Gospel Publishing House, 1969. 103p.

--CHURCH EXTENSION

3968 Assemblies of God, General Council.
Higher goals: National Church Growth Convention digest.

Editorial committee: Gwen Jones, chairman, Ron Rowden,
Mel Surface. Springfield, Mo., Gospel Publishing House,
c1978. viii, 346p. "A condensation of plenary sessions and
seminars conducted at the National Church Growth Convention
in Kansas City, Missouri, Aug. 15-17, 1978." DLC

3969   Hoover, Elva (Johnson)
        Mission U.S.A., by Elva Johnson. Springfield, Mo.,
Gospel Publishing House, c1957. 120p.

3970   Johnson, Daniel E.
        Building with buses [by] Daniel E. Johnson.   Grand Rapids,
Mi., Baker Book House, 1974. 134p. NNUT

3971   Johnson, Daniel E.
        Building with buses [by] Daniel E. Johnson. Stow, Oh.,
New Hope Press, c1974. 33p.

3972   Lebsack, Leland V.
        Ten at the top, by Lee Lesback [!]. Stowe, Oh., New
Hope Press, 1974. 132p. "How 10 of America's largest
Assemblies of God grew." TxWaS

                    --CHURCH WORK

3973   Assemblies of God, General Council.
        How to build and maintain the church library. Springfield,
Mo., 19--. 14p. IKON

3974   Dresselhaus, Richard L.
        The deacon and his ministry [by] Richard L. Dresselhaus.
Springfield, Mo., Gospel Publishing House, c1977. 96p. DLC

3975   Stewart, Marjorie, 1925-
        Women in neighborhood evangelism. Springfield, Mo.,
Gospel Publishing House, c1978. 124p. (Radiant books.)
DLC

                    --CLERGY

3976   Assemblies of God, General Council.
        Theological and functional dimensions or ordination, with
an official position paper on the Assemblies of God view.
Springfield, Mo., Gospel Publishing House, c1977. 59p. DLC

3976a   Harris, Willie Charles, 1927-
        The use of selected leadership, personality, motivational
and demographical variables in the identification of successful
ministers. Tulsa, 1972. 194ℓ. Thesis (Ed.D.)--University
of Tulsa. On graduates of Central Bible College between 1963
and 1970 listed as ministers of the General Council of the Assemblies of God in 1971. OkTU

3977   Thee, Francis Charles Rudolph, 1936-
       The usefulness of Greek in the ministry of the Central
       Bible Institute alumni, by Francis Thee. Springfield, Mo.,
       1959. 86ℓ. Thesis (M.A.)--Central Bible Institute.

--CONTROVERSIAL LITERATURE

3978   Assemblies of God, General Council. Executive Presbytery.
       Official statement on the charismatic movement. In
       Assemblies of God, General Council. Live in the Spirit.
       Springfield, Mo., 1972, 335-336.

--DEVOTIONAL LITERATURE

3979   Bostrom, John H., 1899-
       "Blow upon my garden!" By John H. Bostrom. San
       Gabriel, Ca., Bostrom Publications, 1951. 89p.

3980   Flower, Alice (Reynolds), 1890-
       The altogether lovely one. 4th ed. n.p., 19--. 15p.
       Poems.

3981   Flower, Alice (Reynolds), 1890-
       From under the threshold: devotional heart talks on
       every-day Christianity. Rev. ed. Springfield, Mo., Gospel
       Publishing House, c1947. 111p. OkTOr

3982   Flower, Alice (Reynolds), 1890-
       Threads of gold. Springfield, Mo., Gospel Publishing
       House, 1949. 150p.

3983   Hembree, Charles Ron, 1938-
       Songs in a strange land; inspiring devotionals with Charles
       R. Hembree. Springfield, Mo., Gospel Publishing House,
       1970. 92p.

3984   Lindblad, Frank V.
       A few notes on prayer, by Frank Lindblad. Springfield,
       Mo., Gospel Publishing House, c1927. 64p. DLC

3985   Pearlman, Myer, 1898-1943.
       Windows into the future; devotional studies in the book of
       Revelation. Springfield, Mo., Gospel Publishing House, c1941.
       176p. DLC

3986   Yeomans, Lilian Barbara, 1861-
       The hiding place, by Lilian B. Yeomans. Springfield,
       Mo., Gospel Publishing House, 1940. 64p. DLC

--DIRECTORIES

3987   Assemblies of God, General Council.
        [Official lists of ministers and missionaries and direc-
        tories of churches], 1941-1965. In Library of American
        Church Records, ser. 1, [pt. 1], reel no. 4-7, microfilm.
        NN

--DOCTRINAL AND CONTROVERSIAL WORKS

3988   Anderson, E. Howard
        Receive the Holy Spirit and power.   How you can receive
        the gift of the Holy Spirit and power by faith.   By E. Howard
        Anderson.   Stamford, Ct., 196-.   64p.

3989   Armstrong, Hart Reid, 1912-
        Divine healing, by Hart R. Armstrong.   Springfield, Mo.,
        Correspondence School of the General Council of the Assem-
        blies of God, 19--.   2v.

3990   Armstrong, Hart Reid, 1912-
        Even so come, by Hart R. Armstrong.   Springfield, Mo.,
        Gospel Publishing House, c1950.   128p.

3991   Armstrong, Hart Reid, 1912-
        To those who are left, by Hart R. Armstrong.   Spring-
        field, Mo., 1950.   64p.

3992   Armstrong, Hart Reid, 1912-
        War against God, by Hart R. Armstrong.   Springfield,
        Mo., Gospel Publishing House, 1951.   79p.

3993   Ashcroft, James Robert
        The sequence of the supernatural, and other essays on the
        Spirit-filled life [by] J. Robert Ashcroft.   Springfield, Mo.,
        Gospel Publishing House, 1972.   79p.   TxWaS

3994   Ashcroft, James Robert
        Ways of understanding God's Word, by J. Robert Ashcroft.
        Springfield, Mo., Gospel Publishing House, c1960.   103p.
        DLC

3995   Barham, Wendell S.
        Simple steps to the baptism of the Holy Spirit, by W. S.
        Barham.   San Antonio, Tx., 19--.   19p.   TxWaS

3996   Barney, Kenneth D., 1921-
        Ephesians; teacher's manual.   Springfield, Mo., Gospel
        Publishing House, 1961.   96p.   (Great themes of the Bible.)

3997   Barney, Kenneth D., 1921-
        A faith to live by [by] Kenneth D. Barney.   Springfield,

Mo., Gospel Publishing House, c1976.   125p.   (Radiant books.) DLC

3998   Barney, Kenneth D., 1921-
        The fellowship of the Holy Spirit [by] Kenneth D. Barney.
        Springfield, Mo., Gospel Publishing House, c1977.   96p.
        (Radiant books.)

3999   Barney, Kenneth D., 1921-
        Freedom, a guarantee for everybody; adapted from
        Romans by G. Raymond Carlson [by] Kenneth D. Barney.
        Springfield, Mo., Gospel Publishing House, c1975.   125p.
        (Radiant books.) DLC

4000   Barney, Kenneth D., 1921-
        If you love me [by] Kenneth D. Barney. Springfield,
        Mo., Gospel Publishing House, c1977.   126p.   (Radiant
        books.) "Adapted from Practical Christian living, by Wildon
        Colbaugh." DLC

4001   Barney, Kenneth D., 1921-
        It began in an upper room [by] Kenneth D. Barney.
        Springfield, Mo., Gospel Publishing House, c1979.   128p.
        DLC

4002   Barney, Kenneth D., 1921-
        You'd better believe it! [By] Kenneth D. Barney.
        Adapted from The fundamentals of the faith by Donald Johns.
        Springfield, Mo., Gospel Publishing House, c1975.   126p.
        (Radiant books.) DLC

4003   Bates, A. C.
        The doctrine of the Holy Spirit, by A. C. Bates.   Fort
        Worth, Tx., Manney Printing Co., 19--.   53p.   TxWaS

4004   Bell, Eudorus N., 1866-1923.
        Questions and answers, by E. N. Bell. Springfield, Mo.,
        Gospel Publishing House, 1923.   118p.

4005   Bethany, Edgar W.
        The seven spirits of God, by Edgar Bethany.   n.p.,
        196-.   32p.

4006   Bible. N.T. English. 1957. Worrell.
        The New Testament of our Lord and Saviour Jesus Christ;
        a translation by A. S. Worrell, with notes by the translator.
        Springfield, Mo., Gospel Publishing House, 1957.   iv, 396,
        26p.

4007   Bible. N.T. Acts. English. 1971. Today's English.
        Spirit: good news in action. Springfield, Mo., Assem-
        blies of God, c1971.   106p. "Published for Assemblies of
        God by the American Bible Society."

4008   Bicket, Zenas Johan, 1932-
       Walking in the Spirit; studies in the fruit of the Spirit
       [by] Zenas J. Bicket.   Springfield, Mo., Gospel Publishing
       House, 1977.   94p.   (Radiant books.)   "Originally published
       in the Paraclete."

4009   Bicket, Zenas Johan, 1932-
       We hold these truths [by] Zenas J. Bicket.   Springfield,
       Mo., Gospel Publishing House, 1978.   128p.   DLC

4010   Bostrom, John H., 1899-
       The causes of sickness and how to get well, by John H.
       Bostrom.   Glendale, Ca., Printed by the Church Press,
       Farson & Sons, c1940.   176p.   DLC

4011   Bowman, Elizabeth
       Radiocarbon dating and the word of God.   n.p., c1953.
       20p.

4012   Boyd, Frank Mathews, 1883-
       Ages and dispensations, by Frank M. Boyd.   Springfield,
       Mo., Gospel Publishing House, c1955.   106p.

4013   Boyd, Frank Mathews, 1883-
       Book of the prophet Ezekiel.   Springfield, Mo., Gospel
       Publishing House, 1951.   232p.   DLC

4014   Boyd, Frank Mathews, 1883-
       Book of the prophet Isaiah.   Springfield, Mo., Gospel
       Publishing House, 1950.   248p.   DLC

4015   Boyd, Frank Mathews, 1883-
       The books of the Minor prophets.   Springfield, Mo.,
       Gospel Publishing House, 1954, c1953.   249p.   DLC

4016   Boyd, Frank Mathews, 1883-
       The budding fig tree.   Springfield, Mo., Gospel Publish-
       ing House, c1925.   123p.   (On cover: Pulpit and pew, full
       Gospel series.)   DLC

4017   Boyd, Frank Mathews, 1883-
       Christ; teacher's manual.   Springfield, Mo., Gospel Pub-
       lishing House, 196-.   96p.   (Great themes of the Christian
       faith.)   Cover-title.

4018   Boyd, Frank Mathews, 1883-
       God's wonderful book; the origin, lineage and influence of
       the Bible, by Frank M. Boyd.   Springfield, Mo., Gospel Pub-
       lishing House, c1933.   136p.

4019   Boyd, Frank Mathews, 1883-
       Hebrews and the general epistles, by Frank M. Boyd.
       Springfield, Mo., Berean School of the Bible, 1973.   350p.

4020   Boyd, Frank Mathews, 1883-
        The Holy Spirit; a teacher's manual, by Frank M. Boyd.
Springfield, Mo. , Gospel Publishing House, 195-. 96p.
(Great themes of the Christian faith.)

4021   Boyd, Frank Mathews, 1883-
        Introduction to prophecy, by Frank M. Boyd. Springfield,
Mo. , Gospel Publishing House, 1948. 153p.

4022   Boyd, Frank Mathews, 1883-
        The Kenosis (self-emptying) of the Lord Jesus Christ.
Foreword by J. Narver Gortner. San Francisco, c1947.
38p.

4023   Boyd, Frank Mathews, 1883-
        Old Testament studies, by Frank M. Boyd. Springfield,
Mo. , Berean School of the Bible, 1967. 2v.

4024   Boyd, Frank Mathews, 1883-
        Prophetic light, by Frank M. Boyd. Springfield, Mo. ,
Correspondence School of the General Council of the Assemblies of God, 1948. 77p.

4025   Boyd, Frank Mathews, 1883-
        Prophetic light, by Frank M. Boyd. Springfield, Mo. ,
Berean School of the Bible, 1970. 171p.

4026   Boyd, Frank Mathews, 1883-
        Signs of the times, by Frank M. Boyd. Springfield, Mo. ,
Gospel Publishing House, 1950. 40p.

4027   Boyd, Frank Mathews, 1883-
        The Spirit works today; a Biblical study of the person
and work of the Holy Spirit, by Frank M. Boyd. New ed.
Springfield, Mo. , Gospel Publishing House, c1970. 136p.
First published under title: The Holy Spirit. TxWaS

4028   Boyd, Frank Mathews, 1883-
        Studies in the Revelation of Jesus Christ, by Frank M.
Boyd. Springfield, Mo. , Berean School of the Bible, 1967.
278p.

4029   Brandt, Robert L.
        One way [by] Robert L. Brandt. Springfield, Mo. , Gos-
pel Publishing House, c1977. 128p. (Radiant books.) DLC

4030   Brandt, Robert L.
        The Pentecostal promise [by] Robert L. Brandt. Spring-
field, Mo. , Gospel Publishing House, 1972. 47p. "Previously
published in the Pentecostal Evangel. "

4031   Brandt, Robert L.
        Spiritual gifts, by Robert L. Brandt. Brussels, Inter-
national Correspondence Institute, 1978. 176p.

4032   Brankel, Donald L.
        There is a river, by Don Brankel. n. p. , 1972.   54p.
        TxWaS

4033   Brumback, Carl, 1917-
        Accent on the Ascension! Springfield, Mo. , Gospel Pub-
        lishing House, 1955.   151p.   DLC, TxWaS

4034   Brumback, Carl, 1917-
        "What meaneth this?" A Pentecostal answer to a Pente-
        costal question. Springfield, Mo. , Gospel Publishing House,
        1947.   348p. DLC, NNUT, TxWaS

4035   Buntain, Daniel Newton, 1888-1955.
        The Holy Ghost and fire [by] D. N. Buntain. Springfield,
        Mo. , Gospel Publishing House, 1956.   97p.   KyLxCB, NcD

4036   Cantelon, Willard, 1915-
        The baptism in the Holy Spirit. What is it? Is it for
        today? Is it for everyone? What is the evidence? Spring-
        field, Mo. , Gospel Publishing House, c1951.   34p.   First
        issued in 1951 under title: The Baptism of the Holy Spirit.

4037   Cantelon, Willard, 1915-
        The baptism in the Holy Spirit. Lake Worth, Fl. , Vic-
        toria Press, 19--.   33p.   First issued in 1951 under title:
        The baptism of the Holy Spirit.

4038   Cantelon, Willard, 1915-
        The baptism of the Holy Spirit. What is it? Is it for
        today? Is it for everyone? What is the evidence? Spring-
        field, Mo. , Acme Printing Service, 1951.   33p.   CMlG,
        TxWaS

4039   Cantelon, Willard, 1915-
        El bautismo en el Espíritu Santo. Ed. 3. Springfield,
        Mo. , Editorial Vida, 1955.   46p.

4040   Carlson, Guy Raymond, 1918-
        The Acts story, by G. Raymond Carlson. Springfield,
        Mo. , Gospel Publishing House, 1978.   127p.   Adapted from
        Acts, by Emil Balliet.

4041   Carlson, Guy Raymond, 1918-
        How to study the Bible; student's manual, by G. Raymond
        Carlson. Springfield, Mo. , Gospel Publishing House, 1964.
        40p.   (Great themes of the Christian faith.) Cover title.

4042   Carlson, Guy Raymond, 1918-
        The life worth living [by] G. Raymond Carlson. Spring-
        field, Mo. , Gospel Publishing House, c1975.   127p.   (Radiant
        books.) "Adapted from Gospel of John, by Stanley M. Hor-
        ton. "

4043   Carlson, Guy Raymond, 1918-
          Preparing to teach God's word [by] G. Raymond Carlson.
       Springfield, Mo. , Gospel Publishing House, 1975.   128p.
       DLC

4044   Carlson, Guy Raymond, 1918-
          Romans; teacher's manual, by G. Raymond Carlson.
       Springfield, Mo. , Gospel Publishing House, 1963.   96p.

4045   Carlson, Guy Raymond, 1918-
          Salvation: what the Bible teaches; teacher's manual, by
       G. Raymond Carlson.   Springfield, Mo. , Gospel Publishing
       House, 1963.   96p.   (Great themes of the Christian faith.)

4046   Carlson, Guy Raymond, 1918-
          Salvation: what the Bible teaches;   student's manual, by
       G. Raymond Carlson.   Springfield, Mo. , Gospel Publishing
       House, 1963.   40p.   (Great themes of the Christian faith.)

4047   Carlson, Guy Raymond, 1918-
          Spiritual dynamics: the Holy Spirit in human experience,
       by G. Raymond Carlson.   Springfield, Mo. , Gospel Publishing
       House, 1976.   125p.   (Radiant books.)   DLC

4048   Carter, Howard, 1891-1971.
          The gifts of the Holy Spirit.   Minneapolis, Northern Gos-
       pel Publishing House, 1946.   116p.

4049   Carter, Howard, 1891-1971.
          Spiritual gifts and their operation; anecdotal lectures.
       Springfield, Mo. , Gospel Publishing House, 1968.   96p.
       MnCS

4050   Clark, Earl W. ,   -1933.
          The need of the hour: healing for the body.   Rev. and
       enlarged ed.   Springfield, Mo. , Gospel Publishing House,
       1924.   61p.

4051   Claycomb, Kenneth L.
          Studies concerning the Holy Spirit, by K. L. Claycomb.
       Tallahassee, Fl. , 1971.   74p.

4052   Cockerell, J. M.
          How to be baptized in the Holy Ghost, by J. M. Cockerell.
       Breckenridge, Tx. , c1935.

4053   Collins, Millard E.
          Voices of God, by M. E. Collins.   Fort Worth, Tx. ,
       Manney Printing Co. , 1968.   159p.   TxWaS

4054   Cummings, Robert Wallace, 1892-
          Gethsemane, by Robert W. Cummings.   Springfield, Mo. ,
       Cain Printing Co. , c1944.   64p.

4055   Cunningham, Robert C.
        Filled with the Spirit; what the scriptures say about the
Pentecostal baptism [by] Robert C. Cunningham.   Springfield,
Mo. , Gospel Publishing House, c1972.

4056   Cunningham, Robert C.
        Getting together with Luke and Acts; a guide for group
Bible study, by Robert C. Cunningham.   Springfield, Mo. ,
Gospel Publishing House, 1972.   47p.

4057   Duncan, Mildred H.
        A revelation of end-time Babylon; a verse by verse ex-
position of the book of Revelation, by Mildred H. Duncan.
Edgement, N. D. , 1950.   286p.

4058   Erickson, Clifton O.
        Supernatural deliverance, by Clifton O. Erickson.   Wenat-
chee, Wa. , c1950.   88p.   TxWaS

4059   Evans, William Irvin, 1887-1954.
        This river must flow; selections from the writings and
sermons of W. I. Evans.   Springfield, Mo. , Gospel Publishing House, 1954.   94p.   TxWaS

4060   Ford, Charles William, 1926-
        How to study the Bible: new directions for studying the
word of God [by] Charles W. Ford.   Springfield, Mo. , Gospel
Publishing House, c1978.   128p.   (Radiant books.)   "Adapted
from How to study the Bible, by G. Raymond Carlson. "
        _____.   Teacher's guide.   Springfield, Mo. , Gospel
Publishing House, c1978.   48p.

4061   Ford, Charles William, 1926-
        The inspired scriptures [by] Charles W. Ford.   Spring-
field, Mo. , Gospel Publishing House, c1978.   127p.   (Radiant
books.)   "Adapted from The inspired scriptures, by G. Raymond Carlson. "
        _____.   Teacher's guide.   Springfield, Mo. , Gospel
Publishing House, c1978.   47p.

4062   Foster, Atwood, 1908-
        The magnificent Messiah.   Portland, Or. , Ecclesiastical
Press, c1977.   xvii,334p.   DLC

4063   Frodsham, Stanley Howard, 1882-1969.
        The coming crises and the coming Christ, by Stanley H.
Frodsham.   Springfield, Mo. , Gospel Publishing House, 1936.
64p.   CLamB

4064   Frodsham, Stanley Howard, 1882-1969.
        The life of joy.   Springfield, Mo. , Gospel Publishing
House, 1938.   62p.

4065   Frodsham, Stanley Howard, 1882-1969.
            Rivers of living water; the secret of perpetual Pentecost.
        Springfield, Mo. , Gospel Publishing House, 1934. 80p.
        C LamB

4066   Frodsham, Stanley Howard, 1882-1969.
            Spirit filled, led, and taught; a word to those who desire
        to live a victorious life. Springfield, Mo. , Gospel Publishing
        House, 1936. 61p. TxWaS

4067   Frodsham, Stanley Howard, 1882-
            "Things which must shortly come to pass. " Springfield,
        Mo. , Gospel Publishing House, c1928. 117p. C LamB

4068   Gee, Donald, 1891-1966.
            After Pentecost. Springfield, Mo. , Gospel Publishing
        House, c1945. 111p. Sequel to Pentecost. MSohG, TxWaS

4069   Gee, Donald, 1891-1966.
            All with one accord. Springfield, Mo. , Gospel Publishing
        House, 1961. 61p. TxWaS

4070   Gee, Donald, 1891-1966.
            "Concerning spiritual gifts"; a series of Bible studies.
        Springfield, Mo. , Gospel Publishing House, 1937. xi, 109p.
        C LamB

4071   Gee, Donald, 1891-1966.
            "Concerning spiritual gifts"; a series of Bible studies.
        Springfield, Mo. , Gospel Publishing House, 1947. 119p.
        MnCS

4072   Gee, Donald, 1891-1966.
            Concerning spiritual gifts; a series of Bible studies.
        Rev. ed. Springfield, Mo. , Gospel Publishing House, 1972.
        119p. TxWaS

4073   Gee, Donald, 1891-1966.
            The fruit of the Spirit; a Pentecostal study. Springfield,
        Mo. , Gospel Publishing House, c1928. 95p.

4074   Gee, Donald, 1891-1966.
            The fruit of the Spirit. Springfield, Mo. , Gospel Pub-
        lishing House, 1975, c1928. 78p. (Radiant books.)

4075   Gee, Donald, 1891-1966.
            Fruitful or barren? Springfield, Mo. , Gospel Publishing
        House, 1961. 89p. "Studies in the fruit of the Spirit. "

4076   Gee, Donald, 1891-1966.
            God's grace and power for today; the practical experience
        of being filled with the Holy Ghost. Springfield, Mo. , Gospel
        Publishing House, 1936. 44p.

4077   Gee, Donald, 1891-1966.
        God's grace and power for today; the practical experience
of being filled with the Holy Spirit. Springfield, Mo. , Gospel
Publishing House, 1972, c1936. 48p.

4078   Gee, Donald, 1891-1966.
        God's great gift; seven talks together about the Holy
Spirit. Springfield, Mo. , Gospel Publishing House, 19--.
63p.

4079   Gee, Donald, 1891-1966.
        Is it God? Tests for evaluating the supernatural.
Springfield, Mo. , Gospel Publishing House, 1972. 30p.
Published in 1970 in Paraclete as "Trying the spirits. "

4080   Gee, Donald, 1891-1966.
        The ministry-gifts of Christ. Springfield, Mo. , Gospel
Publishing House, c1930. 110p. Sequel to Concerning spiritual gifts. DLC, MSohG

4081   Gee, Donald, 1891-1966.
        A new discovery. Springfield, Mo. , Gospel Publishing
House, 197-, c1932. 95p. First published under title:
Pentecost. OSW, TxWaS

4082   Gee, Donald, 1891-1966.
        Now that you've been baptized in the Spirit. Springfield,
Mo. , Gospel Publishing House, 1972. 175p. (Radiant books.)
        Contents: pt. 1. Toward Christian maturity. -pt. 2. Gifts
for the church. Pt. 1 first published in 1945 as After Pentecost; pt. 2, in 1940 as The ministry gifts of Christ. KyLoL,
MiBsA, TxWaS

4083   Gee, Donald, 1891-1966.
        Pentecost. Springfield, Mo. , Gospel Publishing House,
c1932. 95p. MnCS, MSohG, TxWaS

4084   Gee, Donald, 1891-1966, ed.
        The phenomena of Pentecost. Springfield, Mo. , Gospel
Publishing House, 1931. 61p. Essays by Donald Gee, Myer
Pearlman, P. C. Nelson, George Jeffreys, and D. W. Kerr.

4085   Gee, Donald, 1891-1966.
        Proverbs for Pentecost. Springfield, Mo. , Gospel Pub-
lishing House, 1936. 83p.

4086   Gee, Donald, 1891-1966.
        Temptations of the Spirit-filled Christ. Springfield, Mo. ,
Gospel Publishing House, c1966. 39p. MnCS

4087   Gee, Donald, 1891-1966.
        This is the way. Springfield, Mo. , Gospel Publishing
House, 1975. 64p. (Radiant books.) First published in

1936 under title: Studies in guidance.

4088   Gee, Donald, 1891-1966.
        Toward Pentecostal unity. Springfield, Mo., Gospel
Publishing House, 19--. 61p. (Radiant books.) First published in 1961 under title: All with one accord. KyWAT

4089   Gee, Donald, 1891-1966.
        A way to escape. Springfield, Mo., Gospel Publishing
House, c1966. 64p. (Radiant books.) First published under
title: Temptations of the Spirit-filled Christ. KyWAT

4090   Gee, Donald, 1891-1966.
        A word to the wise. Springfield, Mo., Gospel Publishing
House, 1975. 78p. First published in 1936 under title:
Proverbs for Pentecost.

4091   Gortner, John Narver, 1874-
        Studies in Daniel, by J. Narver Gortner. With an introd.
by Ernest S. Williams. Springfield, Mo., Gospel Publishing
House, c1948. 204p. DLC

4092   Gortner, John Narver, 1874-
        Studies in Revelation, by J. Narver Gortner. With an
introd. by Frank M. Boyd. Springfield, Mo., Gospel Publishing House, c1948. 276p. DLC

4093   Gortner, John Narver, 1874-
        Water baptism and the Trinity. Studies by J. Narver
Gortner, Donald Gee [and] Hy Pickering. Springfield, Mo.,
Gospel Publishing House, 19--. 62p.

4094   Graves, Arthur H., 1902-1973.
        First and Second Peter; student's manual, by Arthur H.
Graves. Springfield, Mo., Gospel Publishing House, c1965.
96p. (Great themes of the Christian faith.)

4094a   Graves, Arthur H., 1902-1973.
        First and Second Peter; teacher's manual, by Arthur H.
Graves. Springfield, Mo., Gospel Publishing House, c1965.
40p. (Great themes of the Christian faith.)

4095   Hall, John G.
        Dispensations, by John G. Hall. Springfield, Mo., Gos-
pel Publishing House, c1957. viii, 157p. CCmS

4096   Hall, John G.
        Prophecy marches on, by John G. Hall. Springfield,
Mo., Gospel Publishing House, 1962. 2v. CCmS

4097   Hardt, Howard E.
        Christ is the answer, by H. E. Hardt. Dallas, 19--.
150p. TxWaS

4097a   Hardt, Howard E.
            Christ is the answer; an amazing discovery of how to
        enjoy abundant life and happiness, by Howard E. Hardt.
        York, Pa. , 19--.   129p.

4098   Harris, Charles, 1927-
            Proofs of Christianity [by] Charles Harris.   Springfield,
        Mo. , Gospel Publishing House, c1977.   125p.   (Radiant
        books.)   "Adapted from Proofs of Christianity, by Donald F.
        Johns. "   DLC

4099   Harris, Ralph William, 1912-
            The cults; teacher's manual, by Ralph W. Harris.
        Springfield, Mo. , Gospel Publishing House, 1962.   96p.

4100   Harris, Ralph William, 1912-
            The Holy Spirit; student's manual, by Ralph W. Harris.
        Springfield, Mo. , Gospel Publishing House, 19--.   40p.
        (Great themes of the Christian faith.)

4101   Harris, Ralph William, 1912-
            The land of the book, by Ralph W. Harris.   Springfield,
        Mo. , Gospel Publishing House, 1955.   64p.

4102   Harris, Ralph William, 1912-
            Old Testament types, by Ralph W. Harris.   Springfield,
        Mo. , Gospel Publishing House, 1965.   96p.

4103   Harris, Ralph William, 1912-
            Spoken by the Spirit; documented accounts of "other
        tongues" from Arabic to Zulu [by] Ralph W. Harris.   Spring-
        field, Mo. , Gospel Publishing House, 1973.   128p.   DLC,
        TxWaS

4104   Harvey, William Lee, 1880-
            Christianity in action; a lawyer's search for Christian
        reality.   Make deeds of your creeds.   Translate God's word
        into matters of practice.   By William L. Harvey.   Spring-
        field, Mo. , Gospel Publishing House, c1954.   xx, 232p.

4105   Hauff, Louis Harold, 1910-
            Israel in Bible prophecy, by Louis H. Hauff.   Spring-
        field, Mo. , Gospel Publishing House, 1961.   81p.

4106   Hauff, Louis Harold, 1910-
            Israel in Bible prophecy, by Louis H. Hauff.   Spring-
        field, Mo. , Gospel Publishing House, 1974.   v, 84p.   First
        published in 1961.

4107   Hibbard, J. C.
            Are the days of miracles past?   By J. C. Hibbard.
        Dallas, 19--.   171p.   TxWaS

4108   Hodges, Melvin Lyle, 1909-
        The church. Original text [by] Melvin L. Hodges and
        Ralph D. Williams; programmed by L. Jeter Walker. Spring-
        field, Mo. , International Correspondence Institute, 1970.
        222p.

4109   Hodges, Melvin Lyle, 1909-
        Spiritual gifts, by Melvin L. Hodges. Springfield, Mo. ,
        Gospel Publishing House, 1964. 28p. MnCS

4110   Hodges, Melvin Lyle, 1909-
        A theology of the church and its mission: a Pentecostal
        perspective [by] Melvin L. Hodges. Springfield, Mo. , Gos-
        pel Publishing House, c1977. 185p. DLC

4111   Hodges, Melvin Lyle, 1909-
        When the Spirit comes [by] Melvin L. Hodges. Spring-
        field, Mo. , Gospel Publishing House, c1972. 46p. "Chap-
        ters ... previously published in Paraclete and the Pentecostal
        Evangel. "

4112   Holdcroft, Leslie Thomas
        Divine healing: a comparative study, by L. Thomas
        Holdcroft. Springfield, Mo. , Gospel Publishing House,
        c1967. 78p. TxWaS

4113   Holdcroft, Leslie Thomas
        The historical books [by] L. Thomas Holdcroft. Oakland,
        Ca. , Western Book Co. , 1960. iv, 101p.

4114   Holdcroft, Leslie Thomas
        The Holy Spirit: a Pentecostal interpretation [by] L.
        Thomas Holdcroft. Springfield, Mo. , Gospel Publishing
        House, 1979. 252p. DLC

4114a   Holdcroft, Leslie Thomas
        The Holy Spirit from a Pentecostal viewpoint. Santa
        Cruz, Ca. , Bethany Books, c1962. 119p.

4115   Horton, Harold Lawrence Cuthbert, 1880-1968.
        The baptism in the Holy Spirit; a challenge to whole-
        hearted seekers after God, by Harold Horton. Springfield,
        Mo. , Gospel Publishing House, 1956. 23p.

4116   Horton, Harold Lawrence Cuthbert, 1880-1968.
        The gifts of the Spirit, by Harold Horton. 5th ed.
        Springfield, Mo. , Gospel Publishing House, 1953. 228p.

4117   Horton, Harold Lawrence Cuthbert, 1880-1968.
        The gifts of the Spirit [by] Harold Horton. Springfield,
        Mo. , Gospel Publishing House, 1975, c1934. 207p. (Radiant
        books.)

4118   Horton, Stanley Monroe, 1916-
            Bible prophecy, by Stanley M. Horton. Springfield, Mo. ,
        Gospel Publishing House, 1963.   40p.   (Great themes of the
        Christian faith.)

4119   Horton, Stanley Monroe, 1916-
            Desire spiritual gifts ... earnestly; a consideration of
        First Corinthians 12-14 [by] Stanley M. Horton. Springfield,
        Mo. , Gospel Publishing House, 1972.   59p.

4120   Horton, Stanley Monroe, 1916-
            Gospel of John, by Stanley M. Horton. Springfield, Mo. ,
        Gospel Publishing House, c1965.   40p.   (Great themes of the
        Christian faith.)
            _____.   Teacher's manual.   Springfield, Mo. , Gospel
        Publishing House, 1965.   96p.

4121   Horton, Stanley Monroe, 1916-
            Great Psalms, by Stanley M. Horton. Springfield, Mo. ,
        Gospel Publishing House, 1962.   40p.   (Great themes of the
        Christian faith.)
            _____.   Teacher's manual.   Springfield, Mo. , Gospel
        Publishing House, 1962.   96p.

4122   Horton, Stanley Monroe, 1916-
            Into all truth; a survey of the course and content of divine
        revelation, by Stanley M. Horton. Springfield, Mo. , Gospel
        Publishing House, 1955.   145p.
            _____.   Instructor's guide.   Springfield, Mo. , Gospel
        Publishing House, 19--.   62p.

4123   Horton, Stanley Monroe, 1916-
            It's getting late; a practical commentary on the epistles
        to the Thessalonians [by] Stanley M. Horton. Springfield,
        Mo. , Gospel Publishing House, 1975.   iii, 124p.   (Radiant
        books.) DLC

4124   Horton, Stanley Monroe, 1916-
            Panorama of the Bible, by Stanley M. Horton. Spring-
        field, Mo. , Gospel Publishing House, 1961.   96p.   (Great
        themes of the Christian faith.)

4125   Horton, Stanley Monroe, 1916-
            The promise of His coming; a New Testament study of
        the second coming of Christ, by Stanley Horton. Springfield,
        Mo. , Gospel Publishing House, 1967.   128p.

4126   Horton, Stanley Monroe, 1916-
            Ready always; a devotional commentary on the epistles
        of Peter [by] Stanley M. Horton. Springfield, Mo. , Gospel
        Publishing House, 1974.   126p.   (Radiant books.) DLC

4127   Horton, Stanley Monroe, 1916-

Tongues and prophecy; how to know a gift of utterance is
in order [by] Stanley M. Horton. Springfield, Mo. , Gospel
Publishing House, 1972. 28p. "Previously published in
Paraclete as 'When is a gift of utterance in order?' "

4128   Horton, Stanley Monroe, 1916-
Welcome back, Jesus [by] Stanley M. Horton. Spring-
field, Mo. , Gospel Publishing House, 197-, c1967. 120p.
First issued under title: The promise of His coming.

4129   Horton, Stanley Monroe, 1916-
What the Bible says about the Holy Spirit, by Stanley M.
Horton. Springfield, Mo. , Gospel Publishing House, 1976.
302p.

4130   Hoy, Albert L.
The gift of interpretation, by Albert L. Hoy. Battle
Creek, Mi. , 1948. 53p.

4131   Hurst, Duane Vivian, 1923-
The church begins; a study manual on the first 12 chap-
ters of the Acts, by D. V. Hurst and T. J. Jones. Spring-
field, Mo. , Gospel Publishing House, c1959. vii, 136p.
_____. Instructor's guide. Springfield, Mo. , Gospel
Publishing House, 197-. vi, 47p.

4132   Hurst, Duane Vivian, 1923-
Spiritual life--God's gift [by] D. V. Hurst. Springfield,
Mo. , Gospel Publishing House, 1972. 64p.

4133   Instituto Biblico Latino Americano.
Manual de los libros Daniel y Revelación, preparado para
el Instituto Bíblico Latino Americano en San Antonio, Texas,
y para todos los que se intersan en el estudio de la profecía.
San Antonio, La Casa Evangelica de Publicaciones, c1935.
179p. "Copyright ... by Mrs. H. C. Ball. " DLC

4134   Jamieson, S. A.
Pillars of truth, by S. A. Jamieson. Springfield, Mo. ,
Gospel Publishing House, c1926. 105p.

4135   Jeter, Hugh Preston, 1911-
By His stripes [by] Hugh Jeter. Springfield, Mo. , Gospel Publishing House, 1977. 208p. DLC

4136   Johns, Donald Franklin, 1922-
The fundamentals of faith; teacher's manual. Springfield,
Mo. , Gospel Publishing House, 1963. 96p. (Great themes
of the Christian faith.)

4137   Johns, Donald Franklin, 1922-
Proofs of Christianity; teacher's manual. Springfield,
Mo. , Gospel Publishing House, 1965. 96p. (Great themes
of the Christian faith.)

4138   Johns, Donald Franklin, 1922-
        Proofs of Christianity; student's manual.   Springfield,
Mo. , Gospel Publishing House, 1965.   40p.   (Great themes
of the Christian faith.)

4139   Johns, Donald Franklin, 1922-
        Questions you will meet; teacher's manual.   Springfield,
Mo. , Gospel Publishing House, 1964.   96p.   (Great themes
of the Christian faith.)

4140   Johns, Donald Franklin, 1922-
        Questions you will meet; student's manual.   Springfield,
Mo. , Gospel Publishing House, 1964.   40p.   (Great themes
of the Christian faith.)

4141   Kelchner, Herbert B.
        Living your Christianity now in the light of eternity, by
Herbert B. Kelchner.   Scottdale, Pa. , Herald Press, 1974.
2v.

4142   Kerr, Daniel Warren, 1856-1927.
        Waters in the desert, by D. W. Kerr.   Springfield, Mo. ,
Gospel Publishing House, 1925.   139p.   On cover: Pulpit
and pew, full gospel series.   DLC

4143   Lamb, George R.
        Keep the feast: a time for the feast, the hour, and foot
washing at the feast, by George R. Lamb.   Leon, Ia. , Assembly of God Church, 19--.   15p.

4144   Lancaster, John
        The Spirit-filled church.   Springfield, Mo. , Gospel Pub-
lishing House, c1975.   111p.   (Radiant books.)   MoSpE,
TxWaS

4145   Lewis, L. B.
        Believing is receiving.   Wilmington, Ca. , 1956.   64p.

4146   Lindblad, Frank V.
        The spirit which is from God, by Frank Lindblad.
Springfield, Mo. , Gospel Publishing House, c1928.   271p.
DLC

4147   Lindquist, Frank J.
        The truth about the Trinity and baptism in Jesus' name
only, by Frank J. Lindquist.   Minneapolis, Northern Gospel
Publishing House, 19--.   34p.

4148   Lindquist, Frank J.
        The truth about the Trinity and baptism in Jesus' name
only, by Frank J. Lindquist.   4th rev. ed.   Minneapolis,
Northern Gospel Publishing House, 1961.   41p.

4149   Linzey, Stanford E.
        Pentecost in the Pentagon [by] Stanford E. Linzey, Jr.
        Foreword by T. D. Parham, Jr. Hicksville, N.Y., Exposi-
        tion Press, 1975. 103p.

4150   Linzey, Stanford E.
        Why I believe in the baptism with the Holy Spirit, by
        Stanford E. Linzey. Springfield, Mo., Gospel Publishing
        House, c1962. 12p.

4151   Luce, Alice Eveline, -1930.
        The little flock in the last days. Springfield, Mo.,
        Gospel Publishing House, c1927. xii,250p. DLC

4152   Luce, Alice Eveline, -1930.
        Pictures of Pentecost in the Old Testament. Springfield,
        Mo., Gospel Publishing House, 1930. 141p.

4153   Luce, Alice Eveline, -1930.
        Pictures of Pentecost in the Old Testament. Second
        series. Springfield, Mo., Gospel Publishing House, c1930.
        172p. DLC

4154   Luce, Alice Eveline, -1930.
        Pictures of Pentecost in the Old Testament. Springfield,
        Mo., Gospel Publishing House, c1950. 238p. DLC, TxWaS

4155   Lund, Eric, 1852-1933.
        Hermenéutica; o sea, Reglas de interpretación de las
        Sagradas Escrituras, por el dr. E. Lund. San Antonio,
        Casa Evangélica de Publicaciones, 194-. 95p. DLC

4156   Lund, Eric, 1852-1933.
        Hermeneutics; or, The science and art of interpreting
        the Bible; translated from the Spanish by P. C. Nelson.
        Enid, Ok., Southwestern Press, c1934. 140p. DLC

4157   Lund, Eric, 1852-1933.
        Hermeneutics; or, The science and art of interpreting
        the Bible; translated from the Spanish by P. C. Nelson.
        2d ed., with numerous notes, a new chapter and an appendix
        and Scripture index by the translator. Enid, Ok., South-
        western Press, 1938. 159p. DLC

4158   Lund, Eric, 1852-1933.
        Hermeneutics; or, The science and art of interpreting
        the Bible; translated from the Spanish by P. C. Nelson. 3d
        rev. ed., with numerous notes, new chapters and an appen-
        dix and a Scripture index by the translator. Enid, Ok.,
        Southwestern Press, 1941. 207p. DLC, PPDrop

4159   MacDonald, William Graham, 1933-
        Glossolalia in the New Testament, by William G.

MacDonald. Springfield, Mo., Gospel Publishing House,
1964.   20p.   "Originally presented before the annual meeting
of the Evangelical Theological Society, Dec. 28, 1963, in
Grand Rapids, Mich. "   MnCS, MSohG, NRCR

4160   MacDonald, William Graham, 1933-
        Prison and pastoral letters; a study manual for youth.
Springfield, Mo., Gospel Publishing House, 1967.   93p.

4161   Macpherson, Ian, 1912-
        God's plan for this planet.   Springfield, Mo., Gospel
Publishing House, 1977.   91p.

4162   Mallough, Don, 1914-
        Christ; student's manual.   Springfield, Mo., Gospel Pub-
lishing House, 196-.   40p.   (Great themes of the Christian
faith.)   Cover title.

4163   Mallough, Don, 1914-
        Living by faith.   Springfield, Mo., Gospel Publishing
House, c1978.   127p.   (Radiant books.)   DLC

4164   Menzies, William Watson, 1931-
        Understanding our doctrine, by William W. Menzies.
Springfield, Mo., Gospel Publishing House, 1971.   79p.

4165   Menzies, William Watson, 1931-
        Understanding the times of Christ, by William W. Men-
zies.   Springfield, Mo., Gospel Publishing House, 1969.
125p.   DLC

4166   Millard, Amos Daniel, 1923-
        Learning from the apostles; lessons for today from their
lives and witness, by Amos D. Millard.   Springfield, Mo.,
Gospel Publishing House, 1971.   127p.
        _____.   Instructor's guide, by Hugh P. Jeter.   Spring-
field, Mo., Gospel Publishing House, 1971.   131p.

4167   Miller, Elmer C.
        Pentecost examined by a Baptist lawyer [by] Elmer C.
Miller.   Springfield, Mo., Gospel Publishing House, c1936.
131p.   MSohG

4168   Moon, Jesse K.
        Divine healing and the problem of suffering, by Jesse K.
Moon.   Waxahachie, Tx., c1976.   45p.   TxWaS

4169   Moss, Harold H.
        The basis of the Pentecostal message, by Harold H.
Moss.   Springfield, Mo., Gospel Publishing House, 193-.
14p.   PPWe

4170   Needham, George Carter, 1840-1902.

Shadow and substance: an exposition of Tabernacle types, by George C. Needham. Springfield, Mo. , Gospel Publishing House, 1958. 168p.

4171   Nelson, Peter Christopher, 1868-1942.
The baptism in the Holy Spirit; the doctrine, experience, evidence, by P. C. Nelson. Fort Worth, Tx. , Southwestern Press, 1942. 114p. TxWaS

4172   Nelson, Peter Christopher, 1868-1942.
Bible doctrines; studies in the "Statement of Fundamental Truths" as adopted by the General Council of the Assemblies of God, by P. C. Nelson. Enid, Ok. , Southwestern Press, c1934. 75p. "This series of studies first appeared several years ago in Christ's Ambassadors' Monthly, and are reprinted with very slight revision. "-Pref. DLC

4173   Nelson, Peter Christopher, 1868-1942.
Bible doctrines; a handbook of Pentecostal theology based on the Scriptures and following the lines of the Statement of Fundamental Truths as adopted by the General Council of the Assemblies of God. Rev. and enl. by P. C. Nelson ... Introduction by Superintendent E. S. Williams. Enid, Ok. , Southwestern Press, c1936. 177p. DLC

4174   Nelson, Peter Christopher, 1868-1942.
Bible doctrines; a handbook of Pentecostal theology based on the scriptures and following the lines of the Statement of fundamental truths as adopted by the General Council of the Assemblies of God, by P. C. Nelson. Introduction by Superintendent E. S. Williams. 3d ed. Fort Worth, Tx. , Southwestern Press, 1943. 188p.

4175   Nelson, Peter Christopher, 1868-1942.
Bible doctrines; a series of studies based on the Statement of fundamental truths as adopted by the General Council of the Assemblies of God, by P. C. Nelson. Rev. ed. Springfield, Mo. , Gospel Publishing House, 1948. 174p.

4176   Nelson, Peter Christopher, 1868-1942.
Bible doctrines; a series of studies based on the Statement of fundamental truths as adopted by the General Council of the Assemblies of God, by P. C. Nelson. Rev. ed. Springfield, Mo. , Gospel Publishing House, 1962. 160p.

4177   Nelson, Peter Christopher, 1868-1942.
Bible doctrines; a series of studies based on the Statement of fundamental truths as adopted by the Assemblies of God [by] P. C. Nelson. Rev. ed. Springfield, Mo. , Gospel Publishing House, c1971. 160p. Additions and revisions by J. Roswell Flower and Anthony D. Palma. DWT

4178   Nelson, Peter Christopher, 1868-1942.

Doctrinas biblicas; un estudio de la Declaración de verdades funamentales del Concilio General de las Asambleas
de Dios. Springfield, Mo., Editorial Vida, 1954. 180p.
Translation of Bible doctrines. DLC

4179   Nelson, Peter Christopher, 1868-1942.
        Does Christ heal today? Messages of faith, hope and
cheer for the afflicted, by P. C. Nelson. Enid, Ok., Southwestern Press, c1941. 96p. "Appendix: The anointing service ... an abridged chapter from the second edition of 'The
young minister's guide,' by P. C. Nelson": 1ℓ., a-w p. at
end. DLC

4180   Nelson, Peter Christopher, 1868-1942.
        Does Christ heal today? Messages of faith, hope and
cheer for the afflicted, by P. C. Nelson. Fort Worth, Tx.,
c1941. 139p. TxWaS

4181   Nelson, Peter Christopher, 1868-1942.
        The letters of Paul [by] P. C. Nelson. Springfield, Mo.,
Gospel Publishing House, c1976. 143p.

4182   Nelson, Peter Christopher, 1868-1942.
        The life and letters of Paul, by P. C. Nelson. Enid,
Okla., Southwestern Press, c1939. 297p. DLC

4183   Nelson, Peter Christopher, 1868-1942.
        Word studies in Biblical Hebrew, Aramaic, Greek and
Latin, by P. C. Nelson. Enid, Ok., Southwestern Press,
c1941. 81p. DLC

4184   Ness, Henry H.
        Dunamis and the church, by Henry H. Ness. Springfield,
Mo., Gospel Publishing House, 1968. 144p. MB, TxWaS

4185   Nuzum, Mrs. C.
        The life of faith, by Mrs. C. Nuzum. Rev. ed. Spring-
field, Mo., Gospel Publishing House, 1956. 95p. (Radiant
books.) First edition published in 1928.

4186   Orchard, Richard E.
        This is our hope, by R. E. Orchard. Springfield, Mo.,
Gospel Publishing House, c1966. viii, 148p. DLC

4187   Osgood, Howard C.
        God's gift of power, by Howard C. Osgood. Springfield,
Mo., Gospel Publishing House, c1964. 40p. MiBsA, OkTOr,
TxWaS

4188   Palma, Anthony David, 1926-
        Knowing your Bible, by Anthony D. Palma. Springfield,
Mo., Gospel Publishing House, 1970. 78p.

4189   Palma, Anthony David, 1926-
              The Spirit: God in action [by] Anthony D. Palma.
         Springfield, Mo., Gospel Publishing House, 1974.   124p.
         DLC, TxWaS

4190   Palma, Anthony David, 1926-
              Truth: antidote for error [by] Anthony D. Palma.
         Springfield, Mo., Gospel Publishing House, c1977.   128p.
         (Radiant books.)   DLC

4191   Parr, John Nelson, 1886-1976.
              Conditional security, by J. Nelson Parr.   Springfield,
         Mo., Gospel Publishing House, 19--.   62p.   CLamB, MoSpA

4192   Parr, John Nelson, 1886-1976.
              Divine healing, by J. Nelson Parr.   Springfield, Mo.,
         Gospel Publishing House, c1955.   80p.   TxWaS

4193   Pearlman, Myer, 1898-1943.
              Daniel speaks today; a devotional commentary on the
         Book of Daniel.   Springfield, Mo., Gospel Publishing House,
         1943.   118p.

4194   Pearlman, Myer, 1898-1943.
              A trav"és de la Biblia, libro por libro.   San Antonio,
         Casa evangélica de publicaciones, c1940.   438p.   DLC

4195   Pearlman, Myer, 1898-1943.
              The heavenly gift; studies in the work of the Holy Spirit.
         Springfield, Mo., Gospel Publishing House, 1935.   57p.

4196   Pearlman, Myer, 1898-1943.
              Knowing the doctrines of the Bible.   Springfield, Mo.,
         Gospel Publishing House, c1937.   399p.   NjPT

4197   Pearlman, Myer, 1898-1943.
              Knowing the doctrines of the Bible.   Springfield, Mo.,
         Gospel Publishing House, 1939.   399p.   "Second edition. "
         DLC

4198   Pearlman, Myer, 1898-1943.
              Let's meet the Holy Spirit.   Springfield, Mo., Gospel
         Publishing House, [1975].   64p.   (Radiant books.)   First
         published in 1935 under title: The heavenly gift.

4199   Pearlman, Myer, 1898-1943.
              The life and teachings of Christ.   Springfield, Mo.,
         Gospel Publishing House, 19--.   118p.

4200   Pearlman, Myer, 1898-1943.
              Pentecostal truth, by Myer Pearlman and Frank M.
         Boyd.   Springfield, Mo., Correspondence School of the

General Council of the Assemblies of God, 1948. 2v.

4201   Pearlman, Myer, 1898-1943.
        Seeing the story of the Bible ... with diagrams and out-
        lines. Springfield, Mo., Gospel Publishing House, c1930.
        123p. DLC

4202   Pearlman, Myer, 1898-1943.
        The synagogue of the Nazarenes. Springfield, Mo.,
        Gospel Publishing House, 194-. 61p. NN

4203   Pearlman, Myer, 1898-1943.
        Teología bíblica y sistemática. Springfield, Mo., Edi-
        torial Vida, 1958. 472p. Translation of Knowing the doc-
        trines of the Bible. DLC

4204   Pearlman, Myer, 1898-1943.
        Through the Bible book by book. Springfield, Mo.,
        Gospel Publishing House, 1935. 520p.

4205   Pearlman, Myer, 1898-1943.
        Through the Bible book by book. Springfield, Mo., Gos-
        pel Publishing House, 1935. 4v.

4206   Pearlman, Myer, 1898-1943.
        Verdades Pentecostales. Springfield, Mo., Editorial
        Vida, c1954. 56p. TxWaS

4207   Pearlman, Myer, 1898-1943.
        Where is the king of Israel? Springfield, Mo., Gospel
        Publishing House, 1931. 40p.

4208   Pearlman, Myer, 1898-1943.
        Why we believe the Bible is God's book. Springfield,
        Mo., Gospel Publishing House, 1931. 47p.

4209   Pearlman, Myer, 1898-1943.
        Windows into the future; devotional studies in the book
        of Revelation. Springfield, Mo., Gospel Publishing House,
        c1941. 176p. DLC

4210   Perkins, Jonathan Elsworth, 1889-
        The baptism of the Holy Spirit; an explanation of speaking
        in other languages as the Spirit giveth utterance. Los
        Angeles, B. N. Robertson Co., 1945. 69p.

4211   Perkins, Jonathan Elsworth, 1889-
        The rainbow of hope. Springfield, Mo., Gospel Pub-
        lishing House, 19--. 128p.

4212   Perkins, Jonathan Elsworth, 1889-
        What the Bible says about the laying on of hands; or,
        Pentecostal truth defended. Seattle, 19--. 145p. TxWaS

4213   Petts, David
         The dynamic difference. Springfield, Mo., Gospel Pub-
lishing House, 1978. 64p. (Radiant books.) First issued in
1974 in Great Britain under title: Receive power. DLC

4214   Popejoy, Bill
         The case for divine healing [by] Bill Popejoy. Spring-
field, Mo., Gospel Publishing House, c1976. 63p. (Radiant
books.) DLC, TxWaS

4215   Riggs, Ralph Meredith, 1895-1971.
         The Bible's backbone, by Ralph M. Riggs. Springfield,
Mo., Gospel Publishing House, 1945. 140p.

4216   Riggs, Ralph Meredith, 1895-1971.
         Calvinism versus Arminianism, by Ralph M. Riggs.
n. p., North Texas District Ministers Institutes, 1960. 21p.

4217   Riggs, Ralph Meredith, 1895-1971.
         Dispensational studies, by Ralph M. Riggs. Springfield,
Mo., Berean School of the Bible, c1963. 2v.

4218   Riggs, Ralph Meredith, 1895-1971.
         El Espíritu mismo. Springfield, Mo., Editorial Vida,
1956. 208p. Translation of The Spirit Himself. DLC

4219   Riggs, Ralph Meredith, 1895-1971.
         God's calendar of coming events, by Ralph M. Riggs.
Springfield, Mo., Gospel Publishing House, c1962. 62p.

4220   Riggs, Ralph Meredith, 1895-1971.
         Living in Christ; our identification with Him, by Ralph
M. Riggs. Springfield, Mo., Gospel Publishing House, 1967.
96p. DLC

4221   Riggs, Ralph Meredith, 1895-1971.
         The path of prophecy; the revelation of Christ, by Ralph
M. Riggs. Springfield, Mo., Gospel Publishing House, 1937.
227p.

4222   Riggs, Ralph Meredith, 1895-1971.
         The Spirit Himself, by Ralph M. Riggs. Springfield, Mo.,
Gospel Publishing House, 1949. xiv, 208p.
         _____. Instructor's guide. Springfield, Mo., Gospel
Publishing House, 1956. 48p.

4223   Riggs, Ralph Meredith, 1895-1971.
         The story of the future, by Ralph M. Riggs. Springfield,
Mo., Gospel Publishing House, 1968. 174p. DLC, OkTOr

4224   Riggs, Ralph Meredith, 1895-1971.
         We believe; a comprehensive statement of Christian faith.
Springfield, Mo., Gospel Publishing House, 1954. 1v.

(Assemblies of God Cornerstone series, 780.) DLC

4225   Riggs, Ralph Meredith, 1895-1971.
       We believe, by Ralph M. Riggs. Springfield, Mo., Inter-
       national Correspondence Institute, c1969. 110p. An ICI cor-
       respondence course.

4226   Robinson, Charles C.
       The baptism of the Holy Ghost, by Charles C. Robinson.
       Austin, Tx., 19--. 44p. TxWaS

4227   Robinson, Charles Elmo, 1867-1954.
       God and His Bible. Springfield, Mo., Gospel Publishing
       House, 19--. 160p.

4228   Robinson, Charles Elmo, 1867-1954.
       Praying to change things, being a presentation of rules,
       principles and warnings; intended to teach lowly and common-
       place men how to pray effectively. Springfield, Mo., Gospel
       Publishing House, 1928. 144p.

4229   Sandbach, Richard T.
       He shall baptize you. Compiled by R. T. Sandbach.
       Belvidere, Il., 19--. 134p.

4230   Savage, Kenzy Kulman, 1912-
       La Palabra Sanadora, por Kenzy Savage. Roswell,
       N.M., 1951. 126p. TxWaS

4231   Silva, Theodore Joseph, 1909-
       Prophetic types in the book of Esther, by T. J. Silva.
       Kelso, Wa., c1936. 77p. "Building fund edition." DLC,
       IdPI

4232   Smolchuck, Fred
       Tongues and total surrender. Springfield, Mo., Gospel
       Publishing House, c1974. 32p. (Radiant books.) TxWaS

4233   Spittler, Russell Paul, 1931-
       The church [by] Russell P. Spittler. Springfield, Mo.,
       Gospel Publishing House, c1977. 126p. (Radiant books.)
       DLC

4234   Spittler, Russell Paul, 1931-
       The Corinthian correspondence [by] Russell P. Spittler.
       Springfield, Mo., Gospel Publishing House, 1976. 125p.
       (Radiant books.)

4235   Spittler, Russell Paul, 1931-
       God, the father [by] Russell P. Spittler. Springfield,
       Mo., Gospel Publishing House, 1976. 126p. (Radiant books.)
       DLC

4236   Steil, Harry L., 1901-
       A guide to glory land, by Harry J. Steil.   Springfield,
       Mo., Gospel Publishing House, 1938.   63p.

4237   Steil, Harry J., 1901-
       What will happen next?   Heart-to-heart talks about things
       shortly to come to pass, by Harry J. Steil.   Springfield, Mo.,
       Gospel Publishing House, 1938.   60p.

4238   Steinberg, Hardy W.
       The church of the Spirit [by] Hardy W. Steinberg.
       Springfield, Mo., Gospel Publishing House, 1972.   64p.

4239   Stemme, Harry A.
       Speaking with other tongues, sign and gift, by Harry A.
       Stemme.   Minneapolis, Northern Gospel Publishing House,
       1946.   56p.   "A reply to Speaking with other tongues, sign
       or gift, which?"   By T. J. McCrossan.   TxWaS

4240   Stover, Gene
       He shall baptize you with the Holy Ghost.   Conrad, Ia.,
       1933.   77p.   TxWaS

4241   Sumrall, Lester Frank, 1913-
       El catolicismo romano mata, por Lester F. Sumrall.
       San Antonio, Tex., Casa Evangélica de Publicaciones, 1940.
       63p.   Translation of Roman Catholicism slays.   "Este volu-
       men se está publicando simultáneamente en ... inglés y es-
       pañol."--p. [3].   DLC

4242   Sumrall, Lester Frank, 1913-
       Roman Catholicism slays, by Lester F. Sumrall.   Grand
       Rapids, Mich., Zondervan Publishing House, c1940.   61p.
       DLC

4243   Swift, Allan A.
       The Spirit within and upon, by Allan A. Swift.   Green
       Lane, Pa., 19--.   31p.

4244   Teuber, Andrew S.
       Tongues of fire, by Andrew S. Teuber.   n. p., 1966.
       32p.

4245   The victorious Christian life, by an overcomer.   Springfield,
       Mo., Gospel Publishing House, 1938.   63p.

4246   Ward, Alfred George, 1881-1960.
       The Pentecostal testimony according to the scriptures,
       by A. G. Ward.   n. p., 19--.   16p.

4247   Ward, Alfred George, 1881-1960.
       Maintaining the glow, and other studies on the overcoming

life, by A. G. Ward.   Springfield, Mo., Gospel Publishing
House, c1936.   63p.

4248   Ward, Alfred George, 1881-1960.
        Through the days with the Song of Solomon, by A. G.
        Ward.   Springfield, Mo., Gospel Publishing House, 19--.
        144p.   OkTOr

4249   Ward, Charles Morse, 1909-
        There shall be signs, by C. M. Ward.   Springfield,
        Mo., Gospel Publishing House, 1964.   84p.

4250   Ward, Charles Morse, 1909-
        Waiting, by C. M. Ward.   Springfield, Mo., Assemblies
        of God, 1959.   42p.   OkTOr

4251   Ward, Charles Morse, 1909-
        What you should know about prophecy [by] C. M. Ward;
        adapted from Bible prophecy by Stanley M. Horton.   Spring-
        field, Mo., Gospel Publishing House, c1975.   127p.

4252   Wead, Douglas, 1946-
        To another the word of knowledge, by Douglas and Gloria
        Wead with Elaine Cleeton.   Ellendale, S. D., Action Evan-
        gelism, Trinity Institute, 1973.   29p.

4253   Wedgeworth, Ann
        Magnificent strangers.   Springfield, Mo., Gospel Pub-
        lishing House, c1979.   124p.   (Radiant books.)   DLC

4254   Williams, Ernest Swing, 1885-
        Encouragement to faith.   Springfield, Mo., Gospel Pub-
        lishing House, 1946.   64p.

4255   Williams, Ernest Swing, 1885-
        Not I, but Christ; practical thoughts on Christian living,
        by Ernest S. Williams.   Springfield, Mo., Gospel Publishing
        House, 1939.   64p.

4256   Williams, Ernest Swing, 1885-
        Systematic theology.   Springfield, Mo., Gospel Publishing
        House, 1954, c1953.   3v.   DLC

4257   Williams, Ernest Swing, 1885-
        Temptation and triumph, by Ernest S. Williams.   Spring-
        field, Mo., Gospel Publishing House, 19--.   80p.

4258   Williams, Ernest Swing, 1885-
        A word of encouragement to young converts [by] Ernest
        S. Williams.   Springfield, Mo., Gospel Publishing House,
        197-.   23p.   Cover title.

4259   Wilson, Aaron Aubrey

"Things which are most surely believed among us," by
A. A. Wilson. [Kansas City, Mo., 19--] 52p. TxWaS

4260   Womack, David Alfred, 1933-
        Alive in Christ [by] David Womack; adapted from How to
        live the Christian life, by R. L. Brandt. Springfield, Mo.,
        Gospel Publishing House, c1975. 128p. (Radiant books.)

4261   Womack, David Alfred, 1933-
        The wellsprings of the Pentecostal movement, by David
        A. Womack. Written in cooperation with the Committee on
        Advance for the General Council of the Assemblies of God.
        Springfield, Mo., Gospel Publishing House, 1968. 96p.
        DLC, MSohG, TxWaS

4262   Wood, George Oliver, 1941-
        You can't beat the beatitudes [by] George O. Wood and
        William J. Krutza. Springfield, Mo., Gospel Publishing
        House, c1978. 88p. (Radiant books.) DLC

4263   Yeomans, Lilian Barbara, 1861-
        Balm of Gilead. Springfield, Mo., Gospel Publishing
        House, 1935, c1936. 86p. TxWaS

4264   Yeomans, Lilian Barbara, 1861-
        Balm of Gilead [by] Lilian B. Yeomans. Rev. ed.
        Springfield, Mo., Gospel Publishing House, 1973. 80p.
        (Radiant books.)

4265   Yeomans, Lilian Barbara, 1861-
        Divine healing diamonds, by Lilian B. Yeomans.
        Springfield, Mo., Gospel Publishing House, 1933. 96p.
        OkBetC, TxWaS

4266   Yeomans, Lilian Barbara, 1861-
        The great physician [by] Lilian B. Yeomans. Spring-
        field, Mo., Gospel Publishing House, c1961. 72p. First
        published in 1933 under title: Divine healing diamonds.

4267   Yeomans, Lilian Barbara, 1861-
        Healing from heaven, by Lilian B. Yeomans. Spring-
        field, Mo., Gospel Publishing House, 1926. 139p. DLC

4268   Yeomans, Lilian Barbara, 1861-
        Healing from heaven [by] Lilian B. Yeomans. Rev. ed.
        Springfield, Mo., Gospel Publishing House, 1973. 134p.
        (Radiant books.)

4269   Yeomans, Lilian Barbara, 1861-
        Health and healing [by] Lilian B. Yeomans. Springfield,
        Mo., Gospel Publishing House, 1973. 71p. (Radiant books.)
        First published in 1938 under title: The royal road to Health-
        ville.

4270   Yeomans, Lilian Barbara, 1861-
              Resurrection rays, by Lilian B. Yeomans.   Springfield,
        Mo., Gospel Publishing House, 1930.   109p.

4271   Yeomans, Lilian Barbara, 1861-
              The royal road to Health-ville, by Lilian B. Yeomans.
        Springfield, Mo., Gospel Publishing House, 1938.   62p.
        TxWaS

4272   Zimmerman, Thomas Fletcher, 1912-
              He is worthy [by] Thos. F. Zimmerman [et al.]   Spring-
        field, Mo., Gospel Publishing House, c1978.   61p.   (Radiant
        books.)   DLC

        --EDUCATION

4273   Assemblies of God, General Council.   National Sunday School
        Department.
              The Sunday school library.   Springfield, Mo., 19--.   9p.
        IKON

4274   Armstrong, Hart Reid, 1912-
              Administration and organization, by Hart R. Armstrong.
        Springfield, Mo., Gospel Publishing House, c1950.   2v.
        (Sunday school series.)   Vol. 2 has cover title: Administra-
        tion.
              Contents: v. [1] Manual for all workers: Sunday school
        administration. -v. 2. Manual on the administration of the
        Sunday school.

4275   Armstrong, Hart Reid, 1912-
              Manual for workers in the men's Bible class of the Sun-
        day school, by Hart R. Armstrong.   Springfield, Mo., Gospel
        Publishing House, 1951.   144p.

4276   Armstrong, Hart Reid, 1912-
              You should know; a first course for workers' training, by
        Hart R. Armstrong.   Springfield, Mo., Gospel Publishing
        House, 1949.   128p.
        _____.   Instructor's guide.   Springfield, Mo., Gospel
        Publishing House, 19--.   25p.

4277   Bayless, Robert Reaves
              The Assemblies of God educational system: an analysis
        of the perceived and preferred goals in relation to organiza-
        tional theory.   Minneapolis, 1977.   xiv, 313ℓ.   Thesis (Ph.D.)
        --University of Minnesota.   MnU

4278   Brock, Raymond Theodore, 1927-
              Into the highways and hedges; ways of perpetuating evan-
        gelism in and through the Sunday school, by Raymond T.
        Brock.   Springfield, Mo., Gospel Publishing House, c1961.
        117p.   DLC

4279   Bryant, Mary Virginia
        Manual for workers with beginners in the Sunday school,
        by Mary Virginia Bryant and Hart R. Armstrong. Spring-
        field, Mo., Gospel Publishing House, c1950. 112p. (Sunday
        school series.)

4280   Burris, Harold D.
        Extension workers handbook, by Harold D. Burris.
        Springfield, Mo., Gospel Publishing House, c1967. 89p.
        (Sunday school handbook series.)

4281   Burris, Harold D.
        Handbook of Sunday school services of the Assemblies
        of God, by Harold D. Burris. Springfield, Mo., Assemblies
        of God Sunday School Department, 1964. 64ℓ.

4282   Collins, Millard E.
        Establishing and financing higher educational institutions
        in the church body of the Assemblies of God in the U. S. A.,
        by Millard E. Collins. Austin, 1959. 135ℓ. Proposed
        thesis (Ed. D.)--University of Texas. TxWaS

4283   Copeland, Ruth
        Building better vacation Bible schools. Springfield, Mo.,
        Gospel Publishing House, 1961. 112p.
        _____. Instructor's guide. Springfield, Mo., Gospel
        Publishing House, 19--. 488p.

4284   Cunningham, Richard Bruce, 1931-
        An investigation of the use of a taxonomy of education
        as an evaluation device for Assemblies of God overseas Bible
        schools. Salt Lake City, 1974. x, 313ℓ. Thesis (Ed. D.)--
        University of Utah. UU

4285   Currie, Winifred, 1918-
        Creative classroom communications. Springfield, Mo.,
        Gospel Publishing House, 1972. 122p.

4286   Denton, Edith Converse.
        Cradle roll workers handbook. Springfield, Mo., Gospel
        Publishing House, c1963. 82p. (Sunday school handbook
        series.)

4287   Dresselhaus, Richard L.
        Teaching for decision [by] Richard L. Dresselhaus.
        Springfield, Mo., Gospel Publishing House, 1973. 123p.
        DLC

4288   Dresselhaus, Richard L.
        Your Sunday school at work, by Richard L. Dresselhaus.
        Springfield, Mo., Gospel Publishing House, 1970. 79p.

4289   Edge, Findley Bartow, 1916-
        Helping the teacher. Springfield, Mo., Gospel Publishing

House, 1959.   152p.
_____.   Instructor's guide, by Zenas J. Bicket.
Springfield, Mo., Gospel Publishing House, 1965.   54p.

4290   Eggeman, Hazel
       Manual for workers with primaries in the Sunday school,
       by Hazel Eggeman and Hart R. Armstrong. Springfield, Mo.,
       Gospel Publishing House, 1951.   160p.

4291   Eide, David J.
       The study of the discontinuance of students to enrollment
       in sophomore year in Assemblies of God theological schools,
       by David Eide. Springfield, Mo., 1958.   47ℓ. Thesis
       (M.A.)--Central Bible Institute.

4292   Flattery, George Manford, 1936-
       A comparative analysis of Herman Harrell Horne's ideal-
       istic philosophy of education and the philosophy of religious
       education reflected in the adult curriculum of the Assemblies
       of God, 1959-64. Fort Worth, Tx., 1966.   167ℓ. Thesis
       (D.R.E.)--Southwestern Baptist Theological Seminary.   TxFS

4293   Flattery, George Manford, 1936-
       Teaching for Christian maturity, by George N. Flattery.
       Springfield, Mo., Gospel Publishing House, c1968.   123p.

4294   Garlock, John Edward, 1924-
       Teaching as Jesus taught, by John Garlock. Springfield,
       Mo., Gospel Publishing House, c1966.   124p.

4295   Greene, William Washington, 1929-
       A study of the need for and feasibility of elementary and
       secondary schools sponsored by the Assemblies of God, by
       William W. Greene. Athens, 1962.   105ℓ. Thesis (M.A.)--
       University of Georgia.   GU

4296   Guynes, Eleanor R.
       Development of the educational program of the Assemblies
       of God from the school year 1948-49 up to the present time,
       by Eleanor R. Guynes. Dallas, 1966.   vi, 69ℓ. Thesis
       (M.A.)--Southern Methodist University.   TxDaM

4297   Hall, Hayward Glynn, 1935-
       The development of the workers training course of the
       Assemblies of God, by Hayward Glynn Hall, Sr. New Orleans,
       1973.   151ℓ. Thesis (Ed.D.)--New Orleans Baptist Theolog-
       ical Seminary.   LNB

4298   Harrelson, Larry E.
       A survey and evaluation of Assemblies of God college
       libraries, by Larry E. Harrelson. Columbia, 1970.   vi,
       116ℓ. Thesis (M.A.)--University of Missouri.   MoU

4299   Harris, Ralph William, 1912-
        The development of church school curricula of the Assem-
        blies of God during the period, 1954-1969, by Ralph W.
        Harris. Springfield, Mo., 1969. 99ℓ. Thesis (M.A.)--
        Central Bible College.

4300   Hurst, Duane Vivian, 1923-
        And He gave teachers, by Duane V. Hurst. Springfield,
        Mo., Gospel Publishing House, 1955. 185p.
        _____. Instructor's guide. Springfield, Mo., Gospel
        Publishing House, 19--. 64p.

4301   Hurst, Duane Vivian, 1923-
        Mastering the methods [by] D. V. Hurst [and] Dwayne E.
        Turner. Springfield, Mo., Gospel Publishing House, c1971.
        80p. (Fundamentals for Sunday school workers, 4.)

4302   Hurst, Dwayne Vivian, 1923-
        Operation Sunday school; a guide in Assemblies of God
        Sunday school administration, by D. V. Hurst, Ralph W.
        Harris, Bert Webb, Carl Conner, Charles W. Denton, Jim
        Copeland, William G. Eastlake [and] T. F. Zimmerman.
        Springfield, Mo., Gospel Publishing House, c1957. v, 138p.

4303   Jackson, John, comp.
        Senior high workers handbook. Springfield, Mo., Gospel
        Publishing House, c1962. 73p. (Sunday school handbook
        series.)

4304   Jansen, Harris Lloyd, 1927-
        The making of a Sunday school, by Harris Jansen.
        Springfield, Mo., Gospel Publishing House, 1972. 126p.

4305   Johns, Donald Franklin, 1922-
        A philosophy of religious education for the Assemblies
        of God. New York, 1962. xv, 450ℓ. Thesis (Ph.D.)--New
        York University. NNU

4306   Lebsack, Leland V.
        The Ravenna miracle, by Lee Lebsack. Stow, Oh.,
        Creative Communication, 1973. 91p. Cover title. On
        Sunday school methods used successfully by the Assembly
        of God, Ravenna, Ohio.

4307   Pearlman, Myer, 1898-1943.
        Studying the pupil, by Myer Pearlman. Drawings by
        Charles L. Ramsay. Springfield, Mo., Gospel Publishing
        House, c1940. 112p. DLC

4308   Pearlman, Myer, 1898-1943.
        Successful Sunday school teaching. Springfield, Mo.,
        Gospel Publishing House, 1934. 110p.

4309   Pearlman, Myer, 1898-1943.
        Successful Sunday school teaching.   2d ed.   Springfield,
        Mo., Gospel Publishing House, 1935.   109p.

4310   Rasnake, John Samuel, 1932-
        An investigation of the policy of the Assemblies of God
        on glossolalia and its effects on education in their colleges.
        Johnson City, 1965.   v, 88ℓ.   Thesis (M.A.)--East Tennessee
        State University.   TJoS

4311   Reeves, Billy E.
        Beginner workers handbook, by Billy E. Reeves.   Spring-
        field, Mo., Gospel Publishing House, c1963.   93p.   (Sunday
        school handbook series.)

4312   Riggs, Ralph Meredith, 1895-1971.
        A successful Sunday school, by Ralph M. Riggs.   Spring-
        field, Mo., Gospel Publishing House, c1934.   126p.

4313   Sandidge, Jerry L.
        The function of the minister of Christian education in the
        local church of the Assemblies of God, by Jerry L. Sandidge.
        Springfield, Mo., 1964.   113ℓ.   Thesis (M.A.)--Central
        Bible Institute.

4314   Schmidt, Roy Lyn
        Age-group doctrinal training and the Assemblies of God.
        Portland, Or., 1964.   273ℓ.   Thesis (B.D.)--Western Evan-
        gelical Seminary.   OrPW

4315   Sisemore, John Theophilus, 1913-
        The ministry of visitation, by John T. Sisemore.   Spring-
        field, Mo., Gospel Publishing House, c1954.   118p.

4316   Spence, Inez
        Junior high workers handbook, by Inez Mover Spence.
        Springfield, Mo., Gospel Publishing House, c1962.   92p.
        (Sunday school handbook series.)

4317   Steinberg, Hardy W.
        Adult workers handbook, by Hardy W. Steinberg.   Spring-
        field, Mo., Gospel Publishing House, c1963.   87p.   (Sunday
        school handbook series.)

4318   Stetz, Juanita Brown
        Primary workers handbook.   Springfield, Mo., Gospel
        Publishing House, c1962.   90p.   (Sunday school handbook
        series.)

4319   Townsend, Lou Bina
        Nursery workers handbook.   Springfield, Mo., Gospel
        Publishing House, c1963.   v, 98p.   (Sunday school handbook
        series.)

4320   Van Ness, Charles
        Junior workers handbook.   Springfield, Mo., Gospel Pub-
        lishing House, c1963.   92p.   (Sunday school handbook series.)

4321   Vitello, Joseph Louis, 1931-
        A history and evaluation of the attitudes of the Assemblies
        of God toward post-secondary education.   Springfield, Mo.,
        1962.   87ℓ.   Thesis (M. A.)--Central Bible Institute.

4322   Walker, Louise Jeter, 1913-
        A faculty training program for Assembly of God Bible
        schools in Latin America.   Springfield, Mo., 1965.   118ℓ.
        Thesis (M. A.)--Central Bible Institute.

4323   Williams, Maxine
        The eyes have it; a handbook on the use of visual mater-
        ials in Christian teaching.   Springfield, Mo., Gospel Publish-
        ing House, 1962.   145p.   DLC

4324   Wireman, Kenneth, 1932-
        A comparative study of the effect of the teaching of biol-
        ogy on student attitudes toward organic evolution in Assem-
        blies of God church schools.   Salt Lake City, 1971.   xiv,
        294ℓ.   Thesis (Ph. D.)--University of Utah.   UU

                    --EVANGELISTIC WORK

4325   Assemblies of God, General Council.
        Handbook for gospel broadcasters.   Springfield, Mo.,
        Gospel Publishing House, 19--.   34p.

4326   Assemblies of God, General Council.
        Our mission in today's world: Council on Evangelism
        official papers and reports.   Editorial committee: Richard
        Champion, chairman, Edward S. Caldwell, Gary Leggett.
        Springfield, Mo., Gospel Publishing House, c1968.   217p.
        Digest of messages, reports, and seminars of the Council
        on Evangelism, held in St. Louis, August 26-29, 1968.   DLC

4327   Assemblies of God, General Council.   Spiritual Life-
        Evangelism Commission.
        Personal evangelism guide.   Springfield, Mo., Gospel
        Publishing House, 1970.   45p.

4328   Adams, James Edward, 1913-
        Three to win [by] James E. Adams.   Springfield, Mo.,
        Gospel Publishing House, 1977.   125p.   (Radiant books.)
        Adapted from Soul winning, by R. L. Brandt.   DLC

4329   Brock, Raymond Theodore, 1927-
        Into the highways and hedges; ways of perpetuating evan-
        gelism in and through the Sunday school, by Raymond T.

Brock. Springfield, Mo., Gospel Publishing House, c1961.
117p. DLC

4330   Davis, James B.
          Personal soul winning--visitation, by J. B. Davis.
       Springfield, Mo., 19--. 96p.

4331   Edwards, Gene
          How to have a soul winning church. Springfield, Mo.,
       Gospel Publishing House, c1963. 249p.

4332   Fischer, Harold Arthur
          Reviving revivals [by] H. Arthur Fischer. Sheboygan,
       Wi., Gospel Print Shop, 1943. 140p. Cover title. DLC

4333   Fischer, Harold Arthur
          Reviving revivals, by Harold A. Fischer. Introduction
       by Frank M. Boyd. Springfield, Mo., Gospel Publishing
       House, c1950. 229p.

4334   Hurst, Duane Vivian, 1923-
          Ye shall be witnesses, by Duane V. Hurst. Springfield,
       Mo., Gospel Publishing House, 1952. viii, 190p. DLC

4335   Mallough, Don, 1914-
          Grassroots evangelism. Grand Rapids, Baker Book
       House, 1971. 143p. DLC

4336   Riggs, Ralph Meredith, 1895-1971.
          So send I you; a study in personal soul winning, by Ralph
       M. Riggs and others. Springfield, Mo., Gospel Publishing
       House, 1965. 128p.
          _____. Instructor's guide, by D. V. Hurst and
       Robert Myers. Springfield, Mo., Gospel Publishing House
       for Sunday School Department, General Council of the As-
       semblies of God, 196-. vi, 57p.

4337   Stewart, Marjorie, 1925-
          Women in neighborhood evangelism. Springfield, Mo.,
       Gospel Publishing House, c1978. 124p. (Radiant books.)
       DLC

4338   Ward, Charles Morse, 1909-
          Win or lose, by C. M. Ward. Springfield, Mo., Gospel
       Publishing House, c1961. 44p.

4339   Womack, David Alfred, 1933-
          Breaking the stained-glass barrier [by] David A. Womack.
       New York, Harper & Row, 1973. 167p. DLC

                    --FICTIONAL LITERATURE

4340   Frey, Mae Eleanor (Edick), 1865-

The minister, by Mae Eleanor Frey. Springfield, Mo.,
Gospel Publishing House, 1939. 180p. DLC

4341   Pryor, Adel, 1918-
        Tangled paths. Springfield, Mo., Gospel Publishing
House, 19--. 192p. First published in 1959.

4342   Ready, Jewell
        The Connie story. Springfield, Mo., Gospel Publishing
House, c1955. 88p.

4343   Robinson, Charles Elmo, 1867-1954.
        Broken ties. Grand Rapids, Mi., Zondervan Publishing
House, c1940. 212p. DLC

4344   Robinson, Charles Elmo, 1867-1954.
        The governor's choice, an historical romance. Grand
Rapids, Mi., Zondervan Publishing House, c1941. 240p.
DLC

4345   Robinson, Charles Elmo, 1867-1954.
        Guided hearts. Grand Rapids, Mi., Zondervan Publishing
House, c1937. 280p. DLC

4346   Robinson, Charles Elmo, 1867-1954.
        Lifted shadows. Grand Rapids, Mi., Zondervan Publish-
ing House, c1938. 201p. DLC

4347   Robinson, Charles Elmo, 1867-1954.
        Victory! Grand Rapids, Mi., Zondervan Publishing
House, c1936. 208p. DLC

4348   Robinson, Charles Elmo, 1867-1954.
        The winning of Aliene. Grand Rapids, Mi., Zondervan
Publishing House, c1939. 187p. DLC

4349   Russell, Ruth, 1923-
        The locket. Springfield, Mo., Gospel Publishing House,
1952, c1951. 268p. DLC

4350   Warner, Wayne Earl, 1933-
        Letters to Tony [by] Wayne Warner. Springfield, Mo.,
Gospel Publishing House, 1975. 106p. (Radiant books.)
DLC

        --FINANCE

4351   Assemblies of God, General Council.
        [Financial reports] Sept. 1921-1965. In Library of
American Church Records, ser. 1, [pt. 1], reel 2-3, microfilm. NN

4352   Krantz, Patricia Jane, 1941-

Patterns of giving; a study of contributions to four Pentecostal sects, by Patricia J. Krantz. Madison, 1968. 113ℓ. Thesis (M.A.)--University of Wisconsin. Includes Assemblies of God. WU

--GOVERNMENT

4353   Assemblies of God, General Council.
Suggested constitution and bylaws for local assemblies. Springfield, Mo., 1972. 22p.

4354   Dresselhaus, Richard L.
The deacon and his ministry [by] Richard L. Dresselhaus. Springfield, Mo., Gospel Publishing House, c1977. 96p. DLC

4355   Hoover, Mario G.
Origin and structural development of the Assemblies of God. Springfield, Mo., 1968. 214ℓ. Thesis (M.A.)-- Southwest Missouri State College. MoSpS

4356   Hoover, Mario G.
Origin and structural development of the Assemblies of God. Springfield, Mo., 1968, c1970. 214p. Thesis (M.A.) --Southwest Missouri State College, 1968. CSdP, DLC

4357   A visit through headquarters (Filmstrip). General Council of the Assemblies of God.
Made by TV and Film Production Center, Burbank, Calif. 1 roll. color. 35mm. and phonodisc: 2s., 33 1/3 rpm., 15 min. DLC

--HISTORY

4358   Assemblies of God, General Council.
Like a river ...; 50th anniversary. Springfield, Mo., 1964. 75p. DLC

4359   Assemblies of God, General Council. Office of Information.
Early history of the Assemblies of God. Springfield, Mo., 1959. 21p. Prepared by the Assemblies of God "Public Relations Department, with appreciation to Dr. C. C. Burnett for the original research." DLC, MSohG

4360   Assemblies of God, General Council. Office of Information.
In the last days ... an early history of the Assemblies of God. Springfield, Mo., 1962. 32p. "Prepared by the Assemblies of God Public Relations Dept., with appreciation to C. C. Burnett for original research." First issued in 1959 under title: Early history of the Assemblies of God. RPB

4361   Aasen, David Lawrence
        Forty years of New Testament teaching and preaching in
        the General Council of the Assemblies of God, 1914-1954, by
        David L. Aasen. Fort Worth, 1955. 281ℓ. Thesis (Th.D.)
        --Southwestern Baptist Theological Seminary. TxFS

4362   Brumback, Carl, 1917-
        Like a river. Springfield, Mo., Gospel Publishing House,
        c1977. iii, 170p. First published in 1961 as part two of the
        author's Suddenly ... from heaven. DLC

4363   Brumback, Carl, 1917-
        Suddenly ... from heaven; a history of the Assemblies
        of God. Springfield, Mo., Gospel Publishing House, 1961.
        xiv, 380p. DLC, TxWaS

4364   Bufkin, Robert Lee
        The Assembly of God: movement along the continuum
        from cult to church. Fayetteville, 1968. 108ℓ. Thesis
        (M.A.)--University of Arkansas. ArU

4365   Flower, Joseph Roswell, 1888-1970.
        History of the Assemblies of God, by J. Roswell Flower.
        Springfield, Mo., Pearlman Memorial Library, Central Bible
        Institute, 1949. 32ℓ. Paper prepared for use in instruction
        at Central Bible Institute. KyWAT

4366   Flower, Joseph Roswell, 1888-1970.
        The origin and development of the Assemblies of God,
        by J. Roswell Flower. n.p., 193-. [12]p. CU-B

4367   Flower, Joseph Roswell, 1888-1970.
        The origin and development of the Assemblies of God,
        by J. Roswell Flower. Rev. ed. Springfield, Mo., Gospel
        Publishing House, 1948. 24p. TxWaS, WiH

4368   Harrison, Irvine John, -1972.
        A history of the Assemblies of God. Berkeley, Calif.,
        1954. viii, 342ℓ. Thesis (Th.D.)--Berkeley Baptist Divinity
        School. CBBD

4369   Hoover, Mario G.
        Origin and structural development of the Assemblies of
        God. Springfield, Mo., 1968. 214ℓ. Thesis (M.A.)--
        Southwest Missouri State College. MoSpS

4370   Hoover, Mario G.
        Origin and structural development of the Assemblies of
        God. Springfield, Mo., 1968, c1970. 214p. Thesis (M.A.)
        --Southwest Missouri State College, 1968. CSdP, DLC

4371   Kendrick, Klaude, 1917-
        History of the Assemblies of God. Fort Worth, 1948.

97ℓ.   Thesis (M.A.)--Texas Christian University. TxFTC

4372   Kendrick, Klaude, 1917-
       The promise fulfilled: a history of the modern Pente-
costal movement. Springfield, Mo., Gospel Publishing House,
c1961. viii, 237p. On General Council of the Assemblies of
God: p. 73-144.

4373   Menzies, William Watson, 1931-
       Anointed to serve; the story of the Assemblies of God,
by William W. Menzies. Springfield, Mo., Gospel Publishing
House, 1971. 436p. Partially based on thesis (Ph.D.)--
University of Iowa, 1968. DLC, TxWaS

4374   Menzies, William Watson, 1931-
       The Assemblies of God: 1941-1967; the consolidation of
a revival movement, by William W. Menzies. Iowa City,
1968. v, 334ℓ. Thesis (Ph.D.)--University of Iowa. IaU

                --HISTORY AND STUDY OF DOCTRINES

4375   Aubin, Andrew Frederick
       The doctrine of the Holy Spirit and the charismata accord-
ing to the Plymouth Brethren and the Assemblies of God.
New York, 1955. ix, 91ℓ. Thesis (S.T.B.)--Biblical Seminary
in New York. NNBS

4376   Baxter, Yvonne Patricia, 1939-
       Problems arising from a comparison of the Episcopal
prayer book view of the gift of the Holy Spirit with the New
Testament view of the gift which is the Holy Spirit. Springfield, Mo., 1966. 62ℓ. Thesis (M.A.)--Central Bible College.

4377   Bresson, Bernard Lee, 1903-
       Studies in ecstasy [by] Bernard L. Bresson. New York,
Vantage Press, 1966. 127p. DLC, TxWaS

4378   Dalton, Robert Chandler, 1910-
       Tongues like as of fire; a critical study of modern tongue
movements in the light of apostolic and patristic times.
Springfield, Mo., Gospel Publishing House, c1945. 127p.
Based on thesis (B.D.)--Eastern Baptist Theological Seminary,
1940. PPEB, ScCoT, TxWaS

4378a Foster, Fred J.
       Think it not strange: a history of the Oneness movement,
by Fred J. Foster. St. Louis, Pentecostal Publishing House,
c1965. 109p. "The Assemblies of God reject the Oneness
message": p. 65-68.

4379   LaValley, James Francis, 1934-

Mid-century attitudes toward the role of faith in healing as commonly held within the Assemblies of God and the medical profession. Springfield, Mo., 1961. 51ℓ. Thesis (M.A.)--Central Bible Institute.

4380   MacDonald, William Graham, 1933-
Glossolalia in the New Testament, by William G. MacDonald. Springfield, Mo., Gospel Publishing House, 1964. 20p. "Originally presented before the annual meeting of the Evangelical Theological Society, Dec. 28, 1963, in Grand Rapids, Mich." MnCS, MSohG, NRCR

4381   Rasnake, John Samuel, 1932-
An investigation of the policy of the Assemblies of God on glossolalia and its effects on education in their colleges. Johnson City, 1965. v, 88ℓ. Thesis (M.A.)--East Tennessee State University. TJoS

4382   Smeeton, Donald Dean
Perfection or Pentecost: a historical comparison of charismatic and holiness theologies, by Donald D. Smeeton. Deerfield, Il., 1971. 160ℓ. Thesis (M.A.)--Trinity Evangelical Divinity School. Comparison of the teachings of the General Council of the Assemblies of God and the Church of the Nazarene. IDfT

4383   Wellman, David W.
An historical definition of the Assemblies of God doctrine of divine healing as propagated during the interval 1930-1945, by David Wellman. Springfield, Mo., 1961. 90ℓ. Thesis (M.A.)--Central Bible Institute.

4384   Wessels, Roland Heinrich
The doctrine of the baptism in the Holy Spirit among the Assemblies of God, by Roland Wessels. Berkeley, Ca., 1966. vii, 352ℓ. Thesis (Th.D.)--Pacific School of Religion. CBPac

4385   Wyckoff, John Wesley
The doctrine of sanctification as taught by the Assemblies of God. Bethany, Ok., 1972. iv, 90ℓ. Thesis (M.A.)-- Bethany Nazarene College. OkBetC

--HYMNS AND SACRED SONGS

4386   [Assemblies of God, General Council.]
Assembly songs. Springfield, Mo., Gospel Publishing House, 1948. 1v. (unpaged) With music.

4387   [Assemblies of God, General Council.]
Evangel songs. Springfield, Mo., Gospel Publishing House, 1931. 1v. (unpaged) OkBetC

4388   [Assemblies of God, General Council.]
       Evangelistic melodies. Springfield, Mo., Gospel Publish-
ing House, c1959. 1v. (unpaged) Cover title. With music.

4389   [Assemblies of God, General Council.]
       Favorite melodies. Springfield, Mo., Gospel Publishing
House, 1965. 96p. With music. "A Melody publication
compiled by the Gospel Publishing House Music Division,
Edwin Anderson, music editor."

4390   [Assemblies of God, General Council.]
       Full gospel songs. Springfield, Mo., Gospel Publishing
House, 1941.

4391   [Assemblies of God, General Council.]
       Gospel melodies. Springfield, Mo., Gospel Publishing
House, 1961. 1v. (unpaged) With music. "A Melody publication compiled by the Gospel Publishing House Music Division, Edwin P. Anderson, music editor."

4392   [Assemblies of God, General Council.]
       Heart melodies. Springfield, Mo., Gospel Publishing
House, 194-. 65p. Cover title. With music. RPB

4393   [Assemblies of God, General Council.]
       Hymns of glorious praise. Springfield, Mo., Gospel
Publishing House, 1969. 527p. With music. OkBetC

4394   [Assemblies of God, General Council.]
       Melodies of praise. Springfield, Mo., Gospel Publishing
House, 1957. 1v. (unpaged) With music.

4395   [Assemblies of God, General Council.]
       Melody choruses. Springfield, Mo., Gospel Publishing
House, 1963. 1v. (unpaged) With music. "A Melody pub-
lication compiled by the Gospel Publishing House Music
Division."

4396   [Assemblies of God, General Council.]
       Songs of Pentecostal fellowship. Springfield, Mo., Gos-
pel Publishing House, 1924. 1v. (unpaged) With music.

4397   [Assemblies of God, General Council.]
       Songs of praise. Springfield, Mo., 1v. (unpaged) With
music. OkBetC

4398   [Assemblies of God, General Council.]
       Spiritual songs. Springfield, Mo., Gospel Publishing
House, 1930. 1v. (unpaged) With music. OkBetC

4399   Assemblies of God, General Council. Districts. Arkansas.
       Songs of faith and power: old favorites and new melodies
arranged in Southern camp meeting style. Hot Springs, Ar.,

Arkansas District Council of the Assemblies of God, 194-.
1v. (unpaged) With music (shape notes) OkBetC

4400 Ball, Henry Cleo, comp., 1896-
Arpa y voz de salmodia. San Antonio, H. C. Ball,
Casa Evangélica de Publicaciones, c1939. 230p. Without
music. DLC

4401 Ball, Henry Cleo, comp., 1896-
Arpa y voz salmodia. San Antonio, H. C. Ball, Casa
Evangélica de Publicaciones, c1939. [238]p. With music.
DLC

4402 Ball, Henry Cleo, comp., 1896-
Himnos de gloria. San Antonio, 1921. 207p. With
music. IEN, RPB

4403 Ball, Henry Cleo, comp., 1896-
Himnos de gloria. Ed. 2. San Antonio, 1933, c1921.
217p. CaBViP

4404 Ball, Henry Cleo, comp., 1896-
Himnos de gloria. Springfield, Mo., Editorial Vida,
c1949. 233p. KyLxCB

4405 Ball, Henry Cleo, comp., 1896-
Himnos de gloria. Arreglados por H. C. Ball. Springfield, Mo., Casa de Publicaciones Evangelicas, c1949. 1v.
(unpaged) OkBetC

4406 Ball, Henry Cleo, comp., 1896-
Himnos de gloria; cantos de triunfo. Arreglo original:
H. C. Ball. 4. ed. Miami, Fl., Editorial Vida, 1970.
1v. (unpaged) With music.

4407 Revivaltime (Radio program)
Music of the Pentecostal churches. [Phonodisc] Word
W 308 1LP. [196-] 2s. 12 in. 33 1/3 microgroove.
Revivaltime Student Choir, with organ or piano acc.; Cyril
McLellan, conductor. Recorded at the Central Bible Institute
Springfield, Mo., Feb. 26-28, 1959. DLC

--INDEXES

4408 [Gospel Publishing House. Music Department.]
Melody Publications songfinder; music with melody.
Springfield, Mo., 1974- . v. [1]- . Annual.

--JUVENILE LITERATURE

4409 Clark, Clara B.

Slumber time stories, told by Clara B. Clark and Stanley
H. Frodsham (Nemo). Springfield, Mo. , Gospel Publishing
House, c1926. 110p. DLC

4410   Frodsham, Stanley Howard, 1882-1969.
        Around the world with the boomerang boy, by Stanley H.
Frodsham. Springfield, Mo. , Gospel Publishing House,
c1926. 143p. DLC

4411   Frodsham, Stanley Howard, 1882-1969.
        The boomerang boy, and other stories, by Stanley H.
Frodsham. Springfield, Mo. , Gospel Publishing House, 1925.
96p.

4412   Robinson, Charles Elmo, 1867-1954.
        The adventures of Blacky the Wasp. Springfield, Mo. ,
Gospel Publishing House, 1936. 87p.

4413   Robinson, Charles Elmo, 1867-1954.
        The adventures of Hush-wing the Owl. Springfield, Mo. ,
Gospel Publishing House, 1942. 78p.

4414   Robinson, Charles Elmo, 1867-1954.
        The gnat's lifeboat, and other stories, by Charles E.
Robinson. Springfield, Mo. , Gospel Publishing House, 1936.
96p.

4415   Robinson, Charles Elmo, 1867-1954.
        Keo the colt. Springfield, Mo. , Gospel Publishing House,
19--. 89p.

4416   Schickling, Wanda Gail
        My little chatterbox. Springfield, Mo. , Gospel Publish-
ing House, c1950. 111p. DLC

4417   Swinford, Betty, 1927-
        Dark is the forest. Springfield, Mo. , Gospel Publishing
House, 1963. 183p.

4418   Swinford, Betty, 1927-
        Shadow of the hammer. Springfield, Mo. , Gospel Publish-
ing House, 1967. 140p.

4419   Swinford, Betty, 1927-
        Terry and the legend of Indian Joe [by] Betty Swinford.
Illustrated by James Converse. Springfield, Mo. , Gospel
Publishing House, c1977. 125p. (Radiant books.) DLC

        --LITURGY AND RITUAL

4420   Pearlman, Myer, 1898-1943.
        The minister's service book. Springfield, Mo. , Gospel
Publishing House, 19--. 147p.

4421   Pickthorn, William E.
        Minister's manual. Compiled by William E. Pickthorn.
Springfield, Mo., Gospel Publishing House, 1965. 2v.   DLC

        --MISCELLANEA

4422   Favorite recipes of Assemblies of God women: desserts;
2,000 favorite dessert recipes, including party beverages.
        Montgomery, Al., Favorite Recipes Press, 1970. 382p.
DLC

4423   Favorite recipes of Assemblies of God women; holiday cook-
book.
        Montgomery, Al., Favorite Recipes Press, 1971. 286p.
DLC

4424   Favorite recipes of Assemblies of God women: meats, including seafood and poultry.
        Montgomery, Al., Favorite Recipes Press, 1969. 382p.
On cover: 2,000 favorite recipes. DLC

        --MISSIONS

4425   Assemblies of God, General Council. Foreign Missions Department.
        Assemblies of God in foreign lands; a survey ... Spring-
field, Mo., Gospel Publishing House, 1948. 92p.

4426   Assemblies of God, General Council. Foreign Missions Department.
        Missionary manual. Springfield, Mo., 192-. 30p.

4427   Assemblies of God, General Council. Foreign Missions Department.
        Missionary manual. Springfield, Mo., 193-. 32p. CtY

4428   Assemblies of God, General Council. Foreign Missions Department.
        The missionary manual. Springfield, Mo., 1963. 64p.
MoKN

4429   Assemblies of God, General Council. Foreign Missions Department.
        The missionary manual. Springfield, Mo., 1969. 87p.

4430   Assemblies of God, General Council. Foreign Missions Department.
        The missionary manual. Springfield, Mo., Division of
Foreign Missions of the Assemblies of God, 1973. 114p.

4431   Children of the world (Motion picture).
        Cathedral Films in association with the Assemblies of

God Foreign Missions Department, 1967. 30 min. sd.
color. 35mm. With leader's discussion guide. DLC

4432   Cunningham, Richard Bruce, 1931-
            An investigation of the use of a taxonomy of education as
       an evaluation device for Assemblies of God overseas Bible
       schools. Salt Lake City, 1974. x, 313ℓ. Thesis (Ed. D.)--
       University of Utah. UU

4433   Enyart, Ruby M.
            Before their eyes; missionary plays for church and church
       group recreation. Edited by Ruby M. Enyart. Springfield,
       Mo., Gospel Publishing House, 1956. 60p.

4434   Flores, Alfred Lerma, 1943-
            Overseas Christian literature production of the Assemblies
       of God, by Alfred L. Flores. San Luis Obispo, 1974. v,
       138ℓ. Senior project--California Polytechnic State University.
       CSluSP

4435   Hodges, Melvin Lyle, 1909-
            Build my church, by Melvin L. Hodges. Springfield,
       Mo., Gospel Publishing House, 1957. 96p.

4436   Hodges, Melvin Lyle, 1909-
            The indigenous church, by Melvin L. Hodges. Spring-
       field, Mo., Gospel Publishing House, c1953. ix, 157p.
       CLamB

4437   Hodges, Melvin Lyle, 1909-
            The indigenous church, by Melvin L. Hodges. Rev. ed.
       Springfield, Mo., Gospel Publishing House, c1971. 144p.

4438   Hodges, Serena M., ed.
            Look on the fields; a missionary survey. Data supplied
       by Assemblies of God missionaries. Springfield, Mo., Gos-
       pel Publishing House, c1956. 201p. DLC, NNMR

4439   Perkin, Noel, 1893-
            Our world witness; a survey of Assemblies of God foreign
       missions, by Noel Perkin and John Garlock. Springfield,
       Mo., Gospel Publishing House, c1963. 118p.
       _____. Instructor's guide, by George and Billie Davis.
       Springfield, Mo., Gospel Publishing House, 196-. ix, 83p.

                          --MUSIC

4440   Johnson, Darrell Keith
            A study of present day music practices in the Assemblies
       of God. Los Angeles, 1972. iii, 168ℓ. Thesis (M. Mus.)--
       University of Southern California. CLSU

4441   Tanner, Donald Ray, 1931-
        An analysis of Assemblies of God hymnody. Minneapolis,
        1974. viii,250ℓ. Thesis (Ph. D.)--University of Minnesota.
        MnU

4441a   Tanner, Donald Ray, 1931-
        Hymnody of the Assemblies of God [by] Don R. Tanner.
        In Hymn, 31 (Oct. 1980), 252-256, 258.

        --PASTORAL LITERATURE

4442   Assemblies of God, General Council.
        Live in the Spirit; a compendium of themes on the spirit-
        ual life as presented at the Council on Spiritual Life, [Minne-
        apolis, Minnesota, Aug. 14-18, 1972]. Editorial committee:
        Harris Jansen, chairman, Elva Hoover, Gary Leggett. Spring-
        field, Mo. , Gospel Publishing House, 1972. 359p.

4443   Argue, Zelma
        Garments of strength. Springfield, Mo. , Gospel Publish-
        ing House, 1935. 109p.

4444   Bostrom, John H. , 1899-
        What every new convert should know, by John H. Bostrom.
        San Gabriel, Calif. , c1969. 30p.

4445   Brock, Raymond Theodore, 1927-
        The Christ-centered family [by] Raymond T. Brock.
        Springfield, Mo. , Gospel Publishing House, c1977. 124p.
        (Radiant books.) DLC

4445a   Burton, William Frederick Padwick, 1886-1971.
        Where to go with your troubles [by] William F. P. Bur-
        ton. Springfield, Mo. , Gospel Publishing House, 1969. 80p.
        MoSpG

4446   Champion, Richard Gordon, 1931-
        Above and beyond, by Dick Champion. Springfield, Mo. ,
        Gospel Publishing House, 1961. 80p.
        _____. Instructor's guide. Springfield, Mo. , Gospel
        Publishing House, 196-. 23p. Cover title.

4447   Champion, Richard Gordon, 1931-
        Go on singing; how to find joyful living from the Psalms
        [by] Richard G. Champion. Springfield, Mo. , Gospel Publish-
        ing House, 1976. 125p.

4448   Champion, Richard Gordon, 1931-
        What's mine, by Dick Champion. Springfield, Mo. , Gos-
        pel Publishing House, 1962. 96p.

4449   Flower, Alice (Reynolds), 1890-

The business of coat-making. 6th ed. Springfield, Mo.,
19--. 16p.

4450   Flower, Alice (Reynolds), 1890-
        The family altar: what, why, when, how? 4 pertinent
questions answered by Alice Reynolds Flower. Springfield,
Mo., Gospel Publishing House, 19--. 12p.

4451   Flower, Alice (Reynolds), 1890-
        The home, a divine sanctuary. Springfield, Mo., Gospel
Publishing House, 1955. 185p. DLC

4452   Flower, Alice (Reynolds), 1890-
        Jochebed's wages. n.p., 19--. 12p. Cover title.

4453   Flower, Alice (Reynolds), 1890-
        Open windows. Springfield, Mo., Gospel Publishing
House, 1948. 166p. OkTOr

4454   Flower, Alice (Reynolds), 1890-
        The set of your sails, and other twilight chats. Spring-
field, Mo., Gospel Publishing House, 1942. 142p. OkTOr

4455   Flower, Alice (Reynolds), 1890-
        Straws tell, and other twilight chats. Springfield, Mo.,
Gospel Publishing House, 1941. 156p.

4456   Flower, Alice (Reynolds), 1890-
        What mean ye by these stones. n.p., 19--. 16p.
Cover title.

4457   Hanson, Melvin B.
        Present your bodies, by Melvin B. Hanson. Springfield,
Mo., Gospel Publishing House, c1955. 167p. DLC

4458   Harris, Ralph William, 1912-
        Now what? A guidebook for new Christians, by Ralph W.
Harris. Springfield, Mo., Gospel Publishing House, c1964.
24p.

4459   Harris, Ralph William, 1912-
        What's next? New life in Christ; guidebook for children,
by Ralph W. Harris. Springfield, Mo., Gospel Publishing
House, c1971. 24p. First published under title: Helps for
young Christians.

4460   Horban, Michael
        Get with it, man! A fresh look at a man's world. Tor-
onto, Full Gospel Publishing House; Springfield, Mo., Gospel
Publishing House, 1974. 105p. (Radiant books.) DLC

4461   Horban, Michael
        Hanging loose in an uptight world. Toronto, Full Gospel

Publishing House; Springfield, Mo. , Gospel Publishing House,
c1978. 123p. (Radiant books.) DLC

4462   Ludwig, Charles, 1918-
        Say fellows! Springfield, Mo. , Gospel Publishing House,
c1955. 83p.

4463   Sumrall, Lester Frank, 1913-
        Adoradores de la pantalia de plata, por Lester F. Sum-
rall. Prefacio por Edith Mae Pennington. San Antonio, Tx. ,
Casa Evangélica de Publicaciones, c1941. 67p. Translation
of Worshipers of the silver screen. DLC

4464   Sumrall, Lester Frank, 1913-
        Worshipers of the silver screen, by Lester F. Sumrall.
Foreword by Edith Mae Pennington. Grand Rapids, Mi. ,
Zondervan Publishing House, c1940. 64p. DLC

4465   Ward, Charles Morse, 1909-
        Can Christians participate in the $64,000 question? And
37 other questions. By C. M. Ward. Springfield, Mo. ,
Gospel Publishing House, c1955. 39p.

4466   Ward, Charles Morse, 1909-
        Clash, by C. M. Ward. Springfield, Mo. , Gospel Pub-
lishing House, c1955. 32p.

4467   Ward, Charles Morse, 1909-
        The playboy comes home [by] C. M. Ward. Springfield,
Mo. , Gospel Publishing House, c1976. 107p. (Radiant
books.) DLC

4468   Warner, Wayne Earl, 1933-
        Letters to Tony [by] Wayne Warner. Springfield, Mo. ,
Gospel Publishing House, 1975. 106p. (Radiant books.) A
record of correspondence between a teen-age boy and his
pastor on topics such as death, sex, and charismatic experiences. DLC

4469   Williams, Ernest Swing, 1885-
        Your questions ... answered, by Ernest S. Williams.
Springfield, Mo. , Gospel Publishing House, c1968. 85p.
Answers to letters sent to the Pentecostal Evangel. DLC

                        --PASTORAL THEOLOGY

4470   Bicket, Zenas Johan, 1932-
        The effective pastor. Compiled and edited by Zenas J.
Bicket, under the direction of the Assemblies of God Committee on Mission. Springfield, Mo. , Gospel Publishing House,
c1973. v, 184p. DLC

4471   Flower, Alice (Reynolds), 1890-
        Building her house well. Springfield, Mo. , Gospel Pub-
        lishing House, 1949. 152p. For clergy wives.

4472   Gee, Donald, 1891-1966.
        The ministry-gifts of Christ. Springfield, Mo. , Gospel
        Publishing House, c1930. 110p. DLC, MSohG

4472a   Gee, Donald, 1891-1966.
        Spiritual gifts in the work of the ministry today. Spring-
        field, Mo. , Gospel Publishing House, c1963. ix, 101p.
        CLamB, InNd, KyLoS, KyWAT, MnCS, OSW, PGraM, TxWaS

4473   Gilbert, Marvin Glenn
        The decision of Assemblies of God pastors to counsel or
        refer, by Marvin G. Gilbert. In Journal of Psychology and
        Theology, 9 (Fall 1981), 250-256. Based on survey of pastors
        of the West Texas District Council.

4473a   Gilbert, Marvin Glenn
        Variables in the decision by Assemblies of God pastors
        to counsel or refer. Lubbock, 1979. v, 123ℓ . Thesis
        (Ed. D.)--Texas Tech University. TxLT

4474   Hauff, Louis Harold, comp. , 1910-
        Preparation for preaching. Compiled by Louis H. Hauff.
        n. p. [1967] 97p. Contributors include: C. M. Ward, Chas.
        W. H. Scott, Leland R. Keys, Obie L. Harrup, Sr. , O.
        Cope Budge, G. Raymond Carlson, Dwight H. McLaughlin,
        Louis H. Hauff.

4475   Holmes, George
        Toward an effective pulpit ministry. Springfield, Mo. ,
        Gospel Publishing House, 1971. 176p. DLC

4476   Luce, Alice Eveline, -1930.
        El mensajero y su mensaje; manual para obreros cris-
        tianos. Springfield, Mo. , Casa de publicaciones evangelicas,
        c1953. 88p. "Esta edición fué revisada por Benjamín Mar-
        cado. " Translation of The messenger and his message.
        TxDaM

4477   Luce, Alice Eveline, -1930.
        The messenger and his message, by Alice E. Luce.
        Springfield, Mo. , Gospel Publishing House, c1925. ix, 127p.

4478   Luce, Alice Eveline, -1930.
        Messenger and his message; a handbook for young workers
        on the preparation of gospel addresses, by Alice E. Luce.
        San Diego, Ca. , c1930. 191p. TxWaS

4479   Nelson, Peter Christopher, 1868-1942.
        The young minister's guide in conducting funerals,

solemnizing weddings, administering baptism and the Lord's Supper and anointing the sick ... by R. C. Nelson. Enid, Ok. , Southwestern Press, c1932. 67p. DLC

4480   Riggs, Ralph Meredith, 1895-1971.
       The Spirit-filled pastor's guide. Springfield, Mo. , Gospel Publishing House, 1949, c1948. 287p. DLC

4481   Riggs, Ralph Meredith, 1895-1971.
       A successful pastor, by Ralph M. Riggs. Springfield, Mo. , Gospel Publishing House, c1931. 115p.

4482   Ward, Alfred George, 1881-1960.
       The minister and his work, by A. G. Ward. Springfield, Mo. , Gospel Publishing House, c1945. 123p.

4483   Williams, Ernest Swing, 1885-
       A faithful minister; heart-to-heart talks, by Ernest S. Williams. Springfield, Mo. , Gospel Publishing House, c1941. 112p. DLC

4484   Williams, Fred Anthony
       A model for developing pastoral counseling centers primarily for the Assemblies of God. Dallas, 1974. 202ℓ . Thesis (D. Min.)--Southern Methodist University. TxDaM

4485   Zimmerman, Thomas Fletcher, ed. , 1912-
       And he gave pastors: pastoral theology in action. Editor, Thomas F. Zimmerman, associate editors, G. Raymond Carlson, Zenas J. Bicket. Springfield, Mo. , Gospel Publishing House, c1979. 629p. DLC

       --PERIODICALS

4486   Advance. 1- Oct. 1965-
       Springfield, Mo.

4487   Agora. 1- 1977-
       Costa Mesa, Ca.

4488   Assemblies chaplain. 1- 1953-
       Springfield, Mo.

4489   Assemblies of God educator. 1- 1956-
       Springfield, Mo.

4490   Assemblies of God home missions. 1- 19 -
       Springfield, Mo.

4491   La Buona Notizia. 1- 19 -
       Paterson, N. J. Italian and English.

4492   CAM [Campus ambassador magazine]. 1- 1948-
       Springfield, Mo. 1948-1952 as College fellowship bulletin.

4493   Christ's ambassadors. 1- Apr. 1926-1927.
       Springfield, Mo.

4494   Christ's ambassadors monthly. 1- Apr. 1928-1930.
       Springfield, Mo.

4495   Daily devotions. 1- 1941-194-.
       Springfield, Mo.

4496   Dobry Pasterz. 1- 1936-
       South Boston, Ma. NN

4497   Evanhelski Palomnyk. 1- 19 -
       New York

4498   Family altar guide. 1- 1947-
       Springfield, Mo.

4499   Glad tidings herald. 1-27, 1918-1948.
       New York. Title varies.

4500   Glad tidings magazine. 1- July 3, 1925-
       San Francisco, St. Helena, Ca. , Santa Cruz, Ca. 1925-
       19-- as Glad tidings.

4501   Glasnik Puta Spasenja. 1- 19 -
       Detroit

4502   Good news crusades. 1- Aug. 1959-
       Springfield, Mo. 1-9, no. 4, 1959-Aug. 1967 as Global
       conquest.

4503   Good tidings. 1- 1924-
       Springfield, Mo.

4504   Gospel broadcast. 1- 1940-1948.
       Minneapolis

4505   La Guia Dominical. 1- 194 -
       Springfield, Mo.

4506   Hebrew evangel. 1- 195 -
       Chicago

4507   Hi-Call. 1- 195 -
       Springfield, Mo.

4508   Hisway. 1- 1944-
       Springfield, Mo. 1944-197- as Christ's ambassadors
       guide.

4509   Joyas Escogidas. 1- 194 -
        Springfield, Mo.

4510   Just between us. 1- 1953-
        Springfield, Mo.

4511   Licht und Leben. 1- 19 -
        Cleveland, Oh.

4512   Live. 1- 1928-
        Springfield, Mo.   1928-1957 as Gospel gleaners.

4513   La luz apostolica. 1- Sept. 1916-
        Kingsville, Tx. , San Antonio, Tx. , Albuquerque, N. M.

4514   Mission: America. 1- 1970-
        Springfield, Mo.

4515   Missionary monthly. 1- -May 17, 1919.
        Cleveland, Oh.   Merged into Weekly evangel.

4516   Missionettes memos. 1- 1956-
        Springfield, Mo.

4517   Niños Christianos. 1- 194 -
        Springfield, Mo.

4518   Our Pentecostal boys and girls. 1- July 1, 1921-
        Springfield, Mo.

4519   Our Pentecostal little folks. 1- 1922-
        Springfield, Mo.

4520   Paraclete. 1- 1967-
        Springfield, Mo.

4521   Pentecostal evangel. 1- July 19, 1913-
        Plainfield, In. , Findlay, Oh. , St. Louis, Mo. , Spring-
        field, Mo.   1913-1915 as Christian Evangel; 1916-Sept. 11,
        1919 as Weekly evangel.

4522   Poder. 1- 19 -
        Springfield, Mo.

4523   Porlas Ventanas. 1- 194 -
        Springfield, Mo.

4524   Pulpit. 1-7, Aug. 1958-1965.
        Springfield, Mo.

4525   Reach out. 1- 1970-
        Springfield, Mo.

4526   Restoration.   1-   1967-
       St. Louis, Mo., Springfield, Mo.

4527   Reveille.   1-   1941-
       Springfield, Mo.

4528   Soul winner.   1-   19 -
       Spanaway, Wa.

4529   Standard bearer.   1-   1969-
       Neosho, Mo.

4530   Sunday school counselor.   1-   June 1939-
       Springfield, Mo.   1939-Nov. 1955 as Our Sunday school
       counselor.

4531   TEAM [To enlist all men].   1-17, no. 3, Oct. 1954-Sept.
       1970.
       Springfield, Mo.

4532   Word and witness.   1-11, 19 -1915.
       Nashville, Tn., Malvern, Ar., Findlay, Oh., St. Louis,
       Mo.   Merged into Weekly evangel.

4533   World challenge.   1-19, 1944-Mar. 1959.
       Springfield, Mo.   1944-1956 as Missionary challenge.
       Merged into Pentecostal evangel.

4534   Youth alive.   1-   1926-
       Los Angeles; Springfield, Mo.   1926-1967 as Christ's
       ambassadors herald.

4535   Zvestovatel.   1-   19 -
       Chicago

                    --PUBLISHERS AND PUBLISHING

4536   Flores, Alfred Lerma, 1943-
       Overseas Christian literature production of the Assem-
       blies of God, by Alfred L. Flores.   San Luis Obispo, 1974.
       v, 138ℓ.   Senior project--California Polytechnic State Univer-
       sity.   CSluSP

4537   Gospel Publishing House.
       Style manual and specimens of type for editors and
       writers of General Council Assemblies of God departments.
       Springfield, Mo., 1958.   74p.   Edited by Zenas J. Bicket.

4538   Jackson, Russell Rex, 1915-
       The literature program of the Assemblies of God.   Man-
       hattan, 1963.   iv, 223ℓ.   Thesis (M.S.)--Kansas State Uni-
       versity.   KMK

4539   Winehouse, Irwin, 1922-
         The Assemblies of God: a popular survey, by Irwin
       Winehouse. With an introduction by J. Roswell Flower.
       New York, Vantage Press, 1959. 224p. "The Gospel Pub-
       lishing House": p. 157-162. DLC, NNUT, TxWaS

         --RADIO AND TELEVISION BROADCASTING

4540   Ward, Charles Morse, 1909-
         Box 70, by C. M. Ward. Springfield, Mo., Gospel
       Publishing House, c1958. 59p. On the Revivaltime radio
       program.

4541   Winehouse, Irwin, 1922-
         The Assemblies of God: a popular survey, by Irwin
       Winehouse. With an introduction by J. Roswell Flower.
       New York, Vantage Press, 1959. 224p. "The voice of
       'Revivaltime' ": p. 163-177. DLC, NNUT, TxWaS

         --RELATIONS WITH OTHER DENOMINATIONS

4542   A new encounter.
         In Christianity Today, 7 (Feb. 1, 1963), 36-37. On
       meetings between officials of the General Council of the As-
       semblies of God and the Protestant Episcopal Church in the
       U.S.A. in Kansas City, Feb. 16-17, and in Springfield, Mis-
       souri, Nov. 8-9, 1962.

         --SERMONS, TRACTS, ADDRESSES, ESSAYS

4543   Assemblies of God, General Council.
         Filled with the fulness of God. Springfield, Mo., Gospel
       Publishing House, c1930. 62p. TxWaS

4544   Assemblies of God, General Council.
         The Pentecostal pulpit. Springfield, Mo., Gospel Pub-
       lishing House, 1946-19--. 3v. Sermons by Ernest S.
       Williams, J. Narver Gortner, Wesley R. Steelberg, R. M.
       Riggs, J. Roswell Flower, Noel Perkin, W. I. Evans, Myer
       Pearlman, P. C. Nelson, Gayle F. Lewis, Stanley H. Frod-
       sham, Robert Cummings, Harvey McAlister, T. J. Jones,
       William E. Long, Don F. Lehmann, H. C. McKinney, Ben
       Hardin, and Aaron A. Wilson.

4545   Barney, Kenneth D., 1921-
         Christ speaks to the church: practical messages on
       Christ's letters to the seven churches [by] Kenneth D. Barney.
       Springfield, Mo., Gospel Publishing House, c1970. 63p.

4546   Barney, Kenneth D., 1921-

The fourth watch of the night, and other messages for troubled times, by Kenneth D. Barney. Springfield, Mo., Gospel Publishing House, c1973. 95p.

4547   Barney, Kenneth D., 1921-
        Preparing for the storm [by] Kenneth D. Barney. Spring-field, Mo., Gospel Publishing House, 1975. 96p. (Radiant books.) DLC

4548   Barney, Kenneth D., 1921-
        We interrupt the crisis [by] Kenneth D. Barney. Spring-field, Mo., Gospel Publishing House, 1970. 63p. First published under title: Christ speaks to the church.

4549   Bethany, Edgar W.
        The Lord's Day [by] Edgar Bethany. In Sunday; the Magazine for the Lord's Day, 60 (July-Aug. 1974), 3.

4550   Bostrom, John H., 1899-
        Have you forgotten? By John H. Bostrom. Pasadena, Ca., c1945. 44p.

4551   Bostrom, John H., 1899-
        "I saw the Lord!" By John H. Bostrom. Pasadena, Ca., c1941. 31p. DLC

4552   Bostrom, John H., 1899-
        Keep moving! By John H. Bostrom. Pasadena, Ca., c1945. 44p.

4553   Bostrom, John H., 1899-
        The palm tree Christian, by John H. Bostrom. Pasa-dena, Ca., c1941. 30p. DLC

4554   Bostrom, John H., 1899-
        The power of influence, by John H. Bostrom. Pasadena, Ca., c1941. 44p.

4555   Bostrom, John H., 1899-
        The prodigal's brother, by John H. Bostrom. Pasadena, Ca., c1941. 29p. DLC

4556   Bostrom, John H., 1899-
        The scarlet worm, by John H. Bostrom. Pasadena, Ca., c1941. 29p. DLC

4557   Bostrom, John H., 1899-
        There's trouble ahead, by John H. Bostrom. Pasadena, Ca., c1941. 29p. DLC

4558   Bostrom, John H., 1899-
        Twice born, by John H. Bostrom. Pasadena, Ca., 19--. 32p.

4559   Cunningham, Robert C.
            It's the Lord's day [by] Robert C. Cunningham. In
        Sunday; the Magazine for the Lord's Day, 60 (July-Aug.
        1974), 5-6.

4560   Fjordbak, Everitt Merlin, 1921-
            Jonah: a study in God's love for wayward man. From
        three messages delivered at Lakewood Assembly by Pastor
        Everitt M. Fjordbak. Edited by Bob Summers. Dallas,
        Wisdom House Publishers, c1974. 64p. MnMNC

4561   Follette, John Wright, 1883-1966.
            Arrows of truth: sermons and poems. Springfield, Mo.,
        Gospel Publishing House, 1969. 187p.

4562   Follette, John Wright, 1883-1966.
            Broken bread; a book of sermons and poems. Spring-
        field, Mo., Gospel Publishing House, c1957. viii, 216p.
        DLC

4563   Follette, John Wright, 1883-1966.
            Fruit of the land. Springfield, Mo., Gospel Publishing
        House, 19--. 55p.

4564   Jamieson, S. A.
            The great shepherd, by S. A. Jamieson. Springfield,
        Mo., Gospel Publishing House, 19--. 109p. (Pulpit and
        pew, full gospel series.) CCmS, TxWaS

4565   Mallough, Don, 1914-
            Crowded detours. Grand Rapids, Baker Book House,
        1970. 111p. DLC

4566   Mallough, Don, 1914-
            If I were God. Grand Rapids, Baker Book House, 1966.
        109p. DLC

4567   Mallough, Don, 1914-
            Stop the merry-go-round. Grand Rapids, Baker Book
        House, 1964. 97p. DLC

4568   Moody, William E.
            Faith's conquests and other messages, by W. E. Moody.
        Springfield, Mo., Gospel Publishing House, 1931. 134p.

4569   Parker, Charles A.
            Concerning the Holy Spirit, by Charles A. Parker.
        Columbia, Mo., 19--. 46p. Sermons given over Station
        KFRU, Columbia, Missouri.

4570   Perkins, Jonathan Elsworth, 1889-
            The brooding presence and Pentecost. Springfield, Mo.,
        Gospel Publishing House, 1924. 124p. (Pulpit and pew, full
        gospel series.)

4571   Shields, Sidney Guy, 1895-
            Camp-meeting special, by Guy Shields. Amarillo, Tx.,
        1933. 116p. Cover title: Camp meeting echoes.

4572   Shields, Sidney Guy, 1895-
            The moving of the Spirit. Fort Worth, Tx., Manney
        Printing Co., 1935. 88p. "Second printing ... revised."

4573   Sisson, Elizabeth, 1843-
            A sign people. Springfield, Mo., Gospel Publishing
        House, 19--. 15p.

4574   Steil, Harry J., 1901-
            God's diamonds [by] Harry J. Steil. Springfield, Mo.,
        Printed by Midwest Litho and Publishing Co., 1965. 30p.

4575   Ward, Alfred George, 1881-1960.
            Soul-food for hungry saints, by A. G. Ward. Spring-
        field, Mo., Gospel Publishing House, c1925. 141p. (Pulpit
        and pew, full gospel series.) DLC

4576   Ward, Alfred George, 1881-1960.
            A twofold picture of God, and other messages, by A. G.
        and C. M. Ward. Springfield, Mo., Gospel Publishing
        House, 19--. 131p.

4577   Ward, Alfred George, 1881-1960.
            The whirlwind prophet, and other sermons, by A. G.
        Ward. Springfield, Mo., Gospel Publishing House, 1927.
        128p. (Pulpit and pew, full gospel series.) DLC

4578   Ward, Charles Morse, 1909-
            Are you a witness? By C. M. Ward. Springfield, Mo.,
        Assemblies of God, c1960. 47p.

4579   Ward, Charles Morse, 1909-
            Asking no question for conscience sake, by C. M. Ward.
        Springfield, Mo., Gospel Publishing House, c1958. 27p.

4580   Ward, Charles Morse, 1909-
            Campmeeting religion, by C. M. Ward. Springfield,
        Mo., Assemblies of God, c1954. 43p.

4581   Ward, Charles Morse, 1909-
            Choosing rather, by C. M. Ward. Springfield, Mo.,
        Gospel Publishing House, c1958. 28p.

4582   Ward, Charles Morse, 1909-
            Christ was not born on this date, by C. M. Ward.
        Springfield, Mo., Gospel Publishing House, c1955. 25p.

4583   Ward, Charles Morse, 1909-
            Cyprus points to Christ, by C. M. Ward. Springfield,

Mo. , Gospel Publishing House, c1956.   32p.

4584   Ward, Charles Morse, 1909-
          Dr. Wernher von Braun: "The farther we probe into
          space the greater my faith ..." By C. M. Ward. Springfield,
          Mo. , Assemblies of God, 1966.

4585   Ward, Charles Morse, 1909-
          52 complete evangelistic sermons, by C. M. Ward.
          Springfield, Mo. , Revivaltime, c1956.   173p.

4586   Ward, Charles Morse, 1909-
          Five times reprieved, by C. M. Ward.   Springfield,
          Mo. , Gospel Publishing House, c1957.   27p.

4587   Ward, Charles Morse, 1909-
          God speaks today, by C. M. Ward. Springfield, Mo. ,
          Assemblies of God, c1961.   52p.

4588   Ward, Charles Morse, 1909-
          The H-bomb and the battle of Armageddon, by C. M.
          Ward. Springfield, Mo. , Gospel Publishing House, c1956.
          22p.

4589   Ward, Charles Morse, 1909-
          The Holy Spirit is for you, by C. M. Ward. Springfield,
          Mo. , Assemblies of God, 1966.   32p.

4590   Ward, Charles Morse, 1909-
          How far can a mother's prayers reach? By C. M.
          Ward. Springfield, Mo. , Assemblies of God, c1963.   47p.

4591   Ward, Charles Morse, 1909-
          How mean was David's sin? By C. M. Ward. Spring-
          field, Mo. , Gospel Publishing House, c1955.   35p.

4592   Ward, Charles Morse, 1909-
          Is God too good to send anyone to hell and too just to
          keep anyone there forever? By C. M. Ward. Springfield,
          Mo. , Gospel Publishing House, c1956.   22p.

4593   Ward, Charles Morse, 1909-
          Let a man examine himself, by C. M. Ward. Spring-
          field, Mo. , Assemblies of God, c1959.   35p. (The Pulpit
          series.) The story of the communion service former Con-
          federate President Jefferson Davis, a prisoner at Fortress
          Monroe, Virginia, could not share in until he had searched
          his soul.   Vi

4594   Ward, Charles Morse, 1909-
          Life's greatest questions, by C. M. Ward. Springfield,
          Mo. , Gospel Publishing House, c1955.   30p.

4595   Ward, Charles Morse, 1909-
        Most requested radio sermons of 1956, by C. M. Ward,
        Revivaltime speaker. Special ed. Springfield, Mo., Assem-
        blies of God, 1956. 96p. KyWAT

4596   Ward, Charles Morse, 1909-
        My most important health lesson, by C. M. Ward.
        Springfield, Mo., Gospel Publishing House, c1958. 24p.

4597   Ward, Charles Morse, 1909-
        A new name and a number? By C. M. Ward. Spring-
        field, Mo., Gospel Publishing House, 1966. 48p.

4598   Ward, Charles Morse, 1909-
        One taken, the other left, by C. M. Ward. Springfield,
        Mo., Gospel Publishing House, c1955. 34p.

4599   Ward, Charles Morse, 1909-
        Questions and answers, by C. M. Ward. Springfield,
        Mo., Gospel Publishing House, c1954. 37p.

4600   Ward, Charles Morse, 1909-
        Recession or revival? By C. M. Ward. Springfield,
        Mo., Gospel Publishing House, c1958. 28p.

4601   Ward, Charles Morse, 1909-
        Resisting the Holy Spirit, by C. M. Ward. Springfield,
        Mo., Gospel Publishing House, c1955. 32p.

4602   Ward, Charles Morse, 1909-
        Revivaltime pulpit; sermon book number one- [by] C. M.
        Ward. Springfield, Mo., Assemblies of God, National Radio
        Department, 1957- v. 1- .

4603   Ward, Charles Morse, 1909-
        Revivaltime sermons, by C. M. Ward. Grand Rapids,
        Mi., Baker Book House, 1966. 62p. (Dollar sermon li-
        brary.)

4604   Ward, Charles Morse, 1909-
        Right or wrong, by C. M. Ward. Springfield, Mo.,
        Gospel Publishing House, 1957. 40p.

4605   Ward, Charles Morse, 1909-
        Rumors: 1971 prophecy book, by C. Morse Ward.
        Springfield, Mo., Assemblies of God, 1971. 48p.

4606   Ward, Charles Morse, 1909-
        The Sergeant Thompson story, by C. M. Ward. Spring-
        field, Mo., Gospel Publishing House, c1958. 33p.

4607   Ward, Charles Morse, 1909-
        The silent speak, by C. M. Ward. Springfield, Mo.,

Assemblies of God, 1963. 23p. Cites known languages spoken under inspiration by the deaf as initial evidence of the baptism in the Holy Spirit.

4608   Ward, Charles Morse, 1909-
    Space travel foretold, by C. M. Ward. Springfield, Mo., Gospel Publishing House, c1956. 30p.

4609   Ward, Charles Morse, 1909-
    Story-studies of the Bible, by C. M. Ward. Springfield, Mo., Gospel Publishing House, 19--. 56p.

4610   Ward, Charles Morse, 1909-
    The sword of Goliath, by C. M. Ward. Springfield, Mo., Gospel Publishing House, c1955. 42p.

4611   Ward, Charles Morse, 1909-
    These shall be signs, by C. M. Ward. Springfield, Mo., Assemblies of God, c1964. 84p.

4612   Ward, Charles Morse, 1909-
    This child shall be lent unto the Lord, by C. M. Ward. Illustrated by Kim Nettie. Springfield, Mo., Gospel Publishing House, 1967. 32p.

4613   Ward, Charles Morse, 1909-
    The three big lies of communism, by C. M. Ward. Springfield, Mo., Gospel Publishing House, c1954. 32p.

4614   Ward, Charles Morse, 1909-
    The tongue is a fire, by C. M. Ward. Springfield, Mo., Gospel Publishing House, 19--. 11p.

4615   Ward, Charles Morse, 1909-
    The tragedy of mixed marriage, by C. M. Ward. Springfield, Mo., Gospel Publishing House, c1955. 25p.

4616   Ward, Charles Morse, 1909-
    20,000 traps, by C. M. Ward. Springfield, Mo., Gospel Publishing House, c1956. 22p.

4617   Ward, Charles Morse, 1909-
    What are they saying about divine healing? By C. M. Ward. Springfield, Mo., Gospel Publishing House, c1956. 26p.

4618   Ward, Charles Morse, 1909-
    What the Bible says about public divine healing services, by C. M. Ward. Springfield, Mo., Gospel Publishing House, c1955. 40p.

4619   Ward, Charles Morse, 1909-
    Where did Cain get his wife? By C. M. Ward. Spring-

field, Mo., Gospel Publishing House, c1955.   40p.

4620   Ward, Charles Morse, 1909-
       Why I do not pray to the mother of God, by C. M.
       Ward.   Springfield, Mo., Gospel Publishing House, c1958.
       24p.

4621   Ward, Charles Morse, 1909-
       Will the sphinx speak?   By C. M. Ward.   Springfield,
       Mo., Gospel Publishing House, c1955.   24p.

4622   Ward, Charles Morse, 1909-
       World without children!   1970 prophecy book, by C. M.
       Ward.   Springfield, Mo., Assemblies of God, 1970.   48p.
       (The pulpit series.)

4623   Wigglesworth, Smith, 1859-1947.
       Ever-increasing faith.   Springfield, Mo., Gospel Publish-
       ing House, c1924.   160p.   TxWaS

4624   Wigglesworth, Smith, 1859-1947.
       Ever-increasing faith.   Rev. ed.   Springfield, Mo.,
       Gospel Publishing House, 1971.   176p.   CBGTU

4625   Wigglesworth, Smith, 1859-1947.
       Faith that prevails.   Springfield, Mo., Gospel Publishing
       House, 1938.   64p.   OrTOr

4626   Wigglesworth, Smith, 1859-1947.
       Filled with the fullness of God.   Springfield, Mo., Gos-
       pel Publishing House, 1930.   62p.

4627   Williams, Ernest Swing, 1885-
       My sermon notes; the Gospels and Acts, by E. S.
       Williams.   Springfield, Mo., Gospel Publishing House, 1967.
       224p.   DLC

4628   Wilson, Aaron Aubrey
       The gospel reveille: radio sermonettes [by] A. A. Wil-
       son.   [Kansas City, Mo., 19--] 142p.   Delivered on Gospel
       Reveille broadcast.

4629   Wilson, Aaron Aubrey
       "Things which are most surely believed among us," by
       A. A. Wilson.   [Kansas City, Mo., 19--] 52p.   "The mes-
       sages in this book have been given on our 'Gospel Reveille'
       broadcast."   TxWaS

4630   Zimmerman, Thomas Fletcher, 1912-
       The eternal dimension [by] Thos. F. Zimmerman.   In
       Sunday; the Magazine for the Lord's Day, 60 (July-Aug. 1974),
       6.

--WORK WITH CHILDREN

4631   Children of the world (Motion picture).
        Cathedral Films in association with the Assemblies of
God Foreign Missions Department, 1967.   30 min.   sd.
color.   35mm.   With leader's discussion guide.   DLC

4632   Flower, Alice (Reynolds), 1890-
        The child at church.   Springfield, Mo., Gospel Publish-
ing House, 1962.   25p.

4633   Reynolds, Joyce
        Puppet shows that reach & teach children.   Springfield,
Mo., Gospel Publishing House, 1972-1974.   2v.   DLC

4634   Young, Mina Arnold
        Your child's heritage.   Springfield, Mo., Gospel Publish-
ing House, c1971.   10p.   First published in 1956 under title:
Your baby's heritage--God's word.

--WORK WITH DEAF

4635   Lawrence, Edgar Dean, 1932-
        Ministering to the silent minority [by] Edgar D. Lawrence.
Springfield, Mo., Gospel Publishing House, c1978.   92p.
(Radiant books) DLC

4636   Pentz, Croft Miner
        Ministry to the deaf [by] Croft M. Pentz.   n.p., 1978.
91p.

4637   Riekehof, Lottie L.
        Talk to the deaf; a manual of approximately 1,000 signs
used by the deaf of North America, by Lottie L. Riekehof.
Illustrated by Betty Stewart.   Springfield, Mo., Gospel Publishing House, 1963.   145p.   DLC

4638   Stewart, Betty
        A message for the deaf, by Betty Stewart.   Consultant:
Lottie Riekehof.   Springfield, Mo., Gospel Publishing House,
c1966.   31p.

--WORK WITH SERVICEMEN

4639   Jaeger, Harry A.
        Reveille, by Harry A. Jaeger.   Illustrated by Charles L.
Ramsay.   Springfield, Mo., Gospel Publishing House, 1946.
248p.

4640   Plank, David W.
        Called to serve, by David W. Plank.   Springfield, Mo.,
Gospel Publishing House, 1967.   121p.

--WORK WITH WOMEN

4641   Assemblies of God, General Council. Women's Missionary
        Council Department.
          The WMC leader handbook and leadership training.
        Springfield, Mo., Gospel Publishing House, 1967. 121p.

4642   Grams, Betty Jane
          Women of grace; new studies for women on living in the
        Spirit. Springfield, Mo., Gospel Publishing House, c1978.
        127p. (Radiant books.) DLC

4643   Stewart, Marjorie, 1925-
          Women in neighborhood evangelism. Springfield, Mo.,
        Gospel Publishing House, c1978. 124p. (Radiant books.)
        DLC

--WORK WITH YOUTH

4644   Assemblies of God, General Council. Christ's Ambassadors
        Department.
          C. A. manual. Springfield, Mo., Gospel Publishing
        House, 1946. 109p.

4645   Assemblies of God, General Council. Christ's Ambassadors
        Department.
          Camping with Assemblies of God youth; a planning guide
        for directors of Assemblies of God boys and girls camps and
        youth camps. Springfield, Mo., Gospel Publishing House,
        195-. vi, 96p. Cover title: Camp director's manual. Pre-
        pared by the National C. A. Department and the National
        Sunday School Department of the General Council of the As-
        semblies of God.

4646   Assemblies of God, General Council. Christ's Ambassadors
        Department.
          Your ministry to youth. Springfield, Mo., Gospel Pub-
        lishing House, 1962. 96p.

4647   Goulder, Thomas J.
          A study of the national Christ's Ambassadors program
        and its relationships to the characteristics and concerns of
        adolescence, by Thomas Goulder. Springfield, Mo., 1964.
        9ℓ. Outline of proposed thesis (M. A.)--Central Bible Insti-
        tute.

4648   Turner, Dwayne E.
          A survey of Assemblies of God young people to determine
        knowledge of church doctrines [by] Dwayne E. Turner. Den-
        ver, 1966. iii, 77ℓ. Thesis (M. R. E.)--Conservative Baptist
        Theological Seminary. CoDCB

--WORSHIP

4649   Masserano, Frank C.
        A study of worship forms in the Assemblies of God de-
        nomination, by Frank C. Masserano. Princeton, N. J., 1966.
        vii, 124ℓ. Thesis (Th. M.)--Princeton Theological Seminary.
        NjPT

4650   Vick, Arne H.
        How to sit in church and get nothing, by Arne Vick.
        Canoga Park, Ca., 1969. 94p.

--AFRICA

4651   Cunningham, Richard Bruce, 1931-
        An investigation of the use of a taxonomy of education
        as an evaluation device for Assemblies of God overseas Bible
        schools. Salt Lake City, 1974. x, 313ℓ. Thesis (Ed. D.)--
        University of Utah. Administered by author in several schools
        in Africa. UU

4652   Wilson, Elizabeth A. Galley
        History of the Assemblies of God in Africa, including
        Egypt. Fort Worth, 1955. v, 230ℓ. Thesis (M. A.)--Texas
        Christian University. TxFTC

4653   Wilson, Elizabeth A. Galley
        Making many rich. Springfield, Mo., Gospel Publishing
        House, c1955. 257p. Based on thesis (M. A.)--Texas Chris-
        tian University. DLC

        -- --BENIN

4654   Assemblies of God, General Council. Foreign Missions De-
        partment.
        Togo-Dahomey. Springfield, Mo., 1961. 11p. Cover
        title. Christine Carmichael, writer.

        -- --EGYPT

4655   Assemblies of God, General Council. Foreign Missions De-
        partment.
        Egypt. Springfield, Mo., 1961. 11p. Cover title.
        Christine Carmichael, writer.

4656   Assemblies of God, General Council. Foreign Missions
        Department.
        Light along the Nile. Springfield, Mo., 1942. 62p.
        MnMNC

4657   Wilson, Elizabeth A. Galley
        Making many rich. Springfield, Mo., Gospel Publishing

House, c1955.   257p.   Based on thesis (M.A.)--Texas Christian University.   DLC

(Assiut)

4658   Assemblies of God, General Council.   Foreign Missions Department.
          Assiout Orphanage.   Springfield, Mo., 196-.   [12]p.
Cover title.

-- --GHANA

4659   Assemblies of God, General Council.   Foreign Missions Department.
          Ghana.   Springfield, Mo., 1965.   5[7]p.   Cover title.
Christine Carmichael, writer.

-- --LIBERIA

4660   Assemblies of God, General Council.   Foreign Missions Department.
          Liberia.   Springfield, Mo., 1963.   [12]p.   Cover title.
Christine Carmichael, writer.

4661   Assemblies of God, General Council.   Foreign Missions Department.
          Sowing and reaping in Liberia.   Springfield, Mo., 1940.
63p.   NNUT

4662   Shelton, Lois, 1899-
          Tell me.   Mattoon, Il., c1949.   216p.   DLC

(Cape Palmas)

4663   Assemblies of God, General Council.   Foreign Missions Department.
          New Hope Leprosy Mission.   Springfield, Mo., 196-.
10p.   Cover title.

-- --NIGERIA

4664   Assemblies of God, General Council.   Foreign Missions Department.
          Nigeria.   Springfield, Mo., 1961.   15p.   Cover title.
Christine Carmichael, writer.

4665   Phillips, Donald E.
          An examination and evaluation of indigenous principles
in Assemblies of God of Nigeria, by Donald E. Phillips.
Springfield, Mo., 1965.   35ℓ.   Thesis (M.A.)--Central
Bible Institute.

-- --SENEGAL

4666   Collins, William Duane
        An Assembly of God approach to Islam in Senegal, West
        Africa. Bethany, Ok., 1978. vii, 95ℓ. Thesis (M.A.)--
        Bethany Nazarene College. OkBetC

-- --SOUTH AFRICA

4667   Assemblies of God, General Council. Foreign Missions De-
        partment.
            South Africa. Springfield, Mo., 1964. 11p. Cover
        title. Christine Carmichael, writer.

-- --TANZANIA

4668   Assemblies of God, General Council. Foreign Missions De-
        partment.
            Tanganyika. Springfield, Mo., 1964. 10[2]p. Cover
        title. Christine Carmichael, writer.

4669   Assemblies of God, General Council. Foreign Missions De-
        partment.
            Tanzania. Springfield, Mo., 1965. 10[2]p. Cover title.
        Christine Carmichael, writer.

-- --TOGO

4670   Assemblies of God, General Council. Foreign Missions De-
        partment.
            Togo-Dahomey. Springfield, Mo., 1961. 11p. Cover
        title. Christine Carmichael, writer.

--UPPER VOLTA

4671   Assemblies of God, General Council. Foreign Missions De-
        partment.
            The gospel among the Mossi people, French West Africa.
        Springfield, Mo., 193-. 38p. At head of title: The Assem-
        blies of God in foreign lands. NNUT

4672   Assemblies of God, General Council. Foreign Missions De-
        partment.
            Upper Volta. Springfield, Mo., 1961. 15p. Cover
        title. Christine Carmichael, writer.

4673   Assemblies of God, General Council. Foreign Missions De-
        partment.
            A visit to Mosi [!] land, French West Africa. Spring-
        field, Mo., 193-. 22p. Signed: A. E. Wilson. At head of
        title: The Assemblies of God in foreign lands.

4674   Sanders, Raymond Ira, 1917-1951.

Meet the Mossi. [Prepared and edited by Ruby M.
Enyart.   Memorial ed.] Springfield, Mo., Gospel Publishing
House, 1953. 103p. DLC, NNUT

-- --ZAIRE

4675   Berg, Anna Charlotte (Hanson)
       Delivered from the jaws of a leopard.   Springfield, Mo.,
       Gospel Publishing House, 19--. 48p.

4676   Berg, Anna Charlotte (Hanson)
       Jungle trails from which came a little girl without a
       country, by Mrs. Arthur F. Berg.   Springfield, Mo., Gos-
       pel Publishing House, 1930. 228p.

--NORTH AMERICA

-- --BELIZE

4677   Assemblies of God, General Council.   Foreign Missions De-
       partment.
           British Honduras. Springfield, Mo., 1963.   9[3]p.
       Cover title.   Christine Carmichael, writer.

-- --COSTA RICA

4678   Assemblies of God, General Council.   Foreign Missions De-
       partment.
           Costa Rica. Springfield, Mo., 1961. 11p. Cover title.
       Christine Carmichael, writer.

-- --GUATEMALA

4679   Assemblies of God, General Council.   Foreign Missions De-
       partment.
           Guatemala. Springfield, Mo., 1961. 11p. Cover title.
       Christine Carmichael, writer.

-- --HONDURAS

4680   Assemblies of God, General Council.   Foreign Missions De-
       partment.
           Honduras. Springfield, Mo., 1962. 5[7]p. Cover title.
       Christine Carmichael, writer.

-- --MEXICO

4681   Assemblies of God, General Council.   Foreign Missions De-
       partment.
           Mexico. Springfield, Mo., 196-. 11p. Cover title.

-- --UNITED STATES

4682   De Leon, Victor, 1927-
The silent Pentecostals: a biographical history of the
Pentecostal movement among the Hispanics in the twentieth
century. La Habra, Ca., c1979. ix, 206p. Originally pre-
sented as the author's thesis (M.Div.), Melodyland School of
Theology. Includes Assemblies of God. DLC

4683   Lebsack, Leland V.
Ten at the top, by Lee Lesback [!]. Stowe, Oh., New
Hope Press, 1974. 132p. "How 10 of America's largest
Assemblies of God grew." TxWaS

(New York, New York City)

4684   Gardiner, Gordon P., 1916-
The origin of Glad Tidings Tabernacle, by Gordon P.
Gardiner; and, The altar of incense, a sermon by Marie E.
Brown. New York, 1955. vii, 47p.

(New York, Orchard Park)

4685   Reid, Thomas Fenton, 1932-
The exploding church, by Thomas F. Reid, with Doug
Brendel. Plainfield, N.J., Logos International, c1979.
156p. DLC

-- --MIDDLE WEST

4686   Hastie, Eugene N.
History of the West Central District Council of the As-
semblies of God, by Eugene N. Hastie. Fort Dodge, Ia.,
Printed by Walterick Ptg. Co., 1948. 207p. IaU, TxWaS

(Illinois)

4687   Knight, Herbert V.
Ministry aflame, by Herbert V. Knight. Carlinville,
Ill., Illinois District Council, Assemblies of God, c1972.
219p. TxWaS

(Illinois, Springfield)

4688   Lebsack, Leland V.
Ten at the top, by Lee Lesback [!]. Stowe, Oh., New
Hope Press, 1974. 132p. "How 10 of America's largest
Assemblies of God grew." Includes Calvary Temple, Spring-
field, Illinois. TxWaS

(Indiana, South Bend)

4689   Lebsack, Leland V.

Ten at the top, by Lee Lesback [!]. Stowe, Oh., New Hope Press, 1974. 132p. "How 10 of America's largest Assemblies of God grew." Includes Calvary Temple, South Bend, Indiana. TxWaS

(Iowa, Davenport)

4690   Lebsack, Leland V.
Ten at the top, by Lee Lesback [!]. Stowe, Oh., New Hope Press, 1974. 132p. "How 10 of America's largest Assemblies of God grew." Includes West Side Assembly of God, Davenport, Iowa. TxWaS

(Kansas)

4691   Assemblies of God, General Council. Districts. Kansas. Christ's Ambassadors Department.
The harvester, 1913-1955; the historical presentation of the Kansas District Council of the Assemblies of God, Incorporated. Oklahoma City, 1955. 192p.

(Michigan)

4692   Historical Records Survey. Wisconsin.
Inventory of the church archives of Wisconsin. Assemblies of God. Prepared by the Wisconsin Historical Records Survey, Division of Community Service Programs, Work Projects Administration. Sponsored by University of Wisconsin and State Historical Society of Wisconsin. Madison, Wisconsin Historical Records Survey, 1942. 73ℓ. Includes northern Michigan. DLC, WHi

(Missouri, Arnold)

4693   Lebsack, Leland V.
Ten at the top, by Lee Lesback [!]. Stowe, Oh., New Hope Press, 1974. 132p. "How 10 of America's largest Assemblies of God grew." Includes First Assembly of God, Arnold, Missouri. TxWaS

(Missouri, Springfield)

4694   Sizelove, Rachel A.
A sparkling fountain for the whole earth [by] Rachel A. Sizelove. Long Beach, Ca., 19--. folder (11p.) Includes prophecy concerning the importance of Springfield, Missouri, in the Pentecostal movement.

(Nebraska, Ord)

4695   Shields, Sidney Guy, 1895-
Camp-meeting special, by Guy Shields. Amarillo, Tx., 1933. 116p. Cover title: Camp meeting echoes. On

camp meeting held in Clement Grove at Ord, Nebraska, July 27th to August 6th, 1933. "

(Ohio, Cincinnati)

4696   Lebsack, Leland V.
Ten at the top, by Lee Lesback [!]. Stowe, Oh. , New Hope Press, 1974. 132p. "How 10 of America's largest Assemblies of God grew. " Includes Tri-County Assembly of God, Cincinnati, i. e. Fairfield, Ohio. TxWaS

(Ohio, Ravenna)

4697   Lebsack, Leland V.
The Ravenna miracle, by Lee Lebsack. Stow, Oh. , Creative Communication, 1973. 91p. Cover title. On the Assembly of God, Ravenna, Ohio.

(Wisconsin)

4698   Historical Records Survey. Wisconsin.
Inventory of the church archives of Wisconsin. Assemblies of God. Prepared by the Wisconsin Historical Records Survey, Division of Community Service Programs, Work Projects Administration. Sponsored by University of Wisconsin and State Historical Society of Wisconsin. Madison, Wisconsin Historical Records Survey, 1942. 73ℓ. DLC, WHi

(Wisconsin, Milwaukee)

4699   Bach, Marcus, 1906-
The inner ecstasy. Nashville, Abingdon Press, c1969. 199p. Includes description of Bethel Tabernacle in Milwaukee in the 1930s.

4700   Bach, Marcus, 1906-
Report to Protestants; a personal investigation of the weakness, need, vision, and great potential of Protestants today. Indianapolis, Bobbs-Merrill, 1948. 277p. Includes description of Bethel Tabernacle in Milwaukee in the 1930s. DLC, RPB

-- --SOUTHERN STATES

4701   Rasnake, John Samuel, 1932-
Pentecost fully come; a history of the Appalachian District of the Assemblies of God [by] J. Samuel Rasnake. Bristol, Tn. , Westhighlands Church, 1971. viii, 156p. DLC, TxWaS

(Alabama)

4702   Spence, Robert H.

The first fifty years: a brief review of the Assemblies of God in Alabama (1915-1965), by Robert H. Spence. Anniversary ed. [Montgomery, Al., 1965] 115[3]p.

(Arkansas, Russellville)

4703   Booher, Geneva (Taylor)
       Builders together with God: the people speak; an anthology of memorabilia from witnesses who are builders of the kingdom of God at First Assembly of God, Russellville, Pope County, Arkansas, the years, 1914-1972. Russellville, Ar., First Assembly of God, 1972. 161p.

(Arkansas, Siloam Springs)

4704   Adams, Loren W., ed.
       Springs of living water; a history [of the] First Assembly of God, Siloam Springs, Arkansas. n.p., 1977. 97p. TxWaS

(Kentucky)

4705   Rasnake, John Samuel, 1932-
       Pentecost fully come; a history of the Appalachian District of the Assemblies of God [by] J. Samuel Rasnake. Bristol, Tn., Westhighlands Church, 1971. viii, 156p. Until 1935 district included churches in eastern Kentucky. DLC, TxWaS

(Kentucky, Louisville)

4706   Lebsack, Leland V.
       Ten at the top, by Lee Lesback [!]. Stowe, Oh., New Hope Press, 1974. 132p. "How 10 of America's largest Assemblies of God grew." Includes Evangel Tabernacle, Louisville. TxWaS

(North Carolina)

4707   Johnson, Guy Benton, 1928-
       A framework for the analysis of religious action, with special reference to holiness and non-holiness groups. Cambridge, Ma., 1953 [i.e. 1954] iii, 307ℓ. Thesis (Ph.D.)-- Harvard University. Based in part on research in Robeson County, North Carolina, in 1948, 1949 and 1951, which consisted of a survey of ten non-Pentecostal and ten Pentecostal religionists, including one Assemblies of God minister. MH

4708   Rasnake, John Samuel, 1932-
       Pentecost fully come; a history of the Appalachian District of the Assemblies of God [by] J. Samuel Rasnake. Bristol, Tn., Westhighlands Church, 1971. viii, 156p. Until 1945 district included churches in North Carolina. DLC, TxWaS

(Oklahoma)

4709   Hawkins, Leroy Wesley, 1942-
          A history of the Assemblies of God in Oklahoma: the
       formative years, 1914-1929. Stillwater, 1972. v, 127ℓ.
       Thesis (M. A.)--Oklahoma State University. OkS

(Tennessee)

4710   Rasnake, John Samuel, 1932-
          Stones by the river; a history of the Tennessee District
       of the Assemblies of God [by] J. Samuel Rasnake. Bristol,
       Tn., Westhighlands Church, 1975. vi, 195p.

(Texas)

4711   Guynes, Delmar R.
          A study of administrative problems in selected Texas
       secondary schools arising out of religious views held by stu-
       dents and parents of the Assemblies of God faith, by Delmar
       R. Guynes. Dallas, 1966. 72ℓ. Thesis (M.A.)--Southern
       Methodist University. TxDaM

(Texas, Alice)

4712   Alice, Tx. First Assembly of God. Women's Ministries.
          Pentecostal pot-luck. Compiled by Women's Ministries
       of First Assembly of God Church, Alice, Texas. Alice,
       Tx., c1977. 116p. Cover title. TxViHU

(Texas, Dallas)

4713   Lebsack, Leland V.
          Ten at the top, by Lee Lesback [!]. Stowe, Oh., New
       Hope Press, 1974. 132p. "How 10 of America's largest
       Assemblies of God grew. " Includes Oak Cliff Assembly of
       God, Dallas. TxWaS

(Texas, Irving)

4714   Lebsack, Leland V.
          Ten at the top, by Lee Lesback [!]. Stowe, Oh., New
       Hope Press, 1974. 132p. "How 10 of America's largest
       Assemblies of God grew. " Includes Calvary Temple, Irving,
       Texas. TxWaS

(Virginia)

4715   Rasnake, John Samuel, 1932-
          Pentecost fully come; a history of the Appalachian Dis-
       trict of the Assemblies of God [by] J. Samuel Rasnake.
       Bristol, Tn., Westhighlands Church, 1971. viii, 156p. Dis-
       trict includes churches in western Virginia. DLC, TxWaS

(West Virginia)

4716   Rasnake, John Samuel, 1932-
        Pentecost fully come; a history of the Appalachian Dis-
        trict of the Assemblies of God [by] J. Samuel Rasnake.
        Bristol, Tn., Westhighlands Church, 1971. viii, 156p. Dis-
        trict includes churches in West Virginia. DLC, TxWaS

        -- --WESTERN STATES

4717   Tanneberg, Ward M.
        Let light shine out: the story of the Assemblies of God
        in the Pacific Northwest, by Ward M. Tanneberg. n.p.,
        c1977. x, 197p. CBGTU, DLC

        (California)

4718   Balliet, Emil Alexander, 1911-1977.
        A study of the development of the Southern California
        District Council of the Assemblies of God. San Diego, Ca.,
        1969. viii, 48ℓ. Thesis (M.A.)--United States International
        University. CSdI

4719   Muelder, Walter George, 1907-
        From sect to church, by Walter G. Muelder. In Chris-
        tendom, 10 (Autumn 1945), 450-462; abridges in Yinger,
        J. M. Religion, society and the individual. New York, c1957,
        480-488. Compares the institutional development of the As-
        semblies of God with that of the Church of the Nazarene in
        California.

        (California, Glendale)

4720   Hark! The herald.
        In Newsweek, 74 (Nov. 17, 1969), 110. KHOF-TV of
        Glendale, owned and operated by Faith Center, a congregation
        affiliated with the Assemblies of God.

        (California, North Hollywood)

4721   Minimizing future shock.
        In Christianity Today, 17 (Mar. 30, 1973), 46. On prep-
        arations by the First Assembly of God, North Hollywood,
        California, for the Second Coming.

        (California, Pomona)

4722   Garvin, Philip, 1947-
        Religious America. Photographs by Philip Garvin. Text
        by Philip Garvin and Julia Welch. New York, McGraw-Hill
        Book Co., 1974. 189p. "Gifts of the Spirit": p. 141-169;
        includes description of worship of the First Assembly of God,
        Pomona, California.

(California, Wasco)

4723   Goldschmidt, Walter Rochs, 1913-
         Class denominationalism in rural California churches
       [by] Walter R. Goldschmidt. In American Journal of Sociol-
       ogy, 49 (Jan. 1944), 348-355. On Wasco, Kern County,
       California.

4724   Goldschmidt, Walter Rochs, 1913-
         Social structure of a California rural community. Berke-
       ley, 1942. 271ℓ. Thesis (Ph.D.)--University of California.
       On Wasco, Kern County, California. "Religious life": ℓ.
       133-161. CU

(Hawaii)

4725   Assemblies of God, General Council. Districts. Hawaii.
         Light on the past; a history of the Assemblies of God in
       Hawaii. Honolulu, Hawaii Pacific Printers, c1975. 152p.
       TxWaS

4726   Assemblies of God, General Council. Foreign Missions De-
       partment.
         Hawaii. Springfield, Mo., 1962. [12]p. Cover title.
       Christine Carmichael, writer.

(Montana)

4727   Garrett, Harry S.
         A history of the Montana District Council of the Assem-
       blies of God, by Harry S. Garrett. Portland, Or., 1960.
       145ℓ. Thesis (B.D.)--Western Evangelical Seminary. OrPW

4728   Roset, Wilfred Laurier, 1927-
         History [of the] Assemblies of God, Montana District,
       1936-1976, by W. L. Roset. Butte, Mt., Crown Communica-
       tion, c1976. 84p. TxWaS

(Washington, Olympia)

4729   Lebsack, Leland V.
         Ten at the top, by Lee Lesback [!]. Stowe, Oh., New
       Hope Press, 1974. 132p. "How 10 of America's largest
       Assemblies of God grew." Includes Evergreen Christian
       Center, Olympia, Washington. TxWaS

(Washington, Spanaway)

4730   Lebsack, Leland V.
         Ten at the top, by Lee Besback [!]. Stowe, Oh., New
       Hope Press, 1974. 132p. "How 10 of America's largest
       Assemblies of God grew." Includes Assembly of God, Span-
       away, Washington. TxWaS

--WEST INDIES

-- --HAITI

4731   Assemblies of God, General Council.   Foreign Missions De-
       partment.
            Haiti.   Springfield, Mo., 196-.   10p.   Cover title.

       -- --JAMAICA

4732   Assemblies of God, General Council.   Foreign Missions De-
       partment.
            Jamaica.   Springfield, Mo., 1960.   11p.   Cover title.

       --SOUTH AMERICA (including Latin America)

4733   Richardson, James Everett, 1949-
            A study of the leadership training programs of the As-
       semblies of God in Spanish America.   Springfield, Mo., 1974.
       vi, 143ℓ.   Research project (M.A.)--Assemblies of God Gradu-
       ate School.   MoSpA

4734   Walker, Louise Jeter, 1913-
            A faculty training program for Assembly of God Bible
       schools in Latin America.   Springfield, Mo., 1965.   118ℓ.
       Thesis (M.A.)--Central Bible Institute.

       -- --ARGENTINA

4735   Assemblies of God, General Council.   Foreign Missions De-
       partment.
            Argentina.   Springfield, Mo., 1962.   11p.   Cover title.
       Christine Carmichael, writer.

       -- --BOLIVIA

4736   Assemblies of God, General Council.   Foreign Missions De-
       partment.
            Bolivia.   Springfield, Mo., 196-.   [12]p.   Cover title.

       -- --CHILE

4737   Assemblies of God, General Council.   Foreign Missions De-
       partment.
            Chile.   Springfield, Mo., 1961.   [12]p.   Cover title.
       Christine Carmichael, writer.

       -- --COLOMBIA

4738   Assemblies of God, General Council.   Foreign Missions De-
       partment.
            Colombia.   Springfield, Mo., 1963.   11p.   Cover title.
       Christine Carmichael, writer.

4739   Hall, Trella Belle
        A historical sketch of the progress of Protestantism in
        Colombia, South America.   Pittsburg, 1959.   vii, 125ℓ.   The-
        sis (M. S.)--Kansas State College.   Includes Assemblies of
        God: ℓ. 67-69, 118-120.   KPT

4739a   Palmer, Donald C., 1934-
        Explosion of people evangelism, by Donald C. Palmer.
        Chicago, Moody Press, c1974.   191p.   "An analysis of Pente-
        costal church growth in Colombia."   "Assemblies of God":
        p. 83-91.

            -- --GUYANA

4740   Assemblies of God, General Council.   Foreign Missions De-
        partment.
        British Guiana.   Springfield, Mo., 1960.   [12]p.   Cover
        title.

            -- --PARAGUAY

4741   Assemblies of God, General Council.   Foreign Missions De-
        partment.   Paraguay.   Springfield, Mo., 1963.   11p.   Cover
        title.   Christine Carmichael, writer.

            -- --PERU

4742   Assemblies of God, General Council.   Foreign Missions De-
        partment.
        Peru.   Springfield, Mo., 196-.   15p.   Cover title.

            -- --VENEZUELA

4743   Assemblies of God, General Council.   Foreign Missions De-
        partment.
        Venezuela.   Springfield, Mo., 1960.   10[2]p.   Cover
        title.

            --ASIA

4744   Moffett, Samuel Hugh, 1916-
        East Asian Pentecostals [by] Samuel H. Moffett.   In
        Christianity Today, 13 (Aug. 22, 1969), 37.   On the third
        Far Eastern Fellowship Conference of the Assemblies of God,
        held in Seoul, Korea in July.

4745   Osgood, Howard C.
        Four forces in the Far East, by Howard C. Osgood.
        Springfield, Mo., Foreign Missions Department of the Gen-
        eral Council of the Assemblies of God, 195-.   14p.   NNUT

-- --BURMA

4746   Assemblies of God, General Council.   Foreign Missions De-
        partment.
              Burma.   Springfield, Mo., 19--.   7[5]p.   Cover title.

-- --CHINA

4747   Ezzo, Elsie (Bolton), 1930-
              Bought for a dollar, and other exciting stories of China.
        Springfield, Mo., Gospel Publishing House, c1969.   95p.

        (Ninghsien)

4748   Nichols, Nettie D.
              God's faithfulness in Ningpo.   Compiled by Nettie D.
        Nichols and Joshua Bang.   Springfield, Mo., Foreign Mis-
        sions Department, General Council of the Assemblies of God,
        1938.   48p.   NNUT

-- --HONG KONG

4749   Assemblies of God, General Council.   Foreign Missions De-
        partment.
              Hong Kong.   Springfield, Mo., 1962.   8[4]p.   Cover
        title.   Christine Carmichael, writer.

-- --INDIA

4750   Assemblies of God, General Council.   Foreign Missions De-
        partment.
              Opportunities in South India and Ceylon.   Springfield,
        Mo., 19--.   22p.   (Assemblies of God in foreign lands.)
        Compiled largely from information supplied by John H.
        Burgess.   MoSpA

4751   Assemblies of God, General Council.   Foreign Missions De-
        partment.
              South India.   Springfield, Mo., 196-.   15p.   Cover title.

4752   Hillary, Derrick
              Ganges gloom and glory.   Springfield, Mo., Gospel Pub-
        lishing House, 19--.   80p.

4753   Schoonmaker, Violet (Dunham).
              Light in India's night; true stories of India and her peo-
        ple, written especially for young folk.   Springfield, Mo.,
        Gospel Publishing House, c1957.   237p.   DLC

-- --INDONESIA

4754   Assemblies of God, General Council.   Foreign Missions De-
        partment.

Indonesia. Springfield, Mo., 196-. [12]p. Cover title. Christine Carmichael, writer.

-- --JAPAN

4755   Assemblies of God, General Council.   Foreign Missions Department.
Japan. Springfield, Mo., 196-. 15p. Cover title.

-- --KOREA

4756   Assemblies of God, General Council.   Foreign Missions Department.
Korea. Springfield, Mo., 1960. 10[2]p. Cover title.

-- --MALAYSIA

4757   Assemblies of God, General Council.   Foreign Missions Department.
Daybreak in Malay. Springfield, Mo., 193-. 35p. NNUT

-- --MANCHURIA

4758   Assemblies of God, General Council.   Foreign Missions Department.
Gospel rays in Manchoukuo. Springfield, Mo., 1937. [60]p. NNUT

-- --PAKISTAN

4759   Assemblies of God, General Council.   Foreign Missions Department.
Pakistan. Springfield, Mo., 1963. 11p. Cover title. Christine Carmichael, writer.

-- --PHILIPPINES

4760   Assemblies of God, General Council. Foreign Missions Department.
Philippines. Springfield, Mo., 1962. 15p. Cover title. Christine Carmichael, writer.

4761   Sturgeon, Inez
Give me this mountain. Springfield, Mo., Gospel Publishing House, c1960. 175p. TxWaS

-- --SRI LANKA

4762   Assemblies of God, General Council.   Foreign Missions Department.
Opportunities in South India and Ceylon. Springfield, Mo., 19--. 22p. (Assemblies of God in foreign lands.)

Compiled largely from information supplied by John H. Burgess.   MoSpA

-- --TAIWAN

4763   Assemblies of God, General Council.   Foreign Missions Department.
     Taiwan.   Springfield, Mo., 1964.   10[2]p.   Cover title.
Christine Carmichael, writer.

-- --TIBET

4764   Plymire, David, 1921-
     High adventure in Tibet.   Springfield, Mo., Gospel Publishing House, c1959.   225p.   CtY-D, CU, DLC

--EUROPE

-- --BELGIUM

4765   Assemblies of God, General Council.   Foreign Missions Department.
     Belgium.   Springfield, Mo., 1962.   [8]p.   Cover title.
Christine Carmichael, writer.

-- --GREECE

4766   Assemblies of God, General Council.   Foreign Missions Department.
     Greece.   Springfield, Mo., 19--.   11p.   Cover title.

4767   Assemblies of God, General Council.   Foreign Missions Department.
     Italy.   Springfield, Mo., 195-.   [11]p.   Cover title.

-- --SPAIN

4768   Assemblies of God, General Council.   Foreign Missions Department.
     Spain.   Springfield, Mo., 1965.   [12]p.   Cover title.
Christine Carmichael, writer.

--OCEANIA

-- --FIJI

4769   Assemblies of God, General Council.   Foreign Missions Department.
     Fiji.   Springfield, Mo., 1960.   [12]p.   Cover title.

ASSEMBLIES OF GOD IN AUSTRALIA (1937-   )

Formed in 1937 by merger of the Assemblies of God in Queensland and the Pentecostal Church of Australia, the Assemblies of God in Australia resembles its American counterpart both in doctrine and organization. In 1967 when it reported 140 congregations and 4,000 members, the Brisbane-based group was supporting more than fifty missionaries in New Guinea, India, and Japan. The Commonwealth Bible College, founded in 1948, is in Brisbane. The Australian Evangel is the official organ.

--DOCTRINAL AND CONTROVERSIAL WORKS

4770   Duncan, Philip B.
        The Pentecostal path, by Philip B. Duncan. n. p., 19--.
        44p.

--HISTORY

4771   Duncan, Philip B.
        Pentecost in Australia, by Philip B. Duncan. n. p.,
        19--. 93p.

--PERIODICALS

4772   Australian evangel. 1-   1926-
        Richmond, Vict., Brisbane

4773   Glad tidings messenger. 1-   1944-
        Brisbane

ASSEMBLIES OF GOD IN GREAT BRITAIN AND IRELAND (1924-   )

Formed in 1924 by the non-denominational constituency of the Pentecostal Missionary Union, the Assemblies of God in Great Britain and Ireland retains the strong foreign missionary emphasis of the Union. Like its American counterpart, the General Council of the Assemblies of God, from which it borrowed its polity, the British group regards itself as a cooperative fellowship of autonomous churches, not as a denomination. Banded together for missionary, publishing, and worker training programs which would be difficult for congregations individually to maintain, the federated Assemblies in the United Kingdom support over sixty missionaries in Europe, Sierra Leone, Zaire, Kenya, Zambia, South Africa, India, West Pakistan, Malaya, and Japan. The fellowship sponsors a Bible college at Mattersey near Doncaster, Yorkshire, and airs radio broadcasts in the Far East, Africa, and Central America. Redemption

Tidings, the official organ, is issued from headquarters in Nottingham. Donald Gee, a prominent figure in the British Assemblies
from their federation until his death in 1966, was influential in the
formation of the Pentecostal World Conference in 1947. The British
group has wholeheartedly supported the international organization
from the start. In 1975 the fellowship claimed 541 congregations
and about 60,000 members.

4774   Allen, Gillian
        Pentecostalists as a medical minority [by] Gillian Allen
        and Roy Wallis. In Wallis, R., ed. Marginal medicine.
        New York, c1976, 110-137. Based on study of a small
        Scottish congregation affiliated with the Assemblies of God
        in Great Britain and Ireland.

4775   Gee, Donald, 1891-1966.
        The glory of the Assemblies of God. London, Assemblies
        of God Publishing House, 19--. 32p. TxWaS

        --CHURCH EXTENSION

4776   Gee, Donald, 1891-1966.
        The missionary who stayed at home. South Normanton,
        Derbys., South Normanton and District Revival Centre, 19--.
        76p. OkTOr

        --DOCTRINAL AND CONTROVERSIAL WORKS

4777   Burton, William Frederick Padwick, 1886-1971.
        Signs following. 2d ed. Luton, Assemblies of God Pub-
        lishing House, 1950. viii, 40p. L

4778   Carter, Howard, 1891-1971.
        Questions and answers on spiritual gifts. London, As-
        semblies of God Publishing House, c1946. 130p. TxWaS

4779   Carter, John, 1893-1981.
        God's tabernacle in the wilderness and its principal offer-
        ings. Nottingham, Assemblies of God Publishing House, 1970.
        127p. L

4780   Gasson, Raphael
        The challenging counterfeit: a study of spiritualism.
        London, Assemblies of God Publishing House, 19--. 92p.

4781   Gee, Donald, 1891-1966.
        Concerning spiritual gifts; a series of Bible studies.
        Stockport, c1928. 95p. TxWaS

4782   Gee, Donald, 1891-1966.

Studies in guidance. London, Redemption Tidings, 1936. 78p.

4783   Gee, Donald, 1891-1966.
Why "Pentecost"? London, Victory Press, 1944.   56p.
L

4784   Horton, Harold Lawrence Cuthbert, 1880-1968.
The baptism in the Holy Spirit, by Harold Horton. London, Redemption Tidings Bookroom, 19--. 23p. TxWaS

4785   Horton, Harold Lawrence Cuthbert, 1880-1968.
The baptism in the Holy Spirit; a challenge to wholehearted seekers after God, by Harold Horton. London, Assemblies of God Publishing House, 1956. 23p.

4786   Horton, Harold Lawrence Cuthbert, 1880-1968.
The baptism in the Holy Spirit; a challenge to wholehearted seekers after God, by Harold Horton. London, Assemblies of God Publishing House, 1961. 24p.

4787   Horton, Harold Lawrence Cuthbert, 1880-1968.
The baptism in the Holy Spirit; a challenge to wholehearted seekers after God, by Harold Horton. Nottingham, Assemblies of God Publishing House, 19--. 23p.

4788   Horton, Harold Lawrence Cuthbert, 1880-1968.
Chords from Solomon's Song, chapters I, II, III and IV, by Harold Horton. Luton, H. Horton; London, Redemption Tidings Bookroom, 1937. 154p. L

4789   Horton, Harold Lawrence Cuthbert, 1880-1968.
The gifts of the Spirit, by Harold Horton. London, F. J. Lamb, 1934. 211p. L

4790   Horton, Harold Lawrence Cuthbert, 1880-1968.
The gifts of the Spirit, by Harold Horton, Harrow, Middlesex, H. Horton; Luton, Bedfordshire, Redemption Tidings Bookroom, 1946. 224p. "Second edition." DLC

4791   Horton, Harold Lawrence Cuthbert, 1880-1968.
The gifts of the Spirit, by Harold Horton. 5th ed. Luton, Bedfordshire, Assemblies of God Publishing House, 1949 [i. e. 1953] 228p.

4792   Horton, Harold Lawrence Cuthbert, 1880-1968.
The gifts of the Spirit, by Harold Horton. 7th ed. London, Assemblies of God Publishing House, 1962. 228p.
RBaB

4793   Horton, Harold Lawrence Cuthbert, 1880-1968.
The gifts of the Spirit, by Harold Horton. 10th ed. London, Assemblies of God Publishing House, 1971. 216p.

4794   Horton, Harold Lawrence Cuthbert, 1880-1968.
        Receiving without "tarrying," by Harold Horton. Poole,
        19--. 14p.

4795   Horton, Harold Lawrence Cuthbert, 1880-1968.
        Receiving without "tarrying," by Harold Horton. Bourne-
        mouth West, 1960. 14p.

4796   Horton, Harold Lawrence Cuthbert, 1880-1968.
        The sons of Jeshurun; illustrating spiritual types and
        characteristics, by Harold Horton. Luton, Redemption Tid-
        ings Bookroom, 1944. 27p.

4797   Horton, Harold Lawrence Cuthbert, 1880-1968.
        What is the good of speaking with tongues? An enthu-
        siastic vindication of supernatural endowment, by Harold
        Horton. Luton, Redemption Tidings Bookroom, 1946. 34p.
        TxWaS

4798   Horton, Harold Lawrence Cuthbert, 1880-1968.
        What is the good of speaking with tongues? An enthu-
        siastic vindication of supernatural endowment, by Harold
        Horton. London, Assemblies of God Publishing House, 19--.
        35p.

4799   Horton, Harold Lawrence Cuthbert, 1880-1968.
        What is the good of speaking with tongues? An enthu-
        siastic vindication of supernatural endowment, by Harold
        Horton. Nottingham, Assemblies of God Publishing House,
        19--. 35p.

4800   Linford, Aaron
        Baptism in the Holy Spirit. London, 19--. 72p.

4801   Linford, Aaron
        A course of study on spiritual gifts. 2d ed. Nottingham,
        Assemblies of God in Great Britain and Ireland, 19--. 108p.

4802   Martin, S. J.
        The work and personality of the Holy Spirit in the New
        Testament, by S. J. Martin. London, Assemblies of God
        Publishing House, 19--. 28p. TxWaS

4803   Missen, Alfred F.
        Notes on the second coming of Christ, by Alfred F. Mis-
        sen. London, Assemblies of God Publishing House, 19--.
        23p. OkTOr

4804   Missen, Alfred F.
        Problems of a Pentecostal church; a series of articles
        based on the First Epistle to the Corinthians, by Alfred F.
        Missen. London, 19--. 79p. Printed by Assemblies of
        God Publishing House. KyWAT

4805   Rosser, Ivor
        Charismata grace gifts. ----, Monms., c1936. 106p.

4806   Valdez, Alfred Clarence, 1896-
        Divine health in the light of God's word, by A. C. Val-
        dez. London, Assemblies of God Publishing House, 19--.
        73p.

        --EDUCATION

4807   Richards, William Thomas Henry, 1916-1974.
        Reaching the children for Christ through branch Sunday
        schools, by W. T. H. Richards. Slough, Bucks., Ambas-
        sador Productions, 19--. 26p. OkTOr

        --HISTORY

4808   Missen, Alfred F.
        The sound of a going; the story of Assemblies of God as
        told by Alfred F. Missen. Nottingham, Assemblies of God
        Publishing House, c1973. 119p.

        --HYMNS AND SACRED SONGS

4809   Assemblies of God in Great Britain and Ireland.
        Redemption Tidings hymn book: a selected collection of full
        gospel hymns. London, 19--. 181p. With music. KyLoS

4810   Assemblies of God in Great Britain and Ireland.
        Redemption hymnal. 2d ed. Nottingham, Assemblies of
        God Publishing House, 1975. 1v. (unpaged) OkBetC

4811   Assemblies of God in Great Britain and Ireland. "Redemption
        Tidings" hymn book. London, 1935. 64p. L

4812   Assemblies of God in Great Britain and Ireland.
        Redemption Tidings hymn book. Enlarged ed. London,
        1939. 102p. L

        --PASTORAL THEOLOGY

4813   Gee, Donald, 1891-1966.
        Concerning shepherds and sheepfolds; a series of studies
        dealing with pastors and assemblies. London, Assemblies of
        God in Great Britain and Ireland, c1930. 66p.

4814   Horton, Harold Lawrence Cuthbert, 1880-1968.
        Preaching and homiletics; an ideal and a help for all who
        preach "the glorious gospel of the blessed God," by Harold

Horton.   Luton, Assemblies of God Publishing House, 1946.
90p.

4815   Horton, Harold Lawrence Cuthbert, 1880-1968.
         Preaching and homiletics; presenting the scriptural ideal
for all preachers and offering instruction in sermon-making
for those who are seeking it, by Harold Horton.   2d ed.
London, Assemblies of God Publishing House, 1949.   119p.

--PERIODICALS

4816   Missionary messenger.   1-   1931-19--.
         London.

4817   Overseas tidings.   1-   Apr. 1946-19--.
         Luton.   L

4818   Redemption tidings.   1-   July 1924-
         Stockport, London, Nottingham.   L

4819   Redemption tidings ambassador.   1-   1932-
         Stockport.   L

4820   Study hour.   1-10, 1941-1950.
         London.

--SERMONS, TRACTS, ADDRESSES, ESSAYS

4821   Fentimen, Hilda
         Manna.   Birmingham, Kings Norton Press, 19--.   358p.

4822   Horton, Harold Lawrence Cuthbert, 1880-1968.
         Arrows of deliverance, by Harold Horton.   London, As-
semblies of God Publishing House, 19--.   94p.

4823   Horton, Harold Lawrence Cuthbert, 1880-1968.
         Talks on occupying the land; a challenge and a call to
fuller inheritance, by Harold Horton.   Manchester, 1944.
44p.

4824   Horton, Harold Lawrence Cuthbert, 1880-1968.
         Talks on occupying the land; a challenge and a call to
fuller inheritance, by Harold Horton.   Luton, Redemption
Tidings Bookroom, 1944.   43p.

4825   Sheraman, G. T., 1870-1954.
         Some of the secrets of power from on high.   London,
Assemblies of God Publishing House, 19--.   8p.   TxWaS

ASSEMBLIES OF GOD IN MALAYSIA (1957-   )

Although American Assemblies of God missionaries first entered Singapore in 1928 and an English-speaking church was established in Kuala Lumpur, present capital of the Federation of Malaysia in 1930, it was not until the years following World War II that any significant impact was made on the native population. Following a significant revival in 1954, the work spread rapidly, and in the five years following 1962 membership increased from 420 to 1, 077. In 1967 there were eighteen affiliated congregations. Headquarters are in Singapore.

--PERIODICALS

4826   Assemblies of God voice.   1-   1964-
            Singapore.   L

ASSEMBLIES OF GOD IN NEW ZEALAND (1927-   )

Organized March 29, 1927, in Bethel Temple, Wellington, at the end of a series of meetings conducted by A. C. Valdez, an American evangelist, the Assemblies of God in New Zealand modelled its doctrinal statement and church polity after that of the General Council of the Assemblies of God, its American counterpart. Most of the clergy affiliating with the new body came from the Pentecostal Church in New Zealand, among them L. J. Jones, editor of the official periodical which he brought with him. The sluggish growth which characterized the first three decades has apparently quickened. Total membership which stood at 1, 060 in 1961, increased to 2, 028 in 1966, and 3, 599 in 1971. By the latter date the fellowship had 35 affiliated congregations and 39 ordained and lay ministers. The New Zealand Evangel is published in Christchurch. Christian Life Bible College, established at Lower Hutt in 1967, is the recognized center for ministerial training. As early as 1931 the Assemblies of God in New Zealand was giving full or partial support to missionaries in the Congo, Tonga, Fiji, Samoa, and India. Interest in these and other missionary projects has continued unabated. Headquarters are now in Lower Hutt, a suburb of Wellington.

--DOCTRINAL AND CONTROVERSIAL WORKS

4827   [Read, Ralph R.]
            Water baptism: the formula and its meaning; a study of the trinitarian meaning; a study of the trinitarian formula of Matthew 28, v. 19 and the formula of "oneness" teachers: a guide and a refutation. Christchurch, N. Z., Assemblies of God Bookroom, 19--. 12p. Cover title.

--HISTORY

4828   Worsfold, James Evans
        A history of the charismatic movements in New Zealand,
        including a Pentecostal perspective and a breviate of the
        Catholic Apostolic Church in Great Britain, by J. E. Wors-
        fold. Bradford, Yorks., Julian Literature Trust; printed by
        Puritan Press, c1974. xx, 368p. "The Assemblies of God":
        p. 197-223. DLC

        --PERIODICALS

4829   New Zealand evangel. 3, no. 3- Mar. 1927-
        Wellington, Christchurch

ASSEMBLIES OF GOD IN THE PHILIPPINES (1940-   )

        In the 1930s Filipino nationals, trained in Assemblies of God
Bible schools in the United States, returned to their homeland and
raised up a number of churches in Luzon and Panay. Desiring to
form a district council within the American body, the Filipinos found
they could not do so without American representatives in decision-
making roles. As a result, in 1940 they sought and received official recognition from the Philippine government as the Assemblies
of God in the Philippines. Although the thirty churches which composed the group at the time of the registration suffered greatly during the Japanese occupation, the fellowship survived and rebuilt the
post-war body on the foundation of the 1940 agreement. In 1967 the
Philippine Assemblies of God reported 936 congregations and 9, 382
members. With the help of North American workers, it operates
three Bible training schools. Bethel Temple, the headquarters
church in Manila, is next to the largest Protestant congregation in
the Orient.

4830   Cabanilla Esperanza, Trinidad, 1922-
            The Assemblies of God in the Philippines. Pasadena,
        Ca., 1965. iii, 89ℓ. Thesis (M. R. E.)--Fuller Theological
        Seminary. CPFT

        --PERIODICALS

4831   Pentecostal voice. 1- 1963-
        Manila

ASSEMBLIES OF GOD IN QUEENSLAND (1929-1937)

        Organized in 1929 from remnants of the troubled Apostolic

Faith Movement of Australia, the Assemblies of God in Queensland bore a distinct doctrinal and organizational resemblance to its American namesake. Although the fellowship itself enjoyed steady growth, a Bible school established under its sponsorship in 1936, graduated but one class. George Burns, a former Church of Christ minister who served from 1929 to 1931 as president, was succeeded by C. G. Enticknap, who in 1937 led the Queensland Assemblies into union with the Pentecostal Church of Australia. The resulting Assemblies of God in Australia was organized during a joint conference in Sydney.

ASSEMBLIES OF GOD IN SOUTHERN AND CENTRAL AFRICA
    (1932-)
[1932-19-- as Assemblies of God in South Africa.]

An amalgamation of the African constituencies of various North American and European missionary agencies, the Assemblies of God in Southern and Central Africa combines the ministries of Bantu, Coloured and Indian workers with those of Danish, Norwegian, Finnish, Swiss, English, Irish, Canadian, American, and white South African missionaries. The work dates from 1910 when Americans, Hanna James and Mr. and Mrs. R. M. Turney, established the first Pentecostal mission station in Doornkop, Transvaal. In 1917 the American Assemblies received official governmental recognition, the legal foundation upon which the Assemblies of God in South Africa was organized fifteen years later. Although missionaries assist in various evangelistic, educational, and publishing endeavors, administration and leadership of the churches is in the hands of Africans themselves. Nicholas B. H. Bhengu being the best known of the national leaders. In 1967 the fellowship reported 225 congregations and 5, 791 members. At that time the leadership included 163 national and 26 foreign workers. Headquarters are in Johannesburg. Fellowship, the official periodical, is published by Emmanuel Press, Nelspruit, Transvaal.

4832   Dubb, Allie A.
        Community of the saved: an African revivalist church in the East Cape [by] Allie A. Dubb. Johannesburg, Witwatersrand University Press for African Studies Institute, 1976. xvii, 175p. DLC, MH-AH

4833   Moennich, Martha
        God at work in South Africa. In Evangelical Christian, 54 (Aug. 1958), 368.

        --PERIODICALS

4834   Fellowship. 1:1-59/62, Oct. 1952-Sept./Dec. 1957; ns 1-
        1960-
            Nelspruit, Tvl. L

ASSEMBLIES OF GOD, UNITED PENTECOSTAL COUNCIL (1919-192-)

Organized in 1919, the United Pentecostal Council of Assemblies of God was a fellowship of New England congregations. Beginning in December 1920, it published the Apostolic Messenger in Cambridge, Massachusetts. Sometime during the 1920s the United Pentecostal Council merged with the General Council of the Assemblies of God.

--PERIODICALS

4835   Apostolic messenger.   1-   Dec. 1920-
        Cambridge, Ma.

ASSEMBLY OF CHRISTIAN CHURCHES (1939-   )
[Also as La Asamblea de Iglesias Cristianas.]

In 1939, two years following the death of its founder Francisco Olazábal, the Bethel Christian Temple invited other congregations in the New York area to join it in planning a missionary crusade among Spanish-speaking residents in New York and Puerto Rico. Out of this crusade grew the Assembly of Christian Churches. Under Bishop Carlos Sepúlveda, a former Presbyterian minister who headed the group until 1967, the work spread not only to Puerto Rico, but to the U.S. Virgin Islands, the Dominican Republic, Guatemala, Nicaragua, Argentina, and India. Within the United States congregations were organized in Washington, Chicago, and Los Angeles. With the exception of congregations in St. Croix and Bombay which use English, worship is conducted in Spanish. Headquarters and the editorial offices of La Voz Evangélica, the official organ, are in New York. Teachings are similar to those of the General Council of the Assemblies of God. In the mid-1970s about 180 congregations were affiliated with the Assembly of Christian Churches. Of these, 60 churches with a combined membership of 800 were in the continental United States, and 54 churches with a combined membership of 1,200 were in Puerto Rico.

--PERIODICALS

4836   La Voz Evangélica.   1-   19 -
        New York

ASSOCIATION OF CHRISTIAN ASSEMBLIES (1913-1914)

The Association of Christian Assemblies represented a first attempt at cooperative Pentecostal organization in Indiana and other central states. Centered in the Gibeah Bible School and Home at

Plainfield, near Indianapolis, it was organized during a convention held there, June 15-22, 1913. Leaders included D. Wesley Myland and J. Roswell Flower, future Assemblies of God pillars. Flower's Christian Evangel, which began publication in Plainfield a month after the convention, promoted Association activities. With the organization of the General Council of the Assemblies of God the next year, the Association apparently disbanded. The new organization adopted the Christian Evangel as one of two official organs.

--PERIODICALS

4837   Christian evangel.   1-   July 19, 1913-
           Plainfield, In.

BETHEL TEMPLE (1914-   )

Founded in 1914 by W. H. Offiler, a noted writer, Bethel Temple of Seattle is distinctive among Trinitarian bodies in administering baptism in the name of the Lord Jesus Christ. Missionary-minded from its earliest days, Bethel Temple and other independent churches in fellowship with it have for many years supported missionary work in Indonesia. From the start this work, begun in 1921 by two Netherlanders, has operated on indigenous principles. Money and workers sent from America have been used to under gird self-determination. Efforts have been concentrated in two areas: education and publication. Bethel-supported workers established Bible training schools in Java, Sumatra, Celebes and New Guinea, from which national workers were sent out. Printing pressed, located in Java and Sumatra, provided a steady stream of religious literature. So successful was the program that by 1967 the national church, the Geredja Pentecosta di Indonesia, numbered more than a half-million members. In addition, Temple members have evangelized in India, Japan, Taiwan and Colombia, and have worked with United States servicemen stationed in France. In addition to the 300-member mother church in Seattle, there are eleven additional churches in Washington state, two in Minnesota, and one in Wisconsin. Pentecostal Power is published in Seattle, where a Bible training school also is located. In 1975 an estimated $30,000 was given for foreign missions.

--DOCTRINAL AND CONTROVERSIAL WORKS

4038   Offiler, William Henry, 1875-1957.
           God and His Bible; or, The harmonies of divine revelation,
        by W. H. Offiler.   Seattle, Bethel Temple, c1946.   200p.
        DLC

4039   Offiler, William Henry, 1875-1957.
           God and His name; a message for today.   By W. H.

Offiler.   Seattle, c1932.   113p.   (Bethel Bible lectures.)
Cover title.   "This booklet was published in January 1925,
was revised and republished in June 1932. "--Leaf at end.
DLC

--PERIODICALS

4840   Pentecostal power.   1- 19 -
        Seattle.

BIBLE CHURCH OF CHRIST (1961-   )

        Founded March 1, 1961, by Bishop Roy Bryant, the Bible
Church of Christ is at work in the United States and Africa.   In
1978 it reported five churches, nineteen clergy, and 1, 800 members
in the United States.   At that time, however, only 530 were enrolled
in Sunday school.   Headquarters are in New York, from which the
Voice, the official publication, also is issued.

--PERIODICALS

4841   Voice.   1- 19 -
        New York.

BIBLE-PATTERN CHURCH FELLOWSHIP (1940-   )

        Formed during a conference of ministers and deacons in Not-
tingham, November 28-29, 1940, the Bible-Pattern Church Fellowship
resulted from an abortive attempt by George Jeffreys, its founder,
to make democratic reforms in the Elim Foursquare Gospel Alliance,
a movement he also had founded.   Stress is laid on the autonomy of
local congregations.   Doctrinal standards remain identical to those
of the parent body.   Although several of the leaders espoused Anglo-
Israelism, belief in this theory was never made a test of membership.
By 1967 the Fellowship, which had commissioned its first missionary
twenty-two years earlier, was sponsoring six workers in Uruguay,
Puerto Rico, and Spain.   Headquarters are in Birmingham.   The
Pattern, issued in the early years in London, is now published in
Nottingham.   Since the death of the founder in 1962, the movement
has experienced a slow decline.

4842   Jeffreys, George, 1889-1962.
             Healing rays.   3d ed.   London, Henry E. Walter, 1952.
        121p.   DNLM, L

--DOCTRINAL AND CONTROVERSIAL WORKS

4843   Jeffreys, George, 1889-1962.
       Pentecostal rays; the baptism and gifts of the Holy Spirit.
       2d ed. London, Henry E. Walter, 1954.   155p.

--HISTORY

4844   Brooks, Noel, 1914-
       Fight for the faith and greedom.   London, Pattern Book-
       room [1948] 136p.   L

--PASTORAL THEOLOGY

4845   Francis, Gwilym L
       The minister and his ministry, and the Christian worker
       and his work, by Gwilym L Francis.   London, Pattern Book-
       shop, 1964.   11p.   L

--PERIODICALS

4846   Pattern.   1-   1940-
       London, Nottingham.   L

BIBLE STANDARD CHURCHES (1919-1935)

Until 1919 the Lighthouse Temple of Eugene, Oregon, organized
five years earlier following a tent revival, was a branch of the Apostolic Faith Mission.   Led by Fred Hornshuh and Pat Hegan, the founding evangelists, the congregation came to question the claim of the
Apostolic Faith that it was the only true church, and to chafe under
the requirement that remarried divorced persons separate before joining the church.   As a result, the Lighthouse Temple withdrew from
the Portland-based organization and organized the Bible Standard, Inc.,
with Hornshuh as head.   In 1920 it launched the Bible Standard, a monthly
periodical, and in 1925 opened the Bible Standard Theological School.
A number of other congregations affiliated with the movement, and
by 1934 there were groups as far east of Wyoming, Nebraska, and
South Dakota.   It was during visitation of these churches that H. R.
Neat came into contact with the Open Bible Evangelistic Association,
a contact which led to the union of the two groups the next year.   In
1927 the Bible Standard Churches was supporting work in Liberia and
Australia, and in 1930 opened its own mission in Burma.   Sponsorship of the latter continued until 1944, when unsettled conditions
forced its abandonment.

--HISTORY

4847   Hornshuh, Fred, 1884-
        Historical sketches of the Bible Standard Churches, Inc.,
        in 1919 before merging with the Open Bible Churches, Inc.,
        in 1935. Eugene, Or., Eugene Bible College, 1976. vi,
        125p. DLC

--PERIODICALS

4848   Bible standard. 1-16, no. 8, 1920-Aug. 1935.
        Eugene, Or.

BODY OF CHRIST (1952-   )
[Also as B'nai Shalom.]

        Following the death of William Sowders in 1952, the Gospel
of the Kingdom movement separated into several factions. One of
these, the body of Christ, consists of disciples of Elder Reynolds
Edward Dawkins, "apostle and builder of the body of Christ." The
group is composed of dispensationalists who believe that the time of
the gentiles began in 1959. It is governed by "apostolic order," a
schema given to Dawkins by divine revelation. Although charismatic
manifestations occur in the worship of the group, eschatological con-
cerns stand out in its teaching. The Body of Christ regards itself
as the "New Jerusalem" or "natural Israel," serving as the means
whereby the love of God reaches the rest of humankind and deriving
its authority from the Twelve Apostles.

        In the mid-1970s the Body of Christ included eight churches
with about 1,000 members in the United States, and affiliates in Jamaica, Nigeria (eleven churches), the Netherlands, Israel, India,
and Hong Kong. Headquarters are at the Gospel of Peace Camp
Ground in Phoenix, where the Peace Publishers and Company, the
financial arm of the movement, also is located. Since the group
denies that it is a denomination, it refuses to capitalize the word
"body" in its name.

--DOCTRINAL AND CONTROVERSIAL WORKS

4849   Dawkins, Reynolds Edward,   -1965.
        Higher powers. Phoenix, Peace Publishers and Co.,
        19--.   16p.

4850   Dawkins, Reynolds Edward,   -1965.
        The principles of the doctrine of Christ. Phoenix, Peace
        Publishers and Co., 196-.   14p.

4851   Dawkins, Reynolds Edward,   -1965.

Rightly dividing the word of God. Phoenix, Peace Publishers and Co., 19--. 16p.

4852   Tate, Richard
          Alpha and omega. 2d ed. Phoenix, Peace Publishers and Co., 1969. 14p.

4853   Tate, Richard
          The body of Christ. Phoenix, Peace Publishers and Co., 19--. 10p.

4854   Tate, Richard
          In my Father's house. Phoenix, Peace Publishers and Co., 19--. 11p.

          --PERIODICALS

4855   B'nai Shalom. 1- 196 -
          Phoenix.

CALVARY PENTECOSTAL CHURCH (1931-   )

Organized in 1931 at Olympia, Washington, by former Assemblies of God ministers, the Calvary Pentecostal Church set out to achieve the benefits of cooperative action without unnecessary interference from denominational officials. Success was notable, and in 1944 the group reported 20,000 members in 35 congregations. Beginning in the mid-1950s, however, a contest of wills between leading ministers and the Executive Board led to the eventual withdrawal of all but four of the member churches, and the loss of flourishing missionary affiliates in India and Brazil. The remaining United States constituency of approximately 1,500 supports missionary work in the Philippines. Headquarters are in Olympia, Washington.

4856   Calvary Pentecostal Church.
          Constitution and by-laws of the Calvary Pentecostal Church. 16th ed. Olympia, Wa., 1962. 21p.

4857   Moore, Everett Leroy, 1918-
          Handbook of Pentecostal denominations in the United States. Pasadena, Ca., 1954. vii, 346ℓ. Thesis (M.A.)--Pasadena College. "Calvary Pentecostal Church": ℓ. 105-107. CSdP

4858   U.S. Bureau of the Census.
          Census of religious bodies: 1936. Pentecostal assemblies. Statistics, denominational history, doctrine, and organization. Consolidated report. Washington, Government Printing Office, 1940. iv, 49p. Includes Calvary Pentecostal Church. NNUT

--CATECHISMS AND CREEDS

4859   Calvary Pentecostal Church.
         What we believe and why? An examination of the State-
         ment of Faith of the Calvary Pentecostal Church. [Olympia,
         Wa., 19--] 18p. Mimeographed.

--PERIODICALS

4860   Calvary tidings.   1-   1936-
         Olympia, Wa.

CHIESA EVANGELICA INTERNAZIONALE (1969-   )
[Also as International Evangelical Church.]

        The product of the amalgamation of many independent assem-
blies, the Chiesa Evangelica Internazionale is the youngest Pentecostal denomination in Italy.   The group was founded and is led by
John McTernan, a California businessman, who arrived in Italy in
1959.   When threatened in 1966 with loss of his American passport,
McTernan was ready to dedicate the former 1,500 seat Marconi
Theater in Rome as the International Evangelistic Center.   Successful in winning over the official who sought to deport him, McTernan
went on to develop the Chiesa Evangelica Internazionale, which by
the early 1970s claimed 200 congregations and 200,000 members.

        Through its official publication, the Dialogo Cristiano, the
group encourages members to refrain from controversy with other
Christians.   Friendly relations with individual Roman Catholics have
resulted.   A Catholic priest brought McTernan into contact with the
World Council of Churches, an introduction which resulted in applica-
tion by the Chiesa Evangelica Internazionale for membership in that
organization.

--PERIODICALS

4861   Dialogo cristiano.   1-   Feb. 1969-
         Roma.   OkTOr

4862   Pentecoste.   1-7, 1962-Jan. 1969.
         Roma.   OkTOr

CHRIST APOSTOLIC CHURCH (1918-   )
[1916-1922 as Diamond Society; 1922-1931 as affiliate of Faith Tabernacle, Philadelphia; 1931-1939 as affiliate of Apostolic Church; 1939-
194- as Nigeria Apostolic Church; 194 -1942 as United Apostolic
Church.]

The Nigerian Christ Apostolic Church displays a continuity scarcely apparent from its numerous changes in name and affiliation. Beginning in 1922, with one brief, forced retirement from 1957 to 1959, a national pastor, Peter Anim, was its leader even during periods of affiliation with American and British groups.

Since 1931 friendly relations have been sustained with the Christ Apostolic Church in Ghana, and beginning with Joseph Ayo Babalola's visit in 1936, Nigerians have steadily encouraged their brethren in Ghana to increase evangelistic activity.

4863   Peel, John David Yeadon, 1941-
        Aladura: a religious movement among the Yoruba, by
        J. D. Y. Peel. London, Published for the International
        African Institute by the Oxford University Press, 1968.   xiii,
        388p.

CHRIST FAITH MISSION (1939-   )

Organized in 1939 under the leadership of James Cheek in the Old Pisgah Tabernacle in Los Angeles, the Christ Faith Mission is a by-product of the Pisgah Home movement founded by Dr. Finis E. Yoakum. The Herald of Hope, Cheek's paper begun in 1940, is the official organ.   Membership statistics are not kept, but a constituency of approximately 500 supports the Christ Faith Mission Home at the Mountain Ranch near Saugus, and radio ministries in Los Angeles and San Diego.   Foreign editions of the Herald of Hope are produced for distribution in Korea, India, Indonesia, Mexico, and Jamaica.

--PERIODICALS

4864   Herald of hope.   1-   1937-
        Los Angeles.

CHRIST REVIVAL CHURCH (1961-1966)

In 1957 the Church Executive of the Christ Apostolic Church in Nigeria removed Peter Anim from office as general superintendent because of age and replaced him with Pastor D. K. Brifo, a younger man.   Anim returned to Boso, his native village, but chafed continually over his forced retirement.   Determined to regain his position, Anim called a meeting of all church workers and gained their support for reinstatement.   The 1960 meeting of the Church Executive reversed its 1957 decision, removing Brifo and again choosing Anim as general superintendent.   Although permitted to continue as a pastor in Christ Apostolic Church, Brifo decided instead to lead a secessionist movement, and in 1961 founded the Christ Revival Church. The new organization survived five years. In 1966, D. K. Brifo and most of his followers returned to the Christ Apostolic Church.

CHRISTEN-GEMEINDEN ELIM (1926-   )
[Also as Elimgemeinden.]

Founded in 1926 by preachers formerly affiliated with the Christlicher Gemeinschaftsverband GmbH Mülheim/Ruhr, the Christen-Gemeinden Elim differs from the parent body in discountenancing infant baptism and in regarding tongues as the initial evidence of the baptism in the Holy Spirit. Forced from 1938 to 1945 into membership in the Bund Evangelisch-Freikirchlicher Gemeinden in Deutschland, a union of Baptists and Plymouth Brethren, the Christen-Gemeinden Elim reorganized as an independent fellowship following the war. Headquarters are in Hamburg. The Christen-Gemeinden Elim support missionary efforts of the Velberter Mission, a branch of the Arbeitsgemeinschaft der Christen-Gemeinden in Deutschland.

CHRISTIAN CHURCH OF NORTH AMERICA (1927-   )
[1927-1939 as Unorganized Italian Christian Churches of North America; 1939-1942 as Italian Christian Church of North America.]

Tracing its spiritual ancestry to the Pentecostal revival among Italian-Americans of Chicago in 1907, the Christian Church of North America dates its organizational history to the first General Convention of the Unorganized Italian Christian Churches of the United States, held at Niagara Falls, New York, in 1927. Identical in doctrine to the General Council of the Assemblies of God, the group continues to affirm its ethnic origins, yet minister to non-Italians as opportunities present themselves. Fearful of anarchy as well as authoritarianism, the group has moved steadily toward stronger central organization. It incorporated at Pittsburgh in 1948.

The Christian Church of North America has developed a strong missionary outreach. Cooperating in many instances with the General Council of the Assemblies of God and other groups, it has mission projects in seven western European nations and four Latin American areas, as well as Australia, the Philippines, India, and the Ivory Coast. In 1979 the fellowship reported 12,000 members and 101 churches in the United States. Headquarters are in Sharon, Pennsylvania. Official periodicals include Il Faro in Italian and Vista in English.

4865   Christian Church of North America.
           Manual of the General Council [of the] Christian Church
        of North America. n.p., 1950. 66p.

4866   Bongiovanni, Guy
         The Christian Church of North America. Sharon, Pa.,
       Christian Church of North America; distributed by Niagara
       Religious Supply Center, Niagara Falls, N.Y., 197-. 12p.
       Cover title.

4867   Moore, Everett Leroy, 1918-
         Handbook of Pentecostal denominations in the United
       States. Pasadena, Ca., 1954. vii, 346ℓ. Thesis (M.A.)--
       Pasadena College. "Christian Church of North America":
       ℓ. 108-111. CSdP

4868   U.S. Bureau of the Census.
         Census of religious bodies: 1936. Italian bodies. Sta-
       tistics, denominational history, doctrine, and organization.
       Consolidated report. Washington, Government Printing Office,
       1940. iv, 9p. Includes the Unorganized Italian Christian
       Churches of North America. NNUT

--DOCTRINAL AND CONTROVERSIAL WORKS

4869   Fiorentino, Joseph, 1912-
         The new Pentecost and the old. Woburn, Ma., 1971.
       16p.

--HISTORY

4870   Christian Church of North America.
         50; fiftieth anniversary: Christian Church of North
       America, 1927-1977. Sharon, Pa., c1977. 408p.

4871   De Caro, Louis, 1919-
         Our heritage: the Christian Church of North America.
       An historical tracing of the origin and development of the
       General Council, Christian Church of North America. Sharon,
       Pa., General Council, Christian Church of North America,
       c1977. viii, 77p.

4872   Fiorentino, Joseph, 1912-
         In the power of His Spirit: "a summary of the Italian
       Pentecostal movement in the U.S.A. and abroad." Niagara
       Falls, N.Y., Christian Church of North America; distributed
       by Niagara Religious Supply Center, 1968. 17p.

--HYMNS AND SACRED SONGS

4873   Christian Church of North America. Missionary Society.
         Nuovo libro d'inni e salmi spirituali. Pittsburgh, c1959.
       1v. (unpaged) With music. OkBetC

--PASTORAL THEOLOGY

4874   Fiorentino, Joseph, 1912-
       Pulpit ethics and procedures. n. p., 1972. 8p. Caption
       title. "A paper presented at a ministers' seminar at the 45th
       CCNA Convention in Detroit, Michigan, on September 3, 1972."

--PERIODICALS

4875   Il Faro. 1- Aug. 1940-
       Newark, N.J., Erie, Pa., Herkimer, N.Y.

4876   Lighthouse. 1-12, no. 4, 1957-Aug. 1968.
       Beaver Falls, Pa.

4877   Vista. 1- Sept. 1968-
       Beaver Falls, Pa.

CHRISTIAN REVIVAL CHURCH (19 -)

In 1977 the Christian Revival Church with headquarters in
Mokokchung, Nagaland, India, was in cooperative fellowship with
the Assemblies of God in Great Britain and Ireland.

CHRISTIAN REVIVAL CRUSADE (1941-)
[1941-197- as National Revival Crusade; in Australia also as Commonwealth Revival Crusade.]

Founded about 1941 by Evangelist Leo Harris, this Australia-
based movement, strongly devoted to Anglo-Israelism in its first
years, has moderated its emphasis considerably in recent years.
In 1962 there were thirteen congregations in Australia and approximately the same number in New Zealand. Work in each country is
under national leaders. The Australian movement, being older and
larger, is considered the parent. In 1967 the Crusade was supporting six missionaries in New Guinea under the International Church
of the Foursquare Gospel. Headquarters are in Adelaide, where the
Crusade Bible College is located and the official organ, Impact, is
published. Currently, Barry Chant, dean of the Bible college, is
Crusade chairman.

4878   National Revival Crusade.
       Introducing the National Revival Crusade, New Zealand
       and Australia. Wellington, Printed by V. R. Brown, 19--.
       folder.

--HISTORY

4879   Worsfold, James Evans
       A history of the charismatic movements in New Zealand,
       including a Pentecostal perspective and a breviate of the Cath-
       olic Apostolic Church in Great Britain, by J. E. Worsfold.
       Bradford, Yorks., Julian Literature Trust; printed by Puritan
       Press, c1974.   xx, 368p.   "The Christian Revival Crusade":
       p. 292-296.   DLC

--PERIODICALS

4880   Impact.   1-   19 -
       Fullarton, Adelaide.   To 19-- as Revivalist.

CHRISTLICHER GEMEINSCHAFTSVERBAND GmbH MÜLHEIM/RUHR
   (1908-   )

       Organized in 1908, the Christlicher Gemeinschaftsverband is
centered in Mülheim an der Ruhr, a manufacturing city in the Rhineland where many large early Pentecostal conferences were held.
Led by Emil Humburg, the Mülheim alliance reached its zenith in
the years immediately before World War II when it numbered over
600 congregations.   Support of Hitler and abuse of the prophetic office led to the defection of many and the formation of many Freie
Pfingstgemeinden.   Although depleted in numbers, the Christlicher
Gemeinschaftsverband survived.   Closest to the Reformed tradition
of any European or American Pentecostal group, the Mülheim alliance has provided a vehicle for theological dialog with continental
Protestantism.   Its hymnal, Pfingstjubel, is used by German-speaking
Pentecostals around the globe.   Its official organ, Heilszeugnisse, is
published by the Missionsbuchhandlung und Verlag, Altdorf bei Nürnberg.

--DOCTRINAL AND CONTROVERSIAL WORKS

4881   Krust, Christian Hugo
       Was wir glauben, lehren und bekennen.   Unter Mitarbeit
       des Hauptbrüdertages, herausgegeben von Christian Krust.
       Altdorf bei Nürnberg, Missionsbuchhandlung und Verlag, 1963.
       164p.

--HISTORY

4882   Hollenweger, Walter Jacob, 1927-
       The Pentecostals: the charismatic movement in the
       churches [by] W. J. Hollenweger.   Minneapolis, Augsburg

Publishing House, c1972. xx, 572p.   Translation of Enthusiastisches Christentum.   "The attempt to set up a Pentecostal
movement within the Reformation tradition: the Mulheim Association of Christian Fellowships."

4883   Krust, Christian Hugo
        50 Jahre deutsche Pfingstbewegung, Mulheimer Richtung,
        nach ihrem geschichtlichen Ablauf dargestellt, von Christian
        Krust.   Altdorf bei Nurnberg, Missionsbuchhandlung und Ver-
        lag, 1958. 253p.

                    --HYMNS AND SACRED SONGS

4884   Christlicher Gemeinschaftsverband GmbH Mülheim/Ruhr.
            Pfingstjubel.   Altdorf bei Nürnberg, Missionsbuchhandlung
        und Verlag, 1956.   689p.

                    --PERIODICALS

4885   Heilszeugnisse.   1-   1930-1941, 1946-
            Altdorf bei Nürnberg.

4886   Pfingstgrusse.   1-   Feb. 1909-1919.
            Mülheim an der Ruhr.

CHURCH BY THE SIDE OF THE ROAD (1933-   )

        In 1924 some members of a community Sunday school which
met in the Thorndyke School in Seattle received what they believed
to be the baptism in the Holy Spirit.   Although the Pentecostals continued to meet with the community group, contention over their experiences disturbed the unity of the Sunday school and threatened its
continued use of the school facilities.   Realizing this, the charismatic minority withdrew and affiliated with Offiler's Bethel Temple
as a branch mission.   In 1933 the mission became independent, calling itself the "Church by the Side of the Road."   Three years later,
it gave birth to a branch, the Little Chapel of the Church by the
Side of the Road, which in turn later became independent of the
mother congregation.   With a full membership of 175, and an estimated constituency of 500, the Church by the Side of the Road now
works in cooperation with the Northwest District Council of the Assemblies of God.   In addition it supports missionary work in Indonesia.

4887   Church by the Side of the Road.
            Constitution of the Church by the Side of the Road.
        Seattle, 19--.

CHURCH OF CHRIST (Foursquare Gospel) (1950-)

The outgrowth of a mission begun in Avondale in 1946, the Church of Christ (Foursquare Gospel) had by the 1970s become the largest charismatic congregation in New Zealand. The church has been served by one pastor, the Reverend Frederick A. Wilson, during its entire history. Incorporating in 1950, the group built and occupied its own edifice in Mount Roskill the next year. Although several additions have been required to accommodate the present Sunday-night attendance of more than a thousand, the church remains at this site. In 1970 Japanese nationals who had joined the Church of Christ while studying in New Zealand, launched a mission in Osaka, which resulted in the establishment of a permanent work there two years later. In the early 1970s workers were being trained for a similar expansion in New Zealand.

With the exception of Anglo-Israelism, the doctrines promulgated by the Church of Christ (Foursquare Gospel) are identical to those taught by the International Church of the Foursquare Gospel, the Los Angeles-based denomination founded by Aimee Semple McPherson.

--HISTORY

4888   Worsfold, James Evans
        A history of the charismatic movements in New Zealand, including a Pentecostal perspective and a breviate of the Catholic Apostolic Church in Great Britain, by J. E. Worsfold. Bradford, Yorks., Julian Literature Trust; printed by Puritan Press, c1974. xx, 368p. "The Church of Christ, N. Z. (Foursquare Gospel)": p. 304-309. DLC

CHURCH OF GOD:

APOSTOLIC CHURCH OF GOD (1951-)

Founded July 11, 1951, the Apostolic Church of God consists of a single congregation of about sixty members located $4\frac{1}{2}$ miles east of Langley, British Columbia. Formed as a result of the efforts of evangelists associated with the Church of God (Seventh Day) congregation of Vernon, British Columbia, the group keeps Saturday as the sabbath. It stresses the importance of the Ten Commandments, and teaches that Wednesday was the day of Christ's crucifixion and that Saturday was the day of His resurrection. It insists that all holidays not mentioned in Scripture, including Sunday, Easter, Christmas, and Halloween, are pagan relics.

FULL GOSPEL FREE CHURCH OF GOD (1956-)

Incorporated February 14, 1956, the Full Gospel Free Church of God is unique in its polity. D. O. Brown, founder and general overseer, appoints the twelve-member Elders Board, which holds all property. He also appoints all pastors, and may remove any pastor whom he deems disloyal. Headquarters are in Corbin, Kentucky.

IGLESIA DE DIOS, INCORPORADA (1939-)

Unrelated to any other group bearing the Church of God name, the Iglesia de Dios, Incorporada, was founded in 1939 by nine Pentecostal believers of Fajardo, Puerto Rico. It soon spread over the entire eastern end of the island, and eventually to the Virgin Islands and the continental United States as well. The Iglesia de Dios is a sabbatarian, pietistic body, strongly committed to a literal interpretation of the Bible. The organization is directed by a president who resides in San Juan. In 1967 the group claimed 5,500 members twelve years of age and over. That year it reported seventy congregations in Puerto Rico, two in the Virgin Islands, and eighteen in the mainland United States. From 1954 to 1961 affiliated congregations on the mainland were known as the Non-Sectarian Church of God.

4889   Iglesia de Dios.
        Doctrinas Fundamentales de la Iglesia de Dios, Incorporada. 3. éd. Juncos, P.R., Imprenta Junquña, 1966. 28p.

        --PERIODICALS

4890   La Voz Apostólica. 1- 194 -
        San Juan, P.R.

        IGLESIA DE DIOS PENTECOSTAL DE NEW YORK, CONCILIO
        LATINO-AMERICANO (1956-)

The result of work begun in the New York area in 1951 by the Iglesia de Dios Pentecostal de Puerto Rico, the Concilio Latino-Americano de Iglesia de Dios Pentecostal de New York became an autonomous body in 1956. It, however, maintains "affiliation" with the parent body, and continues contributing to its support. By the 1970s the Concilio Latino-Americano had 75 churches and approximately 8,000 members in the New York metropolitan area. Through the New York headquarters are channeled funds for missionary activity in Central America, the Netherlands Antilles, and other areas.

4891   Iglesia de Dios Pentecostal de New York, Concilio Latino-Americano.

Constitución y Reglamento del Concilio Latino-Americano de la Iglesia de Dios Pentecostal de New York, Incorporado. New York, 1958.

IGLESIA DE DIOS PENTECOSTAL DE PUERTO RICO
(1921-   )
[Also as Pentecostal Church of God of Puerto Rico.]

In 1912 Pentecostal missionaries on their way to the Orient stopped in Hawaii long enough to convert a number of Puerto Rican immigrants living at the Government Experimental Station near Honolulu. As a result a Pentecostal congregation was formed, out of which during the next decade several members including the pastor returned to Puerto Rico as missionaries. In 1921 the thirteen congregations gathered by their efforts met in convention at Arecibo and organized the Iglesia de Dios Pentecostal. The body incorporated the next year. Until 1947, when it was refused the status of a domestic district, the Puerto Rican group considered itself part of the General Council of the Assemblies of God. This decision ushered in a period of uncertain fellowship with the mainland body. During these years the situation was made even more difficult by the migration of many islanders to the continental United States, particularly New York. In 1955 the American Assemblies of God offered the organic union it had refused eight years earlier, only to be rejected this time by the Puerto Rican brethren. The next year the Iglesia de Dios Pentecostal de Puerto Rico announced its independence, and granted practical autonomy to its New York area congregations under the name: Concilio Latino-Americano de la Iglesia de Dios Pentecostal de New York. It retained jurisdiction, however, over other stateside work.

Beginning with the Virgin Islands and Haiti in the 1940s, the Puerto Rican denomination has expanded into seven additional Latin American countries as well as Spain and Portugal. Headquarters are at Barrio Caimito, Rio Piedras. By the mid-1970s there were 220 congregations, 600 preaching points, and 20,000 members in Puerto Rico. Ninety-four affiliated congregations in the continental United States had 5,000 members.

4892   Iglesia de Dios Pentecostal de Puerto Rico.
Constitución y Reglamento de la Iglesia de Dios Pentecostal, "The Pentecostal Church of God, Inc." Rev. ed. Rio Piedras, P.R., 1954. 56p.

--EDUCATION

4893   Perez-Torres, Ruben
The pastor's role in educational ministry in the Pentecostal Church of God in Puerto Rico. Claremont, Ca., 1979. x, 111ℓ. Thesis (D. Min.)--School of Theology at Claremont. CCSC

--HISTORY

4894   Lugo, Juan L.
        Pentecostes en Puerto Rico; o, La Vida de un misionero.
        n. p., 1951. 126p.

OPEN BIBLE CHURCH OF GOD (19 -)

The Open Bible Church of God is the Indian affiliate of the
United Full Gospel Ministers and Churches founded in 1951. Willis
M. Clay, founder and president of the Open Bible Church of God,
also served as First treasurer of the Los Angeles-based companion
fellowship. Headquarters are at Tatabad, Coimbatore District,
Madras.

PENTECOSTAL CHURCH OF GOD OF AMERICA (1919-)
[1919-1922 as Pentecostal Assemblies of the U.S.A.; 1922-
   1934 as Pentecostal Church of God.]

Not all those in attendance at and in sympathy with the formation of the General Council of the Assemblies of God in 1914 at Hot
Springs, Arkansas, remained convinced of the commitment of the new
fellowship to congregational autonomy and Biblical orthodoxy. Led
by John C. Sinclair, a Chicago pastor who had been appointed Executive Presbyter following the Hot Springs meeting, and George C.
Brinkman, editor of the Chicago-based Pentecostal Herald, the dissatisfied remnant met December 30, 1919, in Chicago and organized
the Pentecostal Assemblies of the U.S.A. Sinclair became General
Chairman, and Brinkman, secretary. The organization adopted
Brinkman's paper as its official organ.

During the next thirty-two years, the denomination re-located
its headquarters three times, moving to Ottumwa, Iowa, in 1927; to
Kansas City, Missouri, in 1934; and to Joplin, Missouri, in 1951.
In 1933 the Pentecostal Church of God adopted a Statement of Faith
not unlike the Statement of Fundamental Truths of the General Council of the Assemblies of God, which had given the Pentecostal Church
founders such concern. Eventually it also developed a centralized
governmental structure similar to that of the Assemblies. In 1977
the denomination claimed 1,189 congregations in the United States,
with 110,870 members. It was supporting more than fifty North
American workers in fourteen world areas. Since 1927 the official
periodical has been called the Pentecostal Messenger.

4895   Pentecostal Church of God of America.
        General constitution and by-laws, 1926- . Chicago;
        Ottumwa, Ia.; Kansas City, Mo.; Joplin, Mo. v. [1]- .
        Irregular.

4896   Moore, Everett Leroy, 1918-

Handbook of Pentecostal denominations in the United States. Pasadena, Ca., 1954. vii, 346ℓ. Thesis (M.A.)-- Pasadena College. "Pentecostal Church of God of America": ℓ. 93-102. CSdP

4897   Olila, James Howard
Pentecostalism: the dynamics of recruitment in a modern socio-religious movement. Minneapolis, 1968. 57ℓ. Thesis (M.A.)--University of Minnesota. MnU

4898   U.S. Bureau of the Census.
Census of religious bodies: 1936. Pentecostal assemblies. Statistics, denominational history, doctrine, and organization. Consolidated report. Washington, Government Printing Office, 1940. iv, 49p. Includes Pentecostal Church of God of America, Inc. NNUT

--CATECHISMS AND CREEDS

4899   Pentecostal Church of God of America.
Confession of faith, Pentecostal Church of God. In Hardon, J.A. The spirit and origins of American Protestantism: a source book in its creeds. Dayton, Oh., 1968, 246-250.

--CONTROVERSIAL LITERATURE

4900   Porter, William Curtis, 1897-1960.
Porter-Myers debate, between W. Curtis Porter, Monette, Arkansas, representing Church of Christ, and B. Sunday Myers, Opelika, Alabama, representing Pentecostal Church of God. A written discussion: Is the Church of Christ a denomination?, or, Is it the exclusive New Testament church? Monette, Ar., Porter's Book Shop, c1956. 240p.

--HISTORY

4901   Pentecostal Church of God of America.
The Pentecostal Church of God of America. Joplin, Mo., 1969. 96p. At head of title: "For such a time as this." Issued as Pentecostal Messenger, 43:6-7 (July-Aug. 1969).

4902   Moon, Elmer Louis
The Pentecostal Church, a history and popular survey. New York, Carlton Press, 1966. 158p. (A hearthstone book.)

--PERIODICALS

4903   Gospel carrier. 1- 1954-
Joplin, Mo.

4904   Missionary voice. 1- 1958-
        Joplin, Mo.

4905   Pentecostal herald. 1- 1913-1927.
        Chicago.

4906   Pentecostal messenger. 1- 1927-
        Ottumwa, Ia.; Kansas City, Mo.; Joplin, Mo.

        --CALIFORNIA

        -- --LOS ANGELES

4907   Richardson, Robert Porterfield, 1876-
        Pentecostal prophets, by Robert P. Richardson. In
        Open Court, 42 (Nov. 1928), 673-680. On a service at Vic-
        toria Hall, Los Angeles, conducted by "members of Pente-
        costal Church of God."

        -- --SEASIDE

4908   Young, Frank Wilbur, 1928-
        Adaptation and pattern integration of a California sect
        [by] Frank W. Young. In Review of Religious Research, 1
        (Spring 1960), 137-150.

4909   Young, Frank Wilbur, 1928-
        Adaptation and pattern integration of a California sect
        [by] Frank W. Young. In Knudten, R. D., ed. The sociol-
        ogy of religion: an anthology. New York, c1967, 136-146.
        Abridged from Review of Religious Research, 1:4 (1960).

4910   Young, Frank Wilbur, 1928-
        Sociocultural analysis of a California Pentecostal church,
        by Frank W. Young. Ithaca, N.Y., 1954. vii, 163ℓ. The-
        sis (M.A.)--Cornell University. NIC

        PENTECOSTAL EVANGELICAL CHURCH OF GOD, NATIONAL
           AND INTERNATIONAL (1960-)

        Founded in 1960 at Riddle, Oregon, the Pentecostal Evangel-
ical Church of God, National and International, holds to beliefs similar to those of the Assemblies of God. It ordains women to the
ministry. From headquarters in Riddle, it issues two periodicals:
Ingathering and Golden Leaves. A General Convocation meets annually. In 1967, the group reported four churches and fourteen
clergy.

--PERIODICALS

4911   Golden leaves. 1- 196 -
           Riddle, Or.

4912   Ingathering. 1- 196 -
           Riddle, Or.

ROMANIAN APOSTOLIC PENTECOSTAL CHURCH OF GOD OF NORTH AMERICA (19 -)

The Romanian Apostolic Pentecostal Church of God of North America is a small ethnic fellowship of churches much concerned with ministry in Soviet-dominated nations of eastern Europe. In 1972 Emmanuel A. D. Deligiannis, a university professor in California, was general superintendent.

CHURCH OF JESUS AND THE WATCH MISSION (1922-)

In December 1910, after he threw away the cigar he was smoking while walking the streets of New York, George A. Leutjen was converted. Shortly thereafter he received the baptism of the Holy Spirit. Eleven years later Luetjen started preaching in his home in Long Island City, thus beginning a movement which by the 1940s included ministers in eight states and Canada. With a combined membership of only 35 at that time, the Church of Jesus and the Watch Mission had two affiliated congregations: the Israel Gospel Church of Long Island City and the Mizpah Mission of Taft, Florida. Prophetic Age was published in Long Island City.

--PERIODICALS

4913   Prophetic age. 1- 19 -
           Long Island City, N.Y.

CHURCH OF PENTECOST (1953-)
[1953-1957 as Gold Coast Apostolic Church; 1957-1962 as Ghana Apostolic Church.]

In 1952 James McKeown, Apostolic Church missionary in Ghana, was approached by Wings of Healing, an American evangelistic association headed by Thomas Wyatt, with a request for the right to send missionaries to work with the Apostolic Church in the Gold Coast. Although the National Council of the church in the Gold Coast agreed to the proposal, the missionary headquarters in Bradford, England, disapproved it and recalled McKeown. After being dismissed by the English mission authorities, he returned to Africa and the next year established the independent Gold Coast Apostolic Church.

Efforts at reconciliation by the English church failed and McKeown remained leader. In 1960, three years after the Gold Coast achieved independence as Ghana, McKeown returned to Britain for a visit, leaving Anaman, a national pastor, in charge as his deputy. During this absence, Anaman wrote McKeown that President Nkrumah had advised severance of connections with all foreign missionaries. As a result, said Anaman, McKeown was no longer head of the church in Ghana and no longer welcome in that country. McKeown returned, however, and when the National Council discovered Anaman's deception, it reinstated McKeown in office. Anaman and his followers then returned to the parent body. Disputes over property between the secessionists and the British-controlled body were finally resolved in 1962 when the group led by McKeown changed its name from Ghana Apostolic Church to the Church of Pentecost. James McKeown's survival as leader in the face of national independence is nearly unique in the recent church history of Africa.

CHURCH OF THE LORD (ALADURA) (1959-   )

The product of the 1959 merger of two west African groups, both named Church of the Lord, the present body has congregations in Ghana, Sierra Leone, and Liberia. Headquarters are in Kumasi, Ghana.

--HISTORY

4914   Turner, Harold Walter, 1911-
       History of an African independent church, by H. W. Turner. Oxford, Clarendon Press, 1967. 2v. DLC

--HISTORY AND STUDY OF DOCTRINES

4915   Turner, Harold Walter, 1911-
       Profile through preaching; a study of the sermon texts used in a West African independent church [by] Harold W. Turner. London, Published for the World Council of Churches, Commission on World Mission and Evangelism by Edinburgh House Press, 1965. 86p. (C. W. M. E. research pamphlets, 13.) On label: Distributed by Friendship Press, New York, N. Y. DLC

--WORSHIP

4916   Brown, Kenneth I.
       Worshiping with the African Church of the Lord (Aladura)

[by] Kenneth I. Brown. In Practical Anthropology, 13 (Mar. 1966), 59-84.

CONCILIO OLAZÁBAL DE IGLESIAS LATINO-AMERICANO (1936-)

Organized in 1936 and named in honor of Francisco Olazábal, noted Mexican evangelist, the Concilio Olazábal de Iglesias Latino-Americano stresses prayer and fasting as antidotes to bodily desires, and holds to life-long partnership in marriage and conscientious objection to war as convictions of divine origin. In 1967 there were seven churches and 275 members in California and Arizona, and four churches and nearly 100 members in Mexico. Headquarters are at the Tabernaculo Bethesda in Los Angeles. El Revelador Cristiano is the official organ. Although English is used upon occasion, the primary language used in the work of the Concilio Olazábal is Spanish.

--PERIODICALS

4917   El Revelador Cristiano. 1- 19 -
        Los Angeles.

CONGREGAZIONI CHRISTIANI (1910-)

Consisting of 2,500 churches and 500,000 members in 1967, the Congregazioni Christiani of Brazil are the outgrowth of work begun by Luigi Francescan in 1910. Born in Italy in 1866, Francescan migrated to Chicago at age twenty-four. A year after arriving, he converted to Protestantism and joined an Italian Presbyterian church. In 1909, two years followed his espousal of Pentecostalism, he embarked on a mission to Buenos Aires, feeling led to move on to São Paulo the next year. His success as an evangelist to the Italian residents of that city was phenomenal. The movement eventually took hold among the Portuguese-speaking majority, and spread to other areas of southern Brazil as well.

The Congregazioni Christiani manifest several distinctive characteristics attributable to strong dependence on Spirit-guidance in decision making, and to the Italian heritage of their original leaders. Although there is strong distrust of human initiative in interpreting the Bible and preaching (the Holy Spirit chooses ministers to be ordained and gives ministers messages for the people), the group encourages church musicians to seek professional instruction. Orchestras made up of stringed and woodwind instruments are commonly used in public worship. Unlike most Pentecostal bodies, fermented wine is used in communion services and little stress is placed on puritanical standards of conduct. Church buildings often display artistic grace in sharp contrast to the barn-like edifices occupied by

sister fellowships.   Administrative machinery is kept to a minimum
as are contacts with other denominations, even Pentecostal ones.
There is no official periodical.   What centralized direction there is,
is exercised by the central temple in São Paulo. This large church
is the site of a weekly inspirational meeting which draws participants
from all the congregations in the city, undoubtedly helping to unify
the movement thereby.

4918   Willems, Emilio, 1905-
           Followers of the new faith: culture change and the rise
        of Protestantism in Brazil and Chile.   Nashville, Vanderbilt
        University Press, 1967. x, 290p.   On Congregacioni Chris-
        tiani: p. 65, 118-119, 142-144, 148-153, 226.

4918a   Willems, Emilio, 1905-
           Validation of authority in Pentecostal sects of Chile and
        Brazil.   In Journal for the Scientific Study of Religion, 6
        (Fall 1967), 253-258.

CRUZADA NACIONAL DE EVANGELIZAÇÃO DO BRASIL (1946-   )

     The Cruzada Nacional de Evangelização is the outgrowth of
work begun in 1946 by Harold Williams of the Los Angeles-based
International Church of the Foursquare Gospel.   Using tents and the
methods of mass evangelism, it has registered dramatic, sustained
growth.   By 1980, when it had over 30,000 communicant members,
the Cruzada Nacional had become a largely indigenous movement.
Headquarters are in São Paulo.

DAMASCUS CHRISTIAN CHURCH (1939-   )

     The outgrowth of an independent work begun among Spanish-
speaking residents of New York City by Francisco Rosado and his
wife, Leoncia, in 1939, the Damascus Christian Church eventually
spread to neighboring New Jersey, and to the Virgin Islands and
Cuba.   Headquarters are in the Bronx.   By 1962 the group had ten
congregations and about 1,000 members.

DELIVERANCE EVANGELISTIC CENTERS (1966-   )

     The Newark-based Deliverance Evangelistic Centers is unique
among American black organizations for adherence both to Trinitarianism and to a non-Wesleyan understanding of sanctification.   "Apostle" Skinner, the founder, died in 1975.

--PERIODICALS

4919   Deliverance voice.   1-   1966-
        Newark, N.J.

EGLISE PENTECOTISTE DE MADAGASCAR (1962-   )

        Organized in 1962, the Eglise Pentecôtiste gathered into a
continuing fellowship the fruit of the recent revival campaign of
American evangelists M. A. and Jane Collins Daoud in Madagascar.
After five years of existence, the group reported eight congregations,
2,000 members, and an inclusive constituency of 9,000.

EGLISE PENTECOTISTE DU ZAIRE (1960-   )
[1960-1971 as Eglise Pentecôtiste du Congo.]

        Formed in 1960, the Eglise Pentecôtiste du Zaire is the re-
sult of work begun in 1914 by the Congo Evangelistic Mission.   Under national leadership, the church maintains close ties with the
parent agency.   In 1967 the Eglise Pentecôtiste reported 1,012
churches and 46,721 members.   Seven years later, Harold Womersley, a missionary who had observed the movement for half a century, said there were then 2,200 congregations and an inclusive
Christian constituency of over 125,000.

ELIM FELLOWSHIP (1933-   )
[1933-1947 as Elim Ministerial Fellowship; 1947-1972 as Elim Mis-
    sionary Assemblies.]

        The Elim Fellowship is the outgrowth of the Elim Ministerial
Fellowship, which in turn is the product of the Elim Bible Institute.
The school, which was founded in 1924 by Ivan Q. Spencer, produced
a large number of independent workers, who in 1933 formed the Elim
Ministerial Fellowship.   Although its original purpose had been to
serve as an agency for granting ministerial credentials, in 1947 the
organization began admitting churches as well as individuals to membership, and changed its name to Elim Missionary Assemblies.   Missionary outreach, begun with the opening of a field in Kenya in 1940,
included work in twelve world areas thirty-five years later.   In
1973 the group reported 70 churches and 5,000 members.   The United
States constituency is concentrated in New York and Pennsylvania.
Headquarters are in Lima, New York, site of the Elim Bible Institute.   Carlton Spencer, the founder's son, heads both church and
school.

4920   Elim Missionary Assemblies.

Constitution and by-laws. ----, N. Y., 19--.   14p.

4921   Moore, Everett Leroy, 1918-
        Handbook of Pentecostal denominations in the United
        States. Pasadena, Ca., 1954.   vii, 346ℓ.   Thesis (M. A.)--
        Pasadena College. "Elim Missionary Assemblies": ℓ. 111-
        117. CSdP

        --PERIODICALS

4922   Elim herald. 1- 1931-
        Hornell, N. Y., Lima, N. Y.   1931-19-- as Elim Pente-
        costal herald.

ELIM PENTECOSTAL CHURCH (1915-)
[1915-1918 as Elim Evangelistic Band; 1918-1926 as Elim Pente-
    costal Alliance; 1926-1966 as Elim Foursquare Gospel Alliance.]

        Formed in 1915 at Monaghan in Ulster, the Elim Evangelistic
Band first proposed simply to support the efforts of George Jeffreys
and his fellow workers.   In October 1918, the movement incorporated
as the Elim Pentecostal Alliance with headquarters in Belfast.   Gradually Jeffreys spent more and more time in England leaving in the
wake of nearly every meeting a nucleus of converts for the organization of a church.   In 1921 the first of what was to be a circuit of
churches in Essex was organized at Leigh-on-Sea.   This was followed the next year by the opening of Elim Tabernacle, the future
headquarters church, in an abandoned Methodist chapel in Clapham,
southwest London.

        The founding of the Elim Publishing Office in connection with
this church in 1924 signaled a milestone on the road to establishment
of a denominational structure, a development which the founder,
charismatic leader that he was, proved ill-suited to manage.   Ex-
tending his evangelistic itinerary to continental Europe and to the
United States, George Jeffreys developed a warm relationship with
Aimee Semple McPherson, which may explain the new name his organization adopted in 1926.   Despite the similarity in the names and
teachings of the Elim Foursquare Gospel Alliance and Mrs. McPherson's International Church of the Foursquare Gospel, no organizational tie ever existed.

        Although a constitution drawn up in 1934 gave absolute power
to the founder, or principal as he was called, Jeffreys' proclivity
toward congregationalism prevented him from giving the needed organizational direction to the more than 200 congregations formed during the first twenty-five years of his ministry.   His insistence on
the autonomy of local churches affiliated with the movement led to
conflict with headquarters personnel and ultimately to loss of control
over the organization.   The founder's defection along with several

hundred followers to form the Bible-Pattern Church Fellowship in
1940 did little to impede the growth of the Elim Foursquare Gospel
Alliance. It remained the best organized and most aggressive of
British Pentecostal bodies. In 1975 it numbered 310 congregations
and 25,000 members. Having sent its first worker to the Congo
in 1920, the group has an enviable record of missionary outreach.
In 1967 it had 52 missionaries under appointment in twelve world
areas. Headquarters are at Cheltenham, Gloucestershire, where
the Elim Herald, the official organ since 1919, is published.

4923   Elim Pentecostal Church.
            Year book, 19 - . London, Cheltenham, Glos. v. [1]- .

4924   Edsor, Albert W.
            Foursquare revival mirror.   Compiled by A. W. Edsor.
        London, Elim Publishing House, 1936. 64p.

4925   Greenway, Harry William
            Labourers with God, being a brief account of the activi-
        ties of the Elim movement, by H. W. Greenway.   London,
        Elim Publishing Co., 1946. 52p.

4926   Wilson, Bryan Ronald, 1926-
            Sects and society; a sociological study of the Elim Taber-
        nacle, Christian Science, and Christadelphians.   Berkeley,
        University of California Press, 1961. 397p. Based on the-
        sis (Ph. D.)--London School of Economics, 1955. DLC

4927   Wilson, Bryan Ronald, 1926-
            Sects and society; a sociological study of three religious
        groups in Britain. London, Heinemann, 1961. 397p. Based
        on thesis (Ph. D.)--London School of Economics, 1955. CU,
        NIC

4928   Wilson, Bryan Ronald, 1926-
            Social aspects of religious sects: a study of some con-
        temporary groups in Great Britain, with special references
        to a Midland city. London, 1955. 2v. Thesis (Ph. D.)--
        London School of Economics. LE

            --CLERGY

4929   Wilson, Bryan Ronald, 1926-
            Pentecostalist minister: role conflicts and status con-
        tradictions [by] Bryan R. Wilson. In American Journal of
        Sociology, 64 (Mar. 1959), 494-504.

4930   Wilson, Bryan Ronald, 1926-
            The Pentecostalist minister: role conflicts and contradic-
        tions of status [by] B. R. Wilson. In Wilson, B. R., ed.
        Patterns of sectarianism; organization and ideology in social
        and religious movements. London, 1967, 138-157.

--DEVOTIONAL LITERATURE

4931   Boulton, Ernest Charles William,   -1960.
        The garden of unveiling; devotional meditations for each
        day of the month.   London, Victory Press, 1943.   L

4932   Boulton, Ernest Charles William,   -1960.
        Whispers from within the veil.   London, Elim Publishing
        Co. , 1935.   vi, 96p.   L

--DOCTRINAL AND CONTROVERSIAL WORKS

4933   Barratt, Thomas Ball, 1862-1940.
        In the days of the latter rain.   Rev. ed.   London, Elim
        Publishing Co. , 1928.   222p.   L, TxWaS

4934   Boulton, Ernest Charles William,   -1960.
        The focused life.   London, Elim Publishing Co. , 1932.
        vii, 103p.   L

4935   Brewster, Percy S.
        The approach to divine healing; or, Can we expect mira-
        cles today?   London, 1939.   22p.   L

4936   Brewster, Percy S.
        Is lasting revival possible?   London, 1939.   15p.   L

4937   Brewster, Percy S.
        Pentecostal doctrine.   Editor: P. S. Brewster.   [Chel-
        tenham, Glos. , Grenehurst Press], c1976.   400p.   KyWAT

4938   Brewster, Percy S.
        The spreading flame of pentecost [by] P. S. Brewster.
        London, Elim Publishing House, 1970.   ix, 135p.   L

4939   Brumback, Carl, 1917-
        "What meaneth this?"   A Pentecostal answer to a Pente-
        costal question.   London, Elim Publishing Co. , 1949.   348p.
        L

4940   Burton, William Frederick Padwick, 1886-1971.
        Signs following, by W. F. P. Burton.   London, Elim
        Publishing Co. , 1949.   40p.

4941   Canty, George
        In My Father's house; Pentecostal expositions of major
        Christian truths.   Foreword by W. G. Hathaway.   ----,
        Willmer Brothers, 1969.   128p.

4942   Canty, George
        What's going on?   The George Canty viewpoint.   Chelten-
        ham, Glos. , Greenhurst Press, 1977.   iv, 116p.   DLC

4943   Darragh, R. E.
       In defence of His word; being a number of selected tes-
       timonies of dire suffering healed by the power of Christ un-
       der the ministry of Principal George Jeffreys.   Compiled by
       R. E. Darragh.   London, Elim Publishing Co. , 1932.   143p.
       L

4944   Francis, Gwilym L
       The world's next great event--and after.   London, Elim
       Publishing Co. , 1934.   86p.   L

4945   Francis, Gwilym L
       The world's next great event--and after.   Rev. ed.
       London, Victory Press, 1938.   ix, 94p.   L

4946   Gee, Donald, 1891-1966.
       Keeping in touch; studies on walking in the Spirit.   Lon-
       don, Elim Publishing Co. , 1951.   80p.   TxWaS

4947   Gee, Donald, 1891-1966.
       Studies in guidance.   Rev. ed.   London, Elim Publishing
       Co. , 1941.   vi, 74p.   L

4948   Gee, Donald, 1891-1966.
       Trophimus I left sick: our problems of divine healing.
       London, Elim Publishing Co. , 1952.   30p.   L, OkTOr,
       TxWaS

4949   Gorman, Samuel
       Christ--the infallible exemplar.   London, Elim Publishing
       Co. , 1935.   ix, 88p.   L

4950   Gorman, Samuel
       Christ's glorious supremacy.   London, Elim Publishing
       Co. , 1933.   67p.   L

4951   Greenway, Harry William
       This emotionalism, by H. W. Greenway.   London, Vic-
       tory Press, 1954.   ix, 150p.   CCmS, L

4952   Hathaway, William George
       A sound from heaven, by W. G. Hathaway.   London,
       Victory Press, 1947.   104p.   L, TxWaS

4953   Hathaway, William George
       Spiritual gifts in the church, by W. G. Hathaway.   Lon-
       don, Elim Publishing Co. , 1933.   xiv, 123p.   L, TxWaS

4954   Jeffreys, George, 1889-1962.
       Healing rays.   London, Elim Publishing Co. , 1932.
       xiii, 208p.   L

4955   Jeffreys, George, 1889-1962.

The miraculous foursquare gospel--supernatural.   London, Elim Publishing Co., 1929-1930.   2v.   L

4956   Jeffreys, George, 1889-1962.
Pentecostal rays; the baptism and gifts of the Holy Spirit.   London, Elim Publishing Co., 1933.   xv, 255p.   L

4957   Lancaster, John
In spirit and in truth: principles for Pentecostal people. Cheltenham, Glos., Grenehurst Press, 1977.   138p.   KyWAT

4958   Lancaster, John
The Spirit-filled church.   Cheltenham, Glos., Grenehurst Press, 1973.   91p.

4959   Montgomery, Carrie (Judd), 1858-
The prayer of faith.   London, Victory Press, 1930. xviii, 123p.   L

4960   Robinson, Charles Elmo, 1867-1954.
A modern Pentecost.   London, Elim Publishing Co., 1932.   vi, 246p.

4961   Urch, Walter Henry
The place of spiritual gifts in Pentecostal churches. London, Elim Publishing Co., 1955.   30p.   (Pamphlets for the times, 1.)   L

-- --NON-PENTECOSTAL AUTHORS

4962   Pietsch, W. E.
McPherson-Jeffreys Four Square Gospel heresy: a grave warning, by W. E. Pietsch.   Hounslow, Middx., Bible Witness, 1928.   23p.   L

4963   Pollock, Algernon James, 1864-1957.
Modern Pentecostalism, Foursquare Gospel, "healings" and "tongues." Are they of God?   London, Central Bible Truth Depot, 1929.   84p.   L

4964   Pollock, Algernon James, 1864-1957.
Modern Pentecostalism, Foursquare Gospel, "healings," and "tongues." Are they of God?   5th ed.   London, Central Bible Truth Depot, 1929.   80p.   CLamB

--EDUCATION

4965   Greenway, Harry William
Teaching the child.   London, Victory Press, 1947.   78p. L

--HISTORY

4966   Elim Pentecostal Church.
Diamond jubilee [of the] Elim Pentecostal churches.
Cheltenham, Glos., Grenehurst Press, 196-. 32p. MoSpA

4967   Elim Pentecostal Church.
Elim jubilee year souvenir, 1915-1965. London, 196-.
59p. OkTOr

4968   Boulton, Ernest Charles William, -1960.
George Jeffreys, a ministry of the miraculous; a chroni-
cle ... of the Elim Foursquare Gospel Alliance. London,
Elim Publishing Office, 1929. vii, 352p. KyWAT, L

4969   Brooks, Noel, 1914-
Fight for the faith and freedom. London, Pattern Bookroom [1948] 136p. L

--HYMNS AND SACRED SONGS

4970   Hathaway, William George
Elim choruses; words only, nos. 1-18. Compiled by
W. G. Hathaway. Eastbourne, Victory Press, 19--. 62p.
OkBetC

--PASTORAL LITERATURE

4971   Brewster, Percy S.
The convert's handbook. London, 1939. 12p. L

4972   Brewster, Percy S.
Why go to church? London, 1939. L

--PASTORAL THEOLOGY

4973   Elim Foursquare Gospel Alliance.
Elim lay preacher's handbook. London, Elim Publishing
Co., 1946. 112p. L

4974   Gee, Donald, 1891-1966.
Concerning shepherds and sheepfolds; a series of studies
dealing with pastors and assemblies. Rev. ed. London,
Elim Publishing Co., 1952. 88p.

--PERIODICALS

4975   Elim crusader witness. 1- 1928-
London. 1928-1930 as Elim Foursquare crusader. L

4976   Elim evangel. 1- Dec. 1919-
        Belfast, London, Cheltenham, Glos.   To 19-- as Elim
        evangel and foursquare revivalist.   L

4977   Elim missionary courier.   1-   1939-
        London.   L

4978   Elim missionary evangel.   1-   1947-
        London.   L

4979   Elim supplement.   1-3, Aug. -Oct. 1924.
        London.   "Reports from Canada and U. S. A. "   L

4980   Foursquare revivalist.   1, Aug. 3, 1928-May 31, 1929.
        London.   Merged into Elim evangel.   L

4981   Young folk.   1-   19 -
        Cheltenham, Glos.

4982   Young folks' evangel.   1-5, 1926-1930.
        London.   Merged into Elim foursquare crusader.   L

4983   Youth challenge.   1-8, no. 2, 1- , June 1954-Summer 1961,
        1962-July 1966.
        London.   L

                    --SERMONS, TRACTS, ADDRESSES, ESSAYS

4984   Boulton, Ernest Charles William, -1960.
        The challenge of the impossible. London, Victory Press,
        1929.   v, 90p.   L

4985   Boulton, Ernest Charles William, -1960.
        The conquest of the commonplace. London, Victory
        Press, 1930.   vii, 87p.   L

4986   Boulton, Ernest Charles William, -1960.
        Echoes from the sanctuary. London, Elim Publishing
        Co., 1933.   viii, 103p.   L, OkTOr

4987   Boulton, Ernest Charles William, -1960.
        Jewels of the King. London, Victory Press, 1938.   102p.
        L

4988   Boulton, Ernest Charles William, -1960.
        Love's miracles, by E. C. W. Boulton. London, Victory
        Press, 1931.   vii, 88p.   CCmS, L

4989   Boulton, Ernest Charles William, -1960.
        The sanctuary of friendship. London, Victory Press,
        1939.   133p.   L

4990   Brewster, Percy S.
         The revolutionised life. London, Victory Press, 1940.
         46p. L

4991   Greenway, Harry William, ed.
         Power age. Edited by H. W. Greenway. London, Elim
         Publishing Co., 1951. 35p.

EVANGELICAL BIBLE CHURCH (1947-)

In 1947 Frederick Bradshaw Marine of Baltimore organized
the Evangelical Bible Church. Stress is placed on a very detailed
eschatology. Although the group teaches that the Mosiac law, including the Ten Commandments, was abolished by Christ, strict behavioral standards are enforced. Members are committed to non-
combatant service in time of war. Headquarters for the movement,
which consists of three churches in Maryland and a mission in
Pennsylvania, are in Baltimore. There are approximately 250 members in the United States. A church-sponsored missionary project
in the Philippines is known as the Evangelical Church of God.

4992   Evangelical Bible Church.
         Doctrines, teachings, and by-laws of the Evangelical
         Bible Church. Baltimore, 1960. 28p.

EVANGELISTIC AGENCIES:

AMERICAN EVANGELISTIC ASSOCIATION (1954-)

Formed by John E. Douglas and seventeen other independent
ministers in 1954, the American Evangelistic Association is designed
to set professional standards and to license and ordain clergy, also
to coordinated collective missionary, educational, and charitable efforts in foreign countries. In 1968 the Association reported 2,057
members. Although ministers, not churches, are accepted as members, the founder has claimed that the combined membership of congregations served by American Evangelistic Association members is
in excess of 100,000. Membership is concentrated in the vicinity of
Baltimore, the headquarters. Missionary outreach is directed from
offices in Dallas, where World Evangelism, the official organ, is
published. As World Missionary Evangelism, the organization supports mission projects in Haiti, India, Hong Kong, and Korea, and
operates over forty orphanages in various parts of the world. In
1975 the missionary department reported income of approximately
$50,000. At that time it claimed to be giving support to more than
30,000 children overseas.

--PERIODICALS

4993   World evangelism.   1-   1959-
       Dallas

ANCHOR BAY EVANGELISTIC ASSOCIATION (1940-   )

       Organized in 1940, the Anchor Bay Evangelistic Association
is the outgrowth of a single independent congregation in New Baltimore, Michigan. This church, which was begun following a revival
campaign of Mrs. M. B. Woodworth-Etter in 1918, became established under the leadership of Roy John Turner, a local physician,
and his wife, Blanche A. Turner. Although from 1938 to 1940
Turner served as an executive of the International Church of the
Foursquare Gospel in Los Angeles, the New Baltimore congregation
remained independent until the Association organized.

       Work centers in the Anchor Bay Bible Institute, which was
established in the same year as the Association. Here, training in
evangelistic, missionary, and medical techniques is given to prospective home and foreign missionaries. Home missionaries concentrate on ministry to orphans, prisoners, and the poor both inside
and outside of penal and social welfare institutions. The aim of
foreign work is to establish churches and educational projects on
an indigenous, self-supporting basis. In 1975 the Anchor Bay Evangelistic Association had 25 North American workers under appointment in Belize, Mexico, Germany, Turkey, India, Indonesia, and
the Philippines. About $350,000 was contributed for foreign mis-
sions that year.

4994   Anchor Bay Evangelistic Association.
       Articles of faith. New Baltimore, Mi., 19--. 16p.

              --DOCTRINAL AND CONTROVERSIAL WORKS

4995   Dye, M. L.
       The murderous Communist conspiracy, Satan's end-time
       program, by M. L. Dye. New Baltimore, Mi., Anchor Bay
       Evangelistic Association, 19--. 27p.

              --PERIODICALS

4996   Challenge. 1- 1959-
       New Baltimore, Mi.

APOSTOLIC CHALLENGE (1956-   )

Formerly the Southern Maine and New Hampshire section of

the Zion Evangelistic Fellowship, the Apostolic Challenge was organized to coordinate agressive evangelistic activity in the region
after the Zion Fellowship disbanded.   In addition to licensing and
ordaining workers, the Apostolic Challenge is committed to starting
new churches in as many new communities as possible.   As a le-
gally incorporated body, it is authorized to hold title to such property as may be acquired.   Trinitarian in doctrine, it continues to
fellowship Oneness believers also.

BIBLE REVIVAL EVANGELISTIC ASSOCIATION (1962-)
[1962-19-- as Bible Revival, Inc.]

The purpose of the Bible Revival Evangelistic Association,
organized in 1962, is to support and extend the ministry of Evangelist David Nunn.   The Association administers funds given for
radio broadcasting and for missionary projects.   In 1972 Nunn
preached regularly over nineteen stations and budgeted $200,000
for support of national workers and ministerial training in under-
developed nations.   The Healing Messenger, the official periodical,
is published in Dallas.

--PERIODICALS

4997   Healing messenger. 1- 1963-
       Dallas. OkTOr

BOLD LIVING SOCIETY (1961-)

Based in Cloverdale, British Columbia, the Bold Living Society is the principal supporting agency of the evangelistic ministry
of Don Gossett.   In addition to radio broadcasts aired in western
Canada and the West Indies, Gossett conducts traditional revival
campaigns, often in cooperation with congregations affiliated with
the Assemblies of God and the Apostolic Church of Pentecost of
Canada.   Two Canadian churches affiliated with the Society have a
combined membership of approximately 100.   Total individual membership of the organization is approximately 5,000.   Headquarters
of Bold Bible Living, the companion society in the United States,
are in Blaine, Washington.

CALIFORNIA EVANGELISTIC ASSOCIATION (1933-)
[1933-1939 as Colonial Tabernacle.]

Taking its present name in 1939, the California Evangelistic
Association is in essential doctrinal agreement with the General
Council of the Assemblies of God, except that it is amillennial.   It
is the outgrowth of the Colonial Tabernacle of Long Beach, which
was founded in 1933 by Oscar C. Harms, a former Advent Christian

pastor.   Although formation of additional assemblies necessitated
reorganization in 1939, congregations affiliated with the Association
remain autonomous.   In the 1970s there were 62 affiliated churches
and approximately 4, 700 members in California, Oregon, and Washington.   Headquarters are in Long Beach.   The California Evangelistic Association supports missionaries in Italy, Zambia, Brazil,
Colombia, and Mexico.

4998   California Evangelistic Association.
            Constitution and by-laws of the California Evangelistic
        Association, a corporation.   Adopted February 20, 1939.
        Long Beach, 1939.

4999   Moore, Everett Leroy, 1918-
            Handbook of Pentecostal denominations in the United
        States.   Pasadena, Ca., 1954.   vii, 346ℓ.   Thesis (M. A.)--
        Pasadena College.   "California Evangelistic Association":
        ℓ. 103-104.   CSdP

            --PERIODICALS

5000   Berean.   1- 19 -
        Long Beach, Ca.

        CAROLINA EVANGELISTIC ASSOCIATION (1930-   )

        The Carolina Evangelistic Association is the agency through
which the Garr Memorial Church, an independent congregation of
Charlotte, North Carolina, conducts its evangelistic and missionary
outreach.   Established in 1930 by A. G. Garr, pioneer missionary
to Hong Kong, the Garr Memorial Church has sent out more than
one-hundred full-time workers.   In the late 1960s the 1, 000-member
congregation was raising approximately $25, 000 annually for mis-
sions, two-thirds of which went to foreign work.   It contributes
toward the support of workers in Brazil, Jamaica, Germany, Italy,
Okinawa, the Philippines, Hong Kong, and India.   In addition it produces a radio program, "The Morning Thought," and maintains
Camp Lurecrest at Lake Lure, North Carolina, a facility for youth.
Members of the Garr Memorial Church and Faith Chapel, its local
affiliate, are active in ministry to jails and hospitals in the Charlotte area.

5001   Charlotte, N. C.   Garr Auditorium.
            Twentieth anniversary of the Garr Auditorium, 1930-
        1950.   Charlotte, N. C., 1950.   40p.

        CHRISTIAN WORKERS' UNION (-1935)

        Through its official organ, Word and Work published in

Framingham, Massachusetts, the Christian Workers' Union helped
to unify the non-denominational "Finished Work" forces of New
England.   By the late 1920s it was sponsoring an annual camp meeting.   In 1929 this meeting, jointly sponsored by the Union and the
Russian and Eastern European Mission, was held on Oak Street,
Wellesley Park.   In the mid-1930s the Christian Workers' Union
apparently disbanded, most of its constituency being absorbed by
the General Council of the Assemblies of God.

5002   Word and work.   1-57, 1879-1935.
        Springfield, Ma., Framingham, Ma.

COE FOUNDATION (1961-)

Established in 1961, the Coe Foundation is designed to continue the ministry of Evangelist Jack Coe, who died of polio in
1956.   Led by his widow, Juanita, and her second husband, Dan
Hope, the Coe Foundation is successor to Herald of Healing, Inc.
The organization publishes two periodicals, Christian Challenge and
Pentecostal Echoes, and aids foreign missionaries in establishing
churches, Bible schools, and orphanages.   In addition it sponsors
the Jack Coe Memorial Children's Home of Waxahachie, Texas.
Until the early 1970s, Mrs. Coe and Dan Hope continued as pastors
of the Dallas Revival Center.   As the memory of Jack Coe fades,
raising support for Coe Foundation projects becomes increasingly
difficult.

--PERIODICALS

5003   Christian challenge.   1-   1952-
        Dallas.   1952-1954 as Herald of healing; 1955-1962 as
        International healing.   OkTOr

5004   Pentecostal echoes.   1-   196 -
        Dallas.

DEFENDERS OF THE CHRISTIAN FAITH (1925-)

Organized November 27, 1925, at Salina, Kansas, the Defenders of the Christian Faith proposed as an interdenominational
fellowship to mount a defense against the theory of evolution and in
favor of Christian fundamentals.   Gerald B. Winrod, an independent
Baptist who led the movement from its inception until his death in
1957, showed little interest in Pentecostalism.   The Puerto Rican
branch did, however.   Founded by Juan Francisco Rodríguez-Rivera
following a series of missionary conferences conducted by Winrod in
1931, the group included both Pentecostals and Baptists.   Achieving
virtual independence as the Movimiento Defensores de la Fe de
Puerto Rico, the mission never exercised significant influence on
the Wichita-based fellowship.   G. H. Montgomery and Hart Arm-

strong have led the original movement since Winrod's death.   Although both had long served as Pentecostal ministers, neither pursued distinctively Pentecostal themes.   To make up for a significant decline in support following the founder's death, objectives and programs were re-examined.   As a result after 1965 all explicit direction of mission projects from the central office ceased.   Later financial support was limited to direct subsidies for national workers and free literature for public distribution.

--HISTORY

5005   Defender.
            Fire by night and cloud by day: a history of Defenders of the Christian Faith.   Compiled and written by Defenders editorial staff.   Wichita, Mertmont Publishers, 1966.   128p.

--PERIODICALS

5006   Defender. 1- Apr. 1926-
            Wichita, Ks.; Oklahoma City, Ok.; Kansas City, Mo.; Wichita, Ks.

ELBETHEL CHRISTIAN WORK (1912-   )

A society for the deepening of spiritual life, the Elbethel Christian Work originated in Chicago about 1912.   Led at first by Cora Harris MacIlravy, the group soon developed a national, even international constitutency through its journal, Elbethel.   For several decades, the paper has been published in Asheville, North Carolina.

--PERIODICALS

5007   Elbethel. 1- 1912-
            Chicago; Asheville, N.C.

FULL GOSPEL DEFENDERS CONFERENCE OF AMERICA
      (19 -   )

Based in Philadelphia, the Full Gospel Defenders Conference of America places emphasis on Christ's power displayed in signs and miracles.   In the late 1970s Grover S. Smith was general superintendent.

FULL GOSPEL FELLOWSHIP OF CHURCHES AND
      MINISTERS INTERNATIONAL (1962-   )

Formed in September 1962 during a ministerial conference in

Dallas, the Full Gospel Fellowship of Churches and Ministers provides a medium of cooperative action for otherwise independent churches and ministers. "A fellowship of the body of Christ rather than a closed communion," it serves as a credential-granting agency for independent ministers. It pledges "never" to "attempt to exercise a single attribute of power or authority over any church or over the messengers of the churches in such wise as to limit the sovereignty of the churches." Gordon Lindsay, a Dallas-based evangelist, used his paper to urge the establishment of the Fellowship, and although the Christ for the Nations organization, which Lindsay founded, has no organic tie to the Fellowship, a close informal bond exists between the two. By the mid-1970s the Full Gospel Fellowship of Churches and Ministers had 265 affiliated churches, including 56 in Africa, Europe, the West Indies and the Philippines, with a combined membership of 21, 000. Added to this total might be the 30, 000 members of non-affiliated congregations served by 300 member-clergy. Headquarters are in Dallas.

5008   Full Gospel Fellowship of Churches and Ministers International.
        Constitution of the Full Gospel Fellowship of Churches
        and Ministers International. Dallas, 1967.

FULL GOSPEL MINISTER ASSOCIATION (19 -)

An agency for accrediting both ministers and churches, the Full Gospel Minister Association regards ministry as having two aspects: world evangelism and confirmation of the "Word with Signs Following and evidence of the power of God." Members conscientiously object to war. Officers are elected by the membership annually. Headquarters are in East Jordan, Michigan.

5009   Full Gospel Minister Association.
        Constitution and by-laws of the Full Gospel Minister Association. East Jordan, Mi., 19--.

FULL GOSPEL TESTIMONY (1935-1952)

In April 1932, Frederick Squire, Assembly of God pastor at East Kirkby, Nottinghamshire, felt divinely impelled to enter itinerant evangelism. "I distinctly heard," he later recalled, "the words [!] 'Northampton,' and felt at once it was the call of God." A four-week campaign which yielded 631 converts at Northampton that fall, was followed by other successful efforts in the following places in the South Midlands: Wellingborough, Kettering, Rushden, and Nuneaton. Pastor Squire's Full Gospel Testimony Revival Party introduced the Pentecostal message to Ashton-under-Lyne, Fleetwood, Weston-super-Mare, and Falmouth, and greatly strengthened Pentecostal assemblies in Coventry, Norwich, and elsewhere. Squire stressed healing, and the large number of converts claiming cures for physical ailments undoubtedly increased the evangelist's popularity.

Although in complete doctrinal agreement with the Assemblies of God, Squire followed the example of George Jeffreys and other evangelists by organizing the assemblies which resulted from his revivals into a separate fellowship, the Full Gospel Testimony. Headquarters first established in connection with the Full Gospel Publishing House at Southend-on-Sea, were moved to Leamington Spa during World War II. The movement disbanded in the early 1950s, and member congregations joined other groups. The International Bible Training Institute, which Frederick Squire had established at Leamington Spa in 1947, continued as a non-denominational Bible school, however.

5010   Full Gospel Testimony: the revival news. 1-18, no. 2, Apr. 1935-Aug. 1952.
        Southend-on-Sea, Essex. L

GALILEAN ASSOCIATION (195 -   )

With headquarters in Bethany, a suburb of Oklahoma City, the Galilean Association is an extension of the ministry of Louis and Alice Gibbes. Moving to Oklahoma from Memphis, Tennessee, in 1950, the founders established contact with youth, particularly orphans, and others by use of counseling, group study, and radio, television and telephone ministries. In addition to establishing the Healing Waters Center and the Galilean Christian School in Bethany, the Gibbes aided in the founding of the Bethany Guidance Center and in sending a hospital ship staffed by volunteer doctors from Oklahoma City to Honduras. The Gibbes themselves have visited India and Israel as missionary evangelists. As a doctrinal statement the Galilean Association uses a modified version of the Apostles' Creed. Following the affirmation concerning belief in the Holy Ghost, the amended version states belief in "a full gospel, charismatic believing church, the communion of saints, the forgiveness of sins, divine healing, the resurrection of the body, and life everlasting." Several congregations in the Oklahoma City metropolitan area and one in Newkirk, Oklahoma, are members of the Association.

GOSPEL HARVESTER EVANGELISTIC ASSOCIATION (1961-   )

Centered in Atlanta, the Gospel Harvester Evangelistic Association, which was formed on Easter Day, 1961, consists of two congregations, seven clergy, and about 800 members. Founded by Earl P. Paulk, Jr., himself a former pastor and son of a pioneer minister in the Church of God (Cleveland, Tennessee), the group has apparently replaced the holiness emphasis of their former affiliation with stress on divine healing.

5011   Gospel Harvester Evangelistic Association.
        Gospel Harvester Tabernacle. Atlanta, 19--. 8p.

GOSPEL HARVESTERS EVANGELISTIC ASSOCIATION (1962-)

Unrelated to the similarly named group based in Atlanta, the Gospel Harvesters Evangelistic Association adheres to a doctrinal platform in all essential points identical to that of the Gospel Harvester group. Founded in 1962 by Rose Pezzino, an evangelist of Buffalo, New York, the Association reports affiliates in Toronto and Manila. In addition it has many individual supporters in the southern United States. Headquarters are in Buffalo. The organization also maintains an office in Jabalpur, Madhya Pradesh, India. By the mid-1970s the estimated world-wide constituency of the Association was 2,000.

GRACE GOSPEL EVANGELISTIC ASSOCIATION INTERNATIONAL (193 -)

Offended by Arminianism and extremism in the groups of which they were members, a number of West Coast Pentecostals met in the mid-1930s and formed the Grace Gospel Evangelistic Association International. The movement is congregationalist in polity. Affiliated churches sponsor missionary work in Taiwan, Japan, India, Colombia, and Jamaica. Although the movement is concentrated on the Pacific coast, there are member-churches in Oklahoma and Pennsylvania as well. Headquarters are in Longview, Washington. The now defunct Grace Evangel was published by the Association.

--PERIODICALS

5012   Grace evangel. 1- .   -19--.
        Longview, Wa.

INTERNATIONAL EVANGELISM CRUSADES (1959-)

In 1959 Frank E. Stranges, who had gained notoriety as president of the National Investigations Committee on Unidentified Flying Objects, founded the International Evangelism Crusades as a voluntary interracial ministerial fellowship. The primary function of the organization appears to be the issuance of ministerial credentials. Candidates for membership may be either men or women, and need not sever ties with other church bodies or ministerial associations. In 1970 the International Evangelism Crusades claimed a world membership of 6,000. At that time members in the United States and Canada were serving thirty churches with a combined membership of 2,000. Headquarters offices are in Van Nuys, California.

LEROY JENKINS EVANGELISTIC ASSOCIATION (1960-)

In 1960 Leroy Jenkins, a successful Presbyterian businessman

of Atlanta, Georgia, launched an independent ministry as an evangelist. His inspiration came from a miraculous healing he had recently experienced, and from the encouragement of A. A. Allen,
one of the most successful practitioners then in the field. Hand-
some and talented, Jenkins utilized television and radio as well as
personal appearances. By the mid-1970s he had shifted his center
of operations from Tampa, Florida, to Delaware, Ohio. At that
time his Revival of America was regularly being mailed to approximately 100,000 supporters.

--PERIODICALS

5013   Revival of America. 1- 1960-
            Tampa, Fl.; Delaware, Oh. 1960-1961 as Revivals;
        1961-Mar. 1967 as Revival; Apr.-July 1967 as Today with
        Leroy Jenkins.

MIRACLE REVIVAL FELLOWSHIP (1956-1970)

Although the founder claimed that it was in "no sense 'my
organization'," the Miracle Revival Fellowship was in fact the organized constituency of Evangelist A. A. Allen. Formed in 1956,
the Fellowship aimed at providing an instrument for cooperation
"without bondage" for independent Pentecostal ministers and churches,
and to secure legal standing as churches and ministers for affiliated
congregations and individuals. The 500-member first ordination
class bore visible witness to Allen's intention of making the organization an agency for granting ministerial credentials. The evangelist's Miracle magazine became the official organ, and the Miracle
Valley development in southern Arizona, the headquarters of the
movement. Following the founder's death, the Miracle Revival Fellowship apparently disbanded. Don Stewart, the most prominent
of Allen's associates, adopted Miracle magazine as his promotional organ and moved the publication to Phoenix. Although the
Miracle Valley Memorial Campmeeting continued to be held annually,
the Bible college campus was turned over to the Central Latin American District Council of the Assemblies of God, which then opened
the Southern Arizona Bible College, using Hereford, rather than
Miracle Valley, Arizona, as its address. At its height, the Miracle Revival Fellowship claimed 500 affiliated churches with about
10,000 members in the United States and Canada. By the mid-1960s
it had established work in the Philippines, and in Africa and South
America. At that time it was supporting five North American workers in these areas.

5014   Allen, Asa Alonso, 1911-1970.
            Miracle Revival Fellowship, by A. A. Allen. Miracle
        Valley, Az., Miracle Revival Fellowship, 19--. folder
        (10p.)

5015   Allen, Asa Alonso, 1911-1970.
            Prisons with stained glass windows, by A. A. Allen.
        Miracle Valley, Az., A. A. Allen Revivals, c1963.   115p.
        AzFU

        --PERIODICALS

5016   Miracle. 1- 1954-
            Dallas, Tx.; Miracle Valley, Az.; Phoenix, Az.   OkTOr

        OPEN BIBLE EVANGELISTIC ASSOCIATION (1932-1935)

        Following a spectacular revival conducted by Aimee Semple
McPherson in 1927, the sole Pentecostal congregation in Des Moines,
which had been organized only a year before, cast its lot with the
evangelist's International Church of the Foursquare Gospel.   Early
in 1928 the California evangelist returned for a second city-wide
campaign.   So many converts were garnered during this meeting
that the infant Foursquare Gospel Lighthouse congregation bought the
former Grace Methodist Episcopal Church building.   A few weeks
after the meeting construction of a second church building seating
1,500 began.   A third group, which returned to the original location
at Fifth and Grand streets, organized still another branch.   The
Reverend John R. Richey, who came from California to serve as
pastor of this third congregation, distinguished himself as a leader.
In 1930 Richey was instrumental in establishing a Bible training
school in Des Moines, which in turn provided leadership for expansion into other Iowa communities.   In 1932 dissatisfaction over the
tight control exercised by Mrs. McPherson together with embarrass-
ment over sensational publicity generated by the "kidnapping" incident and her subsequent marriage to David Hutton, led Richey and
most Foursquare members in Iowa and Minnesota to sever ties with
the Los Angeles headquarters.   They then formed the Open Bible
Evangelistic Association.   At the first convention of the Association,
forty-six were ordained, including two in absentia.   The Bible school
continued, and the new organization inaugurated its own periodical,
the Open Bible Messenger.   In 1934 the Open Bible Evangelistic Association claimed thirty churches in Iowa, including six in the city
of Des Moines.   The next year the Iowa-based group and the Bible
Standard, an Oregon-based association of churches, united as the
Open Bible Standard Evangelistic Association.

        --HISTORY

5017   Bruland, Gotfred S.
            The origin and development of the Open Bible Church in
        Iowa, by Gotfred S. Bruland.   Des Moines, 1945.   iii,134ℓ.
        Thesis (M.A.)--Drake University.   Includes Open Bible Evan-
        gelistic Association.   IaDmD

--PERIODICALS

5018   Open Bible messenger.   1-3, no. 9, Nov. 1932-Aug. 1935.
        Des Moines

        ORAL ROBERTS EVANGELISTIC ASSOCIATION (1947-   )
        [1947-1956 as Healing Waters.]

        Organized to support the ministry of the evangelist for which
it is named, the Oral Roberts Evangelistic Association has from its
beginning in 1947 mirrored the career changes of its Pentecostal
Holiness founder. From headquarters in Tulsa, the Association has
coordinated the worldwide activity of its Oklahoma-born head, first
as a tent revivalist specializing in healing campaigns, later as an
inspirational writer, television preacher, fund raiser, and university
president. From the beginning the Association has also issued a
periodical and published a continuous stream of books, mostly by
Roberts. In 1959 the evangelist sold his tent. Thereafter he devoted his energies full-time to television preaching, an innovation
introduced in the last years of his itinerant ministry. With the
founding of Oral Roberts University later, Mr. Roberts gave himself
to administration, fund-raising, and television programming of a
new type. In addition to the World Action Singers, a student group,
he frequently used show-business personalities on his broadcasts,
particularly after he joined the Methodist Church in 1968. Presently
he seems preoccupied with the City of Faith Hospital, a holistic
medicine teaching facility in connection with his newly-founded medical school. For popular use, "Evangelistic" was dropped from the
name of the Association in 1969.

5019   Sholes, Jerry
            Give me that prime-time religion; an insider's report on
        the Oral Roberts Evangelistic Association. [Tulsa], Oklahoma
        Book Publishing Co., c1979. xvi, 208p. On spine: Prime-
        time religion. Ok

5020   Sholes, Jerry
            Give me that prime-time religion; an insider's report on
        the Oral Roberts Evangelistic Association. New York, Haw-
        thorn Books, c1979. xv, 208p. DLC, OkBetC

        --HYMNS AND SACRED SONGS

5021   Healing Waters.
            Official song book of Oral Roberts' healing campaigns.
        Tulsa, 1954. 1v. (unpaged) With music (shape notes). OkBetC

        --PERIODICALS

5022   Abundant life. 1- Nov. 1957-

Tulsa. 1947-Aug. 1953 as Healing waters; Sept. 1953-1955 as America's healing magazine; Jan.-June 1956 as Healing.

OSBORN FOUNDATION (1949-   )
[1949-1969 as T. L. Osborn Evangelistic Association.]

Begun in 1949, the organization at first proposed simply to marshal support for the evangelistic activities of T. L. Osborn. The evangelist established headquarters in Tulsa, Oklahoma, and in 1956 started his own promotional paper, the Faith Digest. In addition he inaugurated a book publishing program. Total output by 1967 included literature in eighty languages and 48,000,000 pieces produced annually. Osborn also promoted foreign missions and by 1967 had given support to more than 80,000 national workers through eighty missionary organizations. Gradually literature distribution and fund raising supplanted itinerant evangelism. The new name adopted in 1969 signaled this change. In 1975 the estimated cash income of the Osborn Foundation was $50,000.

--PERIODICALS

5023   Faith digest. 1- 1956-
         Tulsa. OkTOr

TEEN CHALLENGE (1958-   )

Formed in 1958, Teen Challenge gained international attention for its work among drug addicts through The Cross and the Switchblade, an autobiographical account of its founding by David Wilkerson. The founder, an Assemblies of God pastor in Central Pennsylvania, felt divinely led to evangelize deliquent juveniles in New York. He went to the city without any definite plan of action, and after making a number of converts in an ad hoc street ministry, gained the backing of local businessmen and opened an evangelistic drug rehabilitation center in Brooklyn. Through his book published in 1963 and a periodical by the same title, the idea spread and Teen Challenge centers opened in Philadelphia, Chicago, and other major American cities. Enlisting Bible college students and reformed delinquents as workers, the centers depend upon local support, and operate under the direction of local trustees. Teen Challenge also operates a rehabilitation and job training center near Rehnersburg, Pennsylvania, and a worker training program, headed by Wilkerson, near Dallas, Texas. A European program modelled after the American one goes under the name, Continental Teen Challenge. Headquarters for the British arm of this program are in Luton, Bedfordshire. Wilkerson's immense influence on the charismatic movement within mainline denominations was damaged immensely in the early 1970s by his prophecy that Roman Catholic charismatics would soon leave the church.

5024   Wilkerson, David Ray, 1931-
       The cross and the switchblade, by David Wilkerson, with
       John & Elizabeth Sherrill.   New York, B. Geis Associates;
       distributed by Random House, c1963.   217p.   "Gospel Pub-
       lishing House edition."

5025   Wilkerson, David Ray, 1931-
       Hey, Preach--you're comin' through!   Westwood, N.J.,
       Revell, 1968.   160p.   DLC, ICU

5026   Wilkerson, David Ray, 1931-
       Hey, Preach--you're comin' through!   By David Wilker-
       son.   Old Tappan, N.J., Revell, 1971, c1968.   144p.
       (Spire books.)

5027   Wilkerson, Don
       Hell-bound [by] Don Wilkerson, with David Manuel.
       Orleans, Mass., Rock Harbor Press, c1978.   199p.   A
       fictional account of the street ministry of Teen Challenge.
       DLC

           --PERIODICALS

5028   Cross and the switchblade.   1- 1962-
       New York.   OkTOr

           UNITED CHRISTIAN MINISTERIAL ASSOCIATION (1956-)

       An extension of the ministry of Evangelist H. Richard Hall,
the United Christian Ministerial Association is an organization of independent Pentecostal clergy and churches.   It offers ordination to
persons whose ministries have not been recognized by existing church
bodies.   Sixteen orders, including bishop, apostle, evangelist, and
teacher, are conferred.   Although the Association describes itself
as fundamental and Pentecostal, creedal uniformity is not insisted
upon.   By 1972 more than 2,000 candidates had been ordained.

       Headquarters are in Cleveland, Tennessee, where the official
academy, the United Christian Bible Institute, is located, and where
the official organ, the Shield of Faith, is published.

           --PERIODICALS

5029   Shield of faith.   1- 1956-
       Cleveland, Tn.   1956-1960 as Healing broadcast; 1960-
       1962 as Healing digest.

           UNITED PRAYER AND WORKERS LEAGUE (1917-1938)

       Led by Evangelist Raymond T. Richey, the Houston-based

interdenominational United Prayer and Workers League drew together the readership of the Full Gospel Advocate, its official publication, for concerted support of evangelistic endeavors and prayer. Apparently the League disbanded in 1938 when the paper merged into the Gospel Call. The constituency of the United Prayer and Workers League was absorbed by the General Council of the Assemblies of God and other likeminded groups.

--PERIODICALS

5030   Full gospel advocate. 1-23, 1917-1938.
        Houston. Merged into Gospel call.

WINGS OF HEALING (1942-)

The outgrowth of the ministry of Thomas Wyatt, the Wings of Healing organization was formed in Portland, Oregon, in 1942 in connection with Wyatt's temple and radio program, both of which bore the Wings of Healing name. Stressing physical healing and anti-Communism, the organization is strongly opposed to racial discrimination and strongly committed to meeting spiritual, physical, economic, and social needs. In 1959 Thomas Wyatt moved the headquarters to Los Angeles, where since the founder's death in 1964, his wife, Evelyn, has directed the work. Two congregations in Portland and Los Angeles with a combined constituency of 2, 000, underwrite overseas programs of literature distribution, evangelism, and childcare, and sponsor radio broadcasts in Nigeria, South Africa, Sri Lanka (Ceylon), India, and the Philippines, as well as Honduras, El Salvador, Guatemala, and Mexico. In 1975 the group gave $50, 000 to support these ministries. Headquarters issues the March of Faith, and carries on a ministry of intercessory prayer in response to requests sent from constituents.

5031   Wyatt, Thomas, -1964.
            The birth and growth of a world-wide ministry. Los
        Angeles, Wings of Healing, 1960. 16p.

5032   Wyatt, Thomas, -1964.
            Wings of healing. 4th ed. Portland, Or. , Ryder Print-
        ing Co. , 1944, c1943. 204p. TxLoL

5033   Wyatt, Thomas, -1964.
            Wings of healing. 5th ed. , rev. Los Angeles, Wings
        of Healing, 1975, c1943. 62p. KyWAT

--PERIODICALS

5034   March of faith. 1- 1945-
            Portland, Or. ; Los Angeles.

WORLD RENEWAL (1963-   )
[1963-1973 as Berean Fellowship International.]

An outgrowth of the ministry of Warren Litzman, World Renewal, Incorporated, operates on the total "environment" concept.
In 1963 Litzman's congregation in Dallas opened a Bible training
school.   To this eventually were added a day care center and a
home for elderly citizens.   The sponsoring body, known as the
Berean Fellowship International, opened additional total environ-
ments in Wichita, Kansas; Stony Brook, New York; and several
foreign countries.   After nine years the founder resigned and was
replaced by Pete Tovey.   Under his leadership the present name
was adopted and headquarters were moved to Richland, Missouri.

--PERIODICALS

5035   Life in the Spirit.   1-   196 -
        Dallas; Richland, Mo.

WORLD REVIVAL CRUSADE (1935-   )

In 1935 George Jeffreys, the Welsh evangelist who founded
the Elim Foursquare Gospel Alliance, established the World Revival
Crusade as the sponsoring agency of his revival campaigns.   Non-
denominational, the organization was used as a vehicle in establishing the Elim movement, and later the Bible-Pattern Church Fellowship as well.   Until Jeffreys' death in 1962, the organization was
international in scope.   Afterward, its activities were confined to
the homeland.   In 1967 headquarters were in Clapham Park in southwest London.

WORLD-WIDE REVIVAL CRUSADES (1961-1970)

An agency for supporting the evangelistic and missionary
activities of R. W. Culpepper, the World-Wide Revival Crusades
organization held together the evangelist's widely scattered North
American constituency, and garnered financial backing for missionaries and native evangelists.   Culpepper launched on his first overseas evangelistic tour in 1957.   Four years later, he started the
World-Wide Revival Crusades and its official organ, the World-Wide
Revival Reports.   By 1968 the organization was supporting ninety
missionaries and national workers.   Plans to build a headquarters
in Dallas never materialized, and in 1970 Culpepper disbanded the
World-Wide Revival Crusades organization and joined A. C. Valdez
as co-pastor of the Milwaukee Evangelistic Temple.

5036   Culpepper, Richard Weston
        World-Wide Revival Crusades.   35, 000 miles of miracles.

The thrilling story in picture and word of revival in our time.
By R. W. Culpepper. Bellflower, Ca., 1959. 63p.

--PERIODICALS

5037   World-wide revival reports.   1-   1961-1970.
       Dallas.

ZION EVANGELISTIC FELLOWSHIP (1935-1957)

Designed to provide an arena of service for graduates of
Zion Bible Institute, East Providence, Rhode Island, the Zion Evangelistic Fellowship brought together independent churches in at least
a half-dozen northeastern states.   Founded in 1935 by Christine A.
Gibson, the Fellowship marshalled prayer and financial support in
behalf of the school and foreign missions.   In 1953 the 96 affiliated
congregations had a combined membership of 10, 000.   At that time
the Fellowship endorsed 22 foreign missionaries, most of whom
were working in Africa.   Mrs. Gibson died in 1955 and, although
the school continued, the Zion Evangelistic Fellowship was dissolved
two years later.   Shortly thereafter, a portion of the group in New
Hampshire and Maine formed the Apostolic Challenge, a ministerial
association which operated in a fashion similar to the original organization.

5038   Moore, Everett Leroy, 1918-
       Handbook of Pentecostal denominations in the United
       States.   Pasadena, Ca., 1954.   vii, 346ℓ.   Thesis (M.A.)--
       Pasadena College.   "Zion Evangelistic Fellowship": ℓ. 134-
       136.   CSdP

--PERIODICALS

5039   Faith.   1-   June 1, 1915-
       East Providence, R.I.

FAITH CHAPEL (1951-   )

Established in 1951, Faith Chapel is an independent congregation of Zephyrhills, Florida, committed to keeping Saturday as the
sabbath.   Anna and George Rosenberger, the founders, were Swiss
immigrants, who conducted revivals in both the United States and
Switzerland.   Since the death of her husband in 1965, Mrs. Rosenberger has carried forth the ministry alone.   A conservative Bib-
licism characterizes the teaching of Faith Chapel.   Attendance,
which on one occasion reached 128, varies with the season.

FELLOWSHIP OF CHRISTIAN ASSEMBLIES (1922-   )
[1922-1973 as Independent Assemblies of God.]

Known until 1973 as the Independent Assemblies of God, the
Fellowship of Christian Assemblies stands in the congregational tradition of Swedish Pentecostalism.   Formed during a meeting of
Pentecostal ministers at St. Paul, Minnesota, in 1922, the Fellowship strongly affirms the autonomy of local churches.   Cooperation
between congregations is purely voluntary and all general meetings
are convened as free conventions without legislative authority.   In
1948 disagreement over the "Later Rain" revival split the movement,
the pro-revival faction incorporating as Independent Assemblies of
God, International.   The conservatives retained the older name for
another quarter century.   A general meeting held at Madison, Wisconsin, in May 1973, adopted the present designation as descriptive
of the relationship among affiliated churches.   At that time there were
more than ninety churches in twenty states and four Canadian provinces.   Membership totalled more than 10,000.   Cooperative endeavors include publishing and foreign missionary programs.   The
Fellowship Press in Seattle issues Conviction, a monthly magazine,
and member churches sponsor missionary work in Liberia, India,
Japan, and Latin America.   In 1975 for the Liberian work alone,
the churches gave $100,000.   That year 28 North American mis-
sionaries were under appointment in Liberia.

5040   Fellowship of Christian Assemblies.
              The Fellowship of Christian Assemblies: an experience
        in inter-church fellowship.   Seattle, Fellowship Press, 1981.
        9p.   Cover title.   "Fourth revised printing."

5041   Moore, Everett Leroy, 1918-
              Handbook of Pentecostal denominations in the United
        States.   Pasadena, Ca., 1954.   vii, 346ℓ.   Thesis (M.A.)--
        Pasadena College.   "Independent Assemblies of God": ℓ. 117-
        118.   CSdP

                            --PERIODICALS

5042   Conviction.   1-   1963-
              Seattle.

FILADELFIA ASSEMBLY (19 -   )

        The Filadelfia Assembly consists of Armenian residents of
Iran.   In 1967 it reported three churches, two ordained clergy, and
100 members.   Headquarters are in Teheran.

FILIPINO ASSEMBLIES OF THE FIRST-BORN (1933-)

Founded in 1933 by Julian Bernabe, an immigrant clergyman from the Philippines, the Filipino Assemblies of the First-Born sees its mission as ministry to immigrant countrymen. Before the end of 1933, the group moved its headquarters from Stockton, California, its birthplace, to Fresno; in 1942, to San Francisco; and in 1943, to Delano, where it remains. The doctrinal statement is identical to that of the General Council of the Assemblies of God. Although conscientiously opposed to taking up arms, members may serve in noncombatant roles in wartime. By the 1970s there were about 325 members in 32 churches in California and Hawaii. A branch was organized in the homeland in 1947. Its headquarters are at Caba, La Unión.

5043   Filipino Assemblies of the First-Born.
        Constitution and by-laws. Rev. ed. Delano, Ca., 1963.
        23p.

FINNISH PENTECOSTAL CHURCHES OF THE UNITED STATES
    AND CANADA (1925-)
[1925-19-- as Finnish Pentecostal Churches of America.]

An ethnic fellowship established in New York about 1925, the Finnish Pentecostal Churches eventually spread across the entire breadth of the North American continent. First located in New York, the editorial offices of Totuuden Todistaja, the official organ, later moved to Vancouver, British Columbia.

--PERIODICALS

5044   Totuuden todistaja. [1]- 1925-
        New York; Vancouver, B.C.

FIRST DELIVERANCE CHURCH (1956-)

In 1956 William and Lillian Fitch, evengelists who had itinerated seventeen years, established the First Deliverance Church of Atlanta, Georgia. Dedicated to physical as well as spiritual healing, the church places great emphasis on fasting as a pre-condition of miracles. By the 1970s the Atlanta church had 840 members. Affiliated congregations in other towns in Georgia, Florida, Ohio, Oklahoma, and California, carry on similar programs.

"FOURSQUARE CHURCHES" OF THE INTERNATIONAL CHURCH OF
    THE FOURSQUARE GOSPEL, INC., CALIFORNIA, WESTERN
    AUSTRALIA (1953-)
[1953-196- as "Gospel Lighthouse Churches" of the International
    Church of the Foursquare Gospel, Inc., California, Western
    Australia.]

The outgrowth of a single congregation begun in 1953 in
Perth, Western Australia, the Foursquare Churches aggressively
pursue several means of outreach including radio broadcasts, church
planting, and work among the aborigines. Since 1958, the churches
have funded missionary projects in Hong Kong, New Guinea, and the
Ryukyu and Philippine Islands. In 1962 nearly $18,000 was given
for this work. L.I.F.E. Bible College is in Sydney. Headquarters
offices are in Victoria Park, a suburb of Perth. By 1975 there
were sixteen affiliated congregations.

FREE GOSPEL CHURCH (1916-)
[1916-1958 as United Free Gospel and Missionary Society.]

Founded by Frank and William Casley in 1916, the Free Gos-
pel Church consists of 25 churches and about 2,000 members in
Pennsylvania, Ohio, West Virginia, Maryland, and New Jersey.
Known from 1916 to 1958 as the United Free Gospel and Missionary
Society, it sent workers first to Guatemala, later to India, Sierra
Leone, and the Philippines. Although its Guatemalan missionaries,
C. T. Furman and Thomas Pullin, later joined the Church of God
(Cleveland, Tennessee), work in other world areas continues. In
1975 the church had eight North American workers under appoint-
ment and spent $13,835 overseas. Headquarters offices and the
Free Gospel Institute are located in Export, Pennsylvania.

FULL GOSPEL ASSEMBLIES, INTERNATIONAL (1947-)

Founded by Herman Ponge in 1947, the Full Gospel Assem-
blies, International, consists of 105 churches and 2,800 members.
The constituency is concentrated in southeastern Pennsylvania.
Headquarters offices are in Coatesville, Pennsylvania, where the
Charisma Courier, the official periodical, is published and where
in 1980 Charles E. Strauser, denominational president, resided.

                    --PERIODICALS

5045   Charisma courier. 1- 19 -
            Coatesville, Pa.

FULL GOSPEL CHURCHES OF KENYA (19 -)

From 1962 to 1967, the membership of the Full Gospel Churches of Kenya increased from 1, 200 to 6, 885. In the latter year there were 168 congregations. Headquarters are in Kericho.

FULL GOSPEL FELLOWSHIP OF INDIA (19 -)

In 1967 the Full Gospel Fellowship of India consisted of twelve churches and 500 members. Fifteen ordained and 35 lay persons were then engaged in the work which centers in the Bharosa Ghar Mission in Bhagalpur, Uttar Pradesh. Since the death of the American woman who established it, the Mission has been administered solely by Indian nationals. Major activities include direct evangelism, the operation of schools, and the production and distribution of religious literature. Approximately 50, 000 pieces are printed annually.

FULL GOSPEL GRACE FELLOWSHIP (1954-)

Based in Tulsa, Oklahoma, the Full Gospel Grace Fellowship is the outgrowth of pioneer efforts of the Beams of Light Gospel Missionary Society. Church planting activity of the Society resulted in establishment of more than a score of independent churches in the United States. In 1954 several of these congregations united to form the Full Gospel Grace Fellowship. In 1975 the group gave approximately $40, 000 toward the support of mission projects in Ghana and Guyana. Fellowship, a bi-monthly periodical, is issued from the headquarters.

--PERIODICALS

5046   Fellowship.   1-   19 -
           Tulsa.

GENERAL ASSEMBLY AND CHURCH OF THE FIRSTBORN (1907-)

Springing apparently from German Baptist Brethren roots, the General Assembly and Church of the Firstborn is a loosely structured fellowship of autonomous congregations. Many traditional Brethren practices and beliefs including communal meals, footwashing, and conscientious objection to war, have been retained. It rejects the use of medicine in all cases. Emphasis is placed on the family and membership reported in terms of family units rather than individuals. Clergy support themselves by secular employment.

Although a national camp meeting begun near Delores, Colorado, in 1967, draws nearly 1,000 worshippers annually, the fellowship maintains no central organization. Most local congregations are known simply as Church of the Firstborn. In 1978 there were 91 churches in seventeen states, 31 of which were located in Oklahoma, 11 in Indiana, and 9 in California. Of these 18 originated between 1894 and 1907. Led by 117 elders and 34 deacons, the movement consisted of 2,952 family units.

--DIRECTORIES

5047   General Assembly and Church of the Firstborn.
            Directory of churches. Editors: Kenneth and Mary Case. 3d ed. Cushing, Ok., 1978. vii, 94p.

5048   General Assembly and Church of the Firstborn.
            Oklahoma City directory. Editors: Kenneth and Mary Case. Photography: Kenneth Case. Assistant: Randy Herring. 6th ed. Oklahoma City, 1974. vi, 74p.

GEREDJA PENTEKOSTA DI INDONESIA (1923-   )

The outgrowth of missionary work of the Bethel Temple of Seattle, the Geredja Pentekosta di Indonesia, founded in 1923, was first known simply as Pinkstergemeente (Pentecostal Assemblies). In 1937 the name was changed to the Pinksterkerk (Pentecostal Church). Growth has been rapid. By 1956 this highly centralized, indigenous body claimed 250,000 members; a decade later, a half million. Four Bible schools, one each in Java, Samatra, Celebes, and West Irian, train workers, and printing presses in Java and Sumatra produce religious literature. Because Indonesia encompasses over 3,000 islands, the close supervision desired by denominational officials has often been ineffective. Many small splinter groups have resulted.

GOSPEL ASSEMBLY (1927-   )

Strongly dispensational, the Gospel Assembly churches follow the teachings of William Sowders, who in 1927 established the mother church of the movement, the Gospel Tabernacle of Louisville, Kentucky. The movement is committed to the so-called Gospel of the Kingdom doctrine, which was hammered out during the early years in a long service held each Sunday afternoon called the School of the Prophets. This teaching, which includes an elaborate description of the restoration of the Jewish nation and a distinctive theology of the Godhead, forms the ideology of a loosely structured federation of more than ninety assemblies in 22 states and of several splinter groups established following the founder's death in 1952. Member-

ship is approximately 10,000.   There are no headquarters offices.
The Gospel Assembly Ministers' Fund in Norfolk, Virginia, produces
the Ministers' Address Directory "as a guide for those seeking fellowship in the body of Christ. " More than three-fourths of the local
congregations listed in 1970 called themselves Gospel Assembly or
Gospel Assembly Church. The 350-acre Gospel of the Kingdom
campground near Shepherdsville, Kentucky, was purchased in 1935.

--DIRECTORIES

5049   Gospel Assembly Ministers' Fund.
            Ministers' address directory, 1970.   Norfolk, Va. , 1970.
        35p.

--DOCTRINAL AND CONTROVERSIAL WORKS

5050   Goodwin, Lloyd L.
            Mystery Babylon the great, the mother of harlots, by
        Lloyd L. Goodwin.   Des Moines, Ia. , Gospel Assembly
        Church, 19--.   42p.

5051   Goodwin, Lloyd L.
            The mystery of the Godhead, by Lloyd L. Goodwin.   Des
        Moines, Ia. , Gospel Assembly Church, 196-.   26p.

5052   Goodwin, Lloyd L.
            Water baptism that is scriptural, by Lloyd L. Goodwin.
        Des Moines, Ia. , Gospel Assembly Church, 19--.   23p.

5053   Kreis, Janet
            Vexation or visitation.   Coudersport, Pa. , Gospel Assem-
        bly, 19--.   25p.

GOSPEL ASSEMBLY (1965-   )

        In 1965 Tom M. Jolly, pastor of the Gospel of the Kingdom
since 1934, led the Gospel Assembly of St. Louis and a dozen additional congregations in severing ties with the original fellowship.
"An autonomous, independent, unorganized, unaffiliated church" that
"as far as possible" maintains openness to "all Christians, " the new
group apparently holds to the principal teachings of its parent.   In
1970 the fellowship included about thirty congregations and 4, 000
members.   At that time the westernmost church was in Kansas City,
Missouri.

IGLESIA BANDO EVANGELICO GEDEON (1939-   )

        In the early 1920s Wisconsin-born Ernest William Sellers

founded the Gideon Mission in Havana. Assisted by three women, Sellers (known by his followers as Daddy John) soon planted the movement in other parts of the island. Before his death in 1953, the founder established a pattern for future development. In 1939 the group inaugurated its official organ, El Mensajero de los Postreros Dias. Eight years later, Daddy John was named apostle by the annual convention and a three-man board of bishops, all Cubans, was selected to assist him. And in 1950 missionary work was begun in Panama and Mexico. To escape persecution by the Castro regime, the group moved its headquarters to Miami, Florida, in 1969. There it resumed publication of the official periodical, suspended during the last unhappy years in Cuba. In addition it expanded its missionary efforts in Latin America, and to avoid confusion with the Gideons International organization in the United States, substituted "Gilgal" for "Gideon" in the name of the church there.

Committed to keeping the Old Testament law and to sabbatarianism, the church relies strongly on dreams and visions as instruments of prophecy and revelation. Foot washing is practiced as a ritual sign of humility. Clergy are forbidden to engage in political activity.

                    --PERIODICALS

5054   El mensajero de los postreros dias. 1- 1939-
       La Habana; Miami.

IGLESIA CRISTIANA INDEPENDIENTE PENTECOSTÉS (195 -)

Established in its present form in the late 1950s, the Iglesia Cristiana Independiente Pentecostés resulted from the amalgamation of several indigenous Mexican bodies. Andrés Ornelas Martinez who with Raymundo Nieto founded what was to become the mother church of the movement at Pachuca, Hildalgo, in 1922, led the Iglesia Cristiana Independiente until his death in 1958. His successor, Venancio Hernández, resided in Ixmiquilpan in 1971. That year an outside observer reported there were forty congregations with an average of a hundred members each. The Iglesia Cristiana Independiente is noted for its inclusion of traditional Indian concepts and folklore in its theology and worship.

5055   Crouch, Archie R.
       A shoot out of dry ground: the most rapidly growing church in Mexico, by Archie R. Crouch. In New World Outlook, ns 30 (Apr. 1970), 33-35.

5056   Hollenweger, Walter Jacob, 1927-
       Pentecost between black and white: five case studies on Pentecost and politics [by] Walter J. Hollenweger. Belfast,

Christian Journals Ltd. , 1974.   143p.   Includes Iglesia Cristiana Independiente Pentecostés: p. 40-42.

--WORSHIP

5057   Hollenweger, Walter Jacob, 1927-
"Blumen und Lieder"; ein mexikanischer Beitrag zum theologischen Verstehenspozess [von] Walter J. Hollenweger. In Evangelische Theologie, 31 (Aug. 1971), 437-448.

5058   Hollenweger, Walter Jacob, 1927-
Flowers and songs; a Mexican contribution to theological hermeneutics, by Walter J. Hollenweger. In International Review of Mission, 60 (Apr. 1971), 232-244.

IGLESIA CRISTIANA NACIONAL DE LAS ASAMBLEAS DE DIOS (1934-)

Formed in 1934, the Iglesia Cristiana Nacional de las Asambleas de Dios is the result of a split within the Asambleas de Dios en Mexico.   Led from its inception by David G. Ruesga, the group united from 1940 to 1941 and from 1943 to 1946 with the Iglesia de Dios (Cleveland, Tennessee).   Work is concentrated in the Federal District and in the state of Veracruz.   In 1967 the Iglesia Cristiana Nacional reported 630 churches and 12, 727 members.   Headquarters are in Mexico City.

5059   Conn, Charles William, 1920-
Where the saints have trod: a history of Church of God Missions [by] Charles W. Conn.   Cleveland, Tn. , Pathway Press, 1959.   312p.   On union with National Christian Church of the Assemblies of God: p. 123-128.

5060   Hargrave, O. T. , 1936-
A history of the Church of God in Mexico, by O. T. Hargrave.   San Antonio, 1958.   vii, 159ℓ .   Thesis (M. A.)--Trinity University.   On union with National Christian Church of the Assemblies of God: ℓ . 46-77.   TxSaT

IGLESIA DE CRISTO EN LAS ANTILLAS (1935-)

One of the results of the 1934 evangelistic campaign of Francisco Olazábal in Puerto Rico was the formation of an independent church in the barrio La Dolores of Río Grande.   The movement spread and soon twelve additional congregations were established. In 1935 these churches, together with the original congregation at La Dolores of Río Grande, met in general council and organized the Iglesia de Cristo en las Antillas. When a majority of the churches represented at the 1938 assembly voted to change the name to Iglesia de Cristo Misionera, the mother church at La Dolores of Río Grande refused to go along. Instead, it withdrew and began organizing sate-lite congregations under the old name. By the early 1970s it claimed 1,700 members in 17 churches. Headquarters are in Río Grande.

5061   Iglesia de Cristo en las Antillas.
        Constitucíon y Reglamento de la Mision de Iglesias de
        Cristo en las Antillas. Rev. ed. Rio Grande, P. R. , 1963. 9p.

IGLESIA DE CRISTO MISIONERA (1938-)

In the 1938 assembly of the three-year-old Iglesia de Cristo en las Antillas, a majority voted to change the name to Iglesia de Cristo Misionera in order to make the work of the group more in-clusive. Although the mother church of the movement withdrew in protest, the re-named group stepped-up evangelistic activity in other Puerto Rican communities. By the late-1960s the Iglesia de Cristo Misionera had approximately 60 churches and 4,500 members. Head-quarters are in St. Just, a barrio of San Juan.

5062   Iglesia de Cristo Misionero.
        Constitucion y Reglamento de la Iglesia de Cristo Mi-
        sionera. Rev. ed. Río Piedras, P. R. , Nacional Imprenta
        y Offset, 1962.

IGLESIA EVANGÉLICA PENTECOSTAL EN CUBA (1936-)

The outgrowth of work launched in 1920 by the Latin Ameri-can District Council of the Assemblies of God, the Iglesia Evangélica Pentecostal en Cuba has been an autonomous national body since its organization in 1936. An aggressively evangelistic organization, the group claimed 2,746 members in 290 congregations in 1967. La Antorcha Pentecostal, the official organ, was then being published monthly in Havana.

--PERIODICALS

5063   La Antorcha Pentecostal. 1- 1940-
        La Habana.

IGLESIA EVANGÉLICA PENTECOSTAL INDEPENDIENTE (19 -)

After 1930 representatives of the Svenska Fria Missionen

in Mexico, who in earlier years had experienced continual frustration in their evangelistic efforts, witnessed a great influx of converts. By the end of the decade more than 80 congregations with 14,000 members had been established. A national church, the Iglesia Evangelica Pentecostal Independiente, was organized, and a periodical, the Consejero Fiel, was launched. By 1962 there were 300 affiliated churches and 80,000 members.

--PERIODICALS

5064   Consejero Fiel.   1- 19 -
        Mexico. OkTOr

IGLESIA PENTECOSTAL DE JESUCRISTO, INCORPORADA, EN PUERTO RICO (1938-   )

In 1938 a dispute over discipline so provoked the Iglesia de Dios Pentecostal de Puerto Rico congregation in the Balboa barrio of Mayaguez that it left the denomination. The pastor, Felix Rivera Cardona, led the exodus, and became presbyter-general of the council of the Iglesia Pentecostal de Jesucristo, the new body then formed. Augmented the next year by a group at Sabana Grande, the new movement soon spread into the southern and eastern parts of the island and to Haiti. Eventually it followed Puerto Rican immigrants to the mainland United States. By the 1970s the Iglesia Pentecostal de Jesucristo claimed 35 churches, 50 preaching points, and more than 3,000 members in Puerto Rico. In mainland United States it reported churches in New York, Gary, Chicago, and Milwaukee. Headquarters are in Yauco, Puerto Rico.

IGLESIAS PENTECOSTALES AUTONOMAS (19 -   )

In 1962 the Peruvian Iglesias Pentecostales Autonomas reported 75 congregations and 1,000 members. Headquarters were then in Callao.

IGREJA EVANGÉLICA PENTECOSTAL "BRASIL PARA CRISTO" (1955-   )

The outgrowth of the evangelistic work of Manoel de Mello, the Igreja Evangelica Pentecostal "Brasil para Cristo" centers in the founder's own congregation in São Paulo. Mello, a street evangelist from age eleven, decided in 1955 to do the "follow up" on converts which he had previously left to the churches. The result was construction of a 5,000-seat church, designed not so much as a place of worship for Mello's Sunday congregation, but as a training center for street evangelists on weeknights. Enlarged to accom-

modate 25,000 in 1973, a year when central church had 1,496 satellite groups (with 136 fully organized churches) in the São Paulo area
alone, and Brasil para Cristo had more than 4,000 churches, 250,000
baptized members, and one million adherents in the nation as a whole.
Under Mello's program of every-member evangelism, the phenomenal
growth continues unabated.   Hoping that it may learn something
about Christian social action while contributing knowledge about ef-
fective evangelistic work, Brasil para Crist has joined the World
Council of Churches.

5065   Fischer, Ulrich.
          Brasilien für Christus: eine evang.   Herausforderung.
        Neuendettelsau, Freimund-Verlag, 1975.   32p.   DLC

5066   Kostyu, Frank A.
          Will Brazil stay Christian?   By Frank A. Kostyu.   In
        Lamp, 68 (Mar. 1970), 14-19, 27-28.   On Brasil para Cristo:
        p. 18-19, 28.

5067   Mello, Manoel de, 1929-
          Participation is everything; evangelism from the point of
        view of a Brazilian Pentecostal.   In International Review of
        Mission, 60 (Apr. 1971), 245-248.

5068   Pentecostals make marked gains in Brazil.
          In Christian Century, 88 (Jan. 6, 1971), 7.

5069   Read, William Richard, 1923-
          New patterns of church growth in Brazil, by William R.
        Read.   Grand Rapids, Mi., Eerdmans, 1965.   240p.   "Brasil
        para Cristo": p. 144-158.   DLC, OkBetC

5070   Tavares, Levy
          Minha patria para Cristo: discursos e comentarios.
        São Paulo, 1965.   74p.

5071   Tschuy, Théo
          The World Council of Churches and Latin America.   In
        Christian Century, 87 (Mar. 18, 1970), 320-323.

INDEPENDENT ASSEMBLIES OF GOD, INTERNATIONAL (1948-   )

        United as a single unincorporated fellowship from 1935 to
1948, the Independent Assemblies of God trace their origins to the
Pentecostal revival among Scandinavian immigrants in Chicago and
the upper Middle West before World War I.   A deep cleavage developed over the Latter Rain revival movement, and in 1948 under
the leadership of A. W. Rasmussen the pro-revival faction incorporated as the Independent Assemblies of God, International.   While
paying allegiance to the principle of congregational autonomy, the
new organization has been vigorously cooperative and expansionist

from the beginning. Reliance on prophecy is common in decision making. Following one such revelation to Rasmussen, for instance, the system of paying all the tithes to the clergy, rather than into the church treasury, was introduced. The clergy became responsible, in turn, for looking after all local needs, and were expected to pay a tithe of the tithes thus collected to the overseer for support of programs of the International fellowship. In the 1970s the 300 United States and Canadian congregations affiliated with the Independent Assemblies of God, International, were supporting missionary efforts in Germany, the Netherlands, Israel, New Zealand, New Guinea, Korea, India, Tanzania, Kenya, South Africa, Liberia, Argentina, Mexico, and Puerto Rico. Offices of the International fellowship are in San Diego, where the Mantle, the official organ, also is published.

5072   Independent Assemblies of God, International.
        Profile: twentieth century Pentecost, Independent, Assemblies of God, International. San Diego, Ca. , 197-. folder.

--HISTORY

5073   Rasmussen, Andrew W. , 1905-
        The last chapter, by A. W. Rasmussen. Monroeville, Pa. , Whitaker House, c1973. 285p.

--PERIODICALS

5074   Mantle. 1- 1961-
        San Diego.

INDIA CHRISTIAN ASSEMBLIES (1949-)

In 1938 Armas I. Halonen of Finland went to India as a missionary. Not knowing the language, he engaged a national pastor to teach him. The two men became concerned about the large number of destitute children around them, and in 1949 opened an orphanage in Andhra Pradesh in southern India. By 1967 the home had served over 150 children, some of whom became ministers and had established churches which affiliated with the orphanage as India Christian Assemblies. At that time the fellowship consisted of eighteen congregations and 2,500 members. Helluntai-Yestävät, with headquarters in Helsinki, sponsors the group. The official organ, Samajapu Suvartha Prathidwani, is published in Andhra Pradesh.

--PERIODICALS

5075   Samajapu Suvartha Prathidwani. 1- 19 -
        Andhra Pardesh

INTERNATIONAL CHRISTIAN CHURCHES (1943-)

In 1943 Franco Manuel, a Disciples of Christ minister who had migrated to Hawaii from the Philippines, founded the International Christian Churches in Honolulu. The mother church, which is composed mainly of transplanted Filipinos, initiated work in the homeland in 1961, and within a few years seven churches had been organized. Describing itself as "Christian by confession, Pentecostal by persuasion," the group lays stress on traditional Disciples teachings, such as baptism by immersion and the independence of local churches. Affiliated churches are autonomous, free from control by the mother church or other churches.

INTERNATIONAL CHURCH OF THE FOURSQUARE GOSPEL (1927-)

Proclaiming Christ as savior, baptizer with the Holy Spirit, healer, and soon coming king, the International Church of the Foursquare Gospel, which was incorporated December 30, 1927, is the extension of the ministry of Aimee Semple McPherson. The founder, who had itinerated as an evangelist for several years on the east coast, settled in Los Angeles in 1918. Three years later she purchased a church building site across the street from Echo Park in Los Angeles, and formed the Echo Park Evangelistic Association, a legal corporation, to hold title to it. On January 1, 1923, the Angelus Temple, with a seating capacity of 5,300, was dedicated. A month later the L. I. F. E. (Lighthouse of International Foursquare Evangelism) Bible College opened in Room 120 of the building.

Although creation of satellite congregations in North America and abroad necessitated denominational organization, expansion of a local operation into an international one only increased the power of the founder. Mrs. McPherson, her children, and her mother all served as officers of the corporation, and Mrs. McPherson could and did name and remove corporation officers at will. Denominational decisions were made from the top and detailed regulations, such as the one requiring that Foursquare ministers be alumni of the L. I. F. E. Bible College, tended further to centralize power. Upon the founder's death in 1944, her son, Rolf Kennedy McPherson, became president of the church, a position he retains at present.

In 1978 the International Church of the Foursquare Gospel reported 614 congregations and 87,582 members in the United States. More than 5,000 alumni of L. I. F. E. Bible College were in the field, and additional schools were in operation in Vancouver, British Colombia, and Mount Vernon, Ohio. More than $1,500,000 was being spent annually on missionary efforts in 26 world areas. The Bridal Call, launched by Mrs. McPherson in 1917 and now called the Foursquare World Advance, continues as the official organ.

5076   International Church of the Foursquare Gospel.

Articles of incorporation and by-laws.   Los Angeles,
1949. 86p.

5077   International Church of the Foursquare Gospel.
Ministering wholeness, healing, power [and] hope through
the Foursquare Gospel Church.   Los Angeles, Foursquare
Publications, 198-. folder.

5078   Aimee's Four Square behind the war, but she's still not
judgment proof.
In Newsweek, 22 (July 19, 1943), 64.

5079   Bach, Marcus, 1906-
They have found a faith.   Indianapolis, Bobbs-Merrill,
1946. 300p. "The Foursquare Gospel": p. 57-87. DLC

5080   Foursquare with Aimee.
In Time, 83 (Feb. 28, 1964), 62.

5081   McPherson, Aimee Semple, 1890-1944.
Foursquare. In Sunset, 58 (Feb. 1927), 14-16, 80-82.

5082   Moore, Everett Leroy, 1918-
Handbook of Pentecostal denominations in the United States.
Pasadena, Ca. , 1954. vii,346ℓ . Thesis (M. A.)--Pasadena
College. "International Church of the Foursquare Gospel":
ℓ . 57-75. CSdP

5083   Plowman, Edward Earl, 1931-
Foursquare anniversary: in love with Aimee [by] Edward
E. Plowman. In Christianity Today, 17 (Mar. 30, 1973),
50-51.

--CATECHISMS AND CREEDS

5084   International Church of the Foursquare Gospel.
Declaration of faith.   Compiled by Aimee Semple McPherson. Los Angeles, 19--. 30p. Cover title: This we believe. CU-B, TxDaM-P.

--DOCTRINAL AND CONTROVERSIAL WORKS

5085   Britton, Claire
Prophecy. Los Angeles, Lighthouse of International
Foursquare Evangelism, 1928. 3v. in 1. (Foursquare cor-
respondence courses.) CCmS

5086   Courtney, Howard Perry, 1911-
The baptism in the Holy Spirit, by Howard P. Courtney
and Vaneda H. Courtney. Los Angeles, 1963. 40p. OkTOr,
TxWaS

5087   Courtney, Howard Perry, 1911-
         The vocal gifts of the Spirit: tongues, interpretation of tongues, prophecy, by Howard P. Courtney. Los Angeles, 1956. 51p. TxWaS

5088   Duffield, Guy Payson, 1909-
         Salvation and the seventh day, by Guy P. Duffield. Los Angeles, L. I. F. E. Bible College, 19--. 12p. Cover title.

5089   Glover, Kelso R.
         God is in Pentecost, by Kelso R. Glover. Los Angeles, 1946. 35p.

5090   McPherson, Aimee Semple, 1890-1944.
         Awake, America! Los Angeles, Foursquare Publications, 193-. 32p. On cover: America, awake! CU-B

5091   McPherson, Aimee Semple, 1890-1944.
         Behold! Thy king cometh. n. p., c1925. 64p. CU-B

5092   McPherson, Aimee Semple, 1890-1944.
         The foursquare gospel, by Aimee Semple McPherson; collaborator, Georgia Stiffler. Los Angeles, Echo Park Evangelistic Association, 1946. 199p. CtY-D, DLC, TxWaS

5093   McPherson, Aimee Semple, 1890-1944.
         The foursquare gospel [by] Aimee Semple McPherson. Compiled by Raymond L. Cox. Los Angeles, Heritage Committee, International Church of the Foursquare Gospel, c1969. 296p.

5094   McPherson, Aimee Semple, 1890-1944.
         Healing in his wings. n. p., c1925. 64p. CU-B

5095   McPherson, Aimee Semple, 1890-1944.
         The Holy Spirit. Los Angeles, Challpin Publishing Co., 1931. 287p. CLamB, CtY-D, InU, TxWaS

5096   McPherson, Aimee Semple, 1890-1944.
         In remembrance of me. n. p., c1925. 64p. CU-B

5097   McPherson, Aimee Semple, 1890-1944.
         Lost and restored; or, The dispensation of the Holy Spirit from the ascension of the Lord Jesus to His coming descension. Los Angeles, Bridal Call, 192-. 32p. CLU

5098   McPherson, Aimee Semple, 1890-1944.
         Lost & restored; the dispensation of the Holy Spirit from the ascension of the Lord Jesus to His coming descension. Los Angeles, Foursquare Bookshop, c1976. 47p.

5099   McPherson, Aimee Semple, 1890-1944.
         Perfection, can a Christian be perfect? Los Angeles,

Echo Park Evangelistic Association, 193-.   16p.   CU-B

5100   McPherson, Aimee Semple, 1890-1944.
        The second coming of Christ. Is He coming? How is
        He coming? When is He coming? For whom is He coming?
        Los Angeles, c1921. 120p. DLC, TxU

5101   McPherson, Aimee Semple, 1890-1944.
        Symbolon tes pisleos: The Four-square Gospel. Los
        Angeles, 193-. 35p. At head of title: Euangelistike Koinotes,
        "Eko Park. " Title romanized. CU-B

5102   McPherson, Aimee Semple, 1890-1944.
        Tapaö og uppbaett eö a tímabil heilage anda frá burtför
        drottins Jesu til endurkomu hans. Magnús G. Borgfjöro
        býddi. Reykjavík, Prentsmiöjan Gutenberg, 1925. 32p.
        MH, NIC

5103   McPherson, Aimee Semple, 1890-1944.
        The temple of the word. n. p. , 1925. 63p. CU-B

5104   McPherson, Aimee Semple, 1890-1944.
        There is a God; debate between Aimee Semple McPherson,
        fundamentalist, and Charles Lee Smith, atheist. Los Angeles,
        Foursquare Publications, 193-. 46p. Cover title.

5105   McPherson, Aimee Semple, 1890-1944.
        What's the matter with the churches, the pew, the minis-
        try, the old-time religion. Los Angeles, Echo Park Evan-
        gelistic Association, c1923. 29p. CU-B

5106   Walkem, Charles William
        The Jesus only theory; a brief analysis of the Trinity.
        Los Angeles, 19--. 23p. Cover title.

                 -- --NON-PENTECOSTAL AUTHORS

5107   Pietsch, W. E.
        McPherson-Jeffreys Four Square Gospel heresy: a grave
        warning, by W. E. Pietsch. Hounslow, Middx. , Bible Wit-
        ness, 1928. 23p. L

5108   Pollock, Algernon James, 1864-1957.
        Modern Pentecostalism, Foursquare Gospel, "healings"
        and "tongues. " Are they of God? London, Central Bible
        Truth Depot, 1929. 84p. L

5109   Pollock, Algernon James, 1864-1957.
        Modern Pentecostalism, Foursquare Gospel, "healings, "
        and "tongues. " Are they of God? 5th ed. London, Central
        Bible Truth Depot, 1929. 80p. C LamB

5110   Shuler, Robert Pierce, 1880-1965.

"McPhersonism": a study of healing cults and modern day "tongues" movements, by R. P. (Bob) Shuler. Los Angeles, 192-. 63p.

5111   Shuler, Robert Pierce, 1880-1965.
        "McPhersonism": a study of healing cults and modern day "tongues" movements, by R. P. (Bob) Shuler. 2d ed. Los Angeles, 192-. 72p. KyWA

5112   Shuler, Robert Pierce, 1880-1965.
        "McPhersonism": a study of healing cults and modern day "tongues" movements, by R. P. (Bob) Shuler. 3d ed. Los Angeles, 192-. 128p. NN

                --EVANGELISTIC WORK

5113   McPherson, Aimee Semple, 1890-1944.
        Foursquare gospel evangelism. Los Angeles, 1928. 23, 5p. (Foursquare correspondence course.) CCmS

5114   McPherson, Aimee Semple, 1890-1944.
        The silver net; practical helps to soul-winners. Los Angeles, Echo Park Evangelistic Association, 193-. 16p. Cover title. At head of title: The foursquare gospel. CU-B

                --HISTORY

5115   International Church of the Foursquare Gospel.
        50 facts: golden anniversary, International Church of the Foursquare Gospel, 1923-1973. Los Angeles, 1973. folder ([12]p.)

5116   International Church of the Foursquare Gospel.
        Golden anniversary [of the] International Church of the Foursquare Gospel, 1923-1973. Los Angeles, 1973. 24p. Cover title.

5117   International Church of the Foursquare Gospel.
        History of Foursquaredom. Los Angeles, 19--. 9p. Mimeographed.

5118   Kendrick, Klaude, 1917-
        The promise fulfilled: a history of the modern Pentecostal movement. Springfield, Mo. , Gospel Publishing House, c1961. viii, 237p. "International Church of the Foursquare Gospel": p. 152-163.

                --HYMNS AND SACRED SONGS

5119   International Church of the Foursquare Gospel.

Foursquare hymnal. Music editors: Homer R. Hummel [and] James G. Boersma. Los Angeles, c1957. 384p. With music.

5120   International Church of the Foursquare Gospel.
Foursquare hymnal of standard songs of evangelism. Compiled from editorial suggestions submitted by 136 active evangelists and evangelistic music directors. Los Angeles, A. S. McPherson Publishing Co., 1940. 1v. (unpaged) "Supplement containing a large selection of Aimee Semple McPherson's own songs": nos. 180-293. CtY-D

5121   International Church of the Foursquare Gospel.
Living way hymnal. Los Angeles, c1978. 608p. "Published for interdenominational use."

5122   McPherson, Aimee Semple, 1890-1944.
Foursquare favorites. Los Angeles, Echo Park Evangelistic Association, 19--. 1v. (unpaged) Cover title. With music. MBU-T

5123   McPherson, Aimee Semple, 1890-1944.
Foursquare melodies. Los Angeles, Echo Park Evangelistic Association, 192-. 255p. KyWAT

5124   McPherson, Aimee Semple, 1890-1944.
McPherson revival melodies in favorite selections from Victorious service songs. Chicago, Rodeheaver; published for Aimee Semple McPherson, 193-. 1v. (unpaged) With music. OrU

5125   McPherson, Aimee Semple, 1890-1944.
Pearls from paradise; musical gems from the pen of Aimee Semple McPherson. Los Angeles, Echo Park Evangelistic Association, c1940. 20p. Cover title. CU-B

5126   McPherson, Aimee Semple, 1890-1944.
Songs of the crimson road. Los Angeles, Echo Park Evangelistic Association, c1946. 56p. With music. MSohG

5127   McPherson, Aimee Semple, 1890-1944.
Tabernacle revivalist. Los Angeles, Echo Park Evangelistic Association, c1923. 1v. (unpaged) With music. CLU, CaBVaU, ICRL, KyWAT

--OPERAS

5128   McPherson, Aimee Semple, 1890-1944.
The rich man and Lazarus, a sacred opera in nine episodes; words and music by Aimee Semple McPherson. Los Angeles, Echo Park Evangelistic Association, c1938. 2v. Cover title. Reproduced from manuscript. "Edited by Vern Elliott--Local 47--Los Angeles, Cal." DLC

--PASTORAL THEOLOGY

5129   Allen, Chester L.
            Pentecostal preaching is different, by C. L. Allen.
        Los Angeles, G. N. Robertson, Printer, 1961.   104p.
        (The L. I. F. E. Bible College Alumni Association lectureship
        on preaching for 1961.) CPFT, TxWaS

5130   Cox, Raymond Lester, 1924-
            Pentecostal preaching produces Pentecostal churches,
        by Raymond L. Cox. Los Angeles, L. I. F. E.   Bible College,
        1965.   63p.   (L. I. F. E. Bible College Alumni Association.
        Lectureship on preaching for 1965.)

5131   Dorrance, Edythe Guerin
            Operation Pentecost. Los Angeles, c1962. 105p.   (The
        L. I. F. E. Bible College Alumni Association lectureship on
        preaching for 1962.) TxWaS

5132   Duarte, Charles
            Holy Spirit motivated ministers. Los Angeles, L. I. F. E.
        Bible College, 1967.   71ℓ.   (L. I. F. E. Bible College Alumni
        Association.   Lectureship on preaching for 1967.)

5133   Duffield, Guy Payson, 1909-
            Pentecostal preaching, by Guy P. Duffield.   New York,
        Vantage Press, 1957.   100p.   (L. I. F. E. Bible College
        Alumni Association.   Lectureship on preaching for 1956.)
        DLC, KyWAT

5134   Jensen, Elwood Harold, 1919-
            Pentecostal preaching to the second and third generations,
        by Elwood H. Jensen. Los Angeles, L. I. F. E. Bible College
        Alumni Association, 1968.   44ℓ.   (Lectureship on preaching
        for 1967.)

                        --PERIODICALS

5135   Bridal call foursquare.   1-18, no. 1, June 1917-June 1934.
            Savannah, Ga. , Framingham, Ma. , Los Angeles.   1917-
        1923 as Bridal call.   Merged with Crusader to form Bridal
        call crusader.

5136   Crusader.   1- Dec. 2, 1926-1934.
            Los Angeles.   1926-19-- as Foursquare crusader.
        Merged with Bridal call foursquare to form Bridal call cru-
        sader.

5137   Foursquare magazine.   1-37, no. 8, July 4, 1934-Aug. 1964.
            Los Angeles.   July 4, 1934-Sept. 5, 1934 as Bridal call
        crusader (cover title: Foursquare bridal call crusader);
        Sept. 12, 1934-Dec. 11, 1935 as Bridal call-crusader four-

square; Dec. 18, 1935-June 1944 (16, no. 6) as Foursquare crusader. Merged with Foursquare missionary to form Foursquare world advance.

5138   Foursquare missionary. 1- 1923-1964.
        Los Angeles. Merged with Foursquare magazine to form Foursquare world advance.

5139   Foursquare world advance. 1- Sept. 1964-
        Los Angeles. Formed by merger of Foursquare magazine and Foursquare missionary.

--SERMONS, TRACTS, ADDRESSES, ESSAYS

5140   McPherson, Aimee Semple, 1890-1944.
        Divine healing sermons. Los Angeles, Printed by Biola Press, 1921. 146p. CLU, CU-S, DLC, DNLM, InU, Or

5141   McPherson, Aimee Semple, 1890-1944.
        Fire from on high. Los Angeles, Heritage Committee, California, [International Church of the Foursquare Gospel], c1969. 219p.

5142   McPherson, Aimee Semple, 1890-1944.
        Fishers of men. Los Angeles, Echo Park Evangelistic Association, 192-. [12]p. Caption title.

5143   McPherson, Aimee Semple, 1890-1944.
        The foursquare gospel [by] Aimee Semple McPherson. Compiled by Raymond L. Cox. Los Angeles, Heritage Committee, International Church of the Foursquare Gospel, c1969. 296p.

5144   McPherson, Aimee Semple, 1890-1944.
        The ministry of Christ and the ministry of the church; sermon by Aimee Semple McPherson. Los Angeles, Foursquare Gospel Publications, 192-. 26p. Cover title.

5145   McPherson, Aimee Semple, 1890-1944.
        Questions and answers concerning the baptism of the Holy Ghost. Los Angeles, Heritage Committee, International Church of the Foursquare Gospel, 197-. folder ([8]p.) Reprint of tract no. 6 issued in May 1920.

5146   Middlebrook, Samuel Franklin, 1933-
        Preaching from a Pentecostal perspective. Edited by Sam F. Middlebrook. New York, Vantage Press, c1970. 112p. (L. I. F. E. Bible College Alumni Association. Lectureship on preaching for 1959.) Sermons by Howard P. Courtney, Sr. , Guy P. Duffield, Leslie Eno, Paul L. Hackett, Clarence E. Hall, Jack W. Hayford, Sam F. Middlebrook, Donald R. Pickerill, Charles E. Tate and Charles William Walkem. TxWaS

5147   Walkem, Charles William
            The witch of Endor, by Chas. Wm. Walkem. Los
        Angeles, 19--. 7p. OkTOr

            --WORK WITH YOUTH

5148   International Church of the Foursquare Gospel.   Foursquare
        Crusader Youth.
            Officer's handbook. Los Angeles, 1965.   88p.

            --NORTH AMERICA

                -- --UNITED STATES

                (California, Los Angeles)

5149   Church of the Foursquare Gospel.
            The who's-who at Angelus Temple, 1925.   Los Angeles,
        Echo Park Evangelistic Association, 1924.   16p.   (Its Year-
        book, v. 2.) "Issued during third annual convention, January
        2-18 inc. , 1925. " "Convention message [by] Aimee Semple
        McPherson": p. 3-4.   CLU

5150   McPherson, Aimee Semple, 1890-1944.
            Foursquare. In Sunset, 58 (Feb. 1927), 14-16, 80-82.

                (California, Van Nuys)

5151   Hayford, Jack W.
            A West Coast New Testament church [by] Jack W. Hay-
        ford. In West, A. , ed.   The New Testament church book.
        Plainfield, N. J. , 1973, 47-52.   On the Church on the Way,
        Van Nuys, California.

            --SOUTH AMERICA

                -- --COLOMBIA

5152   Hall, Trella Belle
            A historical sketch of the progress of Protestantism in
        Colombia, South America.   Pittsburg, 1959.   vii, 125ℓ .
        Thesis (M. S.)--Kansas State College.   Includes International
        Church of the Foursquare Gospel: ℓ . 80-82, 118-120.   KPT

            --ASIA

                -- --PHILIPPINES

5153   Montgomery, Jim

Fire in the Philippines.   Carol Stream, Ill. , Creation House, c1975.   140p.   First published in 1972 under title: New Testament fire in the Philippines.

5153a   Montgomery, Jim
New Testament fire in the Philippines.   Manilla, C-GRIP (Church Growth Research in the Philippines), 1972.   209p.

INTERNATIONAL CONVENTION OF FAITH CHURCHES AND MINISTERS (1979-   )

Founded in 1979, the International Convention of Faith Churches and Ministers subscribes to the "faith confession" doctrine taught by the Rhema Bible Training Center of Tulsa.   Led by Kenneth Hagin, Sr. , and Kenneth Copeland, evangelists of Tulsa, Oklahoma, and Fort Worth, Texas, respectively, the organization admits both churches and individuals to membership.   In 1980 it claimed a combined total of 200 in the two categories.   The movement is based in Tulsa.

5154   Synan, Harold Vinson, 1934-
Faith formula fuels charismatic controversy [by] Vinson Synan.   In Christianity Today, 24 (Dec. 12, 1980), 65-66.

INTERNATIONAL DELIVERANCE CHURCHES (1962-   )

Founded in 1962, the International Deliverance Churches serves as a coordinating agency for the work of Evangelist W. V. Grant and his associates.   Activities center in the Soul's Harbor Church in Dallas of which Grant is pastor.   Conventions consisting of two weeks of classes are held each summer at headquarters. At the end of each ministers are ordained.   By 1973 the Voice of Deliverance, the official organ, had a circulation of 2,000,000.

--PERIODICALS

5155   Voice of deliverance.   1-   1962-
Dallas.   Aug. 1965-Dec. 1966 as Evangelize.

ITALIAN PENTECOSTAL ASSEMBLIES OF GOD (1932-1940)

Formed under the leadership of Rocco Santamaria, his father, John Santamaria, and Pietro Giordano, in 1932, the General Council of the Italian Pentecostal Assemblies of God aimed at bringing more than two hundred independent Italian-language congregations in the

United States into a single organization. Headquarters offices were in Newark, New Jersey, where Rocco Santamaria, the general super-intendent, resided. Fede, Speranza, Carita was the official organ. In 1936 the group reported sixteen churches and 1,547 members in four northeastern states. All but three of the affiliated congrega-tions were located in New York and New Jersey. Four years later differences over church polity which had barred it from fellowship with like-minded Italian-American brethren were resolved, and the General Council of the Italian Pentecostal Assemblies of God merged into the Italian Christian Church of North America.

5156   U.S. Bureau of the Census.
            Census of religious bodies: 1936. Italian bodies. Sta-
        tistics, denominational history, doctrine, and organization.
        Consolidated report. Washington, Government Printing Of-
        fice, 1940. iv,9p. Includes General Council of the Italian
        Pentecostal Assemblies of God. NNUT

                --PERIODICALS

5157   Fede, speranza, carita. 1- 193 -
            Newark, N.J.

ITALIAN PENTECOSTAL CHURCH OF CANADA (1958-)

        In 1913 a few Presbyterians of Italian descent in Hamilton, Ontario, banded together in prayer and received an experience they believed to be the baptism in the Holy Spirit. Led by Luigi Ippolito and Ferdinand Zaffuto, they initiated an active program of evangelism. As a result independent churches were established in Hamilton, Tor-onto, and Montreal. Although the Montreal congregation received a governmental charter in 1926, the movement as a whole waited thirty-two years before gaining such recognition. Formed to facilitate col-laboration among autonomous congregations, the Italian Pentecostal Church of Canada as a whole works in close cooperation with both the Pentecostal Assemblies of Canada and its American counterpart, the Christian Church of North America, especially missionary efforts in Italy with the latter. Worship is conducted in both Italian and English, and official publications are issued in each language. In 1976 the Italian Pentecostal Church reported sixteen churches and 2,755 members. The Voce Evangelica, the official organ, is pub-lished in Toronto. Headquarters are in Montreal.

                --PERIODICALS

5158   Communicato missionario. 1- 19 -
            Toronto.

5159   Voce evangelica. 1- 1974-
            Toronto. CaOONL

JIYU CHRISTIAN DENDODAN (1950-   )

Founded in 1950, the Jiyu Christian Dendodan is the Japanese branch of the Pinsevennens Ytremisjon, the missionary society of the Pentecostal churches in Norway.   Efforts at church-planting on the island of Honshu have been supplemented by English Bible classes, Sunday schools and child care, literature sales, a radio broadcast, and summer youth camps.   By the mid-1960s the goal of self-support had been reached by only one congregation.   At that time there were fifteen Norwegian and Danish, and ten Japanese workers. Headquarters are in Fukui Shi.

KRISTOVA PENTEKOSTNA CRKVA U. FNR JUGOSLAVIJI (194 -   )

Organized under the leadership of Ludwig Ullen and Dragutin Volf in the years immediately following World War II, the Kristova Pentekostna Crkva is a product of the policy of religious freedom initiated by the Tito regime.   In 1962 the group reported sixty "prayer halls" and 1,600 members.   The larger congregations are located in Osijek, Banat, Novi Sad, Zagreb, and Belgrade.

--CATECHISMS AND CREEDS

5160   Kristova Pentekostna Crkva u. FNR Jugoslaviji.
Temeljne istine Svetog Pisma o vijeri i nauci Kristova Pentekostne Crkve u. FNR Jugoslaviji.   Osijek, 1959.   15p. Processed.

LAMB OF GOD CHURCH (1942-   )

Founded in 1942 by Rose H. Soares, the Hawaiian Lamb of God Church consists of three congregations and about 300 members, all on the island of Oahu.   Doctrinal teachings are similar to those of the Assemblies of God, the former affiliation of the founder. Headquarters offices are in Honolulu, where a Bible training school also is located.

LATTER HOUSE OF THE LORD FOR ALL PEOPLE AND THE CHURCH OF THE MOUNTAIN, APOSTOLIC FAITH (1936-   )

Established in 1936 at Cincinnati, the Latter House of the Lord for All People embodies the teachings of its founder, Bishop L. W. Williams, a former Baptist pastor, who found "enlightenment" while in prayer.   Although shortly after the body was formed Williams claimed only six small congregations, in 1947 he reported four thousand members in several states.

LIGHTHOUSE GOSPEL FELLOWSHIP (1958-   )

Founded in 1958 by Evangelist H. A. Chaney and his wife, Thelma Chaney, the Lighthouse Gospel Fellowship is a loose federation of independent churches.   Headquarters are in Tulsa, Oklahoma. In 1971 there were approximately 100 affiliated churches and 1,000 members.

--DOCTRINAL AND CONTROVERSIAL WORKS

5161   Chaney, Thelma
       Babylon marches again. Tulsa, 19--.   17p.   OkTOr

5162   Chaney, Thelma
       Divorce and remarriage.   Tulsa, 19--.   15p.   OkTOr

5163   Chaney, Thelma
       Harvest time.   Tulsa, Lillian Autry Co., 1953.   92p.
       OkTOr

5164   Chaney, Thelma
       The ministry of women in the church.   Tulsa, H. A. and Thelma Chaney, 1960.   17p.   OkTOr

5165   Chaney, Thelma
       The power of God on exhibition.   Tulsa, TOPService, 1954.   207p.   OkTOr

5166   Chaney, Thelma
       Practical instructions for Christian workers.   Tulsa, 19--.   47p.   OkTOr

5167   Chaney, Thelma
       Sonship, the great break through; foundational truths of this great reformation of the church as taught by the word of God.   Tulsa, All-Hour Business Service, 1965.   85p. OkTOr

5168   Chaney, Thelma
       The way to prosperity.   Tulsa, 19--.   25p.   OkTOr

MISSIONARY SOCIETIES:

ASIAN OUTREACH (1955-   )

Based in Hong Kong, Asian Outreach is an interdenominational charismatic sending and service agency engaged in the production and distribution of Christian literature and audio-visual materials.   In 1975 it was working in Hong Kong, Taiwan, Korea, Japan, Singapore, and Malaysia. That year more than $350,000 was spent in the work. Most of the staff and much of the support is Asian.

--PERIODICALS

5169   Asian report. 1- 19 -
       Hong Kong.

BEAMS OF LIGHT GOSPEL MISSIONARY SOCIETY (19 -   )

Based in Tulsa, Oklahoma, the Beams of Light Gospel Missionary Society specializes in pioneer evangelism and church-planting. Efforts are concentrated in the United States, Guyana, and Ghana. In 1954 several independent churches, which had been organized as a result of the Society's efforts, formed the Full Gospel Grace Fellowship. Sometime before 1975 the Beams of Light Society was absorbed by the Fellowship, which continues its work.

BETHANY MISSIONARY ASSOCIATION (1953-   )

An agency of the Bethany Chapel, an independent congregation in Long Beach founded by David Schoch and his wife in 1953, the Bethany Missionary Association places emphasis on evangelism, church-planting, and development of indigenous leadership. In 1964 the 400-member Bethany Chapel was giving full or partial support to 21 workers in six fields. Eleven years later the congregation was sponsoring eleven missionaries in four fields (Australia, Japan, Brazil and Peru). Estimated income in 1975 was $75,000. A missionary home operated in connection with Bethany Chapel is the setting for the training of prospective workers.

--HYMNS AND SACRED SONGS

5170   Bethany Missionary Association.
          Psalter. 4th ed. Long Beach, Ca. , 1972. ix, 94p.
       With music.

BETHEL FOREIGN MISSION FOUNDATION (1933-   )

Established in 1933, the Bethel Foreign Mission Foundation utilizes direct evangelism, education, literature distribution, and medical assistance in efforts to develop indigenous churches. In 1975 it had 46 American workers under appointment in six fields: Mexico, Guatemala, Haiti, Japan, Korea, and New Guinea. That year it spent $66,500 in these areas. Headquarters offices are in Rockport, Indiana.

CEYLON PENTECOSTAL MISSION (1923-   )

Founded by Alwin R. de Alwis in 1923, the Ceylon Pentecostal Mission is unique in the requirements it makes of the more
than 3,000 ministers affiliated with it.   Prior to recognition by the
Mission, each prospective minister must sell all possessions so
that he may devote himself entirely to Christian work.   All property is held in common.   The results of this program are notable.
In 1963 after forty years of existence the Ceylon Pentecostal Mission had made more than 45,000 converts from Buddhism and other
non-Christian religions, and had established 53 stations in Sri
Lanka, 350 in India, and seven in Malaysia.   Headquarters offices
are in the capital city of Colombo, with branch offices in France,
England, India, and Malaysia.

CHINESE-AMERICAN NEW TESTAMENT MISSIONARY
FELLOWSHIP (1956-   )

In 1956 Missouri-born Hong C. Sit, who previous to being
baptized in the Holy Spirit had served as pastor of a Baptist congregation in Houston, founded the Chinese-American New Testament
Missionary Fellowship as a means of reaching previously untouched
Chinese with the gospel.   The principal methods to be employed
were direct evangelism and church-planting.   To provide financial
backing and worker training, Sit established Grace Chapel and a bilingual Bible school in Houston.   A constituency of 200 supports
missionaries in Taiwan and Hong Kong as well as Japan, Mexico,
Colombia, and Brazil.

CHRIST FOR THE NATIONS (1948-   )
[1948-1967 as Voice of Healing.]

Close allied with the evangelistic and radio ministries of
Gordon Lindsay, Christ for the Nations has throughout its history
carried out an extensive publications program and supported creation of indigenous churches throughout the world.   The Dallas headquarters complex includes the Dallas Christian Center, the Christ
for the Nations Institute, and the editorial offices of Christ for the
Nations, a monthly periodical.   In 1979 the organization raised more
than $1,000,000 for church building and literature distribution over-
seas.

--HISTORY

5171   Lindsay, Gordon, 1906-1973.
            The house the Lord built.   Dallas, Christ for the Nations,
        1972.   111p.

--PERIODICALS

5172   Christ for the nations.   1- 1948-
            Shreveport, La., Dallas.   1948-Feb. 1958 as Voice of
        healing; Mar. 1958-Aug. 1959 as World-wide revival; Sept.
        1959-Mar. 1967 as Voice of healing.

EASTERN EUROPEAN MISSION (1927-   )
[1927-1949 as Russian and Eastern European Mission.]

Founded in Chicago in 1927, the Eastern European Mission
played a significant role in the spread of the Pentecostal movement
in Russia and eastern Europe, particularly in the pre-World War II
era.   Work has centered on publication and distribution of religious
literature and in radio broadcasting in Slavic languages.   Missionaries appointed and fully supported by the Mission train national
workers and Sunday school teachers.   Headquarters are in Pasadena,
California, where the Gospel Call is also published by the Mission.
In 1975 the Eastern European Mission was at work in Greece, Po-
land, the Soviet Union, Yugoslavia, the Federal Republic of Germany,
and the Netherlands.   That year it spent $132,063 overseas.   The
British section, now called the European Evangelistic Society, was
given autonomy in 1952.   In recent years there has been a notice-
able loosening of ties with the Pentecostal churches.

--PERIODICALS

5173   Gospel call.   1- 1927-
            Chicago; Pasadena, Ca.   1927-19-- as Gospel call of
        Russia.   DLC

EUROPEAN EVANGELISTIC SOCIETY (1952-   )
[1952-1961 as Slavic and European Evangelistic Society.]

Granted autonomy in 1952, the Slavic and European Evangelistic Society had been until that date the British section of the Eastern European Mission.   It adopted the present name in 1961.   A
faith mission, the Society aids in the establishment of Slavic-language
congregations, supports in whole or part national workers in several
European countries, and sends Bibles to Russia.   Headquarters are
in Nottingham from which Euroflame, the official periodical, is issued.   It works in cooperation with the Assemblies of God in Great
Britain and Ireland.

--PERIODICALS

5174   Euroflame.   1- 1953-
            Slough, Bucks., Nottingham 1-22, no. 5, 1953-Aug.
        1973 as European herald.

EVANGELIZATION SOCIETY (1920-   )

An agency associated with and complementary to the Pittsburgh Bible Institute, the Evangelization Society operates on unsoli-
cited funds.   Chartered in 1920, the Society developed work in China
and India, now abandoned.   Continuing projects are in Zaire and
Taiwan, where large self-supporting national groups have been gathered.   Centered in Shabunda, Kivu, the work in Zaire consists of more
than 200 churches.   The field headquarters for Taiwan are in Chaiyi.
The number of North American workers under appointment plummeted
from 23 in 1967 to three in 1975.   The official organ, the Record of Faith,
is issued from the central offices in Gibsonia near Pittsburgh.   C. H.
Pridgeon, the founder, was an exponent of the "restoration of all
things" teaching, which denies the doctrine of everlasting punishment
of the wicked.   Although many of his followers did not agree with
Pridgeon in this regard, fellowship between the Evangelization Society and other Pentecostal groups has suffered strain because of it.

--PERIODICALS

5175   Record of faith.   1-   192 -
        Pittsburgh, Gibsonia, Pa.

FULL GOSPEL NATIVE MISSIONARY ASSOCIATION (1958-   )

A fund-raising agency founded in 1958, the Full Gospel Native
Missionary Association supports indigenous churches, pastors, evan-
gelists, schools and orphanages in Korea, the Philippines, Thailand,
Indonesia, India, Sri Lanka, Haiti, and Mexico.   From headquarters
in Joplin, Missouri, the Association issues the Full Gospel Native
Missionary.

--PERIODICALS

5176   Full gospel native missionary.   1-   195 -
        Joplin, Mo.   OkTOr

GLAD TIDINGS MISSIONARY SOCIETY (1950-   )
[1950-196- as Glad Tidings Temple Missionary Society.]

Organized in 1950, the Glad Tidings Missionary Society is an
outgrowth of the Glad Tidings Temple, Vancouver, British Columbia.
In addition to the mother church and a rescue mission in Vancouver,
there are seven "fellowship" churches in British Columbia and Washington state, and six "associated" churches in Alberta, British Columbia, and Washington state.   The combined membership is about
1, 200.   In cooperation with the Bethany Missionary Association, the
Glad Tidings Missionary Society provides full or partial support for
missionaries and national pastors, and subsidies for church-building

projects in Japan, Taiwan, Hong Kong, Singapore, India, Israel, Uganda, Malawi, Jamaica, and Mexico. In 1975 the Society raised approximately $400,000, and had 42 North American workers under appointment. Although trinitarian, the Glad Tidings Missionary Society baptizes converts in the name of the Lord Jesus Christ.

HILFSBUND FÜR DAS LILLIAN-TRASHER-WAISENHAUS (AEGYPTEN) (1961-)
[1961-1963 as Deutsch-Schweizerische Mission.]

Organized in 1961 as the Deutsch-Schweizerische Mission, the Hilfsbund für das Lillian-Trasher-Waisenhaus is, as its name indicates, a fund-raising agency for the orphanage in Assiout, Egypt, founded by Lillian Trasher. Each year the Hilfsbund attempts to raise $25,000 in support of the institution. To this end it makes available to interested groups throughout Switzerland and Germany the film "Die Nilmutter," recounting Miss Trasher's ministry. Administrative offices are in Heilbronn, Baden-Württemberg. The Hilfsbund is a daughter-society of the Schweizerische Missionsgemeinde.

HOME OF ONESIPHORUS (1916-)

In 1916, during a famine in north China, L. M. Anglin and his wife took five Chinese boys into their home in Taian, Shantung. This first Home of Onesiphorus (an Ephesian believer who ministered to Paul in Rome) inspired the establishment of a number of homes in other Chinese cities designed to demonstrate the power of God's love in the lives of the children helped, and to produce strong Christian workers. Following World War II, the society established homes on the original model in Hong Kong, Taiwan, Lebanon, and Israel. In 1975 the Home of Onesiphorus organization spent $165,500 overseas, and had eight North American workers under appointment. Administrative offices are in Chicago. Homes in Israel and Lebanon have distinctive names. The one at Ramallah on the occupied west bank of Jordan is called Home of the Sons; the one in Beirut, the Near East Boys Home. The organization does not characterize itself as Pentecostal now.

--HISTORY

5177   Albus, Harry James, 1920-
Twentieth-century Onesiphorus: the story of Leslie M. Anglis and the Home of Onesiphorus, by Harry J. Albus. Grand Rapids, Mi. , Eerdmans, 1951. 160p. DLC

--PERIODICALS

5178   Onesiphorus harvester. 1- 1921-
Chicago. 1921-19-- as Harvester.

NORSKE PINSEVENNERS YTREMISJON (1910-)

Like their Swedish brethren, Norwegian Pentecostals under
the leadership of Thomas Ball Barratt early committed themselves
to congregationalism. They focused attention on the ministry of the
local church, even in commissioning and supporting foreign missionaries. The first Norwegian workers, Dagmar Gregersen and Agnes
Thelle, went to India in 1910. Following them during the next half-
century were over 300 additional Norwegian missionaries who labored
for extended periods in China, Taiwan, Tibet, Thailand, Nepal,
Japan, and the Congo. By the mid-1960s the 300 churches and
40,000 members, which constituted the home base, were sponsoring
175 workers overseas. The Norske Pinsevenners Ytremisjon coor-
dinates the effort from offices in Oslo.

--HISTORY

5179   Pinsevekkelsen i Norge gjennom 30 år.
        Oslo, Filadelfiaforlaget, 1937.

--PERIODICALS

5180   Bibelsk Tidskrift. 1- 1931-
        Oslo.

5181   Ekko. 1- 196 -
        Oslo.

5182   Korsets Seier. 1- 1904-
        Christiania (Oslo).

PENIEL CHAPEL MISSIONARY SOCIETY (1911-)

As its name implies, the Peniel Chapel Missionary Society is
the agency of a single congregation in West London. Founded in
1911 by Benjamin Griffiths, a Welshman, Peniel Chapel was aggressively evangelistic from the start. It ran its own print shop and
Free Tract Depot, and members actively proselytized at Hyde Park
Corner nearby. Griffiths, who served as pastor until a few months
before his death in 1956, also stressed foreign missions and tithing.
Beginning in 1917 when two women were sent to Africa, a steady
stream of workers have gone forth. Although no collections are
taken, the Society operates under a policy of supporting one foreign
missionary for each ten members of the London congregation. By
the mid-1960s Peniel Chapel was raising $30,000 annually and was
supporting twenty British and twelve national workers in Africa,
Taiwan, Brazil, and Belgium. The cooperative spirit which has
marked Peniel Chapel through the years is illustrated in the case of
the Assemblies of God in Great Britain and Ireland, whose first
General Conference was held there in 1924.

PENTECOSTAL JEWISH MISSION (1931-   )

Founded at Manchester in 1931, the Pentecostal Jewish Mission resulted from the need felt by leaders of the British Assemblies of God and Elim churches for a distinctive witness to Jewish people. Under the leadership of L. T. Pearson, the founder, the Mission confined its activity to voluntary and part-time efforts in Britain. Following World War II, however, it took on new vigor. In 1947 it sent J. Whitfield Foster, a council member, and his wife to Jerusalem, where they took over the already-established Bible Evangelistic Mission. Although they lost the property and were forced to relocate during the war the next year, the work survived. In 1962 the Jerusalem congregation, still known as the Bible Evangelistic Mission, reported 130 members. Emphasis in recent years has been placed on distribution of Bibles in languages native to the thousands of Jewish immigrants arriving from many world areas. Headquarters of the Pentecostal Jewish Mission are in London, where Priority, the official organ, is published.

--PERIODICALS

5183   Priority.   1- 19 -
        London.   L, OkTOr

PENTECOSTAL MISSIONARY UNION (1909-1925)

As in the nineteenth-century Holiness movement, early leaders of the Pentecostal movement, particularly in Britain, encouraged participants to remain in the denominational churches. Collective evangelistic and missionary endeavors were backed by non-denominational associations such as the Pentecostal Missionary Union. Formed in 1909, the Union served as an agency for promoting fellowship and for recruiting, training and sending out "faith" missionaries. Its first leaders were Cecil Polhill, a wealthy Anglican layman who was also a member of the China Inland Mission council, and A. A. Boddy, vicar of All Souls Church, Monkswearmouth, in Sunderland where a major glossolalic revival had broken out a year earlier. The Pentecostal Missionary Union adopted Confidence, a journal Boddy had begun during the 1908 revival, as its official organ. The Whitsuntide conventions held annually from 1908 to 1914 in the All Saints Parish Hall, and for many years thereafter at Sion College on the Thames Embankment near Blackfriars in London, proved a great inspiration and a unifying factor in the movement. The Union sent its first missionaries to India in 1909. That year it also opened a men's Bible training home in Paddington, the next year a similar institution for women in Hackney, both boroughs of London. From 1910 on, most of the missionaries sent out by the Pentecostal Missionary Union were trained in its own schools. Successful evangelism rapidly drew large numbers of the unchurched into the movement, and many independent congregations sprang up. In 1925, the newcomers took the Union with them into the newly-formed Assemblies of God in

Great Britain and Ireland.   Although this action had the tacit ap-
proval of the original leaders, it was accomplished without their
participation.

--PERIODICALS

5184   Confidence.   1-   Apr. 1908-1921.
        Sunderland.

PHILADELPHIA CHURCH MISSION (1922-   )

The agency of a single congregation in Seattle founded in
1922, the Philadelphia Church Mission gives full or partial support
to workers in Japan, Korea, Liberia, Mexico, and Peru.   In Yoko-
hama its mission is known as Firaderufia Kyokai.

SCHWEIZERISCHE MISSIONSGEMEINDE (1941-   )
[1941-1958 as Gemeinde für Evangelisation und Erweckung.]

Founded by Samuel Unger in 1941, the Schweizerische Missionsgemeinde was until 1958 known as the Gemeinde für Evangelisation und Erweckung, the present name being adopted to make apparent the missionary involvement of the organization.   Through its
daughter-society, the Hiftsbund für das Lillian-Trasher-Waisenhaus
(Aegypten), it raises funds for the orphanage in Assiout, Egypt.   In
the mid-1960s it was also supporting workers in Liberia, the Ivory
Coast, and India.   Offices of the Schweizerische Missionsgemeinde
are in Zurich.

SCHWEIZERISCHE PFINGSTMISSIONS-GESELLSCHAFT
     (1921-   )

Formed in 1921, the Schweizerische Pfingstmissions-
Gesellschaft is the agency charged with schooling, sending out, and
supporting missionaries of the Pentecostal churches of Switzerland.
Headquarters are in Basel, where Die Verheissung des Vaters and
Der Ruf, the official periodicals, are published.   The product of
evangelistic work begun before 1910, the Gesellschaft, which in the
mid-1960s claimed 2, 500 members in eighty churches, supports work
in five fields: Lesotho, the Central African Republic, Israel, Japan,
and Peru, the latter in cooperation with the Schweizer Peru-Mission.
More than twenty Swiss missionaries are under appointment.

--PERIODICALS

5185   Der Ruf.   1-   1964-
        Zürich.

5186   Die Verheissung des Vaters.   1- 1909-
        Zürich.

SUOMEN HELLUNTAIYSTÄVIEN ULKOLÄHETYS (1937-)

As in Scandinavian countries, Pentecostals in Finland have
been committed to local church autonomy from the beginning. As a
result, the Finns have spurned denominationalism, yet have cooper-
ated voluntarily in projects, such as foreign missions which tran-
scend local capabilities. In 1912, only a year after the Pentecostal
message was first preached in Finland, the Helluntai-Ystävät, or
Pentecostal Friends as they were called, began supporting workers
abroad, first in East Africa, later in China, India, and in the
Congo. Beginning in 1937 an elected committee from the Finnish
churches, forerunner of the Suomen Helluntaiystävien Ulkolähetys,
took over coordination of the missionary effort, cooperating in particular areas with the Svenska Fria Missionen, the India Christian
Assemblies, and other agencies. Administrative offices are in Helsinki, where the Voitto Sanoma, the official paper, is published.
In 1967 the combined membership of Pentecostal churches in Finland
was approximately 40, 000.

--PERIODICALS

5187   Voitto Sanoma.   1- 1925-
        Helsinki.

SVENSKA FRIA MISSIONEN (1926-)

The fountainhead of studied congregationalism, the Swedish
Pentecostal movement inherited from its founder and long-time
leader, Lewi Pethrus, great evangelistic zeal. Destined to become
the largest free church group in Sweden, its existence as an independent entity dates from 1912, when Pethrus' Filadelfiaförsamlingen
in Stockholm was expelled from the Swedish Baptist Union. The
mother church, in turn, spawned other congregations, which in 1926
formed a loosely-structured coordinating council. Although missionaries had been sent to China as early as 1907, the development of
a central agency, however restricted in its authority, greatly expanded the foreign missionary program. By the mid-1970s, the
93, 000 members in the homeland were represented by 500 missionaries in 24 world areas, and were contributing over $1, 000, 000 an-
nually for foreign missions. Individual congregations continue to
commission and support individual workers. Administrative offices
are in the 6, 500-member Filadelfiaförsamlingen in Stockholm, the
mother of the more than 550 churches which compose the Swedish
movement. Dagen, a newspaper, and the Evangelii Härold, a weekly
journal, are published by the Förlaget Filadelfia in Stockholm.

--GOVERNMENT

5188   Carlsson, Bertil
       Organizations and decision procedures within the Swedish
       Pentecostal movements. [Härnösand, 1979] 131p. Cover
       title. Translation of thesis entitled: Organisationer och
       Beslutsprocesser inom Pingströrelsen, presented to the stat-
       svetenskapliga avdelningen, Stockholm University, 1974.
       MoSpA

--PERIODICALS

5189   Dagen. 1- 1945-
       Stockholm.

5190   Evangelii Härold. 1- Dec. 1915-
       Stockholm.

5191   Den Kristne. 1- 1944-
       Stockholm.

VELBERTER MISSION (1928-   )
[1928-1952 as Vereinigte Missionsfreunde.]

       Taking its present name in 1952 from Velbert, its headquar-
ters city in the Rhineland, the Velberter Mission originated in 1928
as the Vereinigte Missionsfreunde. The Mission has workers stationed in South Africa, Zambia, Nigeria, and India. It operates as
the sending agency for missionary appointees of the Arbeitsgemeinschaft der Christen-Gemeinden in Deutschland.

--PERIODICALS

5192   Missionsnachrichten. 1- 19 -
       Velbert. OkTOr

VOICE OF MIRACLES AND MISSIONS (1955-   )

       Formed in 1955, the Voice of Miracles and Missions serves
as the coordinating agency for the missionary and evangelistic ministries of M. A. and Jane Collins Daoud. Of particular note was
the 1962 campaign of the Daouds in Madagascar, where the evangelists claimed crowds in excess of 30,000 in every meeting. Headquarters are in Dallas, where the Miracles and Missions Digest is
published.

5193   Daoud, Jane (Collins)
       Miracles and Missions and world-wide evangelism.

Dallas, M. A. and J. C. Daoud, c1953.   iv, 138p.

5194   Daoud, Mounir Aziz
        Bringing back the King! God's plan for world evangelisa-
        tion, by M. A. Daoud. Dallas, Voice of Miracles and Mis-
        sions, 1955. 39p. KyWAT

5195   Daoud, Mounir Aziz
        The shooting frontier: revival, by M. A. Daoud. Dallas,
        Voice of Miracles and Missions, 1960. 36p.

        --HYMNS AND SACRED SONGS

5196   Daoud, Mounir Aziz
        Missionary action songs for adults. n. p., 19--. 1v.
        OkTOr

        --PERIODICALS

5197   Miracles and missions digest. 1- 1955-
        Dallas.

    WORLD MISSIONARY ASSISTANCE PLAN (1960-   )

    Founded in 1960, the World Missionary Assistance Plan en-
gages in direct evangelism, worker training, literature production,
and relief work. In 1975 it was supporting 109 North American
workers in sixteen world areas. That year it raised $802, 015 for
all purposes, $153, 000 of which was spent overseas. Union with
the Elim Missionary Assemblies in 1966 was apparently short-lived.
Headquarters are in Burbank, California, where two bi-monthly
periodicals, World MAP Digest and Acts, are published.

        --PERIODICALS

5198   Acts. 1- 197 -
        Burbank, Ca.   OkTOr

5199   World MAP digest. 1- 196 -
        Burbank, Ca.   OkTOr

    WORLD OUTREACH INTERNATIONAL (1932-   )
    [1932-19-- as Slavic and Oriental Mission.]

    Operating in more than a dozen world areas, World Outreach
International is an evangelistic mission engaged in radio broadcasting,
literature distribution, medical work, church planting, and correspondence instruction. In addition it raises support for orphanages

and national workers. First known as the Slavic and Oriental Mission, the organization now concentrates its efforts in the Far East, Africa, and Australia and New Zealand. Administrative offices are in Garland, Texas, where the Evidence, the official organ, is published.

--PERIODICALS

5200   Evidence.   1- Sept. 1938-
       Garland, Tx. OkTOr

WORLD-WIDE MISSIONS (19 -   )

With headquarters in Peoria, Illinois, World-Wide Missions assists independent Pentecostal missionaries in various fields. In the 1960s it was giving assistance to missionaries and mission projects in Mexico and several Asian countries, including Pakistan, India, Indonesia and New Guinea. Work then centered in the overseas evangelistic work of B. G. Drake, Jr. World-Wide Missions serves as an agent for transferring funds raised in the United States directly to the field, without deducting administrative expense. "Firebrand" publications are issued in connection with evangelistic and missionary endeavors of the organization.

WORLD'S FAITH MISSIONARY ASSOCIATION (1894-   )

Founded in February 1894, at St. Louis, and incorporated in December the following year at Shenandoah, Iowa, the World's Faith Missionary Association stressed faith as an operating principle in Christian work, particularly in evangelistic endeavors and in healing the sick. In its first seven years membership increased from seven to more than 300. Led by Dr. Richard R. Hanley, who gave up medical practice to devote himself to ministry, the movement centered in Shenandoah, Iowa, where Hanley had established an independent holiness church and where he published the Firebrand. By 1901, Charles S. Hanley, the founder's son and a newspaperman, had become Association president. Under his leadership the organization apparently tolerated belief in tongues-speech as evidence of the baptism with the Holy Spirit, for J. Roswell and Alice Reynolds Flower, and Flem Van Meter, future Assemblies of God workers ordained in 1913 during a Pentecostal camp meeting at Plainfield, Indiana, received World's Faith Missionary Association credentials.

In 1928 the name was taken by a Missouri corporation, successively known as the Fundamental Ministerial Association and the Evangelical Church Alliance. The latter designation was adopted in 1958. Ministerial credentials held by such well-known evangelists as Kathryn Kuhlman and Alexander Ness were issued by this organization. In 1975 headquarters were in Bradley, Illinois.

--PERIODICALS

5201   Firebrand. 1- June 2, 1887-1920.
        Shenandoah, Ia. Ia-HA

5201a   Missionary world. 1- 1904-1918.
        Shenandoah, Ia.

ZAIRE EVANGELISTIC MISSION (1915-   )
[1915-1971 as Congo Evangelistic Mission.]

    In 1915 James Salter and William F. P. Burton, "faith" mis-
sionaries of Preston, Lancashire, established a mission among the
Baluba people at Mwanza, 400 miles northwest of Elisabethville.
To provide support and additional workers, the Preston Assembly
under the leadership of Thomas Myerscough formed the Congo Evangelistic Mission. The venture was immensely successful. When
independence was proclaimed in 1960, the society had 61 missionaries at work on thirteen main stations. Shortly thereafter Euro-
peans were forced to leave and the Eglise Pentecôtiste du Congo
under national leadership was formed. In 1967 this denomination,
which five years earlier had claimed 20, 715 adult members, reported
46, 721 members and more than a thousand churches. Under the direction of the national church, foreign missionaries concentrate efforts on
the training of workers, production and distribution of gospel literature, and the operation of medical dispensaries and maternity hospitals. Headquarters of the society, which was re-named the Zaire
Evangelistic Mission in 1972, remain in Preston.

        --HISTORY

5202   Burton, William Frederick Padwick, 1886-1971.
        God working with them: being eighteen years of Congo
        Evangelistic Mission history, by W. F. P. Burton. London,
        Victory Press, 1933. xiv, 264p. L, MH-AH, NcD, NNUT,
        WU

5203   Burton, William Frederick Padwick, 1886-1971.
        Missionary pioneering in Congo forests; a narrative of
        the labours of William F. P. Burton and his companions in
        the native villages of Luba-land. Compiled from letters,
        diaries and articles by Max W. Moorhead. Preston, Lancs.,
        R. Seed, 1922. 216p. CtY, InU

5204   Burton, William Frederick Padwick, 1886-1971.
        When God changes a village. London, Victory Press,
        1933. x, 162p. L

5205   Hodgson, Edmund, 1898-1950.
        Fishing for Congo fisher folk, by E. Hodgson. Illustrated

with 80 pen and ink sketches by W. F. P. Burton. London,
Assemblies of God in Great Britain and Ireland, 1934. 182p.
CtY-D, IEN, L, N, OrU

5206   Hodgson, Edmund, 1898-1960.
        Out of the darkness: the story of an indigenous church
        in the Belgian Congo, by E. Hodgson. London, Victory
        Press, 1946. ix, 186p. IEN

5207   Hodgson, Edmund, 1898-1960.
        Out of the darkness: the story of an indigenous church
        in the Belgian Congo, by E. Hodgson. Luton, Beds., As-
        semblies of God Publishing House, 1946. ix, 186p. MoSpA

5208   Womersley, Harold
        Congo miracle: fifty years of God's working in Congo
        (Zaire). Eastbourne, Victory Press, 1974. 160p. DLC,
        L

                        --PERIODICALS

5209   Zaire Evangelistic Mission monthly report. 1- 19 -
            Preston, Lancs. 1-421, 19 -1971 as Congo Evangelistic
        Mission report. OkTOr

MOVIMIENTO DEFENSORES DE LA FE DE PUERTO RICO (1931-   )

        In 1931 Gerald B. Winrod, founder of the Defenders of the
Christian Faith, held a series of missionary conferences in Christian and Missionary Alliance churches in Puerto Rico. As a result
of this tour, Winrod decided to start a Puerto Rican work of his
own. To edit the Spanish edition of his magazine and to open the
first chapel in Arecibo, Winrod chose Juan Rodríguez. The latter
accompanied Francisco Olazábal to the mainland where he assisted the
noted Mexican in an evangelistic campaign in Harlem, a bridgehead
which led to the organization of the first church in New York thirteen
years later. In Puerto Rico Rodríguez continued his endeavors
among Baptist, Methodist, Disciples of Christ, and Christian and
Missionary Alliance groups. As a result churches were formed in
many places. In 1945 a worker-training school, the Defenders Theological Seminary, opened in Rio Piedras. By 1964 when the Puerto
Rican work achieved independence, there were 68 congregations and
about 6,000 members on the island. At that time the New York-
centered work consisted of fourteen churches and missions in seven
states with an estimated membership of 2,000. Each area has a
central committee which directs its affairs. Local branches usually
bear the designation: Iglesia Defensores de la Fe. Puerto Rican
headquarters are in Santurce.

--HISTORY

5210   Defender.
      Fire by night and cloud by day; a history of Defenders
of the Christian Faith. Compiled and written by Defenders
editorial staff. Wichita, Mertmont Publishers, 1966. 128p.

--PERIODICALS

5211   El Defensor Hispano.   1- 193 -
      ----, P.R.

MUSAMA DISCO CHRISTO CHURCH (1922-   )

      Composed of followers of Joseph William Egyanka Appiah,
the Musama Disco Christo Church grew out of the Faith Society, a
prayer group in the Methodist Church at Gomoa Ogwan in the Win-
neba district of Ghana. In 1922 Appiah, who was a minister, and
other members of the three-year-old society were asked to leave
the church, whereupon they formed the present organization. Sometime later, the founder became known as Prophet Jemisimihan Jehu-
Appiah. The Musama Disco Christo Church is among the oldest indigenous churches in West Africa.

5212   Opoku, Kofi A.
      Changes within Christianity: the case of the Musama
Disco Christo Church [by] Kofi A. Opoku. In Fashole-Luke,
E., ed. Christianity in independent Africa. Bloomington,
In., c1978, 111-121.

NATIONAL DAVID SPIRITUAL TEMPLE OF CHRIST CHURCH
UNION (1936-   )

      In July 1936, David William Short together with seven other
pastors and lay delegates organized the National David Spiritual Temple of Christ Church Union. With headquarters in Kansas City,
Missouri, where Short had set in order the first David Spiritual
Temple of Christ Church, December 29, 1932, the body at the time
of incorporation consisted of eleven churches and 1,880 members in
Missouri, Kansas, Oklahoma, and California. Stress was placed on
free exercise of spiritual gifts as well as freedom from "race prejudice and segregation." The Christian Spiritual Voice, published in
Kansas City, Kansas, served as the official organ. In 1949 the St.
David Orthodox Christian Spiritual Seminary offering elementary,
high school, and correspondence courses, was opened in Des Moines
with Bishop Short as president and mentor. Although there is a

National Annual Assembly, the national bishop governs in response
to direct inspiration from God, not in accordance with the desires
of the members. In the mid-1960s the National David Spiritual Temple claimed 66 churches and 40, 816 members. Headquarters at
last report were in Los Angeles. "David" in the names of both the
church and school is a reference to the founder, formerly a Missionary Baptist minister.

--DOCTRINAL AND CONTROVERSIAL WORKS

5213   Short, David William
        The Orthodox Christian Spiritual Church: canon, creed,
        and doctrines. n. p., 1939. 29p.

--HISTORY

5214   Moore, Everett Leroy, 1918-
        Handbook of Pentecostal denominations in the United
        States. Pasadena, Ca., 1954. vii, 346ℓ. Thesis (M. A.)--
        Pasadena College. "National David Spiritual Temple of
        Christ Church Union (Inc.) U. S. A.": ℓ. 119-126. CSdP

--PERIODICALS

5215   Christian spiritual voice. 1- 193 -
        Kansas City, Ks.

NIHON ASSEMBLIES OF GOD KYODAN (1949-)

        In 1949 the Japanese constituencies of the General Council of
the Assemblies of God, the Pentecostal Assemblies of Canada, and
the Assemblies of God in Great Britain and Ireland, came together
to form the Nihon Assemblies of God Kyodan. Kiyoma Yumiyama,
principal of the Bible institute in Tokyo, was elected superintendent,
a position he was to hold for many years. Foreign missionaries
continue in direct evangelism, literature translation, and radio
broadcasting. From 1962 to 1967 membership skyrocketed from
2, 124 to 6, 500. In the latter year headquarters in Tokyo reported
129 churches.

OPEN BIBLE STANDARD CHURCHES (1935-)
[1935-1946 as Open Bible Standard Evangelistic Association.]

        Organized July 26, 1935, the Open Bible Standard Churches
are the result of the union of the Open Bible Evangelistic Association with headquarters in Des Moines, Iowa, and the Bible Standard,

an association of churches centered in Eugene, Oregon. A general conference composed of all ordained and licensed ministers in good standing and one accredited lay delegate from each church, meets annually in Des Moines. Although there are branches in at least two dozen states, membership continues to be concentrated near the original centers in Iowa and Oregon, where strong schools are located. The Inspiration Press and editorial offices of the Message of the Open Bible, the official organ, are in Des Moines. In 1979 the group reported 280 churches and 60,000 members in the United States. At that time it had more than two dozen missionaries under appointment working in nine world areas.

5216   Open Bible Standard Churches.
        Minister's manual containing the policies and principles of the Open Bible Standard Churches, Inc. Des Moines, 1946- . v.[1]- . Cover title: Policies and principles.

--DOCTRINAL AND CONTROVERSIAL WORKS

5217   Pope, Gerald S., ed.
        Bible truth series. Writers: Philip Petersen, W. Ern Bryant, Fred Atwater, and R. Bryant Mitchell. Rev. ed. Des Moines, National Sunday School Department [and] Board of Publications, Open Bible Standard Churches, 1960, c1957. 2v.

5218   Smith, Frank W.
        Pentecostal positives, by Frank W. Smith. Des Moines, Inspiration Press, c1967. 40p.

--HISTORY

5219   Kendrick, Klaude, 1917-
        The promise fulfilled: a history of the modern Pentecostal movement. Springfield, Mo., Gospel Publishing House, c1961. viii, 237p. "The Open Bible Standard Church": p. 164-171.

5220   Moore, Everett Leroy, 1918-
        Handbook of Pentecostal denominations in the United States. Pasadena, Ca., 1954. vii, 346ℓ. Thesis (M.A.)-- Pasadena College. "Open Bible Standard Churches": ℓ. 76-92. CSdP

--HISTORY AND STUDY OF DOCTRINES

5221   Fulton, Everett Paul, 1926-
        An investigation of the changing theological concepts of the ministers of Open Bible Standard Churches, by Everett

P. Fulton. Des Moines, 1964. vii, 194ℓ. Thesis (M. A.)--
Drake University. IaDmD

--PERIODICALS

5222 Message of the open Bible. 1- 1920-
          Eugene, Or., Des Moines. 1-16, no. 8, 1920-Aug. 1935
      as Bible standard; 16, no. 9-25, no. 6, 1935-June 1944.

5223 Overcomer. 1- 195 -
      Des Moines.

5224 Progress. 1- 19 -
      Des Moines.

5225 World vision. 1- 19 -
      Des Moines.

--IOWA

5226 Bruland, Gotfred S.
          The origin and development of the Open Bible Church in
      Iowa, by Gotfred S. Bruland. Des Moines, 1945. iii, 134ℓ.
      Thesis (M. A.)--Drake University. IaDmD

OVERCOMERS CHURCH (1939-)

      Founded in 1939 by James D. Varey, the Overcomers Church
consists of a single 125-member congregation in Toronto. It was
incorporated in 1945. The Overcomers Church is deeply committed
to order in worship. Public exercise of verbal gifts is reserved to
the clergy, who wear clerical collars, preaching gowns, and stoles,
and a specially-designed vestment during the communion service.
Affiliation is maintained with approximately one hundred mission
congregations, mostly in India and Malaysia.

5227 Overcomers Church.
          The manual and constitution of the Overcomers Church,
      and some facts and history concerning the Christian church.
      Toronto, 1951, c1952. vi, 146p. "Authorized by the Inter-
      national Council." MoSCEx

PENTECOSTAL ASSEMBLIES OF CANADA (1919-)

      In 1919 Pentecostal congregations in eastern Canada sought
for and received a dominion charter as the Pentecostal Assemblies

of Canada. Joined two years later by brethren in the four western provinces, who until that time had formed a unit of the United States-based Assemblies of God, the Pentecostal Assemblies of Canada provided a loosely-structured cooperative mechanism for otherwise autonomous local bodies. In doctrine and organization, the Canadian group is in essential agreement with its American and British Assemblies of God counterparts, but more tolerant of minor doctrinal variations than either of them are. In 1978 there were 868 affiliated congregations with a combined membership of 200,000. French, Slavic, German, and Finnish-speaking churches compose ten percent of the total. The Assemblies operate a number of worker-training schools, including Bible colleges for its English language constituents in Saskatoon, Saskatchewan, Peterborough, Ontario, Winnipeg, Manitoba, and Edmonton, Alberta, and schools for ethnic and language minorities in Vancouver, British Columbia, Canwood, Saskatchewan, Moosonee, Ontario, and Montreal and Senneterre, Quebec. The fellowship, which spent $2,000,000 overseas in 1975, had missionaries under appointment in seventeen world areas. Headquarters are in Toronto, where the Full Gospel Publishing House and the editorial offices of the Pentecostal Testimony also are located. Close ties are maintained with the Pentecostal Assemblies of Newfoundland, a like-minded, independent fellowship.

5228   Pentecostal Assemblies of Canada.
        General constitution and by-laws. Toronto, 1974. 80p.
        "Authorized by charter and letters patent 1919. Amended
        and adopted by General Conference 1968, with amendments
        as authorized by General Conference to 1974."

5229   Pentecostal Assemblies of Canada. General Conference.
        Minutes. 1st- 1919- . Ottawa, Ont., London, Ont.,
        Toronto. Biennial. Early publication uncertain.

5230   Pentecostal Assemblies of Canada. Slavic Branches.
        Constitution and by-laws. Toronto, Printed by Gospel
        Mission Publishers, 1957. 29p. Title page in Ukrainian
        and English; text in Ukrainian.

5231   Huffman, James Lamar, 1941-
        Pentecostal growth in Canada [by] James L. Huffman.
        In Christianity Today, 12 (Sept. 13, 1968), 47. On the
        golden-jubilee convention of the Pentecostal Assemblies of
        Canada, held in Windsor, Ontario in August.

5232   McAlister, Walter E.
        Pentecostal Assemblies [by] W. E. McAlister. Revised
        by Tom Johnstone. In Encyclopedia Canadiana. Toronto,
        c1968, VIII, 149-150.

5233   PAOC preaching points.
        In Christianity Today, 16 (Sept. 15, 1972), 58-59. On
        General Conference of the Pentecostal Assemblies of Canada
        held in Halifax, Nova Scotia in August 1972.

5234   Pentecostal gains.
        In Christianity Today, 7 (Oct. 12, 1962), 42. Member-
        ship and missionary activity of the Pentecostal Assemblies of
        Canada as reported to the 23d biennial General Conference in
        Edmonton, Alberta in September.

5235   Pentecostal positions.
        In Christianity Today, 9 (Oct. 23, 1964), 43-44. On the
        General Conference of the Pentecostal Assemblies of Canada,
        held in Montreal in September, stressing discussion of desire
        for access to radio broadcasting time in French Canada.

5236   Tarr, Leslie K.
        Pentecostal action [by] Leslie K. Tarr. In Christianity
        Today, 20 (Sept. 24, 1976), 1336. On the thirtieth national
        convention of the Pentecostal Assemblies of Canada. Actions
        included rejection of ordination of women.

                    --CATECHISMS AND CREEDS

5237   Pentecostal Assemblies of Canada.
        Concerning the faith; a simple explanation of the main
        truths of the Bible for young people and adults, presented in
        the form of questions and answers. Toronto, Full Gospel
        Publishing House, 1951. 94p. Prepared by J. Eustace Pur-
        die. TxWaS

5238   Pentecostal Assemblies of Canada.
        Statement of fundamental & essential truths. Toronto,
        19--. 7p. "Article V of the General constitution and by-
        laws."

5239   Purdie, James Eustace
        What we believe, by J. E. Purdie. Toronto, Full Gos-
        pel Publishing House, 19--. 32p.

                    --DOCTRINAL AND CONTROVERSIAL WORKS

5240   Atter, Gordon Francis, 1905-
        Cults and heresies; an outlined study on the subject of
        cults and heresies of the twentieth century. Prepared for
        personal and classroom use. Peterborough, Ont., Book
        Nook, c1963. 48p. At head of title: The student's hand-
        book. MnCS

5241   Atter, Gordon Francis, 1905-
        Divine healing; an outlined Bible study for personal or
        classroom use. Peterborough, Ont., Book Nook, 1960.
        164p. At head of title: The student's handbook.

5242   Atter, Gordon Francis, 1905-

God's financial plan: a study in tithing.   Peterborough,
Ont., Book Nook, 1961.   29p.

5243   Atter, Gordon Francis, 1905-
Outlined studies on the subject of divine healing, especially prepared for classroom use, with blank pages for additional notes, by Gordon F. Atter.   Peterborough, Ont.,
College Press, c1960.   85p.   At head of title: The student's
handbook on divine healing.   KyWAT

5244   Atter, Gordon Francis, 1905-
Rethinking Bible prophecy (light for the last days); the
students handbook; God's plan of the ages outlined studies in
prophecy for personal or classroom use.   Compiled and ed.
by Gordon F. Atter.   Peterborough, Ont., College Press,
c1967.   xv, 288p.   DLC

5245   Atter, Gordon Francis, 1905-
Rivers of blessing; presenting Pentecostal distinctives,
by Gordon F. Atter.   Toronto, Full Gospel Publishing House,
c1960.   xi, 212p.   "Authorized by the National Publications
Committee, the Pentecostal Assemblies of Canada. "   CaOHM

5246   Barber, Herbert Hanbidge, 1922-
Science and the Christian, by H. H. Barber.   Toronto,
Full Gospel Publishing House, 1960.   21p.   "Publication authorized by the National Publications Committee, the Pentecostal Assemblies of Canada. "

5247   Barber, Herbert Hanbidge, 1922-
What is a Protestant, an Evangelical, a Pentecostal?
By H. H. Barber.   Toronto, National Publications Committee
of the Pentecostal Assemblies of Canada, [1955] 14p.   OkTOr

5248   Bible. N.T. Gospels. English. Harmonies. 1966.
Great is the mystery. Compiled by Bernard T. Parkin-
son.   Toronto, Full Gospel Publishing House, 1966.   294p.

5249   Brown, Victor Gordon, 1914-
The church, historical and contemporary [by] Victor G.
Brown.   Peterborough, Ont., College Press, c1966.   x, 251p.
DLC, OkEG

5250   Brown, Victor Gordon, 1914-
Heal the sick.   Toronto, Full Gospel Publishing House,
19--.   39p.

5251   Brown, Victor Gordon, 1914-
Types of the Holy Spirit, by Victor G. Brown.   n. p.,
1948.   83p.

5252   Brown, Victor Gordon, 1914-
Why I believe in the Lord's Supper.   Toronto, Full Gospel Publishing House, 19--.   17p.

5253   Buntain, Daniel Newton, 1888-1955.
            The Holy Ghost and fire, by D. N. Buntain.   ----, Alta.,
        Rock Publishing Co., 19--. 98p. TxWaS

5254   Cantelon, Willard, 1915-
            The baptism of the Holy Spirit. What is it? Is it for
        today? Is it for everyone? What is the evidence? Toronto,
        Testimony Press, c1951. 33p. Cover title: Speaking with
        God in the unknown tongue.

5254a   Holdcroft, Leslie Thomas
            The Holy Spirit: a Pentecostal interpretation [by] L.
        Thomas Holdcroft. Clayburn, B.C., Western Pentecostal
        Bible College, 1979. iv, 272p. OkTOr

5255   Kulbeck, Earl Nathaniel Oscar
            The threefold ministry of the Holy Spirit, with questions
        and answers, E. N. O. Kulbeck. Woodstock, Ont., c1938.
        51p. OkTOr

5256   McAlister, Robert Edward, 1880-1953.
            God's sovereignty in healing, by R. E. McAlister. Tor-
        onto, Full Gospel Publishing House, 19--. 31p. OkTOr

5257   McAlister, Robert Edward, 1880-1953.
            Heaven's fixed laws, by R. E. McAlister. Toronto,
        Testimony Press, 19--. 39p. OkTOr

5258   McAlister, Robert Edward, 1880-1953.
            The manifestations of the Spirit, by R. E. McAlister.
        Toronto, Full Gospel Publishing House, 1951. 36p. Cover
        title. TxWaS

5259   McAlister, Robert Edward, 1880-1953.
            Pentecostalism, what saith the scriptures? Notes from
        an address by R. E. McAlister. Toronto, Testimony Press,
        19--. 51p. OkTOr

5260   McAlister, Robert Edward, 1880-1953.
            What the Bible teaches concerning apostles and prophets,
        by R. E. McAlister. Toronto, Full Gospel Publishing House,
        196-. 15p. First published under title: Apostles--true or
        false? Prophets--true or false? OkTOr

5261   McAlister, Walter E.
            What every Christian should know concerning the baptism
        with the Holy Ghost, by Walter E. McAlister. Toronto, Full
        Gospel Publishing House, 19--. 10p. Published by the Na-
        tional Publications Committee of the Pentecostal Assemblies
        of Canada under authority of the General Conference. OkTOr

5262   Ratz, Charles Arthur
            The Bible and its supreme authority: a brief study on

how we got our Bible, the supremacy of the Word of God ...
over rationalism, by C. A. Ratz. Peterborough, Ont., Book
Nook, 196-. 58p. (Student's handbook.) OkTOr

5263   Ratz, Charles Arthur
        Bible doctrines of salvation, by C. A. Ratz. Peter-
        borough, Ont., Book Nook, 1961. 40p. (Student's handbook.)
        OkTOr

5264   Ratz, Charles Arthur
        Outlined studies in Hebrews. Peterborough, Ont., Col-
        lege Press, 1956. 312p.

5265   Ratz, Charles Arthur
        Outlined studies in Romans. Brockville, Ont., Standard
        Publishing House, 1948. 175p.

5266   Ratz, Charles Arthur
        Outlined studies in the four gospels; an outlined Bible
        study for personal or class use. Peterborough, Ont., Col-
        lege Press, 1961. 89p. (The student's handbook.)

5267   Ratz, Charles Arthur
        Outlined studies in the Holy Spirit. Peterborough, Ont.,
        College Press, 1963. 136p.

5268   Ratz, Charles Arthur
        The person of Christ. Peterborough, Ont., Book Nook,
        1962. 136p. (The student's handbook.)

        --EDUCATION

5269   Peters, Erna Alma, 1914-
        The contribution to education by the Pentecostal Assem-
        blies of Canada. Winnipeg, 1970. 268ℓ. Thesis (M. Ed.)--
        University of Manitoba. CaMWU

5270   Peters, Erna Alma, 1914-
        The contribution to education by the Pentecostal Assem-
        blies of Canada. Homewood, Man., 1970, c1971. vi, 205p.
        Based on thesis (M. Ed.)--University of Manitoba. DLC,
        TxWaS

5271   Ross, Brian Robert
        James Eustace Purdie: the story of Pentecostal theolog-
        ical education [by] Brian Ross. In Journal of the Canadian
        Church Historical Society, 17 (Dec. 1975), 94-103.

        --GOVERNMENT

5272   Pentecostal Assemblies of Canada.

Local church constitution. Toronto, 19--. 12p.

5273   Lynn, Carman W.
       Saints, bishops and deacons, by C. W. Lynn. Toronto,
       Full Gospel Publishing House, 19--. 20p.

--HISTORY

5274   Atter, Gordon Francis, 1905-
       The third force: a Pentecostal answer to the question
       so often asked by both our own young people and by members
       of other churches: Who are the Pentecostals? By Gordon
       F. Atter. 3d ed., revised. Peterborough, Ont., College
       Press, c1970. xi, 314p. "The Pentecostal Assemblies of
       Canada": p. 95-102.

5275   Kulbeck, Earl Nathaniel Oscar
       A brief history of the Pentecostal Assemblies of Canada.
       Toronto, Testimony Press, 1958. 15p.

5276   Kulbeck, Gloria Grace
       What God hath wrought: a history of the Pentecostal
       Assemblies of Canada. Edited by Walter E. McAlister and
       George R. Upton. Foreword by A. G. Ward. Toronto,
       Pentecostal Assemblies of Canada, 1958. viii, 364p. CaBVU,
       TxWaS, WiH

--MISSIONS

5277   Upton, George R., comp.
       Missionary outreach of the Pentecostal Assemblies of
       Canada. Toronto, Pentecostal Assemblies of Canada, Mis-
       sionary Department, 1957. 72p. NNMR

--PASTORAL LITERATURE

5278   Atter, Gordon Francis, 1905-
       Friendship, courtship and marriage; an outlined study on
       the subject of Christian ethics with regard to friendship,
       courtship, marriage and sex, especially prepared for use in
       Sunday school, church youth meetings and Bible college, by
       Gordon F. and Hope Atter. Peterborough, Ont., Book Nook,
       1961. 54p. At head of title: The student's handbook.

5279   Horban, Michael
       Get with it, man! A fresh look at a man's world.
       Toronto, Full Gospel Publishing House; Springfield, Mo.,
       Gospel Publishing House, 1974. 105p. (Radiant books.)
       DLC

5280   Horban, Michael

Hanging loose in an uptight world. Toronto, Full Gospel Publishing House; Springfield, Mo. , Gospel Publishing House, c1978. 123p. (Radiant books.) DLC

--PERIODICALS

5281   Action. 1- Mar. 1970-
Toronto. Supersedes Know, Dominion outreach, and Missionary outlook.

5282   Chivalry. 1- 19 -
Toronto.

5283   Dominion outreach. 1-7, 1962-1968.
Toronto. Superseded by Action.

5284   Harvest field. 1- Aug. 1976-
South Porcupine, Ont. CaOONL

5285   Know. 1- .   -Feb. 1970.
Toronto. Superseded by Action.

5286   Missionary outlook. 1- .   -1970.
Toronto. First printed issue: no. 25, May 1958.
Superseded by Action. CaOONL

5287   Northland messenger. 1- Dec. 1951-
South Porcupine, Ont.

5288   Pentecostal testimony. 1- Dec. 1920-
London, Ont. , Ottawa, Ont. , Toronto. 1-8, 1920-1927 as Canadian Pentecostal testimony. CaOONL, CtY-D, MnCS

5289   Real living. 1- June 1963-
Toronto. CaOONL

5290   Youth profile. 1- Apr. 1974-
Toronto.

--SERMONS, TRACTS, ADDRESSES, ESSAYS

5291   McAlister, Robert Edward, 1880-1953.
Where do we go from here, and other sermons, by R. E. McAlister. Toronto, Full Gospel Publishing House, 195-. 20p. OkTOr

PENTECOSTAL ASSEMBLIES OF GOD (1924-)

In 1924 Otto and Marian Keller, independent missionaries in Kenya, sought for and received recognition from the Pentecostal

Assemblies of Canada. Under this arrangement additional Canadian
workers went to the field. A strong evangelistic and educational
work resulted. In 1962, when the shift from foreign to national
leadership was in full sway, the Kenya Pentecostal Assemblies of
God reported 60, 000 members. Five years later the number had
increased to 95, 000. At the latter date there were 450 churches.
Although decision-makers are now Kenyans, missionaries continue
to play a significant role in publishing and educational endeavors.
In 1975 the Pentecostal Assemblies of Canada had 66 workers under
appointment. Headquarters are in Nairobi. The Evangel Publishing
House and a strong secondary school are located in Nyanza province
near Lake Victoria.

5292   Pentecostal Assemblies of God.
            The standard of faith and fellowship. Kisumu, Kenya,
        Evangel Publishing House, 1970. 30p. "Parts of this book-
        let adapted from The indigenous church, by Melvin L.
        Hodges." OkTOr

                --CATECHISMS AND CREEDS

5293   Purdie, James Eustace
            567 Christian answers, by J. E. Purdie. Kisumu,
        Kenya, Evangel Publishing House, 1972. 94p. CtY-D

                --EDUCATION

5294   Peters, Erna Alma, 1914-
            The contribution to education by the Pentecostal Assem-
        blies of Canada. Homewood, Man., 1970, c1971. vi, 205p.
        Based on thesis (M. Ed.)--University of Manitoba. "Kenya":
        p. 74-100. DLC, TxWaS

                --PASTORAL LITERATURE

5295   Ratz, Calvin C.
            God's plan for you, by Calvin C. Ratz. Kisumu, Kenya,
        Evangel Publishing House, 1972. 32p. OkTOr

5296   Ratz, Calvin C.
            Light for God's people, by Calvin C. Ratz. Kisumu,
        Kenya, Evangel Publishing House, c1972. 70p. DLC

5297   Ratz, Calvin C.
            The young Christian and witnessing, by Calvin C. Ratz.
        Kisumu, Kenya, Evangel Publishing House, 1972. 96p.
        (Young Christian series, 4.) DLC

--SERMONS, TRACTS, ADDRESSES, ESSAYS

5298   Ratz, Calvin C.
       Sermons for Africa, by Calvin C. Ratz. Kisumu,
       Kenya, Evangel Publishing House, c1972. 32p. (Seed-bed
       series, 1.) OkTOr

PENTECOSTAL ASSEMBLIES OF NEWFOUNDLAND (1925-   )
[1925-1930 as Bethesda Pentecostal Assemblies.]

       The outgrowth of the ministry of Alice Garrigus, an evan-
gelist from Boston who opened the first church, the Bethesda Pentecostal Church in St. John's, on Easter Sunday, 1911, the Pentecostal Assemblies of Newfoundland traces its existence as an organization to 1925, when it gained official recognition from the provincial government. In 1932 the fellowship extended its activities into
Labrador as well. Because until 1949 Newfoundland (and Labrador)
remained independent, the Pentecostal Assemblies of Newfoundland
developed separately from the similarly-named Canadian group,
whose doctrinal statement it shares. Cooperation between the two
bodies is close. A representative of the Pentecostal Assemblies
of Newfoundland sits on the board of the Eastern Pentecostal Bible
College of Peterborough, Ontario, and missionary candidates of the
Newfoundland group go to the field under the auspices of the Canadian fellowship. In 1978 the Pentecostal Assemblies of Newfoundland reported 152 churches and 30,000 members. Headquarters offices are in St. John's, where Good Tidings, the official organ, is
published.

       --PERIODICALS

5299   Good tidings. 1- 194 -
       St. John's, Newf.

5300   Prayer chain bulletin. 1-6, no. 10, 1963-1968.
       St. John's, Newf. CaOONL

5301   Reach. 1- 197 -
       St. John's, Newf.

PENTECOSTAL CHURCH OF AUSTRALIA (1925-1937)

       Formed in 1925 to conserve converts made by the American
evangelist, A. C. Valdez, Sr., the Pentecostal Church of Australia
represents a first attempt at bringing into a single fellowship assemblies in all parts of the commonwealth. Headquarters were in
Richmond, a suburb of Melbourne, where during 1926 and 1927 it

operated the Victorian Bible Institute.   In 1937, under the leadership
of C. L. Greenwood, the Pentecostal Church of Australia united with
the Assemblies of God in Queensland to form the Assemblies of God
in Australia.   The Australian Evangel, the Pentecostal Church paper,
became the official organ of the new body.

--DOCTRINAL AND CONTROVERSIAL WORKS

5302   Valdez, Alfred Clarence, 1896-
        Reply to Dr. McColl's address on "The tongues move-
        ment," by A. C. Valdez.   Melbourne, 1925.

--PERIODICALS

5303   Australian evangel.   1-
        Richmond, Vict.

PENTECOSTAL CHURCH OF NEW ZEALAND (1924-1952)

        Organized December 27, 1924, during a conference in Welling-
ton, the Pentecostal Church of New Zealand brought together the affiliates of the New Zealand Evangelical Mission.   A first effort at
collective fellowship among Pentecostal assemblies in the dominion,
the body at first consisted of thirteen congregations, most of which
had been formed as a result of the evangelistic efforts of Smith
Wigglesworth, an Englishman, and A. C. Valdez, an American.   Difficulties over church order and doctrinal teaching troubled the group.
Unsuccessful attempts to reunite with those of its own number who
in 1927 founded the Assemblies of God in New Zealand, were followed
by overtures to the Elim Foursquare Gospel Alliance of Great Britain.
The latter led to absorption into that fellowship on December 27, 1952.
The New Zealand Evangel, originally the organ of the Pentecostal
Church, continues as the official periodical of the Assemblies of God
in New Zealand.

--DOCTRINAL AND CONTROVERSIAL WORKS

5304   Glover, Kelso R.
        The resurrection both of the just and unjust.   Auckland,
        Seabrook and Farrell, 1925.

5305   Roberts, H. V.
        Beware the new revelation on water baptism.   Auckland,
        Church Army Press, 1946.

5306   Roberts, H. V.
        New Zealand's greatest revival.   Auckland, New Zealand
        Pelorus Press, 1951.

--HISTORY

5307   Worsfold, James Evans
A history of the charismatic movements in New Zealand;
including a Pentecostal perspective and a breviate of the
Catholic Apostolic Church in Great Britain, by J. E. Worsfold. Bradford, Yorks., Julian Literature Trust; printed by
Puritan Press, c1974. xx, 368p. "The Pentecostal Church":
p. 167-190; and "The Elim Church": p. 191-196.

--PERIODICALS

5308   New Zealand evangel. 1-3, no. 2, June 6, 1924-Feb. 1927.
Wellington. 1-2, 1924-1926 as New Zealand evangel of
the apostolic faith. Publication continued under Assemblies
of God in New Zealand.

5309   Pentecostal messenger. 1- . Sept. 1943-Apr./May 1946.
Auckland.

PENTECOSTAL EVANGELICAL CHURCH (1936-)

Organized in 1936, the Pentecostal Evangelical Church functions as an association of churches, a ministerial fellowship, and a
sponsor of orphanages and foreign missions. G. F. C. Fons of
Fort Smith, Arkansas, its first General Bishop, had served from
1934 to 1935 as Moderator of the Pentecostal Church of God of
America. Present headquarters are in Spokane, Washington, where
Gospel Tidings, the official organ, is published. In 1967 its 23 congregations and 1,150 members were supporting twenty North American workers in the Philippines, India, Bolivia, and Guyana.

5310   Pentecostal Evangelical Church.
General by-laws of the Pentecostal Evangelical Church.
Rev. ed. Spokane, Wa., 1966. 20p.

--PERIODICALS

5311   Gospel tidings. 1- 1938-
Fort Smith, Ar., Spokane, Wa.

PENTECOSTAL EVANGELISTIC FELLOWSHIP OF AFRICA (1940-)

An outgrowth of work begun in 1940 by the Elim Missionary
Assemblies, the Pentecostal Evangelistic Fellowship of Africa is an
autonomous, loosely-structured body in Kenya and Tanzania. Esti-

mates of its size vary widely. In 1964 during its annual meeting at Lumuru, Kenya, the Fellowship claimed 640 full-time clergy, 725 churches, and 70,000 members. Three years later, an ecumenical agency reported only 24 churches and 620 members, however. North American workers continue to assist. In 1975 the Elim Fellowship had 38 missionaries under appointment in Kenya alone.

PENTECOSTAL PROTESTANT CHURCH (1958-   )

Separated from the Apostolic Faith Mission of South Africa in the 1950s, the Pentecostal Protestant Church has its headquarters in Isando, Transvaal, where the Pinkster Protestant is published. In the early 1960s the church claimed 10,000 members in eighty congregations.

--PERIODICALS

5312   Pinkster Protestant. 1- 1958-
            Islando, Tvl. Text in Afrikaans and English; summaries in Afrikaans.

PINKSTER CHRISTEN KERK VAN SUID AFRIKA (1950-   )

Originating in 1950, the Pinkster Christen Kerk van Suid Afrika has its headquarters in Boksburg North, Transvaal, where it publishes its official organ, Pinkster-nuus, in both Afrikaans and English.

--PERIODICALS

5313   Pinkster-nuus. 1- 1950-
            Boksburg North, Tvl. Afrikaans and English. L

PISGAH HOME MOVEMENT (1908-   )

The Pisgah Home Movement is the outgrowth of the utopian experimentation of Finis E. Yoakum. The founder, one-time Denver physician and vice president of the Colorado Holiness Association, was healed in a meeting conducted by the Christian and Missionary Alliance in 1894. Moving to Los Angeles, he accepted Pentecostal teaching and in 1908 opened an every-night mission which became known as the Old Pisgah Tabernacle. Attempting to recreate Christian communities similar to those described in the Acts of the Apostles, Yoakum established a series of institutions in and near Los Angeles: the Pisgah Home and the Ark in the city, and Pisgah

Grande and Pisgah Gardens in rural areas east of the city. All who came were accepted provided they refrained from use of alcohol and tobacco. Each institution ministered to a particular need: Pisgah Grande to families and children, the Ark to unwed mothers and their children, and Pisgah Gardens to tuberculars. Yoakum relied on the faith cure as the principal method of treatment of disease. Promotion of the movement was through Pisgah, a journal first published in 1909.

Fearing that the properties might fall into the hands of the founder's children at his death in 1920, Yoakum's followers incorporated as the Pisgah Home Movement. After several years of confused management, the group sold most of the Los Angeles property and purchased what became known as Mountain Ranch near Saugus, California, in the San Bernardino mountains. Editorial offices of the journal moved first to Summit, California, later to the Pisgah Home Camp Ground near Pikeville, Tennessee.

--PERIODICALS

5314　Pisgah. 1- 1909-
　　　Los Angeles, Summit, Ca., Pikeville, Tn.

RAINBOW REVIVAL CHURCH (1957-)

Incorporated in 1957, the Los Angeles-based Rainbow Revival Church carries on a dual program, which includes Sunday services at the headquarters center, and "written church services" and pastoral counseling by mail. Pastors Eldridge and Ruth Plunkett, veterans of fifteen years as evangelists at the church's founding, stress physical healing. They mail out many prayer handkerchiefs each month. The active mailing list of the Rainbow Revival Church consists of more than 6,000 names.

RIDGEWOOD PENTECOSTAL CHURCH (1925-)

On December 6, 1925, a congregation composed of members of the former Full Gospel Mission on Patchen Avenue in Brooklyn, held its first service in a newly acquired hall at 815 Seneca Avenue in the Ridgewood section of the city. Led by Hans R. Waldvogel, a Swiss immigrant, the church expressed a special concern for German-speaking people. It endorsed a number of evangelistic missions by the pastor in Switzerland, Austria, and Germany, and sponsored for more than fifteen years a religious service at the beginning of the German Family Hour over radio station WHOM. From its earliest years, stress was placed on outreach. In 1929 the Ridgewood congregation opened the Woodhaven Faith Home, a residence for ministerial candidates in training under Pastor Waldvogel which also

served as a hostel for ministers and missionaries temporarily in
the New York area. From it sprang a number of branches: the
East Side Pentecostal Church (1933); the Yorkville Gospel Hall (1938);
the Williamsburg Pentecostal Church (1939); the Pelham Pentecostal
Church (1940); the the Canarsie Full Gospel Chapel (1942). Following World War II, the Floral Park Pentecostal Church and the Church
of the Good Shepherd, Ozone Park, also affiliated. In 1946, a year
following its move from the rented hall to a substantial building purchased from another denomination, the Ridgewood congregation opened
Pilgrim Camp at Brant Lake, New York. During this period, the
church supported workers in South Africa, India, and Taiwan, and
initiated a mission effort among blacks and Spanish residents near
it in Brooklyn.

--HISTORY

5315   Brooklyn.   Ridgewood Pentecostal Church.
        Commemorating fifty years of God's blessing and faith-
        fulness to the Ridgewood Pentecostal Church, Brooklyn, N. Y.
        Brooklyn, 1975. ix, 95p. Cover title: Ridgewood Pentecostal
        Church, 1925-1975.

--PERIODICALS

5316   Bread of life. 1- Dec. 1951-
        Brooklyn.

SALAAM CHURCH (1938-)

        Organized in 1938, the Salaam Church of Port Said is the
product of work begun in 1911 by the Swedish Salaam Mission. The
"full gospel" emphasis was introduced by Jack Hardstedt, missionary
of the Filadelfia Church of Stockholm, to whom the Salaam Mission
work was turned over a year before the church was organized.
Since 1946, when all foreign workers left the country, the membership has been entirely Egyptian.

SAMARIA IGLESIA EVANGÉLICA (1947-)

        In 1941 Julio Guzmán Silva was expelled from the Baptist church
in Palmer, Puerto Rico, for claiming to have received "great baths
of the Holy Spirit, " the gift of healing, and the power to exorcise
demons. For the next four years, Silva conducted services in his
home in Palmer. He entered the ministry full time in 1945. The
establishment of the first branch congregation two years later marked
the beginning of the Samaria Iglesia Evangélica as a denomination.
The method used in planting new churches is as follows: first per-

mission is sought to preach in the town plaza, next regular meetings are started in homes, and finally a congregation is organized formally. In the mid-1960s the Samaria Iglesia Evangélica consisted of 25 congregations and 750 members. Headquarters are in Fajardo, Puerto Rico, the founder's birthplace.

SCANDINAVIAN INDEPENDENT ASSEMBLIES OF GOD (1918-1935)

Organized in 1918, the Scandinavian Independent Assemblies of God counted among its early leaders several former Baptist ministers. Among these was A. A. Holmgren, publisher of Sanningens Vittne, a paper which served the movement as a quasi-official organ. Unlike the Independent Assemblies of God, the Scandinavian Independent Assemblies of God was an incorporated body. Desirous of larger fellowship, in 1935 the Chicago-based group dissolved its corporation and united with the unincorporated Independent Assemblies of God.

--PERIODICALS

5317   Sanningens Vittne.   1-   191 -
          Chicago.

SHILOH CHAPEL (194 -   )

Opened in the early 1940s, the Shiloh Chapel is a non-denominational congregation in Colorado Springs. In the early 1970s, it had a membership of approximately 200.

TRUE GRACE MEMORIAL HOUSE OF PRAYER FOR ALL PEOPLE (1962-   )

In 1962 as a result of the court-authorized election of Walter McCollough as successor to "Sweet Daddy" Grace as bishop of the United House of Prayer for All People, twelve members of the dissatisfied minority in the "mother house" in Washington, D.C. withdrew and founded the True Grace Memorial House for All People. They chose Elder Thomas O. Johnson, veteran of twenty-three years in the parent group, as pastor and constructed a new "house" on V Street in northwest Washington. The existence of the new body, which was successful in defeating repeated challenges to its right to use "house of Prayer" in its name, inspired formation of seven additional congregations scattered along the East Coast from New York to Florida. All regard Bishop Grace as their founder. Although they share a common name, local houses have resisted attempts to organize a single body because of differences in worship customs.

UNION DES EGLISES EVANGÉLIQUES DE PENTECÔTE BELGIQUE
(1954-   )

Formed in 1954, the Union des Eglises Evangeliques de
Pentecôte Belgique is the product of efforts dating from 1930 of
workers from Great Britain, Switzerland, United States, Norway,
and Sweden.   After ten years of existence, the fellowship claimed
more than fifty affiliated churches and 2, 052 members.   The Institut
Biblique Emmanuel, established in 1959, is in Andrimont.   The official organ, La Voix Chrétienne, is published in Brussels.   At
least four language groups (French, Flemish, Polish, and Italian)
are represented in its constituency.

--PERIODICALS

5318   La Voix Chrétienne.   1-   1954-
          Bruxelles.

UNION EVANGÉLICA PENTECOSTAL VENEZOLANA (1960-   )

About 1960 Julio Hidalgo and Exeario Sosa were expelled
from the Assemblies of God of Venezuela for participating in political and ecumenical activity.   Soon thereafter they together with several hundred followers organized the Union Evangélica Pentecostal
Venezolana.   The new group demonstrated its commitment to ecumenism by inviting Disciples of Christ missionaries to teach in its
worker training school.   In 1961 twenty congregations were affiliated
with the Union.

UNITED APOSTOLIC FAITH CHURCH (1907-   )
[1907-1926 as Apostolic Faith Church.]

Formed in 1907, the Apostolic Faith Church with headquarters
at Winton, Bournemouth, gave a prominent place to the exercise of
spiritual gifts.   Stress was laid on the gift of prophecy, particularly
in making group decisions.   Alleged excesses of W. O. Hutchinson,
the original leader, lay behind a major exodus and the formation of
the Apostolic Church in 1916.   Missionary advance continued, however, and the group, which had sent out its first missionaries in
1912, established self-governing churches in Canada, Rhodesia, and
South Africa.   Growth at home, where the group apparently embraced
the British Israel teaching, was slow.   As late as 1965 there were
only twelve congregations in the British Isles.   Kent White, husband
of the vitriolic critic of Pentecostalism Alma White, was an early
member of the Apostolic Faith Church in Bournemouth.   Headquarters offices are now in London, where Pentecostal Times and Kingdom Evangel, the official organ, is published.

5319   United Apostolic Faith Church.
         Constitution and decrees. 2d and rev. ed. London,
       1933. 6p. First ed. published in 1927 under title: Consti-
       tution & outline of beliefs. L

5320   United Apostolic Faith Church.
         Constitution & outline of Beliefs. London, 1927. 7p.
       Reproduced from typewriting. L

--CATECHISMS AND CREEDS

5321   Apostolic Faith Church.
         The doctrine and articles of belief of the Apostolic Faith
       Church. Bournemouth, 1916. 2v. L

5322   United Apostolic Faith Church.
         What we believe and teach. London, 1933. 13p. First
       ed. published in 1916 under title: The doctrine and articles
       of belief of the Apostolic Faith Church. L

--DOCTRINAL AND CONTROVERSIAL WORKS

5323   Brooke, James, 1883-1960.
         Light on speaking in other tongues. London, United
       Apostolic Faith Church, 1935. 31p. L

5324   Brooke, James, 1883-1960.
         Light on the baptism of the Holy Ghost. London, King-
       dom Publishing Co., 1937. 48p. L

5325   Brooke, James, 1883-1960.
         Light on the baptism of the Holy Spirit. 2d ed. London,
       Kingdom Publishing Co., 1943. 39p. L

5326   Brooke, James, 1883-1960.
         Light on the baptism of the Holy Spirit. 3d ed. London,
       Kingdom Press, 1951. 39p. L

5327   Brooke, James, 1883-1960.
         The prophetical voice. London, Kingdom Publishing Co.,
       1943. 80p. L

5328   Brooke, James, 1883-1960.
         A testimony concerning Israel in the last days. London,
       Kingdom Publishing Co., 1939. 33p. L

5329   White, Kent, 1860-1940.
         The word of God coming again; return of apostolic faith
       and works now due on the earth. With a sketch of the life
       of Pastor W. Oliver Hutchinson. Bournemouth, Apostolic
       Faith Church, 1919. 296p. L, TxWaS

--PERIODICALS

5330   Hephzibah. [1]- 1920-
        Croydon. L

5331   Missionary news. 1- 1948-
        Bournemouth. L

5332   Pentecostal times and kingdom evangel. 1- 1939-
        London. 1939-19-- as Kingdom evangel. L, OkTOr

5333   Showers. 1- 1910-Apr. 1926, June 1952-
        Bournemouth, London. 1-50, 1910-1926 as Showers of
        blessing. L

UNITED EVANGELICAL CHURCHES (1964-)

        Organized in 1964, the United Evangelical Churches is the
outgrowth of a ministerial association formed five years earlier
under the leadership of two Methodist ministers of Monrovia, California, Charles J. Hardin and Merrill H. Eve. Although Eve died
in 1962, Hardin, who was intent on establishing a fellowship in which
the present leadership of the Holy Spirit would be recognized, joined
with Delbert Hostetter, an Assemblies of God minister, in forming
the United Evangelical Churches. Strongly committed to the exercise of miraculous gifts and ministries, the United Evangelical
Churches, which in 1975 spent more than $40,000 overseas, sends
out workers through the Christians in Action organization. More
than thirty churches, groups, and agencies are affiliated with the
fellowship.

5334   Farah, Charles
        United Evangelical Churches: vision. Monrovia, Ca. ,
        United Evangelical Churches, 19--. 14p.

5335   Pottinger, Ronald R.
        Why U. E. C. ? By Ronald R. Pittinger. Monrovia,
        Ca. , United Evangelical Churches, 1968. folder (3p.)

                --PERIODICALS

5336   Koinonia. 1-4, 196 -
        Monrovia, Ca. OkTOr

UNITED FULL GOSPEL MINISTERS AND CHURCHES (1951-)

        In 1954 the United Full Gospel Ministers and Churches, which
had been incorporated May 16, 1951, consisted of more than fifty

clergy and an undetermined number of churches. The body was
governed by four executive officers, one of whom faced election at
each annual meeting. Arthur H. Collins, first chairman, directed
the organization from Los Angeles. The Open Bible Church of God,
the organization's affiliate in India, had as its founder-president
Willis M. Clay, who also served as first treasurer of the United
Full Gospel Ministers and Churches.

5337   United Full Gospel Ministers and Churches.
        Articles of incorporation and by-laws.   Los Angeles,
        1951.

        --HISTORY

5338   Moore, Everett Leroy, 1918-
        Handbook of Pentecostal denominations in the United
        States. Pasadena, Ca., 1954. vii, 346ℓ. Thesis (M.A.)--
        Pasadena College. "United Full Gospel Ministers and
        Churches": ℓ. 127-129. CSdP

UNITED FUNDAMENTALIST CHURCH (1939-)

        The United Fundamentalist Church was founded by Leroy M.
Kopp in Los Angeles in 1939. Stress is laid on healing and prophecy. "The divine healing of the sick is not only to honor the prayer
of faith, but is to be a sign to confirm the word as it is preached
at home and abroad." In the early years the church sponsored foreign missionary workers under the World-Wide, Signs Following,
Evangelism program. In 1963 it took custody of the Zion Christian
Mission in Jerusalem. Twelve years later it had four North American workers under appointment in Israel. A radio program begun
by the founder in Los Angeles soon after the United Fundamentalist
Church was formed, continues under his son and successor, E. Paul
Kopp. Headquarters offices are in Calvary Temple, Los Angeles.
In 1967 the church reported that about 250 ministers and missionaries
were affiliated with the movement.

        --HISTORY

5339   Moore, Everett Leroy, 1918-
        Handbook of Pentecostal denominations in the United States.
        Pasadena, Ca., 1954. vii, 346ℓ. Thesis (M.A.)--Pasadena
        College. "United Fundamentalist Church": ℓ. 129-130. CSdP

        --PERIODICALS

5340   Christian voice in Israel. 1- 196 -
        Jerusalem.

UNITED HOUSE OF PRAYER FOR ALL PEOPLE, CHURCH ON THE
   ROCK OF THE APOSTOLIC FAITH (1927-   )

In 1903 Charles Emmanuel Grace, nineteen-year-old native of
the Cape Verde Islands, arrived in New Bedford, Massachusetts.
He worked at a variety of jobs: cook, groceryman, and patent medicine salesman.   About 1919 he opened the first House of Prayer in
a building he himself had constructed in West Wareham, Massachusetts.   Grace got a job as cook on a southern railroad and he evangelized as he had opportunity, incorporating the United House of
Prayer for All People, Church on the Rock of the Apostolic Faith
at Washington, D.C. in 1927.   Grace concentrated on poverty-scarred
urban areas, taking "rocks that no one [else] would use and built his
church."   Venerated as "Sweet Daddy" Grace by his followers, he
established centers in New Haven, New York, Buffalo, Philadelphia,
Baltimore, Washington, Newport News, Charlotte, Columbia, Savan-
nah, and Augusta.   Each center provides low-rent housing and employment opportunities in church-related enterprises to members.
Ostracized by sister groups because of its near-worship of Grace,
the United House of Prayer permits unrestrained emotionalism in
worship.   Speaking in tongues, dancing, falling into trances, and un-
controlled jerking of limbs are common occurrences.   The calendar
of yearly observances includes a number of special days commemo-
rating events in the lives of the founder and his successor, Walter
McCollough, known to the faithful as Sweet Daddy Grace McCollough.
The elevation of the latter in 1962 by means of a court-ordered election resulted in the formation of the rival True Grace Memorial
House of Prayer, leaving the original body with approximately 27,500
members in 137 churches and missions scattered from coast to coast.

5341   Alland, Alexander, 1931-
            "Possession" in a revivalistic Negro church.   In Journal
        for the Scientific Study of Religion, 1 (Spring 1962), 204-213.

5342-   Alland, Alexander, 1931-
   3   "Possession" in a revivalistic Negro church.   In Knudten,
        R. D., ed.   The sociology of religion: an anthology.   New
        York, c1967, 83-92.   Abridged from Journal for the Scientific
        Study of Religion, 1 (Spring 1962).

5344   Eddy, George Norman, 1906-
            Store-front religion [by] G. Norman Eddy.   In Religion in
        Life, 28 (Winter 1958/1959), 68-85.   Account of Daddy Grace
        and the United House of Prayer for All People: p. 74-78.

5345   Eddy, George Norman, 1906-
            Store-front religion [by] G. Norman Eddy.   In Lee, R.,
        ed.   Cities and churches; readings on the urban church.
        Philadelphia, c1962, 177-194.   Abridged from Religion in
        Life, 28 (Winter 1958/1959), 68-85.   Account of Daddy Grace
        and the United House of Prayer for All People: p. 182-187.

5346   Whiting, Albert Nathaniel, 1917-
            The United House of Prayer for All People; a case study
        of a charismatic sect, by Albert N. Whiting. Washington,
        1952. xi, 319ℓ. Thesis (Ph. D.)--American University.
        DAU

            --CONTROVERSIAL LITERATURE

5347   The truth and facts of the United House of Prayer for All
        People and the most honorable Bishop W. McCollough, leader.
        Washington, 1968.   viii, 100p.   DLC

            --PERIODICALS

5348   Grace magazine.   1-   19 -
        Washington.

UNIVERSAL CHURCH, THE MYSTICAL BODY OF CHRIST (197 -   )

        An interracial body formed during the 1970s, the Universal
Church, the Mystical Body of Christ sees as its mission the gathering of true Christians into a separate theocratic community, the
144,000 mentioned in Revelation.   A strict code of behavior is observed.   The group, which regards itself not as a denomination but
as the true body of Christ, is led by Bishop R. O. Frazier of Sagi-
naw, Michigan.

            --PERIODICALS

5349   Light of life herald.   1-   197 -
        Saginaw, Mi.

UNIVERSAL WORLD CHURCH (1952-   )
[1952-197- as World Church.]

        The World Church was founded on June 30, 1952, by O. L.
Jaggers, deliverance evangelist and former Assemblies of God minister.   Although through newspaper advertisements the group at one
time reported over 500 ministers, missionaries and workers in Latin
America, Europe, and Asia, the movement in reality consists of a
single congregation in Los Angeles of which Jaggers is pastor.   Official estimates of membership also appear to be undependable.   In
1967 when the founder claimed an active membership in excess of
10,000, an outside observer placed that figure at not more than
1,200.   The World Church is committed to a detailed eschatology

and sees its mission as the gathering of the 144, 000 elect saints
mentioned in Revelation.   Another distinctive teaching is its belief
in transubstantiation.   Four times each year the twenty-four elders,
who constitute the executive committee, participate in an elaborate
ceremony before the golden altar "of changing the bread and wine
into the sacred body and blood of the Lord Jesus Christ."   With
these notable exceptions, doctrinal teachings are nearly identical
to those of the Assemblies of God.   A key figure in the ministry of
the World Church is Velma Jaggers, the founder's wife of twenty-
five years.   Rumor has it that she is his first cousin.

5350   Haines, Aubrey B.
             Miss Velma descends [by] Aubrey B. Haines.   In Chris-
         tian Century, 83 (Aug. 10, 1966), 992, 994.

5351   Martin, Pete
             Faith and fear for $1.07, by Pete Martin.   In Christian
         Herald, 90 (July 1967), 13-14, 42-46, 48-49.

5352   Thrapp, Dan L.
             The background story, by Dan L. Thrapp.   In Christian
         Herald, 90 (July 1967), 15-16, 59.

                    --DOCTRINAL AND CONTROVERSIAL WORKS

5353   Jaggers, Orval L., 1916-
             How to rid the world of Red communism, by O. L. Jag-
         gers.   Los Angeles, Bedrock Press, 1953.   31p.   Cover
         title.   CFlS

5354   Jaggers, Orval L., 1916-
             Life and immortality in the book of St. John, by O. L.
         Jaggers.   Los Angeles, 1959.

                    --HISTORY

5355   Moore, Everett Leroy, 1918-
             Handbook of Pentecostal denominations in the United States.
         Pasadena, Ca., 1954.   vii, 346ℓ.   Thesis (M. A.)--Pasadena
         College.   "World Church": ℓ. 130-134.   CSdP

                    --PERIODICALS

5356   International voice of the World Church.   1- 19 -
             Los Angeles.

5357   Miracle worker.   1- 1952-195-.
             Los Angeles.

5358   World fellowship news.   1-   1956-19--.
        Los Angeles.

2. ONENESS BODIES

        Consolidation of the Finished Work forces under the banner
of the General Council of the Assemblies of God was still a year
in the future when yet another storm of doctrinal controversy broke
over the infant movement.   During the so-called World-Wide Camp
Meeting at Arroyo Seco near Los Angeles in 1913, John G. Scheppe
received new light on baptism and announced his discovery to all
present.   According to this revelation, it is imperative that baptism
be administered in the name of Jesus, as in the earliest Christian
times, rather than in the name of the Father, Son, and Holy Spirit,
as later became common.   Although the camp management did not
accept Scheppe's new insight, many in attendance at the camp meeting did.   Explained more fully by Frank Ewart in a sermon on Acts
2:38 during a tent meeting in East Los Angeles the next spring, the
"New Issue" spread like wildfire, reaching St. Louis, Indianapolis,
Minneapolis, Winnipeg, and Ottawa, within months.   Prominent
preachers, including Frank Ewart, Glenn Cook, George A. Cham-
bers, H. A. Goss, W. E. McAlister, L. V. Roberts, E. N. Bell,
and H. G. Rodgers, were re-baptized, and periodicals designed to
promote baptism in Jesus' name were launched in Los Angeles, Indianapolis, and Eureka Springs, Arkansas.

        Once begun, the reformers did not stop with the formula for
baptism, but reworked the doctrine of God as well.   The resulting
Oneness theology replaced traditional trinitarianism with tri-model
theism: there is one God whose name is Jesus; and His titles are
Father, Son, and Holy Spirit.   The Oneness teaching rent the Finished Work movement asunder.   Appealing to both races, the "New
Issue" nearly emptied the trinitarian Finished Work ranks of blacks.
Both racial harmony and doctrinal unity were short-lived, however,
and the Oneness movement, like its trinitarian counterpart, fractured
repeatedly.

--CONTROVERSIAL LITERATURE

5359   Brumback, Carl, 1917-
        God in three Persons; a Trinitarian answer to the one-
        ness of "Jesus only" doctrine concerning the Godhead and
        water baptism.   Cleveland, Tenn., Pathway Press, 1959.
        192p.   DLC

5360   Gortner, John Narver, 1874-

Water baptism and the Trinity. Studies by J. Narver
Gortner, Donald Gee [and] Hy Pickering. Springfield, Mo.,
Gospel Publishing House, 19--. 62p.

5361   Grant, Walter Vinson, 1913-
       One God, one baptism, by W. V. Grant. Dallas, 19--.
       14p. OkTOr

5362   Lindquist, Frank J.
       The truth about the Trinity and baptism in Jesus' name
       only, by Frank J. Lindquist. Minneapolis, Northern Gospel
       Publishing House, 19--. 34p.

5363   Lindquist, Frank J.
       The truth about the Trinity and baptism in Jesus' name
       only, by Frank J. Lindquist. 4th rev. ed. Minneapolis,
       Northern Gospel Publishing House, 1961. 41p.

5364   Menzies, William Watson, 1931-
       Anointed to serve: the story of the Assemblies of God,
       by William W. Menzies. Springfield, Mo., Gospel Publishing
       House, c1971. 436p. "The new issue (1914-1916)": p. 106-
       121.

5365   [Read, Ralph R.]
       Water baptism: the formula and its meaning; a study of
       the trinitarian formula of Matthew 28, v. 19 and the formula
       of "oneness" teachers: a guide and a refutation. Christ-
       church, N. Z., Assemblies of God Bookroom, 19--. 12p.
       Cover title.

5366   Roberts, H. V.
       Beware the new revelation on water baptism. Auckland,
       Church Army Press, 1946.

5367   Walkem, Charles William
       The Jesus only theory; a brief analysis of the Trinity.
       Los Angeles, 19--. 23p. Cover title.

                    --DOCTRINAL AND CONTROVERSIAL WORKS

5368   Bates, Billy
       The twisted cross. Memphis, Apostolic Publishing House,
       197-. 30p.

5369   Booth-Clibborn, William E.
       The baptism in the Holy Spirit: a personal testimony,
       by William Booth-Clibborn. 3d ed. Portland, Or., Booth-
       Clibborn Book Concern, 1936. 35p.

5370   Booth-Clibborn, William E.
       Too much: the "filled to overflowing" experience, by

William Booth-Clibborn. 2d ed. Portland, Or. , Booth-Clibborn Book Concern, 1944. 64p.

5371   Branham, William, 1909-1965.
Conduct, order, doctrine of the church [by] William Marrion Branham. Jeffersonville, In. , Spoken Word Publications, 1973-1974. 2v. OkTOr

5372   Branham, William, 1909-1965.
An exposition of the seven church ages, by William Marrion Branham. Tucson, Az. , 197-. 381p. IRA, OSteC, OUrC

5373   Branham, William, 1909-1965.
The revelation of the seven seals, as given to our precious brother William Marrion Branham. Tucson, Az. , Spoken Word Publications, 196-. 579p. IRA

5374   Coote, Leonard W.
Acts 2, 4, by Leonard W. Coote. Ikoma, Naraken, Japan, 19--. 48p. Cover title. MoSCEx

5375   Crawford, Mattie
Behold thy King cometh. Indianapolis, c1922. 64p. DLC

5376   Ewart, Frank J. , 1876-
Jesus, the man and mystery. Nashville, Baird-Ward Press, c1941. 165p. DLC

5377   Ewart, Frank J. , 1876-
Jesus, the man and mystery [by] Frank Ewart. Hazelwood, Mo. , Word Afame Press, 197-, c1941. 160p.

5378   Ewart, Frank J. , 1876-
The name and the book. Chicago, Ryerson, c1936. xvii, 174p. WaU

5379   Fitch, Theodore
Authority and power thru Jesus' name. Council Bluffs, Ia. , 19--. 56p. Cover title.

5380   Fitch, Theodore
Deep mysteries now revealed. Council Bluffs, Ia. , 19--. 64p. Cover title.

5381   Fitch, Theodore
God's over-all plan for you. Council Bluff, Ia. , 19--. 48p.

5382   Fitch, Theodore
Lovely titles of Jesus. Council Bluffs, Ia. , 19--. 67p.

5383   Fitch, Theodore
        1, 000 facts about Jesus.   Council Bluffs, Ia., 19--.
        20p.

5384   Fitch, Theodore
        Our afflictions: cause and remedy.   Council Bluffs,
        Ia., 19--.   64p.

5385   Fitch, Theodore
        Our glorious work in the next age.   Council Bluffs, Ia.,
        19--.   71p.

5386   Fitch, Theodore
        Perfect health for Christians.   Council Bluffs, Ia.,
        19--.   51p.

5387   Fitch, Theodore
        Power and authority through the anointing.   Council
        Bluffs, Ia., 19--.   62p.

5388   Fitch, Theodore
        Powerful words of Jesus.   Council Bluffs, Ia., 19--.
        43p.

5389   Fitch, Theodore
        Sex problems between husband and wife.   Council Bluffs,
        Ia., 19--.   48p.   Cover title.

5390   Fitch, Theodore
        Spiritual gifts being restored: our Lord is restoring all
        His gifts and ministries to His church.   Council Bluffs, Ia.,
        19--.   64p.   Cover title.

5391   Fitch, Theodore
        The white race is the true people of Israel.   Sub-title:
        who we are, where we came from, why He chose us, what
        our work is, why our descendants must remain white.   Coun-
        cil Bluffs, Ia., 19--.   64p.

5392   Hall, William Phillips, 1864-1937.
        Remarkable Biblical discovery; or, "The name" of God
        according to the scriptures.   Abridged.   St. Louis, Pente-
        costal Publishing House, c1951.   30p.   Based on 1929 ed.
        "Courtesy of American Tract Society."

5393   Hobbs, Clifford E., 1922-
        Whom say ye that I am?   By Clifford E. Hobbs.   Lansing,
        Il., c1971.   116p.

5394   Jensen, G. K.
        When God became flesh, by G. K. Jensen.   Chilliwack,
        B.C., 19--.   [13]p.

5395   Kolenda, E. J.
        For remission. Know the truth! Hidden truth: truth
is universal! Truth has no fear! Truth destroys tradition!
By E. J. Kolenda. South Bend, In., Apostolic Publishing
Association, 19--. 105p.

5396   Magee, Gordon
        Is Jesus in the Godhead or is the Godhead in Jesus?
Pasadena, Tx., 19--. 32p. Cover title.

5397   Miller, John, 1819-1895.
        Is God a trinity? Hazelwood, Mo., Word Aflame Press,
1975. 144p. Reprint of 1877 ed.

5398   Ooton, L. R.
        Concerning the times and seasons. Tipton, In., c1969.
27p. Cover title.

5399   Ooton, L. R.
        Dimensions and glory of the heavenly Jerusalem, by
L. R. Ooton. Tipton, In., c1966. 24p. Cover title.

5400   Ooton, L. R.
        God's time piece. Tipton, In., c1967. 39p. Cover
title.

5401   Ooton, L. R.
        The sower, the seed and the soil [by] L. R. Ooton.
Tipton, In., c1973. 29p. Cover title.

5402   Ooton, L. R.
        What is time? [By] L. R. Ooton. Tipton, In., c1970.
53p. Cover title.

5403   Paterson, John
        Speaking with tongues. n.p., c1976. 13ℓ. Processed

5404   Prinzing, Raymond Harold
        Converts of the glory, by Ray Prinzing. Boise, Id.,
19--. 236p.

5405   Prinzing, Raymond Harold
        Excellent things, by Ray Prizing. Boise, Id., 19--.
227p.

5406   Prinzing, Raymond Harold
        Redemption--all in all, by Ray Prinzing. Boise, Id.,
19--. 255p.

5407   Prinzing, Raymond Harold
        The triumphant way, by Ray Prinzing. Boise, Id.,
19--. 256p.

5408   Reeves, Kenneth V.
          The Godhead, by Kenneth V. Reeves. Granite City, Ill.,
          c1971. 68p.

5409   Reeves, Kenneth V.
          The great commission re-examined, by Kenneth V.
          Reeves. Granite City, Ill., c1966. 68p. Cover title.

5410   Reeves, Kenneth V.
          The Holy Ghost with tongues, by Kenneth V. Reeves.
          Granite City, Ill., c1966. 44p. Cover title.

5410a   Reynolds, Ralph Vincent
          Dividing the word of truth: a set of Bible doctrine notes,
          divided into twelve units. One year's home study course with
          instructions and review questions. Written and comp. by
          Ralph Vincent Reynolds. 5th ed. Rock Creek, B.C., 1974.
          [148]p. OkTOr

5411   Rowe, G. B.
          Reincarnation of Adam as Jesus Christ. South Bend, In.,
          Apostolic Publishing Association, 19--. 40p.

5412   Small, Franklin, 1873-1961.
          Living waters; a sure guide for your faith. Winnipeg,
          Man., 19--. 106p. Cover title. KyWAT

5413   Springfield, Melvin R.
          Jesus the almighty; a simplified and easy to understand
          study of God in Christ Jesus, by Melvin R. Springfield. 2d
          ed. Portland, Or., Printed by Parry Mail Advertising Ser-
          vice, 1972. 47p.

5414   Two important questions in life: Is Jesus Christ really com-
          ing again? If he does come, will I be ready to meet him?
          Houston, Search for Truth Publications, c1966. [12]p.
          Cover title.

5415   Unto what were you baptized?
          Houston, Search for Truth Publications, c1968. [12]p.
          Cover title.

5416   Urshan, Andrew bar David, 1884-1967.
          The almighty God in the Lord Jesus Christ [by] Andrew
          D. Urshan. Portland, Or., Apostolic Book Pub., 196-.
          166p. KyWAT

5417   Urshan, Andrew bar David, 1884-1967.
          Apostolic faith doctrine of the new birth [by] Andrew D.
          Urshan. Florissant, Mo., Apostolic Book Publishers, 19--.
          14p.

5418   Urshan, Andrew bar David, 1884-1967.

The doctrine of the new birth; or, The perfect way to
eternal life, as taught by our Lord Himself, proclaimed by
His apostles, confirmed by the Holy Spirit and foreshadowed
by the law and the prophets, by Andrew D. Urshan. Cochrane,
Wi., Witness of God, Publishers, 1921. 48p. Cover title.

5419   Weekes, Robert Dodd, 1819-1898.
        Jehovan-Jesus, the supreme God: son of God, son of
man, by Robert D. Weeks [!]. Edited by C. Haskell Yadon.
Twin Falls, Id., c1952. 115p. First published in 1876
(New York, Dodd, Mead) under title: Jehovah-Jesus: the
oneness of God, the true trinity.

-- --NON-PENTECOSTAL AUTHORS

5420   Miller, Luke, 1904-
        A review of the "Jesus Only" doctrine. Austin, Tx.,
Firm Foundation Publishing House, c1959. 25p. Author's
argument in debate with Bishop S. C. Johnson in Florence,
South Carolina.

--HISTORY

5421   Clanton, Arthur Lee, 1915-
        United we stand: a history of Oneness organizations [by]
Arthur L. Clanton. Hazelwood, Mo., Pentecostal Publishing
House, 1970. 207p.

5422   Ewart, Frank J., 1876-
        The phenomenon of Pentecost: a history of the Latter
Rain. Frank J. Ewart, author; W. E. Kidson, collaborator.
Houston, Herald Publishing House, c1947. 111p. First pub-
lished in 1915. OkEG

5423   Ewart, Frank J., 1876-
        The phenomenon of Pentecost; a history of the Latter
Rain, by Frank J. Ewart. St. Louis, Mo., Pentecostal Publishing House, c1947. 110p. TxWaS

5424   Ewart, Frank J., 1876-
        The phenomenon of Pentecost [by] Frank J. Ewart. Rev.
ed. Hazelwood, Mo., Word Aflame Press, 1975, c1947.
207p.

5425   Foster, Fred J.
        "Think it not strange"; a history of the Oneness move-
ment, by Fred J. Foster. St. Louis, Mo., Pentecostal
Publishing House, 1965. 109p.

--HISTORY AND STUDY OF DOCTRINES

5426   Fauss, Oliver F., 1898-

Buy the truth, and sell it not; the history of the revelation of baptism in the name of Jesus, and of the fulness of God in Christ, by Oliver F. Fauss. Hazelwood, Mo., Pentecostal Publishing House, c1965. 72p.

5427   Goodman, Felicitas Daniels, 1914-
Prognosis: a new religion? [By] Felicitas D. Goodman. In Zaretsky, I. I., ed. Religious movements in contemporary America. Princeton, N.J., c1974, 244-254.

5428   McClain, Samuel C., 1889-1969.
Student's handbook of facts in church history [by] S. C. McClaim. Hazelwood, Mo., Pentecostal Publishing House, 1974. 66p. First issued in 1948.

5429   Moore, Everett Leroy, 1918-
Handbook of Pentecostal denominations in the United States. Pasadena, Ca., 1954. vii, 346ℓ. Thesis (M.A.)--Pasadena College. "Oneness Groups": ℓ. 240-241. CSdP

5430   Reed, David Arthur, 1941-
Aspects of the origins of oneness Pentecostalism [by] David Reed. In Synan, H. V., ed. Aspects of Pentecostal-Chrismatic origins. Plainfield, N.J., 1975, 143-168.

5431   Reed, David Arthur, 1941-
Origins and development of the theology of oneness Pentecostalism in the United States. Boston, 1978. xv, 404ℓ. Thesis (Ph.D.)--Boston University. MBU

5432   Rider, James Donald
The theology of the "Jesus only" movement. Dallas, 1956. x, 227ℓ. Thesis (Th.D.)--Dallas Theological Seminary. TxDaTS

5433   Saunders, Monroe R.
Some historical Pentecostal perspectives for a contemporary developmental Pentecost, by Monroe R. Saunders, Sr. Washington, 1974. 146ℓ. Thesis (D.Min.)--Howard University. DHU

--HYMNS AND SACRED SONGS

5434   Booth-Clibborn, Catherine, 1859-1955.
Songs of salvation by the Maréchale and others. Compiled by Victory Booth-Clibborn; Thoro Harris, assistant editor. Chicago, c1915. [126]p. RPB

5435   Crawford, Mattie
The Pentecostal flame. Los Angeles, God's Hospital Publication Office, 19--. 101p.

5436 Hall, L. C., comp.
Pentecostal praises. ----, 1940. 341p.

5437 Harris, Thoro, 1874-1955, comp.
Full gospel songs. Chicago, 192-. 1v. (unpaged) NN

5438 Harris, Thoro, 1874-1955, ed.
Gospel quintet songs. Chicago, 193-. 1v. (unpaged)
With music.

5439 Harris, Theor, ed., 1874-1955.
Gospel songs. Chicago, c1931. [256]p. With music.
DLC

5440 Harris, Thoro, 1874-1955.
Hymns of hope. Chicago, 1922. 1v. (unpaged) With
music. PPiPT

5441 Harris, Thoro, 1874-1955.
Sing His praise. Chicago, 192-. [202]p. Cover title.
With music. KyLoS

5442 Harris, Thoro, 1874-1955.
Songs of His coming. Chicago, 1915. [256]p. Cover
title. With music. ICN

5443 Harris, Thoro, 1874-1955.
Songs of power. Edited by Thoro Harris. Special con-
tributors: L. C. Hall and J. O. Olsen. Chicago, T. Harris,
c1914. 1v. (unpaged) Cover title. With music (shape notes).
ICN, RPB

5444 Harris, Thoro, 1874-1955.
Songs of power. Edited by Thoro Harris. Special con-
tributors: L. C. Hall and J. O. Olsen. Chicago, T. Harris:
for sale by L. C. Hall; Malvern, Ar., E. N. Bell, c1914.
1v. (unpaged) Cover title. With music. OkBetC

5445 Harris, Thoro, 1874-1955.
Songs of power. Revised and enlarged by L. C. Hall.
Thoro Harris, music ed. Chicago, L. C. Hall, c1914. 1v.
(unpaged) With music. OkBetC

5446 Harris, Thoro, 1874-1955.
Songs of summerland. Prepared in cooperation with
Floyd Humble [by] Thoro Harris. Eureka Springs, Ar.,
c1943. 1v. (unpaged) With music. DLC

5447 Ooton, L. R.
Truth in love songs: faith, hope and charity. Tipton,
In., c1965. 17p.

5448 Pentecostal jewels; choice gospel songs for church services,
revivals, and camp meetings.

Houston, Herald Publishing House, c1945. 1v. (unpaged)
With music (shape notes). DLC

--PERIODICALS

5449   Apostolic call. 1- 194 -
        Evansville, In.

5450   Apostolic herald. 1-20, no. 11, 1926-Nov. 1945.
        Louisiana, Mo., Dallas, Houston, St. Louis. Continued
        as Pentecostal herald.

5451   Apostolic standard. 1- 1968-
        Indianapolis.

5452   Blessed truth. 1- 1915-192-.
        Eureka Springs, Ar.

5453   Endtime messenger. 1- 1966-
        Greenville, S.C., Dallas.

5454   Family circle with memory lane. 1- . -197-.
        Fredericton, N.B. Superseded by Pentecostal family
        Christian digest.

5455   Full gospel expositor. 1- 19 -
        ----.

5456   Gospel echoes. 1- Sept. 1, 1957-
        Boise, Id.

5457   Gospel tidings. 1- 19 -
        San Diego, Ca.

5458   Herald of truth. 1- 1945-
        Houston.

5459   Living word. 1- 19 -
        Minneapolis.

5460   Meat in due season. 1- 1914-
        Los Angeles.

5461   Pentecostal family Christian digest. 1- 1972-
        Fredericton, N.B. Supersedes Family circle with mem-
        ory lane. CaOONL

5462   Pentecostal messenger. 1, 192-.
        Fullerton, La. Merged into Blessed truth.

5463   Pentecostal witness. 1- Nov. 1924-1931.
        Port Arthur, Tx., St. Louis, Newark, Oh. Merged into
        Pentecostal outlook.

5464   Revival broadcast.   1-   195 -
        South Bend, In.

5465   Voice in the wilderness.   1-   Apr. 1910-
        Indianapolis.

5466   Witness of God.   1-   1917-
        Cochrane, Wi., Long Beach, Ca., Indianapolis.

        --SERMONS, TRACTS, ADDRESSES, ESSAYS

5467   Branham, William, 1909-1965.
        The spoken word.   Jeffersonville, In., Spoken Word
        Publications, 1972.   196p.   Reprint of messages originally
        published by Spoken Word Publications as vol. 2, nos. 24-28.

5468   Branham, William, 1909-1965.
        The William Branham sermons: how God called me to
        Africa, and other sermons.   Edited by Gordon Lindsay.
        Dallas, Voice of Healing Publishing Co., 195-.   132p.

5469   Brumley, Don
        What must we do?   By Don Brumley.   Visalia, Ca.,
        19--.   [29]p.

5470   Dyson, Charles R., 1922-
        No continuing city, by Charles R. Dyson.   North Little
        Rock, Ar., c1967.   138p.   Includes sermons by M. D. Pad-
        field, Jr. and Tom Fred Tenney.

5471   Ooton, L. R.
        Sermons from the Sermon on the Mount, by L. R. Ooton.
        Tipton, In., c1970.   43p.   Cover title.

APOSTOLIC ASSEMBLY OF OUR LORD AND SAVIOUR JESUS
    CHRIST (19 -   )

        A black congregation located at 1200 West Girard Avenue in
Philadelphia, the Apostolic Assembly of Our Lord and Saviour Jesus
Christ takes official positions against women preachers, military
service, self-defense, and pride in dress or behavior (beauty par-
lors, straightening of hair, toeless shoes, earrings, finger rings,
television, checkers, football, baseball and golf).   In the early 1970s
Bishop W. M. Selby was pastor and general overseer.

        --DOCTRINAL AND CONTROVERSIAL WORKS

5472   Apostolic Assembly of Our Lord and Saviour Jesus Christ.
        Articles of faith.   Philadelphia, 19--.   [13]p.   Caption
        title.   Processed.

5473   McCoy, Larry F.
         The apostolic way of life, by Larry F. McCoy. Rev.
       ed. Philadelphia, Apostolic Assembly of Our Lord and
       Saviour Jesus Christ, 1970. 1v. (unpaged)

5474   Selby, W. M., bp.
         Apostolic facts: who is this that defies and challenges
       the whole religious world on these subjects? Philadelphia,
       Apostolic Assembly of Our Lord and Saviour Jesus Christ,
       19--. 24p. Cover title.

APOSTOLIC CHURCH (1945-)

       The Apostolic Church was organized March 1, 1945, in Bay
City, Texas. According to R. L. Blankenship, the founder and general bishop, the new body became necessary because of church poli-
tics in older groups. In 1954 Blankenship reported between 200 and
300 affiliated ministers. At that time the Apostolic Church Evangel
was being issued monthly "or as often as it seems proper and fit
for the betterment of the church."

5475   Apostolic Church.
         Doctrine and discipline of the Apostolic Church. Bay
       City, Tx., Apostolic Publishers, 19--. 29p.

         --HISTORY

5476   Moore, Everett Leroy, 1918-
         Handbook of Pentecostal denominations in the United States.
       Pasadena, Ca., 1954. vii, 346ℓ. Thesis (M.A.)--Pasadena
       College. "Apostolic Church": ℓ. 270-277. CSdP

         --PERIODICALS

5477   Apostolic Church evangel. 1- 194 -
         Bay City, Tx.

         --SERMONS, TRACTS, ADDRESSES, ESSAYS

5478   Blankenship, R. L.
         Should sinners tithe? By R. L. Blankenship. Bay City,
       Tx., 19--. 7p.

APOSTOLIC CHURCH OF JESUS (1927-)

       Among the converts of Mattie Crawford, an evangelist who

in 1923 visited Pueblo, Colorado, was Antonio Sanches. Soon Antonio's brother, George, was converted also, and together they preached to fellow Spanish-speaking residents, gathering enough followers to organize the Apostolic Church of Jesus in 1927. The group obtained legal incorporation nine years later. The church teaches that the "three-god" or trinitarian doctrine is an error inherited from Roman Catholicism. Led by Raymond P. Virgil, the 300-member denomination consists of bilingual congregations in Pueblo, Trinidad, Walsenburg, Fort Garland, San Luis, Colorado Springs, Denver, and Westminster, Colorado; Verlarge, New Mexico; and San Francisco and Palo Alto, California.

--PERIODICALS

5479   Jesus-only news of the apostolic faith.   19 -
        Pueblo, Co.

APOSTOLIC CHURCH OF JESUS CHRIST (1928-1931)

        Organized in 1928, the Apostolic Church of Jesus Christ was the result of the union of the Emmanuel's Church in Jesus Christ and the Apostolic Churches of Jesus Christ, two of three groups formed four years earlier when many whites left the interracial Pentecostal Assemblies of the World. Headed during its brief history by Oliver F. Fauss and A. H. Beisner, the church was in effect an association of ministers, who by their own membership brought the congregations they served into affiliation. In December 1929, the Pentecostal Witness reported 236 member clergy, 69 percent of whom resided in the states of Texas, Louisiana, Missouri, and Illinois. The next year headquarters, the location of which was determined by the residence of the secretary, moved from St. Louis to Akron. On November 18, 1931, despite opposition from both sides, the Apostolic Church of Jesus Christ and the Pentecostal Assemblies of the World united to form the Pentecostal Assemblies of Jesus Christ.

--HISTORY

5480   Clanton, Arthur Lee, 1915-
        United we stand: a history of Oneness organizations [by]
        Arthur L. Clanton. Hazelwood, Mo., Pentecostal Publishing
        House, 1970. 207p. "The Apostolic Church of Jesus Christ":
        p. 62-69.

--PERIODICALS

5481   Pentecostal witness. 1- Nov. 1924-1931.
        Port Arthur, Tx., St. Louis, Newark, Oh. Merged into
        Pentecostal outlook.

APOSTOLIC CHURCH OF JESUS CHRIST INTERNATIONAL (19 -)

The Apostolic Church of Jesus Christ International holds
membership in the Apostolic World Christian Fellowship.   Bishop
E. G. Valverde of Salinas, California is denominational chairman.

APOSTOLIC CHURCH OF JESUS CHRIST SEVENTH DAY (19 -)

Consisting of a single congregation of fifty or sixty members
in Durant, Oklahoma, the Apostolic Church of Jesus Christ Seventh
Day observes Saturday as the sabbath as its name implies.   Other
distinctive teachings include baptism by immersion in the name of
Jesus Christ and the annual observance of Passover with foot washing as instituted by Christ.   The church publishes the Old Paths
and broadcasts under the same name over a local radio station.

--PERIODICALS

5482   Old paths.   1-   19 -
        Durant, Ok.

APOSTOLIC CHURCH OF PENTECOST OF CANADA (1921-)

On October 25, 1921, Franklin Small and ten others formerly
affiliated with the infant Pentecostal Assemblies of Canada obtained
a Dominion charter as the Apostolic Church of Pentecost of Canada.
The petitioners, which included both clergy and laity, were all committed to the oneness of the Godhead, a position strictly adhered to
by the Apostolic Church of Pentecost for the next thirty-two years.
Union in 1953 with the Evangelical Churches of Pentecost, which included many believers in the tri-unity of the Godhead, resulted in
tolerance of both points of view.   As a result baptism in the name
of Jesus and the eternal security of the believer became principal
emphases.

Membership is concentrated in the prairie provinces.   Headquarters are in Saskatoon, Saskatchewan.   In 1978 the Apostolic
Church of Pentecost reported 120 congregations and 209 clergy.   The
denomination sponsors the Full Gospel Bible Institute, Eston, Saskatchewan, and the Full Gospel Indian Bible School, Fort Qu'Appelle,
Saskatchewan, and supports missionaries in Brazil, Mexico, Guatemala, El Salvador, Ghana, Ivory Coast, Upper Volta, Malawi, South
Africa, Zimbabwe, Israel, India, Taiwan, and Japan.   In 1979 it
spent $255,000 overseas, and had 60 North American workers in
the field.

5483   Apostolic Church of Pentecost of Canada.

General bylaws and articles of faith. Rev. ed. Saskatoon, Sask., 1965.

5484   From the prairie.
       In Christianity Today, 9 (July 2, 1965), 37. On the an-
       nual meeting of the Apostolic Church of Pentecost of Canada.

--DOCTRINAL AND CONTROVERSIAL WORKS

5485   McLean, Glen S.
       Can a genuine believer be lost? By Glen S. McLean.
       Eston, Sask., Full Gospel Bible Institute Press, 19--.

--HISTORY

5486   Larden, Robert A., 1929-
       Our Apostolic heritage [by] Robert A. Larden. [Saska-
       toon, Sask.], Apostolic Church of Pentecost of Canada, 1971.
       192p.

--PERIODICALS

5487   Apostolic advocate. 1- 1926-1927.
       Winnipeg, Man.

5488   Apostolic news. 1- 194 -
       ----.

5489   End times messenger. 1- 1936-
       Regina, Sask., Saskatoon, Sask. 1936-1957 as End times.

5490   Harvest time. 1- 1959-
       Moose Jaw, Sask.

5491   Living waters. 1- 1922-
       Winnipeg, Man.

5492   Missionary messenger. 1- 1950-1957.
       Saskatoon, Sask. Merged with End times to form End
       times messenger.

APOSTOLIC CHURCHES OF JESUS CHRIST (1925-1928)

One of three white groups formed in 1925 in the wake of the
breakup of the interracial Pentecostal Assemblies of the World, the
Apostolic Churches of Jesus Christ was led by W. H. Whittington
and Ben Pemberton. The movement centered in St. Louis where its
official paper, the Apostolic Messenger was published. On October

31, 1928, the Apostolic Churches of Jesus Christ merged with the Emmanuel's Church in Jesus Christ. Apostolic Church of Jesus Christ, the name chosen for the united body, had been the popular designation of the St. Louis-based group all along.

--PERIODICALS

5493   Apostolic messenger. 1- 1925-1928.
        St. Louis.

APOSTOLIC FAITH CHURCH (1924-)

In 1923 Charles and Ada Lochbaum, who had received the baptism in the Holy Spirit a few years before in California, moved to Hawaii. The next year, following a series of tent revivals throughout the islands, they erected a building in the Kaimuki district of Honolulu and founded the first branch of the Apostolic Faith Church. Additional centers were later established in Lahaina, Kahului, Kaunakakai, and Hilo.

Because the names of all believers who receive baptism in the name of Jesus are written in heaven, membership rolls are not kept. The church teaches that victory over sickness has been provided in the atonement. As a result, the Lord's Supper, which is always observed at night, brings healing to all who in partaking "discern the Lord's body." Unlike many similar groups, the Apostolic Faith Church regards conscientious objection to war as disloyalty. A five-member board, which succeeded Charles Lochbaum as trustee in 1959, directs the movement from headquarters offices in the Kalihi district of Honolulu.

--PERIODICALS

5494   Kingdom of God crusader. 1- 195 -
        Honolulu. OkTOr

APOSTOLIC GOSPEL CHURCH OF JESUS CHRIST (1963-)

In 1963 Donald Abernathy organized the First Apostolic Gospel Church in Bell Gardens, a suburb of Los Angeles. Five years later Abernathy drew national attention to himself by reporting a series of visions in which God revealed to him that the entire west coast of North America would soon fall into the ocean as the result of an earthquake. Because the Los Angeles area would be most vulnerable, he advised his followers, which by 1968 included four additional congregations in southern California, to flee eastward to safety. As a result, the group in Avenal moved to Kennett, Missouri; the group in Porterville, to Independence, Missouri; the group in Port Hueneme to Murfreesboro, Tennessee; and the groups in Lompoc and Bell Gardens to Georgia, the latter to Atlanta.   With a combined membership of 540 at the time of migration, the relocated congregations keep contact by letter, telephone, and occasional meetings.   Members depend upon divine intervention for bodily healing to the exclusion of medicine, physicians, and hospitals.   They refrain from taking up arms or supporting those who do.   And they adhere to strict standards of dress and conduct, eschewing the wearing of bathing suits, form-fitting and immodest apparel, jewelry, and contemporary hair styles for both men and women.   Headquarters of the Apostolic Gospel Church of Jesus Christ, also known as Bible Apostolic Churches, are in Atlanta.

5495   Apostolic Gospel Church of Jesus Christ.
           By-laws of the Apostolic Gospel Church of Jesus Christ.
        n. p. , 19--.

        --HISTORY

5496   Run for your life.
           In Time, 92 (Sept. 13, 1968), 58.

ASSEMBLIES OF THE LORD JESUS CHRIST (1952-   )

        In March 1952 at Memphis, Tennessee, the Assemblies of the Church of Jesus Christ, the Jesus Only Apostolic Church of God, and the Church of the Lord Jesus Christ united in a single, racially integrated body, the Assemblies of the Lord Jesus Christ.   Distinctive teachings include opposition to bearing of arms, to membership in any organization which enforces any policy contrary to individual conscience, and to shows, dancing, theatrical performances, and immodest athletic attire in the public schools.   Headquarters and the editorial offices of the Apostolic Witness are in Memphis.   In 1964 the Assemblies of the Lord Jesus Christ had work in 22 states and four foreign countries.   That year it reported 120 churches and 6, 300 members.

5497   Assemblies of the Lord Jesus Christ.
           Constitution--rules--articles of faith.   Rev. ed.   Memphis, Apostolic Publishing House, 1965.

        --PERIODICALS

5498   Apostolic witness.   1-   1952-
           Memphis.   OkTOr

ASSOCIATED BROTHERHOOD OF CHRISTIANS (1933-   )
[1933-194- as Associated Ministers of Jesus Christ.]

The Associated Ministers of Jesus Christ was organized under the leadership of E. E. Partridge and H. A. Riley near Thomas-
town, Mississippi, in 1933. Apparently the inability of the founders
to obtain ministerial credentials in other bodies led to formation of
the new body. To gain exemption from military service the group
incorporated as the Associated Brotherhood of Christians in the
early 1940s. A distinctive teaching of the Brotherhood is that true
communion in the Body of Christ is in the Holy Spirit, not in the
elements of bread and wine. Hence, it refrains from observing the
Lord's Supper. In time of war, members register either as conscientious objectors or as non-combatants. Headquarters for the
Brotherhood, which in the early 1970s included 40 churches, about
100 ministers, and 2,000 members in six states, are in Hot Springs,
Arkansas. The official periodical, Our Herald, is published in
Wilmington, California. The Associated Brotherhood of Christians
holds membership in the Apostolic World Christian Fellowship.

5499   Associated Brotherhood of Christians.
        Articles of faith of the Associated Brotherhood of Chris-
        tians. n.p., 1958. 17p.

        --HISTORY

5500   Moore, Everett Leroy, 1918-
        Handbook of Pentecostal denominations in the United
        States. Pasadena, Ca., 1954. vii, 346ℓ. Thesis (M.A.)--
        Pasadena College. "Associated Brotherhood of Christians":
        ℓ. 281-288. CSdP

        --PERIODICALS

5501   Our herald. 1- 19 -
        Wilmington, Ca.

ASSOCIATION OF SEVENTH DAY PENTECOSTAL ASSEMBLIES
    (1931-   )

Dating from 1931 as an informal fellowship, the Association
of Seventh Day Pentecostal Assemblies remained unincorporated until
1967. The principle of local autonomy is held inviolate and no attempt is made by headquarters in Vancouver, Washington to control
either pastors or members of affiliated churches. Stress is laid on
observance of Saturday as the true sabbath and on baptism by immersion. Although the Association has no stated position in the Oneness/
Trinitarian debate, no minister in the group now holds to an explicitly

Trinitarian position. Work is directed by a seven-man coordinating committee whose members reside in Washington, Oregon, California, and British Columbia. The group sponsors an annual camp meeting at Turner, Oregon. Affiliated assemblies support work in Ghana and Nigeria. The Voice of Truth was at one time published by the group.

--PERIODICALS

5502   Voice of truth.   1-   19 -
        ----.

AUSTRALIAN CHRISTIAN FELLOWSHIP (19 -   )

The Australian Christian Fellowship, whose president is Bishop Bruce Jamieson of St. Peters, New South Wales, holds membership in the Apostolic World Christian Fellowship.

BETHEL APOSTOLIC CHURCH OF THE PENTECOSTAL MOVEMENT ASSOCIATION (19 -   )

In 1980 the Bethel Apostolic Church of the Pentecostal Movement Association, a black body with headquarters in Chicago, held membership in the Apostolic Christian World Fellowship. At that time Bishop D. McCollough was president.

BIBLE WAY CHURCHES OF OUR LORD JESUS CHRIST WORLD WIDE (1957-   )

Formed during a ministers conference in Washington, D. C. , in 1957, the Bible Way Churches of Our Lord Jesus Christ World Wide was organized as the result of widespread complaints of authoritarianism in the Church of Our Lord Jesus Christ of the Apostolic Faith. Elders Smallwood E. Williams, John S. Beane, McKinley Williams, Winfield Showell, and Joseph Moore, and approximately seventy congregations which followed them, were concerned with reform of church government. The theology of the new group is identical to that of the parent. Members are required to attend all church business meetings, and to be present each time the Holy Communion is celebrated. Although the Bible Way Churches require tithing and condemn use of tobacco and alcohol and remarriage of divorced persons while their original partners live, they reject as fanaticism teaching which forbids the straightening and shampooing of hair and the wearing of neckties or shoes without toes or heels. Headquarters offices, a Bible training school, the publishing house, and the residence of Smallwood E. Williams, presiding bishop, are in

Washington, D. C.   In 1970 the denomination reported 350 churches
and 30,000 members.   At that time it was sponsoring work in Jamaica, Trinidad, Tobago, Liberia, and the United Kingdom.   The
Bible Way Churches hold membership in the Apostolic World Christian Fellowship.

--HISTORY

5503   Williams, Smallwood Edmond, 1907-
            Brief history and doctrine of the Bible Way Churches of
        Our Lord Jesus Christ World Wide.   Smallwood, E. Williams,
        ed.   Washington, 195-.   24p.   Cover title.   MoSCEx

--PERIODICALS

5504   Bible Way news voice.   1-   1942-
            Washington.   To 19-- as Bible Way news.

5505   Youth herald.   1-   19 -
            Washington.

--SERMONS, TRACTS, ADDRESSES, ESSAYS

5506   Williams, Smallwood Edmond, bp., 1907-
            Singificant sermons.   Washington, Bible Way Church,
        1970.   164p.   DLC

CHRIST GOSPEL CHURCHES INTERNATIONAL (1963-   )

        In 1963 William Branham, noted healing evangelist, received
by divine revelation knowledge that the "End Time Messenger who
was the Angel to the Seventh Church Age" was present on earth in
the "spirit of Elijah."   Although the evangelist failed to name the
Messenger, his followers believed Branham to be it.   Upon indication from Branham that the Messenger demanded abandonment of denominationalism, the faithful organized the Christ Gospel Churches
International.   Two congregations: the Branham Tabernacle of Jeffersonville, Indiana, and the Tucson Tabernacle of Tucson, Arizona,
led the movement, and following the founder's death on Christmas
Eve 1965, Pearry Green, pastor of the Tucson congregation, assumed leadership.   Green, who visited more than ninety countries
in spreading Branham's message, has reported that in the United
States alone there are more than 300 ministers who believe the de-
ceased evangelist to be the prophet foretold in Malachi 4.   Branham's
followers devote themselves to publishing and distributing his writings.
Some regard his taped sermons as "oral scripture."

--DOCTRINAL AND CONTROVERSIAL WORKS

5507   Branham, William, 1909-1965.
          Conduct, order, doctrine of the church [by] William Mer-
        rion Branham. Jeffersonville, In., Spoken Word Publications,
        1973-1974. 2v. OkTOr

5508   Branham, William, 1909-1965.
          An exposition of the seven church ages, by William Mar-
        rion Branham. Tucson, Az., 197-. 381p. IRA, OSteC,
        OUrC

5509   Branham, William, 1909-1965.
          The revelation of the seven seals, as given to our pre-
        cious brother William Marrion Branham. Tucson, Az.,
        Spoken Word Publications, 196-. 579p. IRA

5510   Branham, William, 1909-1965.
          The spoken word. Jeffersonville, In., Spoken Word Pub-
        lications, 1972. 196p. Reprint of messages originally pub-
        lished by Spoken Word Publications as vol. 2, nos. 24-28.

--PERIODICALS

5511   Christ Gospel messenger. 1- May/June 1963-
          Jeffersonville, In. OkTOr

CHRISTIAN MISSION APOSTOLIC CHURCHES (19 -)

In 1972 W. L. Pye of Philadelphia was bishop of the Northern
Diocese of the Christian Mission Apostolic Churches. At that time Pye,
who was also pastor of the Mount Airy Apostolic Temple, held membership in the Apostolic Ministers Conference of Philadelphia and
Vicinity.

CHURCH OF GOD:

Apostolic Overcoming Holy Church of God (1917-)
[1917-1927 as Ethiopian Overcoming Holy Church of God.]

In 1916 W. T. Phillips, who had been won to the "holiness"
message and ordained by Frank W. Williams three years earlier in
Birmingham, began his career as an evangelist. In March the next
year at Mobile, Alabama, "the Holy Ghost in a body of elders" set
him apart as bishop of the Ethiopian Overcoming Holy Church of
God. The church was incorporated in 1920. Centering in the founder's

own congregation, the Greater Adams Holiness Church of Mobile,
the denomination (re-named the Apostolic Overcoming Holy Church
of God in 1927) was during his lifetime dominated by him as well.
In the early years worship was, outside observers said, simply cha-
otic; institutional development, retarded. Distinctive practices include foot washing as an ordinance and recognition of the equality of
women in the church. Members are forbidden to marry unconverted
persons and to attend services in other churches which are held at
the same hour as those of the Apostolic Overcoming Holy Church of
God. Missionary projects previously sponsored in India, Africa,
and the Caribbean have been abandoned. In 1975, however, three
American workers were sent to Haiti and approximately $50,000 was
raised for work there. In 1956 the denomination claimed 300
churches and 75,000 members. Although branches are located in
nearly every state, membership is concentrated in Alabama, Kentucky, Illinois, Oklahoma, and Texas. Although the two bodies have
no formal connection, the wording of official statements on many
key issues in the disciplines of the Apostolic Overcoming Holy Church
of God and the Church of God (Apostolic) is identical or nearly so.

5512   Apostolic Overcoming Holy Church of God.
         Manual of the Apostolic Overcoming Holy Church of God,
         Inc., founded upon the apostles doctrine: we believe in the
         one true God, Father, Son and Holy Ghost. Read it! To
         know it! Mobile, Al., A. O. H. Church Publishing House,
         196-. 56p. Cover title. MoSCEx

        --HISTORY

5513   Moore, Everett Leroy, 1918-
         Handbook of Pentecostal denominations in the United
         States. Pasadena, Ca., 1954. vii, 346ℓ. Thesis (M. A.)--
         Pasadena College. "Apostolic Overcoming Holy Church of
         God": ℓ. 277-281. CSdP

5514   Phillips, William Thomas, bp., 1893-
         Excerpts from the life of Rt. Rev. W. T. Phillips and
         fundamentals of the Apostolic Overcoming Holy Church of God,
         Inc. Mobile, Al., A. O. H. Church Publishing House, 1967.
         14p.

5515   U. S. Bureau of the Census.
         Census of religious bodies: 1926. Apostolic Overcoming
         Holy Church of God. Statistics, denominational history, doc-
         trine, and organization. Washington, Government Printing
         Office, 1929. 7p. DLC, NNUT

        --PERIODICALS

5516   People's mouthpiece. 1- 19 -
         Mobile, Al.

CHURCH OF GOD (APOSTOLIC) (1897-   )
[1897-1915 as Christian Faith Band.]

In 1897 Elder Thomas J. Cox organized the Christian Faith
Band in Danville, Kentucky, incorporating the body under that name
four years later. Seeking a "more scriptural" name, the group
chose the present title in 1915, but delayed legal incorporation under
it until 1919 because of internal opposition to the change. The
Church of God (Apostolic) teaches the unity of the Godhead and administers baptism in the name of the Lord Jesus. Although it be-
lieves in divine healing, it "does not condemn those who are weak
in faith for using medicine." Women are ordained to the ministry.
The church upholds obedience to the law, but not "in war, nor going
to war." Instantaneous sanctification, it says, will be made evident
in godly living.

The general overseer or apostle, who is also senior bishop,
presides over the general assembly, which is the highest authority.
Headquarters of the Church of God (Apostolic), which in the early
1970s claimed approximately 1,000 members, are in Winston-Salem,
North Carolina. The twenty-five churches are located in Florida,
Georgia, North and South Carolina, Virginia, West Virginia, Pennsylvania, New York, and Michigan. Bishop David E. Smith, general
overseer, lives in Beckley, West Virginia. Similarities in the wording of key passages in the disciplines of the Church of God (Apostolic) and of the Apostolic Overcoming Holy Church of God are coin-
cidental, he says.

5517   Church of God (Apostolic)
            Discipline of the Church of God (Apostolic), Inc.   Beck-
        ley, W. Va., 194-.   40p.

5518   U. S. Bureau of the Census.
            Census of religious bodies: 1926.   Church of God
        (Apostolic).   Statistics, denominational history, doctrine,
        and organization.   Washington, U. S. Government Printing
        Office, 1928.   7p.   DLC

CHURCH OF GOD OF THE APOSTOLIC FAITH ASSOCIATION
(19 -   )

In 1973 the Church of God of the Apostolic Faith Association
held membership in the Apostolic World Christian Fellowship. B. L.
Lumpkins, its presiding bishop, was treasurer of the Fellowship at
that time.

CHURCHES OF GOD IN IRELAND (1955-   )

Formed in 1955, the Churches of God in Ireland, whose
chairman is James Connolly of Belfast, holds membership in the
Apostolic World Christian Fellowship. The movement, which in

1960 included more than 1, 200 who had been baptized in Jesus's name, was established under the leadership of Gordon Magee.   In 1957 Magee married the daughter of W. E. Kidson.   Three years later he migrated to the United States to succeed his father-in-law as pastor of the Houston Gospel Tabernacle.

--DOCTRINAL AND CONTROVERSIAL WORKS

5519   Magee, Gordon
       Is Jesus in the Godhead or is the Godhead in Jesus?
       Pasadena, Tx., 19--.   32p.   Cover title.   Includes "address
       of appreciation" presented to the author upon his departure
       from Ireland: p. 2.

--PERIODICALS

5520   Standard of truth.   1-   1945-
       Ballymena, Northern Ireland.   1945-1946 as Standard
       of truth and call to Pentecost.

CHURCH OF JESUS CHRIST (1927-   )

       The Church of Jesus Christ was founded by M. K. Lawson
in 1927.   Although it claims to be engaged in widespread missionary
work, the principle function of the organization appears to be the
licensing and ordaining of ministers.   Candidates pay for credentials.
In 1975 the headquarters moved to Kingsport from Cleveland, Tennessee.   Five hundred affiliated clergy serve congregations with a
combined membership of approximately 37,500.   Local churches in
some instances modify the name.   The congregation at Stanton, Delaware, for instance, is called Full Gospel Church of Jesus Christ.

--HISTORY

5521   Sapp, R. W.
       Upon this rock I will build my church: the Church of
       Jesus Christ, by R. W. Sapp.   n.p., c1976.   50p.   Cover
       title.   GStG

--PERIODICALS

5522   Messenger.   1-   19 -

--DELAWARE (Stanton)

5523   Jackson, Deborah Bird Rose

The Full Gospel Church of Jesus Christ: a description
and analysis. Newark, 1973. 59ℓ. Thesis (B.A.)--University of Delaware. DeU

CHURCH OF JESUS CHRIST (194 -   )

In the late 1940s some members of the Tennessee-based
Church of Jesus Christ in Indiana and Illinois withdrew and incorporated another body of the same name. After thirty years of separate existence, the new group consisted of twelve ministers and
about 500 members. Its leader at that time was Bishop Ralph Johnson of Bloomington, Indiana.

CHURCH OF JESUS CHRIST MINISTERIAL ALLIANCE (1962-   )

In 1962 disagreement over ministerial courtesy at the time
of Bishop M. K. Lawson's death led to the withdrawal of many ministers and churches from the Tennessee-based Church of Jesus
Christ. No doctrinal issues were at stake in the organization of
the Church of Jesus Christ Ministerial Alliance. The organization
affiliated with the Apostolic World Christian Fellowship. In 1975 it
took the first steps toward reunion with the parent body. At that
time its constituency included 300 ministers, 85 churches, and about
6,000 members. Bishop J. Richard Lee of Portage, Indiana, was
chairman.

CHURCH OF JESUS CHRIST OF GEORGIA (196 -   )

Except for its condemnation of remarriage after divorce
among clergy, the Church of Jesus Christ of Georgia is identical
in all respects to its Tennessee-based parent. Formed in the 1960s,
the two-congregation denomination insists that divorced converts
either return to their original partners or live as single persons.
Four ministers serve a membership of less than a hundred. The
group is headed by Elder Wilbur Childers of Ranger, Georgia.

CHURCH OF OUR LORD JESUS CHRIST OF THE APOSTOLIC
   FAITH (1918-   )
[1918-1931 as Refuge Churches of Our Lord.]

In 1919 the center of activity of the Refuge Churches of Our
Lord, founded the previous year in Columbus, Ohio, shifted to New
York City. At that time Bishop R. C. Lawson, founder of the denomination, opened the Refuge Church of Christ of the Apostolic
Faith in the heart of Harlem, a congregation regarded henceforth

as the headquarters church.   The present name was adopted at the
time of incorporation in 1931.   A major setback occurred in 1957
when seventy congregations followed Elder Smallwood E. Williams
of Washington, D. C. into the Bible Way Churches of Our Lord Jesus
Christ World Wide.   Alleged authoritarianism rather than doctrinal
differences lay behind the dispute.   In fact the Church of Our Lord
Jesus Christ of the Apostolic Faith, itself a splinter of the Pentecostal Assemblies of the World, the oldest Oneness body, differs in
no doctrinal essential with either its parent or its offspring.   In
1954, three years before the Williams-led defection, the church reported 155 congregations and 45,000 members.

5524   Church of Our Lord Jesus Christ of the Apostolic Faith.
            Discipline book of the Church of Our Lord Jesus Christ
        of the Apostolic Faith.   Edited by R. C. Lawson.   New
        York, Church of Christ Printing and Publishing, 1955.   129p.

            --DOCTRINAL AND CONTROVERSIAL WORKS

5525   Lawson, Robert Clarence, bp. , 1883-1961.
            An open letter upon the burning question of marriage and
        divorce, by R. C. Lawson.   Columbus, Oh. , Contender for
        the Faith, 19--.   40p.

5526   Long, C. L.
            Showers of blessing, by C. L. Long.   Washington,
        Greater Scripture Church of Christ, 1979.   34p.

            --HISTORY

5527   Moore, Everett Leroy, 1918-
            Handbook of Pentecostal denominations in the United States.
        Pasadena, Ca. , 1954.   vii, 346ℓ.   Thesis (M. A.)--Pasadena
        College.   "Church of Our Lord Jesus Christ of the Apostolic
        Faith":   ℓ. 289-290.   CSdP

            --PERIODICALS

5528   Apostles' newsletter.   1-   1973-
            New York.

5529   Contender for the Faith.   1-   1918-
            Columbus, Oh. , New York.

CHURCH OF THE LITTLE CHILDREN (1916-   )

        In 1916, having withdrawn from the Baptist ministry because

of doctrinal differences, John Quincy Adams founded the Church of the Little Children in Abbott, Texas. Sometime in the 1930s Adams moved his base of operations to Gunn, Alberta, where in 1951 he died. His wife, who succeeded him as superintendent, returned to the United States, remarried, and settled in Black Rock, Arkansas. Although beginning in 1936 the whole movement met periodically "in congregation," the assemblies no longer are held because of the expense involved. Instead the superintendent maintains a tract ministry by mail. The fellowship holds no property. The eight congregations which have been established in Arkansas, Missouri, Nebraska, Wyoming, Montana, and Saskatchewan, all meet in the homes of members. Combined membership is less than one hundred. The church follows the Bible literally as interpreted by John Quincy Adams. It condemns Trinitarianism, the observance of Sunday as the sabbath, the celebration of Christmas and Easter, the wearing of neckties and the shaving of men's beards, and the use of names of days and months derived from the names of pagan deities, all as vestiges of the phallic worship of Babylon. For believers Christian rites such as baptism in the name of Jesus, frequent observance of the Lord's Supper using unleavened bread and wine, foot washing on the monthly sabbath, speaking in unknown tongues, substitute for pagan-inspired practices. Service in behalf of children who suffer want or hunger is mandatory, as is conscientious objection to military service.

--DOCTRINAL AND CONTROVERSIAL WORKS

5530   Adams, John Quincy, 1891-1951.
        Babylon: just what is it? Gunn, Alta. , 1938.

5531   Adams, John Quincy, 1891-1951.
        Christmas means slaughter. Black Rock, Ar. , Gathering
        Call, 1953.

5532   Adams, John Quincy, 1891-1951.
        Wake up to phallus worship. Gunn, Atla. , Gathering
        Call, 1941.

--PERIODICALS

5533   Gathering call. 1- 19 -
        Gunn, Alta. , Black Rock, Ar.

CHURCH OF THE LIVING GOD, THE PILLAR AND GROUND OF THE TRUTH (1898-   )

Established in 1898 at Cincinnati, the Church of the Living God, the Pillar and Ground of the Truth has been led successively by Bishop F. Ferguson of Cincinnati, Bishop Hood of Chicago, and

Bishop J. W. Woods of Baton Rouge.   Headquarters are in Hammond,
Louisiana.   In 1974 the denomination reported 2,000 members.   At
that time churches were located in New Orleans, Baton Rouge, and
Logansport, Louisiana; Gloster, Mississippi; University City, Missouri; and Cincinnati, Ohio.   Distinctive teachings include baptism
in the name of Jesus according to Acts 2:38, and observance of the
seventh-day sabbath, sunset to sunset.

CHURCH OF THE LORD JESUS CHRIST OF THE APOSTOLIC FAITH (1919-   )

In 1919 Bishop S. C. Johnson, a native of Edgecomb County,
North Carolina, began preaching at 1524 South 17th Street, Philadelphia.   From this beginning grew a substantial congregation, which
on February 28, 1960 dedicated a commodious new edifice at 22d
and Bainbridge Streets.   More crucial in attracting followers, however, was the pastor's radio ministry.   At the time of his death in
1961, Bishop Johnson was being heard weekly over a network of
over seventy church-owned stations in the United States and abroad.
The founder's teaching, which included condemnation of cosmetics,
moving pictures, radio (except his own program), television, smoking and drinking, is continued verbatim by his disciple and successor, Bishop S. McDowell Shelton, who is at times referred to as
"His Excellency" or "His Eminence."   As a result of the radio outreach, branch churches sprang up throughout the United States and
in several foreign countries.   At the time of its 30th National and
4th International Convention in 1963, the Church of the Lord Jesus
Christ of the Apostolic Faith listed 35 affiliates in eighteen states
of the union and seven in five foreign countries.   The headquarters
church in Philadelphia remains the nerve center of the movement.

--DOCTRINAL AND CONTROVERSIAL WORKS

5534   Johnson, Sherrod C. , bp. , 1897-1961.
        The Christmas spirit is a false-spirit, by S. C. Johnson.
        Philadelphia, Church of the Lord Jesus Christ of the Apos-
        tolic Faith, 19--.   folder (6p.)

5535   Johnson, Sherrod C. , bp. , 1897-1961.
        False Lent and pagan festivals, by S. C. Johnson.
        Philadelphia, Church of the Lord Jesus Christ of the Apos-
        tolic Faith, 19--.

5536   Johnson, Sherrod C. , bp. , 1897-1961.
        Is Jesus Christ the son of God now?   Written by S. C.
        Johnson, now being delivered by Bishop S. McDowell Shelton.
        Philadelphia, S. M. Shelton, 19--.   8p.

5537   Johnson, Sherrod C. , bp. , 1897-1961.
        21 burning subjects: who is this that defies and chal-

lenges the whole religious world on these subjects? Written
by S. C. Johnson, [now being delivered by Bishop S. McDowell Shelton]. Philadelphia, Church of the Lord Jesus Christ
of the Apostolic Faith, 196-. 24p. OkTOr

5538   Shelton, S. McDowell, bp. , 1929-
          Let patience have her perfect work. Philadelphia,
        Church of the Lord Jesus Christ of the Apostolic Faith,
        1964. 12p.

-- --NON-PENTECOSTAL AUTHORS

5539   Miller, Luke, 1904-
          A review of the "Jesus Only" doctrine. Austin, Tx. ,
        Firm Foundation Publishing House, c1959. 25p. Author's
        argument in debate with Bishop S. C. Johnson in Florence,
        South Carolina.

--HISTORY

5540   Church of Jesus Christ of the Apostolic Faith.
          Church yearbook and radio history, by S. C. Johnson.
        Philadelphia, 1957. 47p.

5541   Church of the Lord Jesus Christ of the Apostolic Faith.
          Pictorial account of 1963. Philadelphia, 1964. 1v.
        (unpaged) Cover title.

--PERIODICALS

5542   B. S. 1, no. 1-5, 196-.
          Philadelphia. Bible study written by Bishop S. McDowell
        Shelton.

5543   Whole truth. 1- 1947-
          Philadelphia. KU-RH, WiH

COOPERATIVE AGENCIES:

        Apostolic Ministers Conference of Philadelphia and Vicinity
          (1972-   )

        Organized in January 1972, the Apostolic Ministers Conference
of Philadelphia and Vicinity was designed to serve as a means of
fellowship for nine or ten black ministers and their congregations.
Beginning in February that year a combined monthly meeting was
held. The place of meeting changed each month. Bishop Robert
O. Doub served as first president.

5544   Apostolic Ministers Conference of Philadelphia and Vicinity.
        Program book: "Apostolic Day," June 10th, [1972], be-
ing held [at] Blue Horizon, 1314 Broad Street, Phila., Pa.
... Sponsored by Apostolic Ministers Conference of Philadelphia & Vicinity. Philadelphia, 1972. 4[12]p. Cover title.
Processed.

APOSTOLIC WORLD CHRISTIAN FELLOWSHIP (1972-   )

        Formed in 1972, the Apostolic World Christian Fellowship
provides a forum for communication among Oneness organizations.
At the end of its second year of existence, the Fellowship reported
21 member bodies in six countries.   Notable for absence from the
roster of members is the large United Pentecostal Church International.   Headquarters are in South Bend, Indiana, where an international congress is held each May.

                    --PERIODICALS

5545   Clarion.   1-   1979-
        South Bend, In.

EMMANUEL PENTECOSTAL CHURCH OF OUR LORD--APOSTOLIC
    FAITH (19 -   )

        The Emmanuel Pentecostal Church of Our Lord--Apostolic
Faith holds membership in the Apostolic World Christian Fellowship.
M. R. Jackson of Detroit is presiding bishop.

EMMANUEL'S CHURCH IN JESUS CHRIST (1925-1928)

        Organized October 21-23, 1925, during the Trio States Camp
Meeting in Houston, Texas, Emmanuel's Church in Jesus Christ
was one of three white bodies formed that year as the result of a
crisis in the interracial Pentecostal Assemblies of the World.   Although the new church made provision for blacks, decision-making
rested in the hands of a twelve-man, all-white board.   Emmanuel's
Church in Jesus Christ took control of the Pentecostal Witness, a
paper begun a year earlier as the official organ of the Texas District of the Pentecostal Assemblies of the World.   In 1927 negotiations began between the Emmanuel's Church in Jesus Christ and the
Apostolic Churches of Jesus Christ, which resulted in merger of
the two bodies in October the next year.

                    --HISTORY

5546   Clanton, Arthur Lee, 1915-

United we stand: a short history of Oneness organiza-
tions [by] Arthur L. Clanton. Hazelwood, Mo. , Pentecostal
Publishing House, 1970. 207p. "Emmanuel's Church in
Jesus Christ": p. 52-61.

--PERIODICALS

5547   Pentecostal witness. 1- Nov. 1924-1931.
Port Arthur, Tx. ; St. Louis, Mo. ; Newark, Oh.

EVANGELICAL CHURCHES OF PENTECOST (1953-)
[1953-1968 as Full Gospel Ministers Fellowship.]

An amillenialist minority within the Evangelical Churches of
Pentecost stood aloof when that body merged with the Apostolic
Church of Pentecost in 1953.   Zealous for congregational autonomy,
they organized the Full Gospel Ministers Fellowship.   Although after fifteen years it reclaimed the original name, the Evangelical
Churches of Pentecost remained an association of ministers rather
than a federation of congregations.   In the early 1970s all but three
of the 48 pastors, evangelists, and missionaries in the organization
were Canadians.   Nineteen churches in Canada and three in the
United States served by its members, have a combined membership
of more than 3,000. Headquarters are in Vancouver, British Columbia.

EVANGELICAL CHURCHES OF PENTECOST OF CANADA (1927-
1953)
[1927-1946 as Full Gospel Missions.]

In 1927 Pastor A. H. Gillett of Radville, Saskatchewan, who
had led in developing a large camp meeting at Trossacks, Saskatchewan, secured a provincial charter for a group to be known as Full
Gospel Missions.   Eventually this charter, which insured official
recognition of ordinations, was accepted by all four western provinces. In June 1946, the name was changed to the Evangelical
Churches of Pentecost and a dominion charter secured. A distinctive teaching of the body was the eternal security of the believer.
Talks begun in 1949 between the Evangelical Churches of Pentecost
and the Apostolic Church of Pentecost resulted in organic union four
years later. The Full Gospel Bible Institute of Eston, Saskatchewan,
became the officially recognized school of the merged group.

--HISTORY

5548   Larden, Robert A. , 1929-
Our Apostolic heritage [by] Robert A. Larden. [Saska-
toon, Sask.], Apostolic Church of Pentecost of Canada, 1971.
192p. "Unity of the Spirit": p. 169-173.

EVANGELISTIC AGENCIES:

APOSTOLIC EVANGELISTIC ASSOCIATION (1972-)

Incorporated April 11, 1972, at Mobile, Alabama, the Apostolic Evangelistic Association prides itself on its freedom from sectarian control and on its devotion to the scriptures. In 1974 it reported thirteen clergy and three churches. Affiliated congregations with a combined membership of 100 were located in Mobile, the headquarters, and in Vincennes and New Albany, Indiana. Distinctive practices include the observance of Saturday as the true sabbath, dietary laws, and puritanical standards of behavior. Mixed swimming, the wearing of bathing suits, and the frequenting of dance halls and pool halls is forbidden. In 1974 "Evangelist Erma Jones and the Zion Echoes" radio program was being aired each Saturday over a Mobile station. At that time Evangelist Jones was chairman of the Association.

APOSTOLIC MINISTERIAL ALLIANCE (1941-)

The driving force in the Apostolic Ministerial Alliance has been L. R. Ooton, well-known evangelist and gospel singer. Before setting-up the organization in 1941, Ooton had held office in the Pentecostal Assemblies of Jesus Christ. The Apostolic Ministerial Alliance serves as an agency for granting ministerial credentials. Offices are in Tipton, Indiana.

--PERIODICALS

5549   Apostolic advocate. 1- 194 -
       Tipton, In.

APOSTOLIC MINISTERS FELLOWSHIP (1968-)

Formed August 20-22, 1968, in Baton Rouge, Louisiana, the Apostolic Ministers Fellowship represented an alternative to the United Pentecostal Church for many clergy disillusioned by recent trends. The Fellowship regards itself as a haven for ministers disfellowshipped by the parent body, and as a bulwark against moral laxity and worldliness. "We can no longer bear to see good clean men dropped ... because they differed [!] with some organizational policy." It "does not claim to be a church," and makes no attempt to regulate the affairs of local congregations. Ministerial recognition is extended to men and women without distinction. In 1973 members of the Board of Publication resided in the following states: Indiana, Ohio, Missouri, Louisiana, Texas, Colorado, and Nevada, an indication of a geographical distribution not unlike that of the parent body. Traditional "holiness" standards are enjoined. Prohibitions include movies, television, "questionable literature, worldly

sports and amusements, bowling, bingo, ball games," fashionable
dress or hair styles, jewelry "including wedding rings," secret societies, and remarriage after divorce.

5550   Apostolic Ministers Fellowship.
            [Constitution. Melville, La., 1968] 14p.

            --PERIODICALS

5551   Apostolic standard. 1- 1968-
            Indianapolis.

            BETHEL MINISTERIAL ASSOCIATION (1934-   )
            [1934-1960 as Evangelistic Ministerial Alliance.]

            Organized in May 1934, the Bethel Ministerial Association is
the outgrowth of the Bethel Temple of Evansville, Indiana.   The Association, which until 1960 was known as the Evangelistic Ministerial
Alliance, drew together a number of Baptist ministers under the
leadership of A. F. Varnell, the Baptist Temple pastor.   Stress is
placed on baptism by immersion in the name of Jesus and an experience subsequent to conversion in which the believer is possessed by
the Holy Spirit.   Although tongues-speech is permitted, even encouraged, the group emphatically denies that ability so to speak is
evidence of the baptism of the Holy Spirit.   On March 16, 1960, the
body was incorporated under the laws of the state of Indiana.   In
1971 the Bethel Ministerial Association reported 25 churches, 57
clergy, and 5,000 members.

            --PERIODICALS

5552   Words with power. 1- 19 -
            Evansville, In.

            HALL DELIVERANCE FOUNDATION (1956-   )

            The Hall Deliverance Foundation, the corporate arm of the
ministry of Evangelist Franklin Hall, was established in San Diego,
California, in 1956.   The organization moved its headquarters to
Phoenix, Arizona, in 1960.   The founder, who though reared as a
Methodist began itinerating as an independent evangelist during the
depression, identified with the deliverance movement after World
War II.   In this context he enunciated a theory of healing based on
two metaphors: "bodyfelt salvation" and "clothing of power."   The
results of this teaching, he said, were "700% greater than ordinary
healing power," freeing the recipient from all sickness, even body
odor.   The radical implications of Hall's theory has alienated him
from most other evangelists.   In 1970 the Foundation reported 32

affiliated churches with a combined membership of approximately
2, 000.   At that time a "clothing of Power" convention was being
held annually in Phoenix.

--PERIODICALS

5553   Miracle word.   1-   1965-
        Phoenix.

INTERNATIONAL APOSTOLIC FELLOWSHIP (19 -   )

        In 1980 the International Apostolic Fellowship, whose chair-
man was G. D. Peters of Kingsport, Tennessee, held membership
in the Apostolic World Christian Fellowship.   At that time Peters
was also a trustee of the latter organization.

INTERNATIONAL MINISTERIAL ASSOCIATION (1954-   )

        Formed in August 1954 by W. E. Kidson and twenty other
ministers who withdrew from the United Pentecostal Church, the
International Ministerial Association apparently exists to issue credentials to clergy.   Kidson's Herald of Truth, published in Houston,
became the official organ, and Kidson himself served as chairman
of the Association board for the first fourteen years.   By the early
1970s there were 440 individual members in the United States.   At
that time associate membership was held by 117 churches whose
pastors were members.   The International Ministerial Association
is affiliated with the Apostolic World Christian Fellowship.   In 1980
the Association chairman, A. D. Van Hoose of Evansville, Indiana,
was serving also as a trustee of the Fellowship.

5554   International Ministerial Association.
        Constitution.   Houston, 19--.   12p.

--PERIODICALS

5555   Herald of truth.   1-   1945-
        Houston.

FAITH TABERNACLE CORPORATION OF CHURCHES (1924-   )

        In 1936 the Faith Tabernacle in Los Angeles, which had been
formed as a result of a tent revival twelve years earlier, reported
206 members.   After World War II branches sprang up in several
localities making necessary a more comprehensive organization.   In
1980, L. W. Osborne of Portland, Oregon, was presiding bishop.

Faith Tabernacle holds membership in the Apostolic World Christian Fellowship.

FIRST CHURCH OF JESUS CHRIST (196 -   )

The first Church of Jesus Christ was formed in the early 1960s by former members of the Church of Jesus Christ. At the end of its first decade of existence, the group consisted of 40 churches, 43 clergy, and 2,200 members. Bishop H. E. Honea, pastor at Tullahoma, Tennessee, presides.

FULL GOSPEL PENTECOSTAL CHURCH OF CANADA (1933-1946)

Beginning in 1921, many Oneness ministers in the Maritime provinces held credentials with the Apostolic Church of Pentecost of Canada, whose work was concentrated in the western provinces. To remedy the problems occasioned by such distance from other like-minded believers, in 1933 the eastern Canadian brethren formed the Full Gospel Pentecostal Church of Canada. In 1944 this body gained governmental recognition in New Brunswick and Quebec. On May 15, 1946, the annual meeting of the Full Gospel Pentecostal Church voted to merge with the newly-formed United Pentecostal Church, with the proviso that the Canadian churches could withdraw from the St. Louis-based fellowship by a two-thirds vote of their own members. In 1967 the Canadian churches exercised this option and resumed independence.

FULL SALVATION UNION (1934-   )

The Full Salvation Union is unique in that its doctrine of God springs from despensationalism. In its view each personality of the Godhead has acted in one era of history: the Father from creation to the coming of the messiah, the Son during the lifetime of Christ, and the Holy Spirit since Pentecost. In the dispensation of the Holy Spirit, one who rejects the Spirit is at the same time rejecting the Father and Son. Unlike other groups concerned with the tri-unity of the Godhead, the Full Salvation Union regards sacramental ceremonies as antithetical to the spiritual significance they purport to portray. The agency of the Spirit is a key element in teachings concerning the inspiration of scripture and the government of the church. "God has not confined himself to the written word. He still speaks direct [!] to his children." Likewise, "God's simple plan is to have the Spirit reveal his will in business meetings of the church." As a result "there is a spontaneous recognition of what seems good to the Holy Ghost and to those present which the secretary records as the action of the meeting."

The first affiliate of the Full Salvation Union was formed in
Lansing, Michigan, in January 1934.   James F. Andrews, pastor of
the local group, was designated General Pastor of the Union until
twelve elders had joined the movement.   By December that year the
desired quorum of elders had been reached and by a vote of eleven
to one, E. A. Andrews was chosen General Pastor.   Although a
general council was to meet annually, no decisions were made by it.
Rather such actions were the prerogative of the elders who met immediately afterward.   The General Pastor was charged with filling
pastoral vacancies.   In 1954, James F. Andrews, the General Pastor, lived in Kalamazoo, Michigan.

5556   Full Salvation Union.
        Manual. n. p., 1944.   120p.

        --HISTORY AND STUDY OF DOCTRINES

5557   Moore, Everett Leroy, 1918-
        Handbook of Pentecostal denominations in the United
        States.   Pasadena, Ca., 1954.   vii, 346ℓ.   Thesis (M. A.)--
        Pasadena College.   "Full Salvation Union":   ℓ. 290-304.
        CSdP

        --PERIODICALS

5558   Union guide. 1- 19 -
        Kalamazoo, Mi.

GENERAL ASSEMBLY OF APOSTOLIC ASSEMBLIES (1917-1918)

        As a result of the Trinitarian stand taken in October 1916
by the General Council of the Assemblies of God, 156 ministerial
proponents of baptism in Jesus' name found themselves without standing in the fellowship.   In search of a way out of their dilemma, a
number of these ministers gathered in Eureka Springs, Arkansas, on
December 28th.   At 2:30 in the afternoon on January 2d, they began
deliberations which by the end of the following day resulted in formation of the General Assembly of Apostolic Assemblies, the central
purpose of which was to act as a credential-granting agency. D. C. O.
Opperman, H. A. Goss and H. G. Rodgers were to serve as credential
committee.   Opperman's paper, which was published in Eureka
Springs, became the official organ.   On January 22, 1918, at St.
Louis, the group merged with the Pentecostal Assemblies of the
World.   Failure to receive recognition of the government and of the
Clergy Bureau necessary for exemption from military service and
for discounts on rail travel by ministers, prompted union with the
larger interracial body, whose headquarters at that time were in
Portland, Oregon.

--HISTORY

5559   Clanton, Arthur Lee, 1915-
        United we stand: a history of Oneness organizations [by]
        Arthur L. Clanton Hazelwood, Mo., Pentecostal Publishing
        House, 1970. 207p. "The General Assembly of Apostolic
        Assemblies": p. 23-26.

--PERIODICALS

5560   Blessed truth. 1- 1915-192-.
        Eureka Springs, Ar.

GOD'S HOUSE OF PRAYER FOR ALL NATIONS (1964-)

        God's House of Prayer for All Nations is a group of black and
interracial congregations in Illinois.   Several are in the Chicago area.
Each church is an autonomous unit, operating under its own charter.
Although no coordinating agency exists, a similar pattern has emerged
which may be illustrated by God's House of Prayer for All Nations
in Peoria.   This congregation was founded under the leadership of
Tommie Lawrence in 1964.   Although the founder formerly had been
a minister in the Church of God in Christ, a Trinitarian body, the
Peoria church teaches that baptism should be by immersion "in the
name of Jesus Christ, which is the name of the Father, Son and
Holy Ghost."   Lawrence refers to himself as "pastor, chief apostle,
founder, and senior bishop of God's House of Prayer for All Nations."
Reportedly Lawrence's church and several of its sister congregations
use materials published by the Miracle Revival Fellowship, an organization founded by the late A. A. Allen.

HIGHWAY CHURCH OF JESUS OF THE APOSTOLIC FAITH (19 -)

        Congregations affiliated with the Highway Church of Jesus of
the Apostolic Faith are located in the Philadelphia and Washington
metropolitan areas.

5561   Adams, Donald Conrad
        A comparative study of the social functions of the High-
        way Church of Jesus of the Apostolic Faith of T. B. Maryland,
        and the Grace Methodist Church of Chapel Hill, Maryland.
        Washington, 1966. Thesis (B.D.)--Howard University.   DHU

HOLINESS CHURCH OF JESUS CHRIST (195 -)

        Formed in the late 1950s by followers of Bishop L. H. Webb,

the Holiness Church of Jesus Christ consists of between ten and fifteen congregations in four states.   In the early 1970s Bishop Mack G. Arnold was leader of the movement, which was then centered in Kingsport, Tennessee.

HOLY BIBLE MISSION WORKERS (1919-1953)

Founded in 1919, the Louisville-based Holy Bible Mission Workers consisted of a few small churches in Kentucky and Indiana. Distinctive practices included observance of Saturday as the sabbath. Led first by C. T. Adams, later by C. L. Pennington and his wife, the organization dissolved soon after Mrs. Pennington's death in 1953.   Indiana ministers formerly affiliated with the Holy Bible Mission Workers organized the Pentecostal Church of Zion the next year.

IGLESIA APOSTÓLICA DE LA FÉ EN CRISTO JESÚS (1914-   )

The Iglesia Apostólica de la Fé en Cristo Jesús was founded in 1914 by Mexican nationals who, while in the United States, had come into contact with "new issue" Pentecostalism.   During the next fifty years work was established in all regions of Mexico.   In 1964 the Iglesia Apostólica reported over 1,000 clergy.   From headquarters in Mexico City the bishop-president was giving general oversight to churches in twelve administrative districts.

5562   Goodman, Felicitas Daniels, 1914-
        Apostolics of Yucatán: a case study of a religious movement [by] Felicitas D. Goodman. In Bourguinon, E., ed.
        Religion, altered states of consciousness, and social change.
        Columbus, 1973, 178-218.

5563   Goodman, Felicitas Daniels, 1914-
        Disturbances in the Apostolic Church; case study of a trance-based upheaval in Yucatan.   Columbus, 1971.   viii, 244ℓ.   Thesis (Ph.D.)--Ohio State University.   OU

5564   Goodman, Felicitas Daniels, 1914-
        Prognosis: a new religion? [By] Felicitas D. Goodman.
        In Zaretsky, I. I., ed.   Religious movements in contemporary America.   Princeton, N.J., c1974, 244-254.

5565   Goodman, Felicitas Daniels, 1914-
        Disturbances in the Apostolic Church: a trance-based upheaval in Yucatan.   In Goodman, F. D.   Trance, healing, and halucination: three field studies in religious experience.
        New York, 1974.   DLC, RPRC

--HISTORY

5566   Gaxiola, Manuel Jesús, 1927-
       The serpent and the dove; a history of the Apostolic
       Church of Faith in Christ Jesus in Mexico, 1914-1974. Pasa-
       dena, Ca., Fuller Theological Seminary, 1977. iii, 197p.
       (Fuller Theological Seminary. School of World Mission.
       Projects, 1977.) CPFT

5567   Gaxiola, Manuel Jesús, 1927-
       La serpiente y la paloma; analisis del crecimiento de la
       Iglesia Apostólica de la Fé en Cristo Jesús de Mexico [por]
       Manuel J. Gaxiola. South Pasadena, Ca., William Carey
       Library, c1970. xiv, 177p. CPFT, DLC

--HISTORY AND STUDY OF DOCTRINES

5568   Gaxiola, Manuel Jesús, 1927-
       [Theology of liberation]. n. p., 1976. 1v. (various
       pagings) Spanish and English. "Mimeographed notes."
       CPFT

IGLESIA PENTECOSTAL UNIDA DE COLOMBIA (1967-   )

       In its present form the Iglesia Pentecostal Unida de Colombia
dates from a convention held in June 1967 in Cali. Its roots go
back, however, to the arrival of the first Canadian missionary thirty-
one years before. In keeping with the nationalist sentiment which
inspired Colombian leaders, the 1967 constitution assigned to foreign
missionaries a purely advisory role. Reaction to this provision led
in turn to exodus of missionary-led partisans two years later. Despite this, the movement grew rapidly under Superintendent Campo
Elias Bernal S., who nineteen years previously had been the first
Colombian convert to be ordained. During the five years following
1969, membership soared from 50, 000 to 60, 000. Headquarters had
been established in Barranquilla and the church was airing programs
over the Voz del Paraiso, a radio station it had purchased in El
Cerrito. By 1974 the Iglesia Pentecostal Unida de Colombia had
joined the Apostolic Christian World Fellowship, a step its North
American parent refused to take.

5569   Iglesia Pentecostal Unida de Colombia.
       Manual. Barranquilla, 1967.

--HISTORY

5570   Flora, Cornelia (Butler), 1943-

Mobilizing the masses; the sacred and the secular in
Colombia. Ithaca, N. Y., 1970. xiii, 285p. (Cornell University. Latin American Studies Program. Dissertation
series, 25.) Thesis (ph. D.)--Cornell University. Includes
account of the history of the United Pentecostal Church in
Colombia.

5571   Flora, Cornelia (Butler), 1943-
Pentecostal women in Colombia; religious change and
the Status of working-class women [by] Cornelia B. Flora.
In Journal of Interamerican Studies, 17 (Nov. 1975), 411-
425.

5572   Flora, Cornelia (Butler), 1943-
Pentecostalism in Colombia; baptism by fire and Spirit.
Rutherford, N. J., Fairleigh Dickinson University Press,
1976. 288p. Based on thesis (Ph. D.)--Cornell University,
1970. "History of the United Pentecostal Church in Colombia":
p. 33-67.

5573   Palmer, Donald C., 1934-
Explosion of people evangelism, by Donald C. Palmer.
Chicago, Moody Press, 1974. 191p. Based on thesis (M. A.)
--Trinity Evangelical Divinity School. "An analysis of Pente-
costal church growth in Colombia." DLC, MSohG

5574   Palmer, Donald C., 1934-
The growth of the Pentecostal churches in Colombia, by
Donald C. Palmer. Deerfield, Ill., 1972. vi, 196ℓ. Thesis
(M. A.)--Trinity Evangelical Divinity School. IDfT

--PERIODICALS

5575   El Heraldo de la Verdad. 1- 19 -
Barranquilla.

MACEDONIA CHURCHES OF VIRGINIA (19 -)

In 1980 the Macedonia Churches of Virginia held membership
in the Apostolic World Christian Fellowship. At that time Tilmon
Carmichael, Sr., of Gloucester, Virginia, was presiding bishop.

MESSIAH TABERNACLE CHURCH IN AMERICA (1958-)

In 1972 Bishop H. Moore of the Messiah Tabernacle Church
in America was active in the Apostolic Ministers Conference of Philadelphia and Vicinity.

MISSIONARY AGENCIES:

FAR EAST APOSTOLIC MISSION (1918-)

In 1918 Leonard W. Coote, an American businessman who had been converted five years earlier while living in Japan, founded the Far East Apostolic Mission. First established in Osaka and Nara prefectures, the mission concentrated on direct evangelism including street meetings, tent revivals, home visitation and tract distribution. It pursued similar methods in Korea when it opened work there following World War II. It established colleges for training workers in both countries. Post-war successes were followed by slow decline. In Japan, where the organization is known as Nippon Pentekosute Kyodan, membership dropped from 200 to 120 between 1962 and 1967. The Mission works in close cooperation with the Apostolic Church of Pentecost of Canada and the United Pentecostal Church International. In Japan headquarters are in Ikoma, Nara prefecture; in the United States they are in San Antonio, Texas, site of the International Bible College.

5576   Coote, Leonard W.
        Go ye, by Leonard Coote. Ikoma, Japan, 19--. 100p.

        --PERIODICALS

5577   Japan and Korea and Pentecost. 1- 19 -
        Ikoma, Japan, San Antonio. To 194- as Japan and
        Pentecost.

MISSIONARY BODY OF JESUS CHRIST (19 -)

Distinctive in its seventh-day sabbath emphasis, the Missionary Body of Jesus Christ regards itself as a continuation of the revival begun at Jerusalem on the Day of Pentecost and rekindled at Topeka, Kansas in 1901. The leader in 1974 was Maribeth Hunter of Athens, Tennessee.

        --PERIODICALS

5578   Epistle. 1- 19 -
        Athens, Tn.

5579   J. E. S. U. S. bridal call. 1- 19 -
        Athens, Tn.

MOUNT CARMEL HOLY CHURCH OF THE LORD JESUS (19 -)

In 1980 the Mount Carmel Holy Church of the Lord Jesus
held membership in the Apostolic World Christian Fellowship. At
that time William Payne of Camden, New Jersey was general overseer.

MOUNT OF OLIVES INTERNATIONAL BIBLE CENTER (19 -)

In 1980 the Mount of Olives International Bible Center in
Jerusalem held membership in the Apostolic World Christian Fellowship. Shlomo Hizak was then president of the Center.

MOUNT OF ZION GOSPEL CHURCH (19 -)

In 1980, A. U. Eka of Calabar, Nigeria, was president of
the Mount of Zion Gospel Church. At that time the church was a
member of the Apostolic World Christian Fellowship.

NEW BETHEL CHURCH OF GOD IN CHRIST (PENTECOSTAL)
   (1927-)

In 1927, A. D. Bradley was reprimanded by the board of
bishops of the Church of God in Christ for preaching the "Jesus
Only" doctrine. As a result Bradley, his wife, and Lonnie Bates
left the denomination and founded the New Bethel Church of God in
Christ (Pentecostal). Bradley became presiding bishop. Doctrinal
innovations notwithstanding, the New Bethel Church resembles its
parent in many ways. It condemns membership in secret societies.
It regards footwashing as an ordinance. And it disapproves of school
activities which violate a student's religious convictions. Headquarters are in San Francisco.

5580   New Bethel Church of God in Christ (Pentecostal).
           Articles of faith. San Francisco, 19--.

NEW TESTAMENT HOLINESS CHURCH (1966-)

Founded in 1966, the New Testament Holiness Church is a
federation of congregations led by and supportive of the work of
Evangelist David Terrell. Affiliates are concentrated in the southeastern states. Greenville, South Carolina and Dallas, Texas, the
former and present headquarters sites, mark the rough geographical
limits of the New Testament Holiness Church. If Terrell be con-

sidered representative of his followers, the movement places strong emphasis on the gift of prophecy.

--PERIODICALS

5581   Endtime messenger. 1- 1966-
            Greenville, S.C., Dallas.   OkTOr

PENTECOSTAL ASSEMBLIES OF JESUS CHRIST (1931-1945)

The product of the union consummated November 18, 1931, at Columbus, Ohio, between the Apostolic Church of Jesus Christ and the Pentecostal Assemblies of the World, the Pentecostal Assemblies of Jesus Christ was designed as an instrument for restoring the interracial fellowship which had marked the movement in its early years. This goal was not to be realized. The first blow was struck within weeks of the merger. Followers of Bishop Samuel Grimes of the Pentecostal Assemblies of the World met in Dayton, Ohio, and voted to continue the organization under the old charter. Blacks remaining in the Pentecostal Assemblies of Jesus Christ during its first seven years of existence, constituted about twenty percent of the membership. The decision to hold the 1937 conference in Tulsa, Oklahoma, a city with segregated facilities, led to the resignation of Karl F. Smith, the general secretary, and the return of most remaining blacks to the Pentecostal Assemblies of the World. In 1945 the Pentecostal Assemblies of Jesus Christ united with the Pentecostal Church, Incorporated, to form the United Pentecostal Church. At that time it reported 324 churches and 1,028 ministers. The clergy total represented an increase of only 47 over that reported nine years earlier. In its last years headquarters functions were dispersed in five locations: Columbus and Lancaster, Ohio, St. Paul, Minnesota, Kilgore, Texas, and West Tulsa, Oklahoma.

--HISTORY

5582   Clanton, Arthur Lee, 1915-
            United we stand: a history of Oneness organizations [by]
        Arthur L. Clanton. Hazelwood, Mo., Pentecostal Publishing
        House, 1970. 207p. "The Pentecostal Assemblies of Jesus
        Christ": p. 70-86.

5583   U.S. Bureau of the Census.
            Census of religious bodies: 1936. Pentecostal assem-
        blies. Statistics, denominational history, doctrine, and or-
        ganization. Consolidated report. Washington, Government
        Printing Office, 1940. iv, 49p. Includes Pentecostal Assem-
        blies of Jesus Christ. NNUT

--PERIODICALS

5584   Pentecostal outlook.   1-   1932-Oct. 1945.
        Newark, Oh., St. Paul, Mn.   Merged into Pentecostal
        herald.

PENTECOSTAL ASSEMBLIES OF THE WORLD (1912-   )

        Although it held its first General Assembly in Los Angeles
March 25, 1912, the Pentecostal Assemblies of the World did not
take on its definitive role until it merged with the infant General
Assembly of Apostolic Assemblies at St. Louis nearly six years
later. J. J. Frazee of Portland, Oregon, was General Superintendent from 1912 to 1916.   Upon incorporation in 1919, the body moved
its headquarters from Portland to Indianapolis, where Elder G. T.
Haywood headed a large congregation then known as the Apostolic
Faith Assembly Tabernacle.   Most of the black adherents of the denomination lived in the North and most of its white members, in the
South.   Segregation of public facilities in the South made it necessary
to hold denominational meetings in the North.   In 1925 dissatisfaction
over this feature of interracial fellowship led to the exodus of most
white members and the formation of three competing white bodies.
Three years later two of these united to form the Pentecostal Assemblies of Jesus Christ.   Although following Haywood's death in 1931
the Indianapolis-based group formally merged with this body, followers
of Bishop Samuel Grimes voted to continue the original body under the
old charter.   Problems related to segregation again surfaced in the
new body, causing most remaining blacks in the merged body to return to the Pentecostal Assemblies of the World by 1938.

        The Pentecostal Assemblies of the World support missionary
efforts in eleven world areas.   In 1960 the denominations reported
550 churches and 45,000 members in the United States.   It holds
membership in the Apostolic World Christian Fellowship.

5585   Pentecostal Assemblies of the World.
        Manual of discipline of the Pentecostal Assemblies of the
        World, Inc.   New York, Christian Outlook Publishing Co.,
        1945.   v, 54p.

                --DOCTRINAL AND CONTROVERSIAL WORKS

5586   Golder, Morris Ellis
        The confession of sins [by] Morris E. Golder.   Cincin-
        nati, Apostolic Light Press, 19--.   40p.   Cover title.

5587   Golder, Morris Ellis
        The principles of our faith: what we believe [by] Morris

E. Golder. Cincinnati, Apostolic Light Press, 19--. 24p.
Cover title. OkTOr

5588   Haywood, Garfield Thomas, bp., 1880-1931.
Before the foundation of the world; a revelation of the
ages, by G. T. Haywood. Indianapolis, 1923. 76p. "Enlarged and revised edition of the little booklet formerly called
'A revelation of the ages'." DLC

5589   Haywood, Garfield Thomas, bp., 1880-1931.
The birth of the Spirit in the days of the apostles, by
G. T. Haywood. Indianapolis, Christ Temple Book Store,
19--. 40p. Cover title. OkTOr

5590   Haywood, Garfield Thomas, bp., 1880-1931.
Divine names and titles of Jehovah, by G. T. Haywood.
Indianapolis, Voice in the Wilderness, 19--. 19p.

5591   [Haywood, Garfield Thomas], bp., 1880-1931.
Ezekiel's vision; the first chapter of Ezekiel. Indianapolis, Christ Temple Book Store, 19--. 23p. (Behold He
cometh.) Cover title.

5592   Haywood, Garfield Thomas, bp., 1880-1931.
The marriage and divorce question in the church, by
G. T. Haywood. Indianapolis, Christ Temple, 19--. 32p.
Cover title.

5593   Haywood, Garfield Thomas, bp., 1880-1931.
The old and new tabernacle compared by G. T. Haywood.
Indianapolis, Voice in the Wilderness, 19--. 12p.

5594   Haywood, Garfield Thomas, bp., 1880-1931.
The resurrection of the dead, by G. T. Haywood. In-
dianapolis, Christ Temple Book Store, 19--. 20p. (Behold
He cometh.)

5595   Haywood, Garfield Thomas, bp., 1880-1931.
The victim of the flaming sword, by G. T. Haywood.
Indianapolis, Christ Temple Book Store, 19--. 71p. Cover
title. OkTOr

5596   Moore, Benjamin T.
A handbook for saints [by] Benjamin T. Moore. Seattle,
Bethel Christian Ministries, c1974. 67p.

5597   Paddock, Ross Perry, 1907-
The church an organized body, by Ross P. Paddock.
Cincinnati, Apostolic Light Press, 19--. 47p.

5598   Paddock, Ross Perry, 1907-
God's financial plan for the church, by Ross P. Paddock.
Cincinnati, Apostolic Light Press, 19--. 48p.

5599   Paddock, Ross Perry, 1907-
        Marriage and divorce, by Ross P. Paddock. Cincinnati,
        Apostolic Light Press, 19--. 36p.

5600   Paddock, Ross Perry, 1907-
        Restoration, by Ross P. Paddock. Cincinnati, Apostolic
        Light Press, 19--. 24p. Cover title.

5601   Paddock, Ross Perry, 1907-
        Short subjects important to Pentecostals, by Ross P.
        Paddock. Cincinnati, Apostolic Light Press, 19--. 54p.

5602   Smith, Francis L., 1915-
        What every saint should know, by F. L. Smith. East
        Orange, N.J., Lutho Press, 19--. 12p. Cover title.

5603   Smith, Karl Franklin, 1892-1972.
        General outline of the Bible. [Columbus, Oh.], 1941,
        c1947. 175p.

5604   Tobin, R. F.
        The principles of the doctrine of Christ, by R. F. Tobin.
        Indianapolis, Christ Temple, c1945. 31p.

5604a   Wagner, Norman Leonard, 1942-
        Learn to do well [by] Norman L. Wagner. Cincinnati,
        Apostolic Light Press, 19--. 15p.

        --HISTORY

5605   Clanton, Arthur Lee, 1915-
        United we stand: a history of Oneness organizations [by]
        Arthur L. Clanton. Hazelwood, Mo., Pentecostal Publishing
        House, 1970. 207p. "The Pentecostal Assemblies of the
        World": p. 27-34.

5606   Golder, Morris Ellis
        History of the Pentecostal Assemblies of the World [by]
        Morris E. Golder. Indianapolis, 1973. 195p. CPFT

5607   Moore, Everett Leroy, 1918-
        Handbook of Pentecostal denominations in the United States.
        Pasadena, Ca., 1954. vii, 346ℓ. Thesis (M.A.)--Pasadena
        College. "Pentecostal Assemblies of the World": ℓ. 242-
        252. CSdP

5608   U.S. Bureau of the Census.
        Census of religious bodies: 1926. Pentecostal Assem-
        blies of the World. Statistics, denominational history, doc-
        trine, and organization. Washington, U.S. Government Print-
        ing Office, 1929. 9p. DLC, NNUT

5609   U. S. Bureau of the Census.
          Census of religious bodies: 1936. Pentecostal assem-
       blies. Statistics, denominational history, doctrine, and or-
       ganization. Consolidated report. Washington, Government
       Printing Office, 1940. iv, 49p. Includes Pentecostal Assem-
       blies of the World. NNUT

                  --HISTORY AND STUDY OF DOCTRINES

5610   Golder, Morris Ellis
          A doctrinal study of the Pentecostal Assemblies of the
       World. Indianapolis, 1959. 76ℓ. Thesis (M. A.)--Butler
       University. InIB

                  --HYMNS AND SACRED SONGS

5611   The bridegroom songs. 6th ed. , enlarged.
          Indianapolis, Voice in the Wilderness, 192-. [80]p.
       Cover title. KyWAT

5612   The bridegroom songs.
          Indianapolis, Christ Temple Bookstore, 19--. 94p.
       "Christ Temple edition. " With music. "Many of these songs
       are by ... the late Bishop G. T. Haywood. "

5613   Carradine, Beverly, 1848-1931.
          The best of all complete. [Edited by] B. Carradine,
       C. J. Fowler [and] W. J. Kirkpatrick. Indianapolis, Christ
       Temple, 19--. 288p. With music.

5613a Old songs selected.
          Columbus, Oh. , Church of Christ, Apostolic Faith, 19--.
       32p. With music (shape notes). "Prepared and printed by
       Administrative Staff of the Church of Christ, Apostolic Faith. "

                  --MISSIONS

5614   Pentecostal Assemblies of the World. Foreign Missions
       Department.
          We have been there: overseas works of the Pentecostal
       Assemblies of the World, Inc. , led by G. T. Haywood, S. J.
       Grimes, Ross P. Paddock [and] F. L. Smith. Indianapolis,
       1977. 101p. Cover title.

5614a Reeder, Hilda
          A brief history of the Foreign Missionary Department of
       the Pentecostal Assemblies of the World. Indianapolis, For-
       eign Missionary Department, 1951. 76p. DLC, NNUT

--PASTORAL THEOLOGY

5615   Smith, Karl Franklin
        The scriptural view of the Christian pastorate.   Columbus, Oh., 1944. v, 154p. DLC

5615a   Wagner, Norman Leonard, 1942-
        Go ye therefore: an evangelism manual for mass Pentecostal crusades [by] Norman L. Wagner. Youngstown, Oh.,
        Calvary Publications, 197-. 17p. OkTOr

--PERIODICALS

5616   Christian outlook.   1- 1925-
        Indianapolis, New York, Akron, Oh., New York.

5617   Voice in the wilderness.   1- Apr. 1910-192-.
        Indianapolis.

--SERMONS, TRACTS, ADDRESSES, ESSAYS

5617a   Christian stewardship: a story of the tenth.
        Indianapolis, Christ Temple Book Store, 19--. 16p.
        Cover title.

5618   Haywood, Garfield Thomas, bp., 1880-1931.
        Feed my sheep, by G. T. Haywood. Indianapolis, Christ
        Temple Book Store, 19--. 62p. Cover title. OkTOr

5619   Haywood, Garfield Thomas, bp., 1880-1931.
        The finest of the wheat, by G. T. Haywood. Indianapolis,
        Christ Temple Book Store, 19--. 60p. OkTOr

5620   Maynard, Aurora
        The inner guidance. New York, Vantage Press, c1965.
        116p. InIT, OkTOr

--TENNESSEE (Nashville)

5621   Pike, Garnet Elmer
        The rise of a black Pentecostal church in a changing city:
        a historical case study. Nashville, 1972. iv, 105ℓ. Thesis
        (D. Div.)--Vandervilt University. On Greater Christ Temple
        Apostolic Church, Nashville. TNJ-R

PENTECOSTAL CHURCH, INCORPORATED (1925-1945)
[1925-1932 as Pentecostal Ministerial Alliance.]

        The development of this organization fell into two stages, each symbolized by a name. Organized November 3, 1925, in St. Louis, the Pentecostal Ministerial Alliance consisted initially of white ministers recently separated from the Pentecostal Assemblies of the World. Its 1926-1927 roll contained 222 clergy. Although only ministers held membership, an informal fellowship soon developed among congregations served by members. Adoption of a new name and of a plan for district and local church government in 1932, signalled a milestone on the road to denominational order. During the next thirteen years, headquarters of the Pentecostal Church, Incorporated, relocated three times. From Louisiana, Missouri, they moved successively to Dallas, to Houston, and to St. Louis. Short-lived Bible training schools were sponsored in Missouri, Texas, and Idaho. At the time of the merger of the Pentecostal Church, Incorporated, and the Pentecostal Assemblies of Jesus Christ, September 25, 1945, the Pentecostal Church claimed 175 churches and 810 ministers.

--HISTORY

5622   Clanton, Arthur Lee, 1915-
        United we stand: a history of Oneness organizations [by]
        Arthur L. Clanton. Hazelwood, Mo., Pentecostal Publishing
        House, 1970. 207p. "The Pentecostal Ministerial Alliance":
        p. 35-51; and "The Pentecostal Church, Incorporated": p. 87-
        104.

5623   U. S. Bureau of the Census.
        Census of religious bodies: 1936. Pentecostal assem-
        blies. Statistics, denominational history, doctrine, and or-
        ganization. Consolidated report. Washington, Government
        Printing Office, 1940. iv, 49p. Includes the Pentecostal
        Church, Incorporated. NNUT

--PERIODICALS

5624   Apostolic herald. 1-20, no. 11, 1926-Nov. 1945.
        Louisiana, Mo., Dallas, Houston, St. Louis. Continued
        as Pentecostal herald.

PENTECOSTAL CHURCH OF ZION (1954-   )

        The Holy Bible Mission Workers dissolved in 1953 following the death of its president, Mrs. C. L. Pennington. The next year, Luther S. Howard led Indiana ministers formerly affiliated with that group in the formation of the Pentecostal Church of Zion. Distinctive practices include observance of the Jewish sabbath and Levitical dietary laws. The Lord's Supper is regarded as a spiritual meal. Literal observance was discontinued fifteen years ago. By 1974 the total adult membership stood at 77. Churches were located in French Lick, Marengo, Bedford, Burns City, and Sulphur, Indiana,

and in White City, Oregon. At that time Bishop Howard lived in
French Lick.

--CATECHISMS AND CREEDS

5625   Pentecostal Church of Zion.
        What we believe and why. French Lick, In., 1966. 39p.

--PERIODICALS

5626   Word from Zion. 1- 19 -
        French Lick, In.

PENTECOSTAL CHURCHES OF THE APOSTOLIC FAITH ASSOCIA-
TION (1957-   )

        Upon the death of Bishop G. T. Haywood in 1931, a struggle
of many years duration ensued over the office of presiding bishop in
the Pentecostal Assemblies of the World. The principal contenders
were Bishop S. N. Hancock and Bishop Samuel Grimes. In a run-
off vote between the two during the 1952 General Assembly in Baltimore, Bishop Grimes won. Five years later Bishop Hancock made
good repeated threats to leave the organization, when on November
20, 1957, he, together with Bishop Heardie Leaston, Bishop Willie
Lee, and Elder David Collins, incorporated the Pentecostal Churches
of the Apostolic Faith in Wayne County, Michigan. Three of the
four incorporators were residents of the county, the exception being
Bishop Lee of Indianapolis. Personality conflicts were present in
the new body as in the old one. Since the death of Bishop Hancock,
the Pentecostal Churches of the Apostolic Faith Association has fractured three times.

5627   Pentecostal Churches of the Apostolic Faith Association.
        The ministerial record: codified rules of the Pentecostal
        Churches of the Apostolic Faith Association, Inc. n. p., 1960.

PRIMITIVE CHURCH OF JESUS CHRIST (1971-   )

        Organized in 1971, the Primitive Church of Jesus Christ is
an offshoot of the Tennessee-based Church of Jesus Christ. Headquarters are in Inglis, Florida.

SEVENTH DAY PENTECOSTAL CHURCH OF THE LIVING GOD (194 -)

        In the 1940s Charles Gamble, former Roman Catholic and

Baptist, founded the mother church of the Seventh Day Pentecostal Church of the Living God in Washington, D. C. Thirty years later the movement consisted of four churches and 1,000 members in the District of Columbia and nearby states. At that time Bishop Theron B. Johnson of Pleasantville, New Jersey, was general overseer.

UNITED CHURCH OF JESUS CHRIST (1948-)

The United Church of Jesus Christ was organized in 1948 by former members of the Church of Jesus Christ then based in Cleveland, Tennessee. Distinctive practices include invocation of the name of Jesus Christ while the person being baptized is under the water, and use of wine mixed with water in the Lord's Supper. Ministers are addressed as "Reverend." The United Church of Jesus Christ, which consists of 25 congregations, 100 clergy, and approximately 1,250 members. In the early 1970s, W. C. Gibson of Sweetwater, Tennessee, was chairperson.

UNITED CHURCH OF JESUS CHRIST APOSTOLIC INTERNATIONAL (195 -)

Founded in the 1950s by Monroe Saunders, a former Methodist, the United Church of Jesus Christ has congregations in Washington, Baltimore, and other cities in the United States. Saunders, the presiding bishop, lives in Baltimore. The denomination, which claims outreach in Europe and Latin America, holds membership in the Apostolic World Christian Fellowship.

--PERIODICALS

5628   Burning bush. 1- 1976-
            Baltimore.

UNITED PENTECOSTAL CHURCH AUSTRALIA (1956-)

The United Pentecostal Church Australia is the product of missionary work begun in 1956 by the St. Louis-based group of the same name. In 1975 the group, which is centered in Belmore, New South Wales, reported fifteen congregations.

--PERIODICALS

5629   Pentecostal light. 1- 1976-
            Belmore, N. S. W.

UNITED PENTECOSTAL CHURCH INTERNATIONAL (1945-   )
[1945-1973 as United Pentecostal Church.]

Formed September 25, 1945, by union of the Pentecostal Assemblies of Jesus Christ and the Pentecostal Church, Incorporated,
the United Pentecostal Church reassembled white elements once part
of the Pentecostal Assemblies of the World. Well-organized and
aggressive, it has remained at arms length from sister denominations. It has remained outside the Apostolic World Christian Fellowship. Set against combatant service in time of war, the United Pentecostal Church disapproves membership in labor unions and secret
societies. Conservative standards of dress, hair styling, and adorn-
ment are enjoined. Eight Bible colleges prepare both clerical and
lay leaders. Headquarters offices and the Pentecostal Publishing
House are in Hazelwood, Missouri, a suburb of St. Louis. In 1979
the denomination reported 2,830 churches and 450,000 members in
the United States. That year it raised $5,747,516 for foreign mis-
sions and had 187 North American workers under appointment for
service in sixty world areas.

5630   United Pentecostal Church International.
        Manual of the United Pentecostal Church International.
        St. Louis; Hazelwood, Mo., 1945- . v. [1]- . Annual.

5631   Dearman, Marion Veurl
        Christ and conformity: a study of Pentecostal values
        [by] Marion Dearman. In Journal for the Scientific Study of
        Religion, 13 (Dec. 1974), 437-453. A reexamination of Ben-
        ton Johnson's question: "Do holiness sects socialize dominant
        values?" in relation to the United Pentecostal Church.

5632   Dearman, Marion Veurl
        Do holiness sects socialize in dominant values? An em-
        pirical inquiry. Eugene, 1972. 238ℓ. Thesis (Ph.D.)--
        University of Oregon. OrU

--CHURCH WORK

5633   Foster, Fred J.
        Bus ministry manual, by Fred Foster and Charles Glass.
        Hazelwood, Mo., Word Aflame Press, 1974. 32p.

--DOCTRINAL AND CONTROVERSIAL WORKS

5634   United Pentecostal Church.
        This is that. St. Louis, 19--.

5635   United Pentecostal Church.
        What we believe and teach: Articles of Faith of the
        United Pentecostal Church. St. Louis, Pentecostal Publishing
        House, 1946.

5636   Abbey, Albert A.
        Doctrinal handbook for Pentecostal children, by Albert
        A. Abbey. St. Louis, Mo., Pentecostal Publishing House,
        c1960. 37p.

5637   Arnold, Marvin M., 1921-
        The origin and spread of man [by] Marvin M. Arnold.
        Hazelwood, Mo., Word Aflame Press, c1976. 192p.

5638   Bible. English. 1973. Authorized.
        The Holy Bible: Old and New Testaments in the King
        James version; translated out of the original tongues and with
        previous translations diligently compared and revised. Self-
        pronouncing. Hazelwood, Mo., Word Aflame Press, c1973.
        643, 197, 16, 64p. "Doctrines of the Bible": p. 1-22.

5639   Campbell, David, 1927-
        All the fulness. Hazelwood, Mo., Word Aflame Press,
        c1975. 173p.

5640   Curts, Frank E.
        The tabernacle in the wilderness, by F. E. Curts. St.
        Louis, Pentecostal Publishing House, 19--. 144p.

5641   Ewart, Frank J., 1876-
        Jesus, the man and mystery [by] Frank J. Ewart.
        Hazelwood, Mo., Word Aflame Press, 197-, c1941. 160p.

5642   Ewart, Frank J., 1876-
        The revelation of Jesus Christ, by Frank J. Ewart.
        St. Louis, Pentecostal Publishing House, 19--. 46p.

5643   Fauss, Oliver F., 1898-
        Baptism in God's plan; what the scriptures teach about
        baptism in the "name" of Jesus, by Oliver F. Fauss. 2d
        ed. Hazelwood, Mo., Pentecostal Publishing House, 1955.
        40p. Cover title.

5644   Fauss, Oliver F., 1898-
        Buy the truth, and sell it not; the history of the revela-
        tion of baptism in the name of Jesus, and of the fulness of
        God in Christ, by Oliver F. Fauss. Hazelwood, Mo., Pente-
        costal Publishing House, c1965. 72p.

5645   Hall, William Phillips, 1864-1937.
        Remarkable Biblical discovery; or, "The name" of God
        according to the scriptures. Abridged. Hazelwood, Mo.,
        Pentecostal Publishing House, c1951. 30p. Based on 1929
        ed. "Courtesy: American Tract Society."

5646   Johnson, Robert W.
        Miracles in our day. Compiled by R. W. Johnson.
        Hazelwood, Mo., Word Aflame Press, c1973. 80p.

5647   McClain, Samuel C. , 1889-1969.
        Student's handbook of facts in church history [by] Rev.
        S. C. McClain. Hazelwood, Mo. , Pentecostal Publishing
        House, 1974. 66p. First issued in 1948.

5648   Miller, John, 1819-1895.
        Is God a trinity? Hazelwood, Mo. , Word Aflame Press,
        1975. 144p. Reprint of 1877 ed.

5649   Morley, Sallie (Lemons)
        End-time revival, by Sallie Morley. Hazelwood, Mo. ,
        Pentecostal Publishing House, c1973. 64p.

5650   Norris, S. G.
        The mighty God in Christ, by S. G. Norris. St. Paul,
        Mn. , Apostolic Bible Institute, 19--. 20p.

5651   One God.
        Portland, Or. , Apostolic Book Publishers, U. P. C. of
        Portland, 19--. 20p. On cover: Jesus is God.

5652   Paterson, John
        God in Christ Jesus. Hazelwood, Mo. , Word Aflame
        Press, c1966. 71p. First published in 1921 under title:
        Revelation of Jesus Christ. KyWAT

5653   Paterson, John
        God in Christ Jesus. Montreal, c1966. 72p.

5654   Paterson, John
        The real truth about baptism in Jesus' name. Hazelwood,
        Mo. , Pentecostal Publishing House, c1953. 31p. OkTOr

5655   Paterson, John
        La vérité vraie au sujet du baptême au nom de Jésus.
        Saint-Stephen, N. B. , Eglise unie de la Pentecôte, c1960.
        31p. Translation of The real truth about baptism in Jesus'
        name.

5656   Pugh, Jessie Truman, 1923-
        How to receive the Holy Ghost, by J. T. Pugh. Hazel-
        wood, Mo. , Pentecostal Publishing House, 1969. 63p.
        MoSpA

5657   Reynolds, Ralph Vincent
        Truth shall triumph; a study of Pentecostal doctrines.
        St. Louis, Mo. , Pentecostal Publishing House, c1965. 111p.
        MoSpA

5658   Rohn, E.
        Pentecostal Bible study course; 250 lessons with questions
        and index ... as given at the Northwest Bible Training School.
        Caldwell, Id. , c1966. 2v. in 1.

5659   Tenney, Tom Fred, 1933-
            Pentecost: what's that? [By] T. F. Tenney. Hazel-
        wood, Mo., Word Aflame Press, c1975. 192p.

5660   Urshan, Andrew bar David, 1884-1967.
            Apostolic faith doctrine of the new birth [by] Andrew D.
        Urshan. Portland, Or., Apostolic Book Corner, U. P. C.,
        19--. 14p.

5661   Urshan, Andrew bar David, 1884-1967.
            The almighty God in the Lord Jesus Christ, by Andrew
        D. Urshan. Portland, Or., Apostolic Book Corner, U. P. C.
        of Portland, 19--. 95p. Reprint of 1919 ed.

5662   Visker, Jack
            The baptism of the Holy Spirit. Hazelwood, Mo., Word
        Aflame Press, 1975. 21p. (Mustard seed booklet.)

5663   Vouga, Oscar, 1903-
            Nuestro Mensaje Evangelico. n. p., United Pentecostal
        Church, 19--. Translation of Our gospel message.

5664   Vouga, Oscar, 1903-
            Our gospel message. St. Louis, Pentecostal Publishing
        House, 19--. 31p.

5665   Witherspoon, Jet Stallones
            Acts; the amazing story of the early church [by] Jet
        Witherspoon. Hazelwood, Mo., Pentecostal Publishing House,
        1972. 192p. TxFS

5666   Witherspoon, Jet Stallones
            Born in the fire: a study course on the book of the Acts
        of the Apostles. Written by Jet Witherspoon in cooperation
        with General Home Missions Division, United Pentecostal
        Church International. Hazelwood, Mo., United Pentecostal
        Church, 19--. 112p. MoSpA

                -- --NON-PENTECOSTAL AUTHORS

5667   Hawk, Monte Ray, 1936-
            Debate notes on Holy Ghost baptism, for Church of God
        and United Pentecostal arguments. Gadsden, Al., Hawk's
        Publications, 1974. 51p. Notes on a debate with E. J.
        Reynolds of the Church of God, October 15-16, 1973. TMH

5668   Jackson, William Nelsen, 1929-
            The Jackson-Bayer debate on Pentecostalism; or, Dis-
        solving a few Bayer aspirin: a 5 night oral debate held at
        the jr. high school gymnasium, Fulton, Mississippi, July 30-
        August 3, 1979, the participants: William N. Jackson, repre-
        senting the Church of Christ, and R. E. Bayer, representing
        the United Pentecostal Church. Fulton, Ms., Sowing the Seed
        Books, 1980. 328p. DLC

5669   Uar bik nei pawlte.
             Aizawl, Synod Literature Committee, 1977.   88p.   In
        Lushai.   Partial contents: Lalbiakthuanga.   United Pente-
        costal Church.

5670   Vaughn, Ray
             Wallace-Vaughn debate, held at Arvada, Colorado, Sep-
        tember 5-7, 1951, between Ray Vaughn and G. K. Wallace.
        Wire recorded.   Longview, Wa., Telegram Sermons Book
        Co., 1952.   194p.   DLC

             --EDUCATION

5671   McNatt, Elmer E., 1908-
             The Pentecostal Sunday school, by Elmer E. McNatt.
        Nashville? 1952.   201p.   On spine: A Sunday school con-
        cordance.   DLC

5672   Pugh, Jessie Truman, 1923-
             Reaching our generation through the Sunday school.   Com-
        piled by Committee on Teacher Training, General Sunday
        School Department, United Pentecostal Church; author: J. T.
        Pugh.   St. Louis, Pentecostal Publishing House, 1963.   109p.
        OkTOr

5673   Wallace, J. O.
             Team teaching, by J. O. Wallace and D. L. Segraves.
        St. Louis, Mo., Pentecostal Publishing House, c1969.   32p.

             --FINANCE

5674   Krantz, Patricia Jane, 1941-
             Patterns of giving; a study of contributions to four Pente-
        costal sects, by Patricia J. Krantz.   Madison, 1968.   113ℓ.
        Thesis (M.A.)--University of Wisconsin.   Includes United
        Pentecostal Church.   WU

             --HISTORY

5675   United Pentecostal Church International.
             Jubilee!   50th General Conference, United Pentecostal
        Church International, Louisville, Kentucky, October 9-15,
        1974, with scenes from our historic past.   Hazelwood, Mo.,
        1974.   1v. (unpaged)   Cover title.

5676   United Pentecostal Church International.
             The story of the United Pentecostal Church International.
        Hazelwood, Mo., 1974.   1v. (unpaged)   Cover title.   IGreviC,
        MH-AH, OT

5677   Clanton, Arthur Lee, 1915-
        United we stand; a history of oneness organizations [by]
        Arthur L. Clanton. Hazelwood, Mo., Pentecostal Publishing
        House, 1970. 207p.

5678   Foster, Fred J.
        "Think it not strange"; a history of the Oneness Move-
        ment, by Fred J. Foster. St. Louis, Mo., Pentecostal
        Publishing House, 1965. 109p.

5679   Kendrick, Klaude, 1917-
        The promise fulfilled: a history of the modern Pente-
        costal movement. Springfield, Mo., Gospel Publishing House,
        c1961. viii, 237p. "United Pentecostal Church": p. 171-175.

5680   Moore, Everett Leroy, 1918-
        Handbook of Pentecostal denominations in the United
        States. Pasadena, Ca., 1954. vii, 346ℓ. Thesis (M.A.)--
        Pasadena College. "United Pentecostal Church": ℓ. 253-
        269. CSdP

--HISTORY AND STUDY OF DOCTRINES

5681   Williams, O. W.
        What do you think? [By] O. W. Williams. Houston,
        19--. 35p. Cover title. Interview by Cecil Brazell on the
        Talk of Houston radio program.

--HYMNS AND SACRED SONGS

5682   United Pentecostal Church
        Let us praise Him. St. Louis, Pentecostal Publishing
        House, 19--. 1v. (unpaged) Cover title. With music
        (shape notes).

5683   United Pentecostal Church
        Pentecostal praises; a complete church hymnal. Hazel-
        wood, Mo., Pentecostal Publishing House, c1947. 1v.
        (unpaged) With music (shape notes).

5684   United Pentecostal Church
        Pentecostal hymnal revised; a complete church hymnal
        with an exceptionally fine selection of songs for every type
        of service. Hazelwood, Mo., Pentecostal Publishing House,
        c1953. 1v. (unpaged) With music (round notes).

--PASTORAL LITERATURE

5685   Burr, Murray E.
        The hair question, by Murray E. Burr. St. Louis,

Home Missionary Department, United Pentecostal Church,
19--. 16p.

--PASTORAL THEOLOGY

5686   United Pentecostal Church International.
        Magnifying the ministry. Hazelwood, Mo., 197-.   31p.
        Cover title.

5687   Pugh, Jessie Truman, 1923-
        For preachers only [by] J. T. Pugh. Hazelwood, Mo.,
        Pentecostal Publishing House, 1971. 192p. TxFS

--PERIODICALS

5688   Global witness. 1- 19 -
        Hazelwood, Mo. DLC, OkTOr

5689   Home builder. 1- May/June 1979-
        Hazelwood, Mo. DLC

5690   Pentecostal herald. 20, no. 12-Dec. 1945-
        St. Louis; Hazelwood, Mo. Continues Apostolic herald.

5691   Pentecostal homelife. 1- 1971-
        Hazelwood, Mo. DLC, OkTOr

5692   Pentecostal way. 1- 19 -
        St. Paul, Mn.

5693   Tread. 1- 196 -
        St. Louis. OkTOr

--SERMONS, TRACTS, ADDRESSES, ESSAYS

5694   Hanby, Stanley R.
        Do you know? By S. R. Hanby. Hazelwood, Mo.,
        Pentecostal Publishing House, 19--.   leaflet ([4]p.)

5695   Oggs, Allan C.
        Today is the beginning, by Allan C. Oggs, Sr. Hazel-
        wood, Mo., Word Aflame Press, c1974. 128p.

5696   Urshan, Andrew bar David, 1884-1967.
        Timely messages of comfort, by Andrew D. Urshan.
        Portland, Or., Apostolic Book Corner, 1973. 103p. "Second
        printing." Messages preached in Los Angeles in 1918.

5697   Urshan, Andrew bar David, 1884-1967.
        Timely messages of warning, by Andrew D. Urshan.

Portland, Or., Apostolic Book Corner, 1973.   87p.   "Second printing."   First published in 1917.

5698   Urshan, Nathaniel Andrew, 1920-
"Consider Him"; David's son and David's lord, by Nathaniel A. Urshan.   St. Louis, Harvestime, 19--.   30p.

5699   Urshan, Nathaniel Andrew, 1920-
Harvestime sermons, by Nathaniel A. Urshan.   Grand Rapids, Mi., Baker Book House, 1973.   64p.

5700   Urshan, Nathaniel Andrew, 1920-
These men are drunk! (Six messages on the baptism of the Holy Spirit).   Preached on "Harvestime" radio broadcast by Nathaniel A. Urshan.   St. Louis, Harvestime, 19--.   32p.

5701   Willoughby, David, 1945-1973.
What time is it? Hazelwood, Mo., Word Aflame Press, c1974.   126p.

--MINNESOTA (St. Paul)

5702   Holsteen, Melbourne Edward
Controlled resistance to change in a Pentecostal church. Minneapolis, 1968.   iii, 181ℓ.   Thesis (M.A.)--University of Minnesota.   On "Midway Tabernacle" (Apostolic Bible Church, St. Paul, Minnesota).   MnU

--OREGON

5703   Dearman, Marion Veurl
Do holiness sects socialize in dominant values? An empirical inquiry.   Eugene, 1972.   238ℓ.   Based on interviews with United Pentecostal Church members in Springfield, Albany, Corvallis, Roseburg, Ashland, and Portland, Oregon.

WAY OF THE CROSS (1927-)

The mother church of the Way of the Cross is located at 9th and D Street, N.E., Washington, D.C.   Founded by Bishop Henry C. Brooks in 1927, the movement consists of more than two dozen congregations.   It holds membership in the Apostolic World Christian Fellowship.   In 1980 J. L. Brooks was presiding bishop.

WEST INDIAN CANADIAN INTERNATIONAL APOSTOLIC FELLOW-SHIP (19 -)

Headquarters of the West Indian Canadian International Apos-

tolic Fellowship are in Toronto.   In 1980, R. W. Davy was president.
The organization holds membership in the Apostolic World Christian
Fellowship.

YAHVAH TEMPLE (1947-   )
[1947-1953 as Church of Jesus; 1953-1981 as Jesus Church.]

Founded in 1947, the Yahvah Temple has throughout its history sought a name which would indicate its central teaching.   The
body was first known as the Church of Jesus.   "We soon learned, "
however, that "if we are to be called by his name we would have
to take the 'of' out and call ourselves 'The Jesus Church'."   The
present title, which was adopted in early 1982, is intended to iden-
tify Jesus as Yahweh of the Old Testament.   In keeping with this
emphasis, Yahvah Temple observes Saturday as the sabbath.   It is
unique in being the only "Jesus Only" body to spring from the Holiness-
Pentecostal tradition.   Samuel E. Officer, founder and bishop, resides in Cleveland, Tennessee, where the movement originated.   The
official letterhead declares: "Yahvah Temple is governed by the
Melchizedek righteous priesthood."

--CATECHISMS AND CREEDS

5704   Church of Jesus.
        General views and teachings of the Bible.   Cleveland, Tn.,
        1949.   36p.

5705   Jesus Church.
        General views and teachings of the Bible and church.
        Cleveland, Tn., Jesus Church Publishing House, 1953.   49p.

--HISTORY

5706   Moore, Everett Leroy, 1918-
        Handbook of Pentecostal denominations in the United
        States.   Pasadena, Ca., 1954.   vii, 346ℓ.   Thesis (M. A.)--
        Pasadena College.   "The Jesus Church": ℓ. 304-313.   CSdP

--PERIODICALS

5707   Light of the world.   1-   1947-
        Cleveland, Tn.

--SERMONS, TRACTS, ADDRESSES, ESSAYS

5708   Officer, Samuel E., 1908-
        Contend for the faith.   Cleveland, Tn., 19--.   leaflet

5709   Officer, Samuel E., 1908-
        Elohim became man. Cleveland, Tn., 19--. leaflet

5710   Officer, Samuel E., 1908-
        Melchizedek or Christian priesthood? Cleveland, Tn.,
        Gospel Tracts, 19--. folder ([4]p.)

5711   Officer, Samuel E., 1908-
        Messiah returns--1993, by Samuel E. Officer. Cleve-
        land, Tn., Yahvah Temple, 1982. leaflet

5712   Officer, Samuel E., 1908-
        The more excellent way is perfect love. Cleveland, Tn.,
        Gospel Tracts, 19--. folder ([4]p.)

5713   Officer, Samuel E., 1908-
        Sabbath resurrection, by Samuel E. Officer. Cleveland,
        Tn., Yahvah Temple, 1982. leaflet

5714   Officer, Samuel E., 1908-
        Seventh day sabbath. Cleveland, Tn., 19--. leaflet

5715   Officer, Samuel E., 1908-
        Thy kingdom come. Cleveland, Tn., 19--. sheet

5716   Officer, Samuel E., 1908-
        Tithes and offerings. Cleveland, Tn., 19--. leaflet

5717   Officer, Samuel E., 1908-
        Women ministers. Cleveland, Tn., Gospel Tracts,
        19--. leaflet